The Palgrave Handbook of Democracy, Governance and Justice in Africa

Aderomola Adeola · Makau W. Mutua
Editors

The Palgrave Handbook of Democracy, Governance and Justice in Africa

palgrave
macmillan

Editors
Aderomola Adeola
Centre for Refugee Studies
York University
Toronto, Canada

Makau W. Mutua
University at Buffalo, State University
Buffalo, NY, USA

ISBN 978-3-030-74013-9   ISBN 978-3-030-74014-6   (eBook)
https://doi.org/10.1007/978-3-030-74014-6

© The Editor(s) (if applicable) and The Author(s), under exclusive license to Springer Nature
Switzerland AG 2022
This work is subject to copyright. All rights are solely and exclusively licensed by the Publisher,
whether the whole or part of the material is concerned, specifically the rights of translation,
reprinting, reuse of illustrations, recitation, broadcasting, reproduction on microfilms or in any
other physical way, and transmission or information storage and retrieval, electronic adaptation,
computer software, or by similar or dissimilar methodology now known or hereafter developed.
The use of general descriptive names, registered names, trademarks, service marks, etc. in this
publication does not imply, even in the absence of a specific statement, that such names are
exempt from the relevant protective laws and regulations and therefore free for general use.
The publisher, the authors, and the editors are safe to assume that the advice and information in
this book are believed to be true and accurate at the date of publication. Neither the publisher
nor the authors or the editors give a warranty, expressed or implied, with respect to the material
contained herein or for any errors or omissions that may have been made. The publisher remains
neutral with regard to jurisdictional claims in published maps and institutional affiliations.

Cover image: © NSP-RF/Alamy Stock Photo

This Palgrave Macmillan imprint is published by the registered company Springer Nature
Switzerland AG
The registered company address is: Gewerbestrasse 11, 6330 Cham, Switzerland

CONTENTS

1   Africa in Transition: Issues in Democracy, Governance and Justice   1
Aderomola Adeola and Makau W. Mutua
1   Introduction   1
2   Structure of the Book   4
Bibliography   8

2   Election Technology as a Means of Enhancing Democratic Legitimacy: A Case of Kenya   11
Marystella Simiyu
1   Introduction   11
2   Conceptualising Legitimacy   13
3   International Legal Frameworks on Elections   14
4   The Kenyan Experience: Did Election Technology Enhance Democratic Legitimacy in Kenya?   15
  4.1   Reasons for the Adoption of Election Technology in Kenya   15
  4.2   2013 Elections   17
  4.3   2017 Elections   21
5   An Analysis of the Kenyan Experience   27
6   Conclusion   29
Bibliography   30

3   Assessing Cameroon's Elections Against International Standards and Good Practices on Democracy and Human Rights   35
Walters Tohnji Samah and Jespa Ajereboh Tichock
1   Introduction   35
2   Normative Frameworks   36
  2.1   International Frameworks   36

v

vi CONTENTS

	2.2	Regional Frameworks	37
	2.3	National Election Framework	39
3		The Institutional Framework	41
4		The Question of Credibility of Elections in a Democracy	42
5		Overviewing Multiparty Elections Since 1992	43
	5.1	Presidential Elections	44
	5.2	Legislative Elections	45
6		Assessing Cameroon's Elections	47
	6.1	Lack of Independence of Election Management Body	47
	6.2	ELECAM Is Not the Sole Authority on Elections	48
	6.3	Electoral Dispute Resolution	49
	6.4	Timeframe for Filing Election Petitions	49
	6.5	The Conflicting Roles of the Constitutional Council	50
	6.6	Election Campaign Period	50
	6.7	Qualification as a Candidate for Presidential Election	51
	6.8	Unlimited Presidential Terms	52
	6.9	The Question of Multiple Ballot Papers	52
7		Way Forward	53
	7.1	Need for an Independent EMB	53
	7.2	Need for an Independent Constitutional Court	53
	7.3	Election Campaign	54
	7.4	Conditions of Candidacies and Eligibility	54
	7.5	Election Calendar	54
	7.6	Need for Cooperation with International Observers for Free and Fair Elections	54
	7.7	Need for an Enabling Environment for Democratic and Human Rights Expression	55
8		Conclusion	55
		Bibliography	56

4 State Sovereignty and Presidential Term Limits in Africa   61
Kennedy Kariseb

1	Introduction	61
2	State Sovereignty and Presidential Term Limits in Africa	63
	2.1 State Sovereignty: Its Origins, Evolution and Contemporary Interpretations	63
	2.2 Presidential Termism in Africa: Contours, Trends and Prevailing Practices	67
3	Piercing the Doctrine of State Sovereignty: The African Union and Presidential Term Limits in Africa	68
4	Conclusion: Possible Options for Reform by the African Union	71
	Bibliography	72

CONTENTS vii

5 Soldiers in Civilian Uniforms: The Role of the Military in the Pursuit of Third-Termism 75
Trésor Muhindo Makunya and Kwadwo Appiagyei-Atua
1 *Introduction* 75
2 *Soldiers and the Third-Term Agenda* 76
  2.1 *Burkina Faso* 78
  2.2 *Siding with the Incumbent: The Case of Democratic Republic of Congo* 80
3 *Conclusion* 81
Bibliography 81

6 Reflections on the Role of the Pan-African Parliament in Advancing Democratic Governance in Africa 85
Osy Ezechukwunyere Nwebo and Charles Manga Fombad
1 *Introduction* 85
2 *The Vision for the Establishment of the Pap* 86
3 *Interrogating the Parliamentary Status of the Pap* 87
4 *Rationale for the Limited Mandate of the Pap* 91
5 *Objectives, Powers and Functions of the Pap* 93
6 *Strategies for Advancing Democratic Governance in Africa* 96
  6.1 *Oversight Functions* 96
  6.2 *Fact-Finding Missions* 99
  6.3 *Election Observation Missions* 100
  6.4 *Committee Work* 101
  6.5 *Conferences* 102
  6.6 *Model Laws* 103
7 *Conclusion* 104
Bibliography 105

7 Gender Discriminatory Nationality Laws and Childhood Statelessness in Africa: A Reflection on Legislative Interpretations 109
Julie Lugulu
1 *Introduction* 109
2 *The Right to Nationality Under International Law* 111
3 *Legal Frameworks on the Right to Nationality in Swaziland, Libya, Liberia and Sudan* 111
  3.1 *Swaziland* 111
  3.2 *Libya* 113
  3.3 *Liberia* 114
  3.4 *Sudan* 115
4 *Discrimination and Childhood Statelessness* 116
5 *Conclusion and Recommendation* 118
Bibliography 118

viii CONTENTS

8 The Economic Community of West African States and the Mano River Union: Conflict, Cooperation and Accommodation   121
Vandy Kanyako

1	Introduction	121
2	Methodology and Significance	122
3	Analytical Framework	123
4	Historical Context	126
5	The MRU: Reasons for Formation	127
6	Same Goals, Different Missions?	132
7	Challenges in Fostering Closer Ties Between the Two Institutions	132
	7.1 Crisis of Identity	133
	7.2 Different Historical Experiences	133
	7.3 Elusive Peace	134
	7.4 Human Rights and Justice	134
8	Relationship with Ecowas: Why the MRU Matters	134
	8.1 Economic Importance	134
	8.2 Social and Kinship Ties	135
	8.3 Peace and Security Arena	135
9	Attempts at Reforms	136
10	Accomplishments of MRU and ECOWAS	138
11	Areas for Continued Collaboration	140
12	Conclusion	141
	Bibliography	142

9 The Media and Civil Society as Partners in Transitional Justice in Côte D'ivoire   145
Ady Namaran Coulibaly

1	Introduction	145
2	The Media, Conflicts and Transitional Justice in Côte D'ivoire	147
3	Overview of Traditional and Online Media in Côte D'ivoire	150
4	Civil Society Space	151
	4.1 Domestic Regulations on Civil Society Activities	152
5	Transitional Justice Mechanisms in Côte D'ivoire	153
	5.1 Domestic Regulations Governing Operations of the Media	154
6	Media Engagement as a Tool to Further Transitional Justice	156
	6.1 CSOs and Online Media Involved in Transitional Justice	159
	6.2 Interview Responses: Media Engagement by CSOs	160

CONTENTS ix

| | 6.3 | Qualitative Content Analysis: Media Engagement by CSOs in Côte d'Ivoire | 161 |

6.3 Qualitative Content Analysis: Media Engagement
    by CSOs in Côte d'Ivoire   161
7 Summary of Findings and Conclusion   163
Bibliography   166

**10 Genocide, Justice and Democratic Legitimacy: Lessons
from Rwanda's 25-Year Experiment**   171
Noel Twagiramungu
1 Introduction   171
2 Historical and Conceptual Framework   172
   2.1 Background to the 1994 Genocide   172
   2.2 The Quest for Justice   174
   2.3 Transitional Justice   175
   2.4 Limits and Frontiers of Transitional Justice
      in the Real World   176
3 Domestic Responses   176
   3.1 Extrajudicial Responses   176
   3.2 Specialised Chambers   177
   3.3 Gacaca Jurisdictions   178
   3.4 Alternative Punishment and Correctional
      Mechanisms   179
   3.5 Genocide-Centred Lawfare   180
4 International Responses   181
   4.1 ICTR   181
   4.2 Trials in Foreign National Courts   182
   4.3 Extradition Arrangements   182
   4.4 Indictments Against RPF Officers   183
5 The Politics of Justice: Challenges & Controversies   184
   5.1 Genocide Within the Context of Civil War   184
   5.2 Mass Participation in the Genocide   185
   5.3 International Community's Lack of Moral Authority   185
   5.4 The Culture of Victor's Justice   186
6 Conclusion: Looking Back, Reaching Forward   187
   6.1 Looking Back   188
   6.2 Reaching Forward: The Quest for a New Departure   190
Bibliography   191

**11 The Community Court of Justice of the Ecowas
and the Advancement of Human Rights and Social Justice
Reform in West Africa: Three Landmark Cases**   197
Jake Okechukwu Effoduh
1 Introduction   197
2 The Case of Serap v. Nigeria and Anor 2010 ('case 1')   199
3 The Case of Serap v. Nigeria and 8 ORS 2012 ('Case 2')   201
4 The Case of Serap and 10 ORS v. Nigeria and 4 ORS
   2014 ('Case 3')   208

x CONTENTS

5 From the Sub-Regional to the Local—The Correspondence
of Human Rights and Social Justice Norms 213
6 Conclusion 216
Bibliography 217

12 **Contemporary Developments in Human and Peoples' Rights Protection in Africa: Insights from the African Union** 221
Rhuks Temitope Ako and John Gbodi Ikubaje
1 Introduction 221
2 Evolution of Human Rights in Africa 222
3 Normative and Institutional Developments of Human
and Peoples' Rights in Africa 225
4 New Developments on Human and Peoples Rights
in Africa: Mainstreaming Human Rights into Au
Programming 228
5 Conclusion 231
Bibliography 232

13 **Righting the Future from the Past: Four Decades of Human Rights (Illusions) in Zimbabwe** 235
Gift Mwonzora
1 Introduction 235
2 Zimbabwe's 1980 Independence: A 'New Baby is Born' 236
3 Defending the (in) Defensible—Mugabe and the One-Party
State System in Zimbabwe 238
4 A Chronicle of Human Rights Records Under the Regime 239
4.1 The Gukurahundi Massacres (1983–1987)—When
a State Turns Against Its Citizens 239
4.2 State Response to the 1998 Food Riots 241
4.3 'The Emperor Has no clothes'—The 2000 Land
Reform Programme in Zimbabwe 242
4.4 Enduring Human Rights Violations and Erosion
of Democratic Rule 246
4.5 Unleashing Violence Against the Opposition 247
4.6 From Pillar to Post—Human Rights Violations
Under Operation Murambatsvina ('Clear the Filth') 248
4.7 Discovery of Diamonds and Human Rights Violations 249
4.8 The 2008 Election Violence: A Winter of Agony
and Anguish 250
5 Change and Continuity—Human Rights Violations
in the Post-Mugabe Era 251
6 Reaching Forward from the PAST: ARE There Effective
Ways to Re-Write the Future? 253
7 Conclusion 254
Bibliography 255

CONTENTS xi

14 Constitutional Courts as Protection Conduits: The Role of Egypt Supreme Constitutional Court in Advancing Human Rights Protection 259
Mohamed Abdelaal
1 Introduction 259
2 Constitutional Courts as Protection Conduits 261
3 The SCC and Freedom of Belief 265
   3.1 The SCC on Article 2: Towards a Liberal Interpretation 266
   3.2 Litigating Article 2: Women's Rights and Entitlements 267
4 The SCC and Minorities Rights 269
5 The SCC and Civil Liberties (Freedom of Association and Right to Protest) 271
   5.1 Freedom of Association 271
   5.2 Right to Protest 273
6 Conclusion 276
Bibliography 277

15 The Media and Freedom of Expression in Democratic Malawi: A Formality or Reality? 279
Jimmy Kainja
1 Introduction 279
2 Media and Political Landscape 280
3 Legal Framework 283
4 Economic Environment 286
5 Journalists' Standards of Living 288
6 Alternative Media 289
7 Conclusion 290
Bibliography 291

16 The Future in Transition: Realising Respect for Human Rights in the 'New' Gambia 295
Satang Nabaneh
1 Introduction 295
2 Human Rights and Governance Challenges in The Gambia 296
   2.1 Human Rights in The Gambia: An Assessment 296
3 Democratic Transition: A Scorecard 309
   3.1 Equalising the Political Playing Field 309
   3.2 Accountability and Truth Telling 309
   3.3 Constitutional Review Process 311
   3.4 Building a Culture of Human Rights 312
   3.5 'Gambianization' of the Judiciary 314
4 Conclusion 314
Bibliography 315

xii CONTENTS

17 The Psychosocial Well-Being of the African Child in Criminal Proceedings 319
Emma Charlene Lubaale
1 *Introduction* 319
2 *International children's Rights Framework on Participation and Child Psychological Well-Being in Criminal Justice Processes* 322
   2.1 *Participation and Children in Criminal Proceedings* 322
   2.2 *Children's Psychosocial Well-Being in Criminal Proceedings* 325
3 *National Laws in Africa Vis-A-Viz the International Standards on Participation and Child Psychological Well-Being in Criminal Proceedings* 328
   3.1 *Adversarial and Inquisitorial Justice Traditions and Children's Psychological Well-Being in Criminal Proceedings* 329
   3.2 *National Laws and the Psychological Well-Being of Children in Criminal Proceedings* 331
4 *Children's Psychological Well-Being in Criminal Proceedings: Analysis, Conclusion and Recommendations* 342
Bibliography 344

18 Taxation as Protection Finance for the African Child 349
Alexander Ezenagu
1 *Introduction* 349
2 *Taxes as a Strategy to Finance Child Protection* 349
3 *Current Challenges to Effective Tax Regimes* 351
4 *Policy Options for Strengthening the Tax Regime* 355
5 *Conclusion* 357
Bibliography 358

19 Protecting 'Climate Refugees' Under the OAU 1969 Refugee Convention 361
Aderomola Adeola
1 *Introduction* 361
2 *The Global Regulatory Framework* 362
3 *The 1969 OAU Refugee Convention* 367
   3.1 *Expanding Interpretations: The Place of Climate Change Refugees* 368
4 *Conclusion* 371
Bibliography 371

Index 375

LIST OF CONTRIBUTORS

Abdelaal Mohamed Faculty of Law, Alexandria University, Alexandria, Egypt

Adeola Aderomola Centre for Refugee Studies, York University, Toronto, Canada

Ajereboh Tichock Jespa Bamenda, Cameroon

Ako Rhuks Temitope African Union Commission, Addis Ababa, Ethiopia

Appiagyei-Atua Kwadwo Faculty of Law, University of Ghana, Accra, Ghana

Coulibaly Ady Namaran Faculty of Law, Centre for Human Rights, University of Pretoria, Pretoria, South Africa

Effoduh Jake Okechukwu Osgoode Hall Law School, York University, Toronto, ON, Canada

Ezenagu Alexander Hamad Bin Khalifa University, Doha, Qatar

Fombad Charles Manga Faculty of Law, University of Pretoria, Pretoria, South Africa

Ikubaje John Gbodi African Union Commission, Addis Ababa, Ethiopia

Kainja Jimmy University of Malawi, Zomba, Malawi

Kanyako Vandy Conflict Resolution Program, Portland State University, Portland, OR, USA

Kariseb Kennedy School of Law, University of Namibia, Windhoek, Namibia

Lubaale Emma Charlene Faculty of Law, Rhodes University, Makhanda, South Africa

xiv   LIST OF CONTRIBUTORS

Lugulu Julie Faculty of Law, Kabarak University, Nakuru, Kenya

Makunya Trésor Muhindo Faculty of Law, University of Pretoria, Pretoria, South Africa

Mutua Makau W. University at Buffalo, Buffalo, NY, USA

Mwonzora Gift Unit of Zimbabwean Studies, Sociology Department, Rhodes University, Makhanda, South Africa

Nabaneh Satang Human Rights Center & School of Law, University of Dayton, Dayton, Ohio, United States of America

Nwebo Osy Ezechukwunyere Imo State University, Owerri, Nigeria

Samah Walters Tohnji African Union Observer African Mission in the Central African Republic, Bangui, Central African Republic

Simiyu Marystella Faculty of Law, Centre for Human Rights, University of Pretoria, Pretoria, South Africa

Twagiramungu Noel African Studies Center, Boston University, Boston, MA, USA

List of Figures

Chapter 8

Fig. 1   MRU organogram   132

Chapter 10

Fig. 1   ICTR (2014)   182

LIST OF TABLES

Chapter 9

Table 1   Summary of media engagement framework (Centre for Advocacy and Research New Delhi)   157

Table 2   Media engagement framework for CSOs working in TJ in Côte d'Ivoire, adapted from the Centre for Advocacy and Research New Delhi (2012)   158

Table 3   Number of news articles per online news website   160

Table 4   CSO engagement with the media for TJ purposes   162

Chapter 10

Table 1   Formal justice and Gacaca justice in numbers   179

CHAPTER 1

Africa in Transition: Issues in Democracy, Governance and Justice

Aderomola Adeola and Makau W. Mutua

1 INTRODUCTION

The period of independence in many African countries was met with a euphoria of endless possibilities. Africa was rich in resources. It had a wealth of people. And there were great potentials for the newly independent countries. Most of the elites who took over power were charged with ideologies from Marxist inclinations to capitalist ideations. There were examples from various territories on which to hinge the formation of these ideologies, but more importantly, there was hindsight about pre-colonial Africa and the benefits of some modalities of governance within these societal contexts. And while the future was a blank check, there were high hopes that political freedom and the consequent democratic governance were a pertinent step in the right direction. But how has Africa faired over the last six decades? There is an increasing oxymoron across many African countries that reflects an interesting trailer: while more countries are holding regular elections, the governance landscape on a whole is less democratic. Another way of putting this is that in principle, democracy is a popular ideal shared by a vast majority and reflected in the opening lines of constitution as *grundnorm*.

A. Adeola
Centre for Refugee Studies, York University, Toronto, Canada

M. W. Mutua (✉)
University at Buffalo, Buffalo, NY, USA
e-mail: mutua@buffalo.edu

© The Author(s), under exclusive license to Springer Nature
Switzerland AG 2022
A. Adeola and M. W. Mutua (eds.), *The Palgrave Handbook
of Democracy, Governance and Justice in Africa*,
https://doi.org/10.1007/978-3-030-74014-6_1

1

However, the extent to which these principles find expression within national spaces is less reflective of the generality of the idea. Overall to assume that there is democracy across board, while regular elections and political order asserts this, has become hasty generalisation. But what really is the problem with African democracy and how can these issues be fixed? This chapter will not re-harsh existing insights into the narrative. For indeed, there is a plethora of scholarly enterprise on democracy and human rights (Wanyande 1987; Ake 2000; Southall 2003; Murray 2004; Okafor 2007; Iwuji 2007; Mutua 2008: 17–39; Viljoen 2012; Cheeseman 2015; Ibhawoh 2018; Matolino 2018; Harding 2020). But it is useful to assert that the great body of work on these issues presents a reflection of a significantly intertwined ideology—that human rights are integral to the furtherance of democracy and that democracy itself is an exercise of a *demos* participation in a social contract that is constitutionally determined, with strong validation through both multiple tests and experiments across various climes. There are certain conditions for the conditions or parameters, upon which these twin ideations are elevated. While the parameters are never really cast in stone, certain basics are required: multiparty systems and general elections, political participation and representation; gender and youth participation, civic spaces and freedom of expression and human rights protection.

In the 1960s and 1970s, there were general strides towards power consolidation with limited opposition to no opposition with one-party systems and/or military coups (McGowan 2003), for instance, in countries such as Ghana, Tanzania, Central Africa Republic and Algeria. While constitutions were often suspended in military states and as such, there was little to no discussions on fundamental rights and freedoms, in some one-party states such as Malawi and Tanzania, constitutional entrenchment of rights was rejected (Zimba 1984: 113). The presence of one-party systems in some states was premised on the broad-based support liberation movements enjoyed. For instance, in Tanzania, this was an evident reality with the Tanganyika African National Union (Zimba 1984: 115). There were also legacies of the colonial mentality that accompanied these paradigms where winning meant a subjugation of contrary narratives. However, by the 1990s, these systems began to experience evident pressure (Makinda 1996: 555) with an awakening towards inclusive governance. But with the ideation of inclusivity came a new paradox: the incumbency effect, evident, for instance, in countries such as Uganda, Zimbabwe and the Democratic Republic of Congo (DRC). However, the absoluteness of this has begun to ebb in countries such as the Gambia (Adeola 2017), Burkina Faso (Songwe 2014; Wienkoop and Bertrand 2018), Nigeria (Adeola 2019) and Ghana (Cheeseman et al. 2017).

Arguably, there is a new wave of active judiciaries standing up for free and fair electoral processes, for instance, in Kenya (2017) and Malawi (2020). But such evident gains need to be further sustained to become prevalent practice. To the north of the continent, the promise of the Arab spring has also not delivered dividends of multiparty democracy, for instance, in Egypt and

Libya. Tunisia, however, reflects a different paradigm from the spring with two successful general elections and an independent candidate emerging as president. Though one might argue that the Tunisian example, and indeed, also Liberia and Malawi, in more recent years, reflects an emerging appreciation of fairness in electoral processes, such appreciation is not broadly evident across African societies where elections are still form-based than substance-infused, for instance in countries such as Gabon and Equatorial Guinea.

However, there is an emerging acceptance of youth-led governance as a paradigm shift. And while this is mostly in principle, for instance, in Nigeria with the Not-Too-Young-To-Run campaign, the role of women in leadership is gaining traction, for instance, in Liberia with the election of Ellen Johnson Sirleaf. While the continent has indeed witnessed nine women in presidential positions across the continent, there is a need for more inclusion, particularly, beyond appointments into government positions. Much of this success, however, will need to be driven by more active involvement of women in political participation and conscious drive towards addressing stereotypical ideas driven by deep-seat patriarchy. However, advancing political participation also requires characterising democracy as a classless process, particularly through the conscious inclusion of ethnic groups that have been historically repressed. Whether in Kenya or Ethiopia, the down-side of ethnic hierarchies has evidently demonstrated itself as anathema to democratic governance.

But there is something to be said about the consistency in political statements, following elections, where promises are made and democratic values are reinforced. Howbeit, in principle, such rhetoric often includes ending endemic corruption, providing adequate social protection, increasing civic spaces, creating jobs and leading the country into the paradise that erstwhile regimes could not deliver. However, the very same plot of erstwhile regimes finds expression in these administrations. But in response to the revolving plot, the last decades have witnessed a significant surge in vibrant civic spaces. With the advent of technology, these spaces have significantly expanded. But while these spaces are increasingly finding new forms of expression with the emergence of social media as a counter-narrative to traditional forms, that are in some cases captured by states, digital manipulation of the electorate (as with the Cambridge Analytica situation in Kenya and Nigeria) is proving to be a threat to the effectiveness of these platforms. Increasingly, governments are also hijacking these moments to limit expression. In response to fake news, governmental restrictions are beginning to emerge with broad laws such as with the Computer Misuse Act in Uganda (2011) and the Electronic and Postal Communications (Online Content) Regulations in Tanzania (2018).

There are also ebbing commitments towards human rights protection demonstrable through the prevalence of conflict in countries such as South Sudan, Somalia and Libya, generalised violence in places like Mali and Chad, and poor socio-economic conditions in conflict and non-conflict regions including Burundi, Sierra Leone and Comoros. Though human rights norms are constitutionally entrenched in the constitutions of all African countries, compliance with these norms is mixed across various jurisdictions. There are instances where these violations have steered separatist agitations, for instance, in the Anglophone region of Cameroon. However, the practice of human rights starkly contrasts with the elaborate set of principles at various levels of governance—national, regional and continental. Aside from constitutional protection, a plethora of norms has emerged at national level on human rights, including legislations that adopt the African Charter on Human and Peoples' Rights (1981). National jurisprudence giving effect to human rights treaties at regional and continental levels is also replete through the emergence of norms. At the regional continental level for instance, such norms include: African Charter on the Rights and Welfare of the Child (1990); Protocol to the African Charter on Human and Peoples' Rights on the Rights of Women in Africa (2003); African Union Convention for the Protection and Assistance of Internally Displaced Persons in Africa (2009); Protocol to the African Charter on Human and Peoples' Rights on the Rights of Older Persons (2016); Protocol to the African Charter on Human and Peoples' Rights on the Rights of Persons with Disabilities in Africa (2018). However, the fundamental challenge has been one of compliance with these norms. Moreover, compliance with the decisions of regional human rights mechanisms is also an evident challenge, given the prevalence of unimplemented decisions by the African Commission on Human and Peoples' Rights, the African Court on Human and Peoples' Rights and the African Committee of Experts on the Rights and Welfare of the Child. While much is yet to be desired in this regard, there are evident gains towards continental unification in the furtherance of intraregional trade and socio-economic development with the adoption of the African Continental Free Trade Agreement and the Protocol to the Treaty Establishing the African Economic Community Relating to the Free Movement of Persons, Right of Residence and Right of Establishment (2018).

Exploring core questions in democratic governance and justice, this book takes a departure from conventional critiques of Africa. The authors in this book are drawn from a plethora of fields and backgrounds, within governments, international organisations and the academia. There are nineteen (19) chapters in this handbook. A brief outline of the chapters is presented below.

2   STRUCTURE OF THE BOOK

In the discussion of democratic governance and justice, authors in this book raise pertinent discussions in relation to pertinent areas of inquiry including elections, terms limit and governance, human rights, conflict resolution and transitional justice.

In Chapter 2, Marystella Simiyu examines the use of election technology as a means of enhancing democratic legitimacy with specific reference to Kenya. Her article draws out the importance of addressing issues of legitimacy particularly in the use of technology in the furtherance of elections. She focuses on two electoral epochs—the 2013 and 2017 elections—and argues that while technology can facilitate free, fair and credible elections, it is important that there is proper management. As such, it is essential to build in an effective governance structure for the effectiveness of election technology in the furtherance of democratic governance.

In Chapter 3, Walters Samah and Jespa Ajereboh Tichock reflect on the extent to which the electoral process in Cameroon conforms with international standards and good practices on democracy and human rights. Considering various normative frameworks at different governance levels, they assess the Cameroonians' situation and conclude that there is a need to significantly align national norms and practices with relevant standards that Cameroon is also party to and which states adhere with in the furtherance of democratic ideals and human rights protection. Overall, they propose important strategic directions for ensuring conformity including the need for Cameroon to 're-engage with international partners and the international election observation community'.

In Chapter 4, Kennedy Kariseb argues for a reconsideration of the idea of state sovereignty with respect to presidential term limits in Africa. He argues that there is a need for a concerted effort by supranational institutions with respect to the absolute discretion of states to determine the extent of presidential tenure. Given the fact that unconstitutional presidential tenures often trigger conflicts within states, he argues that there is a need to pierce the veil of state sovereignty in regulating the furtherance of supranational regulation of presidential tenures. He makes that, in Africa, the African Union can play a significant role in this regard. He makes the pertinent point that 'the starting point should be a continent-wide intra-State dialogue and diplomatic engagements with each state'.

In Chapter 5, Trésor Makunya Muhindo and Kwadwo Appiagyei-Atua discuss military involvement in democratic governance in Africa through the prism of third-termism across African states. While tracing the nature of this concern and specifically reflecting on the context of Burkina Faso and the Democratic Republic of Congo, they argue that 'it behoves democracy watchers to recognise that the military's involvement in African politics requires a systematic approach towards instilling democratic values across all sectors of the society including the military'.

In Chapter 6, Osy Ezechukwunyere Nwebo and Charles Manga Fombad examine the role of the Pan-African Parliament (PAP) in the realisation of democratic governance in Africa. As an important AU organ, they argue that the PAP holds enormous potential within the regional governance landscape in fostering democracy leveraging on existing frameworks within the African system. They emphasise that 'despite its limited mandate, the PAP is not a mere talk shop'. Through its oversight powers, serving as a consultative and advisory mechanism, they explore viable strategies which PAP can utilise, drawing on initiatives that have also emerged from this regional institution.

In Chapter 7, Julie Lugulu draws a link between gender discriminatory laws and childhood statelessness. This chapter is set against the backdrop of statelessness, which is a concern in Africa, mostly hidden in view of the hidden nature of the situation. Reflecting on four African countries, namely Eswatini, Libya, Liberia and the Sudan, the chapter argues for the need to address the legal gaps to prevent childhood statelessness which may have far-reaching consequences.

In Chapter 8, Vandy Kanyako considers the relationship between the Economic Community of West African States (ECOWAS) and the Mano River Union (MRU). This chapter argues that while these groupings have been in existence for decades, the relationship between the two institutions has not been significantly explored. However, it is imperative that these institutions forge a significant relationship given the interrelatedness of their mandates and the fact that states within the MRU are also ECOWAS member states. While tracing the formation of these institutions and their relevance within the broader political agenda in West Africa, Kanyako argues that 'the protracted and transboundary nature of the challenges experienced in the region would require the concerted efforts of the leading political organisations in collaboration with other civil society stakeholders, both domestic and international, to enable West Africa live up to its expectations'.

In Chapter 9, Ady Namaran Coulibaly discusses the media and civil society as partners in transitional justice. Through a reflection on Côte d'Ivoire, she underscores the importance of this engagement between the media—as an effective platform for advancing narratives—and civil society—as key stakeholders in the furtherance of societal justice. She takes a qualitative approach to the narrative within the Ivorian context and overall, emphasises the need for an effective partnership between these pertinent actors in the furtherance of transitional justice processes.

In Chapter 10, Noel Twagiramungu considers the issue of justice in Rwanda post-1994. Considering the historical narrative of the genocide and the extent of transitional justice processes, he argues that advancing democratic legitimacy is integral to justice, reconciliation and transformation. He argues for a solution that that is cross-cutting, emphasising that 'the Rwandan context requires constitutional and legal arrangements that foster democracy while translating its values into a win–win form of political representation'.

In Chapter 11, Jake Okechukwu Effoduh examines the ECOWAS Court and its exposition on human rights through a consideration of three landmark cases. He significantly reflects on how activist forces have engaged the ECOWAS Court in the furtherance of human rights and consequently, the Court's progressive stance in the furtherance of human rights leveraging on the 1981 African Charter on Human and Peoples' Rights. The analysis in this chapter offers a significant insight into the pertinence of sub-regional courts in furthering the human rights landscape through progressive jurisprudence that holds the potential for continental reverberations.

In Chapter 12, Rhuks Temitope Ako and John Gbodi Ikubaje appraise developments within the African regional system in the furtherance of human rights. They reflect on the pertinence of mainstreaming human rights in regional governance, conflict prevention and post-conflict reconstruction. Tracing the evolution of the human rights narrative in Africa and consequent developments, they accentuate the role of the AU in mainstreaming human rights in programmatic engagements on the continent.

In Chapter 13, Gift Mwonzora examines the landscape on human rights protection in Zimbabwe over the last four decades beginning from the promise of a new era following independence in the 1980s. He argues that the enduring trend of human rights violation unveils the importance of developing measures for re-writing the future. In this regard, he emphasises that it is important for the state to 'improve state-society interactions (engagement of citizens with leadership) without the temptation of always deploying state power (force) in response to citizen disaffection'.

In Chapter 14, Mohamed Abdelaal considers how the Egyptian Supreme Constitutional Court has engaged in the advancement of human rights in Egypt. He demonstrates how the jurisprudence of the Court has moulded the landscape on issues at the fore of human rights challenges in Egypt, specifically, free exercise of religion, freedom of belief, freedom of protest and assembly, women's rights and minorities' rights. He emphasises that the jurisprudence of the Court 'has been extremely influential in the Arab region, not least, in terms of its approaches and methodologies in addressing the constitutionality of legislations, interpreting constitutional provisions and also securing fundamental rights and freedoms'.

In Chapter 15, Jimmy Kainja examines the state of media freedom in Malawi. He argues that while there are constitutional safeguards on freedom of expression including media freedom, there are laws that still impede on the exercise of these freedoms that need to be addressed. Moreover, he argues that it is important to address the social, political and economic dimensions of unfreedom.

In Chapter 16, Satang Nabaneh assesses the state of human rights and governance in the Gambia, reflecting on developments in the furtherance of human rights protection and the potential of the new democratic process in the state post-2016. She underscores the need for political commitment towards human rights standards, a strong judiciary and legal reforms in democratic consolidation. Moreover, she emphasises the fact that the 'government should ensure that laws and their interpretations are in conformity with regional and international standards'.

In Chapter 17, Emma Charlene Lubaale discusses the extent to which the psychological well-being of children in criminal proceedings is being ensured. This reflection is against the backdrop of the cardinality of the best interest principle. She makes the case that while children are interacting with courts in various capacities within the criminal justice system, it is integral to examine the extent to which country law and practice advance children's psychological well-being in such processes. She argues, among others, that there is a need for national legislation on child protection, making the salient point that 'ultimately, ensuring children's psychological well-being in criminal proceedings will rest heavily on states' preparedness to align their laws and practices with current international children's standards than the choice of justice tradition'.

In Chapter 18, Alexander Ezenagu reflects on taxation as a strategy for financing human rights, specifically children's rights in Africa. He makes the point that in addition to providing revenue, taxes can contribute to the furtherance of child protection. He underscores the fact that there is a need for knowledge on how taxation can enhance protection and also emphasises that there needs to be strengthened mechanisms of accountability to ensure that taxes are adequately utilised in the protection of children's rights in Africa. He reflects on policy options in strengthening tax regimes emphasising that issues that impede on its use such as illicit financial flows and base erosions need to be addressed.

In Chapter 19, Aderomola Adeola examines the protection of persons displaced by climate change through lens of the expanded definition of the OAU Convention Governing the Specific Aspects of Refugee Problems in Africa (1969). She argues that the flexibility of the expanded definition is a path for responding to question of protection of persons displaced across borders by climate change. Through the lens of the expanded definition, she argues for 'climate refugees' protection.

Bibliography

Adeola R. 2017. What the rest of Africa can learn from the Gambia's transition to democracy. *The Conversation* March 7.

Adeola R. 2019. Democratic governance and human rights protection in Nigeria from 1999–2019: Obasanjo, Yar'Adua, Jonathan and Buhari's Nigeria. In: Adeola R and Jegede AO (eds) Governance in Nigeria post-1999: revisiting the democratic 'new dawn' of the Fourth Republic. Pretoria University Law Press.

Ake C. 2000. The feasibility of democracy in Africa. Council for the Development of Social Science Research in Africa.

Cheeseman N. 2015. Democracy in Africa: successes, failures and the struggle for political reform. Cambridge University Press.

Cheeseman N, Lynch G, Willis J. 2017. Ghana: the ebbing power of incumbency. *Journal of Democracy*, 28 (2): 92–104.

D'Aiello. 2018. The case of the Gambia: a template for democratic transition? *Foreign Policy Research Institute* August 24.

Harding R. 2020. Rural democracy: elections and development in Africa. Oxford University Press.

Ibhawoh B. 2018. Human rights in Africa. Cambridge university Press.

Iwuji PC. 2007. Beyond Africa's democratic experiments. Author House.

Makinda SM. 1996. Democracy and multi-party politics in Africa. *The Journal of Modern African Studies*, 34 (4): 555–573.

Matolino B. 2018. Consensus as democracy in Africa. African Humanities Program Publications.

McGowan JP. 2003. African military coup d'état, 1956–2001: frequency, trends and distribution. *The Journal of Modern African Studies*, 41 (3): 339–370.

Murray R. 2004. Human rights in Africa: from the OAU to the African Union. Cambridge University Press.

Mutua WM. 2008. Human rights in Africa: the limited promise of liberalism. *African Studies Review*, 51 (1): 17–39.

Okafor OC. 2007. The African human rights system, activist forces and international institutions. Cambridge University Press.

Songwe V. 2014. Africa's democratic transition under construction: some lessons from Burkina Faso. *Brookings* November 6.

Southall R. 2003. Democracy in Africa: moving beyond a difficult legacy. Human Sciences Research Council.

Viljoen F. 2012. International human rights law in Africa. Oxford University Press.

Wanyande P. 1987. Democracy and the one-party state: the African experience. In: Oyugi WO (eds) Democratic theory and practice in Africa. East African Educational Publishers Ltd.

Wienkoop NK and Bertrand E. 2018. Popular resistance to authoritarian consolidation in Burkina Faso. *Carnegie Endowment for International Peace* May 16.

Zimba L. 1984. The origins and spread of one-party states in commonwealth Africa, their impact on personal liberties: a case study of the Zambian model. In: Ndulo M (eds) Law in Zambia, 113–141.

CHAPTER 2

Election Technology as a Means of Enhancing Democratic Legitimacy: A Case of Kenya

Marystella Simiyu

1 INTRODUCTION

There is a general consensus that free, fair and credible elections enhance democracy. However, the mere conduct of elections is not sufficient to achieve this goal. One has to examine how these elections are conducted and whether the process, in its totality, culminates in a genuine representation of the will of the people.

Some governments in Africa have suffered legitimacy crisis when the elections that put them in power were neither demonstrative of the will of the electorate, nor in line with international standards (Sakariyau et al. 2017, 136). In these systems that have been defined as electoral autocracies, elections are held to provide the façade of legitimacy. Authoritarian leaders would establish the necessary formal institutions known to liberal democracies that facilitate political representation but manipulate these systems to deliver flawed electoral wins in their favour (Levitsky and Way 2010; Schedler 2013). In such cases, even though elections are held, and opposition parties are allowed to participate, the ability of authoritarian leaders to fraudulently control the election outcomes negates the possibility of a free and fair process, representative of the will of the people.

M. Simiyu (✉)
Faculty of Law, Centre for Human Rights, University of Pretoria, Pretoria, South Africa
e-mail: mssimiyu@gmail.com

© The Author(s), under exclusive license to Springer Nature Switzerland AG 2022
A. Adeola and M. W. Mutua (eds.), *The Palgrave Handbook of Democracy, Governance and Justice in Africa,*
https://doi.org/10.1007/978-3-030-74014-6_2

Manual electoral systems were and still are highly susceptible to human interference, therefore enabling flawed electoral processes (Gelb and Diofasi 2016). The dissatisfaction of the polity with flawed elections is often expressed in post-election violence, protests, low voter turnout, opposition boycotts, and/or election petitions (Birch 2010). Perceptions of democratic legitimacy are further damaged when the state lacks strong systems of checks and balances that the public can rely on for accountability including an impartial and independent judiciary, electoral management body, free press, vibrant civil society, and competitive political parties (Cheibub et al. 1996).

In light of this, electoral assistance programmes have continuously invested in measures to support democratic elections in Africa including institution building, election technology and other fraud-reducing projects (Goodwin-Gill 2006, 5). African countries are increasingly adopting electronic based systems as one such strategy to address deficiencies of manual electoral systems (Osei-Afful 2019). Election technology provides a more permanent or feasibly long-lasting intervention to enhance the procedural fairness of the electoral process (Osei-Afful 2019).

The integration of technology into elections has been fronted as a way to improve the administration of elections and increase voter confidence because of its perceived levels of accuracy, verifiability and efficiency as compared to manual systems (Cheeseman et al. 2018, 1). Whether these measures have been effective in enhancing democratic legitimacy is largely dependent on the effectiveness of the implementation process and the performance of the government moving forward (Berman et al. 2014, 2–3). Election technology is likely to be more impactful in a country that respects human rights and the rule of law, and actively works towards entrenching democratic principles. (ECES 2019; Alvi, 2011, 135–136). In itself, election technology cannot cure the problems of a flawed electoral system, it is a complementary feature that interacts with various other factors in a democratic society to deliver free, fair and credible elections, including strong and accountable institutions that respect the rule of law (ECES 2019).

This chapter discusses the impact of election technology as a fraud-reducing and legitimacy-enhancing intervention with emphasis on the context in which a country adopts election technology. Kenya is the selected case study with a focus on the 2013 and 2017 elections that were held after the introduction of election technology in the electoral system.[1] In both cases, the failure of aspects of the election technology called into question whether the elections were indeed free and fair as was declared by the Election Management Body (EMB) and international elections observers. This aspect was widely discussed

---

[1] Take note that Kenya had two presidential elections in 2017, following the successful 2017 presidential election petition. However, this article only deals with the general elections and not the repeat presidential election, and the case instituted by Raila Odinga where the issue of election technology was discussed.

in the presidential election petitions that were instituted following these elections, which gives insight on judicial attitudes towards the role of election technology in facilitating credible elections. However, before this discussion, the next section conceptualises the ideation of legitimacy.

2   Conceptualising Legitimacy

Legitimacy is a complex concept that has been the subject of long-standing scholarly debates (Milliken and Krause 2002, 757). It can be defined as a voluntary public acceptance of government (Tyler 2006, 378; Kelman and Hamilton 1989, 6). This manifests in the recognition and acceptance of the political authority, and obedience of the rules and decisions made by this system (Levi and Sacks 2009, 312). It also connotes a belief that the 'source, procedures, goals, values, and performance' of a particular administration are proper (Beetham 2012, 107–116).

Beetham proposes a threefold structure of legitimacy including legality, political justification and consent (Beetham 1991, 3–6). On the principle of legality, he asserts that when political representatives acquire power through accepted norms, rules and procedures, they acquire the authority to exercise this power (Barker 1990, 62). The justification principle points to a 'moral congruency' between the society and state, in that, the actions of the political system conform to the shared societal ideas, values, principles and norms (Beetham 1991, 69). Finally, consent refers to the citizenry's recognition of the authority of that government and acceptance to be bound by the decisions it makes (Beetham 1991, 90).

A normative examination of democratic legitimacy directs one to a discussion of the quality of the consent (Held 2018). Studies have shown that people are more likely to consent to an administration that they believe acceded to power through a free, fair and credible process (Grimes 2006; Rothstein 2009; Rothstein and Teorell 2008; Prud'homme 1992; Taliercio 2004). Furthermore, when people feel that elections are fair, development is good and institutions are effective, their perceptions of democratic legitimacy are bolstered (Williams 1985; Levi and Sacks 2005; Moehler 2005). Critical aspects that impact the quality of consent include the respect for universal suffrage, transparent and fair political competition, meaningful public participation, and integrity of electoral rules and procedures (Diamond and Plattner 2006; Norris 2014; Przeworski 2009). In addition, there should be a strong system of checks and balances to avoid misuse of power within the different levels of government (Dhal 1971; Diamond 1999; Norris 1999, 2–3).

In assessing democratic legitimacy, there is a strong focus on the respect, promotion and fulfilment of human rights and the effectiveness of the institutions (Norris 2005, 2–3). Of key importance is the ability of a government to uphold the tenets of democracy through regular holding of free, fair and credible elections (Donnelly 2003, 43). The integration of election technology into the electoral process can serve as a crucial cog in the wheel in enhancing the quality of the electoral process and consequently the legitimacy of the administration.

3   International Legal Frameworks on Elections

Political rights are provided under Article 21 of the Universal Declaration of Human Rights 1948 (UDHR), and Article 25 of the International Covenant on Civil and Political Rights 1966 (ICCPR). Article 21 of the UDHR states:

1. Everyone has the right to take part in the government of his country, directly or through freely chosen representatives.
2. Everyone has the right to equal access to public service in his country.
3. The will of the people shall be the basis of the authority of government; this will shall be expressed in periodic and genuine elections which shall be by universal and equal suffrage and shall be held by secret vote or by equivalent free voting procedures.

The same spirit is reiterated under Article 25 of the ICCPR, which provides that every citizen has the right and opportunity:

1. To take part in the conduct of public affairs, directly or through freely chosen representatives;
2. To vote and to be elected at genuine periodic elections which shall be by universal and equal suffrage and shall be held by secret ballot, guaranteeing the free expression of the will of the electors;
3. To have access, on general terms of equality, to public service in his country.

In the African context, Article 3 of the Constitutive Act of the African Union provides for the objectives of the AU including the promotion of 'democratic principles and institutions, popular participation, and good governance' (AU Constitutive Act 2000, art 3(g)). Additionally, Article 4 of the AU's guiding principles includes the 'respect for democratic principles, human rights, the rule of law and good governance' (AU Constitutive Act 2000, art 4(m)). With particular reference to the electoral process, Article 4 of the OAU/AU Declaration on the Principles Governing Democratic Elections in Africa provides that in the exercise of these rights, democratic elections should be periodic and free and fair; based on constitutional and legislative frameworks; respecting separation of powers especially independence of the judiciary; and conducted by an impartial, diverse, competent, accountable and well-equipped election institution (OAU/AU Declaration on the Principles Governing Democratic Elections in Africa 2002).

These objectives and principles articulated in these documents are further elaborated by the African Charter on Democracy, Elections and Governance

(ACDEG) (2007). The main purpose of the ACDEG is to reinforce the commitment of AU member states to democracy, rule of law and respect for human rights (2010, 5). In particular, it recognises Africa's tainted political history of undemocratic transitions and explicitly obligates state parties to ensure constitutional rule and 'constitutional transfer of power' (ACDEG 2007, art 5).

The right of a citizen to freely participate in the government of his or her country is also provided in Article 13 of the ACHPR. While the right to vote has not been explicitly mentioned, this has been remedied in the ACDEG, which provides for the right to popular participation through universal suffrage, with no claw-back specifications (ACDEG 2007, art 4(2); Elvy 2013, 64).

State parties to the ACDEG commit to hold regular, transparent, free and fair elections. In achieving this obligation, state parties are required to establish and strengthen independent and impartial Election Management Bodies (EMBs), as well as avenues for redress of election related disputes. Further to this, states are required to ensure equitable access for political parties and candidates to the public broadcaster, and develop a code of conduct for political stakeholders that commits them to accept election results, in the event they are aggrieved, to use legally recognised channels to address their claims (ACDEG 2007, art 17).

Election technology is increasingly influencing the exercise of the right to vote—from the voter registration process, voter identification and verification, and results transmission. In some jurisdictions, the application of election technology has extended to the use of electronic voting machines for the actual voting as well as counting of the votes. In Africa, Namibia was the first country to use electronic voting machines in 2014 (European Parliamentary Research Service Blog, n.d.). In implementing election technologies, state parties to the ACDEG are bound to their commitment to ensure that the elections are 'transparent, free and fair' (ACDEG 2007, art 3(4)).

4   The Kenyan Experience: Did Election Technology Enhance Democratic Legitimacy in Kenya?

4.1   *Reasons for the Adoption of Election Technology in Kenya*

The use of manual electoral systems has historically been a source of electoral dissatisfaction and legitimacy crisis in Kenya with result announcements being preceded and/or followed by protests and violence (CIPEV 2008, 25). This was founded on suspicions of manipulation of votes often in the favour of the incumbent. Following the reintroduction of multiparty rule in 1992, Kenya arguably became an electoral autocracy due to the fact that the possibility of a win against the incumbent was negligible. This was not owing to massive popular support but rather through electoral manipulation.

Kenya's multiparty era was reluctantly ushered in by the despot President Daniel Toroitich Arap Moi following international and national pressure (Adar 2000, 103). Under the Kenya African National Union (KANU) party outfit, President Moi remained in power by undermining elections through skewed voter registration in favour of supporters of the establishment; state-sponsored ethnic clashes; subverting the independence of state institutions; gerrymandering, intimidation, harassment and arrest of dissenters including journalists; and misuse of state resources for electioneering (Adar 2000, 107–109; Commonwealth Observer Group 1993). Further, the establishment applied electoral fraud practices including ballot stuffing, voter bribery, double registration, open voting and importation of voters to ensure a win in favour of Moi (Adar 2000, 107–109). Given the complacency of the EMB in securing a win for the presidency by all costs, voters were increasingly apathetic to exercising their right to vote under the Moi regime. The lack of credible and accountable state institutions was replicated in bodies such as the judiciary, and the police, which failed to play their role in restoring the integrity of the process and public confidence (EU EOM 2008, 1–3).

The 2002 elections that brought to an end the 24 year rule of Daniel Arap Moi can arguably be seen as Kenya's most free and fair election since independence. This may have been influenced by the rallying of opposition as well as the public against the incumbent and the ruling party (KANU). This was further bolstered by the constitutional amendment passed in 1992 that ensured that President Moi could only serve for two terms (Commonwealth Observer Group 2006, 4–5).

Following the advent of multiparty rule in Kenya, the availability of one credible and verifiable register of voters was in serious doubt. Since the 1992 elections, data on voters was captured in manual registers referred to as 'black books' (IREC 2008, 78). Despite the digitisation of the voters roll and proscription of 'black books' in the 2002 elections, these unreliable manual registers resurfaced in the 2007 elections as a backup (IREC 2008, 78). One of the anomalies in the contentious 2007 elections that culminated in the post-election violence that saw the death of about 1300 people and the displacement of over 600,000 people was the circulation of several voters' registers with differing totals (InformAction, n.d.). Other challenges with the electoral roll included unexplained alterations in the number of voters in opposition strongholds, unsatisfactory deletion of dead voters and failure to update the register to reflect relocations (IREC 2008, 86). This was linked to suspicious voter turnouts with some polling stations recording 100% voter turnout (IREC 2008, 86).

In the aftermath of the 2007/2008 post-election violence that was instigated by public outcry against manipulation of the electoral process, the Independent Review Electoral Commission (IREC), popularly referred to as the Kriegler Commission, recommended the introduction of technology in Kenya's electoral system to enhance the accuracy of the register of voters, and improve timely vote counting, tallying and results transmission (IREC 2008,

138). Historically, delays in the release of results, which largely stemmed from poor communication linkages between polling stations, and constituency and national level tallying centres during transmission of results, often triggered suspicions of electoral manipulation, and public unrest (IRI 2008, 23; ECK 2002, 86; 2005, 30).

In view of this historical context, the 2010 constitution sought to address the challenges facing the voting system and democratic culture in Kenya. It has been hailed for its progressive bill of rights, measures to strengthen institutions of accountability, and introduction of devolution to enhance political representation and inclusive governance.[2] The constitution also aims at addressing the challenges that have plagued voting systems in Kenya by tasking the EMB to ensure that[3]:

a. whatever voting method is used, the system is simple, accurate, verifiable, secure, accountable and transparent;
b. the votes cast are counted, tabulated and the results announced promptly by the presiding officer at each polling station;
c. the results from the polling stations are openly and accurately collated and promptly announced by the returning officer; and
d. appropriate structures and mechanisms to eliminate electoral malpractice are put in place, including the safekeeping of election materials.

With the constitution and relevant laws and regulations as the guide, the rebranded EMB, the Independent Electoral and Boundaries Commission (IEBC) was tasked to roll out election technology in the 2013 elections in Kenya.

4.2   2013 Elections

Kenya first used election technology during the 2013 general elections in a bid to enhance electoral transparency and integrity as was recommended by the Kriegler Commission.[4] Of key concern was the credibility of the register of voters, proper identification of voters and effective results transmission.[5] This election cost the country $325 million of which $106.2 million was directed to biometric technology costs (Gelb and Diofasi 2016, 8).

An examination of the process reveals that poor preparation and implementation of the technology compromised the achievement of electoral transparency and integrity (EU EOM 2013, 45). The IEBC used biometric

---

[2] Muna Ndulo, 'Constitutions: The Politics of Constitutional Reform', in *Institutions and Democracy in Africa: How the Rules of the Game Shape Political Developments*, ed. Nic Cheesman (Cambridge: Cambridge University Press, 2018), 119.

[3] Article 86 Constitution of Kenya.

[4] EU EOM, *Kenya General Election 2013 Final Report* (Brussels: EU EOM, 2013) 12.

[5] IREC, *Report 2007*, 78.

technology for voter registration, voter verification and results transmission (ELOG 2013, 5). However, the implementation process was marred with irregularities. The IEBC was embroiled in scandal in the irregular procurement of the Biometric Voter Registration (BVR) kits (Ombati 2017). This delayed the arrival of the kits and limited the time for proper piloting, testing and reconfiguring of the technology not to mention training of staff, and voter education (Carter Centre 2013, 7; ELOG 2013, 10; EU EOM 2013, 12). Additionally, the scandal damaged public perceptions of IEBC's competency, transparency and integrity. The time crunch also marred the BVR process leading to disenfranchisement of about three million voters, especially marginalised communities, women and youth (EU EOM 2013, 1). The period for verification of the voters' register was reduced to two weeks, an inadequate time for such an important process (Carter Centre 2013, 7). The credibility of the roll was still in doubt with allegations of circulation of an illegal manual register rather than the principal register from the BVR (EU EOM 2013, 15). Additionally, it was asserted that the total number of voters in these registers differed (EU EOM 2013, 15).

Looking at voter turnout, the 2013 general elections recorded the highest voter turnout since the reintroduction of multiparty elections (ELOG 2013, 64). Recorded percentages for voter turnout since the 1992 general election are: 68% in 1992 (Wanyande 2006, 67–68), 65.4% in 1997 (IPU, n.d.), 57.2% in 2002 (EU EOM 2003, 31), 69% in 2007 (IRI 2008) and 85.9% in 2013 (ELOG 2013, 64). While the increased turnout cannot be exclusively attributed to election technology, it could be that the increased efficiency of election technology in enhancing the procedural fairness of the process and protecting the integrity of the vote was a strong motivating factor. Even the opposition and its supporters placed significant faith in the ability of the technology to curb election rigging (Cheeseman et al. 2018, 14; Lang'at 2016).

However, the failure of the election technology cast a dark shadow on the integrity of the process. Biometric verification kits broke down in 59.2% of the polling stations, and the results transmission worked in less than half of the polling stations necessitating a reversal to manual systems (ELOG 2013, 5 and 65; EU EOM 2013, 1–2). Despite election observers reporting that the failure of the election technology was one of the biggest challenges of the election, their conclusion was that generally the 2013 general election was credible (ELOG 2013; EU EOM 2013, 1; Carter Centre 2013, 10 and 103). However, this was not a universally shared opinion and for the first time a presidential election petition was instituted under the 2010 constitution challenging the credibility of the 2013 elections.

2013 Presidential Election Petition
Article 140 of the Constitution allows an aggrieved person to file a petition in the Supreme Court of Kenya (SCOK) challenging the election of the president-elect within seven days of the announcement of the election results.

Following the 4 March 2013 presidential election, the IEBC declared Uhuru Kenyatta as the winner of the election with 50.07% of all the votes cast. He was followed by Raila Odinga who received 43.31% of the valid votes (EU EOM 2013, 32). Following the announcement, three petitions were instituted in the SCOK challenging the results (*Raila Odinga & 5 others v IEBC & 3 others*, 2013). These petitions were consolidated into one petition. This chapter focuses on the case of the first, fifth and sixth petitioners who raised questions around the election technology in relation to the credibility of the voters' register, and the failure of the electronic system.

The main issues under determination were the validity of the election of the third and fourth respondents as 'president-elect and deputy president-elect respectively' and whether the elections were 'conducted in a free, fair, transparent and credible manner' as required by the Constitution and relevant laws (*Raila Odinga & 5 others v IEBC & 3 others*, 2013, para 20).

The burden of proof lay on the petitioners but depending on how effectively they discharged it, it shifted to the respondents (*Raila Odinga & 5 others v IEBC & 3 others*, 2013, para 203). The standard of proof was higher than the balance of probability, but lower than beyond reasonable doubt (*Raila Odinga & 5 others v IEBC & 3 others*, 2013, para 203).

Petitioners' Case

The petitioners asserted that the conduct of the general election substantially contradicted the Constitution, and relevant laws and regulations (*Raila Odinga & 5 others v IEBC & 3 others*, 2013, para 9; Constitution of Kenya 2010, arts 10, 81(e), 86, 88 and 138(3)(c); Election (General) Regulations, 2012, secs 59, 60, 61, 62, 74, 79 and 82). It was a key contention of the petitioners that the IEBC failed to deliver a 'simple, accurate, verifiable, secure, accountable and transparent' voting system as mandated by Article 86 of the Constitution. It was their assertion that the failure of the electronic system and IEBC's inability to meet the compulsory requirement to electronically transmit the results, compromised the credibility of the results (*Raila Odinga & 5 others v IEBC & 3 others*, 2013, para 12). This was provided by Section 39 of the Electoral Act and Regulation 82 of the Elections (General) Regulations, 2012. This infraction occasioned irregularities in voter verification and tallying (*Raila Odinga & 5 others v IEBC & 3 others*, 2013, para 135). Electronic results transmission was emphasised during this election because it had been introduced to seal loopholes in manual results transmission, which facilitated election rigging (EU EOM 2013, 1–2).

The voter identification and verification system deleted the name of a person who had voted therefore preventing multiple voting and providing an accurate tally of the persons who had voted (*Raila Odinga & 5 others v IEBC & 3 others*, 2013, para 109). The petitioners asserted that the reversion to manual systems due to failure of this system compromised the accuracy of vote counting (*Raila Odinga & 5 others v IEBC & 3 others*, 2013, para 108; Election (General) Regulations, 2012, sec 69).

Finally, the petitioners cast doubt on the credibility of the voter registration process, which delivered a principal voters' roll whose totals differed materially with the final number of registered voters (*Raila Odinga & 5 others v IEBC & 3 others*, 2013, para 19; Constitution of Kenya 2010, art 83; Election Act 2011, sec 3(2). They averred that there was more than one voters' register in circulation, and an illegal manual voters' roll (*Raila Odinga & 5 others v IEBC & 3 others*, 2013, para 44).

Respondents' Case

The respondents countered that the law allowed IEBC to deploy the technology it deemed appropriate (Elections Act 2011, sec 44; IEBC Act 2011, sec 4(m). It was therefore discretionary on its part whether to use electronic or manual systems or both (*Raila Odinga & 5 others v IEBC & 3 others*, 2013, paras 114–117). Additionally, verification entailed comparing the results from the polling station with those at the constituency tallying centre and national tallying centre, and not necessarily the information in the electronic system (Constitution of Kenya 2010, art 86(c).

The respondents also stated that the manual register (Green Book) and not the electronic register was the principal register. They explained that following auditing of the electronic voters' register, it was discovered that there were inconsistencies with the data in the Green Book (*Raila Odinga & 5 others v IEBC & 3 others*, 2013, para 73). This omission was attributed to the BVR kits and special provisions were made for these voters to prevent their disenfranchisement leading to differing totals (*Raila Odinga & 5 others v IEBC & 3 others*, 2013, para 73).

SCOK's Analysis

In its analysis, SCOK discussed the required standard for annulling election results. It made reference to Section 83 of the Election Act that reflected the common practice (*Morgan and others v. Simpson and another*, 1974, 722):

> No election shall be declared to be void by reason of non-compliance with any written law relating to that election if it appears that the election was conducted in accordance with the principles laid down in the Constitution and in that written law or that the noncompliance did not affect the result of that election.

SCOK recognised that a significant part of the petitioners' case,[6] was based on the failure of the electronic system, interruption of results transmission, and resultant effect on the transparency, security and accountability of the process (*Raila Odinga & 5 others v IEBC & 3 others*, 2013, paras 231–232).

In its unanimous judgement, the Court disagreed that a strict reading of the election laws and regulations revealed that the elections would only be conducted electronically (Elections Act 2011, sec 39; Election (General)

---

[6] Particularly, the 1st, 5th and 6th petitioner.

Regulations, 2012, secs 59, 60 and 82). Rather, it appeared that Kenya's voting system was manual but facilitated by technology (*Raila Odinga & 5 others v IEBC & 3 others*, 2013, para 131). The Court also acknowledged that technology was rarely perfect and given the problems experienced during voting, it was only lawful for IEBC to revert to manual systems (*Raila Odinga & 5 others v IEBC & 3 others*, 2013, paras 233 and 235). It however recognised the weakness in a manual backup framework and recommended reform (*Raila Odinga & 5 others v IEBC & 3 others*, 2013, para 236).

With regard to accuracy of the voters' register, it was SCOK's opinion that though the registration process had many irregularities they were not so substantial to compromise the credibility of the electoral process (*Raila Odinga & 5 others v IEBC & 3 others*, 2013, para 256). It concluded that the process was transparent, accurate and verifiable (*Raila Odinga & 5 others v IEBC & 3 others*, 2013, para 257).

Finally, in disputing the petitioners' contention that the inconsistent application of technology occasioned 'injustice or illegality in the conduct of election', SCOK stated:

> From case law, and from Kenya's electoral history, it is apparent that electronic technology has not provided perfect solutions. Such technology has been inherently undependable, and its adoption and application has been only incremental, over time. It is not surprising that the applicable law has entrusted a discretion to IEBC, on the application of such technology as may be found appropriate. Since such technology has not yet achieved a level of reliability, it cannot as yet be considered a permanent or irreversible foundation for the conduct of the electoral process.

4.3   2017 Elections

In 2017, IEBC was faced with the challenge of addressing the technological problems experienced in the 2013 general election, and avoiding another legitimacy crisis. In doing so, Kenya revamped the electronic system and introduced the Kenya Integrated Elections Management System (KIEMS). KIEMS had four components: BVR, Candidates Registration System (CRS), Electronic Voter Identification (EVID) and Results Transmission System (RTS) (IEBC, n.d.). In enhancing its electoral technology, Kenya's election budget increased to $499 million (Treasury, n.d.). With 19.6 million registered voters, this translated to $25.4 per voter, making it one of the most expensive elections worldwide (The East African 2017).

Procurement challenges revisited Kenya in 2017 during the acquisition of the new electoral technology, and the contentious tender for the supply of election materials (Ogemba 2017). The main concern was lack of competitive procurement and public participation. IEBC was faced with several legal

22   M. SIMIYU

challenges as a result that delayed the implementation and testing of the equipment further compromising its transparency (Carter Centre 2018, 21).

Admittedly, the BVR, and EVID functions of the electoral technology worked better compared to the 2013 general election but there were still critical challenges that the IEBC needed to correct (ELOG 2017, 128). Firstly, the credibility of the voters' register was still in contention (InformAction, n.d.). An audit by KPMG found glaring irregularities in the roll including registrants with invalid details, double registration, amendments to the register after the registration period; data errors, and over one million dead voters (KPMG 2017, 106). While some of these errors were addressed following the audit, IEBC still relied on electronic voter identification to weed out ghost voters (EU EOM 2018, 24). Given the fact that 96.2% of voters were identified biometrically, the biometric identification system may have helped reduce this problem (EU EOM 2018, 24). Additionally, the KIEMS system had notable safeguards against over voting (EU EOM 2018, 28). For example, the system rejected any results where the total number of votes exceeded the number of registered voters in a polling station (Mosoku 2017). Unfortunately, the system failed to exclude cases where the sum of valid votes and rejected votes exceeded the number of registered voters in a polling station (EU EOM 2018, 28).

Secondly, there were challenges in results transmission (EU EOM 2018, 28–29). IEBC was legally required to publish the results forms on an online database accessible to the public (Elections Act 2011, sec 39(IC)(c)). Upon announcement of the presidential election results, the public portal only had three-quarters of the results forms from polling stations (Carter Centre 2018, 27). These affected independent verification of the accuracy of the results (Carter Centre 2018, 27). Additionally, there were allegations of interference with the IEBC systems, which prompted the opposition to decry the accuracy of the results, declaring them as 'computer generated' (Nguta 2017). For a second consecutive election, Kenya was faced with another legitimacy crisis.

Interestingly, the voter turnout in the 2017 general election dropped from 85.9% to 77.5% in the 2017 general election (EU EOM 2018, 66). It is worth considering if this reduction was partly motivated by reduced confidence in the effectiveness of the election technology given its widespread failure in the 2013 elections.[7]

2017 Presidential Election Petition
Following the 8 August 2017 general election, SCOK was faced with another presidential election petition (*Raila Amolo Odinga & another v IEBC & 2*

---

[7] The repeat presidential elections following the successful presidential election petition suffered a significantly reduced voter turnout of 38.84%. This followed a call by Raila Odinga for his supporters to boycott the election. His call to boycott was motivated by the belief that the IEBC had a failed to implement the recommendations of the Supreme Court for electoral reform particularly in addressing the transparency challenges with the election technology. He felt that this system already significantly favoured the incumbent.

others 2017). This followed IEBC's announcement of the re-election of Uhuru Kenyatta, who was again followed by Raila Odinga (*Raila Amolo Odinga & another v IEBC & 2 others* 2017, para 5). The issues before SCOK were premised on whether the 2017 general election was conducted in accordance with the Constitution and relevant laws. Further, whether there were any irregularities, and if so to what extent they affected the credibility of the election (*Raila Amolo Odinga & another v IEBC & 2 others* 2017, para 125). The petitioners raised seven grounds to buttress their claim that the IEBC fundamentally mismanaged the elections in violation of principles of free, fair and credible elections, and the dictates of the Constitution, and relevant laws and regulations (Constitution of Kenya 2010, arts 1, 2, 4, 10, 38, 81, 82, 86, 88, 138, 140, 163 and 249; Elections Act 2011; *Raila Amolo Odinga & another v IEBC & 2 others* 2017, para 14). The discussion below focuses on the effect of failure in the process of relaying and transmitting results electronically.

The burden and standard of proof in this case remained as that in the 2013 presidential election petition (*Raila Amolo Odinga & another v IEBC & 2 others* 2017, para 133).

Petitioners' Case

Generally, the petitioners asserted that the election was marred with irregularities and illegalities that substantially affected its integrity and called for SCOK to annul it (*Raila Amolo Odinga & another v IEBC & 2 others* 2017, paras 18 and 31). They accused IEBC of delivering 'preconceived and predetermined computer generated leaders' who were not a reflection of the will of the people (*Raila Amolo Odinga & another v IEBC & 2 others* 2017, para 17).

To ensure that the voting system met the constitutional requirement under Article 86 of the Constitution and ensure that manipulation is avoided, Section 39(c) of the Election Act was amended. The new section provided for simultaneous electronic transmission of results from the polling stations to the constituency and national tallying centres immediately following tabulation (*Raila Amolo Odinga & another v IEBC & 2 others* 2017, para 24). The petitioners asserted that there was inordinate delay in the transmission of results and even nine days after the election, IEBC admitted to not having all the results from the polling stations and constituencies (*Raila Amolo Odinga & another v IEBC & 2 others* 2017, para 24). They also criticised the IEBC for hosting the KIEMS primary and backup systems abroad therefore compromising its security and negligently exposing it to 'interference and manipulation of results' (*Raila Amolo Odinga & another v IEBC & 2 others* 2017, para 24).

The petitioners also asserted that the 'IEBC failed to electronically collate, tally and transmit the results', and declare them per county therefore concretising the final results at the polling station level (*Raila Amolo Odinga & another v IEBC & 2 others* 2017, para 27). This contradicted the Court of Appeal decision in *IEBC v Maina Kiai & 5 others* (2017) (Maina Kiai case).

Further, the petitioners pointed to inconsistencies between the figures in polling station results forms and constituency results forms contained in the IEBC portal and the physical forms (*Raila Amolo Odinga & another v IEBC & 2 others* 2017, para 26). It was their conclusion that this showed a compromised electronic transmission system (*Raila Amolo Odinga & another v IEBC & 2 others* 2017, para 29). They also directed the Court to the suspicious and constant 11% gap between the results of the first petitioner and the third respondent (*Raila Amolo Odinga & another v IEBC & 2 others* 2017, para 36).

SCOK's attention was also drawn to a notice published by the IEBC prior to Election Day. The notice identified 11 155 out of 40 883 polling stations lacking 3G and 4G network coverage (*Raila Amolo Odinga & another v IEBC & 2 others* 2017, para 221). Presiding officers were therefore required to move with the devices to a place with network or to the constituency tallying centre to send the results in the KIEMS kit (*Raila Amolo Odinga & another v IEBC & 2 others* 2017, paras 43 and 59). The petitioners stated that this notification was delayed in violation of regulations 21, 22 and 23 of the Elections (Technology) Regulations 2017. It should have been done 45 days prior to the elections (*Raila Amolo Odinga & another v IEBC & 2 others* 2017, para 43). Additionally, the figures in the notice of polling stations outside 3G and 4G network coverage contradicted those by the Communications Authority of Kenya (CAK) (*Raila Amolo Odinga & another v IEBC & 2 others* 2017, para 43).

Respondents' Case
The respondents contested the claim that there was need for simultaneous relaying of results from polling centres to the constituency and national level (*Raila Amolo Odinga & another v IEBC & 2 others* 2017, para 57). They stated that according to Section 44A of the Elections Act, the IEBC had the discretion to use a complementary mechanism where technology either fails or is unable to meet the constitutional threshold of a free, fair and credible election (*Raila Amolo Odinga & another v IEBC & 2 others* 2017, para 60).

The respondents also insisted that the data in the KIEMS kit had no legal status and had to be verified by manual constituency and national results forms (*Raila Amolo Odinga & another v IEBC & 2 others* 2017, para 61). They blamed inconsistencies between the information in the KIEMS kit and the physical forms on human error (*Raila Amolo Odinga & another v IEBC & 2 others* 2017, para 62). Finally, they contended that if indeed there were flaws in the electronic transmission of results, they cannot lead to an annulment given the large margin of votes between the candidates (*Raila Amolo Odinga & another v IEBC & 2 others* 2017, paras 223 and 245).

SCOK's Analysis
The majority judgement of the Court underscored one aspect that the respondents consistently ignored. This was the fact that an election was a process

and not an event, and it was made up of various facets including registration of voters, nomination of candidates, voting, counting and tallying of votes, and finally declaration (*Raila Amolo Odinga & another v IEBC & 2 others* 2017, paras 224–226). Therefore, when determining whether an election was free and fair, a judicial body has to examine the whole process (*Raila Amolo Odinga & another v IEBC & 2 others* 2017, para 226).

Reference was made to the *Maina Kiai* case on the finality of polling station results as 'the true locus for the free exercise of the voter's will' (*Raila Amolo Odinga & another v IEBC & 2 others* 2017, para 263). Based on this, the first and second respondents should not have declared the election results without reference to all the polling station results (*Raila Amolo Odinga & another v IEBC & 2 others* 2017, paras 265 and 266).

Evidence showed that on Election Day, the polling centres outside 3G and 4G network transmitted their results manually because the IEBC claimed it was unable to deliver these results electronically. This occasioned the delay in the announcement of the results from these areas (*Raila Amolo Odinga & another v IEBC & 2 others* 2017, para 268). The Court dismissed the IEBC's explanation of failure in technology given it had engaged three internet service providers to ensure there would be no challenges in electronic transmission (*Raila Amolo Odinga & another v IEBC & 2 others* 2017, paras 270 and 272). Even if the presiding officers had to reposition themselves, the delay would just have been a few hours (*Raila Amolo Odinga & another v IEBC & 2 others* 2017, para 272).

Regrettably, IEBC failed to fully comply with an interim court order to provide all the scanned results forms for polling stations and constituency tallying centres to the petitioners for verification, and allow access to its servers and logs (*Raila Amolo Odinga & another v IEBC & 2 others* 2017, para 267). IEBC justified this infraction by stating that allowing access to their servers and logs would pose a security risk to the data therein. It was the Court's view that considering the investment from taxpayers' pockets, IEBC should have invested in an extensive backup system (*Raila Amolo Odinga & another v IEBC & 2 others* 2017, para 277). With this refusal of access, the allegations of hacking and manipulation of presidential election results were neither proved nor disproved (*Raila Amolo Odinga & another v IEBC & 2 others* 2017, para 279). IEBC's contempt of court led to the inference that its IT system was infiltrated and compromised, and the data therein interfered with or internally manipulated (*Raila Amolo Odinga & another v IEBC & 2 others* 2017, para 280). Therefore, the transmission was inconsistent with Section 39(1C) of the Elections Act, and Articles 81 and 86 of the Constitution (*Raila Amolo Odinga & another v IEBC & 2 others* 2017, para 282).

Further, the majority held that simultaneous electronic transmission from the polling station to the constituency tallying centre and finally to the national tallying centre was not only important for verification but also a means of preventing electoral fraud by 'eliminating human intervention' (*Raila Amolo Odinga & another v IEBC & 2 others* 2017, para 288). SCOK also stated that any complementary system should comply with the dictates of Article 86 of the Constitution, which in this case, it failed to do (*Raila Amolo Odinga & another v IEBC & 2 others* 2017, paras 297 and 298). The SCOK disagreed that the conduct of the election fell under the category of 'minor inadvertent errors' as alleged by the respondents (*Raila Amolo Odinga & another v IEBC & 2 others* 2017, para 299).

In considering this particular ground and other anomalies witnessed during the election, SCOK found that the 2017 general election was not conducted in accordance with the principles of the Constitution and relevant laws and was 'neither transparent nor verifiable' and therefore nullified it (*Raila Amolo Odinga & another v IEBC & 2 others* 2017, para 303). The 4 to 2 majority judgement found that the illegalities and irregularities were of such a substantial nature that they could not be seen as the expression of the free will of the people (*Raila Amolo Odinga & another v IEBC & 2 others* 2017, para 379).

In reference to the technological aspect that was so painstakingly canvassed, the majority judgement stated (*Raila Amolo Odinga & another v IEBC & 2 others* 2017, para 400):

> Have we in executing our mandate lowered the threshold for proof in presidential elections? Have we made it easy to overturn the popular will of the people? We do not think so. No election is perfect and technology is not perfect either. However, where there is a context in which the two Houses of Parliament jointly prepare a technological roadmap for conduct of elections and insert a clear and simple technological process in Section 39(1C) of the Elections Act, with the sole aim of ensuring a verifiable transmission and declaration of results system, how can this Court close its eyes to an obvious near total negation of that transparent system?

The SCOK took a bold step in annulling the 2017 presidential election results based on the established illegalities and irregularities. In 2013, the SCOK appreciated the fact that the election technology was still struggling to take root in Kenya's electoral system. Exigencies of the situation in 2013 justified a reversion to manual backup systems upon failure of the technology. This was not an illegal decision on the part of the IEBC. However, in 2017 it was expected that IEBC had put in place proper reforms to prevent a repeat of failure of election technology as experienced in 2013. Certainly, parliament had played its role in amending the law, which was clear on the application of election technology.

The majority judgement of the SCOK took a purposive interpretation to the law underscoring that the legislation provided for election technology to improve the credibility and transparency of the electoral process. This was essential in restoring public trust in the integrity of the process. How it had been implemented did not fulfil these objectives. SCOK faulted IEBC for flouting laws and regulations that provided it with direction on the implementation of election technology purchased on taxpayers' dime. By this judgement, SCOK raised the standard by which the EMB administers elections. Additionally, the contempt in failing to follow Court orders and avail critical evidence was a poor move on the part of IEBC.

5   AN ANALYSIS OF THE KENYAN EXPERIENCE

Kenya introduced election technology to improve election administration and reduce electoral fraud. On the face of it, the election technology helped manage the complexity of the election process especially, voter registration (EU EOM 2018, 24). Even with reported challenges with the election technology, international election observers still concluded that the elections were credible in both the 2013 and 2017 elections (Carter Centre 2013, 103). However, courts received election petitions, including a presidential election petition challenging the results of the elections where questions around the efficiency and effectiveness of the technology and its impact on the final results featured prominently. This led to the annulment of the presidential elections following the 2017 presidential election petition. This was unprecedented in Africa.[8]

The lack of a credible register of voters was of particular concern in Kenya's electoral history and a source of electoral malpractice. To some extent, the BVR improved the accuracy of the voters register but there were still reported inaccuracies especially with regard to existing data on dead voters (KPMG 2017). In 2017, Kenya was able to ameliorate these challenges with its electronic voter identification system that ensured that a significant majority of voters underwent electronic identification (EU EOM 2018, 24). Additionally, the system safeguards in the KIEMS prevented cases of over voting by automatically rejecting votes that exceeded the number of registered voters (Mosoku 2017). This was a laudable aspect of the technology that can be adopted by other countries with further enhancements to reject results where the sum of valid votes and the rejected votes exceed the number of registered voters of a particular voting station.

Election technology is vulnerable to new kinds of digital election fraud. Malicious external and even internal parties may infiltrate the system to manipulate the election results and undermine the election process (Testimony of Daniel Twining 2018, 4). Strong security and backup measures should be in place to prevent external interference and self-serving domestic interests from manipulating election results and undermining the process (Catt 2014, 268). While concerns around hacking of the election technology were raised during the 2017 presidential election petition, this issue was not effectively dealt with

---

[8] It should be noted that there were reported incidences of electoral violence both before and after the elections particularly during the 2017 election. Protests from pro-opposition supporters in many cases were met with harsh state response. K. Tamura, 'Kenya Supreme Court Nullifies Presidential Election', *New York Times*, 1 September 2017, https://www.nytimes.com/2017/09/01/world/africa/kenya-election-kenyatta-odinga.html (accessed 22 April 2020).

in the petition beyond calling into question the suspicious, unwavering 11% gap between the votes of Uhuru Kenyatta and Raila Odinga, which defied the thumb rule of statistics. While IEBC's failure to provide access to their servers and logs undoubtedly inhibited a comprehensive examination of this claim, it is also uncertain whether the applicants had the requisite technical expertise to extrapolate the information and present it in an understandable way to the court as evidence. Moving forward, there is need for political stakeholders to harness their capacities in the presentation of technical evidence on the performance of election technology and implications of technical hitches on the credibility of the process.

After the 2017 election, Kenya held a rating of 43 in the Perceptions of Election Integrity (PEI) index, which was described as low (Norris et al. 2018, 11). In the electoral aspects that touched on technology such as voter registration, voting process and results, Kenya scored 35, 48 and 38 respectively, which still falls under the 'low' category. This was a decline from 2013 where Kenya held a 53 rating on the PEI index, which counts as moderate (Norris et al. 2018, 37). It scored poorly in voter registration and voting process with a rating of 34 and 47, but received a moderate rating of 64 for the results (Norris et al. 2018, 16).

This rating is concerning in the sense that it calls into question the impact of the hefty investment in election technology given that Kenya's rating dropped in the very aspects that the technology was meant to enhance. It is worth considering whether this was as a result of the technology in itself or the institutions responsible for its administration. This emphasises the need to examine the entirety of the elections as a process and hold to account the quality of the different aspects of this process including the integrity and accountability of relevant stakeholders to ensure the transparency and fairness of the process. Additionally, it shows the importance of the context in which election technology is adopted. Therefore, Kenya still needs to reform these areas of its electoral process to fully benefit from election technology.

Kenya had the worst score in the category of election campaign finance in the PEI index at 23 (Norris et al. 2018, 36–38). This illustrates the limitations of election technology in the problems it can solve and those it cannot solve. Other than unchecked campaign financing, it is also not the solution for voter bribery, poor participation of vulnerable groups, misuse of state resources and partisan media (DPI 2011, 3).

As discussed in the beginning of this chapter, the respect, protection and promotion of civil liberties are essential to democratic legitimacy. This is enhanced in the procedural fairness of democratic procedures, such as elections, and the effectiveness of the institutions involved. Given the far-reaching impact of election technology in Kenya's electoral process, including voter registration, voter identification and results transmission, the protection of the integrity of this process is critical to maintaining public confidence that the final vote is indeed the true vote establishing a legitimate government. This resonates profoundly with SCOK's emphasis that an election is a process and not an event. Therefore, procedural fairness should be evident throughout the whole process.

The EMB is a crucial institution in this effect and its conduct should be unimpeachable. The IEBC failed in this regard in the 2017 elections more so than the 2013 elections. The conduct of the 2017 election fundamentally tainted the quality of consent of the electorate and made light of the established norms, rules and procedures. Therefore, in no manner could the government claim legitimacy, necessitating a repeat election.[9] There was also lack of political will in Kenya to harness the advantages of election technology in order to deliver a free, fair and credible process, and enhance democratic legitimacy.

That being said a regression back to a manual electoral system is not the answer given its colossal failure in the past. There is need for stakeholders to relentlessly work towards entrenching a democratic culture in Kenya, particularly in its institutions. However, institutions are made up of people. It is important to ensure that the people in these public positions uphold the principles of integrity in public service. Vetting processes for candidates should be rigorous and include relevant stakeholders. Further, corrupt individuals who seek to disrupt the process should be duly prosecuted, and held accountable.

It also emerged that effective infrastructure is essential to sustaining the performance of election technology. This is closely linked with the need for government to bridge the digital divide and ensure effective access to internet especially in rural areas. Further, government with the support of telecommunications service providers can invest in a Universal Service Access Fund to improve communication and internet networks in rural areas. This is to prevent technical hitches stemming from lack of proper infrastructure.

Finally, towards further entrenching a democratic culture, stakeholders including the EMB and CSOs should effect rigorous voter and democratic education to ensure that the public meaningfully participates in the process, and speak truth to power in the event the quality of their consent is being watered down.

6   CONCLUSION

The evolving influence of technology in elections is a reality in today's democratic scene. Countries therefore that have the state capacity, and political will to capitalise on the benefits of election technology to deliver free and fair elections can reap its optimum benefits. However, as seen in Kenya, it is unlikely that election technology will have a significant impact on the credibility of

---

[9] The 2017 repeat presidential election is not discussed in this article. The repeat presidential election was contested in the Supreme Court largely on the basis that the political environment was not favorable for an election leading to the compromise of the right to universal suffrage. This was because elections did not take place in at least 25 constituencies owing to electoral violence. Election technology was not a key topic in this election petition.

elections and enhance democratic legitimacy if the democratic tenets of the society are encumbered. In itself, election technology is a tool to a particular end, that is, free, fair and credible elections, and it interacts with other facets that are crucial in a democracy to achieve this result.

Overall, should Kenya properly implement electoral technology, then the intended goals of improved integrity and transparency of the process and enhanced democratic legitimacy will likely be realised. Some of the challenges were not caused by technical issues. Poor management of the process by the IEBC also contributed to the malfunction or failure of the technology. Kenya also needs to reform its procurement processes and address integrity and credibility concerns. Unscrupulous individuals who interfere with the process should be prosecuted or otherwise held to account. Additionally, political machinations should not be allowed to compromise expensive electronic investments, and advance fraud.

The courts have played their role in interpreting the law. In 2013, SCOK acknowledged the nascent nature of the technology noting that its reliability was still unsustainable. In 2017, however, the majority judgement acknowledged the increasing significance of election technology in Kenya's elections and called on stakeholders to fulfil the constitutional and statutory requirements in this respect. This shift in judicial attitude from 2013 to 2017 shows a growing appreciation for the impact of technology in facilitating free, fair and credible elections. Elections are the heartbeat of a democracy because it is the vehicle by which the will of the people is expressed, and consequently a source of democratic legitimacy. Therefore, election technology should be seen as an important means of sustaining and strengthening this rhythm.

BIBLIOGRAPHY

Adar, Korwa G. "Assessing Democratisation Trends in Kenya: A Post-mortem of the Moi Regime." *Commonwealth & Comparative Politics* 38, no. 3 (2000): 103–30. https://doi.org/10.1080/14662040008447828.

Alvi, Shahid. "Proceed with Caution: Technology Fetishism and the Millennial Generation." *Interactive Technology and Smart Education* 8, no. 2 (2011): 135–44. https://doi.org/10.1108/17415651111141849.

AU. "African Charter on Democracy, Elections and Governance." African Charter on Democracy, Elections and Governance | African Union, September 11, 2019. https://au.int/en/treaties/african-charter-democracy-elections-and-governance.

AU. "African Charter on Democracy, Elections and Governance." Accessed June 17, 2022. https://au.int/sites/default/files/treaties/36384-treatyafrican- charter-on-democracy-and-governance.pdf.

Barker, Rodney S. *Political Legitimacy and the State.* Oxford: Clarendon Press, 1990.

Beetham, David. *The Legitimation of Power.* Houndmills, Basingstoke, Hampshire: Palgrave Macmillan, 1991.

Beetham, David. "Political Legitimacy." In *The Wiley Blackwell Companion to Political Sociology*, 107–16. Chichester: Wiley, 2012.

Berman, Eli, Michael J. Callen, Clark Gibson, and James D. Long. "Election Fairness and Government Legitimacy in Afghanistan." *Election Fairness and Government Legitimacy in Afghanistan*. NBER, 2014.

Birch, Sarah. "Perceptions of Electoral Fairness and Voter Turnout." *Comparative Political Studies* 43, no. 12 (August 2010): 1601–22. https://doi.org/10.1177/0010414010374021.

Carter Centre. "Observing Kenya's March 2013 National Elections Final Report." Observing Kenya's March 2013 National Elections Final Report. Atlanta: Carter Centre, 2013.

Carter Centre. "Kenya 2017 General and Presidential Elections." Kenya 2017 General and Presidential Elections. Atlanta: Carter Centre, 2018.

Catt, Helena. *Electoral Management Design*. Stockholm: International Institute for Democracy and Electoral Assistance (International IDEA), 2014.

Cheeseman, Nic, Gabrielle Lynch, and Justin Willis. "Digital Dilemmas: The Unintended Consequences of Election Technology." *Democratization* 25, no. 8 (June 8, 2018): 1397–1418. https://doi.org/10.1080/13510347.2018.1470165.

Cheibub, Jose Antonio, Adam Przeworski, Fernando Papaterra Limongi Neto, and Michael M. Alvarez. "What Makes Democracies Endure?" *Journal of Democracy* 7, no. 1 (1996): 39–55. https://doi.org/10.1353/jod.1996.0016.

CIPEV. *Final Report*. Nairobi: GOK, 2008.

Commonwealth Observer Group. "The Presidential, Parliamentary and Civic Elections in Kenya, 1992." *The Presidential, Parliamentary and Civic Elections in Kenya, 1992*. London: Commonwealth Observer Group, 1993.

Commonwealth Observer Group. *Kenya General Election 27 December 2002 The Report of the Commonwealth Observer Group*. London: Commonwealth Secretariat, 2006.

Daniel Twining's testimony. Committee on Foreign Affairs. "Democracy promotion in a challenging world". June 14, 2018 12–14. Accessed 17 June 2022. https://www.govinfo.gov/content/pkg/CHRG-115hhrg30423/pdf/CHRG-115hhrg30423.pdf.

Dhal, Robert. *Polyarchy: Participation and Opposition*. New Haven: Yale University Press, 1971.

Diamond, Larry Jay. *Developing Democracy Toward Consolidation*. Baltimore: Johns Hopkins University Press, 1999.

Diamond, Larry Jay, and Marc F. Plattner. *Electoral Systems and Democracy*. Baltimore: John Hopkins University Press, 2006.

Donnelly, Jack. *Universal Human Rights in Theory and Practice*. New York: Cornell University Press, 2003.

DPI. *Electronic Voting Machines: The Promise and Perils of New Technology*. Vol. 11, 2011.

ECES. "Opportunities and Challenges in the Use of Technology in Elections." ECES. Accessed May 17, 2019. http://www.eces.eu/template/Opportunities%20and%20challenges%20in%20the%20use%20of%20technology%20in%20Elections.pdf.

ECK. "ECK Evaluation of the 2005 Referendum." *ECK Evaluation of the 2005 Referendum*. Nairobi: ECK, 2005.

ELOG. "The Historic Vote: Elections 2013." *The Historic Vote: Elections 2013*. Nairobi: ELOG, 2013.

ELOG. "One Country, Two Elections, Many Voices! The Kenya 2017 General Elections and the Historic Fresh Presidential Election." *One Country, Two Elections,*

Many Voices! The Kenya 2017 General Elections and the Historic Fresh Presidential Election. Nairobi: ELOG, 2017.

Elvy, Stacy-Ann. "Towards a New Democratic Africa: The African Charter on Democracy, Elections and Governance." *Emory International Law Review* 27, no. 1 (July 2013). https://doi.org/10.2139/ssrn.2292733.

EU EOM. "Final Report Kenya General Elections 27 December 2002." *Final Report Kenya General Elections 27 December 2002.* Brussels: EU EOM, 2003.

EU EOM. "Kenya Final Report General Elections 27 December 2007." *Kenya Final Report General Elections 27 December 2007.* Brussels: EU EOM, 2008.

EU EOM. "Kenya General Election 2013 Final Report." *Kenya General Election 2013 Final Report.* Brussels: EU EOM, 2013.

EU EOM. "Final Report Republic of Kenya General Elections 2017." *Final Report Republic of Kenya General Elections 2017.* Brussels: EU EOM, 2018.

Gelb, Alan, and Anna Diofasi. *Biometric Elections in Poor Countries: Wasteful or A Worthwhile Investment?* Vol. 435. Wiley, 2016.

Geoffrey Mosoku. "IEBC Delivers another Blow to Vote Riggers." *The Standard*, August 3, 2017, Accessed May 20, 2019. https://www.standardmedia.co.ke/article/2001250145/iebc-delivers-another-blow-to-voteriggers.

Goodwin-Gill, Guy S. *Free and Fair Elections: International Law and Practice.* Geneva: Inter-Parliamentary Union, 2006.

Grimes, Marcia. "Organizing Consent: The Role of Procedural Fairness in Political Trust and Compliance." *European Journal of Political Research* 45, no. 2 (April 2006): 285–315. https://doi.org/10.1111/j.1475-6765.2006.00299.x.

Grömping, Max, and Ferran M. Coma. *Election Integrity in Africa.* Sydney: University of Sydney, 2015.

Held, David. *Models of Democracy.* Cambridge, UK: Polity, 2018.

IEBC. "KIEMS." IEBC. Accessed May 19, 2019. https://www.iebc.or.ke/election/technology/?KieMS.

InformAction. "Election Watch: Report 6." InformAction. Accessed May 18, 2019. http://informaction.tv/index.php/election-news/item/649-election-watch-report-6.

IPU. "Kenya Parliamentary Chamber: Bunge— National Assembly." Accessed May 17, 2019. http://archive.ipu.org/parline-e/reports/arc/2167_97.htm.

IREC. "Report on the General Elections Held in Kenya on 27 December 2007." *Report on the General Elections Held in Kenya on 27 December 2007.* Nairobi: IREC, 2008.

IRI. "Kenya Presidential, Parliamentary and Local Elections December 27, 2007 Election Observation Mission Final Report." *Kenya Presidential, Parliamentary and Local Elections December 27, 2007 Election Observation Mission Final Report.* Washington: IRI, 2008.

Kelman, Herbert C., and Lee V. Hamilton. *Crimes of Obedience: Toward a Social Psychology of Authority and Responsibility.* New Haven, CT: Yale University Press, 1989.

KPMG. "IEBC Independent Audit of the Register of Voters." *IEBC Independent Audit of the Register of Voters.* Nairobi: KPMG, 2017.

Lang'at, Patrick. "The CORD-Jubilee Divide." *Daily Nation*, December 21, 2016. https://www.nation.co.ke/news/politics/the-cord-and-jubilee-divide/1064-3494410-12m43ey/index.html.

Levi, Margaret and Audrey Sacks. "Achieving Good Government—and, Maybe, Legitimacy." *New Frontiers of Social Policy*, December 2005.

Levi, Margaret, and Audrey Sacks. "Legitimating Beliefs: Sources and Indicators." *Regulation & Governance* 3, no. 4 (2009): 311–33. https://doi.org/10.1111/j.1748-5991.2009.01066.x.

Levitsky, Stephen, and Lucas A. Way. *Competitive Authoritarianism: Hybrid Regimes After the Cold War (Problems of International Politics)*. Cambridge: Cambridge University Press, 2010.

Members' Research Service. "Digital Technology in Elections: Efficiency Versus Credibility?" European Parliamentary Research Service Blog, September 12, 2018. https://epthinktank.eu/2018/09/12/digital-technology-in-elections-efficiency-versus-credibility/.

Milliken, Jennifer, and Keith Krause. "State Failure, State Collapse, and State Reconstruction: Concepts, Lessons and Strategies." *Development and Change* 33, no. 5 (December 2002): 753–74. https://doi.org/10.1111/1467-7660.t01-1-00247.

Moehler, Devra. "Free and Fair, or Fraudulent and Forged: Elections and Legitimacy in Africa?" *Afrobarometer* 55 (2005).

Ndulo, Muna. "Constitutions: The Politics of Constitutional Reform." In *Institutions and Democracy in Africa How the Rules of the Game Shape Political Developments*, edited by Nic Cheeseman. Cambridge: Cambridge University Press, 2018.

Nguta, Judy. "We Will Not Accept Computer-Generated Leaders, Raila Says as NASA Opts to Go to Court." *The Standard*, August 16, 2017. https://www.standardmedia.co.ke/article/2001251594/we-will-not-accept computer-generated-leaders-raila-says-as-nasa-opts-to-go-to-court.

Norris, Pippa. *Critical Citizens: Global Support for Democratic Government*. OUP Oxford, 1999.

Norris, Pippa. *Critical Citizens: Global Support for Democratic Government*. New York: Oxford University Press, 2005.

Norris, Pippa. *Why Electoral Integrity Matters*. New York: Cambridge Univ. Press, 2014.

Norris, Pippa, Sarah Camero, and Thomas Wynter. *Corruption and Coercion: The Year in Elections 2017*. Sydney: University of Syndney, 2018.

OAU/AU, "Declaration on the Principles Governing Democratic Elections in Africa." Accessed June 17, 2022. https://archives.au.int/bitstream/handle/123456789/572/AHG%20Decl%201%20%28XXXVIII%29%20_E.pdf?sequence=1&isAllowed=y.

Ogemba, Paul. "Courts, Procurement Board Scrutinise IEBC Blunder." *The Standard*, May 31, 2017. https://www.standardmedia.co.ke/article/2001241669/courts-procurement-board-scrutinise-iebc-avoid-blunders.

Ombati, Cyrus. "Chickengate Scandal Suspects James Oswago and Trevy Oyombra Arrested, to Appear in Court." *The Standard*, February 8, 2017. https://www.standardmedia.co.ke/article/2001228648/chicken-gate-scandal-suspects-james-oswago-and-trevy-oyombra-arrested-to-appear-in-court.

Osei-Afful, Rhoda. "Solutions or Problems? The Increasing Role of Technology in African Elections." Africa Up Close. Accessed May 13, 2019. https://africaupclose.wilsoncenter.org/solutions-or-problems-the-increasing-role-of-technology-in-african-elections/.

Permanent Forum of Arab-African Dialogue on Democracy and Human Rights. *The African Charter on Democracy, Elections and Governance: The Role of NHRIs*. Paris: UNESCO, 2010.

Prud'homme, R. "Informal Local Taxation in Developing Countries." *Environment and Planning C: Government and Policy* 10, no. 1 (February 1992): 1–17. https://doi.org/10.1068/c100001.

Przeworski, Adam. "Constraints and Choices." *Comparative Political Studies* 42, no. 1 (July 2009): 4–30. https://doi.org/10.1177/0010414008324991.

Rothstein, Bo. "Creating Political Legitimacy." *American Behavioral Scientist* 53, no. 3 (December 2009): 311–30. https://doi.org/10.1177/0002764209338795

Rothstein, Bo, and Jan Teorell. "What Is Quality of Government? A Theory of Impartial Government Institutions." *Governance* 21, no. 2 (April 2008): 165–90. https://doi.org/10.1111/j.1468-0491.2008.00391.x.

Sakariyau, Tunde R., Sani A. Mohd, and Zakuan A. Ummu. "Nigeria's Electoral Politics and the Legitimacy Crisis in the Fourth Republic: An Overview." *Asian Journal of Multidisciplinary Studies* 5, no. 6 (June 6, 2017): 136–44.

Schedler, Andreas. *The Politics of Uncertainty: Sustaining and Subverting Electoral Authoritarianism.* Oxford: Oxford University Press, 2013.

Taliercio, Robert R. "Administrative Reform as Credible Commitment: The Impact of Autonomy on Revenue Authority Performance in Latin America." *World Development* 32, no. 2 (February 2004): 213–32. https://doi.org/10.1016/j.worlddev.2003.08.008.

The East African. "Kenya Poll One of the Most Expensive in the World." *Daily Nation*, July 17, 2017. https://www.nation.co.ke/news/Kenya-holds-one-of-the-most-expensive-elections/1056-4018144-10vpg41/index.html.

Treasury. "Pre-Election Economic and Fiscal Report." Accessed May 19, 2019. http://www.treasury.go.ke/fiscalreport2017/PREELECTION%20ECONOMIC%20AND%20FISCAL%20REPORT%202017.pdf.

Tyler, Tom R. "Psychological Perspectives on Legitimacy and Legitimation." *Annual Review of Psychology* 57, no. 1 (2006): 375–400. https://doi.org/10.1146/annurev.psych.57.102904.190038.

Wanyande, Peter. "Electoral Politics and Election Outcomes in Kenya." *Africa Development* 31, no. 3 (2006).

Williams, John T. "Systemic Influences on Political Trust; the Importance of Perceived Institutional Performance." *Political Methodology* 11 (1985): 125–42.

CHAPTER 3

Assessing Cameroon's Elections Against International Standards and Good Practices on Democracy and Human Rights

Walters Tohnji Samah and Jespa Ajereboh Tichock

1   INTRODUCTION

Since independence more than half a century ago, Cameroon has been ruled by only two presidents, Amadou Ahidjo (1960–1982) and Paul Biya, in power for nearly four decades. During this period, there has been no regime change through the ballot as Biya took over following Ahidjo's resignation on 6 April 1982. Under the one-party system that was established in 1966, elections which were managed entirely by the Territorial Administration Ministry were a mere formality since they offered voters only one choice (Dicklitch 2002, 152–176). However, with the demise of the Cold War, which transformed the international landscape, democratisation became a strategic objective and relevant benchmark in bilateral and multilateral relations. Consequently, international partners and donors leveraged better governance and liberal-democratic reforms as a political conditionality for foreign assistance (Emmanuel 2010, 856–877; Fomunyoh 2001, 39; Park 2019). This, coupled with growing pressure for change at the national level, led to the introduction of multiparty politics, and the organisation of the first presidential elections in

W. T. Samah (✉)
African Union Observer African Mission in the Central African Republic, Bangui, Central African Republic
e-mail: samahwalters@gmail.com

J. Ajereboh Tichock
Bamenda, Cameroon

© The Author(s), under exclusive license to Springer Nature Switzerland AG 2022
A. Adeola and M. W. Mutua (eds.), *The Palgrave Handbook of Democracy, Governance and Justice in Africa*,
https://doi.org/10.1007/978-3-030-74014-6_3

35

1992. What this illustrates is that the opening of political space was not the outcome of a genuine political will from President Paul Biya to democratise the country, but the result of domestic and international pressures.

2   NORMATIVE FRAMEWORKS

2.1   International Frameworks

As a member of many international and regional inter-governmental organisations, notably the United Nations (UN), African Union (AU), the Commonwealth and *La Francophonie*, Cameroon is a State Party to various international instruments on democracy and human rights. Consequently, it is expected to conduct its elections following the minimum international standards and good practices established by these organisations. Generally, these international standards on elections stem from political rights and fundamental freedoms established by universal and regional treaties and political commitments. For example, international principles on elections recognise the right of every citizen to take part in the conduct of public affairs, the right to vote and to be elected (OHCHR, 2022).

Chief among international instruments on human rights is the Universal Declaration of Human Rights (UDHR), adopted by the United Nations on 10 December 1948. According to the UDHR, the will of the people shall be the basis of the authority of the government, which shall be expressed in periodic and genuine elections that shall be universal and equal suffrage. It shall be held by a secret vote or by equivalent free voting procedures (Art. 21, UDHR.). Though the UDHR was drafted and adopted as a non-binding instrument, the UDHR remains a powerful tool and the single most invoked human rights instrument worldwide (Steiner and Alson 1996; Glendon 1998, 1153–1190), and many of its provisions are now considered binding due to customary international law (Davis-Roberts and Carroll 2010, 416 –441).

Another critical international instrument on democracy and human rights is the International Covenant on Civil and Political Rights (ICCPR). The multilateral treaty was adopted by the United Nations General Assembly Resolution 2200A (XXI) on 16 December 1966 and entered into force on 23 March 1976. The ICCPR, which Cameroon has ratified, empowers every citizen of the world to take part in the political affairs of their country, directly or through freely chosen representatives. It also accords every citizen the right to vote and to be elected at genuine periodic elections by universal suffrage through secret ballot, guaranteeing the free expression of the will of the electorate (Art. 25 ICCPR). Relatedly, it highlights the importance of the freedoms of association, assembly, movement and opinion or expression. Article 40 of the ICCPR expands the rights and freedoms of individuals to participate in elections, to include the quality of elections and the independence of institutions involved in the electoral process, such as the election management body and the judiciary. Other relevant international instruments with salient provisions on elections, democracy and human rights are the Convention on the Elimination of All Forms of Racial Discrimination (ICERD), the Convention on the Elimination of All Forms of Discrimination against Women (CEDAW), the Convention on the Political Rights of Women (CPRW) and the Convention on the Rights of Persons with Disabilities (CRPD).

ICERD was adopted by the UN General Assembly resolution 2106 (XX) of 21 December 1965 and entered into force on 4 January 1969. It obliges State Parties to prohibit and eliminate racial discrimination in all its forms. It further obliges them to guarantee the right of everyone, without distinction as to race, colour, national or ethnic origin, to vote and to stand for election, based on universal, equal suffrage, to take part in the government as well as in the conduct of public affairs (Art. 5 ICERD). It was ratified by Cameroon on 24 June 1971.

CEDAW was adopted by the UN General Assembly on 18 December 1979 and entered into force as an international treaty on 3 September 1981. It obliges State Parties to take all appropriate measures to eliminate discrimination against women in the political and public life of the country and, in particular, to ensure to women, on equal terms with men, the right to vote in all elections and public referenda and to be eligible to all publicly elected bodies (Art. 7 CEDAW). Cameroon ratified it on 23 August 1994. Concerning the CPRW, it was adopted by the UN General Assembly on 18 December 1979 and entered into force as an international treaty on 3 September 1981. It obliges states to ensure women are entitled to vote in all elections on equal terms with men, without any discrimination (Art. I). According to this Convention, women are eligible for elections to all publicly elected bodies established by national law, on equal terms with men, without any discrimination (Art. II). Cameroon ratified the Convention on 23 August 1994.

Finally, the CRPD was adopted by the UN General Assembly on 13 December 2006 and entered into force on 3 May 2008. States Parties to this Convention reaffirm that persons with disabilities have the right to recognition everywhere as persons before the law (Art. 12). This, therefore, implies that such persons have to be treated equally with others before the Constitution and other relevant electoral laws of a country. They cannot, therefore, be denied the opportunity to vote or be voted because of their disabilities. Their freedom of expression and opinion, being fundamental political rights, must be guaranteed by states (Art. 21). It was signed by Cameroon on 1 October 2008 but is still pending ratification.

2.2   *Regional Frameworks*

At the regional level, the most important legal instruments on democracy and human rights are African Charter on Human and Peoples' Rights (ACHPR), the Constitutive Act of the African Union and the African Charter on Democracy, Elections and Governance (ratified by Cameroon on 24 August 2011).

The ACHPR is the continent's principal human rights instrument. It guarantees several rights and freedoms with significant implications on elections, including the right to equality of every individual before the law and equal protection before the law (Art. 3 ACHPR), the right of every citizen to participate freely in the government of his country, either directly or through freely chosen representatives under the provisions of the law and the right to have equal access to the public service of his/her country (Art. 13 ACHPR).

The Constitutive Act of the African Union seeks, among other objectives, to promote democratic principles and institutions, popular participation and good governance; and to promote and protect human and peoples' rights as expressed in the ACHPR and other relevant human rights instruments (Art. 3, Constitutive Act). Member States of the African Union, including Cameroon, are therefore expected to conduct political affairs in general and elections in particular in transparent and democratic fashions which uphold and promote the objectives of the African Union.

In fostering democracy, good governance and human rights, African leaders adopted the African Charter on Democracy, Elections and Governance (ACDEG) at the 8th Ordinary Session of the Assembly, held in Addis Ababa, Ethiopia, 30 January 2007. The Charter aims to institutionalise legitimate authority and democratic change of governments by promoting the holding of regular free and fair elections (Art. 2(3)). It also seeks to encourage the establishment of the necessary conditions to foster citizen participation, transparency, access to information, freedom of the press and accountability in the management of public affairs (Art. 2(10)). In this regard, State Parties including Cameroon are required to hold regular, transparent, free and fair elections (Art. 3), establish and strengthen independent and impartial national electoral bodies and establish and strengthen national mechanisms that redress election-related disputes promptly (Art. 17).

Complementing the above regional instruments is the OAU/AU Declaration on the Principles Governing Democratic Elections in Africa, adopted by African Heads of State and Government on 8 July 2002 in Durban, South Africa. Fundamental principles of this Declaration include: that democratic elections are the basis of the authority of any representative government; that the holding of democratic elections is a vital dimension in conflict prevention, management and resolution; and that democratic elections should be conducted freely and fairly, under democratic constitutions and in compliance with supportive legal instruments and by impartial, all-inclusive competent accountable electoral institutions staffed by well-trained personnel and equipped with adequate logistics (AU Declaration 2002).

Furthermore, there is the Protocol to the African Charter on Human and People's Rights on the Rights of Women in Africa, adopted at the 2nd Ordinary Session of the Assembly of the African Union in Maputo on 11 July 2003. Based on the principles of equality, peace, freedom, dignity, justice, solidarity and democracy, the Protocol, among other things, guarantees African women's right to participation in political and decision-making process. It demands State Parties to take specific positive action to promote participative governance and the equal participation of women in the political life of their countries through affirmative action. In this regard, it encourages states to pass legislation and take other measures to ensure that women participate and are represented equally without any discrimination at all levels in the electoral process (Art. 9 Protocol). While international law obliges states to let their citizens take part in political decision-making and conduct free elections, it allows for a diversity of political systems in executing these obligations (Fahner 2017, 321–341).

2.3   National Election Framework

The Cameroon Constitution (1996)
It recognises the value of human rights and freedoms and international human rights law instruments in its Preamble which states that:

> We, the people of Cameroon, ...affirm our attachment to the fundamental freedoms enshrined in the Universal Declaration of Human Rights, the Charter of the UN, the African Charter on Human and Peoples' Rights and all duly ratified International Conventions thereto, in particular, to the following principles: all persons shall have equal rights and obligations ...; the state shall ensure the protection of minorities and shall preserve the rights of indigenous populations ...; no person may be prosecuted, arrested or detained, except in the cases and according to the manner determined by law; the law shall ensure the right of every person to a fair hearing before the courts.... (Preamble 1996 Constitution)

The Constitution also provides for presidential, legislative, regional and municipal elections and referenda. As per Article 6(1) of the Constitution, the President of the Republic is elected for a seven-year term by universal suffrage and by direct, equal and secret ballot. It also provides that a single-round majority ballot elects the President and the candidate with the majority of the votes cast should be declared the winner. However, the Cameroon Constitution does not have any presidential term limit, which provides for seven years per term presidential term. Though regional and international instruments only provide for periodic elections, without any specification on the number and the duration of the term of office, the good practice in many countries across the world including Nigeria, Ghana, Benin, Kenya and Liberia is for a two-term limit, and four-five years per term.

The Constitution empowers the Constitutional Council to ensure the regularity of presidential elections, parliamentary elections and referendum and to announce the results and adjudicate electoral disputes (Art. 48). International and regional human rights institutions prescribe judicial bodies to be independent and impartial. In Cameroon, however, the Constitutional Council has a conflicting role as it is responsible for both declaring election results and addressing appeals by competing parties. Beyond declaring the results and adjudicating related disputes, the Constitutional Council also directly participates in the electoral process by appointing its member to ensure the regularity of elections and to become the chairperson of the vote-counting commission. Getting involved in election management does not allow for an independent appeals process. Another factor that undermines the Constitutional Council's independence and impartiality is the fact that its members are appointed by the President (Art. 51, 1996 Constitution). President Paul Biya has used this provision to select his most devout CPDM party members to the Council, such as the appointment, on 15 April 2020, of Joseph Owona, the former Secretary-General of the Presidency and former Minister of Education, as member of the Constitutional Council.

They are expected to serve for a period of six years renewable.

The Electoral Code (2012)

The Cameroon Electoral Code has legal provisions for the creation of an election body and other institutions mandated to carry out various election-related responsibilities. Under Section 3 of the Electoral Code, the 'organisation, management and supervision of all election and referendum operations shall devolve upon Elections Cameroon, abbreviated as ELECAM'.

Despite giving ELECAM this broad mandate, the Electoral Code also provides for the creation of various joint electoral commissions charged with 'preparing electoral activities, organising and supervising election operations, polling operations and the final counting of votes' (Section 49). Furthermore, it empowers the President of the Republic to call for elections and spell out the duties of the Constitutional Council in the electoral process, including the hearing and deciding of election petitions and proclaiming election results (Sections 132–139). Significantly, the Electoral Code limits the voting age to 20 years, provides for public funding of election, referendum campaigns and penal provisions for electoral malpractices.

The Diaspora Voting Law (13 July 2011)

It enfranchises eligible Cameroonians living abroad to participate in the election of the President of the Republic and referendums (Section 1 Diaspora Voting Law). According to this law, to take part in an election, Cameroonians settled or residing abroad would have to enter their names on electoral registers opened at the diplomatic representations and consular posts in their respective countries of residence (Section 3). In this regard, the law requires the election management body to draw up and revise voter registers abroad in consultations with Cameroon diplomatic representations and political parties and to set up a commission responsible for the issuance and distribution of voters' cards, and local polling stations. Though this law gives Cameroonians in the diaspora the opportunity to vote and is in line with the international standard of universal suffrage, it also raises some issues. Firstly, putting diplomatic representations and consular offices at the centre of the external voting may lead to abuse of the process including voter intimidation and coercion, given that these institutions are beholden of the regime in power and are headed by appointees of President Paul Biya (Tande 2011). Secondly, it prevents thousands of people of Cameroon origin with dual/multiple nationalities from taking part in elections.

Public Funding of Political Parties and Election Campaign Law (2000)
It directs the government to subsidise campaign costs of political parties. This law has raised mixed feelings in Cameroon. According to Dibussi Tande, though the law is relatively straightforward, its implementation is characterised by a lack of transparency (Tande 2009). He argues that instead of specific parliamentary allocation based on an objective assessment of the political landscape, the funds allocated for elections are arbitrarily decided upon by the government (Tande 2009).

Other Subsidiary Laws with Implications on the Electoral Process
There exist other subsidiary laws with a direct and indirect impact on election, democracy and human rights processes. Key among these laws are those on political parties, freedom of association, freedom of mass communication, maintenance of law and order, public meetings and processions (popularly known as the 1990 Liberty Laws) and the anti-terrorism law (Law n°2014/028). The anti-terrorism law, for example, has been widely criticised by various national and international stakeholders as being a tool used by the government to restrict fundamental rights protected under the Cameroon Constitution and international human rights law. It has been used by President Biya to shrink the civic and political space. Following of review of the law by Amnesty International, the organisation concluded that 'the law sets out an overly broad definition of terrorism, which could be used to criminalise peaceful political activities, and infringes the rights to freedom of association and assembly' (Amnesty International, October 2017). Amnesty International has since then been calling for the law to be amended to bring it in line with international human rights standards.

3   THE INSTITUTIONAL FRAMEWORK

Besides the election management body, ELECAM, that is responsible for organising, managing and supervising all elections and referendum operations in Cameroon, there are several other institutions directly or indirectly involved in the election process, top of which is the Constitutional Council. Its primary function is to determine electoral disputes relating to legislative and presidential elections in Cameroon. Also, the Council is responsible for ensuring the regularity of legislative and presidential elections and operations and proclaims the results (Section 48(1 and 2) Electoral Code). It also participates in counting final votes and appoints its member as the Chairperson of the National Commission for the Final Counting of Votes (Section 68(1) Electoral

Code). Before the Constitutional Council went operational in 2018, its role in the electoral process, particularly in handling election disputes and proclaiming the results, was played by the Supreme Court. Other state institutions with an assigned role in the electoral process include the Territorial Administration and Justice Ministries and the Presidency of the Republic.

Under the one-party state, the Territorial Administration Ministry (popularly known by its French acronym MINAT) was the sole authority responsible for conducting elections in Cameroon. Even with the advent of multipartyism and the creation of election management bodies, MINAT has continued to have an undue influence in all elections. As per the Electoral Code, MINAT is also responsible for granting accreditation to all national and international election observers (Section 296(2) Electoral Code). The fact that this Ministry has always been headed by a member of the ruling party and close ally to President Paul Biya has made many election stakeholders—notably, opposition leaders, to question its independence and continued role in elections. According to Fombad, the most contentious issue surrounding elections in Cameroon has been the role the laws confer on the Territorial Administration Ministry (Fombad 2003, 34). Concerning the Justice Ministry, it appoints Presidents of High Courts that serve as chairpersons of the Divisional Supervisory Commissions responsible for supervising elections in all the administrative divisions in the country (Section 64(1) Electoral Code).

Lastly, there is the President of the Republic who has the constitutional authority to convene electors by a presidential decree (Section 86 Electoral Code). Unlike in other democratic countries in Africa, such as Ghana and Kenya, where the incumbent President has little discretion over the electoral calendar, in Cameroon, the law gives the President, who in the case of Paul Biya is also the chairperson of the ruling party, an undue advantage. According to the African Elections Database Initiative, elections conducted in Cameroon since independence can be divided into four main periods, namely restricted democratic practice (1960–1966); one-party state (1966–1990); multiparty transition (1990–1992); and restricted democratic practice (African Elections Database Initiative, n.d.).

4   The Question of Credibility of Elections in a Democracy

Elections are a crucial pillar of liberal democracies—political systems characterised by regular and free elections in which candidates through political parties compete to form the government, and where virtually all adult citizens can exercise their civil and political rights, including the right to vote, freedoms of expression, association and the press (Sandbrook 1988, 240–267; Adejumobi 2000, 59–73; Diamond et al. 1989; Sorensen 1993). According to Alfred Maurice de Zayas, United Nations Independent Expert on the Promotion of a Democratic and Equitable Order, democracy is the correlation between the will of the people and the actions of its elected representatives (Report of the Independent Expert 2012). In assessing the credibility of elections, the expression of 'free and fair' has most often been espoused internationally as the baseline (Boda 2011). As Beco puts it, the expression of free and fair is used to 'mean ideal and excellent conduct of an election, a means by which citizens exercise their democratic right to vote leaders of their choice in a representative democracy' (Beco 2013, 380–397). According to the United Nations, 'even in countries where the electoral process has been seriously flawed or where elections have not resulted in a change of regime ... the holding of "free and fair" competitive elections has become the universal standard' (United Nations 1997, 5).

As a cornerstone of liberal democracy, human rights are an essential consideration in assessing the conduct of elections. As Aidoo asserts, the struggle for democracy also denotes a struggle for human rights (Aidoo 1993, 703–715). According to the UN Centre for Human Rights Geneva, elections are human rights events because they give voice to the political will of the people involved (UN Centre for Human Rights 1994). For elections to be tryly free and fair, they must be conducted in an atmosphere which is respectful of fundamental human rights consistent with international standards (United Nations 1994). By this token, measures that undermine the people's will or violate the UDHR renders an election unfair (United Nations, *United Nations Human Rights and Elections*, 10). Another term that is increasingly being used to assess elections is 'genuine'. According to Farer et al., the minimum requirements for a genuine election are the absence of unreasonable restrictions on the ability of an individual to participate as a candidate or a voter, respect for political freedoms prior to the elections in a manner sufficient to allow individuals to obtain information about the process and also, respect for the integrity of the process (Farer et al. 1988, 505–518).

For an election to be considered credible, genuine, free and fair, it should allow every eligible voter to participate, and each vote must carry equal weight. Additionally, there should be an independent electoral commission; the electoral process must be transparent; the results should reflect the number of votes cast; and dissatisfied candidates must be allowed to challenge the results before an independent court or tribunal (Abuya 2009). Besides, there exist several globally accepted electoral best practices on conducting free, fair and genuine elections that can be used to assess Cameroon's electoral procedures and practices. For instance, the public display of election results is widely recognised as the best practice needed to ensure verifiable vote-counting and tabulation processes (Davis-Roberts and Carroll, 430).

5   Overviewing Multiparty Elections Since 1992

Cameroon has conducted several presidential, legislative and municipal elections since the return to multiparty democracy in 1990 (African Elections database Initiative, n.d.). However, given that the stakes of municipal elections and elections for the Senate do not aptly reflect most of the issues covered in this chapter, this section will focus on the presidential and legislative elections into the National Assembly.

5.1 Presidential Elections

Since 1992 up until 2020, Cameroon has conducted five presidential elections (1992, 1997, 2004, 2011 and 2018), all of which were characterised by numerous criticisms and allegations of irregularities and contested before the electoral tribunal. Perhaps the most contested was the 11 October 1992 presidential election, which many observers believed was won by John Fru Ndi, Chairman of Social Democratic Front (SDF) and presidential candidate of the Union for Change alliance (Konings 2004, 8). However, the National Vote Counting Commission announced the incumbent Paul Biya as the winner with 39.9% of the votes. Rejecting the election results, Fru Ndi held a press conference in his party's stronghold of Bamenda on 21 October 1992 and declared himself the legitimate winner of the elections, stating that, 'I have accepted the verdict of my people and I declared myself ready to assume the mission of President of the Republic that they have just confided in me' (Tande 2010). Two days after, Biya's victory was confirmed by the Supreme Court, acting in place of the Constitutional Council, sparking massive street demonstrations particularly in Anglophone, Littoral and Western regions. Furthermore, John Fru Ndi was kept under house arrest and a state of emergency imposed on his Anglophone stronghold of Northwest Province (Konings 2004, 8; Fonchingong 1998, 119–136).

The elections were widely criticised as fraudulent by both national and international observers, pointing to widespread irregularities (Kelley 2010, 158–172). For instance, in its report on the 1992 presidential election, the US-based National Democratic Institute (NDI) reported of a flawed and heavily rigged electoral process (NDI, November 1993). It noted that President Biya and his government retained control over the appointment of every elected official, issued every electoral decree, established all vote-counting procedures, staffed every electoral bureaucracy and strictly controlled governmental release of partial results—for which no provision existed in the Electoral Code (NDI, November 1993). It concluded in the absence of a democratic political system in which political leaders can contest elections fairly and work within the political system whether they win or lose, Cameroon was likely to regress into an authoritarian rule (NDI, November 1993). According to Y. Morse of the University of Connecticut, who has written extensively on authoritarian regimes in sub-Saharan Africa, 'Biya's survival in the 1992 election depended on leveraging his control of the administration and security services' (Morse 2018, 114–129).

Paul Biya won the presidential election of 1997, which was boycotted by major opposition parties. The 11 October 2004 presidential election was also marked by many irregularities. As soon as the election results were released, the opposition candidates disputed them, claiming 'widespread fraud' had been committed. Speaking on behalf of Catholic observers, the Archbishop of Douala described the election as a 'masquerade'. On its part, the Commonwealth Observer Group, in its overall assessment, concluded that the electoral process was poorly managed and lacked credibility (Commonwealth 2004, 42–43). Noting that the Territorial Administration Ministry was the principal obstacle to the holding of credible elections in Cameroon, it recommended as an overriding priority the establishment of an independent election management body that can organise and conduct all aspects of the electoral process (Commonwealth 2004, 45). However, such recommendations for free and fair election formulated by international observation missions to Cameroon have mostly been disregarded by the Cameroon government, leaving the electoral landscape largely unchanged since the 1990s. This could partly explain why major international organisations that frequently deploy international election observation missions in sub-Saharan Africa such as European Union, Commonwealth, the Carter Center, NDI and Transparency International have been absent in recent elections in Cameroon.

In 2008, President Biya quickly pushed for the revision of the 1996 Constitution that scrapped the two presidential term limits, which cleared the way for him to run for the 2011 and subsequent presidential elections. The *change* also increased *the term length* from five to seven years. Since then, Biya has comfortably won all presidential elections, assisted by various forms of fraud and intimidation (Albaugh 2011). For instance, in the presidential election held on 7 October *2018, Paul Biya's victory was* contested by the opposition leaders, particularly Maurice Kamto of the Cameroon Renaissance Movement (Signe 2018; International Crisis Group 2018), who filed complaints before the Constitutional Council alleging vote fraud and irregularities (International Crisis Group 2018). However, *the complaints were all* dismissed. Having failed to use the ballot box to bring about political change and to achieve a reform of the Electoral Code, Kamto has since been calling for nationwide peaceful demonstrations against President Paul Biya, as a means to force him to resign and allow for electoral reforms (Foute 2020; Krippahl 2019).

5.2 Legislative Elections

Cameroon has a bicameral legislature comprising a Senate with 100 members and a National Assembly made up of 180 members elected by direct and secret universal suffrage for a five-year term of office (Art. 15(1) 1972 Constitution as amended in 1996 and 2008). Seven legislative elections have taken place in Cameroon since the return to multiparty democracy for seats in the National Assembly (1992, 1997, 2002, 2007, 2011 and 2020) and only one for the Senate, all of which have been dominated by the ruling CPDM party. Like the presidential elections, these legislative elections have also been widely criticised for irregularities and other electoral malpractices. According to British human rights organisation named Article 19 (Global Campaign for Free Expression), the 1992 legislative elections were marred by the lack of opposition participation and the fairness which resulted in a ruling party majority, leading to national and international observers questioning its credibility (Article 19, 1997, 2–3).

The 9 February 2020 legislative elections took place amid security challenges in Cameroon's two English-speaking North West and South-West regions, opposition boycotts and lack of enthusiasm towards the voting process which consequently greatly affected voter turnout (Herrmann 2020). As was widely expected, the ruling CPDM party of President Paul Biya won 167 out of the 180 seats in the National Assembly. Allegations of fraud and rigging, notably in the two English-speaking regions, led to at least forty electoral petitions to the Constitutional Council from 15 political parties. On 25 February 2020, the Council ordered for re-run elections for the remaining 13 constituencies, 11 of which were in English-speaking regions (Ndi 2020). The re-run election was held on 22 March 2020 (Decision no. 0471/D/ELECAM/DGE, 7 March 2020), against the backdrop of continued fighting between the military and armed separatists. It, therefore, triggered further criticisms from national and international stakeholders, including Amnesty International, which questioned the rationale for holding elections under such challenging circumstances (Amnesty International 2020).

From the foregoing, the credibility of elections conducted in Cameroon since the return to multiparty politics in 1990 has been questioned by national and international actors, due to widespread allegations of fraud and other irregularities. For instance, in its report on the first multiparty presidential election of 11 October 1992, the NDI documented widespread irregularities that called into question the validity of the outcome (NDI 1993). According to International IDEA, elections have been used in Cameroon and other African countries such as Angola, Chad, Equatorial Guinea, Eritrea, The Gambia, Sudan, Uganda and Zimbabwe to legitimise undemocratic regimes (International IDEA 2019, 67).

Writing about election irregularities in Cameroon, F. B. Nyamnjoh noted that 'Since 1990, rigging elections have been perfected to the ridiculous level, making the theme a standing joke among satirical comedians, critical journalists, opposition politicians, and ordinary Cameroonians who have mostly given up on expectations of change under the current regime' (Nyamnjoh 2002). Other scholars have talked of a failed electoral system and failed democratic transition in Cameroon (Dicklitch 2002, 152–176; Yanou 2013: 303–320; Brown 2001, 725–739). For example, 'M. Yanou blames this failure on the bodies and institutions managing elections in Cameroon' (Yanou 2013: 303–320).

To S. Browns, elections that fall short of international standards of free and fair account for the prolonged stay in power of most authoritarian regimes in Africa despite the frequent holding of elections (Brown 2001, 725–739). Due to these factors, Cameroon is one of the countries in sub-Saharan African that is experiencing 'democratic backsliding'. According to Rep. Bass, 'democratic backsliding includes but not limited to degradation of free and fair elections, infringement of freedom of speech, impairment of political opposition to challenge the government and hold it accountable, the weakening of the rule of law such as limiting the autonomy of the judiciary, manufacturing and over-emphasising national security threat that allows the government to malign critics' (US Congress 2020).

6   ASSESSING CAMEROON'S ELECTIONS

In this section, Cameroon's elections are assessed against international standards and good practices on democracy and human rights. The focus will be on critical elements of the electoral landscape that are in stark contrast to acceptable international and regional standards and good practices on democracy and human rights. Amnesty International has pointed out that Cameroon repeatedly violates its obligations under international human rights law, including the International Covenant on Civil and Political Rights (ICCPR) (Amnesty International, 16 September 1997). In 2019, it reported that peaceful protests in Yaoundé and other main cities, held by political activists to contest alleged irregularities in the 2018 electoral process that led to the re-election of President Biya for a 7th term, were severely repressed (Amnesty International 2019).

6.1   *Lack of Independence of Election Management Body*

Key international and regional human rights law instruments such as the ICCPR and the ACDEG require that state institutions involved in managing elections be independent (General Comment 25, Para 20 ICCPR; Art. 17(1) ACDEG). Such independence must be absolute for two reasons: to enable the institutions to perform their duties without any interference in delivering free, fair and genuine elections, and to instil and sustain trust and confidence in the voters about the electoral process. To fulfil this critical requirement, Cameroon's Electoral Code provides that the election management body 'shall be an independent body responsible for the organisation, management, and supervision of all election and referendum operations' (Section 4(1) Electoral Code). However, ELECAM is not truly independent, de jure and de facto as per international standards for an independent election management body. Currently, all its eighteen members, including its head, are named by the President (Section 12(3) Electoral Code).

In granting the Cameroonian President such constitutional powers, the Electoral Code did not provide any safeguards to ensure that incumbents do not act arbitrarily. As a result, President Paul Biya has exploited this provision by appointing members to the ELECAM that mostly suit his political or electoral calculus. For example, before his appointment in 2011 as the Chairman of the Electoral Board of *ELECAM,* Samuel *Fonkam* Azu'u was a Central Committee Member of the ruling CPDM (Yanou, 311). Similarly, before she was appointed Member of the Electoral Board of ELECAM, Dorothy Limunga Njeuma was a prominent CPDM politburo member. Born in Buea Anglophone Southwest region on 26 June 1943, her membership of the ruling party dates back to the years of President Ahmadou Ahidjo, who appointed her Vice Minister of National Education in 1975. The Cameroonian President also appoints the Director-General and Deputy Director-General of ELECAM who are responsible for running of the body and the provision of technical and operational support for elections (Yanou, 313; Section 24 Electoral Code).

In a context like Cameroon with a history of flawed elections, the appointment of high-level ruling party members into ELECAM undermines the credibility, independence and impartiality of the institution and its members. Moreover, it contradicts the practice in many countries across Africa, such as in Kenya, Ghana and Nigeria that have established non-partisan electoral bodies by excluding from their membership all those who actively had previously taken part in partisan party politics (Jinadu 1997, 1–11). It is therefore not surprising that President Biya's appointment in 2011 of *Fonkam* Azu'u as Board Chairman and Dorothy Limunga Njeuma as Board Member were met with scepticism and criticism from national and international actors, despite the public announcement of their decision to renounce their membership of the ruling party (Commonwealth 2011).

6.2   *ELECAM Is Not the Sole Authority on Elections*

Although the Electoral Code states that ELECAM is 'an independent body responsible for the organisation, management, and supervision of all election and referendum operations', it does not have the sole and exclusive authority over election matters. This is because the same Electoral Code also provides for the creations of various ad hoc commissions, namely the Local Polling Commissions, the Divisional Supervisory Commissions and the National Commission for the Final Counting of Votes (Sections 50–69), which are in charge of different aspects of the election operations. The majority of the members of these commissions, which are established before an election, are representatives of various state institutions that are headed by appointees of the Cameroonian President. For example, the National Commission for the Final Counting of Votes is made up of one representative of the Constitutional Council; two representatives of the Supreme Court; five representatives of the Ministry of Territorial Administration; five representatives of ELECAM; and one representative of each candidate or political party taking part in the election (Section 68 Electoral Code). Other state institutions with specific duties and responsibilities relating to the electoral process are the Constitutional Council and the Presidency. With the law assigning these bodies and institutions with most of the core elections-related operations and responsibilities, ELECAM is left to playing what appears to be a mere coordinating role in the conduct of elections in Cameroon.

6.3   Electoral Dispute Resolution

The credibility of an electoral process is determined mostly by the state's capacity to resolve electoral disputes effectively (The Carter Center, n.d., 178). The ICCPR provides for everyone to be entitled to a competent, independent and impartial tribunal to determine his or her right (Art. 14 of ICCPR). However, the Constitutional Council in charge of resolving electoral disputes relating to legislative and presidential elections in Cameroon (Art. 48(1) 1996 Constitution) and protecting fundamental rights and freedoms also plays several other roles that undermine its impartiality and neutrality in settling electoral petitions. More so, its members are all appointed by the Cameroonian President, who is the chairperson of the ruling party. Also, the majority of its 11 members many of whom are former cabinet ministers have ties to the ruling party (presidential decree no. 2018/105, 7 February 2018). This was further attested when President Biya, on 15 April 2020, appointed to the Constitutional Council one of his most faithful loyalists and CPDM central committee member, former Minister Joseph Owona (Presidential Decree no. 2020/194 of 15 April 2020).

Assessing the independence and impartiality of the Constitutional Council, C. M. Fombad observes that the Council which is 'designed to determine disputes between the organs of state and to protect fundamental rights and freedoms is an obsolete and discredited body that is likely to remain under the control of the President of the Republic' (Fombad 1998, 172–186). On its part, Freedom House observes that the creation of the Constitutional Council compromises the independence and integrity of Cameroon's electoral framework as the Council has the powers to validate election results and adjudicate election disputes (Freedom House 2020). Freedom House goes further to point out that the Council rejected all 18 petitions filed by opposition parties requesting the cancellation of the 2018 presidential election results, despite fraud and intimidation allegations (Freedom House 2020).

6.4   Timeframe for Filing Election Petitions

According to Section 133(2) of the Electoral Code, candidates or political parties unsatisfied with the results of the legislative and presidential election must file petitions within 72 hours of the close of the poll. Nevertheless, petitioners must specify the alleged facts and evidence, or stand the risk of having their petitions rejected by the Constitutional Council. Once notified of any petition, the opposing party has only 24 hours to submit a response (Section 133(3) Electoral Code). Both timelines fall short of international human rights law standard for fair trials, which requires the elections tribunal to allocate reasonable time for litigants or petitioners to prepare their cases. The Constitutional Council also has the powers to unilaterally issue a 'reasoned decision' rejecting any petition it considers inadmissible or based on objections that cannot influence the outcome of the election (Section 134 of Electoral Code). Such broad powers have led to many electoral petitions being rejected in Cameroon. For example, for the February 2020 legislative elections, over 30 petitions demanding the partial or total cancellation of the elections due to fraud were rejected (Kindzeka, Voice of America, 26 February 2020).

By the very complex nature of elections in Cameroon, involving many remote locations or constituencies from where issues must be collected, including evidence, election petitions are uniquely demanding. Given this reality, M. Yanou argues that 'it is impracticable for a candidate who contested a nationwide election for the presidency to effectively collect all the evidence of malpractice in the entire country, prepare his pleadings, and file his action in Yaoundé within 72 hours' (Yanou, 317). Underscoring the importance of timelines in electoral dispute resolution and in maintaining electoral integrity, Chief Justice Georgina Theodora Wood of Ghana (2007–2017) stated that 'in our contemporary world, in a representative democracy, the timeliness with which a judiciary decisively determines electoral disputes without fear or favour, affection or ill-will, is part of the package of mirrors through which civilised societies view a people' (The Judicial Service of Ghana 2012; Nkansah 2016, 98).

6.5 The Conflicting Roles of the Constitutional Council

The Constitutional Council's primary roles in the electoral process include leading final vote-counting, including correcting any clerical errors in the counting of votes (Sections 68 and 69 of Electoral Code), determination of election petitions and the proclamation of the results. However, for a Council that has scrutinised, validated and proclaimed the election results to turn around and adjudicate on the same results is in stark contrast to the independence of the judiciary and against natural justice, which requires that *nemo judex in causa sua* (no-one should be a judge in his/her own cause). To retain its impartiality, neutrality and independence, the Council should not get involved in the management of elections.

6.6 Election Campaign Period

The Cameroon Electoral Code prescribes two weeks of electoral campaigns before an election (Section 87 of the Electoral Code)—a timeframe that is too limited for any reasonable campaign to take place. There is no specific timeframe established by any international human rights instruments on the duration of electoral campaigns. However, free, fair and genuine elections by international human rights law require that the electorates are well informed of the manifestos of candidates in order to make informed choices. According to Reisman, Professor of International Law at the Yale Law School, 'the whole idea of an election is to provide the voting body and or electorate with an adequate opportunity to inform itself of the issues and options available to it and to permit it to form an enlightened opinion....' (Reisman 1992, 1–48). Reisman further notes that this involves the freedom of candidates to move about the territory in which the election is to be held, to have access to places where they can meet and share their views with the electorate.

Considering the size of Cameroon, with its 10 Regions, 58 Divisions and 360 Sub-divisions, and logistical challenges, opposition political parties and candidates have faced tremendous challenges campaigning throughout the country within two weeks. The limited campaign period, therefore, gives undue advantage to the ruling party. This is particularly true considering that in Cameroon, the ruling CPDM controls state resources, including senior government officials who are deployed for campaigns long before the official launch of the campaign period. Confirming this fact, the Commonwealth Expert Team, in its report on the 2011 presidential election in Cameroon, pointed out that:

> The official campaign period for the 2011 presidential election commenced on 25 September 2011 and lasted until 8 October. Some opposition parties complained that the ruling party began its campaign before the official start. Cameroon Radio and Television (CRTV) [State-owned] announced the launch of president Biya's campaign website on 13 September 2011, 12 days before the official start date. (Commonwealth 2011, 13)

6.7 Qualification as a Candidate for Presidential Election

Though the Cameroon Electoral Code provides for both political parties and independent candidates in presidential elections (Section 121(1) Electoral Code), the provision raises three main issues. The first relates to the conditions to qualify as an independent candidate. According to the Code, any individual wishing to become an independent candidate must submit a list of at least 300 signatures, with at least 30 from each of the ten regions of the country. These signatures which must be authenticated by the relevant administrative authorities should be among dignitaries such as Members of Parliament, Members of the Chamber of Commerce, municipal authorities and traditional rulers or chiefs (Section 121(2) Electoral Code). On the number and calibre of individuals required to back an independent candidate, the ICCPR states that 'if a candidate is required to have several supporters for the nomination, this requirement should be reasonable and not act as a barrier to candidacy' (Para. 17 of the General Comment No. 25 of ICCPR).

The second issue is the sum of 30,000,000 FCFA that any presidential candidate must pay into the state treasury, as required by Section 124(1) of the Electoral Code. Both conditions are onerous and against the standards established by ICCPR, which states that conditions relating to nomination dates, fees or deposits should not be discriminatory (General Comment No. 25 of ICCPR). This requirement of the Code does not give every eligible citizen and potential candidates a level playing field. Thirdly, the Code does not allow nor mention independent candidates for the legislative elections (national assembly and Senate) and therefore requires all candidates to be nominated only by political parties (Section 164(4) Electoral Code). This provision of the Electoral Code violates the ICCPR which states that the right of persons to stand for election should not be limited unreasonably by requiring candidates to be members of parties or specific parties (Para 17 of General Comment No. 25 of ICCPR).

6.8 *Unlimited Presidential Terms*

The Cameroon Constitution provides for *unlimited* 7-year *terms*. Though *International Human Rights Law* (IHRL) provides for periodic elections, it does not specify how often elections should hold, stating vaguely that it 'should probably not be unduly long, but limited to a maximum of 5–7 years' (NEEDS, n.d.). Without any legal clarity on presidential term limit, recourse should be on best practices worldwide. A four five-year term renewable only once is the generally accepted and considered reasonable worldwide in the twenty-first century. Conversely, an extended stay in power lasting decades like in the case of Cameroonian President Paul Biya naturally leads to authoritarianism, demagoguery and damaging repercussions on the democratisation process and human rights situation of the country. To promote democratic consolidation and foster the peaceful transfer of executive power across the continent, several pro-democracy advocacy institutions led by the NDI, Kofi Annan Foundation, Africa Forum *and the Open Society Initiative for West Africa* (OSIWA), met in Niamey, Niger, from 2 to 4 October 2019, pushing for constitutional amendments to presidential term limits (Niamey Declaration, 4 October 2019).

6.9 *The Question of Multiple Ballot Papers*

Cameroon's electoral system uses multiple ballot papers for its legislative and presidential elections. No international human rights instrument specifies the use of multiple or single ballot papers for elections. However, the growing best practice is to use a single ballot paper for all presidential candidates or candidates for other elections within the same constituency. The primary objective of preferring the single ballot paper is to curb fraud, especially ballot stuffing. According to the Commonwealth Expert Team, the use of multiple ballot papers rather than a single ballot was one of the constraints that plagued the 2011 presidential election in Cameroon (Commonwealth 2011). As a result, Cameroon's electoral authorities, among other things, have been encouraged to adopt the single ballot papers system.

Printing and Storage of Ballot Papers
Giving Cameroon's history of disputed elections, how ballot papers are printed, stored and distributed on polling day is a crucial issue to be examined. In many emerging democracies in Africa, the general practice is to build confidence and trust in the electoral process by ensuring impartial and transparent conduct of elections, including ballot printing, storage and distribution. In this regard, and as a best practice, ballot papers should be printed by an independent company approved by the electoral stakeholders including civil society. The ballot papers should contain security serial numbers, and the printing, distribution, transportation and storage should also be monitored and observed by all relevant stakeholders. At present, ballot papers are produced by the National Printing Press in Yaoundé, under the supervision of its director *who* reports to the Minister of Communication and Government's Spokesperson. Staunch members of the ruling party have always held this position. For instance, the current Communication Minister is Emmanuel *René* Sadi, former Territorial Administration Minister and former Secretary-General of the Central Committee of the CPDM (CPDM, n.d.; *Cameroon Tribune* 2019).

7   Way Forward

7.1   *Need for an Independent EMB*

Cameroon needs a genuinely independent election management body with the sole responsibility for organising, managing and monitoring the entire electoral process, including voter registration; the announcement of an electoral calendar; management of election materials; accreditation of national and international observers; and the proclamation of results. To protect it from political influence, the appointment of its members or commissioners should follow a vigorous and impartial process. Further, the independent election body should be allowed to elect its leadership.

7.2   *Need for an Independent Constitutional Court*

The role of the judiciary in enhancing electoral processes in Africa has been exemplified in countries such as Kenya and Malawi where Supreme Courts annulled presidential elections due to irregularities after the election results had already shown the incumbent as the winners. Taking a cue from such practices, the Constitutional Council should be independent and free from partisan influence. As such, appointment of its members should follow a rigorous and transparent process as this will ensure that only politically neutral persons with integrity become members of the Council. To retain the Constitutional Council's integrity as the sole authority on electoral petitions, it should refrain from directly participating in final vote-counting and proclamation of election results.

7.3 Election Campaign

The current official campaign period of two weeks is too short for political parties and candidates to carry out enough campaigns within their constituencies and within the national territory in presidential elections. It should be extended to two (2) or three (3) months. The timeframe of 72 hours, after polls close, for lodging complaints or petitions should be extended to 10–15 days to give aggrieved parties or candidates reasonable time to prepare their case.

7.4 Conditions of Candidacies and Eligibility

For the presidential election, the requirement of at least 3000 signatures from dignitaries from each of the ten regions of Cameroon should be reduced to 300 or more signatures from ordinary citizens. Furthermore, the candidacy application fee of 30,000,000 FCFA (approximately USD52,000) is considered excessive and should be reduced to a reasonable amount. The law should be reviewed to allow interested eligible Cameroonians to participate in national assembly elections as independent candidates. The seven-year term for the President should be reduced to four or five years, and the unlimited term should be scrapped and limited to two terms.

7.5 Election Calendar

International good practices and standards are for the details of electoral calendars with fixed election dates to be contained in the Constitution or the electoral law (Bleck and Van De Walle 2019). This will help prevent the party in power from calling anticipated elections for partisan political gains, thereby helping to level the playing field for all parties. In this regard, the Parliament of Cameroon should pass new legislation or amend the current Electoral Code setting fixed election dates so that future elections can follow a regular cycle with dates and timelines publicly known to all the stakeholders.

7.6 Need for Cooperation with International Observers for Free and Fair Elections

Despite its apparent biases and other shortcomings (Kelley 2010; Lappin 2009; Lynge-Mangueira 2012), election observation undertaken by renowned international organisations can be a valuable tool for improving the quality of elections. It can help detect and deter electoral irregularities; promote and protect the civil and political rights of citizens in elections; build public trust and confidence in the electoral processes; mediate disputes; and bridge distrust among rival political contenders, thus preventing and mitigating electoral violence and enhancing the legitimacy of the governments that emerge from those elections (Chand 1997; Smidt 2016). **Besides, international election observation** can assess whether an election is in line with international standards, highlight specific recommendations for improvement and demonstrate the support of the international community for genuine democratic elections, thereby spreading international electoral norms (Open Election Data Initiative 2022). Based on this reality, international election observation can be particularly relevant to countries like Cameroon, with a protracted history of flawed elections and where a sizable part of the population lacks trust in the electoral system. In this regard, the Cameroon Government should proactively re-engage international organisations—notably, the European Union, the Commonwealth, the Carter Center, NDI and Transparency International to solicit technical support in future elections, including through the deployment of election observation missions.

7.7 Need for an Enabling Environment for Democratic and Human Rights Expression

The civil society can play multi-faceted roles in improving electoral processes—including domestic observation and monitoring, voter education, training of electoral officers and conflict prevention. The government of Cameroon should create a more enabling environment for all electoral stakeholders, including the general populace to function and contribute to credible elections. This would require amending laws related to freedom of association, freedom of mass communication, maintenance of law and order, public meetings and processions and anti-terrorism laws that have provisions that are repugnant to democratic practices protected under the Constitution and international human rights law.

8   CONCLUSION

Holding credible, free and fair elections is an essential element by which states can uphold and promote democratic principles of democracy and human rights. Unfortunately, this is an area in which Cameroon has not made any significant progress. This is because elections conducted in the country over the past three decades have fallen short of the minimum international standards. Characterised by *voting* irregularities and fraud, these elections have been highly contested and disputed in court by opposition *leaders and widely criticised by civil society organisations and national and international* election observers. A major factor responsible for this lack of progress is the electoral legal framework, which is defective and void of essential international human rights law safeguards for elections. This development is taking place against a general backdrop of an erosion of democracy in Cameroon as the country continues to retreat from core democratic practices. To change this dynamic, several recommendations have been formulated. Unless there is a reform of the legal framework to reflect international and regional standards and good practices, elections in Cameroon will continue to be flawed and are unlikely to offer any real opportunities for change of government or renewal of political leadership. The government of Cameroon also needs to re-engage international partners and the international election observation community for support. These measures would contribute to restoring confidence in state institutions, particularly the election management body and the Constitutional Court.

BIBLIOGRAPHY

Abuya, Edwin Odhiambo, "Consequences of a Flawed Presidential Election," *Legal Studies*, Vol. 29, no. 1 (March 2009): 127–158.

Adejumobi, Said, "Elections in Africa: A Fading Shadow of Democracy?," *International Political Science Review*, Vol. 21, no. 1 (2000): 59–73.

African Union, "African Union Constitutive Act," Addis Ababa: African Union, 2002.

Aidoo, Akwasi, "Africa: Democracy Without Human Rights?," *Human Rights Quarterly*, Vol. 15, no. 4 (November 1993): 703–715.

Albaugh, Ericka A., "An Autocrat's Toolkit: Adaptation and Manipulation in 'Democratic' Cameroon," *Democratisation*, Vol. 18, no. 2 (April 2011): 388–414.

Amnesty International, "Amnesty International Submission for the Universal Periodic Review of Cameroon," October 2017, https://www.amnesty.org/en/get-involved/take-action/cameroon-protect-our-rights/.

Amnesty International, "Cameroon: Blatant Disregard for Human Rights," 1997, https://www.amnesty.org/en/wpcontent/uploads/2021/06/afr170161997en.pdf, Index Number: AFR 17/016/1997.

Amnesty International, "Cameroon: Opposition leader and more than a hundred supporters face the death penalty," 2019, https://www.amnesty.org/en/latest/news/2019/02/cameroon-opposition-leader-and-more-than-a-hundred-supporters-face-thedeath-penalty/.

Amnesty International, "Cameroon Protect Our Rights: They Still Count in the Fight against Terror!" n.d. https://www.amnesty.org/en/get-involved/take-action/cameroon-protect-our-rights/.

Amnesty International, "Cameroon: Rise in Killings in Anglophone Regions Ahead of Parliamentary Elections," 6 February 2020, https://www.amnesty.org/en/latest/news/2020/02/cameroon-rise-in-killings-in-anglophone-regions/.

Article 19, "Cameroon: A Transition in Crisis," October 1997, https://www.article19.org/data/files/pdfs/publications/cameroon-a-transition-in-crisis.pdf.

BBC, "Cameroon's President Paul Biya Wins Seventh Term," BBC News, 22 October 2018, https://www.bbc.com/news/world-africa-45940414.

Beco, D. G., "Human Rights Indicators: From Theoretical Debate to Practical Application," *Journal of Human Rights Practice*, Vol. 5 (2013): 380–397.

Bleck, Jaimie and Van De Walle, Nicolas, *Electoral Politics in Africa Since 1990: Continuity in Change*, New York: Cambridge University Press, 2019.

Boda, Michael D., "A New Generation in Election Observation: International Law as a Standard for Electoral Practice", PhD Thesis, Johns Hopkins University, 2011.

Brown, Stephen, "Authoritarian Leaders and Multiparty Elections in Africa: How Foreign Donors Help to Keep Kenya's Daniel Arap Moi in Power," *Third World Quarterly*, Vol. 22, no. 5 (2001): 725–739.

Cameroon Tribune, 7 January 2019, https://www.cameroon-tribune.cm/article. html/23421/fr.html/rene-emmanuel-sadi-desormais-la.

Cameroon's People Democratic Movements, n.d., http://www.rdpcpdm.cm/les-sec retaires-generaux-du-comite-central-du-rdpc/.

Chand, Vikram K., "Democratisation from the Outside In: NGO and International Efforts to Promote Open Elections," *Third World Quarterly*, Vol. 18, no. 3 (1997): 543–561.

Commonwealth Secretariat, "Cameroon Presidential Election 11 October 2004. Report of the Commonwealth Observer Group."

Commonwealth Secretariat, "Report of the Commonwealth Expert Team, Cameroon Presidential Election," 9 October 2011.

Commonwealth, https://thecommonwealth.org/our-member-countries/cameroon/ history.

Davis-Roberts, Avery and David J. Carroll, "Using International Law to Assess Election," *Democratisation*, Vol. 17, no. 3, (June 2010): 416–441.

Diamond, Larry, Juan J. Linz and Seymour Martin Lipset (eds.), *Democracy in Developing Countries: Latin America*, Boulder: Lynne Rienner, 1989.

Dicklitch, Susan, "Failed Democratic Transition in Cameroon: A Human Rights Explanation," *Human Rights Quarterly*, Vol. 24, no. 1: (February 2002): 152–176.

EC-UNDP, "Compendium of International Standards for Elections," https://www. ec-undp-electoralassistance.org/wp-content/uploads/2018/08/undp-contents-pub lications-compendium-of-int-standards-for-elections-English.

Emmanuel, Nikolas George, "Undermining Cooperation: Donor-Patrons and the Failure of Political Conditionality," *Democratisation*, Vol. 17, no. 5 (2010): 856–877.

Farer, Tom J., et al. "The Human Right to Participate in Government: Toward an Operational Definition," *Proceedings of the Annual Meeting (American Society of International Law)*, JSTOR, Vol. 82 (1988): 505–518.

Fahner, Johannes Hendrik, "Revisiting the Human Right to Democracy: A Positivist Analysis," *The International Journal of Human Rights*, Vol. 21, no. 3 (2017): 321–341.

Fombad, Charles Manga, "Election Management Bodies in Africa: 'Cameroon's National Election Observatory' in Perspective," *African Human Rights Law Journal*, Vol. 3, no. 1 (2003): 25–51.

Fombad, Charles Manga, "The New Cameroonian Constitutional Council in a Comparative Perspective: Progress or Retrogression?," *Journal of African Law*, Vol. 42, no. 2 (1998): 172–186.

Fomunyoh, Christopher, "Democratisation in Fits and Starts," *Journal of Democracy*, Vol. 12, no. 3 (2001): 37–50.

Fonchingong, Tangie Nsoh, "Multipartyism and Democratization in Cameroon," *Journal of Third World Studies*, Vol. 15, no. 2 (1998): 119–136.

Foute, Franck, "Cameroon: Opposition Leader Kamto Calls for 'Anti-Biya' Protest," *The Africa Report*, 22 September 2020, https://www.theafricareport.com/42612/ cameroon-opposition-leader-kamto-calls-for-anti-biya-protest/.

Freedom House, "Freedom in the World 2019: The Annual Survey of Political Rights and Civil Liberties," *Freedom House*, 2020, 978-1538134566.

GARDAWORLD News Alert, "Cameroon: Incumbent Party Wins 22 March Partial Legislative Elections Re-run/Update 4," https://www.garda.com/crisis24/news-alerts/330376/cameroon-incumbent-party-wins-march-22-partial-legislative-electi ons-rerun-update-4.

Glendon, Mary A., "Knowing the Universal Declaration of Human Rights," *Notre Dame Law Review*, Vol. 73, no. 5 (1998): 1153–1190.

Gros, Jean-Germain, "The Hard Lessons of Cameroon", *Journal of Democracy*, Vol. 6, no. 3. (1995): 112–127.

Herrmann, Clarissa, "Cameroon Elections: A Vote Marked by Violence and Absten-tion," *Deutsche Welle* (DW), 8 February 2020, https://www.dw.com/en/cam eroon-elections-a-vote-marked-by-violence-and-abstention/a-52304640.

International Crisis Group, "Uncertainties Deepen in Cameroon After Divisive Elec-tion," 5 November 2018, https://d2071andvip0wj.cloudfront.net/5nov18-uncert ainties-deepen-in-cameroon-after-divisive-election.pdf.

International IDEA, *The Global State of Democracy 2019: Addressing the Ills, Revising the Promise*, Stockholm: International IDEA, 2019.

Jinadu, L. Adele "Matters Arising: African Elections and The Problem of Electoral Administration," *African Journal of Political Science*, Vol. 2, no. 1 (June 1997): 1–11.

Kelley, Judith, "Election Observers and Their Biases," *Journal of Democracy*, Vol. 21 (3 July 2010): 158–172.

Kevin, Brenda, Stone Sam ad Maclean Ruth, "Biya Wins Again in Cameroon as Crackdown Disrupts Anglophone Vote," *The Guardian*, 22 October 2018, https:// www.theguardian.com/world/2018/oct/22/paul-biya-cameroon-85-year-old-pre sident-wins-reelection-landslide.

Kindzeka, Moki Edwin, "Cameroon Courts Orders Partial Elections Rerun in Trou-bled English-Speaking Regions," *Voice of America*, 26 February 2020, https:// www.voanews.com/africa/cameroon-court-orders-partial-election-re-run-troubled-english-speaking-regions.

Konings, Piet, "Opposition and Social-Democratic Change in Africa: The Social Democratic Front in Cameroon," *Commonwealth & Comparative Politics*, Vol. 42, no. 3 (November 2004): 1–23.

Krippahl, Cristina, "Cameroon: Opposition Vows to Defy Paul Biya's Government", *Deutsche Welle* (DW), 28 January, 2019, https://www.dw.com/en/cameroon-opp osition-vows-to-defy-paul-biyas-government/a-47266478.

Lappin, Richard, "Why Observe Elections? Reassessing the Importance of Credible Elections to Post-conflict Peacebuilding," *Peace Research, Canadian Journal of Peace and Conflict Studies*, Vol. 41, no. 2 (2009): 85–117.

Lynge-Mangueira, Halfdan, *Why 'Professionalising' International Election Observa-tion Might Not Be enough to Ensure Effective Election Observation*, Stockholm: International IDEA, 2012.

Mehler, Andreas, "Political Parties and Violence in Africa: Systematic Reflections Against Empirical Background," In Matthias Basedau, Gero Erdmann, and Andreas Mehler (eds.) *Votes, Money and Violence: Political Parties and Elections in Sub-Saharan Africa*, Durban: University of KwaZulu-Natal Press, 2007, 194–223.

Micah, Eddy, "No Dictatorship Considers Protests Legal, Cameroon's Opposition Politician Says," *Deutsche Welle* (DW), 22 September 2020, https://www.dw.com/ en/no-dictatorship-considers-protests-legal-cameroons-opposition-politician-says/a-55013976.

Morse, Yonatan L., "Electoral Authoritarianism and Weak States in Africa: The Role of Parties Versus Presidents in Tanzania and Cameroon," *International Political Science Review*, Vol. 39, no. 1 (2018): 114–129.

National Democratic Institute for International Affairs (NDI), "An Assessment of the 11 October 1992 Election in Cameroon," 1993, https://www.ndi.org/sites/def ault/files/060_cm_assessment.pdf.

National Democratic Institute for International Affairs, "Declaration in Support of Constitutionalism for Democratic Consolidation and the Peaceful Transfer," 4 October 2019, https://www.ndi.org/publications/declaration-support-constitution alism-democratic-consolidation-and-peaceful-transfer.

Ndi Eugene Ndi, "Cameroon Court Orders Parliamentary Polls Repeated in the Anglophone Regions," *The East African*, 26 February 2020.

NEEDS (EU), "Compendium of International Standards for Elections," Brussels: European Commission, n.d.

Nkansah, Lydia Apori, "Dispute Resolution and Electoral Justice in Africa: The Way Forward," *Africa Development*, Vol. 41, no. 2 (2016): 97–131.

Nyamnjoh, Francis B., "Cameroon: Over Twelve Years of Cosmetic Democracy," 2002, https://www.academia.edu/3033234/Cameroon_Over_twelve_years_of_cos metic_democracy.

Office of the High Commissioner for Human Rights, "OHCHR and elections and human rights," 2022, https://www.ohchr.org/en/elections.

Open Election Data Initiative, "Electoral Integrity: The Role of Election Observation, Open Election Data Initiative," 2022, https://openelectiondata.net/en/guide/ele ctoral-integrity/election-observation/.

Park, J.-D., "Assessing the Role of Foreign Aid, Donors and Recipients," In *Re-Inventing Africa's Development*, Cham: Palgrave Macmillan, 2019, pp. 37–60.

Reisman, Michael W., "International Election Observation," *Pace University Law Review: Yearbook of International Law*, Vol. 4, no. 1 (1992): 1–48.

Sandbrook, Richard, "Liberal Democracy in Africa: A Socialist-Revisionist Perspective," *Canadian Journal of African Studies*, Vol. 22, no. 2 (1988): 240–267.

Signe, Landry, "Cameroon's Contentious Elections Come at a Precarious Time in the Country's History," *Quartz Africa*, 6 October 2018, https://qz.com/africa/141 6006/cameroon-election-2018-everything-you-need-to-know/.

Siobhán, O'Grady, "Divided by Language: Cameroon's Crackdown on Its English-Speaking Minority Is Fueling Support for a Secessionist Movement," *Washington Post*, 5 February2019, https://www.washingtonpost.com/graphics/2019/world/ cameroon-anglophone-crisis/.

Smidt, Hannah, "From a Perpetrator's Perspective: International Election Observers and Post-electoral Violence", *Journal of Peace Research*, Vol. 53, no. 2 (2016): 226–241.

Sorensen, Georg, *Democracy and Democratisation: Processes and Prospects in a Changing World*, New York: Avalon Publishing, 1993.

Steiner, Henry and Philip Alson, *International Human Rights in Context, Law, Politics, Morals*, London: Oxford University Press, 1996.

Takougang, Joseph, "The 2002 Legislative Election in Cameroon: A Retrospective on Cameroon's Stalled Democracy Movement," *Journal of Modern African Studies*, Vol. 41, no. 3 (2003): 421–435.

Tande, Dibussi, "Biyaism Without Biya? The Battle for Regime Change in Cameroon," 20 January 2020, https://www.dibussi.com/2008/01/biyaism-without.html?cid=98206294.

Tande, Dibussi, "Issues and Questions About Cameroon's Diaspora Voting Act (Part II)," *Scribbles from the Den*, 10 August 2011, https://www.dibussi.com/2011/08/-cameroons-diaspora-voting-act-part-ii.html.

Tande, Dibussi, "Memory Lane (October 1992): A Tale of Two Presidents—Paul Biya and John Fru Ndi," *Scribbles from the Den*, 4 December 2010, https://www.dibussi.com/2010/12/memory-lane-october-1992-a-tale-of-two-presidents-.html.

Tande, Dibussi, "State Funding of Political Parties: A Democratic Imperative or Hush Money for the Opposition?," In *Essays on Politics and Collective Memory in Cameroon*, African Books Collective, 2009.

The Judicial Service of Ghana, *Manual on Adjudication*, Second Edition, Accra, DPI Print Ltd, 2012.

United Nations, *Elections: Perspectives on Establishing Democratic Practices*, New York: UN, 1997.

United Nations, *Report of the Independent Expert on the Promotion of a Democratic and Equitable International Order*, Alfred Maurice de Zayas, A/HRC/21/45 (2012).

United Nations Centre for Human Rights, *United Nations Human Rights and Elections: A Handbook on the Legal, Technical and Human Rights Aspects of Elections*, Geneva: UN Centre for Human Rights, 1994.

US Congress, "Hearing on Democratic Backsliding in Sub-Saharan Africa," Subcommittee on Africa, Global Health, Global Human Rights and International Organizations, 30 September 2020, https://foreignaffairs.house.gov/hearings?ID=4163F3C7-9249-4A48-9784-5D0A33FDEBF6.

US Government, "2019 Country Reports on Human Rights Practices: Cameroon," https://www.state.gov/reports/2019-country-reports-on-human-rights-practices/cameroon/.

Yanou, Michael A., "Democracy in Cameroon: A Socio-Legal Appraisal," *Law and Politics in Africa, Asia and Latin America*, Vol. 46, no. 3 (2013): 303–320.

CHAPTER 4

State Sovereignty and Presidential Term Limits in Africa

Kennedy Kariseb

1   INTRODUCTION

Over the past decade, there has been increased and sustained discussions about presidential term limits in Africa and beyond (Wiebusch & Murray, 2019). The heightened effect of scholarly and practical discussions on this subject should come as no surprise given the challenge in democratic governance (Claude, 1991; Jean-Francois, 1993) with a particular relevance to Africa. Africa, more than any other continent, despite some considerable efforts, continues to struggle democratically. The causes and underlying challenges for this phenomenon are diverse and cumbersome, both in a political and legal context. Practices and political trends in most parts of Africa reveal that democratic consolidation and good governance remains subverted by reactionary political practices that undermine popular aspirations for peace and political stability on the continent (Hengari, 2015). Perhaps one of the most manifest illiberal political practices that has fraught Africa is the unlawful (or even lawful) extension of presidential terms.

Although most post-1990 constitutions in Africa provide for presidential term limits, often with two terms, these have frequently been violated by incumbent regimes. Hence, much of the political unrests on the continent has been as a result of incumbent presidents refusing to relinquish political power

---

K. Kariseb (✉)
School of Law, University of Namibia, Windhoek, Namibia
e-mail: kkariseb@unam.na

© The Author(s), under exclusive license to Springer Nature Switzerland AG 2022
A. Adeola and M. W. Mutua (eds.), *The Palgrave Handbook of Democracy, Governance and Justice in Africa*,
https://doi.org/10.1007/978-3-030-74014-6_4

after the expiration of their constitutionally mandated presidential terms. One may only make terse reference to the post-electoral violence that erupted in early 2007 in Kenya as a notable example (Mbondeny et al., 2015). As Vencovsky (2007: 17) rightly states, in fledgling democracies, as is the case with most of Africa, the 'main importance of term limits stems from its positive impact on power alternation which, in turn, contributes to democratic consolidation'. Accordingly, there is some sort of justification for placing limitations on presidential terms. Term limits are premised on the 'principle of rotation' and even distribution of political power and 'derives its efficacy from the liberal principle that leadership is inherently a shared, public, participatory and transitory function' (Omondi, 2015: 1).

The limitation of presidential terms, whether in Africa or beyond, has consequences on State sovereignty. These consequences may be positive or negative depending on the context within which they are to be understood. Furthermore, constraints brought about by presidential tenure limitations can be viewed as an expression of the sovereignty of the people in a particular State. But such intrusion can be viewed, as a limitation on the sovereign right of a State to regulate its domestic affairs, including its governance systems. Accordingly, the question of State sovereignty, though an old one, is quite paradoxical and charged, raising more contestations than solutions for governance processes, especially in Africa.

This chapter seeks to advance the ongoing discourse on the sovereign rights of States to regulate their internal affairs vis-à-vis the limitations placed on presidential tenure given the challenges it may have on governance systems in Africa. A central question that is considered here is whether the supranational regulation of presidential terms in Africa by an intergovernmental entity such as the African Union (AU) is an intrusion on the sovereign rights of States to regulate their internal affairs. This is an important question worth considering.

Often the scholarly discourse on presidential term limits in Africa places central focus on the need for some sort of regulation on this matter without considering the counter argument that it could be an intrusion on State sovereignty. This approach may undermine not only the rights of States but could also lead to unprecedented impersonation of Western models of democracy that may not always be suitable to the African context. This chapter therefore seeks to juxtapose the State sovereignty argument within the existing literature on presidential term limits in Africa. This is not to suggest that States have an absolute sovereign right to regulate their internal affairs and therefore have the sole discretion as to how they deal with presidential term limits in their governance systems. On the contrary, this chapter addresses the question of State sovereignty, showing how it is mutilating, both as a concept and in its practical application internationally. It argues therefore that States no longer have an absolutist discretion over how they manage their internal affairs.

Consequently, State sovereignty should not be the basic premise for legitimising the extension of presidential terms, even if such a measure is validated through constitutional means. To this end, I argue that State sovereignty ought to be understood within the context of its evolving character and presidential terms needs to be regulated at the international level, constraining State sovereignty to certain limitations. The AU as the supranational body to which African States subscribe has a role to play towards this endeavour.

2 STATE SOVEREIGNTY AND PRESIDENTIAL TERM LIMITS IN AFRICA

2.1 State Sovereignty: Its Origins, Evolution and Contemporary Interpretations

One of the fundamental basis of international law has been the inviolability of State sovereignty; that is that States or supranational bodies are not allowed to 'intervene in matters which are essentially within the domestic jurisdiction of States'. The core basis of this principle in international law is aptly captured by Perrez (2000: 13) in his proposition:

> [t]hat sovereignty is the most important if not the only structural principle of international law that shapes the content of nearly all rules of international law, that the international legal order is merely an expression of the uniform principle of external sovereignty, that sovereignty is the criterion for membership in the international society, and that sovereignty in sum is the 'cornerstone of international law' and the 'controlling principle of world order'.

Since States form the soul of international law, their sovereignty forms an essential element of their existence and interaction in the international system. To this end international law has developed on the understanding that States are equal in their exercise of rights and duties and has the absolute supremacy over what goes on within their borders. Despite this relatively common appreciation, State sovereignty, as a concept, has had diverse meanings, or, at the very least, has attracted kilometric interpretations.

In practice, the concept of State sovereignty has a long history pre-dating the Post World War II period (Hinsley, 1986; Bartelson, 1995; Jackson, 2007). Its interpretation has long also been influenced by the political developments over the centuries. What is however clear is that there has been a reorientation of State sovereignty in the theory and practice of the international legal system, which as Kofi Annan (1999: 352) once held, is 'not least by the forces of globalization and international co-operation'. Therefore today, State sovereignty cannot be curtailed in a neat definition but rather as broadly as a reference to the wide rights and privileges which a State enjoys over its territory and population. Accordingly, Cassese (2005: 49) expatiates that state sovereignty includes more or less the following sweeping powers and rights:

> The power to exercise authority over all the people living in a particular territory; the power to freely use and dispose of the territory under the state's jurisdiction and to perform all activities deemed necessary or to the benefit of

the population living there; the right that no state intrude in the state's territory; the right to immunity from the jurisdiction from foreign courts for acts or actions performed by the state in its sovereign capacity and for execution measures taken against the use or planned use of public property or assets for the discharge of public functions; the right to immunity for state representatives who act in their official capacity and the right to respect for the State's nationals and its officials abroad.

Though a feasible reflection of the wide powers and rights of a State, Cassesse's assertion is surely not exhaustive and may overtime, and as globalisation is taking its toll the world over, be expanded. The epistemological parameters of what we know today as State sovereignty has drastically altered over the years. Fundamentally, State sovereignty was understood in absolutist terms. Robert Jenning's (2002) narration of the work of Jean Bodin as depicted in his *De Republica* treaties published in 1576 is illustrious of how given the realities in Continental Europe at the time, States opted for an absolutist appreciation of State sovereignty, that is premised on the idea of absolute power being deposited in the hands of a sovereign who had the power to make laws and was not bound by the law it made. The sovereign, according to Jean Bodin's jurisprudence, was a reference to the State and its supremacist ruler imbued with authority to make incontestable laws that were not binding to him.

According to Jean Bodin (tr by Franklin 1992), the concept of sovereignty primarily entails the absolute and sole competence of law making within the territorial boundaries of a state and that the state would not tolerate any other law-creating agent above it. He maintains that sovereignty, as the supreme power within a state, cannot be restricted except by the laws of God and by natural law (Franklin, 1992). No constitution could limit sovereignty and therefore a sovereign was regarded to be above positive law. Similarly, Bodley (1993: 419) argued that '[S]overeignty is the most extensive form of jurisdiction under international law. In general terms, it denotes full and unchallengeable power over a piece of territory and all the persons from time to time therein'. This narration of State sovereignty affirms 'international legal sovereignty', which is concerned with establishing the status of a political entity in the international system (Krasner, 2002).

In the nineteenth century, however, concepts around State sovereignty took an overhauled turn; one that recognised the imminent power of the citizenry. In terms of this reconceptualisation, sovereignty was viewed as power emanating from people who commune to form a State. The State therefore became an essential element of sovereignty and a fundamental actor of the international legal order that followed. The 1648 Peace of Westphalia consensus, which marked the end of political tensions in most of Continental Europe also further bought into the idea of State *based* sovereignty.

An important element of this conception of sovereignty was the principle of 'non-interference in matters falling within the territorial jurisdiction of a

State'. Modern international law, though building on these earlier conceptions of State sovereignty slowly began to dilute it, in that it recognised the equality of nation-States and more importantly called for a new international legal order premised on hegemonic stability. That this approach became more appropriate, especially after the end of World War II with the emergence of Super Powers who yielded more political command in the international legal regime, was compelled by the political developments of the time. By the time the United Nations (UN) was instituted in 1945, most of sub-Saharan Africa was still under colonial rule. This in practice meant that those nations under colonial rule or placed under the trusteeship system of the UN could not exercise sovereignty. This reality prompted a rethinking in international law that questioned State sovereignty because in practice some nation-States did not enjoy sovereignty contrary to the ideals of the UN Charter. State sovereignty as a result evolved from its formative roots which were premised on individual anarchic sovereignty to absolutist State sovereignty, to more contemporary understandings that relegate and subject sovereignty to certain limitations under international law. In other words, the understanding today is that States are sovereign entities firstly by virtue of being subjects of international law and thus only subject to it and not to the domestic whims of any other State. State sovereignty is therefore in one of its contemporary facets a reference to a State's legal independence from other States (Ansong, 2016).

Within the African regional system, there is also a growing trend, both in terms of practice and theory, that supports the dilution of absolute sovereignty; a somewhat surprising development. This is because the formation of the Organisation of African Unity (OAU) was deeply rooted in State sovereignty, and in its practice, the OAU took an 'inflexible stance on sovereignty' (Warner, 2017).That State sovereignty remained a core determinant in the identity and practice of the OAU is not surprising given its political history at the time. The hard won independence against colonial imperialism and racial segregation among others could only be appraised because it gave African States leverage with their former colonial masters.

The post-2002 reformation in the OAU however came with new paradigm shifts; one of which was to do away with an absolutist orientation of State sovereignty. Perhaps given the atrocities that permeated the African continent for the larger part since the early 1980s, the newly formed African Union (AU) ushered in a more relaxed stance on State sovereignty. One of the most overt illustrations of the relaxation of State sovereignty within the AU framework is visible in Article 4 (h) of the AU Constitutive Act of 2002, which provides for:

> ...the right of the Union to intervene in a Member State pursuant to a decision of the Assembly in respect to grave circumstances, namely: war crimes, genocide, and crimes against humanity.

The primary impact of this Article, as explicated from its wording is that it empowers the AU an unprecedented right of intervention in a member State in cases of war crimes, genocide and crimes against humanity. An acute problem however with this provision is the question whether prior UN Security Council authorisation is required (Amvane, 2005). The answer is not a settled one, however, the 2003 amendments to the AU Constitutive Act may serve as a hint on the possible interpretation that should be given. In terms of these amendments, the AU extended the right of intervention to what it termed '…a serious threat to a legitimate order to restore peace and stability to the member state of the Union upon the recommendation of the Peace and Security Council', (African Union 'Protocol on Amendments to the Constitutive Act of the African Union', 2003) clearly ousting UN Security Council authorisation. Furthermore, States may, on the basis of this provision interfere in the domestic policies and laws of other States where there is an imminent threat to the collective security of the AU Member States, or, gross violations of the fundamental human and peoples' rights of its citizens.

Another development within the African regional human rights system that can serve as an indicator of the flexing character of State sovereignty in Africa is the common position taken by the AU concerning unconstitutional changes to governments. In early 2007, the AU Assembly of Heads of State and Government adopted the African Charter on Democracy, Elections and Governance in Africa (ACDEG). The primary objective of the ACDEG is to "promote adherence, by each State party, to the universal values and principles of democracy and respect for human rights" (Article 2(1) of the ACDEG) (Article 2 (1) of the African Charter on Democracy, Elections and Governance in Africa, 2007). Viewed in this light, the ACDEG is a forerunner in terms of the AU legal instruments with a direct and immediate mandate aimed at addressing democratic deficits in AU Member States.

One of the pressing provisions of the ACDEG is located in article 23, which deals with sanctions in cases of unconstitutional changes of government. Described in terms of the Lomé Declaration as an 'unacceptable and anachronistic act', the AU has introduced a firm policy position aimed at condemning and prohibiting illegitimate transitions to State authority. Accordingly, once a situation of an unconstitutional transition of government in any AU Member State occurs the AU has through its policy undertaken to embark on one or more of the following action (Souare, 2009; Vunyingah, 2011): (a) a public condemnation by either the chairperson of the African Union Commission (AUC) or the chairperson of the AU Assembly of Heads of State and Government and a plea for the return of constitutional order in the State concerned; (b) convening of an urgent meeting by the Peace and Security Council of the AU to discuss and strategise about the illegitimate transition; (c) immediate suspension (preliminary for a period of six months) of the affected State (and consequently its representatives) from all policy organs of the AU; and (d) after a period of six months of suspension, and depending on the political climate in the affected State, introduce a range of limited yet targeted sanctions against any regime that refuses to restore constitutional order.

The policy position of the AU referred to above is not only a form of international delegation but equally a manifestation of the changing attitudes towards the exercise of absolute State sovereignty in African States. The mere fact that the AU can institute targeted sanctions against its Member States is an indication of the influential role the continental body has assumed and the delineation of State power on the part of African States. The intrusion on State sovereignty may be discerned from the fact that the AU can undertake practical action against one of its Member States based on a violation of a treaty obligation.

As is evident from the above analysis, State sovereignty is not what it used to be, whether understood from a theoretical or practical position. In this context, the international community no longer recognises absolutist sovereignty of a political ruler or State. Furthermore, as a result of the repositioning of the international order caused primarily by determinants such as globalisation and changes in political, legal and economic value systems, States cannot evade their duties, both to their citizens and to the international community solely on account of the exercise of sovereignty.

2.2   Presidential Termism in Africa: Contours, Trends and Prevailing Practices

Presidential term limits and extensions have largely been regarded as matters of domestic policy making in Africa (Hengari, 2015). As a result, most African States continue to reinforce sovereignty as the underlying basis for extending presidential terms. It is therefore not surprising that there has not been a holistic approach in dealing with presidential terms domestically in African States. This is the case despite the fact that in all African States presidential terms limits are dealt with in national constitutions.

Most African countries entrench two five-year terms for presidents. This includes countries such as Algeria (since 2016 Constitutional reforms), Angola (since 2010 Constitutional reforms), Burundi (since 2005 Constitutional referendum), Benin, Botswana, Burkina Faso, Cape Verde, Central African Republic (since 2015 Constitutional reforms), Ivory Coast (since 2000 Constitutional reforms), DRC (since 2005 Constitutional referendum), Congo (since 2015 Constitutional referendum), Kenya (since 2013 Constitutional reforms), Madagascar (since 1992 Constitutional referendum), Malawi (since 1992 Constitutional referendum); Mali (since 1992 Constitutional referendum); Mauritania (since 1991 Constitutional referendum), Mozambique (since 20,014 Constitutional referendum); Namibia (since its founding Constitution adopted in 1990); Niger (since 1999 Constitutional referendum); Rwanda (since 2015 Constitutional reforms); Sao Tome and Principe; Senegal (since 2016 Constitutional reforms); South Africa; Tanzania (since 1977 Constitutional reforms); Tunisia (since 2014 Constitutional reforms); Zambia (since 2006 Constitutional reforms) and Zimbabwe (since 2013 Constitutional reforms).

A considerable number of States, although few, make reference to more than five-years two term presidential limits. This is the case with countries such as Liberia (six-year two consecutive terms); Ethiopia (two six-year consecutive terms for the prime minister) with Gabon providing for unlimited seven years presidential terms. Equatorial Guinea, unlike Gabon, provides for two consecutive seven years presidential term limit. Nigeria, Egypt and Ghana are the only three countries providing for two four-year presidential term limits. Seychelles is the only country on the continent stipulating three consecutive five-year presidential term constraints since its 1991 constitutional reforms.

Eight African countries place no limitation on the holding of presidential office. Comoros, Gabon, Chad, Cameroon (since 2008 Constitutional reforms), Mauritius, South Sudan, Togo and Uganda provide for renewable five-year presidential terms. The omission of presidential term limits in these States therefore means by necessary implication that one can presumably hold political office as president for a life time.

Trends from different parts of the continent also reveal numerous occasions in which incumbent presidents successfully amend their constitutions to extend their stay in power. At least seven cases lend support to this fact. (Former) Presidents Sam Nujoma (Namibia); Omar Bongo (Gabon), Blaise Compaore (Burkino Faso); Idriss Deby (Chad); Lansa Corte (Guinea); Gnassingbe Eyadema (Togo) and Yoweri Museveni (Uganda) all successfully enabled constitutional reforms that secured their prolonged presidency.

Another visible pattern has been one of unsuccessful attempts of constitutional tempering aimed at securing third presidential terms contrary to constitutional provisions. Despite constraints from national Constitutions Presidents Chiluba (Zambia), Muluzi (Malawi) and Obasanjo (Nigeria) sought constitutional reforms, albeit unsuccessfully, directed at reversing tenure limits. The failed attempts in Zambia, Nigeria and Malawi have prompted some analysts to argue that there is 'clear scope for meaningful action by civil society organizations (and perhaps the broader international community) to yield pressure on incumbents from using their political muscles to secure tenures for themselves' (Vencovsky D., 2007). One thing however remains certain, and that is, at least from the above exposition it is clear that Africa has a mixed account of trends and practices relating to presidential tenures; and that equally there cannot be a uniform approach that can be regarded as a remedying method.

3   Piercing the Doctrine of State Sovereinty: The African Union and Presidential Term Limits in Africa

The challenges arising out of the domestic regulation of presidentialism in Africa, which are for the most premised in the sole discretion that States have in regulating their own domestic affairs, has prompted international reactions and responses. Intergovernmental entities such as the AU therefore gradually began to address the kilometric hold of power visibly in certain parts of the continent.

AU norms and standards relating to governance generally are enormous. These are however often generally framed with strong probabilities of no binding effect. A cursory reading of the African governance architecture clearly reveals a regional deficit of standards relating to presidential tenure. While the AU has been proactive in denouncing unconstitutional changes in governments in Africa (Souare, 2009), it has to date no official correspondence dealing explicitly with the visible extension of presidential term limits on the continent.

Much iteration has been centred around principles of good governance, peace and security. Agenda 2063: The Africa we want, one of the pertinent governance architecture of the AU adopted at its 24th Ordinary Summit in Addis Ababa in January 2015, reiterates in its fourth aspiration continental 'peace and security' (AU Agenda 2063: The Africa We want, 2015). Article 23 (1) of the African Charter on Human and Peoples' Rights provides for the right to national and international peace and security. Similarly, right from the start, in its preamble, the AU Constitutive Act echoes the determination of the African people 'to promote and protect human and peoples' rights, consolidate democratic institutions and culture, and to ensure good governance and the rule of law' (See AU Constitutive Act, 2002). Furthermore, Article 3 (f) and (g) obligates the AU to 'promote peace, security, and stability on the continent'and to 'promote democratic principles and institutions, popular participation and good governance'. These provisions may be authoritative and compelling to 'read into' the possible limitation or bar on unauthorised extension of presidential tenure. However, their protracted and vague wording may not necessarily be satisfactory to argue against the elongations of constitutionally set out presidential terms.

Perhaps the closest the AU standards and norms have peeled on presidential tenure is in Article 23 (5) of the African Charter on Democracy, Elections and Governance of 2012. Article 23 (5) provides as follows:

Article 23

States parties agree that the use of, inter alia, the following illegal means of accessing or maintaining power constitute an unconstitutional change of government and shall draw appropriate sanctions by the Union:

(5) any amendment or revision of the constitution or legal instruments, which is an infringement on the principles of democratic change of government.

This provision evidently bars any attempt aimed at Constitution tampering with the aim of undermining settled standards of democratic governance. It seems therefore that Article 23 (5) prohibits law makers, including sitting heads of state, from amending or undertaking constitutional reforms aimed at extending their political grip in governance. Any violation of Article 23

(5) can give rise to the AU Security Council imposing sanctions on States as contemplated in Article 24 of the African Charter on Democracy, Elections and Governance. Certainly, Article 23 (5) should be sufficient for the AU to take action against an incumbent president attempting to alter term limits.

The AU rightly prides itself as the primary regional organ responsible for the maintenance of peace and security on the continent. Article 3 (f) and (g) of the AU Constitutive Act reiterates this point by stating that one of the primary objectives of the AU is to 'promote peace, security, and stability on the continent' and the promotion of 'democratic principles and institutions, popular participation and good governance'. Given the reality that much of the political unrest on the continent is as a result of disputes relating to excessive presidential incumbency, it is only logical and necessary that the AU through its governance architecture adopts a framework regulating presidential terms.

The question often asked is: Whether there is any justification for the AU to regulate presidential terms? Is such intervention not an unwarranted intrusion on sovereignty of States and the margin of appreciation bestowed on States to regulate their internal affairs? Is the limitation on presidential terms a means to an end? These are broad, yet important questions; that are context-dependent. Suffice to say, that there are compelling arguments and validations for the regularisation of presidential terms because of the inordinate effects of centralised presidentialism.

The risks and danger associated with the non-regulation and extension of presidential terms is adamant since it centralises power in a small pool of political elite, to the detriment of the masses, with the probability of abuse of political power. As Roger (2006) rightly stated, Africa in particular, is in dire need of term limits due to the continents' past history which has shown the tendency of ambitious leaders to extend their tenure and at times even declare themselves 'president for life' to the detriment of their nations.

The extension of presidential terms in Africa often triggers civil strife and unrest, violence and gives rise to coups (Vencovsky, 2007). The absence of mechanisms, domestically but equally also on a regional level, through which alternation of power is to be affected, often leads to civilian frustration, which in the long run, translates into assassinations and coup *d' ètats*, as has been the case with some African heads of States, such as Kwame Nkrumah (1966), Idi Amin (1979), Hilla Limann (1981), Samuel K. Doe (1990), Dawda Jawara (1994), Mobutu Sese Seko (1997), Hosni Mubarak (2011), Ben Ali (2011) François Bozizé (2003) and Robert Mugabe (2017).

Often as a result of overstay in the presidency, political accountability becomes eroded and state machinery privatised. Term limits, offers some sort of security of political change, and subsequently offers possibilities of reformations in government. It may be one of possibly many explorations aimed at putting cheques and balances which help counteract the primordial mentality of holding power in perpetuity.

Given the above negative consequences of unlimited presidential tenure and, or, extension of presidential term limits; and further taking into account the AU's primary mandate of ensuring, *inter alia*, 'regional peace and security', clearly regional interventions in the form of standard setting may be warranted to gradually level the playing field as far as excessive presidential tenure is concerned. The proposed intervention by the AU can come in many forms. Ideally, three are advanced here. First, it could be either in the form of a broad interpretation of the existing provisions of the ACDEG without the need of an amendment. This could easily be achieved through a General Comment to existing provisions of the ACDEG, by the African Union Commission (AUC), the body tasked with the responsibility of the monitoring the implementation of the ACEDG. Alternatively, the AUC can through a purposive interpretation of existing provisions to States during periodic reporting and the subsequent concluding observations to State reports make pronouncements on the issue of presidential tenure. The second avenue that could be explored is an amendment of the ACEDG. Under this option, either existing provisions of the ACDEG could be identified and amended to include an explicit provision regulating presidential terms of office. Alternatively, an entire provision could be added to the text of the ACEDG that explicitly deals with presidential tenure. The third, and perhaps the least appealing option that can be undertaken is to introduce a treaty on presidential tenure in Africa. Given the backlashes of rights ritualism, time bound and the kilometric nature of producing international treaties, the third option may not be desirable. It is however also an option available to the AU for consideration. What the exact substantive content of the three proposals made here will entail goes beyond the scope of this chapter contribution. In fact, it can be a matter for further research, building on the narrations made in this and related discourses on this subject matter. For now, the case is made that supranational bodies, such as the AU should look into this overdue matter and make concerted efforts to address the democratic deficits brought about by the hiccups in presidential tenures in Africa.

Although one should accept that the AU should as a matter of principle steer towards introducing a normative framework that should regulate presidential term limits, primarily because of the adverse effects of non-regulation, caution should be made on how this exercise should be undertaken. It should be done in a cohesive-gradual manner, taking into account the historical, cultural, political and socio-economic indifferences of each of the 55 African States. Surely, the starting point should be a continent-wide intra-State dialogue and diplomatic engagements with each state. The AU as the intergovernmental body bringing these States together should ideally spearhead such a process.

4   Conclusion: Possible Options for Reform by the African Union

The trends and practices relating to presidential terms in Africa have proven to be charged as this chapter illustrates. For the most part, disputes arising out of expanded presidential terms, whether constitutionally or otherwise, serves as an incentive for conflict and political unrest on the continent. An immediate consequence of this has been that the peace and security of the continent is threatened. This calls for a concerted effort, and intervention on the part of supranational bodies, such as the AU. Suggestions for such an intervention, as this chapter does, are not misplaced. On the contrary, such intervention can be a peripheral, yet important initiative, aimed at fostering a culture of constitutionalism and the respect for the rule of law on the continent.

Furthermore, intervention is warranted because as shown in this chapter, while international law recognises the ultimate power of States to regulate their internal affairs such sovereignty is not absolute. There has been a gradual change in both conception and practice about State sovereignty. Whether this gradual alteration concerning State sovereignty has reached customary international status is not settled. Certainly, in the midst of such ambiguity there remains compelling arguments for such a status change at the international level. The abuses of State power through unconstitutional presidential tenure is one such consideration that may warrant the relaxation of State sovereignty and justify supranational intervention in domestic State affairs. The argument advanced here is that presidential tenure is an issue that should be regulated at the international level. In the case of African States, by the AU. The time for such concerted effort, intervention and reforms on the part of the AU is now more than in the past compelling.

BIBLIOGRAPHY

African Union 'Protocol on Amendments to the Constitutive Act of the African Union'. (2003, July 11).

Alex Ansong. (2016). "The Concept of Sovereign Equality of States in International Law". *Ghana Institute of Management and Public Administration Law Review, 2* (1), 23.

Amvane, G. (2005). "Intervention pursuant to Article 4 (h) of the Constitutive Act of the African Union without United Nations Security Council authorization,". *African Human Rights Law Journal, 15*(2), 282–298.

Annan, K. (1999, September 18). "Two Concepts of Sovereignty". *The Economist*, 352. https://www.economist.com/international/1999/09/16/two-concepts-of-sovereignty. (Last accessed on 1 June 2019).

Article 2 (1) of the African Charter on Democracy, Elections and Governance in Africa. (2007, January 30).

Attorney-General of Guyana v Cedric Richardson, CCJ 17 (AJ) 1, CCJ Appeal No. GYCC 2017/008. (The Supreme Court 2018).

AU Agenda 2063: The Africa We want. 2015. Retrieved from 2015: http://arc hive.au.int/assets/images/agenda2063.pdf. Last accessed and retrieved on 24 June 2016.

B, J. F. (1993). *The State in Africa: The Politics of the Belly*. New York: Longman.

Bartelson, J. (1995). *A Genealogy of Sovereignty*. Cambridge: Cambridge University Press.

Bodin, J. (1992). *On Sovereignty: Four Chapters from the Six Books of the Commonwealth*. (b. J. Franklin, Trans.).

Bodley, A. (1998). Weakening the Principle of Sovereignty in International Law: The International Tribunal for the Former Yugoslavia. *New York University Journal of International Law and Politics, 31*, 419.

Cassese, A. (2005). *International Law*. Oxford: OUP Oxford.

Claude, A. (1991). "Rethinking African democracy". *Journal of Democracy, 2*, 32–44.

DM & Simons, C. (2017). 'The Institutionalisation of Power Revisited: Presidential Term Limits in Africa'. *Africa Spectrum, 52* (2), 79–102.

Hengari, A. (2015). 'Presidential Term Limits: A New African Foreign Policy Challenge'. *Southern African Institute International Affairs Policy Brief*, 2.

Heyl, C. (2019). "Senegal (1970–2016): presidential term limit reforms never come alone". In C. Heyl, & A. &. A Baturo (Ed.), *The politics of presidential term limits* (pp. 339–361). Oxford University Press.

Hinsley, F. (1986). *Sovereignty*. Cambridge: Cambridge University Press.

Human rights and democratic governance in Kenya: A post-2007 Appraisal. (2015). In M. Mbondeny, & T. K. E Owiye-Asaala (Ed.).

Jackson, R. (2007). *Sovereignty: Evolution of an Idea*. Cambridge: Polity Press.

Jennings, R. (2002a). *"Sovereignty and International Law"*. (G. Kreijen, Ed.) Oxford: Oxford University Press.

Jennings, R. (2002b). "Sovereignty and International Law". In G. Kreijen (Ed.), *State Sovereignty and International Governance* (p. 29). Oxford: Oxford University Press.

Krasner, S. D. (2002). "Sovereignty: Organized hypocrisy". In A. &. Steiner, *International Human Rights in Context: Law, Politics, Morals* (pp. 575–577).

Mbondeny, M. (2015). *Human rights and democratic governance in Kenya: A post-2007 Appraisal*. (T. K. E Owiye-Asaala, Ed.).

Omondi, G. (2015). 'The New Assault on Presidential Term Limits in Africa: Focus on Burundi'. *African Security Studies*, 1. http://www.africanleadershipcentre.org/index.php/2014-10-22-15-44-06/alc-newsletters/sept-2015-issue/385-the-new-assault.

Perex, F. (2000). Cooperative Sovereignity From Independence to Interdependence in the Structure of International Law. 13.

Roger, T. (2006). Politics and Presidential Term Limits in Uganda. In *Leadership Change and Former Presidents in African Politics* (pp. 175–176).

See AU African Union Constitutive Act. (n.d.). Retrieved from 2002: http://www.au.int/en/sites/default/files/ConstitutiveAct_EN.pdf (Last accessed and retrieved on 25 June 2016).

Souaré, I. (2009). The AU and the Challenge of Unconstitutional Changes of Government in Africa. In M. Vunyingah. (Ed.), *Institute for Security Studies Policy Paper*, (pp. 1–16).

Souare, I. (2009). 'The PSC and Unconstitutional Changes of Government in Africa: A Critical Assessment'. *Institute for Security Studies Policy Brief* , 1–4.

U.S Term Limits, Inc v Thornton , 115 S.C Ct (The Supreme Court 1995 at 1842).

UN Charter in Article 2 (7). (1948, December 10).

Vencovsky, C. D. (2016). 'Presidential Term Limits in Africa'. In V. Goundon, *Conflict Trent* (p. 15). https://www.google.com.na/#q=d+vencovsky+presidential+term+limits+in+africa (Last accessed and retrieved on 25 June).

Vencovsky, D. (2007). 'Presidential Term Limits in Africa'. In *V Goudon Conflict Trent* (p. 17).

Vunyingah, M. (2011). "Unconstitutional Changes of Government in Africa: An Assessment of the Relevance of the Constitutive Act of the African Union". *Africa Institute of South Africa Policy Brief*, (pp. 1–8).

Warner, J. (2017). "The African Union and Article 4 (h): Understanding Changing Norms of Sovereignty and Intervention in Africa Through an Integrated Levels-of-Analysis Approach". In E. Sahle (Ed.), *Democracy, Constitutionalism, and Politics in Africa*.

Wiebusch, M. (2019). 'Presidential Term Limits and the African Union'. *Journal of African Law, 63*(1), (pp. 131–160).

CHAPTER 5

Soldiers in Civilian Uniforms: The Role of the Military in the Pursuit of Third-Termism

Trésor Muhindo Makunya and *Kwadwo Appiagyei-Atua*

1 INTRODUCTION

"Third termism" refers to the phenomenon of altering or removing presidential term limits to allow an incumbent president to seek a third or unlimited terms of office. Term limits were introduced as a tool to address the proclivity among African leaders for life presidential terms. (Mangu, 2014a: 748–757; Mangu, 2014b: 133–147).

While the subject has attracted a lot scholarly attention, most literature on the rise of third-termism in Africa fail to persuasively explain the role of the African military in supporting the phenomenon (Mangala, 2020; Odinkalu & Osori, 2018; Fombad, 2017: 52). This chapter seeks to fill that gap using Burkina Faso (under Blaise Compaoré) and the Democratic Republic of Congo (under Joseph Kabila) as case-studies.

T. M. Makunya (✉)
Faculty of Law, University of Pretoria, Pretoria, South Africa
e-mail: tresormakunyamuhindo@gmail.com

K. Appiagyei-Atua
Faculty of Law, University of Ghana, Accra, Ghana
e-mail: KAppiagyeiAtua@ug.edu.gh

© The Author(s), under exclusive license to Springer Nature
Switzerland AG 2022
A. Adeola and M. W. Mutua (eds.), *The Palgrave Handbook of Democracy, Governance and Justice in Africa*,
https://doi.org/10.1007/978-3-030-74014-6_5

2   Soldiers and the Third-Term Agenda

African States have experienced three generations of constitution-making since the time of independence (Shivji, 2000: 1–19; Fombad, 2016: 23–20).[1] More than three-thirds of African countries gained independence through political deals entered into with the former colonisers and less through violent military confrontation with the departing colonial administration (Thompson, 2010). Consequently, the first era of constitution-making was negotiated with the departing colonialists and was built on the rule of law, separation of powers, respect for human rights and multi-party democracy (Shivji, 2000). However, these constitutions did not last long. Many African states rejected these constitutions as 'the starting point in the process of consolidation of the people's power'. Thus, between 1960 and 1962, before the Organisation of African Unity (OAU) was born in 1963, 13 newly independent African states, beginning with Ghana, amended or replaced their independence constitutions (Prempeh, 2007).

The second generation of post-independence constitutions focused on purging the constitutional features what were considered as 'schisms' that African leaders argued were inserted to impede 'speedy development' and the attainment of national unity in the new independent states. This constitutional approach saw African presidents entrenching themselves in power through mainly the concept of African socialism and military dictatorship (Muhindo, 2017: 14). African socialism and authoritarian constitutions were built around presidential systems, imperial or life presidency (Mboya, 1963: 17–19; Dwyer, 2019). A few exceptions where democracy remained undisturbed were The Gambia, Botswana, Senegal and Mauritius (Jackson & Rosberg, 1985: 293–305).

The third, as noted above, is the adoption of new constitutions in the 1990s wave of democratisation that swept across Africa (Fombad, 2016: 23–30). In all of these scenarios, the role of the militarism has been evident.

In the first generation of constitution-making, the focus of discussion of the military in politics revolved around the conditions of democracy and civilian control of the military (Luckham, 1994: 13–75). In reality, the role of the military in African politics at this stage was largely limited to promoting the traditional notion of security with the state as the sole referent object (Hama, 2017: 1–19). The nation-state inherited from colonialism was weak and fragile and needed strong military presence to keep it in place from both internal and external threats (Baynham, 1975). Early studies of newly formed African armies and police establishments saw themselves as part of an institutional transfer of western paradigms of governance as military professionalism was considered integral to the neo-colonial enterprise of transferring power to elites.

---

[1] 'Constitution' is used here broadly to mean both written and unwritten laws which constitute the supreme law of the land out of which other laws derive their legitimacy, force and validity from.

It did not take long for the military to establish its foothold in African politics in a more overt fashion, a major factor responsible for the unravelling of the democratic experimentation negotiated for independence and for Africa to enter its second generation of constitution-making. The underlying factor was the closure of space by African socialist leaders for inclusive politics which provided very limited space for political dissent, pluralism and peaceful change in government through the ballot box. In this political equation, the military was engaged as gatekeepers for dictatorial regimes. However, in most cases, it was not the entire military set-up but the development of an elitist reserve force that maintains absolute loyalty to the political establishment in consideration for political and economic favours.

This gatekeeper arrangement gave way to direct involvement of the military in politics through *coups d'état* to effect regime change (Kuehn, 2017:787–788). Consequently, Matlosa and Zounmenou observe that 'a few years into self-government Africa became a theatre of military coups in which governance by the bullet took centre stage, postponing democratisation and jettisoning rule by the ballot' (Matlosa & Zounmenou, 2011: 95). Nearly three-fourth of African leaders who left power in the 1960s and 1970s did so through a coup, a violent overthrow or an assassination (McGowan, 2003: 368). Powell and Thyne record the occurrence of 206 coups attempts in Africa from 1950, of which 105 failed and 100 succeeded (Powell & Thyne, 2011: 249–259).

Apart from *coups d'état*, mercenarism—the employment or enlisting of non-nationals to overthrow by force or arms or by any other means a government of another nation (OAU Convention for the Elimination of Mercenaries in Africa 1972, art 1)—also reared its ugly head as another form of militarisation of African politics. This phenomenon led to the adoption of the OAU Convention for the Elimination of Mercenaries in Africa in 1972.

The role of the military in politics is classified as constituting unconstitutional changes in government by the then OAU in its Lome Declaration of July 2000 on the framework for an OAU response to unconstitutional changes of government[2] which came up with four grounds which reflects this reality:

i) military coup d'etat against a democratically elected Government;
ii) intervention by mercenaries to replace a democratically elected Government;
iii) replacement of democratically elected Governments by armed dissident groups and rebel movements;
iv) the refusal by an incumbent government to relinquish power to the winning party after free, fair and regular elections.

The Economic Community of West African States (ECOWAS) has also taken steps to deal with unconstitutional changes in government and the role of military in politics. Thus, in its Protocol Relating to the Mechanism

[2] (AHG/Decl.5 (XXXVI).

for Conflict Prevention, Management, Resolution, Peacekeeping and Security adopted in 1998, article 25(e) of the Protocol provides that one of the conditions for its application shall include a situation that involves 'an overthrow or attempted overthrow of a democrati-cally elected government'. A Supplementary Protocol was adopted three years later which expresses '[z]ero tolerance for power ob-tained or maintained by unconstitutional means' and considers the armed forces an 'apolitical' body that 'must be under the command of a legally constituted political authority'.

Between 1990 and 2010, more than twenty countries made transitions to democracy or to something away from authoritarianism. However, the process was not always smooth as some military regimes were unwilling to give up power but resorted to the strategy of 'civilianising' themselves to contest for office while manipulating the process to remain in power. However, the nature of military involvement has morphed to supporting incumbents within the context of third-termism.

These unconstitutional means of regime change were later endorsed by the AU and embodied in the African Charter on Democracy, Elections and Governance which added a fifth element that relates to third-termism. That is, [a]ny amendment or revision of the constitution or legal instruments, which is an infringement on the principles of democratic change of government. With the appetite for *coups d'etat* or any of the covert militarism now gone down, the military has resorted to its gatekeeper role, in this context, through support for third-termism. The situations in Burkina Faso and the Democratic Republic of Congo reflect this reality.

2.1   *Burkina Faso*

Blaise Compaoré came to power in 1987 through a military coup staged against Captain Thomas Sankara (Sampana, 2015:34; Frère & Englebert, 2015: 295). For 27 years, Compaoré's regime survived, in part, due to the loyalty he enjoyed from the *Régiment de Sécurité présidentiel* (RSP) (Sampana, 2015: 34). The democratic legitimacy of Compaoré's regime sprung from the 1991 presidential elections where he gained a seven year-term despite large boycott by opposition parties and lower voter turn-out (Natielse, 2013: 320–323). Subsequent elections, he won, took place in 1998 and his second term was to expire in 2005. However, in between, Compaoré managed to amend the country's Constitution. Constitutional Amendment Act 003–2000/AN of 11 April 2000 reduced the duration of the president's term from seven to five years and limited presidential terms to two and non-renewable (Keré, 2017: 1–2).

The RSP is notoriously known for its unalloyed and avowed commitment to Compaoré who used it to do various known dirty jobs for the regime, including acts of torture of opponents, brutal repression of protests and quelling of dissent. From a comparative perspective, dictatorships with ethnically fragmented security forces are less likely to support transition to democracy (Allen & Grewal, 2019). Also, Allen argues somewhere else that 'the interaction between military rule and ethnic stacking facilitates three predominant democratisation patterns. Africa's military regimes are nearly always ethnically stacked, which leads to frequent but often short-lived transitions to democracy. When non-military-led regimes stack the armed forces with co-ethnics, the result is most often a blocked transition. Only non-military-led regimes that do not ethnically stack their armie tend to result in stable democratic rule'. (Allen, 2019, 247–268).

RSP's loyalty was based on a number of grounds, including the ethnic factor as well as the economic and political benefits bestowed upon them. Above, it has also been argued that the military is likely to be unwilling to support change where they have very bad human rights record to protect. Therefore, until and unless they are assured that democracy will not threaten their institutional status, they are more likely to side with the regime in power.

Despite his ability to secure his election in 2005 and 2010, power bulimia continued to hunt Compaoré and his Congress for Democracy and Progress (CDP). An attempt was made in June 2014 to have a referendum organised to allow him to stand for election in the 2015 presidential race though Article 37 of the Constitution barred him (Bjarnesen & Lanzano, 2015: 3). The plan met with resistance by civil society organisations, opposition political parties and large numbers of the Burkinabé citizenry (Hagberg, 2015: 115–116). This time, however, the insurrections of 30 and 31 October 2014 on the streets of Ouagadougou and other main cities across the country would result in the resignation from office of Blaise Compaoré and his fleeing to Cote d'Ivoire to seek refuge there (Signé, 2014).

What accounts for the success of this transition is that 'the military is less likely to maintain loyalty to the regime in power when protesters are more united and organised across religious, ethnic or economic lines. Armies that recruit their lower ranks from marginalised socioeconomic groups or that are broadly representative of society find it particularly challenging to stop large protests', citing the example of the fall of dictators in Sudan, Ethiopia and Algeria (Allen & Noyes, 2019). When militaries are tightly linked to those in power, democratic change is likely to come more slowly and requires some kind of agreement and concessions to the old regime.

In the end, Burkina Faso's military was divided between the faction loyal to President Compaoré and those who were on the side of change. Compaoré himself made this clear some days after he was ousted. He blamed his Army Chief of Staff, Honoré Nabéré Traoré whom he accused of having colluded with opposition leaders to oust him (Yahmed, 2014). Compaoré's disappointment revealed that he no longer had sufficient control over units of the regular military apart from his loyal RSP. This is, in part, why army officials outside the RSP shifted their support and allegiance to the insurrection. The positions of loyalty within Burkina Faso's army (re)defined the attitude they adopted during the October 2014 insurrection. Unlike the RSP, particularly its leadership, which owed all to Compaoré and to whom the defence of a regime seemed more important than allowing citizens to voice their concerns through democratic process, the regular military believed otherwise and sided with change. The latter was convinced that their interests and that of Burkina Faso and burkinabés will be better off if a new regime took over. The regular army, unlike the RSP, for obvious reasons, understood that the interests of the citizens and that of the country were more important than those of the outgoing president. Therefore, the position taken by the military determined the success or failure of third-termism in Burkina Faso.

The Burkinabé situation, however, is in sharp contrast to what happened in Democratic Republic of Congo (DRC) where both the regular army and the presidential guards sided with the incumbent as the next section demonstrates.

2.2   Siding with the Incumbent: The Case of Democratic Republic of Congo

Joseph Kabila became president when Laurent-Désiré Kabila was assassinated in January 2001 (Mangu, 2004: 13; Appiagyei-Atua, 2017: 340). A Brigadier General, Joseph Kabila was the Army Chief of Staff at the time of his appointment by the National Security Council as interim president. The young soldier groomed into president successfully led the country to the post-war free and fair elections in which the erstwhile warring factions participated in, namely, the Movement for the Liberation of Congo (MLC) led by Jean-Pierre Bemba and the Congolese Rally for Democracy (RCD) led by Azarias Ruberwa. The 18 February 2006 Constitution ushered the country into a new democratic era in which the Head of State was to be elected for a five-year term renewable once. However, the 'military god complex' soon caught up the young soldier, who begun as far back as 2009 (Reybrouck, 2014: 654),[3] to engineer constitutional amendment to remain in power for life. Attempts to remain in power attained their peak between 2015 and 2018 but was met with severe domestic and international resistance (Muhindo, 2017: 26–33).

As a soldier in civilian uniform, Kabila relied on the military to coerce anti-third term campaigners. The coercion was mostly done through repression of protests. Between 8,000 to 10,000 soldiers were trained overseas on 'techniques of urban guerrilla warfare' and poured into the police force to give a semblance of legality to their actions (Rigaud, 2017) and to suppress protests and demonstrations in violation of the principle that '(m)embers of the armed forces can only be used for law enforcement in exceptional circumstances and where strictly necessary'.[4] The United Nations Joint Office for Human Rights

---

[3] In September 2009, Joseph Kabila instituted a commission to examine possibilities of extended from five to seven years, the duration of presidential term and of repealing the two term limit.

[4] African Commission on Human and Peoples' Rights, General Comment 3 on the Right to Life.

observed that soldiers were used to quell demonstrators, including the Presidential Guard Unit (GR) and regular army, which led to excessive use of force (United Nations Joint Office for Human Rights, 2017; Mangu, 2016: 217), mainly in Kinshasa (the country's capital city) where the mobilisation was rife.

Unlike Compaoré, Kabila remained politically legitimate in the eyes of the army. The military's cost and benefit assessment, to wit, what senior military officials may gain or lose should other political leaders takeover indicated that the survival of Kabila's regime entailed the continuation of corruption in the army, patron-client relations, exploitation and control of mining resources and illicit selling and acquisition of ammunition.

3   Conclusion

The chapter sought to trace the role of the military in politics in Africa from the time of independence to date in order to situate the discussion in the context of the role of the military in supporting third-termism or otherwise. Though designed as apolitical institutions, the political landscape inherited from colonialism and which morphed into African socialism and one-party dictatorship and attendant cases of maladministration, corruption and inept governance practices, created an avenue for the military to move from a passive to a more covert and direct role in politics in most African countries. Yet, rule by the bullet has not proven to be as effective as rule by the ballot.

However, so long as Africa continues to struggle to consolidate its democratic gains, the military sees a space it can occupy to influence the process and exploit it for its own good. Thus, the return to democracy in the post-Cold War era has seen the re-emergence of the role of the military in politics as gatekeepers of the old order in many parts of Africa. Therefore, it behoves democracy watchers to recognise that the military's involvement in African politics requires a systematic approach towards instilling democratic values across all sectors of the society including the military. Political parties, non-governmental organisations and inter-governmental organisations should therefore be interested in monitoring the basis and criteria for recruitment into the security forces, especially the military and to make sure the military remains apolitical.

Bibliography

Allen, N. & Grewal, S. (2019). Can Sudan's Military Be Convinced to Support Democracy? https://warontherocks.com/2019/06/can-sudans-military-be-convinced-to-support-democracy/.

Allen, N. & Noyes A.H. (2019). African Dictators Have Been Losing Power—Some to Democratic Governments. Militaries Can Tip the Scales Toward Democracy https://www.rand.org/blog/2019/09/african-dictators-have-been-losing-power-some-to-democratic.html.

Allen, N. (2019). Authoritarian Armies and Democratizing States: How the Military Influences African Transitional Politics. *Democratization* 26/2, 247–268.

Appiagyei-Atua, K. et al. (2017). State Security, Securitisation and Human Security in Africa: The Tensions, Contradictions and Hopes for Reconciliation. *Global Campus Human Rights Journal* 1, 340.

Baynham, S.J. (1975). *Politics and the Military in Africa*. https://www.krigsvide nskab.dk/politics-and-the-military-in-africa.

Bjarnesen, J. & Lanzano, C. (2015). Burkina Faso's One-Week Coup and its Implications for Free and Fair Elections. *Nordiska Afrikainstitutet Policy Note 10*, 3.

Dwyer, M. (2019). *The Military in African Politics*. In Cheeseman, N. *The Oxford Encyclopedia of African Politics* (Oxford: Oxford University Press).

Fombad, C.M. (2016). The Evolution of Modern African Constitutions: A Retrospective Perspective. In Fombad, C.M. *The Separation of Powers in African Constitutionalism* (Oxford University Press).

Fombad, C.M. (2017). Presidential Term Limits Through Constitutional Amendments in Africa: Deconstructing Legitimacy. In Materson, G. & Meirotti, M. *Checks and Balances: African Constitutions and Democracy in the 21st Century* (Johannesburg, EISA).

Frère, M.-S. & Englebert, P. (2015). Briefing : Burkina Faso-The fall of Blaise Compaoré. *African Affairs* 114/455, 295.

Hagberg, S. (2015). Thousands of new Sankara: Resistance and struggle in Burkina Faso. *Africa Spectrum* 3, 115–116.

Hama, H.H. (2017). State Security, Societal Security, and Human Security. *Jadvpur Journal of International Relations* 21(1), 1–19.

Jonathan, P. & Thyne, C. (2011). Global Instances of Coups from 1950-Present. *Journal of Peace Research* 48(2), 249–259.

Keré, B. (2017). Avant-Propos. https://www.wipo.int/edocs/lexdocs/laws/fr/bf/bf017fr.pdf.

Kuehn, D. (2017). Midwives or Gravediggers of Democracy? The Military's Impact on Democratic Development. *Democratisation* 24(5), 787–788.

Luckham, R. (1994) The Military, Militarization and Democratization in Africa: A Survey of Literature and Issues. *African Studies Review* 37(2), 13–75.

Mangala, J.R (2020). *The Politics of Challenging Presidential Term Limits in Africa* (London, Palgrave Macmilan).

Mangu, A. M. (2004). DR Congo: The Long Road From War to Peace and Challenges for Peaceful Transition and National Reconstruction. *Africa Insight* 34(2/3), 31.

Mangu, A.M. (2014a). Constitutionalisme, constitutions, et limitation des pouvoirs et des mandats présidentiels en Afrique. in Aïvo, F.J. (2014a). *La Constitution béninoise du 11 décembre 1990 : Un modèle pour l'Afrique ? Mélanges en l'honneur de Maurice Ahanhanzo-Glélé* (L'Harmattan): 748–757.

Mangu, A.M. (2014b). Inconstitutionnalité d'un troisième mandat présidentiel: leçons de la Cour constitutionnelle du Bénin à d'autres Cours constitutionnelles africaines. *African Journal of Democracy and Governance* 1(4), 133–147.

Mangu, A.M. (2016). MK Tshiabo Auguste Les sanctions ciblées américaines contre des responsables congolais violent le droit international, 2016. *African Journal of Democracy* 3(3), 217.

Matlosa, K. & Zounmenou, D.D. (2011)The tension between militarisation and democratisation in West Africa: A comparative analysis of Niger and Guinea. *Journal of African Elections* 10(2), 95.

Mboya, T. (1963). African Socialism. *Transition* 8, 17–19.

McGowan, P.J. (2003). African military coups d'état, 1956–2001: Frequency, trends and distribution. *Journal of Modern African Studies* 41(3), 368.

Meredith, M. (2013). *The State of Africa: A History of the Continent Since Independence. Martin Meredith* (London New York Sydney Toronto New Delhi: Simon & Schuster).

Natielse, K.J. (2013). Le Burkina Faso de 1991 à nos jours: entre stabilité et illusionnisme démocratique. *PhD Thesis, University Montesquieu Bordeaux IV*: 320–323. https://tel.archives-ouvertes.fr/tel-00869173/document (accessed 17 August 2019).

Nyarko, M.G. & Makunya, T. (2018). Selected developments in human rights and democratisation during 2017: Sub-Saharan Africa. *Global Campus Human Rights Journal* 2(1), 154–155.

OAU Convention for the Elimination of Mercenaries in Africa O.A.U. Doc. CM/433/Rev.L, Annex 1 (1972).

Odinkalu, C. & Osori, A. (2018). *Too Good to Die: Third Term and the Myth of the Indispensable Man in Africa* (Lagos, Prestige).

Prempeh, K.H. 'Africa's "constitutionalism revival": false start or new dawn?' (2007) 5(3) *International Journal of Constitutional Law* 469–506.

Reybrouck, D.V. (2014). *Congo. Une Histoire* (Babel).

Rigaud, C. (2017). RDC: Joseph Kabila peut-il compter sur son armée. http://afrikarabia.com/wordpress/rdc-joseph-kabila-peut-il-encore-compter-sur-son-armee/ (accessed 17 August 2019).

Robert H. Jackson & Carl G. Rosberg (1985, Winter). "Democracy in Tropical Africa: Democracy Versus Autocracy in African" in Politics *Journal of International Affairs* Vol. 38, No. 2, Dilemmas of Democracy, pp. 293–305.

Sampana, L. (2015). La demilitarisation paradoxale du pouvoir politique au Burkina Faso. *Les Champs de Mars* 28(3), 34.

Shivji, I.G. (2000). Three Generations of Constitutions in Africa: An Overview and Assessment in Social and Economic Context (University of Dar es Salaam). http://repository.udsm.ac.tz:8080/xmlui/bitstream/handle/20.500.11810/2118/Three_Generations_of_Constitutions_in_Af.pdf?sequence=1&isAllowed=y (accessed 26 September 2020).

Signé, L. (2014). Four reasons why Burkina Faso's long-ruling dictator fell. (web page) *The Washington Post* 10 November 2014. https://www.washingtonpost.com/news/monkey-cage/wp/2014/11/10/four-reasons-why-burkina-fasos-long-ruling-dictator-fell/?noredirect=on&utm_term=.c96eacf1fea0 (accessed 17 August 2019).

United Nations Joint Office for Human Rights, March 2017 Report on the main trends of human rights violations in DRC (April 2017). https://www.undp.org/content/dam/unct/rdcongo/docs/UNCT-CD-BCNUDH-Note-mars%202017.pdf (last accessed 17 August 2019).

Vohito, S. (2020). COVID-19 and unamendable limits on duration of presidential and legislative terms in the Central African Republic. http://constitutionnet.org/news/covid-19-and-unamendable-limits-duration-presidential-and-legislative-terms-central-african (accessed 9 September 2020).

Yahmed, M.B (2014). Burkina Faso: Blaise Compaoré, sa version des faits … https://www.jeuneafrique.com/39106/politique/burkina-faso-blaise-compaor-sa-version-des-faits/ (accessed 9 September 2020).

CHAPTER 6

Reflections on the Role of the Pan-African Parliament in Advancing Democratic Governance in Africa

Osy Ezechukwunyere Nwebo and Charles Manga Fombad

1 Introduction

Beyond the level of domestic or national parliaments, international parliamentary institutions have mushroomed since the World War II. These institutions are endowed with powers and functions that enable them carry out parliamentary functions to the extent defined in their founding treaties. Today a number of international parliamentary institutions are legally established as legislative bodies of international organisations with mandate to promote constitutionalism and democratic governance both in the parent organisations and in their respective member states.

This chapter is based on the fourth chapter of thesis titled: 'The role of the Pan African Parliament in Promoting Constitutionalism and Democratic Governance in Africa: Lessons from Other Supranational Parliaments' submitted by OsyEzechukwunyere Nwebo in February 2019 in fulfilment of the requirement for the degree of Doctor Legum (LLD) in the Faculty of Law, University of Pretoria, South Africa.

O. E. Nwebo
Imo State University, Owerri, Nigeria

C. M. Fombad (✉)
Faculty of Law, University of Pretoria, Pretoria, South Africa
e-mail: charles.fombad@up.ac.za

© The Author(s), under exclusive license to Springer Nature
Switzerland AG 2022
A. Adeola and M. W. Mutua (eds.), *The Palgrave Handbook of Democracy, Governance and Justice in Africa*,
https://doi.org/10.1007/978-3-030-74014-6_6

The Pan-African Parliament (PAP) is a regional legislative body in this genre, with the aim of promoting the African Union (AU) agenda on constitutionalism and democratic governance. This chapter examines avenues through which PAP can advance democratic governance in Africa. In advancing the discussion, this chapter interrogates the legislative status of the PAP, the vision for its establishment, powers and functions, the rationale for the limited mandate of the PAP, the assessment of the activities it has carried out so far and those it can effectively carry out within its powers and functions under the PAP Protocol. This chapter argues, that despite its limited mandate, the PAP is not a mere talk shop, but possesses the attributes of a classical parliament that has been undertaking activities within its mandate. There is however room for improvement in undertaking its activities more effectively especially in promoting democratic governance in Africa.

2   The Vision for the Establishment of the PAP

The visionary founders of the AU understood from the very beginning that the parliamentary dimension of the AU governance architecture is a *sine qua non* for the effective realisation of the aims and objectives it has set out for itself. This is even particularly critical in the promotion of its agenda on constitutionalism and democratic governance and in achieving continental integration. The establishment of the PAP is therefore informed by the understanding of African leaders that the people of Africa need to be represented and fully involved in the programmes and policies of the AU for their effective implementation. This vision is clearly expressed in Article 17 of the Constitutive Act which provides that: 'In order to ensure the full participation of African peoples in the development and economic integration of the continent, a Pan-African Parliament shall be established' (AU Constitutive Act 2000, art 17).

The PAP was therefore foreseen as the institution that can represent the people of Africa and their grassroots organisations as well as constitute a common platform for the people of Africa to articulate their views on the challenges facing the continent. The establishment of the PAP was a clear demonstration of determination and commitment of African leaders to realise the ideals of pan-Africanism and African renaissance. Enamoured by the vision of the AU in establishing the PAP and guided by its mandate and set of objectives in the Protocol, the PAP formulated a strategic plan for itself, informed by its own vision, mission, mandate and core values as well as the developmental challenges facing the continent (PAP Strategic Plan 2014–2017, 2014). The PAP envisions a continental institution harnessing 'One Africa one voice'.

The PAP's vision has a long-term horizon and envisions a Pan-African Parliamentary institution that will provide a common platform for African peoples to fully participate in the decision-making processes of the AU for the political and socio-economic development and integration of the African continent. This is to be promoted through the harmonisation and coordination of national and regional policies and laws in order to promote a sense of unity and common destiny among the peoples of Africa. Based on the foregoing, the PAP proposed six strategic objectives as follows (PAP Strategic Plan 2014–2017, 2014):

> To strengthen its legislative parliamentary functions;
> To provide a platform to mainstream African voices and those in diaspora into the AU policy making process;
> To promote human rights, democracy, and good governance in Africa;
> To promote peace, security and stability;
> To promote integration and development in Africa; and
> To strengthen the institutional capacities of the PAP

It is clear that the PAP's vision and strategic objectives are in tandem with the AU vision in establishing the institution, particularly with regard to its agenda on constitutionalism and democratic governance. However, the question is whether the parliament has been effectively delivering on its mandate, to what extent and how can it be more effective. We argue that despite its challenges, the PAP has not only recorded appreciable accomplishments and growth but has also acquired global influence and prominence. Indeed, the parliament has emerged as an indispensable institution in strengthening Africa's democratic institutions, democratic culture, good governance, transparency and rule of law in Africa. Thus, the vision of African leaders in establishing the PAP is being realised despite its teething challenges.

3   Interrogating the Parliamentary Status of the PAP

In interrogating the parliamentary status of the PAP, we note that various academics and commentators on the role of the PAP have expressed the view that the institution is a mere 'talk shop', a name described as 'befitting of an institution that undertakes workshops, seminars and conferences largely for the benefit of the parliamentarians' (Dinokopila, 2016). The role of the institution has been undermined to the extent of asking whether it 'will ever be a real continental legislature—or will it remain forever a glorified talk shop?' (Fabricius, 2016; Zambara, 2009; Dinokopila, 2016).

Unfortunately, comments by some members of the PAP themselves tend to be in agreement with the above opinion. For instance, at the 2017 October session, some members of the PAP expressed their frustrations regarding the slow pace in the ratification of the PAP revised Protocol and having struggled to make their voices heard, were prompted to ask themselves: 'What are we for?' 'Every time we're here, we obsess over the same things. If we are not making laws, then what's the point of being here?' (News24, 2017). Similar comment was made by Hon Floyd Shivambu, a parliamentarian from South

Africa when he said thus: 'This forum is not a parliament it is just a discussion platform that does not have any legislative powers. This institution is still wobbly', 'As it is, it is a waste of resources'. More significantly, the president of the PAP, at the time, observed that without the power to take concrete action, the parliament is doomed to continue as a talking shop (News 24, 2017). These types of comments, especially coming from members of the PAP casts doubt as to capacity of this institution to effectively deliver on its mandate under the PAP Protocol.

However, we argue that there is evidence to the fact that PAP is an important continental parliament and not just a mere talking shop. What is indeed required is for the parliament to clearly understand the enormity of its powers under the PAP Protocol and how it can harness its potentials in achieving its objectives. In order to buttress our argument, it is considered apposite to first examine the legal basis for its existence and authority to carry out parliamentary functions. The authority of the PAP to exist and function as a parliament can be ascertained by examining the provisions of the relevant sections of the following source documents, namely: the Constitutive Act of the African Union; the Protocol to the Treaty Establishing the African Economic Community Relating to the Pan-African Parliament; and the Rules of Procedure of the Pan-African Parliament.

The basic source document authorising the establishment of the PAP is the Constitutive Act of the African Union (the Act) which provides in Article 17 as follows:

1. In order to ensure the full participation of African peoples in the development and economic integration of the continent, a Pan-African Parliament shall be established.
2. The composition, powers, functions and organization of the Pan-African Parliament shall be defined in a protocol relating thereto.

Pursuant to Article 17 of the Act,[1] the Protocol to the Treaty Establishing the African Economic Community Relating to the Pan-African Parliament (the Protocol) formally established the PAP. The Protocol therefore constitutes the instrument which established the PAP and define its composition, powers, functions and organisation accordingly. On whether the PAP performs the traditional functions of a classical parliament, this can be determined by considering the role parliaments play in modern democratic societies *vis a vis* that of the PAP and by drawing inferences from that. To begin with, in contemporary usage, parliaments are strictly speaking, the democratically elected body of representatives constituting one of the three main branches of government whose traditional role is to represent the people; to make laws and to oversee the main constitutional functions of the other arms of government. The crux

---

[1] The Act provides that 'the powers and functions of the Pan-African Parliament shall be defined in a Protocol'.

of the argument of those who opine that the PAP is not a parliament in the strict sense of the term is the apparent lack of authority to make laws like in the case of classical parliaments. This is based on the restriction of the PAP to advisory and consultative powers only (The Protocol 2001, art 2(3)).

On this issue, we argue that this apparent restriction to advisory and consultative role cannot be interpreted to mean that the PAP cannot carry out legislative functions. This simply means that the PAP on its own cannot, in the interim, make laws that can have binding effect on the AU, hence the attribution of legislative competence will be in phases as may be determined by the AU Assembly. Our argument is fortified by the clear provision that 'the ultimate aim of the parliament shall be to evolve into an institution with full legislative powers...' (The Protocol 2001, art 2(3)). This provision, in our view, assumes that the PAP to all intents and purposes is a parliament, though with limited legislative powers, *ad interim*.[2] In any case, it must be borne in mind that the law-making process is not the exclusive preserve of the legislature rather it involves the role of some other authorities in one form or the other and at one stage or the other.[3]

It is instructive to note that there are various forms of law and law-making processes which include rule making. In this connection, reference is made to the provisions of Article 11 of the PAP Protocol on the powers and functions of the PAP (particularly paragraph 8) which empowers the parliament to adopt its own Rules of Procedure without restriction. Thus, Article (8) gives wide powers to the PAP in exercising its oversight, investigative, consultative and advisory functions to adopt any rule which it deems necessary to achieve its objectives as set out in Article 3 of the Protocol and to exercise its powers as set out in Article 11 of the Protocol. This in our view constitutes a form of law-making power by the PAP, albeit in the form of rules of procedure.

Undoubtedly, the PAP cannot be equated to a fully developed parliament due to its special circumstance as an evolving continental parliamentary institution. Evidently, it does not possess all the attributes of a well-developed supranational parliament like the European Parliament. However, modern constitutional democracies, beyond the classical role of law-making, also vest parliaments with oversight functions as the people's watch-dog against the abuse of executive office. By virtue of this oversight function, parliaments take steps to ensure that the principle of constitutional supremacy and the core elements of constitutionalism and democratic governance are adhered to. Members of parliament carry out oversight functions by investigating, requesting for documents and reports, debating issues (in the plenary or in

---

[2] The legal maxim which states that 'equity sees that as done what ought to be done' supports this argument.

[3] For instance, in some national constitutions the chief executive can propose government bills to be debated and passed by the parliament. He can also sign bills into law or even veto a bill subject however to the power of the parliament to override such veto. In international organisations like the European Union, the European Parliament shares this role with the Council.

committees of the House as the case may be) and also by making their findings available to the appropriate agency for necessary action. It is clear from the provisions of Article 11 of the PAP Protocol grants the PAP parliamentary oversight powers, particularly, consultative and advisory powers.

However, some commentators on the role of the PAP are of the opinion that the oversight powers of the PAP are not concrete in view of its limited mandate as a merely advisory and consultative institution. Hence, the result of its oversight functions ends up in making recommendations. In our view, this opinion wrongly assumes that it is within the powers of parliaments to implement recommendations. This is because even in classical parliamentary institutions, their role does not include the execution of laws or implementation of recommendations made by them. This comes within the traditional role of the executive arm of government.[4] Therefore, the oversight role of the PAP is not materially different from that of classical state parliaments with the exception that the state executive is accountable to the state parliament, which usually has the power to pass a vote of no confidence on the executive in appropriate circumstances, and can also invoke its impeachment powers to remove the executive in accordance with the state constitution. Considering the powers and functions of the PAP particularly as provided for in Article 11 (1) (2) and (5), it can be argued that its oversight role is very clear and not materially different from that of classical parliaments and cannot be undermined for the reason only that its recommendations may not be implemented as expected.

With regard to the representative role of a parliament, it is instructive to note that Article 17 (1) of the Protocol states that the PAP is established in order to ensure the full participation of African peoples in the development and economic integration of the continent. Furthermore, the preamble to the PAP Protocol states that the establishment of the PAP is informed by a vision to provide a common platform for African peoples and their grassroots organisations to be more involved in discussions and decision-making on the problems and challenges facing the continent. Accordingly, one of the strategic objectives of the PAP is to provide a platform to mainstream African voices and those in the diaspora into the AU policy making processes. Based on the above, the representative role of the PAP cannot equally be disputed. In the final analysis, we conclude that to all intents and purposes, the PAP is a parliament and that it carries out the traditional functions of a classical parliament albeit, with limited legislative powers.

---

[4] In classical parliaments, for instance, the oversight powers of the legislature are meant to expose corruption, inefficiency or waste and not designed to enable the legislature usurp the general investigative functions of the executive or the adjudicatory function of the judiciary (Senate of National Assembly v Tony Momoh, 1983).

4 Rationale for the Limited Mandate of the PAP

In defining the powers and functions of the PAP, Article 11 of the Protocol states that 'the Pan-African Parliament shall be vested with legislative powers to be defined by the Assembly. However, during the first term of its existence, the Pan-African Parliament shall exercise advisory and consultative powers only' (PAP Protocol 2001, art 11). This provision has generated some debate on the extent of the powers and functions of the PAP and whether the PAP is indeed a parliament in the classical sense. The perceived ineffectiveness of the PAP (especially in influencing the direction of the AU governance through its recommendations) though arguable, has been attributed to this limitation. Though these questions have earlier been addressed,[5] the rationale for the limited mandate of the PAP remains puzzling and calls for examination in order to understand the circumstances warranting the imposition of the limitation. This examination is approached from two considerations, that is, the political perspective and the institutional capacity perspective.

In examining the political dimension, the African political and economic environment is taken into consideration. This is with a view to assessing whether the current political climate is conducive for the establishment of a supranational legislative institution with full continent-wide legislative powers. In this connection, the impact of the plural character of the African continent in terms of its diverse cultures, religion, language and other differences must first be recognised. These diversities pose serious challenges which are difficult to overcome and therefore require a strategic but gradual process to manage. The effective harmonisation and management of these differences must precede the adoption of any collective initiative no matter how positive. Politically, it must be noted that African states have achieved decolonization and are still struggling to come to terms with the challenges of self-governance and are at different stages of democratisation and development. Due to internal crisis, there are also concerns with state fragility on the continent.

The scepticism as a result of Africa's past experience of colonial economic exploitation and political domination have negative impact on the willingness of African states to concede power to a supranational parliamentary institution to legislate for the whole continent. At independence, African states were preoccupied with the preservation of their hard-worn independence and territorial integrity.[6] However, the AU is currently embarking on the gradual process of consolidation and bridge building for continental integration and at the same time struggling to overcome the reluctance of member states to ratify the AU shared values instruments.

---

[5] See Sect. 2 above titled: The Vision for the Establishment of the PAP.

[6] However, the convergence of values is an internal logic of supranationalism (Nwezi, 2014, 489). In other words, without a set of common democratic values that support integration, supranationalism cannot be achieved.

With regard to the institutional capacity dimension, the point is that in determining whether to arrogate full legislative powers to a supranational parliament, the preparedness of the institution to take up the mammoth task of law-making and the responsibilities required in terms of specialisation, research and knowledge competencies is critical (Nzewi, 2014). Therefore, the question is whether at its formative stage, considering the AU's experience in regionalism, capacity and competency issues, a supranational parliament with full legislative powers is ideal. The argument is that with limited capacity in technical, research and human resources, a supranational parliament will find it challenging to effectively undertake full legislative activities. AU leaders understood these challenges. Hence, they opted for limited legislative powers for the PAP in the interim. This was to allow the PAP to evolve into a parliament with full legislative powers with time. Aside from capacity challenges in the AU governance system, a limited legislative power was also a compromise option in view of sovereignty concerns of member states.[7] In addition, the PAP is to operate in a competitive environment with existing parliamentary assemblies within regional economic communities (RECs) and national parliaments as well, each of which is struggling for political space to assert its influence on the activities of the executives. The evolution of the PAP into a parliament with full legislative powers was therefore linked to the gradual process of the African continental integration agenda. The PAP is therefore expected to grow as the AU moves towards supranational governance.

However, it is interesting to note that the Protocol empowers the PAP to determine its own Rules of Procedure thereby giving it a level of responsibility for its own institutional growth. The Rules of Procedure acts as both a control and coordinating instrument for the PAP in undertaking its activities. The optimal exploitation of the Rules of Procedure has the potential to promote an internal shared vision and mechanism that will enable the PAP to build its own capacity, grow and strengthen inter-institutional relationships as well as build on its complementary roles and the other non-legislative functions (Nzewi, 2014). This implies that the PAP is expected to develop its capacity to deliver on its mandate to acquire credibility and legitimacy that are necessary for it to deserve incremental attribution of legislative powers. Thus, the question is whether at this stage, in its development, the realities on ground justify increased legislative powers. This question will be subsequently addressed based on what the PAP has been doing to achieve its objectives within the limit of its powers and functions under the Protocol.

---

[7] AU member states may fear that ceding legislative powers to PAP will amount to subjecting the law-making powers of national parliaments to that of a regional parliament, thereby compromising the legislative sovereignty of the former.

5   OBJECTIVES, POWERS AND FUNCTIONS OF THE PAP

The Constitutive Act and the preamble to the PAP's Protocol give a clear indication of what African leaders intend to achieve by establishing the PAP. Thus, Article 17 of the AU Constitutive Act states that the PAP was established 'in order to ensure full participation of African peoples in the development and economic integration of the continent' (AU Constitutive Act, 2000, art 17). On the other hand, the preamble to the Protocol states that the establishment of the PAP is informed by a vision to provide a common platform for African peoples and their grassroots organisations to be more involved in discussions and decision-making on the problems and challenges facing the continent.

More specifically, Article 3 of the PAP Protocol sets out nine objectives of the PAP. In specific terms, Article 3 of the Protocol provides that the objectives of the PAP shall be to:

1. Facilitate the effective implementation of the policies and objectives of the OAU/AEC and, ultimately, of the African Union;
2. Promote the principles of human rights and democracy in Africa;
3. Encourage good governance, transparency and accountability in Member States;
4. Familiarise the peoples of Africa with the objectives and policies aimed at integrating the African Continent within the framework of the establishment of the African Union;
5. Promote peace, security and stability;
6. Contribute to a more prosperous future for the peoples of Africa by promoting collective self-reliance and economic recovery;
7. Facilitate cooperation and development in Africa;
8. Strengthen Continental solidarity and build a sense of common destiny among the peoples of Africa;
9. Facilitate cooperation among Regional Economic Communities and their Parliamentary fora.

The powers and functions of the PAP are as provided for in Article 11 of the Protocol which states that the PAP shall be vested with legislative powers to be defined by the Assembly. However, during the first term of its existence, the PAP shall exercise advisory and consultative powers only. In this regard, it may:

1. Examine, discuss or express an opinion on any matter, either on its own initiative or at the request of the Assembly or other policy organs and make any recommendations it may deem fit relating to, inter alia, matters pertaining to respect of human rights, the consolidation of democratic institutions and the culture of democracy, as well as the promotion of good governance and the rule of law.

2. Discuss its budget and the budget of the Community and make recommendations thereon prior to its approval by the Assembly.
3. Work towards the harmonization or co-ordination of the laws of Member States.
4. Make recommendations aimed at contributing to the attainment of the objectives of the OAU/AEC and draw attention to the challenges facing the integration process in Africa as well as the strategies for dealing with them.
5. Request officials of the OAU/AEC to attend its sessions, produce documents, or assist in the discharge of its duties.
6. Promote the programmes and objectives of the OAU/AEC, in the constituencies of the Member States.
7. Promote the coordination and harmonization of policies, measures, programmes and activities of the Regional Economic Communities and the parliamentary fora of Africa.
8. Adopt its Rules of Procedure, elect its own President and propose to the Council and the Assembly the size and nature of the support staff of the Pan-African Parliament.
9. Perform such other functions as it deems appropriate to achieve the objectives set out in Article 3 of this Protocol.

The power to discuss its budget and the budget of the Community and make recommendations thereon prior to its approval by the Assembly (The Protocol 2001), art 11(2) is a very important oversight power which allows the PAP to debate the budget and make necessary input by way of recommendation to the policy organs before the budget of the Community is approved. This is a strong oversight power which enables the parliament to scrutinise the budget, though in its advisory and consultative capacity only, as it has no power to ensure that its recommendation is taken into consideration before the approval.

The Protocol empowers the PAP to request officials of the OAU/ African Economic Community (AEC) to attend its sessions, produce documents or assist in the discharge of its duties (The Protocol 2001, 11(5). This is another important oversight power which avails the parliamentarians an opportunity to ask questions or seek clarification on matters under their discussion. This enables the members to carry out informed debate on the issues before passing their resolutions and making recommendations thereby enhancing the effective exercise of their mandate.

Pursuant to its powers under Article 11 (8) of the Protocol, the PAP adopted its Rules of Procedure confirming and elaborating on its powers and functions with a view to operationalising its consultative and advisory powers which are already detailed in the Protocol. For instance, Rule 4 of the Rules of Procedure provides that in its consultative and advisory role and in accordance with the provisions of articles 3, 11 and18 of the Protocol, parliament shall carry out its functions. The article substantially repeats the provision of

Article 3 of the Protocol (dealing with the objectives of the PAP), Article 11 (which deals with the functions and powers of the PAP) and Article 18 (which deals with the relationship between the PAP and the parliaments of Regional Economic Communities (RECs) and National parliaments or other deliberative organs). Rule 5 makes provisions for the powers of Parliament in the discharge of its functions as provided for in Article 4 as follows:

In discharge of its functions provided in Rule 4, Parliament shall have powers to:

(a) Oversee the development and implementation of policies and programmes of the Union;
(b) Organise debate on the objectives, policies, aims, programmes and activities of Regional Economic Communities, on all matters relating to the proper functioning of organs and the life of the African Union.
(c) Examine, discuss or express an opinion or give advice on its own initiative or at the request of any of the Organs of the African Union, a Regional Economic Community or the Legislative Body of any Member State;
(d) Make recommendations and take resolutions on any matters relating to the African Union and its organs, Regional Economic Communities and their respective organs, Member States and their organs and institutions;
(e) Issue invitations to the representatives of the Organs of the African Union, Regional Economic Communities and their organs, Member States and their organs and institutions to furnish explanations in plenary on issues affecting or likely to affect the life of the African Union;
(f) Exercise all other powers as are incidental or auxiliary to the discharge of its functions.

Further to the above, the Rules of Procedure also makes some important provisions authorising the parliament to carry out its oversight functions. For instance, Rule 73 provides that all decisions of the AU Assembly and the AU Executive Council and programmes of organs of the AU shall be submitted to PAP. Rule 74 provides that the President may, after consulting the Bureau, invite the Chairperson of the AU Assembly, the Chairperson of the AU Executive Council, or the Chairperson of the AU Commission, to make a statement to PAP after each meeting of the AU Assembly, or of the AU Executive Council, explaining the main decisions taken and that statement shall be followed by a debate by Members.

Rule 75 makes provisions requiring that Annual reports and other reports of AU organs to be submitted to the parliament to enable it realise its objectives in terms of Article 3. The said Rule provides as follows:

1) Annual reports and other reports of Organs of the Union shall be submitted to Parliament in order to enable Parliament make contributions in terms of Article 3 of the Protocol.
2) Annual reports and other reports of Organs of the Union shall be referred to the appropriate Permanent Committees which will deliberate upon them and submit reports with recommendations to Parliament.
3) The reports submitted to Parliament shall be debated by Parliament which will pass resolutions on them for consideration by the Executive Council.

The power of the PAP under the above rule is very important considering the fact that the parliament can only act with information gathered from the relevant authorities for the effective execution of its mandates. In other words, the Annual reports and other reports of AU organs are the material sources of information upon which the parliament can base its recommendation in an advisory and consultative manner. This power is consistent with the provision of Article 3(u) of the Statutes of the AU Commission which requires the Commission to prepare and submit an Annual Report on the activities of the Commission to the AU Assembly, the AU Executive Council and the PAP. This no doubt implies that the organs of the AU are subjected to the oversight powers of the PAP albeit in its consultative and advisory capacity.[8] Having examined the powers and functions of the PAP, it is relevant to examine strategies which PAP can utilise in the furtherance of democratic governance in Africa. In considering this issue, the next section will examine some of the ways through which PAP has been engaging in the promotion of constitutionalism and democratic governance.

6   Strategies for Advancing Democratic Governance in Africa

While PAP exists as a formidable institution for the furtherance of democratic governance in Africa, it is imperative to examine strategies through which it may advance such in Africa.[9] Drawing on its mandate, this section considers ways in which it has advanced issues and what lessons can be put forward in the furtherance of democratic governance in Africa.

6.1   Oversight Functions

Parliamentary oversight is a major parliamentary function in any modern democratic political organisation. The oversight activities of the PAP in this

---

[8] This means that whatever emerges from the PAP by way of report or recommendations from the PAP remains advisory and the PAP has no power to enforce the implementation or hold the organs accountable.

[9] The PAP was inaugurated on 18 March 2004.

regard are therefore important in the assessment of its role as a parliament and its potentials to perform more effectively within the framework of its powers and functions under the Protocol. For the purpose of a discussion on this issue, the relevant powers of the PAP are those provided for in the Protocol.[10] These are examined with particular reference to those matters pertaining to the respect for human rights, the consolidation of democratic institutions as well as the promotion of good governance and the rule of law.

Empowered by its mandate under the Protocol and its rules of procedure as highlighted above, the PAP has made significant efforts in deepening democratic governance, sustaining Africa's democratic ideals and promoting the principles of human rights, transparency and accountability in member states of the AU. Though Viljoen expresses the view that the PAP serves mainly as an ineffectual 'talk shop' (Viljoen, 2012), he, however, acknowledges that the PAP has passed a number of resolutions and recommendations aimed at the attainment of the AU's objectives by invoking its power to examine 'any matter' and to make any recommendations aimed at the attainment of the AU's objectives (Viljoen, 2012, 175).

With specific reference to the oversight powers of the PAP over AU organs and institutions to promote good governance, transparency and accountability, the Protocol empowers the PAP to oversee the AU budget preparation before its approval. Pursuant to the above, the PAP annually requests the chairperson of the AUC to attend the parliament's sessions to present the draft budget of the AU for discussion. This request is in conformity with the provision under the Protocol which authorises the PAP 'to discuss the AU budget and the budget of the Community and make recommendations thereon prior to its approval by the Assembly of the African Union' (The Protocol 2001, art 11(2); PAP Rules of Procedure, Rule 75). This provision enables the PAP to play its role as the representative of the people of Africa to ensure the judicious spending of the peoples' wealth. The challenge, however, is that there is no mechanism provided in the AU governance architecture for the PAP to monitor and ensure that its input and recommendations are reflected in the approved budget, thereby questioning the effectiveness of the whole exercise.

As part of its oversight functions, the PAP receives reports on the status of the implementation of the assessment missions in the countries that have undergone an APRM review.[11] This is in compliance with the APRM base document which provides that 'six months after each country review report (CRR) has been considered by the Heads of State and Government of the participating member countries, it should be formally and publicly tabled in key regional and sub-regional structures such as the Pan-African Parliament' (APRM Base Document, 2001, para 25). By necessary implication, the report

---

[10] These are as provided for in art 11 of the Protocol.

[11] See for instance, the report of the work of the Pan-African Parliament for the period January to December 2007, Addis Ababba, Ethiopia, 28–29 January 2008, PAP/S/RPT/72/08, 9.

will not only be tabled, but will be debated by the PAP MPs before adoption (Dinokopila, 2013, 302–323).

In fact, this practice has become a regular feature during PAP sessions. Such reports are debated by the parliamentarians and recommendations adopted *vis a vis* the position of the Parliament on the issues raised for possible adoption in the future to improve on the governance record of the countries reviewed.[12] Through such debates, each country's representatives in the parliament is afforded the opportunity to make an input when the reports are debated at the national level (Dinokopila, 2013). It is the practice of the PAP to routinely invite the APRM and the other AU governance institutions to attend its sessions and to present the reports of their activities before the parliament.[13]

In the same vein, the chairperson of the PSC routinely attends the PAP sessions and presents reports to the plenary on the prevailing security situation in Africa and the activities of the council in response to such situations.[14] In connection with the oversight functions of the PAP, it is instructive to recall that the leaders of European Union and the AU launched the Joint Africa-EU Strategy (JAES) at the Africa–EU Summit in Lisbon in 2007, setting out the intention of both continents to move beyond a donor/recipient relationship towards long-term cooperation on jointly identified, mutual and complementary interests (Joint Africa-EU Strategy, 2007).[15] In a subsequent implementation framework, it was emphasised that the PAP and the EP, national and regional parliaments, as well as the civil societies on both continents were to be fully involved in decision-making at their respective levels in order to ensure that there is proper transparency and accountability to all

[12] The PAP has, for example, received Malawi's APRM report. In the case of Ghana, Rwanda and Kenya, it is indicated that 'the PAP, upon extensive deliberations, exhorted African leaders to accede to the APRM review and implement its findings'.

[13] For instance, at the Second Session of the Fourth Parliament held from Tuesday, 3 to Friday 13 May, 2016 at the precincts of PAP at Midrandin Johannesburg, South Africa the APRM Country Reports, African Governance and the Ibrahim Index of African Governance were presented and debated.

[14] For instance, Sierra Leone's Ambassador to the Federal Democratic Republic of Ethiopia and Permanent Representative to the AU, Osman Keh Kamara, made a presentation on behalf of the African Union PSC at the 3rd Ordinary Session of the 4th Parliament of the Pan-African Parliament which took place on Thursday 13 October, 2016 in Sharm El-Sheikh, Egypt (Kamara, 2016).These reports are debated and recommendations made where necessary on how to more effectively address some of the security challenges.

[15] The Heads of state and Government of the EU and AU, the President of the European Council, the President of the European Commission, the President of the AU and the Chairperson of the AU Commission, met in Brussels on 2–3 April 2014, on the theme of 'Investing in People, Prosperity and Peace', committed to enhance Africa-EU cooperation adopted the implementation framework for the 2014–2017 period and further agreed that the implementation of the Joint Strategy shall focus on the following priority areas. These are: Peace and Security; Democracy, Good Governance and Human Rights; Human development; Sustainable and inclusive development and growth and continental integration; and Global and emerging issues.

citizens involved in the process (Joint Africa-EU Strategy: Roadmap 2014–2017). In particular, the role of the PAP and the EP is to carry out joint monitoring and evaluation on the implementation of the JAES. The two parliaments also issued joint declaration which they presented to the summit of the Heads of State and Government of the two continental organisations to guide their discussions (Declaration of the EP-PAP, 2014). This is a significant joint oversight function over the activities of the executive organs of the two continental organisations. At this juncture we note that there is a memorandum of understanding guiding the collaboration and cooperation between the two parliaments.[16] Evidently, the oversight functions of the PAP will no doubt draw attention to situations of non-compliance and enable PAP to propose necessary recommendations to ensure implementation.

6.2 Fact-Finding Missions

The PAP has played a critical role in promoting peace and security in Africa by participating in fact-finding missions in countries with underlying security and human rights challenges. Several fact-finding missions to a number of countries have been undertaken by the PAP, with reports of such missions tabled before the PAP, debated, resolutions passed and recommendations made to the appropriate AU executive organs. The PAP through this process has interacted with relevant stakeholders on the ground and issued reports, resolutions and recommendations to the plenary on conflict situations in a number of African countries. For instance, concerned about the violence in the war-torn Darfur region of Sudan, the devastating effects of human security and human rights violations, PAP sent a fact-finding mission in 2004 to assess the situation. The PAP Darfur report was debated at the plenary and appropriate resolution on the crises was passed with recommendations to the AU policy organs as part of its annual activity report. The recommendation contained in the report of the PAP was particularly useful in the proactive intervention of the AU in Darfur with a view to resolving the crisis.

In 2005, the PAP, acting under rule 5(1)(a) of its Rules of Procedure, passed a resolution to undertake a peace mission to Côte d'Ivoire and the Democratic Republic of Congo (DRC). The other countries where the PAP has undertaken peace missions include the Central African Republic, Mauritania, Libya, Tunisia, Sierra Leone, Liberia and the Saharawi Arab Democratic Republic. The PAP recommendations following these missions assisted the AU in appreciating the realistic humanitarian dimensions of the conflicts and have further resulted in assisting the AU in adopting better informed measures for the resolution of these conflicts. In respect of the crisis in the

[16] A delegation of the EP attended the PAP May session and had a bilateral meeting with the Bureau on how to strengthen their relationship and concluded negotiation on strategies for their joint oversight role in the implementation of the JAES and called for the acceleration of the ratification of the Revised Protocol. See the PAP Activity Report for the 2017 May Session.

Saharawi Arab Democratic Republic,[17] the PAP collected information from members of the government, state organs, national political groups and civil society organisations on the situation of Western Sahara. This informed PAP's recommendations on the need to facilitate the liberation of the state.

6.3   Election Observation Missions

The PAP regularly engages in election observation missions (EOM) as a means of achieving one of its objectives of promoting constitutionalism and democratic governance in Africa. The report of the election observation team is usually presented to the parliament for debate following which resolutions and recommendations are submitted to the AU for necessary action.

For instance, against the backdrop of the political crisis and controversy in Zimbabwe and subsequent to the outcome of the elections held on 29 March 2008 that failed to produce an outright winner, the PAP resolved to send an election observation to the Presidential run-off elections rescheduled for 27 June 2008. This was with a view to assessing whether the elections met the guidelines set out in the OAU/AU Declaration on Principles Governing Elections in Africa and whether they were conducted in accordance with the country's constitutional provisions. PAP's objective and evidence-based report and recommendations brought to the fore irregularities that needed to be addressed (Pan-African Parliament, 2008). However, this did not enjoy support from Zimbabwe's government and the leadership of the AU.

Subsequently, the AU decided on a joint EOM with the PAP to avoid conflicting reports and to manage cost as against the normal practice of independent EOM by the PAP (AU Executive Council, 2010). This practice has remained a challenge to the PAP which has been uncomfortable with the whole administrative arrangements. Consequently the PAP passed a resolution on the holding of Autonomous EOM which, among other things, resolved to call for the institution of autonomous election observation missions.[18] At the 31st ordinary session of the Executive Council, the Council deliberated on the PAP's activity report and decided that EOM organised in member states should remain a joint AU activity organised by the AUC in collaboration with the PAP and that it should be governed by the relevant financial and administrative regulations (AU Executive Council, 2017).[19] It is instructive to

---

[17] The mission took place from 11–16 July 2011. See the PAP Activity Report for the October 2011 session (available at the PAP Documentation Unit).

[18] PAP.4/PLN/RES/06/MAY.17.

[19] Accordingly, within the framework of the joint election observation missions of the AU, the PAP continues to maintain collaborative engagement with the AUC and members of the Parliament are deployed to election observation missions to various parts of Africa. Thus, the PAP has participated in EOM in many African countries including: Burkina Faso, Côte d'Ivoire, Tanzania, Comoros, Niger, Benin, Capo Verde, Republic of Congo, Djibouti, Chad and Equatorial Guinea, Angola, Ghana, Senegal, Gambia, Congo, Libya, Burkina Faso, Sierra Leone, Djibouti, Equatorial Guinea and Cape Verde, Nigeria, Ghana,

note that the credibility of elections has bearing on the quality of governance. Therefore, EOM is important in that it enables independent assessment of the level of compliance with democratic principles before, during and after elections especially based on the African Charter on Democracy, Elections and Governance. The report enables the country observed to reappraise its processes based on the observed lapses that are recommended to be addressed. In this way, democratic governance can be advanced.

6.4   *Committee Work*

Parliamentary committees are indispensable organs for the effective performance of the role of parliaments. In fact, committees constitute the engine hub of parliamentary activities. Thus, the oversight powers granted to the PAP under the Protocol and indeed the general activities of the parliament cannot be effectively exercised without functional committees. This is the principle which forms the basis for the provision in Article 11 (8) of the Protocol which empowers the PAP to adopt its own Rules of Procedure. This implies that the PAP is authorised to adopt any rule which it deems necessary to attain its objectives as set out in Article 3 of the Protocol and to exercise its powers as set out in Article 11 of the Protocol. Pursuant to the authority under Article 11 (8), the PAP adopted its Rules of Procedure. For the purpose of carrying out the business of the parliament, the PAP established parliamentary committees in terms of Rule 22 of the Rules of Procedure.

In terms of the procedure of the committees, Rule 23 confers on the committees, the power to receive evidence, call witnesses and require the production of papers and documents. This rule also provides for the presentation of reports to the parliament for debate. The modalities are as outlined in Rule 24 in order to allow committees to perform their functions effectively. Rule 25[20] provides that the president of the PAP shall on the advice of the Bureau[21] determine the general business to be handled by the committees and that committees shall handle business that is ordinarily handled by the corresponding Specialised Technical Committee responsible to the Executive Council in accordance with Article 14 of the Constitutive Act. Rule 26 makes provisions for specific functional domain for each of the specified Committees to assist the Parliament to oversee particular areas or departments.

D.R Congo, the Gambia and Kenya, to mention but a few. This process has established a good foundation for sustaining Africa's democratic ideals by formulating independent positions and making recommendations that contribute to the strengthening of democracy and stable governance on the continent. Through these activities, the PAP promotes conflict resolution in troubled parts of Africa, peaceful, free fair and credible elections in Africa, in line with the Governance Charter.

[20] The resolution was adopted on18 October 2012. See the PAP Activity Report of May 2013 (available at the PAP Documentation Unit).

[21] The 'Bureau' means the Bureau of the PAP and it is composed by the president and vice presidents of the PAP: See art 1 of the Protocol on definitions.

The functional terms of reference of the committees are wide enough to deal with the corresponding specialised technical committees of the AUC. One significant and proactive measure taken by the PAP was to adopt a resolution to align its committees with that of the AUC in order to enhance effective cooperation and facilitate its oversight functions. The purpose of its activities, the committees are empowered to request for reports and may call for the production of papers and documents from relevant AU Officials regarding the subject matter of the investigation or oversight. The committees then debate and consider the evidence, papers and documents to make their findings, adopt their recommendations and submit their reports to Parliament for presentation and debate at the plenary. These are debated at the plenary and if adopted are communicated to the AU Assembly for consideration, adoption and possible implementation.[22]

6.5 *Conferences*

Pursuant to Article 18 of the Protocol which requires the PAP to work closely with Parliaments of Regional Economic Communities (RECs) and National Parliaments or other deliberative bodies of member states, the PAP instituted an 'Annual Speakers Conference'. Through this conference, the PAP has strengthened its relationship with regional and national parliaments. The objectives of the conference are to sensitise the speakers of national and regional parliaments on AU decisions especially the legal instruments and the need to achieve their speedy ratification, domestication and implementation by member states. Many of these instruments relate to governance, democracy and human rights and provide a solid foundation for peace and security on the continent. The forum also considers the report of the PAP on its activities and on the state of integration in the continent.

The 8th in the series of the conference was held in Midrand, South Africa from 4 to 5 August 2016. The Conference brought together parliamentarians from national parliaments and regional (RECs) parliaments to discuss the dynamics relating to the ratification of African Union (AU) treaties in particular the Revised Protocol establishing the Pan-African Parliament (Malabo Protocol). The theme of the conference, 'From Adoption to Ratification of the African Union Treaties, in Particular the New Protocol of the Pan-African Parliament: What are the Advantages for Africa', is particularly significant in view of the drive for the ratification of the Revised Protocol.

The focus of the conference was on how ratification of AU treaties could be brought into the core of the priorities of national parliaments, the obstacles to the speedy ratification of AU treaties and benefits that member states could gain from the ratification of AU treaties. It reviewed the progress made by the parliaments in pushing for the ratification, domestication and implementation

---

[22] Rule 76 of the Rules of Procedure provides that the President shall present to the Assembly the resolutions and reports of Parliament.

of AU treaties, particularly the Revised Protocol and suggested measures to accelerate ratification.[23]

It is apposite to note that the acceleration of the ratification, domestication and implementation of the AU instruments fall within the PAP's mandate to facilitate the effective implementation of the policies and objectives of the AU and ipso facto part of its promotional mandate. Against this background, the AU specifically called upon the PAP to take up this responsibility.[24] The PAP responded by initiating a campaign dubbed '11before2011' to raise awareness on the ratification of the African Charter on Democracy, Elections and Governance (ACDEG) by the end of 2011.This campaign was carried out in conjunction with the Political Affairs Department of the AUC through several regional consultative meetings[25] and within one year the required additional ratifications were obtained leading to the coming into force of the ACDEG in 2012. Through the various conferences, the PAP brings parliamentarian at various governance levels and other deliberative bodies of member states to a forum where they are sensitised on the existence and importance AU decisions especially the legal instruments aimed at advancing democratic governance and the need for their domestication and implementation.

6.6   Model Laws

The Protocol allows PAP a good deal of discretion in adopting Rules of Procedure to enable it effectively carry out the various functions and powers given to it under the Protocol. This in our view is a law-making process which is justified based on the functionalist theory. Further to the above, we argue that nothing stops the PAP from developing and adopting model laws that it deems necessary for the effective realisation of its objectives and that of the AU, for possible adoption by the Assembly.

---

[23] On the side lines of the conference of speakers of the African national and regional parliaments it was agreed among others that the inter-regional Parliamentary meetings should be organised on a rotational basis. The meeting also recommended that the PAP, EALA, ECOWAS, SADC-PF, and CEMAC as regional Parliaments need to synergize in the pursuit of the ratification of the Revised Protocol and the promotion of integration agenda.

[24] See the decisions of the AU, particularly those taken during the Assembly of Heads of State and Government at Sharm el Sheikh as well as the Executive Council's Decision EX.CL/DEC. 526(XVI) which called on the PAP to assist in advocacy and in the sensitisation of Member States so as to accelerate the process of signing/ratification/accession to the OAU/AU Treaties.

[25] The PAP organizes annual Regional Consultative Meetings hosted by any willing member state from each region whose turn it is to host in conjunction with the PAP and supported by funding partners for the promotion of the ratification, domestication and implementation of the AU legal instruments especially the revised PAP Protocol. During such meetings stakeholders including government officials and civil society groups are sensitized on the need to support the programmes and policies of the AU especially with respect to the AU shared values instruments.

Over the years, the PAP has been active in proposing model laws which member states can adopt for effective implementation of the AU agenda.[26] Some of these actions are evident in the following instances: the PAP has partnered with NEPAD and developed a model law on the Drugs and Pharmaceutical sector in Africa, namely 'Model law on Medical Products Regulation and Harmonization in Africa'; recently, the PAP adopted a resolution on the development of a 'Model Police Law for Africa and Model Mutual Assistance Treaties for Police Cooperation in Africa'[27]; 'the African Union Model Law on the Protection of Cultural Property and various other Charters and conventions aimed at effectively protecting cultural property and heritage in times of war and armed conflicts'[28]; and are currently developing draft model law on free movement of people in Africa and the African passport in conjunction with the AUC.[29] The foregoing shows clearly that the PAP has been active in proposing model laws which member states can adopt for effective implementation of the AU agenda. Against this background, PAP can propose model laws which are aimed at advancing democratic governance in Africa, for adoption by the AU Assembly.

7 Conclusion

This chapter has advanced the increasing acceptance of the fact that democracy and good governance are not a luxury, but fundamental requirements for the achievement of sustainable development (United Nations Economic Commission for Africa, n.d.). In this connection, parliaments (national or supranational) as the democratically elected representatives of the people have pivotal functions of legislation, representation and oversight to perform on

[26] These efforts are indicated and explained in Sect. 8 above: Promotion of Constitutionalism and Democratic Governance by Model Law Making.

[27] PAP.4/PLN/RES/02/MAY.17. The resolution on the development of a 'Model Police Law for Africa and Model Mutual Assistance Treaties for Police Cooperation in Africa' mandated the PAP Committee on Human Rights and Justice, with the technical support of its partners at the African Policing Civilian Oversight Forum, to develop a Model Police Law for Africa and a Model Treaty for Mutual Legal Assistance for police cooperation in Africa for consideration by the Plenary for debate and adoption.

[28] This was in line with the Executive Council Decision EX.CL/974(XXIX) on the development of the African Union Model Law on the Protection of Cultural Property and various other Charters and conventions aimed at effectively protecting cultural property and heritage in times of war and armed conflicts the PAP also resolved to devise ways and means for the full protection and preservation of cultural property and heritage and accordingly prepared model Law as a guide for AU member states.

[29] The PAP passed a resolution on the free movement of people in Africa and the African passport which among others undertook to popularise and demystify of the concept of 'African Passport', set up a mechanism for monitoring progress on free movement of persons, right of residence and to development and draft model law on free movement of people in Africa and the African passport in conjunction with the AUC This is contained in the Activity Report for the 2016 October Session, available at the PAP Documentation Unit.

behalf of the citizens. Therefore, strong and effective parliaments play crucial roles in gauging, collating and presenting the views and needs of the people, articulating their expectations and aspirations in determining the national or regional development agenda. The general perception is that the PAP is ineffective, powerless and does not possess the capacity to promote democratic governance in Africa has been examined. However, it has been demonstrated in this chapter, that so far, the PAP has been playing positive roles in advancing democratic governance in Africa by adopting different options including creatively undertaking advisory, consultative and oversight functions, especially through its committee works, fact-finding missions, election observation missions, proposing model laws and making necessary recommendations for adoption by the AU Assembly.

It has also been demonstrated, that democratic governance can be advanced in African states through PAP's initiated interactions between the PAP, RECs and state authorities which aim to popularise regional standards of legal and democratic norms adopted by the Assembly and the necessity to have them ratified and domesticated by member states. In this way, democratic norms of regional standards can be inculcated in the collective consciousness of international and domestic actors thereby advancing democratic governance. In order to effectively achieve the advancement of the AU democratic governance agenda, member states are encouraged to come out of their silo mentality engendered by the outmoded state sovereignty conundrum and embrace supranationalism. Thus, the capacity of the AU governance institutions and mechanisms, especially the PAP which is the pivotal organ of the AU with democratic governance advancement mandate can be further strengthened for greater effectiveness.

BIBLIOGRAPHY

African Civil Society Organisation and the Pan-African Parliament Consultative Dialogue Report on building effective mechanisms for civil society engagement with the Pan-African and Regional Institutions, Gallagher Estate, Midrand, South Africa (7–8 May 2007) http://www.southernafricatrust.org/docs/PAP%20Dialogue-dft5.pdf.

APRM Base Document, 2001.

Constitutive Act of the African Union (2000/2001).

Dinokopila B Ramadi 'The role of the Pan-African parliament in the promotion of human rights in Africa' (2016) LLD Thesis, University of Pretoria, Pretoria.

Dinokopila R Bonolo 'The Pan-African Parliament and African Union human rights actors, civil society and national human rights institutions: The importance of collaboration' (2013) 2 *African Human Rights Law Journal* 302–323.

Declaration of the EP-PAP Parliamentary Summit to the IVth Africa-EU Summit (2014) http://www.africa-eu-partnership.org/sites/default/files/userfiles/final_en.pdf.

Executive Council Decision: EX. Cl/Dec.534 (XVI) adopted during the 16th Ordinary Session in February 01, 2010.

EX.CL/Dec. 979 (xxx1), 31st Ordinary Session of the Executive Council, 27 June to 01 July 2017, Addis Ababa.

Fabricius Peter 'Will the Pan African Parliament ever be worthy of its name?' *ISS Today* 5 May 2016.

Fagbayibo Babatunde 'Towards the harmonisation of laws in Africa: is OHADA the way to go?' (2009) 42(3) *Comparative and International Law Journal of Southern Africa* 309.

Fombad Manga Charles 'Some Reflections on the Prospects for the Harmonization of International Business Laws in Africa: OHADA and Beyond', Vol. 59, No 3 (Spring 2013), pp. 51–80, Indian University Press.

'ISS Today: Does Africa really want a continental parliament?' *Daily Maverick* 19 October 2017. https://www.dailymaverick.co.za/article/2017-10-19-iss-today-does-africa-really-want-a-continental-parliament/#.WxBNtzko_IU.

Joint Africa-EU Strategy https://ec.europa.eu/europeaid/regions/africa/continental-cooperation/joint-africa-eu-strategy_en.

Joint Africa-EU Strategy: Roadmap 2014–2017h http://www.africa-eu-partnership.org/en/documents/joint-africa-eu-strategy-roadmap-2014-2017.

LebaleNorbet et al (2009), Economic Development in Africa Report: Strengthening Regional Economic Integration for Africa's Development UNCTAD, Geneva.

Mpanyane Saki 'Transformation of the Pan-African Parliament: A part to Legislative Body?' (2009) *ISS Paper 181* March 2009 https://www.files.ethz.ch/isn/99267/PAPER181.pdf.

News24 'Pan-African Parliament in grip of existential crisis' 17 October 2017 https://www.news24.com/Africa/News/pan-african-parliament-in-grip-of-existential-crisis-20171017.

Nzewi Ogochukwu 'Influence and Legitimacy in African Regional Assemblies: The Case of the Pan-African Parliaments Search for Legislative Powers' (2014) *Journal of Asian and African Studies* Vol. 49(4) 488–507 p 489.

Presentation of the Peace and Security Council of the African Union to the Pan African Parliament on the Status of Peace and Security in Africa by Ambassador Osman Keh Kamara, Permanent Representative of Sierra Leone to the African Union, Sharm-El-Sheikh, Egypt (13 October 2016).

Protocol to the Treaty Establishing the African Economic Community Relating to the Pan-African Parliament 2001.

Protocol to the Constitutive Act of the African Union Relating to the Pan-African Parliament 2014.

Senate of National Assembly v Tony Momoh (1983) 4 NCCR 269.

Submission from Civil Society Organizations to the Pan-African Parliament on the Proposal for Continental Government 14 May 2007, Gallagher Estate, Midrand, South Africa, http://www.afrimap.org/english/images/research_pdf/CSO_SubmissionPAPMay2007.pdf.

The Pan-African Parliament election observer mission to the Presidential run-off and parliamentary by-elections in Zimbabwe, 1 July 2008 https://reliefweb.int/report/zimbabwe/pan-african-parliament-election-observer-mission-presidential-run-and-parliamentary.

United Nations Economic Commission for Africa 'The role of parliament in promoting good governance' https://www.uneca.org/sites/default/files/Publicati onFiles/role-of-parliament-in-promoting-good-governance.pdf.

Viljoen Frans *International Human Rights in Africa* (2012).

Zambara Webster 'Pan African Parliament must stop its 'talk-shop' and get down to real business' *Cape Times* 2009.

CHAPTER 7

Gender Discriminatory Nationality Laws and Childhood Statelessness in Africa: A Reflection on Legislative Interpretations

Julie Lugulu

1 INTRODUCTION

Nationality is the legal bond between a person and a state which requires the person to perform civic obligations while the state provides diplomatic protection (*Nottebohm* case, 13; Edwards 2014, 12–14). Nationality may be acquired through various means including birth on the territory (jus soli), descent (jus sanguinis), marriage or through naturalisation. While states retain the sovereignty to determine their nationals they must comply with international law.

Article 1(1) of the 1954 Convention Relating the Status of Stateless Persons (1954 Stateless Convention) defines a stateless person as 'a person who is not considered as a national by any state under the operation of its law'. Consequently, a stateless child is not considered as a national of any state under the operation of its law (African Committee of Experts on the Rights and Welfare of the Child *The Institute For Human Rights And Development In Africa And The Open Society Justice Initiative (On Behalf Of Children Of Nubian Descent In Kenya)* v Kenya (2011) (*Kenyan Nubian Minors Decision* 2011), para 44). Statelessness is a global concern which affects millions of people around the world and every ten minutes a stateless child is born (UN

J. Lugulu (✉)
Faculty of Law, Kabarak University, Nakuru, Kenya
e-mail: juleslugulu@gmail.com

© The Author(s), under exclusive license to Springer Nature
Switzerland AG 2022
A. Adeola and M. W. Mutua (eds.), *The Palgrave Handbook of Democracy, Governance and Justice in Africa,*
https://doi.org/10.1007/978-3-030-74014-6_7

109

Refugee Agency '*I am here, I belong. The urgent need to end childhood statelessness*', n.d.). Nationality is an enabling right which enables children access other rights; statelessness hinders children from fully enjoying socioeconomic rights predisposing them to discrimination and exploitation (de Chickera and Whiteman, 2017, 102; UNCEF and Institute on Statelessness and Inclusion, n.d., 10; Feller 2020, 103; Frye 2015, 181). Childhood statelessness is caused by discrimination on ethnic, social or religious grounds; as seen in Kenya (*Kenyan Nubian Minors Decision*, 2011, para 55) and the Dominican Republic (*Case of the Yean and Bosico v Dominican Republic* 2015, para 172). Childhood statelessness is also attributed to gender discriminatory nationality laws which deny women equal right as men to confer nationality to their children (Fisher, 2017, 186). This is evident in Eswatini, Liberia, Libya and Sudan and twenty other countries around the world that have gender discriminatory nationality laws which perpetuate childhood statelessness (UN Refugee Agency, Submissions by the United Nations High Commissioner for Refugees for the office of the High Commission for Human Rights compilation Report Universal Periodic Review: 36th Cycle, 2020). Discriminatory nationality laws cause childhood statelessness where a mother is unable to confer nationality due to discrimination while the child's father is stateless or unknown or has abandoned his family or died before conferring nationality to their child (UN Refugee Agency, 2021; Ujvari 2017, 105–114). Intergenerational statelessness forced migration and obstacles to birth registration may also contribute to childhood statelessness (UNCEF and Institute on Statelessness and Inclusion, n.d., 2).

This chapter focuses on the nexus between gender discriminatory laws and childhood statelessness in Eswatini, Libya, Liberia and Sudan, as case studies of African countries which uses such laws. The justification of focusing on these African countries is that they are part of the few African countries which do not provide gender equality on the conferral of nationality.[1] Although, the said countries have legislative provisions which recognise the child's right to a nationality, within their respective Constitutions: their nationality laws contain gender discriminatory laws which results into childhood statelessness. It will use the terms citizenship and nationality interchangeably and further use the names Swaziland or Eswatini to refer to the Kingdom of Eswatini. It argues that gender discriminatory nationality laws in Eswatini, Libya, Liberia and Sudan cause and perpetuate childhood statelessness in contravention with these countries' international obligations. This article is divided into three parts; the first part discusses the right to nationality under international law, the second part discusses the legal framework on the right to nationality in Swaziland, Libya, Liberia and Sudan, the third part focuses on discrimination and childhood statelessness. Lastly, the paper provides a conclusion.

---

[1] Somalia, Togo and Burundi nationality laws do not allow women to confer nationality to their children and spouses on equal basis as men.

2 THE RIGHT TO NATIONALITY UNDER INTERNATIONAL LAW

Everyone has a right to acquire a nationality enshrined in the Universal Declaration of Human Rights (UDHR, art 2), the International Convention on the Elimination of All Forms of Racial Discrimination (ICERD, art 5d.iii), the Convention on the Elimination of All Forms of Discrimination Against Women (CEDAW, art 9(1)) and the International Convention for the Protection of All Persons from Enforced Disappearance (ICPPED, art 25(4)).

The child's right to acquire a nationality is recognised in the International Covenant on Civil and Political Rights (ICCPR, art 24(3)) which recognises every child's right to acquire a nationality. Similarly, the Convention on the Rights of the Child (CRC, art 7(1)) provides for the child's right to be registered immediately after birth, have a name and acquire a nationality. The right to a name and nationality of migrant worker's children is provided for in the International Convention on the Protection of the Rights of All Migrant Workers and Members of their Families (ICPRMWF, art 29).

Regionally, the child's right to acquire a nationality is provided for: in the African Charter on the Rights and Welfare of the Child (ACRWC, art 6(3)), the Protocol to the African Charter on Human and Peoples' Rights on the Specific Aspects of the Right to a Nationality and the Eradication Of Statelessness in Africa (draft Protocol to ACHPR, art 3(2a)), the American Convention on Human Rights (art 20), the European Convention of Nationality (art 7), the Convention on the Rights of the Child in Islam (art 7), the Commonwealth of Independent States Convention on Human Rights and Fundamental Freedoms (art 24(1) and (2)), the European Convention of Nationality Convention on the Elimination of all forms of Discrimination (art 5) and the 1961 Convention on the Reduction of statelessness (the 1961 Convention, arts 1–4).

3 LEGAL FRAMEWORKS ON THE RIGHT TO NATIONALITY IN SWAZILAND, LIBYA, LIBERIA AND SUDAN

This section will reflect on the legal frameworks on the right to nationality in Swaziland, Libya, Liberia and Sudan. In this regard, this chapter reflects on the legislative interpretation of nationality provisions of Eswatini, Libya, Liberia and Sudan in line with international and regional human rights obligations.

3.1 Swaziland

Swaziland Constitution 2005
The Swaziland Constitution 2005 (Swaziland Constitution) provides for the acquisition of Swazi citizenship after the commencement of the Act through

112   J. LUGULU

descent; one acquires Swazi citizenship by birth if born in Swaziland and if at the time of birth their father was a Swazi national (art 43(1)). A person born abroad is Swazi if at the time of birth their father was a Swazi citizen (art 43(2)). These provisions discriminate against Swazi female's ability to confer nationality to their children because it only allows citizenship to be conferred through a male Swazi, thus children born to Swazi mothers with stateless fathers or of unknown parentage are put at risk of becoming stateless.

A child born outside wedlock to Swazi citizens, if not claimed by his or her father in accordance with the Swazi customs shall acquire Swazi citizenship by birth through the child's mother (art 43(4)). This provision allows Swazi mothers to pass nationality to their children born out of wedlock, the provisions aim to prevent childhood statelessness among children born out of wedlock.

Citizenship may be acquired through adoption (art 43(5)). The Swaziland Constitution recognises that foreign women can acquire Swazi citizenship through marriage to male Swazi nationals. This provision is discriminatory because it fails to allow Swazi women equal opportunity to confer citizenship to foreign men through marriage. Consequently, children born to Swazi females with foreigners may be stateless if their fathers cannot confer citizenship to them. It is commendable that the Swaziland Constitution confers Swazi nationality to foundlings below 7 years, this provision prevents childhood statelessness by providing nationality to children of unknown parentage.

Swaziland Citizenship Act 1992
The Swaziland Citizenship Act (1992) (SCA) provides for the acquisition of citizenship through descent.

The SCA recognises acquisition of Swazi citizenship before the commencement of the Act to a person in Swaziland or abroad if at the time of their birth, his or her parent was a Swazi citizen (sec 6(1)). This is a gender-neutral provision which grants Swazi nationality to persons whose parents were Swazi nationals. Persons born in Swaziland after the commencement of the Act acquire Swazi nationality if their father was a Swazi national (sec 7(1)). While a person born outside Swaziland after the commencement of the Act becomes a Swazi national if at the time of their birth the persons' father was a Swazi national (sec 7(2). After the commencement of the Act, the acquisition of nationality to persons born in Swaziland or abroad is discriminatory as it can only be acquired through the father, these provisions do not allow female Swazi nationals to pass nationality on their children born abroad or within territory on the same basis as the male counterparts. This may result in childhood statelessness if the child is born between a Swazi woman and a foreigner, or stateless persons or with unknown parentage.

The SCA only recognises Swazi females' ability to confer nationality to their children if born out of wedlock and have not been claimed by their fathers in accordance with customary law (sec 7(4)). A woman married to a Swazi national can acquire Swazi citizenship through marriage (sec 8). The provisions on acquisition of Swazi citizenship are discriminatory because they do not allow women to confer nationality to their children or husbands on equal basis as Swazi males.

The SCA attempts to prevent childhood statelessness by providing that: children born after the death of their fathers shall be deemed to be Swazi citizens by birth (sec 46). Additionally, Section 17 of the SCA provides for citizenship by birth for children of unknown parentage. This provision is commendable because it prevents childhood statelessness among foundlings.

It is commendable that SCA grants nationality to foundlings in compliance with the 1961 Convention on the Reduction of Statelessness which obligates state parties to grant citizenship to foundlings as a way of reducing childhood statelessness (art 2).

3.2   Libya

Libyan Nationality Law no 24 for 2010/1378
Nationality law in Libya is governed by the Libyan Nationality law no 24 of 2010/1378 (Libyan Nationality Law). Libyan nationality is mainly acquired through male descent, it can be granted through birth on the territory for foundlings and through naturalisation (Section 9).

Section 3 of the Libyan Nationality law provides that a Libyan is one born in Libya to a Libyan father, if the father acquired his citizenship through birth or naturalisation. Persons born abroad can acquire Libyan nationality, if born to a Libyan father and registered with relevant offices within a year. A child born in Libya to a Libyan mother and an unknown father or stateless father is considered Libyan. This section fails to recognise children born to Libyan mothers and foreign fathers (Human Rights Watch: *Libya: Step Ahead for Women on Nationality Rights*).

Section 3 of the Libyan Nationality law indicates that citizenship is granted through descent and conferred through the father whether the person is born in Libya or abroad. This provision does not recognise the ability for Libyan mothers to also pass their nationality to their children. It is noteworthy that, Section 3 that Libyan mothers are allowed to pass nationality to their children if the father of the child is stateless or of unknown nationality. While this provision acts as a safeguard in curing childhood statelessness, Libyan women are not allowed to confer nationality to their children born in Libya or abroad on the same basis as men thus making it discriminatory. It is commendable that Section 3 provides for foundlings to be granted Libyan citizenship, this provision provides a safeguard against childhood statelessness.

Children of Libyan women and non-Libyan nationals can be granted Libyan nationality in Section 11 of the Libyan Nationality Act on a discretionary basis. This provision prevents childhood statelessness by allowing Libyan women to confer nationality to their children born with foreigners. Conversely, the

114   J. LUGULU

granting of the nationality by Libyan women is on a discretionary basis, while Libyan men automatically confer nationality to their children.

Section 12 provides for the loss of Libyan nationality if acquired through fraud, if a father loses his nationality after acquiring it fraudulently, his children will also lose their nationality. This provision causes childhood statelessness because it does not base the deprivation of the father's nationality on the acquisition of a new nationality. Thus, it causes statelessness for the father and his child.

It is commendable that the Libyan Nationality law grants nationality to foundlings in compliance with the 1961 Convention on the Reduction of Statelessness which obligates state parties to grant citizenship to foundlings as a way of reducing childhood statelessness (art 2).

3.3   Liberia

Liberia Constitution
Article 27 of the Liberian Constitution provides for the acquisition of Liberian citizenship and only limits the citizenship to Negroes or persons of Negro descent (art 27). This provision is discriminatory based on race.

The Liberian Constitution grants citizenship through descent to any person whose father or mother was a Liberian citizen at the time of their birth (art 28). This provision recognises both the fathers and mothers' ability to confer citizenship (art 28). The Liberian Constitution provides for both genders to confer nationality to their children, but the Aliens and Nationality law only confines this right to Liberian fathers.

Aliens and Nationality Law 1973
The Aliens and Nationality law provides for the acquisition of Liberian citizenship at birth to persons who are Negros or of Negro descent (sec 20.1). Persons born abroad to Liberian fathers are also recognised as Liberian citizens at birth (sec 20.1(b)). Children born abroad to Liberian fathers are also Liberian citizens if their father resided in Liberia before the birth of the child (sec 20.1(b) (iii)). The law only recognises that fathers can confer nationality to their children by birth this is discriminatory and may result in childhood statelessness in cases where the father is stateless, or refuses to confer citizenship, is dead or if the father is unknown hence may create childhood statelessness. Unlike the Constitution, the Aliens and Nationality law does not uphold gender equality in the conferral of citizenship to children.

The only remedy for children abroad to Liberian mothers and non-Liberian fathers is to naturalise when they attain adulthood. Section 21.31 of the Aliens and Nationality law does not allow children born abroad to Liberian mothers in or out of wedlock to be granted Liberian citizenship while Liberian fathers can confer nationality to their children whether born in Liberia or abroad.[2] This provision is discriminatory and creates childhood statelessness if the father of the child is unable to confer his citizenship.

3.4 Sudan

Sudan Constitution 2019
Sudanese nationality is conferred through descent to a child born to either a Sudanese mother or father (art 45). This provision prevents childhood statelessness by allowing mothers and fathers to can confer citizenship to their children.

Sudan Nationality Law 1994
Sudanese nationality is mainly granted through descent (Abdulbar 2011, 160), but an applicant can also acquire citizenship through naturalisation (Sudan Nationality Law 1994, art 4(4) and 7(1)) and marriage (Sudan Nationality Law 1994, art 8(a) and (b)). One can acquire Sudanese nationality after the commencement of the Act if the applicants' father is Sudanese by birth at the time of the applicants' birth (Sudan Nationality Law 1994, art 4(3)). This provision is discriminatory because it does not allow Sudanese women to pass nationality to their children on the same basis as the Sudanese men which may result in childhood statelessness if the father of the child is unable or unwilling to confer citizenship to his child.

A person could acquire Sudanese nationality after the commencement of the Act, if the person was born to a father who is Sudanese citizen (Sudan Nationality Law 1994, art 4(2)). While a person born to a Sudanese mother can only acquire Sudanese nationality if the person applies for it (Sudan Nationality Law 1994, art 4(3). While these provisions recognise the right of both Sudanese fathers and mothers to confer nationality to their children, while Sudanese fathers can automatically confer nationality to their children, children of Sudanese mothers meet a different threshold which requires them to make an application. Therefore, these provisions are discriminatory based on gender.

While the Sudanese Constitution adopts the principle of non-discrimination in granting citizenship, the Sudanese Nationality Act has discriminatory provisions which contravene the Sudanese Constitution. It is commendable that the Sudanese Nationality Act provides safeguards against childhood statelessness by presuming Sudanese nationality for foundlings (Sudan Nationality Law 1994, art (5)) in compliance with the 1961 Convention on the Reduction of Statelessness.

---

[2] The Institute on Statelessness and Inclusion, Global Campaign for Equal Nationality Rights and Equality Now ' Joint Submission to the Human Rights Council at the 36th Session of the Universal Periodic Review Liberia' accessed December 10, 2021 https://files.institutesi.org/UPR36_Liberia.pdf.

4   DISCRIMINATION AND CHILDHOOD STATELESSNESS

The Human Rights Committee General Comment No 18 on Non-Discrimination (1989) defines discrimination as the preference made on certain grounds which impedes everyone's ability to enjoy equal rights and freedoms. Gender discriminatory laws in Eswatini, Libya, Liberia and Sudan prevent children from access to the right to acquire a nationality resulting into childhood statelessness.

Discrimination in the acquisition of nationality is prohibited in international human rights instruments; the ICERD prohibits racial discrimination in the right to acquire a nationality (art 5(d) iii). State parties to ICCPR are tasked to ensure that individuals enjoy the rights in the ICCPR without distinction on race, colour, sex, birth or other status (arts 2(1) and 26) including the right for a child to acquire a nationality (ICCPR, art 24(3)). More importantly, the CEDAW obliges state parties to grant women equal rights with men regarding the nationality of their children (art 9). Lastly, the CRC outlines core guiding principles that state parties applied when dealing with child rights; the principle of non-discrimination (article 2), the best interest principle (article 3), the right to survival life and development (article 6) and respect for the views of the child (article 12). Being state parties to the CRC Eswatini, Libya, Liberia and Sudan have an obligation to apply these principles to ensure that all children acquire a nationality without discrimination (CRC, arts 2 and 7(1)) since statelessness is antithesis to the best interests of the child (*Kenyan Nubian Minors Decision* 2011, para 46).

Eswatini, Libya and Liberia are state parties to CEDAW. The CEDAW obliges state parties to grant women equal rights as men when granting nationality to their children. As earlier discussed the Swaziland Constitution and SCA have gender discriminatory provisions which only allow Swazi males to pass nationality to their children, hence children born to Swazi females are at risk of becoming stateless if their fathers are unknown, unable or unwilling to confer nationality to them. As a state party to the CEDAW, the discriminatory citizenship laws contravene Eswatini's obligations under CEDAW resulting into childhood statelessness. Similarly, as a state party to the ICCPR, Eswatini contravenes the obligations under ICCPR with tasks it to ensure that nationality is enjoyed without distinction on race, sex or 'other status'. Lastly, the CRC obliges Eswatini to ensure that all children enjoy the right to acquire a nationality without discrimination. The gender discriminatory laws contravene the principle of non-discrimination and the best interests of the child principle. Therefore, the gender discriminatory laws in Eswatini contravene the provisions of the CEDAW, ICCPR and CRC resulting into childhood statelessness.

The Libyan Nationality law does not recognise children born to Libyan mothers and fathers' who possess a foreign nationality, in instances where the fathers are unable to confer nationality, thus putting these children at risk of becoming stateless. Also, Libyan Nationality law does not allow women to pass nationality to their children on the same basis as the Libyan men. Being a state party to CEDAW, ICCPR and the CRC, Libya contravenes the provisions of these treaties putting the Libyan children at risk of becoming stateless. The gender discriminatory laws in the Libyan Nationality law are incompliant with the CRC's principle of non-discrimination, best interests of the child principle, the child's right to life survival and development and respect for the views of the child.

Similarly, Liberia is a state party to the CEDAW, ICCPR and the CRC. The Aliens and Nationality law recognises that only fathers can confer nationality to their children by birth. This provision is discriminatory and may result in childhood statelessness in cases where the father is stateless, dead, unknown or refuses to confer citizenship to their child hence may create childhood state-lessness. Unlike the Liberian Constitution which does not have discriminatory provisions, the Aliens and Nationality law does not uphold gender equality in the conferral of citizenship to children thus does not comply with the provisions of CEDAW, ICCPR and the CRC. The gender discriminatory laws in the Liberian Nationality laws contravene the principle of non-discrimination, best interests of the child principle, the child's right to life survival and development and respect for the views of the child.

Sudan is not a state party to CEDAW. The Sudanese Nationality Act allows Sudanese men and women to confer nationality to their children. Sudanese women are required to confer their Sudanese nationality to their children through an application process while Sudanese automatically grant citizenship to their children. This provision is discriminatory because it requires women to meet a higher threshold in order to confer their Sudanese nationality to their children. The gender discriminatory laws in the Sudanese nationality laws contravene the principle of non-discrimination, best interests of the child principle, the child's right to life survival and development and respect for the views of the child. These provisions contravene the provisions of the ICCPR and the CRC because Sudanese women cannot confer Sudanese nationality to their children on equal footing with men.

Regional human rights instruments also provide for the right of the child to acquire nationality without discrimination. Article 6(3) of the ACRWC provides for every child's right to acquire a nationality. Just like the CRC, the ACRWC has core principles which guide the implementation of child rights: the principle of non-discrimination (article 3), the best interests of the child (article 4) and survival and development (article 5), while Article 6 of the ACRWC provides for every child's right to a name and nationality. The General Comment on article 6 of the ACRWC highlights the importance of article 6 in preventing and reducing statelessness. Eswatini has signed the ACRWC, while Libya, Liberia and Sudan are state parties to the ACRWC. Libya, Liberia and Sudan are state parties to the ACRWC thus have an obligation of ensuring that they adopt gender-neutral laws which will allow women in their countries to confer nationality on equal basis with men in order to promote the child's right to acquire a nationality in accordance with the provisions of the ACRWC.

Eswatini, Libya and Liberia have all ratified the African Charter on Human and People's Rights on the rights' of Women in Africa (Maputo Protocol) which obliges them to adopt gender-neutral provisions.

5   CONCLUSION AND RECOMMENDATION

Most of the countries studied have made effort to reform their nationality laws by enacting gender-neutral laws. Eswatini has a gender-neutral provisions which grants Swazi nationality to persons whose parents are Swazi nationals. While that Libya allows Libyan mothers to pass nationality to their children if the father of the child is stateless or of unknown nationality. In addition, Libya grants nationality to foundlings of unknown parentage. It is also commendable that the Liberian and Sudanese Constitutions provide for both genders to confer nationality to their children in their recent Constitutions. Conversely, these constitutional provisions have not been reflected in the Liberian Aliens and Nationality law of 1973 and Sudan's 1994 Nationality Act.

With twenty-five countries around the globe not allowing women to confer nationality to their children, gender discriminatory nationality laws remain one of the major causes of childhood statelessness. According to the UNHCR, a stateless child is born every ten minutes. The brief discussion above of the nationality laws of Eswatini, Libya, Liberia and Sudan shows that gender discriminatory nationality laws cause childhood statelessness. If Eswatini, Libya, Liberia and Sudan continue to contravene their international and regional obligations that require them to grant all children the right to acquire a nationality without discrimination; gender discriminatory laws will continue to perpetuate childhood statelessness. Adopting the principle of non-discrimination when enacting nationality laws in Eswatini, Libya, Liberia and Sudan will help prevent, reduce and eliminate childhood statelessness.

BIBLIOGRAPHY

Abdulbar, Nasredeen "Citizenship Rules in Sudan and Post-Secession Problems," *Journal of African Law*, 55 no 2 (October 2011): 160 https://www.cambridge. org/core/journals/journal-of-african-law/article/abs/citizenship-rules-in-sudan-and-postsecession-problems/E9C50F9B07C70584D0B44BCD8560287D.

African Committee of Experts on the Rights and Welfare of the Child *The Institute For Human Rights And Development In Africa And The Open Society Justice Initiative (On Behalf Of Children Of Nubian Descent In Kenya) v Kenya* (2011) (*Kenyan Nubian Minors Decision* 2011) https://www.acerwc.africa/decisions-on-communications/.

African Union, "General Comment on Article 6 of the African Charter on the Rights and Welfare of the Child" paragraph 83 accessed December 14, 2021h https://vio lenceagainstchildren.un.org/file/2292/download?token=9MytNzjQ.

Case of the Yean and Bosico v. Dominican Republic (2015) (Inter-American Court of Human Rights – IACtHR).

de Chickera, Amal and Whiteman, Joanna "Addressing statelessness through the rights to equality and non-discrimination" in *Solving statelessness,* ed. Melanie Khanna and Laura Van Waas (Netherlands: Wolf Legal Publishers, 2017).

Edwards, Alice "The meaning of nationality in International law in the era of human rights," in *Nationality and Statelessness under International Law,* ed. Alice Edwards and Laura Van Waas (UK: Cambridge University, 2014).

Feller, Erika "The Right to a Nationality: No Time to Be Complacent," *Brown Journal of World Affairs,* 26 no 2 (Spring/Summer 2020) https://bjwa.brown.edu/26-2/the-right-to-a-nationality-no-time-to-be-complacent/.

Fisher, Betsy "Gender and birth discrimination and childhood statelessness," in *The World's Stateless Children,* ed. van Waas, Laura and de Chickera, Amal (Netherlands: Wolf Legal Publishers, 2017) 186.

Frye, J Susan, "Nationality Laws and Statelessness after State Breakup: A Comparative Look at the Former SFRY and Sudan, and a Prediction for Post-conflict Syria," *Tulane Journal of International and Comparative Law,* 23 no 1 (2015) https://heinonline.org/HOL/LandingPage?handle=hein.journals/tulicl23&div=10&id=&page.

Human Rights Committee 1989 Paragraph 7 Thirty-seventh session (1989) "General comment No. 18: Non-discrimination," accessed December 14, 2021 https://www.refworld.org/docid/453883fa8.html

Human Rights Watch, "*Libya: Step Ahead for Women on Nationality Rights,*" accessed November 11, 2021 https://www.refworld.org/docid/4c8df27cc.html.

Nottebohm Case (Liechtenstein v Guatemala) Second Phase Judgment of 6 April 1955, p 13.

The 1961 Convention on the Reduction of Statelessness.

The Institute on Statelessness and Inclusion, Global Campaign for Equal Nationality Rights and Equality Now " 'Joint Submission to the Human Rights Council at the 36th Session of the Universal Periodic Review Liberia" accessed December 10, 2021 https://files.institutesi.org/UPR36_Liberia.pdf.

Ujvari, Blanka "The Causes of Statelessness," *Hungarian Yearbook of International Law and European Law* (2017): 105–114.

UNHCR, "Background note on gender equality, nationality laws and statelessness 2021," accessed December 20, 2021 https://www.refworld.org/docid/604257d34.html.

UNHCR, "I am here, I belong. The urgent need to end childhood statelessness," accessed December 10, 2021 https://www.unhcr.org/ibelong/the-urgent-need-to-end-childhood-statelessness/.

UNHCR, "Submissions by the United Nations High Commissioner for Refugees for the office of the High Commission for Human Rights compilation Report Universal Periodic Review: 36th Cycle," accessed December 14, 2021 https://www.uprinfo.org/sites/default/files/document/session_36_may_2020/unhcr_upr_submission_on_liberia_36th_session.pdf.

UNICEF and Institute for Statelessness and Inclusion (n.d.), *The Child's Right to a Nationality and Childhood Statelessness. Texts and Materials* ISBN: 9789082836653, accessed December 14, 2021 https://files.institutesi.org/crn_texts_materials.pdf.

UNICEF and Institute on Statelessness and Inclusion (n.d.), *The Child's Right to a Nationality and Childhood Statelessness. Texts and Materials* ISBN: 9789082836653, accessed December 14, 2021 https://files.institutesi.org/crn_texts_materials.pdf.

CHAPTER 8

The Economic Community of West African States and the Mano River Union: Conflict, Cooperation and Accommodation

Vandy Kanyako

1 INTRODUCTION

A defining feature of West Africa is the presence and influence of its two main politico-institutions: the Mano River Union (hereafter MRU) and the Economic Community of West African States (hereafter ECOWAS). Because of their growing influence in shaping economic, social and political policies, to understand West Africa's trajectory one needs to understand its two leading intergovernmental institutions. The relationship between the two has been influenced by the region's political economy, history and geography that have shaped and continue to impact the growth and evolution of its institutions. On the one hand, the subregion is of growing strategic importance to the global economy as a result of the ongoing discovery of commercial hydrocarbons, specifically oil and gas. The foreign direct investment—largely concentrated in the extractive industry—offers critical socio-economic opportunities for job creation in both the formal and informal economies and for forging closer ethnic and kingship linkages—two key goals of both the MRU and ECOWAS. On the other hand, however, despite its vast mineral resources, fertile agricultural land and a sizeable offshore fishing industry, West Africa is still one of the least developed subregions in the world. The situation in the MRU

V. Kanyako (✉)
Conflict Resolution Program, Portland State University, Portland, OR, USA
e-mail: vkanyako@pdx.edu

© The Author(s), under exclusive license to Springer Nature Switzerland AG 2022
A. Adeola and M. W. Mutua (eds.), *The Palgrave Handbook of Democracy, Governance and Justice in Africa*,
https://doi.org/10.1007/978-3-030-74014-6_8

states of Sierra Leone, Liberia, Guinea and Côte d'Ivoire epitomises a region-wide problem where vast mineral wealth has not translated into economic development for its 41 million citizens. Furthermore, the unique historical experiences of its individual member states coupled with the geographical obstacles presented by a poorly demarcated and sometimes rugged and inhospitable terrain make the border regions of the MRU states one of the most under-governed in the region. Given the transboundary nature of the issues affecting the region (transboundary diseases such as Ebola and onchocerciasis, trade, human and arms smuggling, terrorism etcetera), what therefore happens in the Mano River Union states is of concern, and rightly so, to the much larger and better-resourced ECOWAS. Tackling these complex issues requires a more robust engagement between the MRU and ECOWAS. This chapter maps the history, growth and evolution of the transnational relationship between the two political entities.

2 METHODOLOGY AND SIGNIFICANCE

Transnational political organisations are of growing interest to various fields of discipline in the social sciences. Their genesis and role, especially in global governance and in managing conflict and resolving various types of disputes among state and nonstate actors, have garnered attention from academics and policymakers. Both the MRU and ECOWAS are part of an expanding group of regional integration schemes that have become a key feature of international politics. The European Union is perhaps the best known of these regional and subregional institutions, but most certainly not the only one. This chapter is therefore informed by the growing body of theories and frameworks that focuses on the subregional institutions of governance. The chapter has also been enriched by extensive field research over the last two decades in West Africa in general and the Mano River Union states in particular.

In April 2015 and August 2017, respectively, I spent a combined total of six weeks conducting fieldwork with various stakeholders in the regions on the theme of natural resources, boundaries, conflict and peace. In my tour of the region, I held discussions with a cross section of stakeholders: farmers, oil merchants, petty traders, human rights activists, border police, politicians, students and professional civil society in countries as diverse as Nigeria, Ghana, Liberia, Sierra Leone, Guinea and Equatorial Guinea. Over the last several years, I have had the opportunity of working with young professionals from Chad, Burkina Faso, Mali, the Gambia and Senegal. In 2015, I spent a week at the ECOWAS Secretariat observing the daily operations of the organisation. In that time, I spoke with various officials at the Secretariat in Abuja (from security guards to managers) to gain a deeper understanding of the workings of the organisation. The insights gained from those engagements and fieldwork inform this chapter.

This chapter is important for several reasons. The first is that there is a gap in the general literature about the importance and effect of the 'near neighbourhood' phenomenon on small and weak states. To explore this theme in-depth, the chapter is guided by three main questions: How and why do intrastate organisations behave the way they do? In the larger global governance framework, weak states, such as the ones that dominate West Africa, find strength in numbers. Umbrella intrastate institutions provide them the platform to advocate and pursue common interests with various stakeholders, both domestic and global. As such, the theoretical and practical pertinence of supranational organisations such as ECOWAS and the MRU offers an interesting laboratory for the examination of regional integration efforts (Adkisson 1984, 2). Furthermore, what does all of these regional efforts at integration portend for the principle of sovereignty and for peace and stability? Brauer (2013) provides part of the answer '...most studies and policy recommendations and actions remain focused on the afflicted state itself and far less on the region within which it is located'. Yet what happens in the neighbourhood could have an adverse effect in areas such as income growth, especially for neighbours. The European Union, which started off as the European Coal and Steel Commission (ESCS) is today credited with unifying and bringing peace to Western Europe. What lessons could be extrapolated from the European model of integration to make West Africa a stable and prosperous region? In short, the role and behaviour of a country's neighbour and the regional context are important to understanding why states behave the way they do.

3   ANALYTICAL FRAMEWORK

This chapter uses a subregional approach as opposed to a global approach to analyse the relationship between the two intra-political institutions referenced earlier. The 'region' that is the unit of analysis in this case is West Africa. Though the term 'West Africa' lacks geographic precision, it is used here to refer to the westernmost region of sub-Saharan Africa. The region has a total area of approximately 1,974,103 squares miles and had an estimated population of 362 million in 2016. Politically, West Africa includes 16 countries,[1] which are also the countries that belong to ECOWAS. The subregion is as varied politically as it is culturally, economically or topographically. Geographically, West Africa is predominantly plains, with numerous rivers, including the Niger, Senegal, Gambia and the Kolenté (also known as the Great Scarcies) (World Atlas 2019).

The MRU on the other hand is both politically and geographically a subset of ECOWAS, consisting of only four countries—two anglophone

---

[1] Benin, Burkina Faso, Cape Verde, Ivory Coast, the Gambia, Ghana, Guinea, Guinea-Bissau, Liberia, Mali, Mauritania, Niger, Nigeria, Senegal, Sierra Leone and Togo. Additionally, the region also includes two British Overseas Territories: Saint Helena and Ascension and Tristan da Cunha.

(Sierra Leone and Liberia) and two francophone countries (Guinea and Côte d'Ivoire). In this sense, therefore, all members of the MRU are members of ECOWAS but not all ECOWAS member countries are members of the MRU. Whereas the MRU membership was formed more gradually: from two to three and eventually four, that of ECOWAS on the other hand was more purposeful about its membership from its inception. Membership in ECOWAS is open to all West African states.

The thrust of the chapter is on the evolving but symbiotic relationship between the two main political institutions (the MRU and ECOWAS) that operate in West Africa. The focus is on the collective relational policies of these two institutions and the impact of such policies on interstate relations within and outside the subregion. At the heart of the analytical framework is the notion that every nation state, large or small, developed or underdeveloped, strong or weak is concerned with what happens in their immediate vicinity. Poor, weak and small countries such as the ones that constitute West Africa are often more attuned to going on in their geographical surroundings (see Fig. 1) for the simple fact that (hostile or friendly) neighbours can make or break a regime. This is largely because these states lack the means (military, economic or diplomatic) to project power and influence outside of their immediate neighbourhood. The micro-subregional level (represented in the diagram below as the 'near neighbourhood') is therefore important to understanding why West African countries behave the way they do. This is because when all is said and done the immediate neighbourhood presents both an opportunities and challenges, and in some cases even an existential threat to the regime in power. Foreign policy is therefore local.

The theory of transnational integration is important to helping us understand the rationale, motivations and drivers for the formation of both the MRU and ECOWAS. David Mitrany is often considered as the father of integration theory. His theory of functional integration, first propounded in 1943 in a series of essays, has formed the basis of the study of integration across various disciplines, from sociology to political science to international relations. Having lived through both the First and Second World Wars, he saw intense rivalry and military alliances as a critical root cause of armed conflicts. As a result, he came to see integration, especially at the politico-institutional and non-military levels, as critical conflict prevention tools. The incentive for conflict decreases the more states feel vested in the affairs of those around them. The Romanian-born Mitrany believed that 'One of the primary causes of conflict – salient, nationalist identity and the loyalties derived from it – can be ameliorated by the creation of cross-cutting forms of allegiance manifested through a web-like system of interdependencies' (Mitrany, quoted in Adkisson 1984, 8).

One scholar who was influenced by the functionalist theory of Mitrany is the Norwegian Sociologist, Mathematician and one of the architects of the field of peace and conflict studies, Johan Galtung. In his seminal work titled 'A Structural Theory of Integration', Galtung (1968) described integration in simple, unsophisticated yet poignant terms. It is according to him 'the process whereby two or more actors form a new actor. When the process is completed, the actors are said to be integrated' (Galtung 1968, 377). He sees integration as a process involving not only the constituent actors but also their environment, especially their external environment. No doubt Galtung's definition is limited in scope and rather simplistic. For integration is not just a means but a process. In the lifespan of supranational organisation, such a process can be long, drawn out and sometimes messy.

A more comprehensive definition of integration is that proffered by Duffy and Feld (1980, 510). For them, integration refers to:

> The means through which various states within a region, in a peaceful and noncoercive manner, collectively seek to resolve conflicts in either a preemptive or reactive response. Moreover, it is a vehicle through which member states maximize, or attempt to maximize, their national interests on a long-range basis through the creation of supranational institutions and the evolution of regional policies.

For Duffy and Feld (1980), states often view interaction with others through a very practical realpolitik lens. They look after their own interests either bilaterally or as a group. Through such prism, states come to view neighbours as representing a double-edged sword. Cooperative neighbours can be a blessing as they could help promote closer ties and, in the process, strengthen one another, with various economic, social and political benefits. Conflicting or noncooperative neighbours could, however, be a curse and thus can become a drain and impose burdens on each other. In the interests of long-term, sustainable peace, it is important for countries to pre-plan for the likelihood of a neighbour requiring assistance and to help prevent conflict by committing resources to such assistance (Brauer 2003).

But states do not just limit their vision to their immediate vicinity, as important and practical as that approach is. Even small nations are concerned with what happens outside of their immediate neighbourhoods. In the case of the MRU states for example, they cast their vision on what happens in West Africa and beyond. This helps to explain why all members of the MRU and ECOWAS are also members of much larger entities such as the African Union of the United Nations. Part of the reason has to do with how states view their position in the larger global community. The need to belong is innate in states as it is in humans. In doing so however, small and weak states are often aware of their strengths and most importantly their limitations. As such, their foreign policy aspirations are cast very wide in the near neighbourhood. It gets narrower and more realistic as they view the far horizon.

4   HISTORICAL CONTEXT

Both the MRU and the ECOWAS schemes are products of historical circumstances. Except for Liberia, all of the other countries in the region were once under British or French domination for more than a century. The colonial influence which lasted until the 1960s was to have a lasting influence on the subregion as well as on future relations between the newly independent states and their political leaders. For example, whereas leaders such as Houphouët-Boigny of the then Ivory Coast favoured strong individual states, others such as Leopold Senghor of Senegal and Kwame Nkrumah of Ghana favoured pan-African unity, or where that is not feasible at the very least some kind of a federation. The result is that West Africa was carved up into small political units. A key starting point therefore to understanding both ECOWAS and the MRU rests with analysing their origins, mandates and modus operandi and with their evolving relationship with one another.

Colonial rule not only divided the region into small political entities, it also imposed a francophone-anglophone divide (which was not just confined to language but to culture and style of governance and even cuisine). Nearly half of the countries in West Africa are French speaking. The French preferred form of administering their colonies was more direct, with all key policies directed from Paris. For example, apart from Guinea, all the former French colonies[2] used the Communauté Financière Africaine (CFA) currency and maintained very close ties with Paris. The British on the other hand introduced the so-called indirect rule system by which they governed their territories through traditional institutions such as chiefs. The anglophone countries,[3] on the other hand, minimised their interaction with the British government post-independence. None of them chose to use the pound sterling after independence, opting instead to use their national currencies, which in itself became a source of national pride.

The socio-political and economic legacies made it difficult or at least complicated the process of creating any kind of intrastate organisation around which members could coalesce. This helps to partly explain why it took nearly 14 years to establish ECOWAS and the MRU. It was not helped by the fact that the African leaders were divided about their vision for Africa. Some leaders such as Sékou Touré preferred a radical brand of pan-Africanist socialism, with closer inter-Africa ties and very minimal ties to the colonial masters. Others such as Houphouët-Boigny preferred a more gradualist approach with policies set by the individual African governments.

Despite these historical, political and interpersonal challenges, several factors favoured the creation of a political entity of some sort. The deplorable economic situation in the subregion at independence meant that it was just a

---

[2] Senegal, Mali, Burkina Faso, Guinea, Côte d'Ivoire, Niger, Mauritania, Togo.

[3] Nigeria, Sierra Leone, Gambia, Ghana.

matter of time before they started having discussions about creating an inter-state economic organisation to address those pressing needs. Furthermore, the African unity dreams of pan-Africanist leaders such as Nkrumah never really disappeared, even in the period following independence. A politico-economic institution would represent an actualisation of that vision. Of equal importance was the aftermath of the Nigerian civil war which lasted from 1968 to 1970. The war divided the subregion with at least Gabon and Côte d'Ivoire openly supporting the Biafra secessionists. With Nigeria eventually winning the war, an opportunity to heal the wounds of the war and reunite the region was seen through the creation of an intrastate organisation with the common goal of re-uniting a subregion fragmented by colonialism and inter-state rivalry.

5 THE MRU: REASONS FOR FORMATION

The reasons for the formation of ECOWAS are not much different from that of its smaller subregional counterpart. If ECOWAS exists to promote regional trade, and political integration among its member countries, the MRU exists to do the same, albeit on a smaller scale. Both institutions see regional trade and economic integration as critical to its success and to lifting its people out of poverty. The MRU exists to foster peace, security, stability as well as economic cooperation among its member states. The subregional interstate institution was initially established in 1973 with Sierra Leone and Liberia as the founding members. Guinea joined in 1980 and Côte d'Ivoire, some 26 years later, in 2008. Organised in relation to the members' shared connection to the Mano River, the MRU Declaration provides that:

> the aims and objectives of the Union shall be: to expand trade by the elimination of all barriers to mutual trade; by cooperation in the expansion of interna-tional trade; by the creation of conditions favourable to an expansion of mutual productive capacity, including the progressive development of a common protec-tive policy and cooperation in the creation of new productive capacity. (MRU Declaration 1973, 266)

The Mano River (also called Bewa or Gbeyar), from which the MRU gets its name, is a river that originates in the Guinea Highlands in Liberia and flows through the so-called Parrot's Beak area of Guinea, through Liberia's Lofa County and the Kono and Kailahun District of eastern Sierra Leone. The river directly links three of the four MRU countries and forms more than 90 miles (145 km) of the Liberia–Sierra Leone border (McKenna 2015).

Subregional peace and other forms of security concerns played a central role in the formation of the MRU. The Mano River Union was borne out of a desire to keep the peace and consummate a non-aggression pact between Sierra Leone and Liberia at a time when military coups, armed dissident mili-tary invasions and other forms of political instability were of major concerns in sub-Saharan African countries as a whole, following independence. As a result, it was not uncommon for dissidents from various countries to seek refuge and support in neighbouring countries, often among their kith and kin. Sesay (1980, 167) alluded to the nature of mutual suspicions that guided the relations among the political leaders at the time:

> Relations between Guinea and Sierra Leone were neither cordial nor collaborative in the period from 1961-64. This was mainly due to leadership incompatibility. In Freetown, Sir Milton was a conservative and passionately pro-West, and disliked radical politics. Like Tubman and Sir Abu Bakar [Tafawa Balewa], he too was opposed to Pan- African political union and favoured instead, a functional approach starting with economic and cultural links among neo-colonies in Africa. Guinea was thus perceived as a bridge through which socialist influence from the East would filter through to Freetown and other moderate states in West Africa.

Sierra Leone's relations with Liberia was no better. The political leadership of the two countries detested each other. Sesay (1980, 171) again:

> Albert Margai did not care much about relations with Tubman and Liberia. If ideological affinity brought Tubman and Sir Milton together, ideological and personality incompatibility between Tubman and Albert Margai drew both leaders apart. There was no incentive in Freetown to improve relations with Monrovia. Albert Margai instead identified himself closely with radical Toure and Nkrumah both of whom were already suspect in Liberia because of their radicalism. But diplomatically, they remained correct because Albert Margai favoured regional cooperation and in particular, both countries were involved in negotiations for the creation of the Free Trade Area.

It was therefore hoped that a regional organisation, especially one focused on non-aggression, good neighbourliness and the harmonisation of cross-border trade would ease the tense interactions that characterised the relationship among the countries in the region. The end result was a Non-aggression Pact and Good Neighbourliness Treaty between the initial two members and later Guinea and Côte d'Ivoire, with the latter joining after the civil wars of the 1990s.

That the four countries formed/joined a politico-economic union of sorts is at face value not surprising. The idea had been toyed with before, prior to the formation of the MRU. As Sesay (1980, 177) notes, the four countries had previously banded together in 1964 to propose a West African Free Trade Area (WAFTA), not dissimilar to the aims and objectives of what eventually became known as the MRU. In fact, it is not a stretch to state that the WAFTA idea was in many ways the precursor to the MRU. It was the seeds that germinated into the MRU some 10 years later (Sesay 1980, 80–82). What is even more interesting is that right from the outset the MRU founders left the door open for other countries in the subregion to join. The 1973 MRU Declaration provides that:

having regard to the great importance of extending economic cooperation within Africa, the Union shall be open for participation to all States in the Western African Sub-Region which subscribe to the aims and objectives of the Union. (MRU Declaration 1973, 267)

Closely related to peace and security as causal factors for the formation of the MRU, economic integration also played a critical role. The four countries share similar socio-economic features. As littoral states with access to the Atlantic Ocean, all four countries have good fishing resources. Furthermore, agricultural potentials are relatively good in all four countries. As Robson observed 'of Liberia's available 24 million acres, only 1–3 million are in use, while of Sierra Leone's available 4–5 million acres, only 1million are under cultivation. Sierra Leone has good fishing resources, and both countries possess extensive forests. Considerable potential exists for hydro-electric power from the Mano River' (Robson 1982, 615). In short economic integration holds a lot of potential for the small economies of various countries in the region.

Mano River Union	*Economic Community of West African States*
Year founded: 1973	Year founded: 1975
Members: Sierra Leone, Liberia, Guinea and Côte d'Ivoire (one article in the Declaration however leaves the door open for other states in the region to join)	Members: Membership open to all countries in West Africa
Aims (summary):	Aims (summary):
• Establishment of a Customs Union/to be done in two phases	• Promote the economic and political well-being of its 16 regional members
• Expand/ promote cross-border trade	• Equality and interdependence of member states
• Foster non-aggression and good neighbourliness among its members	• Solidarity and self-reliance
• Establish a customs training school	• Interstate cooperation and harmonisation of policies and integration of programmes
• Establish a joint Ministerial Committee	
• Open to all members in the subregion[a]	• Non-aggression among member states[b]
Headquarters: Freetown, Sierra Leone	Headquarters: Abuja, Nigeria
Working languages: English, French	Working languages: English, French, Portuguese
Population: 41 million (2016)	Population: 362 million (2016)

[a] The Original Declaration signed in 1974 had 9 aims
[b] The Fundamental Principles have about 14 aims and objectives

West Africa, like most of sub-Saharan Africa, also faced serious economic challenges at independence in the 1960s. With the transfer of power to indigenes, the political leaders of the newly independent countries had to come to terms with the harsh realities of governance, especially with regard to providing economic security for their citizens. The pressing tasks included overseeing economies that were relatively small, largely agricultural, rural, underdeveloped and to the chagrin of some of the leaders, still heavily dependent on the European powers who provided the bulk of the aid, financial and technical assistance. For example, Guinea's total G.N.P. in 1979 was $1,484 million and the G.N.P. per capita amounted to $280 (Sesay 1980, 617).

With a very weak industrial base, the newly independent nations were heavily dependent on their natural resources, including mining, for foreign exchange. For example, in Nigeria, oil (which had been discovered in 1953) accounted for more than 80% of its GDP in the 1960s. Elsewhere across the subregion, the economic outlook and lack of diversification in its economic regions were similar. Sesay (1980, 164) gave the example of Sierra Leone to illustrate the nature of the issues facing the subregion at the time the two organisations came into being.

> At independence, most of the country's trade links were with the West and Britain, the erstwhile colonial metropole, in particular. In 1961, for instance, the United Kingdom accounted for 44 % of total imports and 78 % of exports. By 1967, the figures had dropped to 27 and 71 % respectively.

In addition to the economy and relations with external powers, security, especially in the form of contagion military coup d'états, was a major issue in the subregion. For example, between 1963 and 1977, Benin, one of the smallest countries in the subregion, experienced no fewer than five military coups. From 1966 to 1987, Burkina Faso experienced about six military coups. The same number was recorded in Ghana from the period 1966–1981. From 1966 to 1985, Nigeria also witnessed six military coups. Though coups and counter-coups were common in the whole of sub-Saharan Africa but evidence, based on a 2003 database developed by McGowan, shows that the menace was more pervasive in West Africa. McGowan (2013, 355) outlined the West African-specific nature of the problem:

> With 16 states, West Africa has one-third of all independent SSA states, yet with 85 failed and successful coups out of 188 (45-2 %), it has been the African region most prone to PI. All of the 16 states in this region apart from Senegal have experienced from one to six (Benin, Burkina Faso, Nigeria) successful coups and all have had at least one failed coup attempt. ...much of this activity occurred in Ghana, Sierra Leone, Benin, Nigeria and Burkina Faso. To the extent that coup contagion exists in SSA, it would appear strongest in West Africa.

McGowan's data shows that between 1956 and 2001 West Africa recorded 85 coups; North Eastern Africa 53; Central Africa 26; Southern Africa 11; Indian Ocean 13 (McGowan 2013, 356). Most of these coups were violent, leaving in some cases hundreds dead. Others such as in Nigeria led to pogroms, which eventually paved the way for the 1968–1970 Biafra Civil War that claimed more than a million, mostly civilian lives. The MRU states were not spared either. Sierra Leone experienced two successful coups in the 1960s. Liberia's first coup was in April of 1980. The bloody nature of the coup, which saw the President William Tolbert and his entire cabinet executed, contained the seeds for the civil wars that eventually engulfed the subregion in the 1990s.

Without a doubt, the menace of violent military takeover precipitated the decision of African leaders to create institutions that would promote stability, non-aggression and good neighbourliness. In sum, it is safe to state that security and economic concerns as well as the need to establish closer social ties all contributed to the formation of these two political institutions. There were also cultural factors responsible for the creation of the two institutions. The desire to promote cultural ties which the artificial borders divided resonated very well for the pan-African elements within West Africa's leadership. Most of West Africa's borders was established in the wake of the 1884–1885 Berlin Conference. The borders were set up largely based on the territorial interests of the French and British colonial powers as opposed to the interests of the ethnic groups that inhabited the areas. In the case of the Niger-Nigeria border for example, Aker et al. (2013, 5) highlighted the challenge:

> The border that emerged in 1906 divided the Hausa, Fulani and Kanuri ethnic groups between the two countries. It also created a Niger that included eight primary ethnic groups (Hausa, Songhai/Zarma, Toureg, Fulani, Kanuri, Arab, Toubou and Gourmantche) that were, for the most part, situated in geographically distinct regions.

This ethnic border anomaly (dividing lines between geographically contiguous areas that are homogenous in ethnic composition) came with its own administrative, security and business challenges. Aker et al. (2013, 8) highlight the challenges to cross-border trade at independence.

> Despite the absence of natural or political barriers to trade between the two countries, there are several potential barriers to trade in agro-pastoral goods at the international border. One possible source of trade friction arises from currency exchange costs between the Communauté Financière Africaine (CFA) franc of Niger and the Nigerian Naira. Furthermore, there are often costs due to delays at the border (e.g. due to waiting for customs papers) or bribes paid to police officers and customs' officials. Finally, linguistic differences (between the official languages of Niger and Nigeria, French and English, respectively) may also add to transaction costs if trade is conducted in these languages.

Evidently, ECOWAS was a welcome development. It was established by treaty in 1975 to promote the economic and political well-being of its then 16 contiguous states in West Africa. Unlike the MRU whose membership is restricted, membership in ECOWAS is open to all West African states. In promoting the socio-economic and political welfare of its membership states, its core mandate is not much different from that of the MRU.

Fig. 1 MRU organogram

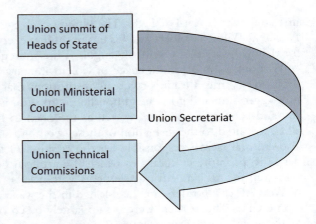

6   Same Goals, Different Missions?

If the historical circumstances that gave rise to the two institutions were somewhat similar, the governance structure that the two institutions went on to develop were very different. Given its small membership, the MRU was lean (see Fig. 1 from the outset, depending largely on consensus for decision-making). The only full-time administrative organ in the MRU is the Freetown-based Secretariat which undertakes the daily administrative tasks that keep the organisation functional. In that regard, therefore, the Secretariat is the most important of the union. Though the most important policy decisions are still made by the Heads of States through the Union Summit, the Secretariat is the nerve centre, the technical and administrative instrument through which the union pursues its objectives. It interfaces with donors and development partners as well as represents the union at various international forums. All of the other organs only meet intermittently. With a permanent presence, the Secretariat is the face of the organisation.

ECOWAS, on the other hand, is administratively 'denser' compared to the MRU. It comprises three arms of governance, namely the Executive, the Legislature and the Judiciary. The Chairman of the Authority of Heads of State and Government is the official head and is appointed by fellow Heads of State and Government (ECOWAS Annual Report 2012).

7   Challenges in Fostering Closer Ties Between the Two Institutions

To make the relationship, ECOWAS and the MRU, more sustainable in the years ahead, there are a few challenges that the two institutions have to address. These challenges are examined in this section.

7.1 Crisis of Identity

Right from its conception, the MRU has struggled both in terms of an identity crisis and in terms of it overarching mission and goals. To start with, the Mano River which unites Sierra Leone, Liberia and Guinea is geographically nowhere near Côte d'Ivoire. Secondly, its relationship with the ECOWAS was never fully established. Is it a branch, an arm of ECOWAS? What are the best mechanisms that the two institutions can develop to complement the work of each other? The histories of the four countries are also very different, two anglophone and two francophone countries. While Sierra Leone, Liberia and Guinea share boundaries, only Liberia and Guinea share boundaries with Côte d'Ivoire. There is very little direct trade between Sierra Leone and Côte d'Ivoire. These crises (of both identity and capacity) mean that the organisation has never managed to live up to its full capacity.

Not surprisingly, by 1975, the MRU was subsumed into the ECOWAS, the main regional body that brings together the sixteen countries of West Africa. The MRU has sometimes been the weak link in the peace and security sector of the region. Despite this haphazardly undefined and sometimes confusing relationship, the MRU is important both to its members and indeed to the larger ECOWAS. The fact that the organisation continues to exist more than four decades after its establishment continues to underscore its security, socio-cultural, economic and symbolic importance to West Africa.

7.2 Different Historical Experiences

There is the language barrier and varied historical experiences of the respective countries. The subregion consists of francophone, anglophone and lusophone countries. These linguistic differences have played a role in shaping the evolution of the relations among the various countries. France has been much more involved in the affairs of its former colonies, than has the United Kingdom, or the other European countries that had colonies in Africa. For example, the CFA is pegged to the French Franc. France has been involved in some direct military coups against regimes that have fallen out of favour. France has intervened militarily more than 50 times on the continent, since independence (Powell 2020). Under the guise of protecting its national interests, France has militarily and diplomatically intervened in Guinea, Mali, Togo, Gabon and Chad. This is in sharp contrast to London which has largely maintained a hands-off approach to its former colonies. Some have argued, with some justification, that France's interventionist policies (especially those that prop up unpopular regimes such as in Chad) undermine peace and stability in the subregion.

7.3 Elusive Peace

Instituting sustainable peace remains a core challenge in the subregion. The Boko Haram insurgency in north-eastern Nigeria has not only claimed 50,000 lives (peaking in 2014) and disrupted life in that part of the country, it is also becoming a subregional problem (Global Terrorism Index 2019). Chad, Niger and Cameroon have all been affected by the insurgency. Threats from Islamic fundamentalists are not just confined to these countries. Burkina Faso is also facing its own challenges in that regard. According to the United Nations Refugee Agency (UNHCR), the region is subjected to 'mixed migratory movements' (2008, 2 one in which people, in the form of refugees, traders and other transient populations, are always on the move. It is mainly a region of origin and/or transit and, to a lesser extent, of destination.

7.4 Human Rights and Justice

Human rights violations continue to be a source of concern in the subregion. Basic rights such as freedom of movement, of association and of speech continue to come under stress. In different countries in the region, including Sierra Leone, Côte d'Ivoire and Nigeria, political tensions and ethnic rivalries continue to undermine human rights and justice. The two organisations would need to collaborate to address impunity and enhance human rights norms.

8 Relationship with Ecowas: Why the MRU Matters

8.1 Economic Importance

The MRU is of immense economic and financial importance, both to its members and indeed to the ECOWAS. As outlined already, the subregion is endowed with abundant natural resources. The MRU countries are home to vast resources capable of transforming the subregion. The MRU zone is endowed with fertile agricultural land, vast offshore fishing industry and perhaps most importantly, all sorts of in-demand mineral resources, including oil, diamonds and bauxite. West Africa accounts for 15% of the iron ore production in Africa, with most mines located in Liberia, Sierra Leone and Guinea. Guinea has the largest Bauxite reserves in the world, estimated at over 40 billion tons. Sierra Leone is very well renowned for both the quantity and quality of its diamonds. Côte d'Ivoire is one of the largest economies in West Africa. It is the centre of cocoa production. Liberia is richly endowed with mineral resources such as diamond, iron ore and gold. The country also has abundant water resources, forests and a climate that favours agriculture. Liberia has a long history of artisanal gold mining, peaking at over 30,000 oz per annum in the 1940s. Between 2008 and 2012, gold production averaged 20,000 oz per annum (Owuor 2019).

8.2 Social and Kinship Ties

With its close ethnic and social kinship links, social and cultural matters help define the MRU. The subregion's plateau is inhabited by several groups, including the Kpelle (Guerze), Malinke and Kisi peoples. The Fulas, Mandingoes and Susus are found in all four countries. These groups are divided by artificial borders, which fortunately have not prevented them from cross-border engagements. Though communities along the borders have historically been marginalised in terms of social, political and economic developments, the MRU also has a lot of potential, especially in promoting cooperation and strengthening kinship ties (Poole and Mohammed 2013). Another element that binds the countries of the subregion is food and culinary habits. The staple food crops are rice, cassava and maize, with bananas, coffee, pineapples, palm kernels, groundnuts and citrus fruits as the principal commercial crops. Guinea has a small manufacturing sector in which several of the enterprises are relatively large in scale. They include factories for textiles, food and agricultural processing, cement and a construction materials plant, although their economic performance has been uniformly slow (Robson 1982, 617).

8.3 Peace and Security Arena

In the security arena, all four members of the MRU have experienced various levels of violent conflicts in the last two decades. Sierra Leone, Liberia and Côte d'Ivoire have all experienced full-blown civil wars. While the war in Côte d'Ivoire was the shortest (2002–2004; 2011) and claimed the least number of lives and destruction (around 3000), the carnage in both Sierra Leone and Liberia lasted more than a decade, claiming more than 400,000 lives and displacing millions in the process. While Guinea has not experienced a major domestic armed conflict, its southern forest region was greatly exposed to the conflict in the neighbouring countries and continues to experience sporadic localised inter-communal violence (International Alert 2010). Conciliation Resources, a London-based NGO, summarised the conflict security nexus best:

> The Mano River basin has experienced violent conflict since the late 1980s. The conflicts have caused an estimated 300,000 deaths in Liberia and Sierra Leone, brought massive social dislocation, devastated the countries' infrastructure, eroded the social fabric and led to crippling economic hardship for the majority of the population. (Poole and Mohammed 2013)

The wider implications of these conflicts were felt well beyond the confines of the four MRU countries. The civil wars of the early 1990s started in West Africa through its Mano River member states. In fact, it is as a result of these brutal wars, which started in Liberia in December 1989 and that eventually spread to other parts of the subregion that prompted ECOWAS to focus its attention on security and conflict management. In 1993, the ECOWAS treaty was revised to include 'preventing and settling regional conflict', giving the organisation an explicit security and conflict function (ECOWAS Revised Treaty 1993, 36). The brutal civil wars of the 1990s in Sierra Leone and Liberia became a litmus test for the organisation's capacity to manage armed conflicts. Despite some nagging challenges, relating to funding and logistics, evidence shows the organisation has succeeded in containing some of these protracted conflicts. For example, border tensions between Guinea and Sierra Leone over the border town of Yenga—a tiny town on the banks of the Makona River in Kailahun district on the Sierra Leonean side of the border— have been a burning issue ever since the end of the Sierra Leone Civil War in 2002.

Given the geographical, socio-cultural ties and economic importance of the MRU to the West African region, what therefore transpires in the union is of utmost concern to the ECOWAS. That is partly because most of the challenges that the subregion faces (illegal weapons smuggling, diseases such as Ebola, smuggling of contraband, etc.) are transboundary in nature which means that what happens in one country could quickly spread to other parts of West Africa, especially given the region's porous borders. The MRU basin countries are of immense importance to the general well-being of the subregion and there is an evident symbiotic relationship between the two institutions.

9   ATTEMPTS AT REFORMS

The call for reforms has been a recurring theme ever since the two institutions were established. Every major crisis in the region and in the MRU states (of which there have been quite a few) is often followed by calls for changes. One of the earliest of such calls for reform came in 1976 when the Union's Ministerial Council called for a comprehensive external review in a bid to assess the viability of the organisation with specific emphasis on its structures, procedures and performance. The ensuing review report was less than complimentary of the organisation's operations. It questioned the appropriateness of the structures and called for streamlining of decision-making. Robson (1982, 619) summarised the main accomplishments of the recommendations:

> considerable emphasis was placed on the necessity for the activities of the Union to be integrated with national development plans, and for a more effective two-way process of interaction to be devised than had hitherto been the case. To this end, recommendations were made for improving the capacity of the Secretariat.

This was just the beginning of several changes that the organisation was subjected to following this initial external review. In response to the complex transnational post-war challenges faced in the region, and in the face of considerable dissatisfaction with the operations, both the MRU and ECOWAS embarked on a series of reforms designed to plan and coordinate in a bid to better respond to various forms of transborder challenges. With the end of the war in Sierra Leone and in Liberia in 2002 and 2003, respectively, the

MRU mandate was revised on 20 May 2004, and subsequently, in 2008, Côte d'Ivoire was invited to join. With this new addition, several new protocols were adopted to make the union nimbler and to equip it with the necessary tools to better respond to emerging threats.

One of the most notable of these protocols by which members vowed to revitalise the Union is the 15th Protocol signed by the Union's Heads of State on 19 May 2000. Officially known as the 15th Protocol to the Mano River Declaration, it called on the MRU to work for the maintenance of peace, security and stability in its three member states. It incorporated a mechanism to monitor the common borders, with the aim of preventing, controlling, discouraging, forestalling and averting security-related problems. It has since been politically re-affirmed, with the Heads of State of all four countries once more pledging their commitment to the philosophy of the MRU and a coordinated approach to security, trade and development. The 15th Protocol was also important for other reasons. For the first time, it gave the MRU Secretariat an intergovernmental role in conflict prevention. Early warning was also mainstreamed, and a special technical committee was established to monitor and investigate border security and related issues.

These reforms were followed by several other high-profiled, largely security-related meetings on a few occasions organised by the MRU member countries and on other occasions in concert with ECOWAS. On 10 December 2008 for example, union member states held a mini Summit in Freetown to address security, agriculture and financing of the MRU Secretariat. A Joint Security Committee and Joint Border Security and Confidence Building Units were also activated as a result of this meeting. A few years later, in June 2011, ECOWAS organised a meeting in Freetown on Cross-Border Cooperation and Cross-Border Initiatives, where delegates endorsed the MRU to serve as the subregional organisation to coordinate ECOWAS cross-border programmes among its MRU member states. In March 2012, at Abidjan, union members approved the establishment of the Peace and Security Unit within the MRU Secretariat. Member states also agreed to second security officers on a rotational basis to run the unit (Small Arms Survey 2012).

Civil society, both local and international, played a multifaceted role in promoting human security, accountability and human rights in West Africa. Both ECOWAS and the MRU recognise this input and as such has formalised relationships with various civil society actors. Civil society is listed as one of the ten 'sectors' within ECOWAS. Organisations such as the Centre for Accountability and Rule of Law (CARL); the Coalition for Justice in Liberia, National Human Rights Centre of Liberia, Mano River Women's Network for Peacebuilding; and the International Centre for Transitional Justice (ICTJ) were instrumental in pushing for political, civil and social accountability. The ECOWAS Commission works mainly through the West African Civil Society Forum (WACSOF). Partly through ECOWAS funding, WACSOF commissioned studies aimed at broadening the knowledge base of civil society and enhancing their participation in the ECOWAS integration programme

(ECOWAS 2016). Despite these remarkable achievements, as International Alert (2010) observes, 'Civil society is still generally weakly developed', partly caused by a host of factors including lack of funding and constant government interference.

10 Accomplishments of MRU and ECOWAS

Despite its limitations, the two institutions have recorded some notable successes that have helped to consolidate the peace and improve the lives of ordinary West Africans. Cross-border cooperation has delivered relative security in the subregion. The institution of a joint border patrol and the joint use of security assets in the MRU has yielded some dividends. The security-development nexus is seen as critical to moving the subregion to economic development, social integration and stability.

The various countries continue to collaborate on issues of importance to economic development, peace and stability and the promotion of democracy. For example, the ECOWAS Political Affairs Directorate, together with the Secretariat of the Mano River Union (MRU), and the Office of the United Nations for West Africa and the Sahel (UNOWAS), organised a two-day workshop for the promotion of peaceful and credible elections in Liberia in Monrovia on the 28th and 29th of August 2017 (ECOWAS Press Release 2017).

The relationship between ECOWAS and the MRU oscillates between formal and informal. The two engage each other through multiple avenues ranging from consultations, trainings, monitoring and evaluations of each other's activities. Given their size and budget, the two organisations are by no means equal. As such, most of the strengthening and capacity building are carried out by ECOWAS sometimes in collaboration with other external actors, including the United Nations, the African Union and the European Union. Such a working relationship is inevitable, as the two complement each other even as they undertake various mandates, sometimes independently. As already mentioned, all members of the MRU are founding members of ECOWAS which means that they are part of the policy decisions that are made in Abuja. ECOWAS also engages with member states of the MRU through bilateral means, especially around issues of good governance. For example, ECOWAS election monitors played a pivotal role in the 2018 elections in both Liberia and Sierra Leone. MRU states also work with various other domestic stakeholders such as traditional leaders and civil society groups that ECOWAS engages. This creates cross-fertilisation of ideas at the grassroots level.

One of the earliest accomplishments for the MRU countries was the Mano River bridge, the first tangible symbol of the Union, which was completed in 1976. It reduced the distance between the Freetown and Monrovia from 630 to 340 miles, thereby greatly helping to improve the infrastructure for promoting trade and relations between the two founding members (Robson

1982, 14). In many ways, the bridge has offered the opportunity to strengthen the economic and social ties of the two countries.

Perhaps one of the most significant of the steps being made to reintegrate the economies of the countries in ECOWAS and the MRU is the proposed introduction of a common currency, to be called the Eco. The key architects behind this landmark fiscal policy are the West African Monetary Zone (WAMZ), formed in 2000 and which consists of Gambia, Ghana, Guinea, Nigeria, Sierra Leone and Liberia. After the introduction of the ECO, the goal is to merge the new currency with the West African CFA franc (used by the French-speaking members of ECOWAS since 1945) at a later date. This merger will create a common currency for much of West Africa. This has taken several years, but when it eventually launches it would represent a major step in further integrating and harmonising West Africa's economies. This follows on the footsteps of the establishment of a customs union among the MRU states (Robson 1982, 620).

The introduction of the ECO is expected to confer several advantages. It will boost economic development in the region and improve cross-border trade. It is also expected to facilitate the exchange of goods and services by creating country-specific specialisations. Another advantage highlighted by Salaudeen (2019) is that the single currency will address the region's monetary problems like the difficulty in converting some of its currencies and the lack of independence of central banks.

The outbreak of Ebola in 2013 demonstrated the importance of such intrastate organisations. The disease started in the forest region of Guinea and quickly spread to neighbouring Sierra Leone, Liberia, Côte d'Ivoire and Nigeria. By the time it was contained in 2016, it had claimed more than 11,000 lives in more than 6 countries. Without even the rudimentary organisational structure provided by both ECOWAS and the MRU, which the international community, including the WHO, was able to tap into, it would have been much worse.

But perhaps the biggest achievement of all, and one for which the organisation is best known for, is in the peace and security sectors. This is perhaps a bit of an irony given that the organisation started first and foremost as an economic entity, and only much later did it evolve into a security outfit. Osadolor (2011, 87) explains this anomaly in stating that 'Although ECOWAS is basically an economic grouping, its desire to promote peace and stability in the overall interest of integration and cooperation for development provides a better understanding of the threat perception of member states on war and security'.

The ECOWAS Monitoring Group (ECOMOG) was the result of these efforts (the need to merge security and economic objectives), which built on the 1978 non-aggression pact and the 1981 and 1999 mutual aggression protocol and conflict prevention mechanisms, respectively. ECOMOG played an active role in resolving the conflict in Sierra Leone, Liberia, Côte d'Ivoire and to a lesser extent Guinea Bissau. In Côte d'Ivoire, ECOMOG sent 1500 troops to maintain the peace following the election crisis. All countries of the MRU played critical roles in helping establish and sustaining ECOMOG. The first operational headquarter was established in Lungi, Sierra Leone. Sierra Leone and Guinea contributed troops while Côte d'Ivoire, which was not yet a member of the Union, played host to some of the peace talks, especially regarding the Sierra Leone Civil War.

11   Areas for Continued Collaboration

Both the MRU and ECOWAS need each other. Their collective fortunes (and misfortune) are intertwined in more ways than one. In the immediate and distant future, ongoing transnational challenges would require continued collaboration between the two institutions. One such area is the planned common currency. This will be a litmus test given that the MRU states, except for Côte d'Ivoire, are among the poorest in the subregion. For the monetary union to work the way it is designed to do, all countries would have to meet the 'convergence criteria' which among other potential benefits ensure that members 'benefit from reduced transaction costs, end of the beggarthy-neighbor policies, the elimination of exchange rate uncertainty, and more transparent price among other things' (De Grauwe 2000). But such accrued benefit comes at a cost as articulated by Kaminsky et al. (p. 91). They posit that 'Loss of country's sovereignty over monetary policy, especially loss of control over monetary policy instruments/shock absorbers such as exchange rate and interest rate, is one of the major potential costs for the membership of monetary union'. Beetsma and Giuliodori (2010) outlined how the European Monetary Union helped keep the inflation rate of its member states at 2%, despite critics.

Another area for continued collaboration between the two institutions is in the borderlands of the MRU Basin in particular. This sometimes rugged and inhospitable terrain where legitimate trade exists side by side with the illegitimate trade in human trafficking, narcotic drugs, counterfeit goods and precious minerals is an important trade link and a lifeline for vulnerable communities. Cross-border trade and the exchange of goods and services is a powerful conflict resolution tool. Such cross-border interaction not only provides sources of livelihoods, but the exchange of goods and services also generates solidarity between border communities and thus critically contributes to promoting peace and stability (African Development Bank 2012).

Human security challenges will also continue to dominate the agenda of the two organisations. Most of the subregion's nagging issues: communicable diseases, arms and people smuggling, are transnational in nature. As Gustavsen et al. (2016) point out 'Diseases don't respect borders, so efforts to control and eliminate diseases must also be flexible and adaptable enough to effectively reach the populations that live in the areas around national frontiers' (Gustavsen et al. 2016, 1). The transboundary nature of the challenges in the subregion means the interests and mandates of the two organisations are best fulfilled through collaboration and compromise.

Freedom of movement and economic well-being will also be an area of continued convergence. The dream of the founders of the regional body was to ensure the unhindered movement of community citizens. The crisscross movements of people, services and goods, including formal and informal, legitimate and illegitimate trade in livestock, agricultural and manufactured goods, illegal weapons, drugs and handicrafts, to name but a few, continue to have profound effects (both positive and negative) on the subregion in general.

The ongoing discovery of oil (and gas) in the subregion will also have an impact on MRU and ECOWAS relations. Oil and natural gas, two of the world's most profitable natural resources, have been discovered in commercial quantities in large parts of West Africa. For a region saturated with weak states, fledgling civic institutions and a history of protracted resource-based conflicts, the rapid and unchecked expansion of Petro-capitalism into its sizzling political economy is a recipe for instability. Oil and gas also present the perfect opportunity for cooperation among the various stakeholders, including governments, international oil and gas companies and host communities. To manage oil-related conflicts, the two organisations would need to continue to work together constructively.

Security threats from religious extremist groups including Boko Haram, which had been raging in the Lake Chad basin since 2009, and the political instability in countries like Mali, continue to plague the subregion. A robust engagement (both military and diplomatic) between the two organisations is needed to manage conflicts and prevent the Boko Haram insurgency from spreading beyond Nigeria, Cameroon, Niger and Chad.

12   Conclusion

This chapter has discussed the evolving relationship between the MRU and ECOWAS. It has argued that the two organisations have played an indispensable role in fostering political, social and economic integration. The end of the armed conflicts of the 1990s and the ensuing peace should ideally create an avenue for both the MRU and ECOWAS to finally achieve their original mandates: peace, stability, good governance, development and economic prosperity. But as with most political organisations of this nature, the efficacy of these intergovernmental institutions is partly contingent upon a host of internal and external factors. The chapter argues that the protracted and transboundary nature of the challenges experienced in the region would require the concerted efforts of the leading political organisations in collaboration with other civil society stakeholders, both domestic and international, to enable West Africa live up to its full potential.

Bibliography

Adkisson, Stephen C., "Integration in West Africa: An Empirical Examination of ECOWAS." Dissertations and Theses. Paper 3277, Portland State University MA thesis, 1984.

Afrika, Jean-Guy K., and Gerald Ajumbo, 2012, "Informal Cross Border Trade in Africa: Implications and Policy Recommendations." *African Development Bank* 3, no. 10.

Aker, Jenny C., Michael W. Klein, Stephen A. O'Connell, and Muzhe Yang, "Borders, Ethnicity and Trade." Boston, Massachusetts, Tufts University, 2013, Accessed June 2, 2019, http://sites.tufts.edu/jennyaker/files/2010/02/Niger_Border-March-2013.pdf.

Beetsma, Roel, and Massimo Giuliodori, "The Macroeconomic Costs and Benefits of the EMU and Other Monetary Unions: An Overview of Recent Research." *Journal of Economic Literature* 48, no. 3 (2010): 603–641. https://doi.org/10.1257/jel. 48.3.603.

Brauer, Jurgen, "Introduction." *Defence and Peace Economics* 14, no. 3 (2003): 151–153. [Introduction to special issue: Economics of Conflict, War, and Peace in Historical Perspective.].

Brauer, Jurgen, "Neighbours: A Blessing Or a Curse?" Stockholm International Peace Research Institute, 2013, Accessed May 7, 2019. https://www.sipri.org/commentary/blog/2013/neighbours-blessing-or-curse.

De Grauwe, Paul, "Monetary Policies in the Presence of Asymmetries," *Journal of Common Market Studies*, Wiley Blackwell, 38, no. 4 (2000): 593–612, November.

Duffy, Charles A., and Werner J. Feld, eds., "Whither Integration Theory?" In *Comparative Regional Systems*, edited by Werner J. Feld and Gavin A. Boyd. New York: Pergamon Press, 1980.

ECOWAS, "Annual Report 2012", Accessed July 7, 2019. http://www.events.ecowas.int/wp-content/uploads/2013/03/2012-Annual-Report_Annexes_English_final.pdf.

ECOWAS Press Release, "ECOWAS Partners UNOWAS and MRU on Peaceful Elections in Liberia-2016", Accessed June 10, 2019. https://www.ecowas.int/ecowas-partners-unowas-and-mru-on-peaceful-elections-in-liberia/.

ECOWAS "Revised Treaty 1993", Accessed Jul 1, 2022. https://ecowas.int/?page_id=82

ECOWAS "Community Strategic Framework 2016", Accessed July 1, 2022. https://ecodocs.ecowas.int/wpcontent/uploads/2016/04/COMMUNITY-STRATEGIC-FRAMEWORK.pdf,

Galtung, Johan, A Structural Theory of Integration, *Journal of Peace Research* 5, no. 4 1968: 375–395.

Gustavsen, Kenneth, Yao Sodahlon, and Simon Bush, "Cross-Border Collaboration for Neglected Tropical Disease Efforts—Lessons Learned from Onchocerciasis Control and Elimination in the Mano River Union." *Globalization and Health*, 2016.

Human Rights Watch, 2020, Accessed August 17, 2020. https://www.hrw.org/africa/liberia.

Institute for Economics and Peace, "Global Terrorism Index, 2019: Measuring the Impact" Sydney: Australia, Accessed January 15, 2020. http://visionofhumanity. org/app/uploads/2019/11/GTI-2019-briefingweb.pdf.

International Alerts, 2010, "Human Security in the Mano River Union, Empowering Women to Counter Gender-based Violence in Border Communities." Accessed July 10, 2019. https://www.international-alert.org/publications/human-security-mano-river-union.

Kaminsky, Graciela, Amine Mati, and Nada Choueiri "Thirty Years of Currency Crises in Argentina: External Shocks or Domestic Fragility?" *Economía* 10 (Fall 2009), no. 1.

Mano River Union Declaration, 1973, Accessed July 1, 2022. https://wits.worldbank.org/GPTAD/PDF/archive/MRU.pdf,

McGowan, Patrick J., "African Military Coups D'état, 1956–2001: Frequency, Trends and Distribution." *The Journal of Modern African Studies* 41, no. 30 (2013): 339–370.

McKenna, Amy, Mano River, 2015, Accessed on July 1, 2022. https://www.britannica.com/place/Mano-River.

Mitrany, David, *A Working Peace System*. Chicago: Quadrangle Books, 1966.

Nagourney, Eric, August 19, 2020, Mali Military Coup: Why the World Is Watching, accessed August 17, 2020. https://www.nytimes.com/2020/08/19/world/africa/Whats-happening-Mali-coup.html.

Osadolor, Osarhieme Benson, "The Evolution of Policy on Security and Defence in ECOWAS 1978–2008." *Journal of the Historical Society of Nigeria* 20 (2011): 87–103.

Owuor, Sophy, "What Are the Major Natural Resources of Liberia?" 2019, Accessed August 17, 2020. https://www.worldatlas.com/articles/what-are-the-major-natural-resources-of-liberia.html.

Poole, Maureen, and Janet Adama Mohammed, "Border Community Security Mano River Union Region." *Conciliation Resources*, London: United Kingdom, 2013.

Powell, Nathaniel, "The Flawed Logic Behind French Military Interventions in Africa." Department of War Studies, University of London, 2020. https://theconversation.com/the-flawed-logic-behind-french-military-interventions-in-africa.

Robson, Peter, "The Mano River Union." *The Journal of Modern African Studies* 20, no. 4: 613–628. Cambridge: Cambridge University Press, 1982.

Salaudeen, Aisha, Cable News Network, "West African Countries Choose New 'ECO' Single Trade Currency," accessed July 15, 2019. https://www.cnn.com/2019/07/01/africa/single-trade-currency-ecowas/index.html.

Sesay, Amado, "Conflict and Collaboration: Sierra Leone and her West African Neighbours, 1961–80." In *Afrika Spectrum*, Hamburg, 1980.

Small Arms Survey, "2012 Annual Report", Accessed July 7 2019. http://www.smallarmssurvey.org/de/tools/ro-poa/profiles-of-regional-organizations/africa/mru.html.

The Economist, "Quietly impressive; West Africa's Regional Club." p.40EU. Business Collection, 2010, Accessed July 2, 2019. http://link.galegroup.com/apps/doc/A222026477/ITBC?u=s1185784&sid=ITBC&xid=4bc1dc78.

United Nations High Commission for Refugees, "Refugee Protection and International Migration in West Africa, Statement by the Assistant High Commissioner—Protection." UNHCR Regional Conference on Refugee Protection and International Migration in West Africa Dakar, 13–14 November 2008.

United Nations, "Liberia and Sierra Leone: The Mano River declaration." *United Nations Treaty Series* 952 (1974): 265–275.

World Atlas, "What Are the Major Rivers of West Africa?" Accessed July 5, 2019. https://www.worldatlas.com/articles/which-are-the-major-rivers-of-west-africa.html.

World Bank Treaty Series, "MRU Declaration," 1974, accessed July 15, 2019. https://wits.worldbank.org/GPTAD/PDF/archive/MRU.pdf.

CHAPTER 9

The Media and Civil Society as Partners in Transitional Justice in Côte D'ivoire

Ady Namaran Coulibaly

1 INTRODUCTION

The media has too often been ignored and perceived as 'an afterthought' in transitional justice (TJ) processes (Price and Stremlau 2012). The inclusion of the media in transitional justice processes in some countries such as Kenya and Liberia, however, demonstrates that the use of appropriate media channels and active involvement of media professionals in such processes should be encouraged. In an article titled *Kenya's Search for Truth and Justice: The Role of Civil Society*, Kemunto and Lynch (2014, 256) analysed the key role played by civil society organisations (CSOs) in the realisation of objectives of truth and reconciliation (in 2003 and from 2008 to 2013) and the impact of their exchanges with the media, international donors, state actors and other stakeholders on these processes. For instance, the Kenya Transitional Justice Network (KTJN), formerly known as the Multi-Sectoral Task Force (MSTF), carried out advocacy campaigns for the enactment of truth, justice and reconciliation (TJRC) legislation, and launched a media campaign to ensure rapid passing of the legislation (Songa 2018, 27).

In Liberia, the media was also instrumental in accountability for civil war atrocities. Liberian Women's Initiative (LWI) recorded instances of rape of

A. N. Coulibaly (✉)
Faculty of Law, Centre for Human Rights, University of Pretoria, Pretoria, South Africa
e-mail: adinamaran@yahoo.com

© The Author(s), under exclusive license to Springer Nature Switzerland AG 2022
A. Adeola and M. W. Mutua (eds.), *The Palgrave Handbook of Democracy, Governance and Justice in Africa*, https://doi.org/10.1007/978-3-030-74014-6_9

145

women and girls for the purposes of war, as well as the massive recruitment of child soldiers, and published media releases on these violations (Dhizaala 2018, 46). The Transitional Justice Working Group (TJWG), a technical committee made of up several CSOs in Liberia, also held media briefings with radio, television and newspaper outlets to explain the functions and powers of the Liberian Truth and Reconciliation Commission (LTRC), three months prior to the launch of this Commission (Dhizaala 2018, 53).

These country-specific examples demonstrate the various ways through which transitional justice mechanisms have made use of the media, particularly through advocacy campaigns, and as a communication tool to provide information to the public and relevant institutions involved in the implementation of TJ processes. Although the Kenya and Liberia examples depict how TJ processes and actors channelled information through the media, the media itself can also play an active role in providing key insights into TJ processes. This can be achieved when media professionals are trained so as to be able to explain TJ processes to the public and go on to initiate publicity campaigns (Price and Stremlau 2012, 1077). The media's capacity to do so should be strengthened, considering that a well-informed public is better able to engage in and support initiatives which seek to enable a post-conflict society to redress past wrongs. The media constitutes a key pillar of TJ projects, especially when it comes to shedding light on heinous crimes and violations perpetrated against populations at a particular time in a country's history. Through information provided by the media, citizens could be kept abreast of key issues and also participate in post-conflict processes such as reconciliation, reparations and accountability.

The need to include the media in TJ processes cannot be overemphasised, all the more because in some African countries, the media is known to have played a non-negligible role in outbreak of conflict. In Côte d'Ivoire, the media has over the years been blamed for the role it played in fuelling and exacerbating crisis in the country through the lack of professionalism and the promotion of animosity, xenophobia and tribalism. Instances of the media's shortcomings with regard to conflict prevention have been recorded by the national monitoring body for press freedom and ethics (*l'Observatoire de la Liberté de la Presse, de l'Ethique et de la Déontologie*, OLPED), which recorded 2,025 ethical blunders in local newspapers through monitoring of the Ivorian media landscape between 1995 and 2000. Specifically, OLPED highlighted shortcomings of newspapers, magazines, radio and television relating to insults, inciting tribalism, racism and xenophobia; and fuelling revolt and violence among other unprofessional conduct (Zio 2012, 12). Such a bleak media landscape prior to the two major crisis the country underwent (the 2002 civil war & 2011 post-electoral crisis) could be said to have provided fertile ground for further polarisation of the media in the years ahead. An October 2010 report by Reporters Without Borders following monitoring of four local newspapers (*Fraternité Matin, Le Nouveau Réveil, Notre Voie and Le Patriote*) foreshadowed the media's role in the conflict which erupted in 2011.

According to the organisation, these four privately-owned media had made use of inflammatory language against political candidates, thereby violating professional norms.

The media undoubtedly influences conflicts and is negatively impacted by conflicts, and adverse effects of conflicts on the media are worse when the media toes partisan lines. The media could, however, constitute a double-edged sword in conflict and post-conflict periods: they could contribute to the promotion of transitional justice (TJ) elements such as peace and reconciliation; or fuel and deepen division and hatred within the nation. Even where the media is involved in TJ processes, the path they chart could lead to either positive or negative outcomes, depending on the media environment and political landscape.

CSOs in Africa also face a number of challenges, as a result of the conflict history in most countries on the continent, and governments' concerns about the power which civil society wields (Brankovic and Hugo van der 2018). Bah (2013), however, argues that despite the precarious position of the Ivorian media vis-à-vis conflict and post-conflict issues and obstacles CSOs may face in dealing with the state, they play an invaluable problem-solving role in post-conflict building and reconstruction. The role of the media as a platform 'to address past wrongs and define a new future' has also been highlighted as pre-eminent in the success of TJ processes (Price and Stremlau 2012, 1077).

It is against this backdrop that this chapter seeks to assess the various ways through which the media and CSOs in Côte d'Ivoire have combined forces for the realisation of the country's TJ objectives. Specifically, the chapter explores two dimensions of civil society and media engagement in TJ processes in Côte d'Ivoire. This includes: identifying major CSOs and online news media involved in TJ processes, and exploring ways in which civil society organisations have engaged media professionals and made use of online news media to further TJ objectives. Also, the chapter examines ways in which civil society organisations have engaged media professionals, made use of online news media to further TJ objectives and how coverage and reporting on TJ processes by online news media reflect the media's role in these processes. The analysis on CSO and media engagement in TJ processes will be preceded by an overview of media, conflicts and TJ in Côte d'Ivoire; traditional and online media; the civil society space and TJ mechanisms.

2 THE MEDIA, CONFLICTS AND TRANSITIONAL JUSTICE IN CÔTE D'IVOIRE

The Ivorian media has been a key player in the country's politics from the period of the French colonial rule. The media, especially the press, was used as a powerful mobilisation tool to galvanise support for the independence agenda, which became a reality on 7 August 1960 (Adjue 2016). Despite the key role played by the media in the country regaining independence, successive years did not record a robust and plural media landscape. As a stark example, during the one-party system under the country's first president, Félix Houphouët-Boigny, there were only two daily newspapers and two weekly magazines operating in the country (Adjue 2016).

Côte d'Ivoire transitioned to a media-friendly environment when popular revolt led to the establishment of multiparty democracy and democratic transition in 1990 (Bah 2017). This multiparty system has been enshrined in article 13 of Côte d'Ivoire's 2016 Constitution, guaranteeing the establishment of political parties and groups and their right to operate freely so long as they abide by the laws of the country, and by 'principles of national sovereignty and of democracy' (Constitution of Côte d'Ivoire 2016, art 25). The introduction of the multiparty system in 1990, a year labelled the 'springtime of the media', led to the establishment of about 100 political parties by 1996, with the media landscape recording a total of 178 daily newspapers that same year (Zio 2012, 2).

Although it proved beneficial in terms of media pluralism, this newly found multiparty democratic system of the year 1990 did not usher in an era of free, fair and level playing field in the political scene of the country. The Democratic Party of Côte d'Ivoire (*Parti Democratique de la Côte d'Ivoire*, PDCI), which had held the reins of power since 1960, still came out victorious in the 1995 elections with Henri Konan Bédié, the successor of former President Félix Houphouët-Boigny as candidate, through oppression of political opponents (Bah 2017). Eventually, the PDCI was ousted in 1999 through a military coup orchestrated by General Robert Guéï, who organised elections in 2000 which again resulted in popular uprisings due to alleged rigging. Subsequently, Laurent Gbagbo, leader of the *Front Populaire Ivoirien* (FPI) and presumed winner of the 2000 elections, came into power.

Côte d'Ivoire has known two main crises: 2002 to 2003 and 2011. The 2002 to 2003 crisis involved attacks by northern-based rebel groups of strategic locations in Abidjan and Bouaké and Korhogo, which are major towns in the north of the country (Malu 2019, 162). Retaliation from the government culminated in various human rights violations being committed by security forces, involving rape, summary executions, detention, arbitrary arrests, extortion and enforced disappearances, with similar violations also carried out by the rebels in the north (Human Rights Watch 2015).

After the country had turned the page of that brutal period through the Ouagadougou Political Agreement signed in 2007 by the parties, presidential elections were held in October 2010 (Malu 2019, 162). The election, which had as main candidates—Alassane Ouattara, Laurent Gbagbo and Henri Konan Bedie—led to a run-off between Gbagbo and Ouattara in November 2010 (Malu 2019, 163). Competing electoral victory claims after the run-off between Ouattara and Gbagbo plunged the country into a crisis characterised by deep ethnic, political and religious divisions. Grave human rights violations were committed by forces loyal to each of these presidential candidates, leading to the death of at least 3,000 people (Human Rights Watch 2019). With the arrest of Gbagbo on 11 April 2011, the crises finally came to an end on 21 May 2011, when Alassane Ouattara was sworn in as president.

Efforts towards post-conflict reconstruction and reconciliation were made by the newly elected government of Ouattara from 2011, through the establishment of national mechanisms such as a truth and reconciliation commission. These initiatives were part of efforts to take the nation on the path to transitional justice. The African Union Transitional Justice Policy (AUTJP) adopted in February 2019 at the 32nd Ordinary Session of the Assembly of the Union established eleven 'indicative elements' of transitional justice (African Union Commission 2019).

According to the AUTJP, elements which are indicative of societies in transition are peace processes; transitional justice commissions; African traditional justice mechanisms; reconciliation and social cohesion; reparations; redistributive (socio-economic) justice; memorialisation; diversity management; justice and accountability; political and institutional reforms; and promotion and institutionalisation of a human rights culture (African Union Commission 2019). These elements are extensive and create a framework that includes all CSOs working in any of these areas within the domain of TJ. In the same vein, an international NGO involved in issues of TJ, the International Center for Transitional Justice (ICTJ) describes approaches to transitional justice as inclusive of criminal prosecutions, truth commissions, reparations, programmes, gender justice, security system reform and memorialisation efforts. The African Commission on Human and Peoples' Rights (ACHPR) has also identified five approaches to TJ in Africa: accountability through criminal prosecutions; truth, reconciliation and social healing processes; reparation and redistributive measures; institutional and political reform; and local and indigenous justice mechanisms.

These classifications are useful in gaining an overview of TJ processes in Côte d'Ivoire. According to Malu (2019, 210), mechanisms established to achieve post-conflict reconstruction and reconciliation in Côte d'Ivoire include the Dialogue and Reconciliation Commission (CDVR); National Commission for Reconciliation and Compensations for Victims; and the National Programme for Social Cohesion. Others include the National Commission of Inquiry (*Commission nationale d'enquête*, CNE); the National Social Cohesion programme; Special Investigative Unit; and the Ministry of Solidarity, Social Cohesion and Victims' Compensation.

The establishment of these mechanisms constitutes a milestone towards national reconciliation and peace building. As key stakeholders, the media and CSOs ought to spearhead the promotion, implementation and popularisation of TJ processes. The first guiding principle of the European Union for engagement in TJ, which seeks to ensure that TJ processes are 'nationally owned, participative, consultative and include outreach' lists public acknowledgement as crucial for TJ processes (European Union 2015). Specifically, it recommends that:

Outreach activities, including public consultation, media engagement and the dissemination of information should thus inform the public about the purpose and design of transitional justice mechanisms... (European Union 2015)

The media possesses tremendous potential for the promotion of conflict prevention and transformation, so long as they engage in fair and accurate journalism, and non-governmental organisations can boost this potential by 'co-operating with the media and promoting pluralism in the communication environment and ethical standards in journalism' Melone et al. (2002).

3 Overview of Traditional and Online Media in Côte D'ivoire

Côte d'Ivoire's press freedom rating improved slightly between 2018 and 2019. From occupying the 82nd place in 2018, the country moved to the 71st position in 2019 (World press freedom Index 2019). This could signify the opening up of the Ivorian media space to increased freedom of expression and press freedom in general.

In the early 1960s, the government of Côte d'Ivoire ensured tight control of the media, allegedly to prevent national divisions along ethnic lines (Adjue 2016, 73). This rigid media landscape, between 1960 and 1990, resulted in only two daily newspapers and two weekly magazines in the country: *Fraternité Matin* and *Ivoir' Soir*, and *Fraternité Hebdo*, and *Ivoire Dimanche*, respectively (Adjue 2016, 73). The fact that the country had only four print media during an entire 30-year period could be a reflection of the lack of freedom of expression and press censorship during that period.

The Ivorian media agency (*L'Agence Ivoirienne de Presse*, AIP) was created in 1961, the same year in which radio was established in the country, and two years later, the government-owned television station (*Radiodiffusion Television Ivoirienne*, RTI) was established (Adjue 2016, 74). Prior to 1990 which marked the beginning of multiparty politics in the country, the Ivorian media was expected to follow instructions and directives from the Félix Houphouët-Boigny led PDCI government, which was in power from 1963 to 1993 (Adjue 2016, 74).

The subsequent transformation of the political landscape and introduction of multiparty politics in the early 1990s led to the establishment of about 100 political parties by 1996 (Zio 2012, 11). This development proved to be fertile ground for the media, as the country recorded 178 daily newspapers in 1996 (Zio 2012, 11). This new media environment was necessary to allow for diversity in opinions and the entrenchment of a culture of democracy.

The opening up of the media landscape to numerous outlets, however, came with dire consequences. Various opposition parties in the country began establishing media outlets since 1999, leading to the use of information for partisan purposes and to the fuelling of political violence (Bah 2017, 11). This media landscape did not provide a space for fruitful exchanges. Instead, it offered a tool to partisan interests seeking to advance their individual agendas. These challenges notwithstanding, the presence of diverse media outlets in Côte d'Ivoire offered tremendous opportunities to reach out to the public and to promote societal transformation.

Aside from traditional media such as radio, newspapers and television, digital media (e.g. online media, web radio, web television) also provides a platform for societal transformation. The online media landscape in Côte d'Ivoire is composed of media which are solely available online, and newspapers which have online/digital versions. A prime example of such newspaper with strong online presence is the government-owned newspaper, *Fraternité Matin*. The network of online media professionals in Côte d'Ivoire (Réseau des professionnels de la presse en ligne, REPRELCI), which is composed of producers of online information, was established in September 2006. As a sign of growing interest in this sector, REPPRELCI set up a regulatory body for digital media in 2015, known as Observatory of Digital Media in Côte d'Ivoire (*Observatoire des médias numériques de Côte d'Ivoire*, OMENCI), with the backing of the government. Based on a census it embarked on between 2013 and 2014, REPPRELCI recorded 41 newspapers with online presence; 10 online news web portals; 4 web televisions; 1 web radio; and 3 online press agencies (UNESCO-funded study). Information on online media in Côte d'Ivoire demonstrates its economic potential, with the sector said to employ more than 386 personnel, including 186 professional journalists; 80% of online news websites employ at least 1 journalist, and 61% of online media have physical offices.

4   CIVIL SOCIETY SPACE

The Centre for Research and Action for Peace (CERAP) undertook a study titled *Mapping the contribution of civil society organisations to sector governance in Côte d'Ivoire*. Based on the 2017 data from the Directorate General for Territorial Administration (Direction Generale de l'Administration du Territoire, DGAT), CERAP recorded 8,227 registered CSOs in Côte d'Ivoire, out of which 2,089 are associations and 1,549 are NGOs (CERAP 2018, 17). Just like the media landscape, the civil society space in Côte d'Ivoire blossomed after the instauration of multiparty democracy in 1990. This meant that CSOs could operate freely and bring about societal transformation. However, CSOs were also negatively impacted by the post-electoral violence in 2011. The crisis culminated into deep politicisation, instrumentalisation and polarisation of CSOs (CERAP 2018, 17).

According to CERAP, CSOs in Côte d'Ivoire have been described as playing six major roles: participation in public life; participation in the formulation of public policies; inclusive and sustainable growth; prevention of conflicts, consolidation of peace and state building; service provision; and transparency and accountability (CERAP 2018, 17). In terms of conflict prevention and peace building, the study revealed that CSOs have faced a major obstacle, that of an absence of dialogue with public authorities, and confrontation with the state.

CERAP's 2018 survey on CSO participation in governance in Côte d'Ivoire involving 1,315 CSOs and 290 local administrative and government authorities revealed pertinent details about the relationship between CSOs and the state: more than 80% of CSOs affirmed having working relations with public authorities, and more than 90% of public authorities also said they work with CSOs. In this same study, when asked to explain how they perceive their role, civil society actors identified seven elements, namely: (a) improvement of living conditions; (b) support to populations; (c) local development; (d) promotion of human rights; (e) fight against poverty; (f) advocating for specific causes; and (g) contributing to social cohesion (CERAP 2018, 6). Despite the supposed collaborative relations between the public sector and CSOs, and the key issues which CSOs identified as the role they play in society, these organisations highlighted some areas as problematic, risky or 'forbidden', such as advocacy for human rights and transparency in electoral processes (CERAP 2018, 8). These are challenges which could hinder civil society efforts towards transitional justice in the country.

Data on CSOs which operate in the field of TJ in Côte d'Ivoire is readily available, following a European Union project known as Leadership and Initiative of Non-state Actors (*Leadership et Initiatives des Acteurs Non Etatiques*, LIANE) implemented from 2012 to 2015 with the aim of boosting the capacities of CSOs. The database provides names of CSOs, the region within which they are located, the issues they focus on, email and telephone numbers of resource persons.

4.1 Domestic Regulations on Civil Society Activities

The existing law on associations, which regulate activities of CSOs in Côte d'Ivoire, dates as far back as the 1960s. This law has been described as archaic and not suited to the massive changes which have since taken place as far as the development of CSOs is concerned (CERAP 2018, 7). As part of a project between the Ivorian government and the European Union on strengthening capacities of non-state actors, an outcome document dubbed 'Proposals for the improvement of the legal framework of Ivorian civil society organisations' made recommendations which were presented to the government in 2016. Some of the issues raised include the fact that the 1960 law on associations did not take into account new categories of CSOs and was unclear as to basic concepts such as non-profit.

On the bright side, the 2016 Constitution of Côte d'Ivoire contains several provisions which positively impact the civil society space, such as the guarantee of freedom of association, assembly and peaceful protests (Law N° 2016-886 of 8 November 2016). Specifically, article 26 identifies civil society as a key component of democracy and acknowledges that civil society organisations contribute to the 'economic, social and cultural development' of the country.

The Ivoirian Constitution of 2016 can therefore be considered as a primary legal instrument for the growth of CSOs in the country.

In addition to the 1960 law on associations and the 2016 Constitution of Côte d'Ivoire, there are two laws which strengthen the legal framework for the operations of CSOs. These are Law N ° 2014-388 of 20 January 2014 on the promotion and protection of human rights defenders and its decree N ° 2017-121 of 22 February 2017 on modalities of implementation. Another key law is Law N° 2012-1132 of 13 December 2012 on the establishment, attribution, organisation and functioning of the National Human Rights Commission (*Commission Nationale des Droits de l'Homme de Côte d'Ivoire*, CNDHCI). By virtue of article 7, Law N° 2012-1132 of 13 December 2012 on the CNDH, the Human Rights Commission is composed of a central committee with 16 members having voting rights, out of which eight are CSOs.

5   TRANSITIONAL JUSTICE MECHANISMS IN CÔTE D'IVOIRE

Mechanisms established to achieve post-conflict reconstruction and reconciliation in Côte d'Ivoire include the Dialogue and Reconciliation Commission CDVR (2012); National Commission for Reconciliation and Compensations for Victims (2015); National Commission for Reconciliation and Indemnification of Victims (2015); and National Programme for Social Cohesion (2015) (Malu 2019, 197). Others include National Commission of Inquiry (*Commission nationale d'enquête*, CNE) set up in May 2011; the National Social Cohesion Programme; Special Investigative Unit; and the Ministry of Solidarity, Social Cohesion and Victims Compensation. TJ processes in Côte d'Ivoire have therefore included accountability mechanisms; truth, reconciliation and healing processes; and reparations and redistributive measures.

According to the African Union Transitional Justice Policy, various countries going through transitions have utilised criminal prosecutions for the purpose of accountability and re-establishing the rule of law (AUTJP 2019, 9). In the case of post-conflict reconstruction in Côte d'Ivoire, national courts and the International Criminal Court (ICC) have been used as accountability mechanisms. National courts have been able to prosecute 150 persons during a five-year period (2010 to 2015) for crimes which were committed during the country's major conflicts (Malu 2019, 197).

Côte d'Ivoire signed the Rome Statute on 30 November 1998, ratified it on February 2013 and has given the ICC jurisdiction to prosecute crimes which date back to 1 July 2002 (Bah 2017, 12).

In terms of dissemination of information about the Court's activities in the country, the ICC has, to a great extent, made use of local media, an approach which helps to mitigate challenges such as financial constraints and reaching huge numbers of victims (Malu 2019, 249). A study conducted on perceptions and attitudes about security and justice in Abidjan, Côte d'Ivoire, on the basis of consultations and a survey of 1,000 randomly selected respondents revealed high levels of awareness by respondents about the ICC which, according to the researchers, 'likely reflects good access to media' (Pham and Vinck 2014).

The Special Investigative and Examination Cell (*La Cellule Spéciale d'Enquête et d'Instruction*, CSEI) was set up in 2011 by the government of Côte d'Ivoire, composed of judges and prosecutors tasked with investigating crimes which were perpetrated during the 2010 post-election crisis (Human Rights Watch 2015). According to the Human Rights Watch (2015), the CSEI brought charges against more than 20 alleged perpetrators of human rights violations of the post-election period. The National Commission of Inquiry (*Commission Nationale d'Enquête*, CNE) was established as a mechanism for the identification and documentation of crimes committed between 2010 and 2011.

The Dialogue, Truth and Reconciliation Commission (*Commission Dialogue, verité et reconciliation CDVR*), whose three-year mandate expired on 28 September 2013, was established through Decree N° 2011-85 of 13 May 2011, which was later replaced by Decree N° 2011-167 of 13 July 2011. The CDVR was birthed in 2011, as a body that would focus on reconciliation efforts as well as investigate human rights violations which were carried out in the heat of the country's two major conflict periods (Malu 2019, 181). According to Malu (2019), its focus in terms of communication was hinged on inclusion, diversity and participation, where inclusion means providing access to public information in citizens' own languages, through the media and new technologies such as the internet. In terms of diversity, the commission aimed to respect all opinions emanating from public discourse, and for participation, the CDVR had the goal of ensuring that all opinions are heard, with the possibility for citizens to dialogue with decision-makers (Malu 2019).

The National Program for Social Cohesion (*Programme National de Cohésion Sociale*, PNCS) was established to handle reparation programmes. The country also has a ministry of solidarity, social cohesion and victims' compensation. According to Amnesty International (2016), the National Commission for Reconciliation and Compensation for Victims (*La Commission Nationale pour la Réconciliation et l'Indemnisation des Victimes des crises survenues en Côte d'Ivoire*, CONARIV) was set up in March 2015 as a continuation of the reconciliation efforts of the CDVR, with emphasis on registration of unidentified victims of post-electoral violence.

5.1 Domestic Regulations Governing Operations of the Media

In Côte d'Ivoire, the legal and regulatory framework for the operation of the media is provided for in the Constitution and decrees issued by the government. French laws on media freedom and functioning of the media were in force in Côte d'Ivoire prior to the year 1991 (Gueudeu 2012). With consensus from various stakeholders on the need for the country to adopt its own laws, a number of laws were passed in 1991 to regulate operations of the media (these are Law N° 91–1001 of 27 December 1991 relating to audio-visual communication; Law N° 91–1033 of 31 December 1991 on the press; and Law N° 91–1034 of 31 December 1991 on the legal status of professional journalists). These laws have since gone through various amendments, including the law regulating the press. Such amendments have sought to decriminalise press offences and to ensure autonomy and independence of media regulatory bodies (Gueudeu 2012).

On the whole, laws regulating the media in Côte d'Ivoire can be said to be forward-looking and promote access to information, media freedom and pluralism. For instance, the government passed a Law on Access to Information of Public Interest in December 2013, which provides for the right to access, without discrimination, by persons or institutions, of public interest information and public documents of state institutions [Article 3, Law N° 2013-867 of 23 December 2013 on Access to Information of Public Interest].

Similarly, article 31 of the law regulating the press provides for the freedom of journalists in the gathering, processing, publishing and dissemination of information, subject to legal and regulatory laws in force, as well as ethical codes of the profession [Article 31, Law N° 2017-867 of 27 December 2017 on the press]. These laws are laudable, since journalists can be hindered in carrying out their duties when they are compelled to work in environments where information meant for public consumption is a scarce resource.

Media freedom is also enshrined in the 2016 Constitution of Côte d'Ivoire, by virtue of article 101, where it is stipulated that 'the law sets forth rules concerning citizenship, civil rights and fundamental guarantees granted to citizens for the exercise of public freedoms, as well as "freedom, pluralism and independence of the media"'.

In addition, the legal framework promotes professionalism within media practice. This is evident in article 8 of the 2017 law regulating the press (including digital media), which clearly states that the head of publication, the managing editor, the assistant editor and majority of the editorial team must be professional journalists [Article 8, Law N° 2017-867 of 27 December 2017 on the press]. This provision is laudable, as it might reduce the likelihood of untrained personnel holding managerial and editorial positions in the media, and therefore promote higher levels of professionalism.

The 2017 law regulating the Ivorian press also provides that the press shall be free to benefit from financial support from the state, publicity tax and from development partners towards the training of journalists and communication specialists; printing, dissemination and distribution; development of the press and production of digital information [Article 75, Law N° 2017-867 of 27 December 2017 on the press].

Activities of the media are overseen by an independent national body in charge of regulating the press, known as the National Press Authority (*Autorité nationale de la presse*, ANP), through a 2017 amendment of the law regulating the press.[1] This body is mandated to ensure freedom and pluralism of the press, adherence by the media to ethical codes of the profession; to act as a disciplinary mechanism for actors in the press; and to promote respect for the laws relating to the establishment, ownership and resources of press houses [Article 41, Law N° 2017-867 of 27 December 2017 on the press].

In recognition of the role of digital media in the promotion of freedom of expression and citizenship, it was recommended, following a study of the press, online media, radio and television in Côte d'Ivoire, that digital media should be taken into account during the drafting of media laws in Côte d'Ivoire. Perhaps, as a result of this recommendation, digital media was subsequently included in the press law of December 2017, with article 3 stating that 'this law relates to the print media as well as production of digital information' [Article 3, Law N° 2017-867 of 27 December 2017 on the press].

A code of ethics for journalists in Côte d'Ivoire, an amendment of the 1992 Journalists' Code of Ethics, was adopted at the Press House (Maison de la Presse, MPA) on 23 February 2012 in the presence of representatives of journalists in Côte d'Ivoire. This code of ethics, which lays out 22 responsibilities and 10 rights of journalists, calls on journalists, in article 14, to refrain from fuelling tribal sentiments, xenophobia, revolt, violence and crimes, war crimes and crimes against humanity.

6 MEDIA ENGAGEMENT AS A TOOL TO FURTHER TRANSITIONAL JUSTICE

Media engagement by CSOs working in the domain of TJ could procure significant benefits for these organisations. Media engagement creates working relations with media practitioners and representatives, which could be harnessed in times when information needs to be relayed urgently. Despite the positive contribution it could bring to the success of TJ efforts, media engagement in TJ is not always a simple and fluid process, as there may exist several hurdles to the media's effective participation in such processes. Difficulties arise for instance in countries where the media itself has either triggered or fuelled violence. This could be a result of several circumstances, such as media ownership by political and business figures who aim to advance their own interests (Price and Stremlau 2012, 1078). Media approach to covering TJ processes also poses a considerable challenge, especially where the media polarises or inflames identity issues. The media can therefore be a double-edged sword in TJ processes: it could lead to increased divisions or help in resolving conflicts.

---

[1] This body was initially known as the National Press Council (Conseil nationale de la presse, CNP) and was renamed National Press Authority (Autorité nationale de la press, ANP) through a 2017 amendment in Article 40 of Law N° 2017-867 of 27 December 2017 on the press.

A media engagement framework designed following a study on human rights, sexual orientation and gender identity in South Asia (India, Nepal and Bangladesh) provides insights into key issues that should be included in media engagement (UNDP 2013, 2). The framework covers engagement with communities, stakeholders and the media, on the basis of three issues: providing scope for initiatives; shaping evidence; and connecting community with media.

Below is the media engagement framework as presented in the study (Table 1):

Elements of the above framework which focus specifically on the media guided analysis of interviews for this chapter. These elements are: 1 (c) tracking and monitoring media; 1 (d) use of online media; 2 (c) creating media-friendly products; 3 (c) sensitising media; and 3 (d) sustaining meaningful relationships. The media engagement framework designed by the Centre for Advocacy and research New Delhi is reproduced below with additional inputs, for the purpose of defining elements of engagement, key activities and expected outcomes for media engagement by CSOs in Côte d'Ivoire (Table 2).

The above media engagement framework guided the preparation of an interview guide, and interviews were conducted with representatives from seven (7) CSOs operating in Côte d'Ivoire.

Analysis of Abidjan.net, acknowledged as the top online news media in Côte d'Ivoire, was useful in aggregating news from several local news websites. The phrase *justice transitionnelle* (transitional justice) was typed in the search tool of Abidjan.net, and all articles published from 2011 to September 2019 were selected for analysis. This period was chosen because 2011 marked the

Table 1 Summary of media engagement framework (Centre for Advocacy and Research New Delhi)

1	Provide the scope of the initiative	a. A regular mechanism for communication exchange between stakeholders; b. Monitoring and stimulating ground-level community responses; c. Tracking and monitoring media; and d. The use of online media
2	Shape evidence	a. Using epidemiological evidence; b. Documenting good practices and challenges; and c. Creating media-friendly products
3	Connect community with media	a. Training community representatives; b. Ensuring crisis management capacity; c. Sensitising media; and d. Sustaining meaningful relationships

Table 2 Media engagement framework for CSOs working in TJ in Côte d'Ivoire, adapted from the Centre for Advocacy and Research New Delhi (2012)

Element of engagement	Key activities	Expected outcome
Tracking and monitoring of media	– Identifying key outlets and tracking how various issues are presented – Identifying practitioners/media who shape evidence and coverage of TJ issues	Forging understanding of various perspectives on TJ
Use of	– Online media (news websites, blogs, social media, etc.)	Reaching huge numbers of the population and diverse segments
Creating media-friendly products	– Campaign briefs, backgrounders, events hand-outs – Database to provide key information on trends, practices and other important details on TJ	– Encourage free flowing discourse – Develop media interest in key issues
Sensitising media	– Providing training on TJ, professionalism, media ethics to media practitioners and influencers – Award schemes to initiate frontline cadre of reporters and journalists on TJ who can be positive models – Site visits – Engage with professional media associations and sustain active dialogue and exchanges with these platforms	Boost capacities of media professionals/develop journalists who can be role models in the domain
Sustaining meaningful relationships	– Carrying out regular and constant media campaigns – Marking special days, celebratory events and ensuring media coverage	The creation of close links with the media

establishment of several transitional justice mechanisms in the country, and by 2015, some of these mechanisms had published reports on their activities.[2]

Findings from the content analysis of Abidjan.net web portal and interviews with representatives of CSOs are presented in the next sections.

---

[2] For example, the Dialogue, Truth and Reconciliation Commission (CDVR) published its final report of 125 pages in December 2014, and the National Commission on Enquiry (CNE) published a 35-page report on violations of human rights and international humanitarian law in July 2012.

6.1 CSOs and Online Media Involved in Transitional Justice

In total, 14 CSOs were mentioned in the 72 selected TJ-related news articles generated through the search engine of Abidjan.net. Out of these 14, only two are international CSOs: the International Center for Transitional Justice and the Open Society for West Africa. The tally of the frequency of their appearance in these news articles produced the following results:

1. *19 mentions*—International Center for Transitional Justice (ICTJ);
2. *5 mentions*—Actions for the Protection of Human Rights (Actions pour la protection de droits de l'homme, APDH) —APDH was established in 2003 and has Observer Status before the African Commission on Human and Peoples' Rights;
3. *5 mentions*—The Observatory of Transitional Justice (L'Observatoire de la justice transitionnelle de Côte d'Ivoire, OJT-CI, established in 2013);
4. *1 mention*—Press Editors Association (Groupement des éditeurs de presse de Côte d'Ivoire (GEPCI);
5. *2 mentions*—Journalists Union of Côte d'Ivoire (l'Union nationale des journalistes de Côte d'Ivoire, UNJCI);
6. *1 mention*—PLAYDOO;
7. *5 mentions*—The Alliance to rebuild Governance in Côte d'Ivoire (l'Alliance pour refonder la gouvernance en Afrique, ARGA);
8. *1 mention*—The Working Group on Transitional Jusitce (Groupe de travail sur la justice transitionnelle (GTJT), composed of APDH, MIDH, RAIDH and Wanep-Ci);
9. *3 mentions*—Ivorian Human Rights Mouvement (Mouvement ivoirien des droits de l'Homme, MIDH);
10. *2 mentions*—Group of victims in Côte d'Ivoire (Collectif des victimes en Côte d'Ivoire, CVCI);
11. *3 mentions*—Action, Justice and Peace Network (Le réseau Action, Justice et Paix, RAJP);
12. *2 mentions*—Open Society for West Africa (OSIWA);
13. *3 mentions*—Confederation of organisations of victims of the Ivorian crises (Confédération des organisations de victimes de la crise ivoirienne, COVICI); and
14. *3 mentions*—Ivorian Human Rights League (Ligue ivoirienne des Droits de l'Homme, LIDHO).

During analysis of selected articles on TJ in the web portal Abidjan. net, articles from 7 other online news aside Abidjan. net itself were produced. It was also possible to record the number of articles published by each of these online news media. These are presented in descending order (Table 3).

Table 3 Number of news articles per online news website

	Number of articles on TJ	News website
1	30 articles	AIP
2	11 articles	APA
3	10 articles	L'intelligent d'Abidjan
4	9 articles	Abidjan.net
5	3 articles	Le Patriote
6	3 articles	Le Democrate
7	2 articles	Le Temps
8	2 articles	Abidjan24h

6.2   Interview Responses: Media Engagement by CSOs

A total of seven (7) interviews were conducted with representatives of CSOs, with a view to finding out the various ways through which they engage the media in their activities. These CSOs are:

1. Ligue ivoirienne des Droits de l'Homme (LIDHO) established in 1987;
2. Femme en action-CI founded in 1992;
3. The International Center for Transitional Justice (ICTJ) created in 2001;
4. Service for Peace Bouaké (SFP) created in 2002;
5. Convention de la Société Civile ivoirienne (CSCI) established in 2003;
6. Aide, Assistance et Developpement Communautaire de Côte d'Ivoire (ADC-CI) founded in 2006;
7. CIVIS Côte d'Ivoire (CIVIS—CI)) established in 2015.

The interview guide focused on five key components, namely tracking and monitoring of media; use of online media; the creation of media-friendly products; media sensitisation; and sustaining meaningful relationships with the media. Information gathered during the interviews is presented below and is supplemented with information from desktop research conducted on each CSO.

ICTJ revealed that it engages four main actors involved in TJ processes in Côte d'Ivoire: the government, victims, CSOs and the media. ICTJ engages with government because it is the main entity responsible for the implementation of TJ processes and mechanisms. Engagement with the government involves capacity building for representatives of TJ mechanisms and provision of technical support. Engagement with victims was identified as essential, considering that TJ is about victims having access to redress and reparations. ICTJ's engagement with victims focuses on capacity building to help them understand the various TJ processes and promote their participation. The organisation provides technical support to CSOs and training in advocacy strategies to empower them to push for reforms and participate in implementation processes.

In terms of media engagement, the ICTJ representative noted that the organisation provides training for media associations and media professionals, as well as technical support. Essentially, it strives to assist journalists in identifying issues related to TJ and writing them from a human rights perspective. In addition, training is provided to the media on how to scrutinise the various TJ processes, prepare feature articles and news stories from a victim-centred perspective, and engage national actors for TJ to benefit society. ICTJ has provided such capacity building by holding a series of workshops with media associations. ICTJ has also carried out special programmes on community radios which enable victims and experts to share ideas. These radio programmes are usually recorded and shared with radio stations in other regions of the country.

ADC-CI is an NGO founded in 2006 based in Yamoussoukro, which focuses on the promotion of human rights and democracy, good governance, peace and security. CIVIS-CI is an NGO which works in peace processes, reconciliation and social cohesion, human rights, political and institutional reforms, governance, rule of law, democracy and elections. According to Kouamé Christophe, president of the organisation, CIVIS-CI has engaged radio, the press, online news media, social media and community radios.

LIDHO deals with human rights, reconciliation and social cohesion, rural lands, political and institutional reforms among other issues. SFP is involved in community disarmament and reinsertion of youth, reconciliation and social cohesion, and its media engagement has mainly targeted online news media, posters and pamphlets.

Femme en action-CI is an NGO which works in the area of peace and reconciliation, issues of women, children and youth, and reproductive and sexual health. CSCI is a platform made up of 166 local civil society organisations, involving religious organisations, professional bodies, groups and NGOs. Its objective is to influence the political, economic and social processes for the well-being of populations in Côte d'Ivoire, and its mission is to promote rule of law, good governance, human rights and participatory democracy.

Table 4 summarises responses from CSOs concerning engagement with the media on TJ processes.

6.3 *Qualitative Content Analysis: Media Engagement by CSOs in Côte d'Ivoire*

Qualitative content analysis of 72 news articles on activities of CSOs and the media derived from Abidjan.net provided useful insights into the various ways through which CSOs have engaged the media over the years. Melone et al. (2002) categorise media projects geared towards conflict transformation into three: projects targeting journalists; projects dealing with the content of media; and projects which seek to shift the political context. Media-related activities

Table 4 CSO engagement with the media for TJ purposes

Element of engagement	Key activities reported by CSOs
Tracking and monitoring media	– Monitor information in the media to identify the key issues making headlines in the area of TJ – Target media which publish information about the areas of intervention of the organisation – Identify relevant media practitioners on TJ
Use of online news media	– Providing articles to online news media on CSO activities on TJ – Participation in events organised by online news media – Use of social media platforms for publishing information on TJ
Creating media-friendly products/activities	– Printing of brochures and pamphlets, which contain details on key areas of intervention and activities of CSOs – Issue press statements and organise public events where the media is invited to provide coverage
Sensitising media	– Train media on TJ processes reporting and coverage of TJ – Award of outstanding journalists in the area of human rights and TJ
Sustaining meaningful relationships with media	– Granting media interviews and speaking on media platforms on TJ-related issues

of CSOs working on TJ with emphasis on projects targeting journalists and media content are presented below.

Projects Targeting Journalists and Media Content

ICTJ organised a workshop for the association of newspaper editors in Côte d'Ivoire (Groupement des éditeurs de presse de Côte d'Ivoire, GEPCI) in April 2013 to provide them with fundamental information on TJ; strengthen their capacities in writing reports and news articles on TJ mechanisms. The workshop covered three thematic areas: TJ in Côte d'Ivoire, the media's role in TJ and coverage of TJ issues. This workshop, according to Mohamed Suma (head, International Center for Transitional Justice Côte d'Ivoire office), was one of many such workshops held at the behest of journalists, who emphasised that it was necessary for editors to also be trained on TJ, so as to facilitate cooperation between editors and journalists.

Journalists and press correspondents were trained on the theme of 'criminal justice in transitional justice' in February 2014 by ICJT. A workshop was organised by the national journalists' union (L'Union nationale des journalistes de Côte d'Ivoire, UNJCI), ICTJ and OSIWA to strengthen the capacities of about 30 journalists between 8 and 9 November 2012.

ICTJ and CONARIV jointly organised a workshop for the journalists working in the press, online media and community radios on the policy of reparation for victims in June 2015. Journalists were also called upon to avoid broadcasting or publishing sensitive information about witnesses and victims during hearings, at a workshop organised by ICTJ in June 2015 on the role and limits of the media in the protection of witnesses.

The United Nations Operation in Côte d'Ivoire (UNOCI) held a workshop for CSOs and the media in June 2011, to strengthen social cohesion and reconciliation, and on TJ. The article published with regard to this event is very informative, as it presents the components of the module taught at the workshop, such as the values of the culture of peace, transitional justice, human rights, dignity and non-violence.

CSOs and international organisations also organised workshops to strengthen the capacities of other CSOs in the area of TJ. A seminar was organised for about 60 CSOs by LIDHO, the United Nations and the CDVR on TJ mechanisms in April 2012.

Analysis of articles also revealed the use of radio for the purpose of advancing TJ in Côte d'Ivoire. Specifically, the Action, Justice and Peace Network (Le réseau Action, Justice et Paix, RAJP), together with Goethe-Institut, ICTJ and UNICEF, presented a radio programme aimed at giving a platform to youth affected by the crises to tell their stories. This information is in line with information provided on the website of ICTJ, which states that the ICTJ has 'worked with RAJP youth leaders to broadcast victims' testimonies on local airwaves, broadening dialogue around reparations'. Workshops organised to train media on writing and reporting on issues of TJ are also projects which seek to transform and impact media content.

7 SUMMARY OF FINDINGS AND CONCLUSION

This chapter had two main objectives: to identify major CSOs and online news media involved in TJ processes, and explore ways in which civil society organisations have engaged media professionals and made use of online news media to further TJ objectives.

Engagement by CSOs on TJ has been quite extensive, considering that it involved a wide range of actors in TJ processes, some of which include traditional leaders, war victims, the government, media associations and media professionals. This is a positive and encouraging development which could forge greater collaboration among all stakeholders for the realisation of transitional justice in Côte d'Ivoire.

The approach to using radio programmes (especially on community radio) in addressing TJ issues is commendable and demonstrates a desire to reach and engage grassroots populations. Special media projects on radio or television hold significant potential for post-conflict transformation.

As concerns achievements of media engagement efforts, CSOs recorded increased access to media coverage for their events, greater collaboration with the media and ease of reaching journalists. A key hindrance to effective partnership with the media was highlighted as the failure of media professionals to ensure in-depth analysis and reportage of TJ issues covered by CSOs. Most often, media professionals mainly focus on reporting of TJ events. This factor motivated several international and local CSOs in Côte d'Ivoire to hold capacity-building workshops for journalists and media practitioners to promote understanding of TJ issues. Most of these were organised by ICTJ and other civil society organisations with funding from the European Union and the United Nations. These workshops were aimed at empowering the media with notions of transitional justice, and to boost their capacity to write detailed reports on TJ processes.

Through content analysis, the following emerged as elements of the media's engagement by CSOs in Côte d'Ivoire: capacity-building workshops, feature articles, interviews, press releases and special media projects. Feature articles which explain TJ and its various processes were written by either experts in TJ, or journalists. One such article, titled *Un instrument de paix au service des pays fragiles*, explained the significance of the different elements of TJ in post-conflict reconstruction. An extensive feature article written by the Head of ICTJ Côte d'Ivoire in commemoration of the International Day of Justice demonstrates the relevance of such feature articles, in terms of enabling citizens understand components of TJ.

Interviews with opinion leaders, CSO representatives and experts on TJ conducted by journalists offered key insights into major TJ issues in the country. Only three such interviews were identified in selected news articles. One of such interviews was granted by the president of APDH, who placed emphasis on the role of repentance in justice and forgiveness. An interview was also granted by the vice-president of the West Africa Civil Society Forum, who addressed issues surrounding justice and reconciliation in Côte d'Ivoire. Another interview was held with the president of MIDH, in which he explained the danger in giving priority to reconciliation and leaving justice on the back burner. Press releases constitute a key source of information for the media. Press releases were used by journalists to write articles on TJ programmes.

In view of the aforementioned, the following recommendations are offered to CSOs and the media:

Civil society organisations

- The holding of workshops by CSOs for the media demonstrates that CSOs acknowledge the media as a key pillar in the success of TJ processes. These workshops also provide an opportunity of forging closer links and greater collaboration between CSOs and the media, which could be beneficial ensuring adequate and professional coverage of TJ issues by within the media. Such workshops should be multiplied, as they enable the media to grasp key elements of TJ and also forge closer links between the media and CSOs.

- The lack of websites by some CSOs included in this chapter was a challenge in terms of acquiring credible information on these organisations. As a result, news articles containing information about these CSOs were consulted. CSOs should therefore prioritise the creation, maintenance and regular updates of their organisation's website, to provide the media and the public with pertinent information about their activities.
- Through the expertise they gain in the field of TJ, CSO representatives ought to write and publish feature articles in the press and online media. These articles will inform the public and also provide the media with key concepts on TJ issues. It will also promote greater interest of the media in TJ.
- CSOs should take advantage of the commemoration of days which are related to TJ to bring TJ issues to the limelight within the media landscape.

The media

- Most articles written about TJ by journalists focused on reports of happenings and events on transitional justice. There is the need to forge greater understanding and appreciation of TJ processes within the media, to enable journalists develop and write feature articles and reports covering the various processes and mechanisms of TJ. The media should therefore harness available opportunities to participate in workshops and seminars organised by CSOs, so as to build their capacity in covering TJ processes.
- Journalists ought to be proactive in their coverage of TJ issues. Specifically, such coverage could include interviews with opinion leaders and experts in the field of TJ, so as to ensure that the public gets detailed and in-depth information on TJ processes.
- CSOs perceive the Ivoirian media as deeply polarised based on political affiliation. This, according to some CSO representatives interviewed, hinders collaboration and media engagement. It is recommended that media associations and journalists in Côte d'Ivoire give pride of place to professionalism and adhere to code of ethics.

BIBLIOGRAPHY

Abidjan.net website: https://abidjan.net/.

Abidjan.net. «17 juillet, Journée Internationale de la Justice: La Côte d'Ivoire sur le pendule de la Justice» https://news.abidjan.net/h/437425.html (accessed October 1, 2019a).

Abidjan.net. «Côte d'Ivoire: les responsables de victimes de guerre formés sur le monitoring et la conduite des consultations» https://news.abidjan.net/h/615977.html (accessed October 1, 2019b).

Abidjan.net. «Des journalistes ivoiriens se forment aux notions de la justice transitionnelle, jeudi.» https://news.abidjan.net/h/486951.html (accessed October 1, 2019c).

Abidjan.net. «Des leaders communautaires de Toulépleu instruits sur la justice transitionnelle» https://news.abidjan.net/h/637233.html (accessed October 1, 2019d).

Abidjan.net. «Hervé Gouaméné, président de l'APDH: "La réconciliation vraie ne pourra se faire sans la justice et le pardon qui s'obtient après une repentance» https://news.abidjan.net/h/402438.html (accessed October 1, 2019e).

Abidjan.net. «Justice transitionnelle: Une table ronde pour renforcer les capacités des médias,» https://news.abidjan.net/h/457956.html (accessed October 1, 2019f).

Abidjan.net. «Les professionnels des médias formés sur la réparation des victimes des crises» http://news.abidjan.net/h/556384.html (accessed October 1, 2019g).

Abidjan.net. «Me Drissa Traoré, président du MIDH: "Il ne faut pas sacrifier la justice pour la réconciliation» https://news.abidjan.net/h/402437.html (accessed October 1, 2019h).

Abidjan.net. «Médias-Justice: les journalistes ivoiriens appelés à s'abstenir de diffuser des informations sensibles sur des témoins et victimes» https://news.abidjan.net/h/555701.html (accessed October 1, 2019i).

Abidjan.net. «Nathalie Koné-Traoré, Vice-présidente du FOSCAO: Il n'y a pas de dichotomie entre la justice et la réconciliation» https://news.abidjan.net/h/402 571.html (accessed October 1, 2019j).

Abidjan.net. «Séminaire de l'Onuci sur l'engagement des leaders d'opinion pour le renforcement de la cohésion sociale et la réconciliation: l'éducation à la culture de la paix, selon Dr Doumbia Diénéba» https://news.abidjan.net/h/402769.html (accessed October 1, 2019k).

Abidjan.net. «Un instrument de paix au service des pays fragiles» https://news.abidjan.net/h/402302.html (accessed October 1, 2019l).

Abidjan.net. «UNJCI/Formation des journalistes:Les acteurs de la presse et des médias à l'école de la justice transitionnelle» https://news.abidjan.net/h/444589.html (accessed October 1, 2019m).

Abidjan.net. «Yamoussoukro / Mécanisme de justice transitionnelle pour le retour à la paix: ONG et société civile instruites par la LIDHO et l'ONUCI» https://news.abidjan.net/h/430744.html (accessed October 1, 2019n).

Adjue, A. J. (2016) Histoire de la communication en Côte d'Ivoire: épreuve d'une épistémologie. *Communication en Question*, no. 7 (November/December): 63–83.

African Commission on Human and Peoples' Rights. (2019) Study on Transitional Justice and Human and Peoples, https://www.achpr.org/news/viewdetail?id=185.

African Press Agency (APA) website: https://apanews.net.

African Union. (2019) "Transitional Justice Policy" (African Union Commission), https://au.int/sites/default/files/documents/36541-doc-au_tj_policy_eng_web.pdf.

Agence ivoirienne de presse (AIP) website: https://aip.ci/.

All You Can Read 'Top 12 Côte d'Ivoire Newspapers and News Media', https://www.allyoucanread.com/ivory-coast-newspapers/.

Amnesty International (2016) *Amnesty International Report 2015/16 – Côte d'Ivoire*, 24 February (accessed September 28, 2019) https://www.amnesty.org/download/Documents/POL1025522016ENGLISH.PDF.

APDHCI website. https://www.apdhci.org.

Bah, Abu Bakarr. (2013). Civil Non-state Actors in Peacekeeping and Peacebuilding in West Africa. *Journal of International Peacekeeping* 17, nos. 3–4: 313–336. https://doi.org/10.1163/18754112-1704008.

Bah, Abu Bakarr. (2017). Seeking Democracy in Côte d'Ivoire: Overcoming Exclusionary Citizenship. Global Centre for Pluralism.

Bosire, L. K., & Lynch, G. (2014). Kenya's Search for Truth and Justice: The Role of Civil Society. *International Journal of Transitional Justice*, no. 8: 256–276.

Brankovic, Jasmina, & van der Merwe Hugo, eds. (2018). *Advocating Transitional Justice in Africa: The Role of Civil Society*. Cham: Springer.

Centre for Advocacy and Research New Delhi. (2012). A Framework for Media Engagement on Human Rights, Sexual Orientation and Gender Identity in South Asia: Regional Framework, Literature. Review and Country Case Studies, India.

Christophe Kouamé (president, CIVIS-CI) in discussion with the author, October 10, 2019.

Coalition for the ICC 'Côte d'Ivoire'. http://www.coalitionfortheicc.org/country/cote-divoire.

Commission Dialogue, vérité et reconciliation. (2014). Rapport final (December), 9, http://www.gouv.ci/doc/presse/1477497207RAPPORT%20FINAL_CDVR.pdf.

Convention de la société civile ivoirienne *Présentation génerale de la convention de la société civil ivoirienne* (accessed September 25, 2019), http://csci.group/vision neuse/web/viewer.html?file=http://csci.group/documents/201807101presentat iondelacscisiteweb2018.pdf.

Convention de la société civile ivoirienne «Présentation génerale de la convention de la société civil ivoirienne,» http://csci.group/visionneuse/web/viewer.html?file=http://csci.group/documents/201807101presentationdelacscisiteweb2018.pdf (accessed September 25, 2019).

Dhizaala, J. T. (2018). Transitional Justice in Liberia: The Interface Between Civil Society Organisations and the Liberian Truth and Reconciliation" in *Advocating Transitional Justice in Africa: The Role of Civil Society* edited by Jasmina Brankovic & van der Merwe, 43–63. Cham: Springer.

Djadou, P. (2015a). *Comprendre la presse en Côte d'Ivoire: des origines a nos jours'* (July 1, 2015a) http://www.100pour100culture.com/media/dossier-comprendre-la-presse-en-Côte-divoire-des-origines-a-nos-jours-2/.

Djadou, P. (2015b). Comprendre la presse en Côte d'Ivoire: des origines à nos jours (www.100pour100culture.com1 July 2015b) (accessed September 16, 2019). http://www.100pour100culture.com/media/dossier-comprendre-la-presse-en-Côte-divoire-des-origines-a-nos-jours-2/.

European Union. (2015). The EU's Policy Framework on Support to Transitional Justice (November), 8, http://recom.link/wp-content/uploads/2015/11/The-EU%E2%80%99s-Policy-Framework-on-support-to-transitional-justice.pdf.

For More Details on the Organization: http://www.pantheonsorbonne.fr/fileadmin/IREDIES/Projets_de_recherche/Rapport_du_sondage_sur_le_processus_de_r%c3%a9conciliation_nationale_et_la_CVDR.pdf (accessed October 1, 2019).

Fraternité Matin is online at https://www.fratmat.info.

GEPCI Launched a Digital News Website in February 2018, available here https://www.pressecotedivoire.ci/ (accessed October 1, 2019).

Gueudeu, Y. P. (2012). *The Law and the Media in Côte d'Ivoire*. Accra: Media Foundation for West Africa.

Human Rights Watch. (2015). To Consolidate This Peace of Ours: A Human Rights Agenda for Côte d'Ivoire' (December 8) https://www.hrw.org/report/2015/12/08/consolidate-peace-ours/human-rights-agenda-Côte-divoire

Human Rights Watch "Côte d'Ivoire: No Amnesty for Serious Crimes of 2010–11 Crisis" (https://www.hrw.org/news/2018/08/07/cote-divoire-no-amnesty-serious-crimes-2010-11-crisis).

Human Rights Watch, "Making Justice Count: Lessons from the ICC Work in Côte d'Ivoire" (https://www.hrw.org/report/2015/08/04/making-justice-count/lessons-iccs-work-cote-divoire).

Human Rights Watch, "To Consolidate This Peace of Ours: A Human Rights Agenda for Côte d'Ivoire," https://www.hrw.org/report/2015/12/08/consolidate-peace-ours/human-rights-agenda-cote-divoire (accessed September 23, 2019).

Human Rights Watch. (2019). "World Report 2019: Côte d'Ivoire Available" https://www.hrw.org/world-report/2019/country-chapters/cote-divoire.

International Center for Transitional Justice «Côte d'Ivoire: ICTJ's role https://www.ictj.org/our-work/regions-and-countries/c%C3%B4te-divoire (accessed October 1, 2019).

International Center for Transitional Justice, "Espoirs déçus: traitement judiciaire des violences postélectorales en Côte d'Ivoire," 5 (April 2016), 5, https://www.ictj.org/sites/default/files/ICTJ-Report-CDI-Prosecutions-2016-French.pdf.

International Center for Transitional Justice, "Transitional Justice Factsheet," https://www.ictj.org/about/transitional-justice (accessed September 22, 2019).

Kemunto, B. L., & Lynch, G. (2014). Kenya's Search for Truth and Justice: The Role of Civil Society. *International Journal of Transitional Justice* 8, no. 2 (July): 256–276, https://doi.org/10.1093/ijtj/iju002.

L'intelligent d'Abidjan website: https://www.lintelligentdabidjan.info/.

Laplante, L. J., and Phenicie K. (2009). Mediating Post-Conflict Dialogue: The Media's Role in Transitional Justice Processes. *Marquette Law Review* 93: 251–283.

Law N ° 2013-867 of 23 December 2013 on Access to Information of Public Interest, Côte d'Ivoire.

Law N ° 91–1001 of 27 December 1991a relating to audiovisual communication, Côte d'Ivoire.

Law N ° 91–1033 of 31 December 1991b on the press, Côte d'Ivoire.

Law N ° 91–1034 of 31 December 1991c on the legal status of professional journalists, Côte d'Ivoire.

Law No 2012-1132 of 13 December 2012 on the establishment, attribution, organisation and functioning of the National Human Rights Commission (Commission Nationale des Droits de l'Homme de Côte d'Ivoire, CNDHCI).

Law of 60–315 of 21 September 1960 on associations, Côte d'Ivoire.

LIANE «Cahier de propositions pour l'amélioration du cadre juridique des organisations de la société civile ivoirienne», LIANE, http://rcliane.cerap-inades.org/content/loi-sur-les-associations-en-c%C3%B4te-divoire-la-soci%C3%A9t%C3%A9-civile-fait-ses-propositions (accessed September 25, 2019).

LIDHO website: www.lidho-ci.org.

Lucini, B. A., & Kalvin, B. (2017). Country Overview: Côte d'Ivoire, Driving Mobile-Enabled Digital Transformation (April) 3. https://www.gsmaintelligence.com/research/?file=d1553a76179408fc82301b75174bc281&download (accessed September 21, 2019).

Malu, L. N. (2019). *The International Criminal Court and the Peace Process in Côte d'Ivoire*. In *The International Criminal Court and Peace Processes*, 159–187. Cham: Palgrave Macmillan.

Melone, S., Terzis, G., & l Beleli, O. (2002) *Using the Media for Conflict Transformation: The Common Ground Experience*. Berghof Research Center for Constructive Conflict Management. http://edoc.vifapol.de/opus/volltexte/2011/2588/pdf/melone_hb.pdf.

MIDH was established in 2000, website: http://www.midhci.org/.

Mohamed Suma (Head, International Center for Transitional Justice Côte d'Ivoire office) in discussion with the author on October 7, 2019.

OSIWA website: http://www.osiwa.org.

Phuong N. Pham, & Vinck, P. (2014). Fragile Peace, Elusive Justice: Population-Based Survey on Perceptions and Attitudes About Security and Justice in Abidjan, Côte d'Ivoire (Harvard Humanitarian Initiative, 2014), v, http://www.peacebuildingdata.org/sites/m/pdf/Abidjan_2014_Fragile_Peace_Elusive_Justice.pdf.

Price, M., & Stremlau, N. (2012). Media and Transitional Justice: Toward a Systematic Approach. *International Journal of Communication* 6 (23): 1077–1099

Radiodiffusion-Télévision ivoirienne (RTI) « Médias: Le nouveau code de déontologie du journaliste ivoirien adopté" https://www.rti.ci/info/societe/138/medias-le-nouveau-code-de-deontologie-du-journaliste-ivoirien-adopte (accessed September 21, 2019).

RCLIANE.CERAP, What Is the LIANE Project?, http://rcliane.cerap-inades.org/content/quest-ce-que-le-projet-liane (accessed September 25, 2019).

Reporters Without Borders. (2019). *2019 World Press Freedom Index* (accessed September 15), https://rsf.org/en/2019-world-press-freedom-index-cycle-fear.

Reporters Without Borders, «Monitoring des médias: dérapages inquiétants dans la presse écrite privée» (https://rsf.org/fr/actualites/monitoring-des-medias-derapages-inquietants-dans-la-presse-ecrite-privee) Reporters sans frontiers, https://rsf.org/fr/ (accessed September 16, 2019).

RTI *Mise en place d'un organe d'autorégulation des médias numériques: la tutelle félicite le RPPRELCI* Radiodiffusion-Télévision ivoirienne, https://www.rti.ci/infos_societe_15210_mise-en-place-d-un-organe-d-autoregulation-des-medias-numeriques-la-tutelle-felicite-le-repprelci.html.

Songa, A. (2018). Locating Civil Society in Kenya's Transitional Justice Agenda: A Reflection on the Experience of the Kenya Transitional Justice Network with the Truth, Justice and Reconciliation Commission. In *Advocating Transitional Justice in Africa: The Role of Civil Society* edited by Jasmina Brankovic & van der Merwe, 17–41. Cham: Springer.

170 A. N. COULIBALY

The Centre for Research and Action for Peace. (2018). *Cartographie de la contribution des organisations de la société civile à la gouvernance sectorielle en Côte d'Ivoire* (December) https://eeas.europa.eu/sites/eeas/files/tome_1-reduzed.pdf.

The Constitution of the Republic of Côte d'Ivoire, Law N ° 2016-886 of 8 November 2016.

The Constitution of the Republic of Côte d'Ivoire, Law N° 2016-886 of 8 November 2016 (Article 101), Original text: [La loi fixe les règles concernant: – la citoyenneté, les droits civiques et les garanties fondamentales accordées aux citoyens pour l'exercice des libertés publiques, la liberté, le pluralisme et l'indépendance des medias…].

The International Criminal Court, "Gbagbo and Blé Goudé Case: The Prosecutor v. Laurent Gbagbo and Charles Blé Goudé", The International Criminal Court, https://www.icc-cpi.int/cdi/gbagbo-goude (accessed September 20, 2019).

The New Humanitarian 'Analysis. (2012). Côte d'Ivoire Needs Top Down Reconciliation' IRIN (20 December) http://www.irinnews.org/analysis/2012/12/20/côte-divoire-needs-top-down-reconciliation.

The website of ARGA http://www.afrique-gouvernance.net/index_fr.html.

UNDP. (2013). *A Framework for Media Engagement on Human Rights, Sexual Orientation and Gender Identity in South Asia*, 2. New Delhi: Centre for Advocacy and Research.

UNESCO, *Etude-Diagnostique de la Situation des Medias: Presse, Presse En Ligne, Radio est Télévision, Entrave A La Proffessionalisation et Mesures Correctives*, http://www.caidp.ci/uploads/3af05f87c7a98e4ba0b790c018e5f39b.pdf.

UNJI's website (www.unjci.net) was not active as at 1 October 2019.

WANEP Côte d'Ivoire was established in 2003 https://www.wanep.org/wanep/index.php?option=com_content&view=category&layout=blog&id=39&Itemid=56.

Zio, Moussa. (2012). *The Media and the Political Crisis in Côte d'Ivoire*. Media Foundation for West Africa 1: Legon, Ghana.

CHAPTER 10

Genocide, Justice and Democratic Legitimacy: Lessons from Rwanda's 25-Year Experiment

Noel Twagiramungu

1   INTRODUCTION

The injury that a crime inflicts upon the social body is the disorder that it introduces into it: the scandal that it gives rise to, the example that it gives, the incitement to repeat it if it is not punished, and the possibility of becoming widespread that it bears within it.

—Foucault (1995: 92)

Can there be justice after genocide? (Twagiramungu 2014b). Building on Michel Foucault (1995)'s broader understanding of justice as a collective and holistic response to 'the injury that a crime inflicts upon the social body', this chapter examines the meaning and impact of the domestic and international efforts devoted to the pressing demands for justice in post-genocide Rwanda. Findings show mixed results, pitting the hope to eradicate impunity against the reality of instrumentalising justice for the sake of legitimising state capture (World Bank 2000).

The study builds on a vast range of empirical data and contending narratives gathered from oral and written sources as well as the author's long-standing exposure to, and familiarity with, the issues at hand. All along the analysis,

---

N. Twagiramungu (✉)
African Studies Center, Boston University, Boston, MA, USA
e-mail: notwa14@gmail.com

© The Author(s), under exclusive license to Springer Nature
Switzerland AG 2022
A. Adeola and M. W. Mutua (eds.), *The Palgrave Handbook of Democracy, Governance and Justice in Africa*,
https://doi.org/10.1007/978-3-030-74014-6_10

171

evidence reveals a paradoxical success for the ruling party, the Rwandan Patriotic Front (RPF)[1] whose successful efforts to impose victor's justice conflict with the official commitment to fulfil the triple goal to 'end impunity', 'promote reconciliation' and establish the 'real truth of what happened during the Genocide' (Twagiramungu 2014b). The chapter concludes that Rwanda's 25-year experiment amounts to an unfinished business of a society rising from the ashes of genocide yet still lacking democratic legitimacy necessary to 'confront the crimes of the victors' (Gahima 2013: 158) and thus heal and reconcile the nation as a whole.

The chapter proceeds into five parts. Part one gives an overview of the historical and conceptual framework, which lays the foundations for better understanding of the puzzle of justice in post-genocide Rwanda. Parts two and three examine respectively the domestic and international responses to the 1994 genocide. Part four accounts for the politics of justice with emphasis on the limits of domestic and international responses to the demands for justice in Rwanda and beyond. As a way forward, part five makes a case for democratic legitimacy as a precondition for the brand of reconciliatory justice and collective healing that post-genocide Rwanda and other societies in comparable situations need to heal, reconcile and move forward.

2   Historical and Conceptual Framework

2.1   Background to the 1994 Genocide

In the spring of 1994, a brutal genocide threatened to wipe out the entire Tutsi population of Rwanda and forced nearly half of the Hutu population into exile, leaving the then six-million people country as a skeleton of itself (Twagiramungu and Sebarenzi 2018). While the drivers of these horrors are too complex to tolerate any logic of simple causality, they can be best conceived of as the ultimate, though not inevitable, endgame of a deadly cyclical 'struggle over power and resources' (Coser 1957)—a struggle pitting the elites from the two main social groups, the Hutu (85%) and the Tutsi (14%), against one another at the expense of the society as a whole including the often marginalised Twa (<1%). To properly account for the complexity of the dynamics leading to this bloodshed, something needs be said of the critical junctures that Rwanda has evolved through since its coming into existence as a nation-state in the seventeenth century. Five key factors of interest with enduring consequences are worth mentioning here: pre-colonial social structures; colonial racist policies; post-independence ethnopolitics; post-cold war pressures for democratisation; and the 1990–1994 civil war (Twagiramungu 2014b).

---

[1] The Rwandan Patriotic Front (RPF) is a rebel group formed in Uganda in 1987 and which invaded Rwanda in October 1990 and seized power in Kigali in July 1994 and has since then dominated the political arena in the country. For a comprehensive account, see Nyakabwa (2002) and Twagiramungu (2014a: 78–90).

To begin with, pre-colonial Rwanda was an 'archaic kingdom, hierarchically organized, where kingship served as the main focus of popular loyalties' (Lemarchand 1970). Its social and political structures were so fascinating that 'by the time of European arrival in the late nineteenth century, Rwanda and Burundi became identified as paradigmatic of the social organisation in Africa's Great Lakes region' (Newbury 2001: 258). After Rwanda fell under colonial domination, first German from 1894 to 1916, then Belgian from 1917 to 1962, traditional state-society relations were profoundly altered, with the racist policies embedded in the Hamitic myth[2] favouring the aristocratic class (Tutsi) at the expense of the commoners (Hutu).

During the struggle for independence, a Hutu uprising overthrew the Tutsi-dominated monarchy and established a Hutu republic that forced thousands of Tutsis into exile in the 1960s. For the subsequent decades, ethnic exclusion and political marginalisation of the Tutsi became one of the pillars of the Hutu Republic. It was in response to this situation that a group of Tutsi guerrillas who had helped Museveni to seize power in Uganda in 1986 took up arms and invaded Rwanda on 1 October 1990.

Meanwhile, the post-cold war detente led the Western donor community to impose democratisation as a precondition for aid. Confronted with external invasion and pressing demands for democratisation, General Habyarimana's regime adopted an in-group versus out-group scheme (Brewer 2001: 17–41) to revive the antagonism Hutu-Tutsi as a strategic weapon in his quest to solidify his Hutu base. For a while though, the vast majority of the Rwandan social and political forces rejected this Manichean dichotomy (Kimonyo et al. 2004; Twagiramungu 2014a: 67–68). This became particularly evident with the emergence of independent civil society groups and political parties (ROR 1991), whose combined pressures obliged Habyarimana to form a pluralistic government in April 1992 and to negotiate a power-sharing agreement with the RPF. At the end of the day however, it became obvious that the entourage of neither President Habyarimana—referred to as *akazu* (Musabyimana 2008)—nor the RPF's strongman, General Paul Kagame, had interest in the implementation of a peace agreement signed in Arusha, Tanzania, on 4 August 1993. Nor were the UN peacekeepers—UNAMIR—led by General Romeo Dallaire strong enough to force the peace agreement on the unwilling parties (Dallaire 2004). After eight months of increasing polarisation and military build-up on both sides, President Habyarimana's plane was fatally shot down on 6 April 1994. His entourage used this event as a much-needed pretext, first to decapitate the political opposition to the ruling party, MRND, and then to wipe out the Tutsi people qua people collectively seen as the RPF

---

[2] The Hamitic myth is a racist belief claiming that major traditional ruling classes in Africa like the Tutsis in Rwanda and Burundi belonged to an African population supposedly distinguished by its race—Caucasian—and its language family, from the Negro inhabitants of the rest of Africa below the Sahara. See Sanders (1969) and Twagiramungu (2016).

'fifth colon'. Meanwhile, the RPF resumed war and eventually defeated the then Hutu government and its armed forces and seized power in July 1994.

Much has been written about the horrors that befell Rwanda in 1994 (Des Forges 1999). But as a Rwandan observer has forcefully argued, these horrors are beyond imagination:

> Despite the various excellent studies on the Tutsi genocide, these works can never properly put into words the scale of such horrifying experiences. These pains go beyond words. I can't manage it myself. And if history stammers, it is because its witnesses mumble when it comes to describing the terrifying power of evil in everyday life. (Rurangwa 2009)

In fact, the genocide literally destroyed the country to the extent that, to quote a keen observer who visited the country in the early 1995, 'Rwanda was not just a country full of skeletons, it was a skeleton of itself' (Twagiramungu 2014a: 1). The notion of a 'skeleton-nation' can seldom be an exaggeration for a country which saw nearly 20% of its 6 million population savagely slaughtered and up to 50% forced into massive exile whereas the remaining 30% were IDPs—the vast majority being orphans, widows, old people and invalid men. Such was the country that the RPF-led government inherited. Among other priorities, the demands for justice were overwhelming.

2.2 *The Quest for Justice*

The concept of justice implies, among other goals, that the perpetrators of criminal acts are held accountable and punished. This notion stems from the perception of criminal act as 'eviance [which] makes people more alert to the interests they share in common and draws attention to those values which constitute the 'collective conscience' of the community' (Vidmar 2001: 1). Durkheim underscores the role of deviant acts in cementing collective solidarity, stating, 'Because they are found in all consciences, the infraction committed arouses in those who have evidence of it or who learn of its existence the same indignation' (Durkheim quoted in Vidmar 2001: 1). From a more philosophical perspective, Foucault sums up the reason why we need a collective and holistic response to criminal acts:

> The injury that a crime inflicts upon the social body is the disorder that it introduces into it: the scandal that it gives rise to, the example that it gives, the incitement to repeat it if it is not punished, and the possibility of becoming widespread that it bears within it. (Foucault 1995: 92)

Applied to post-conflict contexts, this imperative calls for efforts to respond in a comprehensive and effective way to the legacies of past wrongs. Justice is said to be retributive when the focus is on judicial investigations of the alleged crimes and punishment of those found guilty beyond reasonable doubt. It is said to be restorative when the focus is on reconciliatory and/or reparative mechanisms. In the case of Rwanda, the empirical reality speaks to the necessity of combining the two approaches in achieving a balance 'between vengeance and forgiveness' (Minow 1999). Such a combination is consistent with the emerging mechanism of transitional justice.

2.3 Transitional Justice

Since the 1990s, the paradigm of transitional justice has emerged as a promising 'array of processes designed to address past human rights violations following periods of political turmoil, state repression, or armed conflict' (Olsen et al. 2010: 11). The starting point for this analysis rests upon the premise that:

> The universe of transitional justice can be broadly or narrowly defined. At its broadest, it involves anything that a society devises to deal with a legacy of conflict and/or widespread human rights violations, from changes in criminal codes to those in high school textbooks, from creation of memorials, museums and days of mourning, to police and court reform, to tackling the distributional inequities that underlie conflict. A narrow view can be criticized for ignoring root causes and privileging civil and political rights over economic, social and cultural rights, and by so doing marginalizing the needs of women and the poor. On the other hand, broadening the scope of what we mean by transitional justice to encompass the building of a just as well as peaceful society may make the effort so broad as to become meaningless. (Arriaza 2006: 1).

While there is no 'one-size-fits-all' blueprint for transitional justice mechanisms, there is now a minimum consensus on what it can take for societies confronting past atrocities to decide—through cross-cultural and critical dialogue—what is most important to accomplish and the morally best ways to do so (Crocker 1999: 43). To be effective, the minimum framework must be able to help us, in Crocker's words:

> identify and clarify (1) the variety of ethical issues that emerge in reckoning with past wrongs, (2) widespread agreements about initial steps for resolving each issue, (3) leading options for more robust solutions of each issue, and (4) ways to weight or trade off the norms when they conflict. (Crocker 1999: 43)

To this end, Crocker outlines eight goals on which transitional justice mechanisms should focus, namely truth; a public platform for victims; accountability and punishment; the rule of law; compensation to victims; institutional reform and long-term development; reconciliation; and public deliberation (Crocker 1999).

2.4 Limits and Frontiers of Transitional Justice in the Real World

One of the major difficulties in fulfilling the promises of transitional justice as a remedy tool is the possibility that it cannot adequately address all the past wrongs. This shortcoming is particularly vexing in societies like Rwanda emerging from genocidal violence whose roots date back to colonial, if not pre-colonial times. To this end, establishing transitional justice comes down to answering three fundamental questions: (1) Which abuses can be addressed? (2) When might the abuses have taken place? (3) Who can be held accountable for the abuses committed?

In legal terminology, these questions hint at the four major jurisdictional limits, namely jurisdiction ratione materiae or matter-subject jurisdiction; jurisdiction ratione temporis or temporal jurisdiction; jurisdiction ratione loci or territorial jurisdiction; and ratione personae or the personal reach of the courts' jurisdiction. Jurisdiction ratione materiae is about 'the jurisdiction over the nature of the case and the type of relief sought; the extent to which a court can rule on the conduct of persons or the status of things' (USLegal 2003). Implicit in this definition is the notion that a court of law is legally tasked to deal with specific crimes. Jurisdiction ratione temporis 'refers to the jurisdiction of a court of law over a proposed action in relation to the passage of time' (USLegal 2003). Regarding jurisdiction ratione personae, this paradigm further narrows the scope of crimes under consideration by specifying the nature and extent of 'criminal responsibilities as regard to modalities of participation in the commission of crimes' (Cassese 2006: 274). With this historical and conceptual background in mind, the next section discusses how the government of Rwanda responded to the demands of justice for the genocide and other related crimes.

3 Domestic Responses

The RPF-led government responded to the demands of justice in a variety of ways, which can be grouped into five main categories: extra-judicial responses; specialised chambers; Gacaca jurisdictions; alternative correctional mechanisms; and genocide-centred lawfare.

3.1 Extrajudicial Responses

Throughout its road to power and shortly after defeating the genocidaire forces in July 1994, the RPF's dominant justice motto was: 'kill the killers, rescue the victims'.[3] After UN agencies, human rights groups and some officials including the then Minister of Justice (Alphonse-Marie Nkubito) and the Minister of Internal Affairs (Seth Sendashonga) started denouncing

---

[3] The author personally heard about this motto from many RPF soldiers, rank and file alike, in different parts of the country between August and November 1994.

these 'purification' killings,[4] RPF soldiers abandoned massive summary executions to embark on a new campaign of massive arrests and detentions in all corners of the country. In response to local and international concerns over the abuses and dramatic consequences associated with illegal detentions, the newly appointed Parliament adopted on 9 June 1995 legislation suspending the procedural rules relating to remand in custody. However, this political response to demands of justice was so flagrant that the Supreme Court declared it unconstitutional on 26 July 1995. It was in this context of prolonged impasse that the government convened an 'International Conference on Genocide, Impunity and Accountability' in Kigali from November 1 to November 5, in an effort to examine the appropriate ways and means to respond to the increasing demands for justice.

3.2   Specialised Chambers

One of the Conference's recommendations was to establish a solid legal framework that empowered the Rwandan judicial system to adjudicate the crime of genocide. As one expert observes however, '[the] task of legislating was arduous, as it was necessary to find a way forward while taking account of the magnitude of the crimes, the rights of the victims seeking justice and the process of national reconciliation' (de Beer, 1997: 19). The task was overwhelming as the 1996 official statistics suggested that more than 92,000 genocide suspects languished in detention, most without charge. The official response came in the form of an organic law drafted by Rwandan and foreign jurists between 1995 and 1996, and promulgated in September 1996 under the name 'Organic Law No 08/96 of 30 August 1996 on the Organization of Prosecutions for Offences Constituting the Crime of Genocide or Crimes against Humanity Committed since 1 October 1990' (ROR 1996) This law established specialised chambers in each of the 12 provincial jurisdictions as well as in the military courts—a major innovation. The genocide trials commenced in December 1996[5] and culminated in the public executions of 22 genocide perpetrators on 24 April 1998. According to one local

---

[4] For instance, on 23 September 1994, in a report known as 'Gersony Report' which was subsequently suppressed, UN High Commissioner for Refugees alleged that the RPA killed between 25,000 and 45,000 persons in reprisal attacks between April and 1 August 1994. See Des Forges (1999).

[5] The author had the privilege to closely monitor and/or supervise monitoring of most the genocide trials during the period 1996–1999. For instance, he monitored the very first trial that took place in Kibungo on 27 December 1996 and which lasted four hours, resulting in two death sentences. He was then working with the UN High Commissioner for Human Rights Office Field Operation in Rwanda. He went on to serve as Coordinator for a 'Genocide Trials Monitoring' Project jointly set up by Human Rights Watch and the Umbrella of Rwandan civil society groups (Cladho) during the period 1997–1998. Later on, he was tasked by Liprodhor to put in place and lead the 'Center for Information and Documentation on Genocide Trials [CDIPG].'

178   N. TWAGIRAMUNGU

leading human rights group, the specialised chambers put on trial 9,721 geno-cide suspects between 1996 and 2003; 775 were sentenced to death penalty, 2,441 were sentenced to life imprisonment, and 2,090 were found innocent (Liprodhor 2002). As succinctly summarised by one expert, the results of the specialized chambers are mixed at best, 'More than five years after their incep-tion', states Meierhenrich, 'the Chambres Specialisées had adjudicated barely six percent of those incarcerated for their alleged participation in the 1994 genocide' (Meierhenrich 2009: 19). Per Human Rights Watch's estimates, "By 1998, the total prison population had reached about 130,000, but only 1,292 people had been tried. It became apparent that it would take decades to pros-ecute all those suspected of involvement in the genocide" (HRW, 2014; see also Des Forges and Longman 2004: 59).

In this context, the slow pace of prosecution suggested that it would take more than a century to deal with the pending criminal cases. In response to these pessimistic prognostics, the government made it clear that an alternative was needed. This came in the form of Gacaca jurisdictions.

3.3   Gacaca Jurisdictions

Between May 1998 and June 1999, President Pasteur Bizimungu initiated national consultations to discuss the most pressing problems and possible solutions, including the option of reviving the traditional mechanism of conflicting resolution known as Gacaca.[6] During the discussions, partici-pants raised a number of concerns. Some were worried that Gacaca would minimise the genocide to a family quarrel, because Gacaca was traditionally used for these matters. Others doubted whether ordinary people could real-istically be expected to carry out trials of genocide in an appropriate way. Others still expressed concern about the Hutu population's willingness to actually speak the truth. Not least, international experts wondered whether Gacaca would conform to international standards. Eventually, the arguments favouring Gacaca outweighed those opposing it, and the lack of another alter-native convinced the participants that Gacaca was the only viable mechanism by which Rwanda could deal with the aftermath of the genocide (ROR 1996; Clark 2014; Twagiramungu 2005a, 2005b).

The newly installed National Gacaca Commission designed a bill that served as the basis on which the Rwandan Parliament adopted on 12 October 2000 the law establishing the new Gacaca jurisdictions. The law was offi-cially promulgated in January 2001 (ROR 2002). On the eve of the official launch of Gacaca jurisdictions in February 2001, President Kagame reminded his fellow citizens that the cardinal goals of Gacaca was to 'end impunity', 'pro-mote reconciliation' and establish the 'real truth of what happened during the

---

[6] While Gacaca is now one of the most popular themes in the academic literature, it had received scant attention until the 1994 genocide. Notable exceptions include: Ntampaka (1984: 139–148) and Reyntjens (1990: 916–1973).

Table 1 Formal justice and Gacaca justice in numbers

#/ Category	Courts	Judges	Cases tried	Duration (years)	Trials/ year	%
Regular courts	12	50	9,721	6	1,620	0.01
Gacaca courts	12,000	50,000+	1,958,634	6	326,442	99.99

Source Statistics compiled from various sources

Genocide' (Burnet 2008: 189). Following the 2001–2002 pilot phase, which yielded meagre results, and after a long pause during the 2003 presidential and legislative elections, the Gacaca law was amended and a new organic law was promulgated on 19 June 2004.

The Gacaca jurisdictions as such began operating nationwide in January 2005. The process consisted of two major phases, namely investigation and trials. During the investigation phase (2005–2006), the Gacaca jurisdictions identified 761,000 genocide suspects (Lemon 2007; Reyntjens 2005: 1–26). Once this step was reached, the process of trials went so quickly that, by December 2007 official statistics showed that 712,723 of more than 1.12 million cases had been completed (Radio 10, 2010). The vast majority of Gacaca jurisdictions concluded the trials in 2009, and the government officially closed them on 18 June 2012 (Radio 10, 2010) (Table 1).

Without engaging the polarised and polarising debates about the ups and downs of Gacaca, one can candidly acknowledge that the Gacaca justice is an innovative justice experiment with mixed results. A keen observer underscores this point, asserting:

> Since 2005, just over 12,000 community-based *gacaca* courts [...] have tried approximately 1.2 million cases. They will leave behind a mixed legacy. Some Rwandans have welcomed the courts' swift work and the extensive involvement of local communities, stressing that *gacaca* has helped them better understand what happened in the darkest period of the country's history and has eased tensions between the country's two main ethnic groups (the majority Hutu and minority Tutsi). Others are more skeptical: some genocide survivors complain that not all perpetrators were arrested or punished adequately for their crimes. Some of those convicted and sentenced to decades in prison maintain that trials were seriously flawed, that private individuals and government authorities manipulated the course of justice, that *gacaca* became politicized over the years, and that ethnic tensions remain high. On both sides, there are doubts, as well as tentative hopes, about *gacaca*'s contribution to long-term reconciliation. (HRW 2011)

3.4   *Alternative Punishment and Correctional Mechanisms*

Another original contribution of the government of Rwanda to the transitional justice system is evident in two innovative punishment mechanisms. The first mechanism called Community Service for Prisoners and widely known under its French acronym TIG (Travaux d'Intérêt Général) is 'an alternative penalty to imprisonment' which was introduced in 2005 to allow 'people convicted of participating in the genocide to serve part of their sentences doing community services' (ROR 2005).[7] In addition to performing community work including the construction of classrooms and houses for vulnerable genocide survivors, the TIG participants (aka Tigistes) also receive training in literacy, numeracy, hygiene and other subjects which are deemed vital to facilitate their social reintegration.

Building on the lessons learned from the TIG experiment, the government established in 2010 a permanent mechanism called the Rwanda Correctional Service (RCS), combining the TIG Community Services with the former National Prisons Service (NPS). Established with the aim 'to ensure reformation, rehabilitation and reintegration of inmates', the long-term goal being 'to become an income generating institution with the view to become self- reliant in all its needs and requirements rather than relying only on the government budget' (Gahonzire 2015). As of April 2016, the RCS operated through 14 correctional centres employing 1604 prison guards who were in charge of 52,926 inmates and 744 Tigistes.

3.5   Genocide-Centred Lawfare

Like any post-genocide society, Rwanda has been marred by negationism, or genocide denial. In response, the government has adopted an impressive arsenal of legal instruments and political measures meant to deal with the discourses and practices of ethnicity, discrimination, hate speech or incitement to genocide. The first step was a 2001 law criminalising 'offenses of discrimination and sectarianism' (ROR 2011). According to reliable sources close to RPF, this law was adopted in response to a move taken by former President Pasteur Bizimungu, who defied the RPF and founded a new political party after being forced into resignation and replaced by Paul Kagame in 2000 (Sebarenzi 2009). 'Because he was a Hutu', suggests one RPF insider 'there was fear that he would mobilize his fellow Hutu countrymen against Kagame' (Twagiramungu 2014a).

The letter and spirit of the 2001 law were later incorporated into the 2003 Constitution (ROR 2003) in the wake of the transition endgame marked by the 2003 presidential and legislative elections. Specifically, Article 13 of the 2003 Constitution criminalises 'revisionism, negationism, and trivialization of

---

[7] While this form of alternative punishment was new in Rwanda, it has a long history notably in the West. Per Michel Foucault (1995): "The use of prisoners in public works, cleaning city streets or repairing the highways, was practised in Austria, Switzerland and certain of the United States, such as Pennsylvania. These convicts, distinguished by their 'infamous dress' and shaven heads, 'were brought before the public. [...].To prevent them from returning injuries which might be inflicted on them, they were encumbered with iron collars and chains to which bombshells were attached, to be dragged along while they performed their degrading service, under the eyes of keepers armed with swords, blunderbusses and other weapons of destruction."

genocide', whereas article 9 commits the government to 'fighting the ideology of genocide and all its manifestations' (ROR 2003).

In the same year, Rwanda adopted a new genocide law that criminalises 'any person who will have publicly shown, by his or her words, writings, images, or by any other means, that he or she has negated the genocide committed, rudely minimized it or attempted to justify or approve its grounds' (ROR 2003). Finally, in anticipation of the 2008–2010 electoral marathon, Rwanda adopted a new law making punishable the crime of 'Genocide Ideology' (ROR 2008).

4   INTERNATIONAL RESPONSES

Shocked by the magnitude of the 1994 genocide and embarrassed by its failure to stop the carnage, the international community vowed to help in rendering justice. Four instances of international justice are worth mentioning here: the United Nations-sponsored International Criminal Tribunal for Rwanda (ICTR); trials in Western domestic courts; extradition cases; and indictments against RPF officers.

4.1   ICTR

The ICTR was established on 8 November 1994 by the Resolution 955 in order to try people responsible for genocide and other serious violations of international law in Rwanda, or by Rwandan citizens in nearby states, between 1 January and 31 December 1994. Located in Arusha, Tanzania, since 1995, the tribunal's results have been mixed at best. Its historic achievements include that of being the first international tribunal to find guilty and punish a perpetrator of genocide. Moreover, the ICTR established precedent that rape can be a crime constitutive of genocide.[8] Despite its enormous resources however, the tribunal's quantifiable results read as follows (Fig. 1):

The ICTR delivered its last trial judgement on 20 December 2012 before handing over its residual functions to a closing strategy known as the Mechanism for International Criminal Tribunals whose one key function 'is the tracking and arrest of the three accused who remain fugitives[9] from justice' (ICTR 2014).

While the crimes allegedly committed by RPF soldiers fall within the ICTR jurisdiction, the RPF-led government built enormous obstacles in the path to investigating and eventually prosecuting these crimes. The difficulties first

---

[8] In the case Prosecutor against Jean-Paul Akayesu, the tribunal established, among other facts, that "the acts of rape and sexual violence, as other acts of serious bodily and mental harm committed against the Tutsi, reflected the determination to make Tutsi women suffer and to mutilate them even before killing them, the intent being to destroy the Tutsi group while inflicting acute suffering on its members in the process". See ICTR (1998).

[9] Those are: Félicien Kabuga (who was later arrested in France) and Protais Mpiranya and Augustin Bizimana who have to date evaded justice.

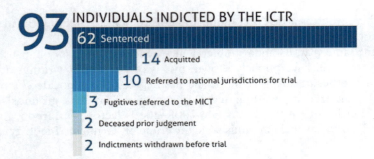

Fig. 1 ICTR (2014)

started when Rwanda deceived the international community by opposing the resolution establishing the ICTR. While the ICTR 'recognized the need to investigate the RPF cases' (Peskin 2011: 178) from the start, the first successive chief prosecutors—Richard Goldstone and Louise Arbour—opted for 'maintaining good relations' with Kigali. However, when a new chief prosecutor, Carla Del Ponte, resolved to 'pursue the RPF file with the most vigor' (Peskin 2011: 178), the RPF-led government first suspended its cooperation with the tribunal, then paralysed the tribunal by blocking witnesses from travelling to Arusha, and finally managed to pressure the UN to sacrifice Del Ponte. 'The high drama surrounding Del Pontes' dismissal from the ICTR', concludes Peskin, 'showed the limits of prosecutorial independence and the obstacles to moving beyond victor's justice' (Peskin 2011: 178). It thus came as no surprise that the new prosecutor, Hassan Jallows, bowed to pressures from Kigali and thus reinforced the prevailing image of the ICTR as an instance of 'prosecution of the vanquished' (Cruvellier 2012).

4.2 Trials in Foreign National Courts

In addition to support and cooperation with the ICTR, a number of Western countries prosecuted genocide suspects in the West. As of January 2020, more than 20 people accused of genocide have been put on trial by national jurisdictions, with notable trials held in Belgium, Canada, France, Netherlands, Norway, Sweden, Switzerland and the USA.

4.3 Extradition Arrangements

In other countries including the UK, the USA, France and Canada, instead of putting suspects on trial to establish their responsibilities in the genocide in Rwanda, domestic courts limited themselves to decide whether the conditions were met to extradite the suspects to Rwanda. As of July 2019, only the USA and Canada had extradited suspects to Rwanda whereas other countries including France and the UK ruled out that option. For instance, in July

2017, the British High Court ruled against extraditing five genocide suspects to Kigali on the grounds that they would not receive a fair trial in Rwanda: '[Celestin Mutabaruka, 63, from Kent; Vincent Brown, also known as Vincent Bajinya, 59, from Islington, north London; Celestin Ugirashebuja, 66, from Essex; Charles Munyaneza, 61, from Bedford; and Emmanuel Nteziryayo, from Manchester' (*Guardian* 2019).

4.4 Indictments Against RPF Officers

As of October 2020, there have been three notable attempts to hold RPF members accountable for their crimes in foreign national courts. The first case, and the one which drew the most attention, was the 'Bruguière Report' (Bruguière 2006). The so-called report concerns an international arrest warrant issued by French judge, Jean-Louis Bruguière, for eight leading RPF members close to President Kagame in connection with the assassination of former President Habyarimana on 6 April 1994. In response to this arrest warrant, Rwanda severed diplomatic ties with France in November 1996 and, on 5 August 2008, retaliated by producing its own report—known as Mucyo Commission Report—which accused 33 current and former French officials of involvement in the 1994 genocide. Under pressures from both Kigali and powerful pro-RPF lobby groups in France, the French government re-negotiated the restoration of diplomatic relations and a new judge was appointed to re-examine the charges.

The second case began in Spain on 8 February 2008, when a Spanish magistrate issued an indictment for forty Rwandan military officers on charges of genocide, crimes against humanity, war crimes, terrorism and other crimes committed in Rwanda and in the Democratic Republic of Congo between 1990 and 1998.

The third case began in the USA on 30 April 2010, when three attorneys led by Peter Erlinder filed a wrongful death lawsuit in an Oklahoma City federal court, alleging that Rwandan President Paul Kagame ordered the political assassinations that triggered the 1994 Rwandan genocide. The lawsuit was filed on behalf of the widows of former President Habyarimana of Rwanda and Ntaryamira of Burundi who both perished in the plane shot out of the sky on 6 April 1994. At first glance, the case seemed flimsy, especially given the controversies surrounding Erlinder's arrest and subsequent release on bail in Rwanda.

However, it took a serious turn that obliged Kigali to mobilise significant resources and political lobbyists. This came after the court declared a default judgement in favour of the plaintiffs, alleging that the defendants failed to answer the complaint within the time allowed. To appeal the judgement, Kagame called upon a prominent lawyer, Pierre Richard Prosper, who ironically once served as the US ambassador-at-large for war crime issues from 2001 to 2005. Meanwhile, on 29 August 2011, the US State Department filed a report entitled 'Suggestion of Immunity Submitted by the United States of

America', which requested immunity for Rwandan President Paul Kagame. In response, the plaintiffs appealed to the US Supreme Court, filing their objections to the State Department 'Suggestion of Immunity on Behalf of Rwanda's President Kagame'. In their objections, they 'cited the State Department statement of interest of the United States of America, No. 1,104 CV 1360 (Feb. 14, 2011) (LMB), declaring that immunity is only applicable to "official acts by a sitting government"' (Bay View National Black Paper 2013). The Supreme Court finally rejected the plaintiffs' objections in March 2013.

5 THE POLITICS OF JUSTICE: CHALLENGES & CONTROVERSIES

The sad duty of politics is to establish justice in a sinful world.

—Reinhold Niebuhr quoted in Shapiro (1977)

Over the last 25 years, the government of Rwanda has engineered several innovative mechanisms to tackle the horrors of the 1994 genocide and its aftermath. In addition to supporting Rwanda by providing funds, logistics and technical expertise needed to carry out the government's ambitious initiatives, the international community heeded the call for justice by establishing the ICTR whereas some Western countries allowed their courts of law to prosecute the suspect genocidaires on their soils. Despite notable achievements and breakthroughs registered at both domestic and international levels, the responses to the demands of justice in the wake of the 1994 genocide have suffered a host of challenges and controversies that speak volume about the problematic relationship between justice and politics and more so in the aftermath of the horrors of genocide. In this regard, this chapter's findings show that Rwanda's 25-year experiment can be best described as a paradigmatic example of what the American Theologian Reinhold Niebuhr has termed 'the sad duty of politics [...] to establish justice in a sinful world' (Shapiro 1977). To make this case, four major political challenges are worth examining briefly: the context of civil war; mass participation; the international community's lack of moral authority; and the culture of victor's justice.

5.1 Genocide Within the Context of Civil War

In the language of Article 2 of the 1948 Convention on the Prevention and Punishment of the Crime of Genocide, genocide means any act 'committed with intent to destroy, in whole or in part, a national, ethnical, racial or religious group, as such'. While the reality of 'Hutu, Tutsi, Twa' in Rwanda defies the conventional 'protected groups' in the language of the genocide convention, it is now common knowledge that the state-led campaign of mass killings targeted the Tutsi people as a whole. However, given the multiplicity of other heinous crimes including politicides, war crimes and crimes against humanity committed before, during and after the genocide by the two belligerents, the choice of which perpetrators to hold accountable and for which crimes became a matter of hot politics and controversy. To illustrate this puzzle, consider for instance remarkable variation in the ratione temporis by the Government of Rwanda and the ICTR. The ICTR is competent to handle the crimes committed between 1 January and 31 December 1994 whereas Rwandan courts have been mandated to prosecute the crimes committed between 1 October 1990 and 31 December 1994. This variation has serious political and judicial implications when it comes to defining and categorising the acts of genocide. While the common knowledge is that the Rwandan genocide refers to the brutal campaign of massacring Tutsi people and moderate Hutu in the wake of the assassination of President Juvénal Habyarimana on 6 April 1994, the RPF-led government took exception to this view and imposed a powerful narrative with a dual aim: to legitimise the RPF invasion of Rwanda on 1 October 1990, as a liberation war, and to paint any efforts to oppose the so-called liberation war as an act of genocide. It is in this context that one can understand how and why the RPF-led government is still applying the label 'genocidaire' to several Rwandan military officers and government officials who had no involvement in the 1994 genocide as such. Of great concern in this case is the fate of former officials like André Ntagerura who was tried and found innocent by the ICTR in 2004 but is still languishing in a 'safe house' in Tanzania alongside other 8 former co-detainees, waiting for a host country (Justiceinfo.net 2020).

5.2 Mass Participation in the Genocide

Another uniqueness of the Rwandan genocide—limited here to the killings that targeted the Tutsi between April and July 1994—is its 'popular' character—what makes some analysts to call it 'the popular genocide' (Kimonyo 2008) or [the work of] 'Killing Neighbours' (Fuji 2009). This uniqueness begs a balance between the ambitious goal to hold all and every perpetrator accountable and the danger of putting the whole nation at trial.

5.3 International Community's Lack of Moral Authority

The impotence and failure of the international community during the genocide compromised the moral authority along with manoeuvrability for international actors to restore order and justice in Rwanda. No wonder that the international justice has thus far done little more than bowing to the RPF's warfare and thus reinforcing the one-sided, victor's justice aka 'justice for some' (Twagiramungu 2014b). The impotence of international justice is aggravated by the lack of any reliable mechanism of reparation and compensation, which raises the serious puzzle of the place of the victims and the survivors in the post-genocide justice system.

5.4   The Culture of Victor's Justice

Whatever approach one chooses—broad or narrow—and whatever goals one sets, transitional justice is first and foremost a political matter. To underscore this reality, one is reminded of the words of theologian Niebuhr, 'the sad duty of politics is to establish justice in a sinful world' (Quotationsbook.com 2013).

The RPF responded to the demand of justice in post-genocide Rwanda through a combination of non-judiciary, judiciary, political and international lobbies in an effort to legitimise and consolidate its monopolistic hold on power. Among these responses, the Gacaca jurisdictions proved an extraordinarily innovative, cheap and swift response to the burden of holding accountable thousands of genocide suspects.

For its admirers like Phil Clark (2010), Gacaca appeared as a 'rough road to justice and reconciliation' which, thanks to its genuine 'engagement through popular participation', fulfilled the promise of 'mending hearts and minds' and thus put the Rwandan society on a painful, but sure path of 'healing and forgiveness'. Beneath the surface, however, such claims are seriously undermined by Gacaca's failure to move beyond what a legal scholar and formal architect of the post-genocide justice system in Rwanda has summed up in a telling phrase: 'Untold story, unfinished business: Confronting the crimes of the Victors' (Gahima 2013: 158–186).

Another scholar sheds light on the dual problem of 'the imposition of collective guilt on Hutu and the lack of official accountability for RPF war crimes' (Waldorf 2011: 51) to show how the RPF 'hijacked the process [of transitional justice] and used it as just another tool of repression' (Habimana 2011: 355). This form of justice instrumentalisation underscores a growing consensus among keen observers that Rwanda is moving from genocide to political vengeance. As a Rwandan human rights activist and jurist observes:

> Failure of the ruling elite to assume its share of responsibility has had several consequences. For one, it has left the whole judicial process grappling with issues of perception and legitimacy, raising questions about whether genocide suspects properly face the long arm of justice or are subject to political vengeance. It has also resulted in one of the worst types of post-conflict discrimination, leaving some victims to fend for themselves while allowing a selected group of perpetrators to walk free as heroes. (Habimana 2011: 355)

Echoing this assessment, another keen observer describes Gacaca as a textbook case of what Burnet (2008) has termed 'the injustice of local justice'. Referring to 'local perceptions of widespread injustice in the Gacaca process' in areas where community-based organisations had managed to re-establish or build new cross-ethnic relationships, Burnet observes that 'Gacaca has not only deepened the cleavages between Hutu and Tutsi but also made some Tutsi genocide survivors increasingly mistrustful of the current government and of the RPF' (Burnet 2008: 188).

The notion of 'political vengeance' is also apparent in the legal arsenal officially meant to deal with genocide, but which actually has served a wide range of political ends from silencing local and international critics to constraining political parties and punishing dissidents and opponents. For instance, on the eve of the 2003 elections, the only opposition party, MDR, was banned following an accusation that it promoted 'divisionism' and 'genocide ideology'. In response to widespread denunciations of the abuses that marred the elections, including 'disappearances, arrests, threats, intimidation and co-option of human rights defenders' (Frontline 2004), the RPF-led government concocted a report through a Parliament commission which:

> not only leveled accusations of genocidal ideology against the usual targets (the sole independent human rights organization, LIPRODHOR, and the last independent newspaper, Umuseso), [...but] also named CARE, Trócaire, BBC, VOA, and a multitude of Christian churches as several the charges of and divisionism. (Frontline 2004)

The cases that attracted the most attention included that of a prominent human rights activist and Rwandan genocide expert, the late Alison Des Forges, who was accused of becoming 'a spokesperson for genocide ideology' in 1998 and declared persona non grata in Rwanda after she criticised the law on genocide ideology, calling it an abusive tool intended to punish any criticism of the RPF (Waldorf 2011: 51).

A former Speaker of the Rwandan Parliament, who prides himself on being 'the first prominent Tutsi to flee the so-called Tutsi-dominated government', sums up: 'Rwanda is increasingly seen not as a nation emerging steadily out of the division of the past but as a country at risk of another cycle of violence' (Sebarenzi 2009: 351).

To sum up with a remark by a world's leading human rights activist, '[by] instrumentalizing the genocide --through gacaca and its genocide ideology campaigns--to maintain its hold on power', the RPF runs the risk to 'trivialize the genocide and fuel further negationism' (Waldorf 2011: 49).

6   Conclusion: Looking Back, Reaching Forward

The political nature of the demands for justice in post-genocide Rwanda points to a thorny question: Can there be justice without democratic legitimacy in a violently divided society? By democratic legitimacy, I mean a system of governance in which citizens have the right to freely chose and hold accountable their leaders. Addressing this question comes down to recognising two important facts: (1) democratic legitimacy in the Lincolnian sense of 'a government of the people, by the people, and for the people' has no precedent in Rwanda; (2) far from being a radical break from the past, the post-genocide government still has much in common with its predecessors (Straus and Waldolf 2011; Uvin 1998; Twagiramungu 2014).

In fact, since achieving independence in 1962, Rwanda has continued to suffer from the horrors of successive cycles of victor's justice and political revenge. Each regime rose to power in hope and moderation, vowing to reckon past injustices and heal the nation, only to end up becoming autocratic, militarised and ethnic-centred. Consequently, each regime failed to fulfil the primary duty of every government: to protect peoples' lives, liberties and properties. Despite the achievement of a relative stability and economic development, each government generally led to tragic loss of human lives and unequal opportunities among Rwandans. The loss of human lives and unequal opportunities were in part consequences of the 'winner-takes all' politics, which is unsuitable for an ethnically polarised country. Such politics has created an ethnic security dilemma that continues to generate a fierce competition for power between Hutu and Tutsi elites on the one hand, and within factions of the ethnic group in power on the other hand. A quick look into past trajectories underscores this point.

6.1   Looking Back

Many in the West know Rwanda because of the 1994 genocide. However, while the intensity and destructive scale of the genocide were unprecedented, the dynamics underlying it are an integral part of the horrors of ethnic violence that started in the late 1950s, as Rwandans struggled to achieve independence and establish a democratic republic. The first republic, led by MDR-Parmehutu of President Grégoire Kayibanda, came to power with the goal of healing the wounds left by both colonialism and the monarchy system. At the onset, a Hutu elite backed by the colonial administration overthrew a decaying Tutsi-dominated monarchy. The overthrow and related ethnic violence forced into exile former rulers, their followers and many ordinary Tutsi.

Yet, in the face of the threats posed by exiled Tutsi insurgents, President Kayibanda consolidated his regime, not as a *res publica* or a motherland for all its sons and daughters, but as a republic of the Hutu at war with the Tutsi. As a result, some Tutsi were summarily executed, others were deported whereas the remainder were reduced to the status of second-class citizens. In the process, the MDR-Parmehutu regime used the 'Tutsi peril' as a pretext to silence its rivals notably the APROSSOMA, RADER and AREDETWA, killing some of their leaders and co-opting others. This move that culminated in a de facto one-party system since 1965 further erased democratic hopes and aspirations born out of independence.

To its credit, Kayibanda's MDR distinguished itself by undertaking important reforms in terms of economic development—much of which has been popularised by Paternostre de la Mairieu (1972). Ironically, Kayibanda's regime distinguished itself, not by upholding the democratic values it promised to cultivate, but by assuming the old monarchic leadership style it had vowed to eradicate. 'Like the mwami', Lemarchand observed, talking about

Kayibanda in 1970, 'the president is inaccessible, inviolate and unaccountable. His inaccessibility enables him to avoid taking up overt positions on specific issues, and thus to create around his position and his policies an atmosphere of ambiguity which makes them immune from criticism' (Lemarchand 1970: 270–271). It thus came as little surprise that, on the eve of President Kayibanda's expiration of his legal term in office in 1973, his associates who had excelled in singing his praises embarked on the fatal path of calling for constitutional amendments to allow him seek a third term in office as 'the only leader able to preserve stability and prosperity'.[10] More ironically still, instead of taking seriously the then simmering north-south conflict as a problem of power struggle among the Hutu elites, the regime sponsored another wave of anti-Tutsi pogroms. Yet, this scapegoating strategy proved counter-productive and paved the way for the July 1973 coup d'état that sadly led to the gruesome death of President Kayibanda and his close aides.

The coup leader, Major General Juvenal Habyarimana, took over and vowed to build the second republic regime around the triple goal of 'Peace, Unity, and Development'. For many years, the triple goal translated into relative stability and economic development that made the Habyarimana regime (along with his single-party system, MRND) a darling of the donor community. Paradoxically, despite his much-vaunted merits as the architect of 'the Switzerland of Africa' or 'a model of African development', Habyarimana failed to tackle vital challenges, including two related issues: the Hutu-Tutsi conflict and the refugee problem. As a result, the unresolved refugee problem paved the way for the 1990–1994 war and, ultimately, the assassination of the president himself and his close aides on 6 April 1994. This criminal act sparked the 1994 genocide from which Kagame's RPF emerged as the new ruling force which took power by force in July 1994 and became the third republic.

Like its predecessors, the new government put forth impressive objectives, including reconciliation and national unity, good governance, and resolution of the refugee problem. Yet the government soon proved to be another authoritarian regime, centred around one man, Paul Kagame. In addition to being responsible for serious human rights violations at home and abroad, the RPF-led regime gradually became a de facto single-party system, with no intention to respect term limits, while growing extremely intolerant of dissents.

As of today, it is common knowledge that democratic spaces in Rwanda have dramatically shrunk including within the ruling RPF formal structures (Nyamwasa et al. 2010; Reyntjens 2013; Twagiramungu and Sebarenzi 2019). This situation has forced independent thinkers and alternative voices into silence (Frontline 2004), thus reducing the country's chances of embarking on a transformational path.

---

[10] Fascinating parallels in the logic underlying the case for constitutional change to allow the incumbent president seek a third term in office under Kayibanda and Kagame are particularly of great interest here.

Worse still, like its predecessors, the RPF-led regime appears to be convinced that ethno-militarist autocracy is necessary to reckon past wounds and build a stable and prosperous country. In fact, former governments concentrated powers in the hands of a tiny Hutu politico and military elite, ostensibly to preserve the 1959 Revolution in the face of a feared 'Tutsi peril'. Kagame has walked in the footsteps of his predecessors by concentrating powers in the hands of a tiny Tutsi politico and military elite, presumably to prevent another genocide. Yet, experience has shown that these types of policies are wrong and ineffective and are recipes for disaster, not only for the Rwandan people as a whole but also for autocrats themselves. Predictably, while history is not doomed to repeat itself, experience shows that the more an autocrat concentrates all the powers in his hands, the more likely he becomes poised to be violently replaced by another autocrat.

In this regard, while most of the rivals and critics of the RPF present themselves as legitimate and viable alternatives, past experiences caution us that any mere change of the guards in the absence of deep structural transformations is doomed to result in the proverbial scenario where the dancers change, but the dance style remains the same. Suffice it to recall that, as a result of that extreme violence the country has endured since October 1990, every Rwandan family has been affected, directly or indirectly, at the hands of fellow Rwandans. Rwandans of all backgrounds (ethnic, regional, age, gender, etc.) have lost family members, were or have been forced into exile, arbitrarily imprisoned and relegated to second-class citizens. The cycle of violence has gone from generations to generations. Furthermore, there are victims and perpetrators among Rwandans of all backgrounds. Ironically, some victims have become perpetrators and vice versa (Mamdani 2002). This widespread victimisation has made Rwanda into a wounded nation, a situation that fits well within Foucault's definition of a criminal act as an injury inflicted upon the society as a whole.

6.2   Reaching Forward: The Quest for a New Departure

Given that Rwandan conflicts are fundamentally political, the solutions must also be political. But since the conflict has taken on dangerous ethnic dimensions, political solutions must consider the needs, fears and interests of each community: Hutu and Tutsi. Over the last 25 years, the international community has encouraged the government of Rwanda to embrace democratic norms. But what does democracy mean to Rwandans in the first place? As Lijphart (1999: 6) notes, 'there is a surprisingly strong and persistent tendency in political science to equate democracy solely with majoritarian democracy'. This tendency is of great concern in the context of Rwanda where post-independence politics blurred the lines between ethnic majority and majoritarian democracy. As a result, since the conflict between Hutu and Tutsi has crystallised ethnic identities to the detriment of national identity, Hutu elites tend to understand the term *democracy* as synonymous with Hutu domination whereas Tutsi elites are keen on conceiving of majoritarian democracy as an existential threat against the Tutsi people as a whole (Twagiramungu and Sebarenzi 2018). To break the cycle of bloody competition resulting from these divergent views of democracy, the Rwandan context requires constitutional and legal arrangements that foster democracy while translating its values into a win-win form of political representation. The intended alternative political system that can guarantee true justice echoes Lijphart (1999)'s concept of consociational democracy, based on inclusive representation, accountability and ethics.

Seen from a transitional justice perspective, the democratic legitimacy that Rwanda needs should be innovative and inclusive to meet the fears of the two rival ethnic groups: fear among Tutsis who feel caught between the rooming peril of another genocide and the 'deep blue sea' of political marginalisation due simply to being in a numerical minority, and fear among Hutus to continue to pay the bill for the genocide committed by people from their community, and to remain being onlookers in the political management of the country despite their numerical majority.

By providing security and reassurance to the two communities and thus putting an end to the cycle of vengeful violence, consociational democracy and the resulting legitimacy would constitute a foundation for the healing of the Rwandan society as a whole (Rudasingwa 2013). Such is the governance system that Rwanda desperately needs to get rid of the tyranny of fear embedded in the endemic Hutu-Tutsi security dilemma.

BIBLIOGRAPHY

Arriaza, N.R. (2006). *The Pinochet Effect: Transnational Justice in the Age of Human Rights*. Philadelphia: University of Pennsylvania Press.

Bay View National Black Paper. (2013). "Obama Requests Immunity for Kagame Rwanda Genocide and Congo Wars." *Bay View National Black Paper*, September 14.

Brewer, M. (2001). "Ingroup Identification and Intergroup Conflict, When Does Ingroup Love Become Outgroup Hate?" In *Social Identity, Intergroup Conflict, and Conflict Reduction*. Eds. R.D. Ashmore, L. Jussim, & D. Wilder. Oxford: Oxford University Press.

Bruguière, J.L. (2006). The Report by French Anti-Terrorist Judge Jean-Louis Bruguière on the Shooting Down of Rwandan President Habyarimana's Plane on 6 April 1994. http://cirqueminime.blogspot.com/2007/10/completed-bruguire-report-translated.html

Burnet, J. (2008). "The Injustice of Local Justice. Truth, Reconciliation, and Revenge in Rwanda." *Genocide Studies and Prevention* 3 (2).

Cassese, A. (2006). *International Criminal Law*. New York: Oxford University Press.

Clark, P. (2010). *The Gacaca Courts. Post-Genocide Justice and Reconciliation in Rwanda. Justice Without Lawyers*. London: Cambridge University Press.

Clark, P. (2014). Bringing the peasants back in, again: State power and local agency in Rwanda's gacaca courts." *Journal of Eastern African Studies*, 8 (2): 193–213.

Coser, L. (1957). *The Functions of Social Conflict*. Glencoe, IL: Free Press.

Crocker, D. (1999). Reckoning with Past Wrongs: A Normative Framework. *Ethics & International Affairs* (13): 43–64.

Cruvellier, T. (2012). *Court of Remorse: Inside the International Criminal Tribunal for Rwanda*. Translated by Chari Voss. Madison: Wisconsin University Press.

Dallaire, R. (2004). *Shake Hands with the Devil: The Failure of Humanity in Rwanda* Da Capo.

de Beer, D. (1997). *The Organic Law of 30 August 1996 on the Organization of the Prosecution of Offences Constituting the Crime of Genocide or Crimes against Humanity. Commentary*. Kigali: Alter Egaux Editions.

Des Forges, A. & Longman, T. (2004). "Legal Responses to Genocide in Rwanda." In *My Neighbor, My Enemy. Justice and Community in the Aftermath of Atrocity*. Eds. E. Stover & H.M. Weinstein. Cambridge: Cambridge University Press.

Forges, A. (1999). *Leave None to tell the story. Genocide in Rwanda*. New York: HRW.

Foucault, M. (1995). *Discipline & Punish: The Birth of the Prison*. Vintage Books.

Frontline. (2004). *Front Line Rwanda. Disappearances, Arrests, Threats, Intimidation and Cooption of Human Rights Defenders 2001–2004*. Dublin, Ireland: Front Line.

Fujii, L. A. (2009). *Killing Neighbors: Webs of Violence in Rwanda*. Cornell University Press.

Gahima, G. (2013). *Transitional Justice in Rwanda: Accountability for Atrocity*. Routledge.

Gahonzire, M. (2015). The Rwanda Correctional Service: Challenges and the Way Forward on Managing Risk in Contemporary Correctional Systems. *ICPA Annual General Meeting*. Melbourne, Australia.

Habimana, A. (2011). "The Dancing Is Still the Same." In *Remaking Rwanda. State Building and Human Rights After Mass Violence*. Eds. Scott Straus & Lars Waldorf. Madison: The University of Wisconsin.

Human Rights Watch. (2011). Rwanda: Mixed Legacy for Community-Based Genocide Courts. *News Release*. https://www.hrw.org/report/2011/05/31/justice-com promised/legacy-rwandas-community-based-gacaca-courts.

ICTR. (2014). The ICTR in Brief. https://unictr.irmct.org/en/tribunal.

ICTR. (1998). The Prosecutor v. Jean Paul Akayesu (Trial Judgement). ICTR964T. http://www.unhcr.org/refworld/docid/40278fbb4.html.

Justiceinfo.net. (2020). ICTR Acquitted Languish in Confinement. https://www.jus ticeinfo.net/en/tribunals/ictr/44024-ictr-acquitted-languish-in-confinement.html.

Kimonyo, J.P. (2008). *Rwanda, un génocide populaire*. Paris: Karthala.

Kimonyo, J. P., Twagiramungu, N., & Kayumba, C. (2004). *Supporting the Postgenocide Transition in Rwanda. The Role of the International Community*. The Hague: ClingendaelCRU.

Lemarchand, R. (1970). *Rwanda and Burundi*. New York, Washington, DC, London: Praeger Publishers.

Lemon, C. (2007). Rwanda's Troubled Gacaca Courts. https://userpages.umbc.edu/ ~davisj/rwanda.pdf.

Lijphart, A. (1999). *Patterns of Democracy—Government Forms and Performance in Thirty-Six Countries*. New Haven and London: Yale University Press.

Liprodhor. (2002). *L'état des lieux des procès de génocide 1996–2001*. Kigali: CDIPG.

Mamdani, M. (2002). *When Victims Become Killers. Colonialism, Nativism, and the Genocide in Rwanda*. Princeton: Princeton University Press.

Meierhenrich, J. (2009). Lawfare. Gacaca Jurisdictions in Rwanda. *Manuscript.* Cambridge: Harvard University.

Minow, M. (1999). *Between Vengeance and Forgiveness: Facing History after Genocide and Mass Violence.* Boston: Beacon Press.

Musabyimana, G. (2008). *Rwanda. Le mythe des mots. Recherche sur le concept «Akazu» et ses corollaires.* Paris: L'Harmattan.

Newbury, D. (2001). "Precolonial Burundi and Rwanda. Local loyalties, Regional Royalties." *The International Journal of African Historical Studies,* 34 (2): 258

Ntampaka, C. (1984). "La place de la coutume dans la législation Rwandaise–état actuel." In *Revue Juridique Du Rwanda, 8:* 139–148

Nyakabwa, R. (2002). Stateless and the Batutsi Refugees' Invasion of Rwanda, 1990–94. Ph.D. Diss., University of London.

Nyamwasa, K., Karegeya, P., Rudasingwa, T., & Gahima, G. (2010). Rwanda Briefing. http://musabyimana.be/uploads/media/Rwanda_Briefing_August2010.pdf

Olsen, T., Payne, L.A., & Reiter, A.G. (2010). *Transitional Justice in Balance. Comparing Processes, Weighing Efficacy.* Washington, DC: USIP.

Paternostre de la Mairieu, B. (1972). *Le Rwanda: Son effort de développement. Antécédents historiques et conquêtes de la révolution rwandaise.* Bruxelles: Editions de Boek.

Peskin, V. (2011). The uneasy relationship between the ICTR and Gacaca. In: Straus, S. and Waldorf, L. *Remaking Rwanda State Building and Human Rights after Mass Violence.* Madison: Winsconsin University Press.

Radio 10. (2003). Inkiko Gacaca zasoje imirimo yazo. http://www.radio10.rw/?p=2770

Radio 10. (2010). Inkiko Gacaca zasoje imirimo yazo. http://www.radio10.rw/?p=2770

ROR [Republic of Rwanda]. (1991). *Raporo ya Komisiyo y'igihugu ishinzwe gutegura ivugurura rya politiki. Inyandiko ya 1.* Kigali: Perezidansi ya Repubulika y'u Rwanda.

ROR. (1996). Organic Law No. 08/96 of August 30, 1996 on the Organization of Prosecutions for Offences constituting the Crime of Genocide or Crimes against Humanity committed since October 1, 1990 Organic Law.

ROR. (2002). Law No. 47/2001 of 18/12/2001 Instituting Punishment for Offences of Discrimination and Sectarianism. *Journal Officiel* No.4 (February 15).

ROR. (2003). Constitution of the Republic of Rwanda. *Journal Official Special of June.*

ROR. (2005). Arrêté présidentiel n° 10/01 du 7 mars 2005 déterminant les modalités d'exécution de la peine alternative à l'emprisonnement de travaux d'intérêt général. https://www.ilo.org/dyn/natlex/natlex4.detail?p_isn=71583&p_lang=fr.

ROR. (2008). Law No.18/2008 of 13/7/2008 Relating to the Punishment of the Crime of Genocide Ideology.

ROR. (2011). Law No. 47/2001 of 18/12/2001 Instituting Punishment for Offences of Discrimination and Sectarianism. Journal Officiel No.4, February 15, 2002. http://www.grandslacs.net/doc/4040.pdf

Reyntjens, F. (1990). "Le gacaca ou la justice du gazon au Rwanda", *Politique Africaine,* 40: 31–41.

Reyntjens, F. (2005). "Chronique politique du Rwanda et du Burundi 2003–2005." In *L'Afriques des Grands Lacs. Annuaire 2004–2005.* Paris: L'Harmattan, 1–26.

Reyntjens, F. (2011). "Constructing the Truth, Dealing with Dissent, Domesticating the World: Governance in Post-genocide Rwanda." *African Affairs* (110:438):1–34. https://doi.org/10.1093/afraf/adq075

Reyntjens, F. (2013). *Political Governance in Post-Genocide Rwanda*. Cambridge University Press.

Rudasingwa, T. (2013). *Healing A Nation: A Testimony: Waging And Winning A Peaceful Revolution To Unite And Heal A Broken Rwanda*. North Charleston, SC: CreateSpace Independent Publishing Platform.

Rurangwa, R. (2009). *Genocide, My Stolen Rwanda*. London: Reportage Press.

Sanders, E. (1969). "The Hamitic Hypothesis. Its Origin and Functions in Time Perspective." *The Journal of African History*, 10 (4):521–532. https://doi.org/10.1017/S0021853700009683.

Sebarenzi, J. (2009). *God Sleeps in Rwanda. A Journey of Transformation*. New York: Atria.

Sebarenzi, J. (2011). "Justice and Human Rights for All Rwandans." In Remaking *Rwanda. State Building and Human Rights After Mass Violence*. Eds. S. Straus & L. Waldorf. Madison: The University of Wisconsin Press.

Shapiro, H. (1977). A Conversation With Jimmy Carter. *The New York Times*.

Straus, S. & Waldorf, L. (2011). *Remaking Rwanda State Building and Human Rights after Mass Violence*. Madison: Winsconsin University Press.

The Guardian. (2019). Met Police Investigate Five Men over Rwandan Genocide Claims. https://www.theguardian.com/uk-news/2019/apr/09/met-police-investigate-five-men-over-rwandan-genocide-claims

Twagiramungu, N. (2005a). Gacaca or Grassroots Justice. Its Basis in International Law and Implications for Human Rights in Post-genocide Rwanda. Unpub. Thesis. Utrecht: Utrecht University.

Twagiramungu, N. (2005b). "Burundi." In *How Mass Atrocities End*. Studies from Guatemala, Burundi, Indonesia, the Sudans, Bosnia-Herzegovina, and Iraq. Ed. B. Conley-Zilkic. Cambridge University Press.

Twagiramungu, N. (2008). Démocratisation et édification des états en Afrique. Enjeux et perspectives vus d'en bas. Montréal- Canada: Symposium Forum Africa-Canada. http://www.ccic.ca/e/docs003_acf_2008_acf_democratization_afiquebis1.pdf.

Twagiramungu, N. (2014a). *Two Roads to Power: Explaining variation in the Transition from genocidal Violence to Rebel Governance in Contemporary Rwanda and Burundi*. Medford, MA: Tufts University.

Twagiramungu, N. (2014b). "Can there be Justice After Genocide? Lessons from Rwanda." In *Al Jazeera English Magazine* (Special Issue).

Twagiramungu, N. (2016). "Burundi: Anatomy of Mass Violence Endgames." In *Bridget Conley-Zilkic* (ed.), How Mass Atrocities End. Cambridge University Press.

Twagiramungu, N. (2018). "Rwanda." In *Oxford Bibliographies in African Studies*. Ed. Thomas Spear. New York: Oxford University Press.

Twagiramungu, N., & Sebarenzi, J. (2018). Rwanda Can't Achieve Reconciliation Without Fixing Its Democracy. *The Conversation*.

Twagiramungu, N., & Sebarenzi, J. (2019). Rwanda's Economic Growth Could Be Derailed by Its Autocratic Regime. *The Conversation*. https://reaction.life/author/noel-twagiramungu-jospeh-sebarenzi/.

USLegal. (2003). Legal Definitions & Legal Terms Defined. http://definitions.uslegal.com.

Uvin, P. (1998). *Aiding Violence. The Development Enterprise in Rwanda*. West Hartford, CT: Kumarian Press.

Vansina, M. J. (2004). *Antecedents to Modern Rwanda*. The Nyiginya Kingdom. Madison: The University of Wisconsin Press.

Vidmar, N. (2001). Retribution and revenge. In *Handbook of justice research in law*. Eds. J. Sanders & V. L. Hamilton (pp. 31–63).

Vidmar, N. (2011). Retributive Justice: Its Social Context. In *The justice motive in everyday life*. Eds. M. Ross & D.T. Miller. Cambridge: Cambridge University Press.

Waldorf, L. (2011). "Instrumentalizing Genocide. The RPF's Campaign Against 'Genocide Ideology'." In *Remaking Rwanda. State Building and Human Rights after Mass Violence*. Eds. Scott Straus & Lars Waldorf. Madison: The University of Wisconsin Press.

World Bank. (2000). *Anticorruption in Transition: Contribution to the Policy Debate*. Washington, DC: World Bank Publications.

Zorbas, E. (2011). *Reconciliation in Post-genocide Rwanda: Discourse and Practice*. London: LAP LAMBERT Academic Publishing.

CHAPTER 11

The Community Court of Justice of the Ecowas and the Advancement of Human Rights and Social Justice Reform in West Africa: Three Landmark Cases

Jake Okechukwu Effoduh

1 INTRODUCTION

The human rights mandate of the ECOWAS Court can be traced to article 4(g) of the ECOWAS Revised Treaty which affirms the agreement made by the ECOWAS Member States to adhere to the recognition, promotion and protection of human and peoples' rights in accordance with the provisions of the African Charter on Human and Peoples Rights (ACHPR). The ECOWAS Court is the only sub-regional international court that applies as its primary instrument, a regional instrument, that has been explicitly incorporated into its body of 'law' (Alhaji Tidjani v. FRN, 2007). Since the Court applies the rights catalogued in the ACHPR, it is not surprising that most applications that the Court has taken up were brought under the ACHPR. In this chapter, the judgement of the ECOWAS Court in three (3) prominent cases will be reviewed. These three cases border on environmental and/or socioeconomic justice pursuits instituted by 'activist forces' before the ECOWAS Court. The term 'activist forces' recognises the role of local activism in international law (Okafor 2007). While Okafor uses this concept to describe a broad range of actors (especially as they engage with the African Commission), here, the expression will be used to mostly describe NGOs, especially as they engage with the ECOWAS Court. Coincidentally (and impressively too), the three

---

J. O. Effoduh (✉)
Osgoode Hall Law School, York University, Toronto, ON, Canada
e-mail: effoduh@gmail.com

© The Author(s), under exclusive license to Springer Nature Switzerland AG 2022
A. Adeola and M. W. Mutua (eds.), *The Palgrave Handbook of Democracy, Governance and Justice in Africa*,
https://doi.org/10.1007/978-3-030-74014-6_11

197

(3) cases were instituted by the same activist force: an NGO named the Socio-Economic Rights and Accountability Project (SERAP). By analysing these cases, this chapter will offer an insight into the character of the jurisprudence and norms of the ECOWAS Court especially as they relate to environmental and socioeconomic justice reform. The sources of literature that is used for this case-study analysis include (but are not limited to) case files from the Court's registry, factums of the parties, law reports, the ECOWAS Revised Treaty, ECOWAS Court Protocol (including the Supplementary Protocol) and treaty provisions from the laws cited in the judgements of the Court. The jurisprudence from the three (3) cases reviewed in this chapter will reveal how the ECOWAS Court in each case adjudicated on one or more of the following justice issues:

- The *locus standi* of activist forces to institute human rights cases relating to environmental and/or socioeconomic justice pursuits in West Africa.
- The justiciability of environmental and socioeconomic rights, and the interpretation of the specific kinds of environmental and socioeconomic rights contained in the ACHPR as the primary 'human rights treaty' of the ECOWAS Court as well in other International Human Rights Law (IHRL) sources such as: the Universal Declaration of Human Rights (UDHR), the International Covenant on Civil and Political Rights (ICCPR), the International Covenant on Economic Social and Cultural Rights (ICESCR), the Convention on the Elimination of All Forms of Discrimination against Women (CEDAW), the Convention on the Rights of the Child (CRC), etc.
- The ECOWAS Court's application of some key principles and standards in IHRL as they relate to environmental and socioeconomic justice. For example, the right of a people or community to exercise 'free, prior and informed consent (FPIC)' in situations where industrial action (like natural resource extraction) takes place in their community. This is to accord local and indigenous communities (like the people of the Niger Delta in this case), the ability to give or withhold consent to a project that may affect them or their territory.
- The application of damages (and other judicial remedies) in human rights cases that relate to environmental and socioeconomic justice.

The above list is not exhaustive. They will also not be addressed in the order listed above. The three (3) cases within the focus of this chapter will be analysed one after another, by addressing the above issues when they apply to the particular case at hand. This chapter will also reveal the unique norms, processes and procedures of the ECOWAS Court system and its 'law'. The chapter reveals how activist forces have utilised the ECOWAS Court in the efforts to pursue environmental and socioeconomic justice reforms in Nigeria, and it also assesses the Court's jurisprudence on these issues. The 'door' of the

ECOWAS Court is directly open to activist forces. This is unlike some other supranational courts that do not accept direct lodgement of cases and may require a commission to screen a petition before it is deemed admissible, or may require a state to accept the court's jurisdiction. For example, for a case to be admissible before the African Court on Human and Peoples' Rights, the applicant must, inter alia, exhaust local remedies, subject to certain exceptions. Access to the ECOWAS Court is not conditioned on the ratification by a state of a protocol allowing activist forces to engage the court. Although the Court's jurisdiction is extensive and does not have the benefit of an institution with powers of coercion to enforce its judgements, the ECOWAS can rely on the pressure generated by the political arms of the community; the indulgence of national executives; and the goodwill of domestic courts to bring to help advance the struggle for socioeconomic rights in the sub-region. The ECOWAS Court offers West African activist forces a way to minimise the obstruction, haggling and delay that may be experienced if they stuck only with the domestic or continental human rights system. Through sub-regional litigation on 'non-justiciable' rights, activist forces are opening up a reformist path, away from the limited avenues of legal recourse available to victims of socioeconomic and environmental rights violations in domestic courts in West Africa. In 2019, the Court declared that it recorded the highest number of decisions since its inception. Many of the cases have been initiated by activist forces (Independent, 13 January 2020).

2 THE CASE OF SERAP V. NIGERIA AND ANOR 2010 ('CASE 1')

This was the first case instituted by SERAP before the ECOWAS Court. Before the case was instituted, SERAP had consulted with other activist forces in and out of the region, and then decided to 'test' the 'progressive' jurisdiction of the ECOWAS Court system (Anaba 2016). As a human rights NGO with interest in public accountability, transparency and socioeconomic rights, SERAP initiated this case based on a tip from a whistle-blower, and consequent upon an investigation they carried out themselves on the activities of Nigeria's Universal Basic Education Commission (UBEC), an administrative body established by the government with the aim of ensuring basic primary education in Nigeria. They submitted their investigation as a petition to the Independent Corrupt Practices Commission and Other Related Offences Commission (ICPC) who took action on the case and produced a report alleging 'massive corruption' based on the discovery of embezzlement, misappropriation and the mismanagement of funds allocated to UBEC, which were meant for the education sector (SERAP Online 2017). To confront what they claimed is a violation of several rights: the right to quality education, the right to human dignity, the right of peoples to their wealth and natural resources, and the right of all peoples to socioeconomic development, SERAP challenged Nigeria and UBEC before the ECOWAS Court claiming a breach of five (5) of the provisions of ACHPR (articles 1, 2, 17, 21 and 22). SERAP estimated that, as a direct consequence of corruption, more than five million children in Nigeria would now lack access to primary education (UNICEF 2007).

SERAP relied on article 4(g) of the 1993 Revised Treaty of ECOWAS, as well as the provisions in articles 2, 17, 21 and 22 of the ACHPR as grounds to challenge Nigeria's alleged violation of the right to education, including positing that the right to education within the African Charter is intrinsically linked to the right of the people's economic and social development. SERAP sought six (6) reliefs from the ECOWAS Court:

1. A declaration that every Nigerian child is entitled to free and compulsory education by virtue of Article 17 of the African Child's Rights Act, Sect. 15 of the Child's Rights Act 2003 and Sect. 2 of the Compulsory Free and Universal Basic Education Act 2004;
2. A declaration that the diversion of the sum of 3.5 billion naira from the UBE fund by certain public officers in 10 states of the Federation of Nigeria is illegal and unconstitutional as it violates Articles 21 and 22 of the ACHPR;
3. An order directing the defendants to make adequate provisions for the compulsory and free education of every child forthwith;
4. An order directing the defendants to arrest and prosecute the public officers who diverted the sum of 3.5 billion naira from the UBE fund forthwith;
5. An order compelling the government of Nigeria to fully recognise primary school teachers' trade union freedoms and to solicit the views of teachers throughout the process of educational planning and policy-making;
6. An order compelling the government of Nigeria to assess progress in the realisation of the right education with particular emphasis on the Universal Basic Education: appraise the obstacles, including corruption, impeding access of Nigerian children to school; review the interpretation and application of human rights obligations throughout the education process ('Case 1').

Two of the above reliefs were granted by the court. The Court granted the first and the third one and dismissed the other four (4).

On recognising the right to education as a fundamental right that should be enforceable despite domestic constitutional limitations, the ECOWAS Court held (and for the first time ever) that:

[E]very Nigerian child is entitled to free and compulsory basic education. What the first defendant [Nigeria] said was that the right to education was not justiciable in Nigeria, but the court... in this case, decided it was justiciable under the ACHPR. The applicant is saying that following the diversion of funds, there is insufficient money available to the basic education sector. We have earlier referred to the fact that embezzlement or theft of part of the funds allocated to the basic education sector will have a negative impact; this is normal since shortage of funds will disable the sector from performing as envisaged by those who approved the budget. Thus, whilst steps are being taken to recover the funds or prosecute the suspects, as the case may be, it is in order that the first defendant [Nigeria] should take the necessary steps to provide the money to cover the shortfall to ensure a smooth implementation of the education programme, lest a section of the people should be denied a right to education. (para 26, 28. Emphasis mine)

For the first time, the Nigerian government was held responsible by a supranational adjudicatory body for its non-fulfilment of the right to primary education of its people. The ECOWAS Court in this case dismissed the 'excuse' of non-justiciability of the right to primary education and affirmed the justiciability of socioeconomic rights (including the right to education) in Nigeria (and in the rest of West Africa).

The ECOWAS Court was progressive in establishing three (3) things in this case: one, that Nigeria is obligated under IHRL to fulfil the right to education of its people, beyond its domestically non-justiciable, albeit constitutional, fundamental objectives and directive principles of state policy; two, that the failure of Nigeria to investigate and address the systemic corruption in the UBEC amounted to a breach of her legal 'responsibility to protect' the human rights of its people. As the Court noted, this was deeply 'a failure to seriously address all allegations of corruption at the highest levels of government and the levels of impunity that facilitate corruption... lest a section of the people should be denied a right to education'; and three, that the socioeconomic right to education is justiciable.

3 THE CASE OF SERAP V. NIGERIA AND 8 ORS 2012 ('CASE 2')

This suit is built upon many years of activist pursuits and struggles. The backdrop and origins of this claim for environmental and socioeconomic justice in the Niger Delta region can be traced to the movement-building of local activist forces that took place in the sixties in Nigeria (Platform London). The consideration by SERAP to use litigation and human rights law to secure environmental and socioeconomic justice for the 'Niger-Deltans' came from the human rights-consciousness that had built up over the years (Obi and Rustad 2011). The 'engagements' of activist forces who desired environmental and socioeconomic justice produced similar desires for justice, in and out of the region. Activist forces such as the Movement for the Survival of the Ogoni People (MOSOP), Social and Economic Rights Action Center (SERAC) and Center for Economic and Social Rights (CESR) from north America transmitted ideas around a 'network' of human rights activists. This 'network'

202   J. O. EFFODUH

leveraged on their desire to challenge the unparalleled environmental and socioeconomic injustice that existed and still exists in the country, and these activist forces gradually won more people into their fold. They converged at community workshops, seminars, focus groups, town hall meetings, etc., and they designed, facilitated, oiled and consolidated ideas for similar justice causes, including to challenge the military regime at the time (Ibeanu 2006).

In 1996, they decided to approach the African Commission. The reason and outcome from exploring the African Commission as a mechanism for seeking justice for the people of the Niger Delta were briefly recounted, by one of the activist forces in a case study, as follows:

> Between 1996 and 1998... Nigeria was still ruled by a brutal military dictatorship, which had replaced the bill of rights and other important constitutional provisions with draconian military decrees. Under the decrees the authority of the courts to intervene in human rights or political cases was drastically limited. Thus, the prospect of judicial intervention was dim, and the military junta would have probably ignored any judicial order... For these reasons, SERAC along with community leaders decided not to rely on litigation as their primary tactic. The possibility of using international and regional human rights mechanisms was also considered. In 1996, in collaboration with the Center for Economic and Social Rights, SERAC filed a communication with the Banjul-based African Commission on Human and Peoples' Rights regarding massive violations of the economic, social, and cultural rights of the Ogoni community in the oil-rich Niger Delta region... However, the commission's highly politicized history, and its well-known delay in processing cases, did not inspire any confidence in its capacity to issue an unbiased and timely judgment. In any event, the commission's lack of compulsory jurisdiction and capacity to enforce its decisions also made that prospect unappealing. (Morka 2014)

On the communication about the issues in the Niger Delta which was initiated by SERAC and CESR at the African Commission, the Commission held Nigeria to be in violation of articles 2, 4, 14, 16, 18, 21 and 24 of the ACHPR. The African Commission 'appealed' to the Nigerian government to ensure protection of the environment, health and livelihood of the people of Ogoniland by ceasing attacks on the community, investigating human rights violations and prosecuting offenders. The African Commission also asked Nigeria to provide adequate compensation to victims and ensure appropriate environmental and social impact assessments are prepared for any future oil development. Specifically, the African Commission requested Nigeria to:

> Stop all attacks on Ogoni communities and leaders by the Rivers State Internal Securities Task Force and permit citizens and independent investigators free access to the territory; Conduct an investigation into the human rights violations and prosecute officials of the security forces, Nigerian National Petroleum Corporation (NNPC) and relevant agencies involved in human rights violations; Ensure adequate compensation to victims of the human rights violations, including relief and resettlement assistance to victims of government sponsored

raids, and undertake a comprehensive cleanup of lands and rivers damaged by oil operations; Ensure that appropriate environmental and social impact assessments are prepared for any future oil development and that the safe operation of any further oil development is guaranteed through effective and independent oversight bodies for the petroleum industry; and then providing information on health and environmental risks and meaningful access to regulatory and decision-making bodies to communities likely to be affected by oil operations. (ACHPR Communication 115/96, 69)

The Commission urged Nigeria to keep the Commission abreast of the development in the region:

The African Commission urges the government of the Federal Republic of Nigeria to keep the African Commission informed of the outcome of the work of: The Federal Ministry of Environment which was established to address environmental and environment related issues prevalent in Nigeria, and as a matter of priority, in the Niger Delta area including the Ogoniland; The Niger Delta Development Commission (NDDC) enacted into law to address the environmental and other social related problems in the Niger Delta area and other oil producing areas of Nigeria; and The Judicial Commission of Inquiry inaugurated to investigate the issues of human rights violations. (Communication 115/96)

This communication gained global attention, but activist forces decry that even after a decade of the communication, 'no progress' was made to resolve or end the environmental and socioeconomic injustice inflicted on the Niger Delta and its people (Amnesty International 2014). The activist forces in the pursuit of environmental and socioeconomic justice for the region had to return to the drawing board.

Though progressive, the communication made by SERAC and CESR to the African Commission exposes two long-standing impediments to accessing pursuits of ESJ in the region. First, article 56 of the ACHPR requires the prior exhaustion of domestic remedies in order to approach the African Commission. The rationale for the exhaustion of local remedies is to give the domestic courts an opportunity to decide upon cases before they are brought to an international forum, thus avoiding contradictory judgements of law. For example, under the African Charter, the exhaustion of local remedies rule is applicable in respect of all communications submitted against a state. The exhaustion of local remedies rule could also be to conserve the application of quasi-judicial and judicial resources. The African Commission held in four of its previous communications that a state party should be given notice of any human rights violation within its jurisdiction so as to have the opportunity to remedy the violation before being called to account by an international tribunal (ACHPR Communications 25/89, 47/90, 56/91 and 100/93).

The above two limitations have been extinguished from the West African supranational adjudicatory procedure; hence, they do not apply under the ECOWAS system (Protocol A/P.1/7/91 as amended by Protocol A/SP.1/01/05 art 9). Therefore, as SERAC had 'fought for the Niger-Deltans' before the African Commission and had 'contributed its own bit in the struggle' for environmental and socioeconomic justice, SERAC figuratively handed the baton to SERAP (note that they have similar names but are different organisations) to continue the pursuit of environmental and socioeconomic justice for the people of the Niger Delta (Nnimmo 2017). SERAP took up the pursuit by instituting 'Case 2' before the ECOWAS Court. Before launching this case, SERAP (and other activist forces) had carried out advocacy on the environmental and socioeconomic conditions of the Niger Delta. Various activist forces had engaged with the press; with other activist forces; the government (in both public private meetings); and some international stakeholders about this issue (Grant 2015). The Nigerian public and the ECOWAS Court itself were 'aware' of the environmental and socioeconomic justice problems in Niger Delta.

SERAP in this case ('Case 2') sought environmental and socioeconomic justice for the people of the Niger Delta. It instituted this case in 2009 against the Nigerian government and seven (7) oil companies operating in the Niger Delta region (as co-defendants). In its originating application at the ECOWAS Court, SERAP described the aspect of the Niger Delta that the case was concerned with thus:

> On 28 August 2008, a fault in the Trans-Niger pipeline resulted in a significant oil spill into Bodo Creek in Ogoniland. The oil poured into the swamp and creek for weeks, covering the area in a thick slick of oil and killing the fish that people depend on for food and for livelihood. The oil spill has resulted in death or damage to a number of species of fish that provide the protein needs in the local community. Video footage of the site shows widespread damage, including to mangroves which are an important fish breeding ground. The pipe that burst is the responsibility of the Shell Petroleum Development Company (SPDC). SPDC has reportedly stated that the spill was only reported to them on 5 October of that year... However, the leak was not stopped until 7 November.
>
> On 25 June 2001 residents of Ogbobo in Rivers State heard a loud explosion from a pipeline, which had ruptured. Crude oil from the pipe spilled over the surrounding land and waterways. The community notified Shell Petroleum Development Company (SPDC) the following day; however, it was not until several days later that a contractor working for SPDC came to the site to deal with the oil spill. The oil subsequently caught fire. Some 42 communities were affected as the oil moved through the water system. The communities' water supply, which came from the local waterway, was contaminated... People in the area complained of numerous symptoms, including respiratory problems. The situation was so dire that some families reportedly evacuated the area, but most had no means of leaving... Hundreds of thousands of people are affected, particularly the poorest and other most vulnerable sectors of the population, and those who rely on traditional livelihoods such as fishing and agriculture. ('Case 2', para 18)

The above testimony is quoted from SERAP's factum before the ECOWAS Court, describing the situation in the region. This account may have been the umpteenth time that an activist force had had to recount the environmental and socioeconomic condition of the Niger Delta in Nigeria. As far back as 1995, SPDC admitted that its infrastructure needed work and that corrosion was responsible for 50 per cent of oil spills. Yet, in the same year, 1995, Ken Saro-Wiwa (a prominent activist force and the then president of MOSOP) was hanged by the military dictatorship for his activism (Roy and Falola 2016).

SERAP made several demands before the ECOWAS Court: They sought a declaration that Niger-Deltans are entitled to environmental protection and socioeconomic development; that the complicity of the Nigerian government is a violation of IHRL; that the failure of Nigeria to monitor the human impact of oil exploration is a violation of the ACHPR, the ICCPR and the ICESCR; and that the systematic denial of access to information to the people of the Niger Delta is also a violation of the ACHPR, the ICCPR and the ICESCR. SERAP sought orders from the ECOWAS Court to direct the defendants to fulfil the environmental and socioeconomic development rights of the people and secure their justice from violations of environmental and socioeconomic development rights. Finally, SERAP sought an effective clean-up to the environmental pollution of the region and monetary compensation of $1,000,000,000 (one billion USD) to the victims of human rights violations in the Niger Delta.

Nigeria challenged this case on grounds of jurisdiction (Nigeria maintained that the ECOWAS Court has no jurisdiction to examine the alleged violations of the ICCPR and the ICESCR as those are none of the court's instruments), *locus standi* (Nigeria maintained that SERAP is not a victim or an aggrieved party hence has no 'standing' to sue), and that the case was statute barred (the Nigerian government contended that some of the facts pleaded by the plaintiffs occurred before 1990, 1995, 2001, 2003 and 2005. These dates fell outside the three-year statutory period for submitting a communication as required by article 9(3) of the 2005 Supplementary Protocol (A/SP.1/01/05). This provision states that 'any action by or against a Community Institution or any member of the Community shall be statute barred after three (3) years from the date when the right of action arose'. All three claims by Nigeria were thrown out by the ECOWAS Court.

First: on jurisdiction, the ECOWAS Court justified its reliance on IHRL (especially the ICCPR and the ICESCR) despite being a sub-regional court with no normative instrument of its own. According to the Court:

> Even though ECOWAS may not have adopted a specific instrument recognizing human rights, the Court's human rights protection mandate is exercised with regard to all the international instruments, including the African Charter on Human and Peoples' Rights, the International Covenant on Civil and Political Rights, the International Covenant on Economic, Social and Cultural Rights, etc., to which the Member States of ECOWAS are parties. ('Case 2', para 28)

206   J. O. EFFODUH

The Court did have solid justification for this conclusion. It supported its stand, by citing the Protocol that establishes the Court.

> The new Article 9(4) of the Protocol on the Court as amended by Supplementary Protocol A/SP.1/01/05 of 19 January 2005 provides: "The Court has jurisdiction to determine cases of violation of human rights that occur in any Member State." This provision, which gives jurisdiction to the Court to adjudicate on cases of human rights violation, results from an amendment made to the 6 July 1991 Protocol A/P1/7/91 on the ECOWAS Court. The *raison d'être* of this amendment is Article 39 of the 21 December 2001 Protocol A/SP1/12/01 on Democracy and Good Governance, which provides: "Protocol A/P1/7/91 adopted in Abuja on 6 July 1991 relating to the Community Court of Justice, shall be reviewed so as to give the Court the power to hear, inter-alia, cases relating to violations of human rights... ('Case 2')

The Court held that by agreeing to this Protocol, Nigeria is bound by the human rights law 'contained in international instruments, with no exception whatsoever' (emphasis mine). The Court also noted that any individual or organisation is free to have recourse to any court or institution established within the framework of an IHRL instrument. The preamble of the Supplementary Protocol as well as paragraph (h) of its article 1 stipulates the principles of constitutional convergence common to the Member States, which provides:

> The rights set up in the African Charter on Human and Peoples' Rights and other international instruments shall be guaranteed in each of the ECOWAS Member States ; each individual or organisation shall be free to have recourse to the common or civil law courts, a court of special jurisdiction, or any other national institution established within the framework of an international instrument on Human Rights, to ensure the protection of his/her rights.

Second: on *locus standi*, the ECOWAS Court referred to the initial SERAP Case before it, establishing the competence of activist forces to institute action before the Court in representative capacity ('Case 1').

Third: on the case being statute barred, the ECOWAS Court noted that the Protocol does stipulate a 3-year time frame for action to be instituted before the court (2005 Protocol, article 9). And facts that occurred before the Protocol came into force in 2005 cannot be taken into consideration because the said Protocol cannot be applied retroactively. However, in this case, the Court distinguishes between an isolated human rights violation and a persistent and continuous violation that lasted until the date the complaint was filed with the Court and is still ongoing:

> It is trite law that in situations of continued illicit behaviour, the statute of limitation shall only begin to run from the time when such unlawful conduct or omission ceases. Therefore, the acts which occurred after the 2005 Protocol

came into force, in relation to which the Federal Republic of Nigeria had a conduct considered as omissive, are not statute barred. ('Case 2' para 62)

In effect, the ECOWAS Court establishes that for this case, the problem has been enduring, and the failure of Nigeria to prevent the damage or hold anyone to account was continuing; hence, the suit was not time-barred.

The ECOWAS Court emphasised that the Nigerian government has a duty to ensure that the activities (by any other person) within its jurisdiction and control do not cause damage to the environment and the people. Any derogation from that duty is a violation. The ECOWAS Court provides its own description of the environment as follows:

> The environment... is *not an abstraction but represents the living space, the quality of life and the very health of human beings, including generations unborn...* It must be considered as an indivisible whole, comprising the *biotic and abiotic natural resources, notably air, water, land, fauna and flora and the interaction between these same factors.* The environment is essential to every human being. The quality of human life depends on the quality of the environment... [E]very State [is] to take every measure to maintain the quality of the environment understood as an integrated whole, such that the state of the environment may satisfy the human beings who live there, and enhance their sustainable development. ('Case 2' para 100, 101)

The ECOWAS Court unprecedentedly connects environmental rights to socioeconomic survival of people. In arriving at its holding above, the Court interestingly relied on three documents: ACHPR (particularly article 24 of the ACHPR which provides thus: 'All peoples shall have the right to a general satisfactory environment favourable to their development'); ICJ Advisory Opinion of 8 July 2006 (which provides the general obligation of States to ensure that activities within their jurisdiction and control respect the environment of other States and is now part of the corpus of international law); and the International Law Institute's Resolution of 4 September 1997 (which provides the breach of an obligation of environmental protection established under international law and engages responsibility to re-establish the original position or to pay compensation). By virtue of the above international environmental standards, and articles 1 and 24 of the ACHPR, Nigeria's omission to act, to prevent damage to the environment of the people of the Niger Delta, and to hold the oil companies responsible characterises violation of Nigeria's obligations under the ACHPR. The ECOWAS Court held Nigeria in violation of twenty-nine (29) different articles from a string of IHRL instruments including the UDHR ('Case 2' para 91).

'Case 2' is celebrated for its ground-breaking feat and precedent-setting value to human rights adjudication and for its impact in the recognition of environmental and socioeconomic justice in the region. This is the most cited case decided by the ECOWAS Court.

4   THE CASE OF SERAP AND 10 ORS v. NIGERIA AND 4 ORS 2014 ('CASE 3')

> I am from Bundu waterfront and I was shot at home. I had earlier heard gunshots, went outside and learnt soldiers were shooting. I was in the house when the bullet hit me on the leg and I was taken to Teme Clinic, where my leg was operated on. I was admitted for about four days and discharged while the iron they put in my leg was left inside for about 6 months. I was a student and I lost a school-year due to the injury. ('Case 3')

The above is part of the testimony from PW3, one of the five (5) plaintiff witnesses who testified on the facts alleged by SERAP in this case. She was one of the several indigenes who was shot by security agents sent by the government to quell the protesters of Bundu Ama. The locals were protesting against the implementation of the decision of the government of Rivers State to carry out demolition in preparation for the 'urban renewal' project in their community. The plaintiff witness (like many others in the community) was in her home when a bullet fired by one of the security officials hit her.

From the factums submitted by both parties to the court, the Rivers State government of Nigeria was planning a large-scale demolition of the villagers' waterfront settlement without adequate consultation with the relevant communities. At this point, it is important to highlight what 'adequate consultation' entails in IHRL especially for when the government plans to take over land in an indigenous or local community, or where the government is aiming for an 'urban renewal project' like in this case.

The Njemanze waterfront was one of the waterfronts close to the Bundu Ama area in Rivers State which was demolished in August of 2009. SERAP claimed that between 13,800 and 19,000 people were forcibly evicted from their homes and that this was done without adequate notice, compensation, alternative accommodation or legal remediation ('Case 3', para 20). According to the plaintiffs, on the morning of the 12th of October 2009, government authorities accompanied by security agents, including the army and the Nigerian Police, went to Bundu waterfront community to conduct the planned enumeration exercise and assess the structures earmarked for demolition, when they met some of local activists including women and children singing and chanting songs in protest. An armoured vehicle from the security agents drove into the crowd and without notice, soldiers began to shoot. They chased the protesters and shot at them from behind, injuring many, including people who were in their homes but sustained wounds from bullets permeating the structures they lived in. The security agents were described in the statement of claim by SERAP as wearing regular army camouflage uniforms and camouflage head gear; camouflage uniforms and red berets; mobile police uniforms, mobile police uniforms and 'RSVG' flak jackets; police uniforms and 'S.O.S'/swift

Ops Squad flak jackets, and plain clothes agents wearing "JTF" flack jackets' ('Case 3', para 21).

The defendants alleged that the waterfront settlements earmarked for demolition were densely populated and were used as hideouts by hoodlums and miscreants. The defendants also stated that the landlords of the waterfront had been invited for several meetings and were in support of the demolition on satisfactory terms. They alleged that the surveyors who were sent to the community to ascertain the number of structures, take census and calculate the value of properties were beaten up by hoodlums. They posit that when they sent another set of surveyors, they met a confrontation with barricades and villagers blocking the entrance to Bundu. While attempting to remove the barricade, a conflict ensued which led the defendants to call for security back up and led to some villagers getting shot and injured ('Case 3' paras 19–29; 30–51).

This case touches on several civil and political rights (such as the right to life; the right to dignity of the human person; the right to peaceful protest and demonstration; freedom of assembly and association; and freedom of expression, to mention but a few). These rights are fundamental and enforceable as domestic constitutional rights. They are also protected rights under the ACHPR, as well as under the ICCPR and other IHRL instruments (ACHPR articles 1–6, 10–14 and 16; UDHR articles 2, 3, 5, 7, 9, 12, 13, 17, 20, 21 and 25; ICCPR articles 2, 3, 6, 9, 10, 12, 22 and 26; ICESCR articles 2, 3, 5, 10 -12). The right of everyone to adequate shelter and housing has been broadly interpreted to include the right to live in security, peace and dignity (A/HRC/7/16, February 2008). Nigeria has a duty towards the people of Bundu Ama to ensure a degree of security of tenure, which guarantees their legal protection against any form of forced evictions, or threats, or harassments. Forced evictions constitute prima facie violations of a wide range of internationally recognised human rights and can only be carried out under exceptional circumstances and in full accordance with IHRL.

According to the *Principles and Guidelines on the Implementation of Economic, Social and Cultural Rights* in the ACHPR (adopted by the African Commission on 24 October 2011), reference is made to the prohibition of forced evictions and guidance provided in the basic principles and guidelines on development-based evictions and displacement. According to the guidelines, states have an obligation to provide all, regardless of their type of tenure, a degree of security of tenure which guarantees legal protection against forced eviction, harassment and other threats. 'Urban renewal' projects premised on 'public interest', or 'public good' as a ground for development-based evictions or displacement need to conform to a number of conditions or standards of human rights. A balance also needs to be struck between the necessity of developmental projects and the rights of people who are likely to be displaced from same. This is critical for African states especially as development projects are a root cause of internal displacement in the region (Adeola 2021).

In 2014, the OHCHR released a fact sheet on forced evictions in 2014 listing the conditions for displacement on grounds of 'urban renewal' or development projects which should include the following—that it must be 'reasonable' and must be carried out as a last resort when no alternative is available; it must also be 'proportional' (evaluation of the decision's impact on and potential benefit for various groups, including through an eviction impact assessment) and need to promote the general welfare of the people and show evidence of such an outcome; it must be 'foreseeable' and defined in law, and non-discriminatory in both law and practice; it must be subject to control to evaluate their conformity with the constitution and the State's international obligations; and finally, it must also be subject to consultation and participation, with effective recourse to mechanisms that should be available for those directly or indirectly affected (UN Habitat Fact Sheet No. 25/Rev.1).

The ECOWAS Court did not address this case from a 'right to shelter' or a 'right to housing' perspective. One hypothesis for this gap could be that SERAP did not approach the court seeking a socioeconomic and environmental remedy. From the six reliefs sought by SERAP, only one of the reliefs (the fourth one) mentioned the 'urban renewal' plan by the government as not in conformity with IHRL.

1. A declaration that the indiscriminate shooting into the crowd of unarmed protesters is unlawful and unjustifiable under any circumstance and a violation of international human rights obligations and commitments.
2. A declaration that the indiscriminate shooting was unlawful and a violation of the right to life and dignity of the human person, the right to security and health.
3. That the failure of the Defendants and their agents to investigate and prosecute the perpetrators of the incident is unlawful.
4. An order of injunction restraining the Defendants and their agents from implementing any plan to carry out any enumeration in preparation for the 'urban renewal' as non-conformity to the requirements under international human rights law would lead to further violation of the plaintiffs guaranteed human rights.
5. An order directing the Defendants and their agents to promote, respect, secure, fulfil and ensure the rights of the 2nd-11th plaintiffs previously listed.
6. An order directing the Defendants and their agents to pay adequate monetary compensation in the sum of $100,000,000 (one hundred million dollars) to the plaintiffs for violation of their rights and to provide other forms of reparation which may take the form of restitution, satisfaction or guarantees of non-repetition ('Case 3').

SERAP did not ask for a declaration from the court to pronounce the 'urban renewal' project as inimical to the protection of the right to shelter and the right to environment of the Bundu Ama people. Instead, SERAP sought an injunction to restrain the defendants from implementing the plan to carry out any demolition in preparation for the 'urban renewal' as non-conformity to the requirements under international human rights law would lead to further violation of the peoples' guaranteed human rights. As in the common law systems (such as Nigeria's), the court is likened to an umpire, she will not add to a claim or descend into the case between both parties; here also, the ECOWAS Court worked only with the application brought before her. SERAP's claim focused on the civil and political rights of the people to assembly, association, dignity, consultation and a compensation for arbitrary abuses suffered.

While the applicable human rights law of the Court (the ACHPR) does not have a specific provision on the right to 'housing' or 'shelter', it is inferred from a combination of several articles of the ACHPR such as articles 14, 16 and 18 which provides for the right to enjoy the best attainable state of mental and physical health; the right to property; and the protection of family life, respectively (which in interpretation extends to the protection of family shelter from destruction). This corollary linkage and intersection of the three (3) ACHPR provisions to establish the socioeconomic right to shelter under the ACHPR are not new. The African Commission had interpreted and established this nexus in 2001 (Communication 155/96). Through the Commission's communication on SERAC and CESR, the African Commission underscored two elements for realising the right to housing under the Charter: first, that state parties should not forcibly evict people from their houses and second, that state parties should not obstruct the efforts by individuals and communities to rebuild lost homes: 'The right to housing goes beyond having a roof over one's head. It extends to embody the individual's right to be let alone and live in peace-whether under a roof or not' (para 61). Any obstruction to the enjoyment of the contents of the right to housing therefore is a violation of the ACHPR.

The right to adequate shelter and housing is protected by article 17 of the ICCPR, article 11 of the ICESCR, article 14(2) of CEDAW, and articles 16(1) and 27(4) of the CRC. Nigeria has ratified all of the above-cited human rights treaties. The UN Committee on Economic, Social and Cultural Rights, in its General Comment No 4, stated that the right to housing should be interpreted broadly beyond a structure, and that instances of forced eviction are *prima facie* incompatible with the requirements of the ICCPR (CESCR, General Comment No 4, Right to Adequate Housing, 13/12/91, para 6, 7). The State must refrain from forced evictions and ensure that the law is enforced against its agents or third parties who carry out forced evictions (para 8).

The ECOWAS Court did not leverage on any of the above standards to protect and advance the shelter and environmental rights of the people of Bundu Ama. What the Court then does in this case (and uniquely so since the plaintiffs did not institute this action as a socioeconomic rights issue) is to award equitable compensation to the victims by taking into consideration all the events including the injuries, distress and the loss they may have incurred from being out of work or employment. The right to work is clearly a socioeconomic right and it is categorically provided for under the ACHPR in Article 15. An award of equitable compensation to the victims is a socioeconomic justice reparation. The Court first ordered compensation of five hundred thousand naira (500, 000) to each of the 10 plaintiffs (2nd to 11th) for the violation of their rights to assembly. It also awarded three million naira (3, 000, 000), two million naira (2, 000, 000) and one million naira (1,000, 000), respectively, to the plaintiffs who had suffered various socioeconomic injustices during the incident at issue here.

The ECOWAS Court noted that the 'urban renewal' objective by the government which would clearly alter the environmental and socioeconomic rights of the poor communities which lived by the waterfront, even though with good intentions towards 'development' still needed to conform to requirements of IHRL ('Case 3', para 78–79).

The ECOWAS Court used this case to emphasise that it is not subject to any domestic 'stand-still' by articulating its unique jurisdiction and mandate as a court of first and direct recourse when it comes to human rights. The defendant had claimed that the current case was an abuse of court process, being similar to a suit pending before the National Court. The ECOWAS Court rejected this claim by holding thus:

> [T]his Court has stressed that its jurisdiction cannot be in doubt once the facts adduced are related to human rights violation... The mere allegation that there has been a violation of human rights in the territory of a Member State is sufficient *prima facie* to justify the jurisdiction of the Court... The Community Court of Justice cannot give up its jurisdiction in favour of a domestic court.... (paras 71, 72, 74)

The ECOWAS Court had earlier held in the case of *Valentine Ayika v. Republic of Liberia* (ECW/CCJ/APP/07/11) that the pendency of a suit before a domestic court cannot oust its jurisdiction to determine a case of an alleged human rights violation. This is not the case with some other sub-regional adjudicatory systems which require the exhaustion of domestic remedies before approaching them. For example, under article 15(2) of the Protocol on the Southern African Development Community (SADC) Tribunal, provision is made that no person may bring an action against a Member State unless he or she has exhausted all available remedies or is unable to proceed under the domestic jurisdiction. The European Convention on Human Rights and Fundamental Freedoms of 1950 (the European Convention) provides, in article 26, that the European Commission of Human Rights 'may only deal with a matter after all domestic remedies have been exhausted, according to the generally recognized rules of international law'. Even the ACHPR provides, in article 50, that the African Commission can only deal with a matter submitted to it after making sure that all local remedies, if they exist, have been exhausted, unless it is obvious to the African Commission that the procedure of achieving the remedies would have been unduly prolonged.

A remarkable point made by the ECOWAS Court in this case is the emphasis that NGOs as activist forces have been the most active players in advancing justice causes within the framework of the ACHPR. As referenced in the judgement of 'Case 3', the ECOWAS Court held that the Court must show respect to NGOs who have been lodging complaints 'on behalf of individuals, who for any reasons, are deprived of means to have access to justice' ('Case 3' para 59). The Court took two (2) of the pages of the decision to affirm this point and to counter the defendant's objection to the plaintiff's standing to sue. By citing the previous SERAP case as precedent ('Case 2'), the Court held that an NGO may enjoy standing to file a complaint (or even join one) even when they have not been directly affected by the violation complained of. Quoting the presiding Justice B.M. Ramos:

> In the African context and in the framework of the African Charter... it is worthy to note that since inception, the African Commission on Human and Peoples' Rights has not been raising any objection to Non-governmental organizations standing to lodge complaints on behalf of individuals... As recognized by the doctrine, *"Although the African Charter in Article 55, by referring to communications other than those State Parties' does not specifically identify or recognize the role of NGOs in the filing of complaints regarding human rights violations, in practice the complaints procedure before the Commission has been used mainly by NGOs who have filed complaints on behalf of individuals or groups alleging violation of human and peoples' rights enshrined in the African Charter"-* **The African Charter on Human and People's Rights, The System in Practice 1986-2000, page 257.** The same favourable approach to the NGO's standing to lodge complaints for human rights violations, even when they are not direct victims, can be found in Rule 33, Section 1, paragraph (d) of the African Court on Human and Peoples' Rights Rules. (para 60)

The ECOWAS Court recognises the struggles, pursuits and contribution made by activist forces (especially NGOs) who have for many years worked hard to advance human rights in the sub-region and the continent. NGOs have been 'brokering and facilitating the 'correspondence' of human rights awareness and the reliance of human rights norms' at the level of the African Commission, the ECOWAS Court and within Nigeria (Okafor 2007, 251).

5   FROM THE SUB-REGIONAL TO THE LOCAL—THE CORRESPONDENCE OF HUMAN RIGHTS AND SOCIAL JUSTICE NORMS

Okafor's quasi-constructivist account emphasises the role of norms in the formation of the characteristics and interests of actors but he agrees with

Sikkink's theory on the effectiveness of International Human Rights Institutions (IHI Effectiveness) that local or international networks can be influential within states because they can contribute to a 'reformulation in the understandings of a human rights discourse' especially at opportune moments when conventional or 'traditional understandings of sovereignty and national interest' are interrogated by international events (Finnemore and Sikkink 1998). The strands of judicial, executive and legislative alterations to environmental and socioeconomic issues in Nigeria did not occur by happenstance but spiked at the same time when the barometer for socioeconomic and environmental justice was reading at a high pressure both internationally and sub-regionally. Activist forces leveraged on the opportunity and pursued their causes or supported same depending on their activist roles, e.g. as individuals, media practitioners, lawyers, funders or NGOs.

What may have started with grassroots activism by individuals in local Nigerian villages grew into several coordinated meetings with other local activist forces across states of the federation. These activist forces, comprising mostly of CSAs, became aware of justice struggles around the world and gained human rights-consciousness from the political and socioeconomic realties around them at the time. Through workshops, town hall meetings and seminars, the virtual network of these activist forces in Nigeria grew stronger and they began to engage with other activist forces from the West. With varied forms of activism (some succeeded, and some did not), some of these activist forces decided to submit a complaint to the African Commission which was at the time 'ripe' to deliberate on environmental justice causes (SERAC and their Western counterpart, CESR instituted the communication before the African Commission). The result was ground-breaking: the African Commission held Nigeria liable for environmental and socioeconomic injustice in the Niger Delta of Nigeria. This 'win' made many scores around advocacy spaces, courts, media institutions and even academia. The situation in the Niger Delta, however, remained with 'no progress'.

Several years later, some activist forces, also in their 'resistance character', and what can be described as a no-giving-up attitude leveraged on the unique jurisdiction of the ECOWAS Court to institute an action (Okafor 2007, 3). A local activist NGO represented the people of the Niger Delta region, and then, the foreign activists they engaged with filed amicus curiae brief in support of the claim before the court. Worthy of note is the 'engagement' and allyship between local and foreign activist forces on both occasions and in both levels of adjudication. At the African Commission, SERAC (local) and CESR (foreign) activist forces both filed the complaint before the African Commission, and at the ECOWAS Court, SERAP (local) and Amnesty International (foreign) filed the action and amicus brief to support the plaintiffs, respectively. After several cases before the court recognising environmental and socioeconomic justice, the struggles so far may not have refurbished the dwelling spaces of Niger-Deltans, or ordained the people with the socioeconomic and environmental justice entitlements they deserve, but this process has effectuated normative changes in key domestic institutions in Nigeria by effecting action at the level of the Nigerian Legislature, Executive and Judiciary. The struggles so far may not have resulted into a constitutional amendment in Nigeria (to make all socioeconomic and environmental rights as justiciable as the civil and political rights), and neither had it facilitated a codification of the ICESCR in a separate single domestic document. However, the environmental and socioeconomic justice struggles analysed in this work have given credence to Okafor's theory of 'correspondence' in IHRL which demonstrates a need for a modest expansion of the conventional 'compliance' optics through which international human rights institutions are assessed.

For the first time (as analysed in 'Case 1'), the Nigerian government was held responsible by a supranational adjudicatory body for its non-fulfilment of the right to primary education of its people. The ECOWAS Court dismissed the 'excuse' of non-justiciability of the right to primary education and affirmed the justiciability of socioeconomic rights (including the right to education) in West Africa and Nigeria (despite domestic constitutional limitations). This was the first time that a court pronounced education in Nigeria as an enforceable and fundamental human right. In 'Case 2', the ECOWAS Court also held that by Nigeria agreeing to the Protocol of the Court, the state is bound by the human rights law 'contained in international instruments, with no exception whatsoever' (Judgement of 'Case 2' at para 27). The Court emphasised that the Nigerian government has a duty to ensure that the activities (by any other person, including corporations) within its jurisdiction and control do not cause damage to the environment and the people. A rationale the court provided for this decision included the Court's description of the environment as representing the living space, the quality of life and the very health of human beings, including generations unborn. Therefore, according to the Court, the Niger Delta must be considered as an indivisible whole, comprising the biotic and abiotic natural resources, notably air, water, land, fauna and flora and the environmental and socioeconomic interaction between these factors. In awarding damages for human rights violations, the ECOWAS Court in 'Case 3' awarded equitable compensation to the victims by taking into consideration all the events that affected the victims, including the injuries, distress and the loss they may have incurred from being out of work or employment as the latter amounts to an infringement of their socioeconomic right to occupation.

The unprecedented outcomes from the ECOWAS Court in 'Case 1', 'Case 2' and 'Case 3' were facilitated by SERAP's action before the Court in its pursuit for environmental and socioeconomic justice in Nigeria. The progressive prospects and the unique jurisdiction of the ECOWAS Court attracted SERAP to approach the court with its pursuits of challenging environmental and socioeconomic injustice in Nigeria, thereby initiating the three cases analysed in this work. As an open access court, SERAP was able to approach the Court first-hand (the Court grants direct access to individuals as well as activist forces in representative capacity, to challenge human right violations in any of the Member States). Also, with the funding SERAP receives as an NGO, and their support and strategy from their 'networks', including their competence in litigation, all of these components contributed towards the outcome of the three (3) cases analysed in this chapter.

The case studies in this work highlighted some successes, but also underscored some challenges (e.g. the Court's indisposition to address 'Case 3' from a 'right to shelter' or a 'right to housing' perspective). Analysing these cases also provided insight on the practice and procedures of the ECOWAS Court and how its normative influence has supported SERAP's pursuit of environmental and socioeconomic justice in West Africa.

6   CONCLUSION

This chapter evidences the pursuits and struggles of some activist forces who have in some ways used the ideas, spaces, networks, knowledge and the strategies available to them to advance human rights and social justice causes from the ECOWAS Court. More specifically, this chapter features an activist force (SERAP, an NGO) who has worked within and with the jurisdiction of the ECOWAS Court, a sub-regional international court in West Africa, to pursue environmental and socioeconomic justice in Nigeria, especially for the benefit of poor and marginalised people/communities like the Niger Delta region of Nigeria where natural resource extraction has been largely unfavourable to the well-being and development of the people. Through the analysis of three important cases from the court, this chapter explored the conceptions and standards of environmental justice and socioeconomic rights within the ambit of three (3) levels of human rights law, viz. international human rights law, regional human rights law (in Africa) and the domestic laws of Nigeria, albeit with major focus on the African regional system. This is because the African Charter on Human and Peoples Rights is considered a primary 'human rights treaty' of the ECOWAS Court. The analysis of the decisions from the ECOWAS Court in this work has highlighted the jurisprudence from the Court, and its successes in the relevant respects, and also underscored some challenges and proffered some ideas regarding the pursuit of environmental and socioeconomic justice in Nigeria (and West Africa). Analysing these cases also provided insight on the practice and procedures of the ECOWAS Court and how its modest but significant normative influence supported the pursuit of human rights and social justice in Nigeria.

This chapter contributes to the legal literature on regional human rights systems in Africa. By deploying *Okafor*'s theory of 'correspondence', the work also affirms and exemplifies the quasi-constructivist model for estimating the extent of the 'internalisation' of human rights norms (without abandoning the regular 'compliance' model for assessing the fulfilment by states of their international human rights law obligations). This work shows the broad conditions of how the ECOWAS Court (as a sub-regional IHI 'International Human Rights Institution') modestly helped in shaping and/or reshaping the 'logics of appropriateness, conceptions of interest, and self-understandings' around environmental and socioeconomic justice in Nigeria.

Bibliography

Adeola, Romola. *Development-induced Displacement and Human Rights in Africa: The Kampala Convention*. Routledge, 2021.

African Charter on Human and People's Rights (Ratification and Enforcement Act) Cap A9, LFN 2004.

African Charter on Human and Peoples' Rights, 1997.

African Commission on Human and Peoples' Rights, ACHPR Communications *25/89*.

African Commission on Human and Peoples' Rights, ACHPR Communications *47/90*.

African Commission on Human and Peoples' Rights, ACHPR Communications *56/91*.

African Commission on Human and Peoples' Rights, ACHPR Communications *100/93*.

African Commission on Human and Peoples' Rights, Decision on communication of The Social and Economic Rights Action Center and the Center for Economic and Social Rights/Nigeria (155/96), para 9. Decision made at the 30th Ordinary Session of the African Commission of Human and Peoples' Rights (Banjul, 13–27 October 2001), ACHPR, http://www.achpr.org/communications/decision/155.96/>.

Alhaji Tidjani v. Federal Republic of Nigeria [ECW/CCJ/APP/01/06].

Amnesty International. "No Progress: An Evaluation of the Implementation of UNEP's Environmental Assessment of Ogoniland, Three Years On." (2014).

Anaba Eze, "The SERAP v Nigeria Case" *Nigerian Chronicles: Media Activists in the News* (2016), 3.

CESCR, General Comment No. 4, *The Right to Adequate Housing*, 13/12/91.

Compulsory Free and Universal Basic Education Act, 2004

Constitution of the Federal Republic of Nigeria, 1999 (as amended).

Corrupt Practices and other Related Offences Act, 2000.

Doron Roy & Toyin Falola, *Ken Saro-Wiwa*. Ohio University Press, 2016.

ECOWAS Community Court of Justice Protocol A/P.1/7/91.

ECOWAS Court Practice Direction, 2012.

ECOWAS Court Rules of Procedure, 2002.

ECOWAS Protocol on Democracy and Good Governance A/SP1/12/01.

ECOWAS Revised Treaty.

ECOWAS Supplementary Protocol A/SP.1/01/05.

Environmental Impact Assessment Act (EIA Act) Cap E12 LFN 2004.

Federal Ministry of Environment, "Ogoniland: Background" http://environment.gov.ng/index.php/ogoni.

Finnemore Martha and Sikkink Katherine, "International Norm Dynamics and Political Change" (1998) 52 International Organisation.

Grant, Evadne, "International courts and environmental human rights: re-imagining adjudicative paradigms." *Research handbook on human rights and the environment*. Edward Elgar Publishing, 2015.

Ibeanu Okechukwu, "Insurgent Civil Society and Democracy in Nigeria: Ogoni Encounters with the State, 1990 – 1998" *Research Report for ICSAG Programme of the Centre for Research and Documentation (CRD), 1999, Kano.*

Ibeanu, Okechukwu, "Civil Society and Conflict Management in the Niger Delta" (2006) CLEEN Foundation Monograph Series (2), 13.

Independent, "Agency Report: ECOWAS Court Says It Recorded Highest Number Of Decisions In 2019 Since Inception" (13 January 2020), https://www.ind ependent.ng/ecowas-court-says-it-recorded-highest-number-of-decisions-in-2019-since-inception/

Joseph Onyekwere, "Court Declares Free Compulsory Education Enforceable Right" *The Guardian* (2 March 2017) https://guardian.ng/news/court-declares-free-com pulsory-education-enforceable-right/.

Morka Felix, "A Place to Live: Resisting Evictions in Ijora-Badia, Nigeria" *How African Activists Reclaim Human Rights to Challenge Global Poverty* ed. Lucie E. White & Jeremy Perelman (Stanford University Press: 2014), 66.

Nnimmo Bassey, "Economic Social and Cultural Rights in the Niger Delta" *The Guardian* (12 June 2017), 34.

Obi Cyril and Rustad Siri Aas, Oil and Insurgency in the Niger Delta: Managing the Complex Politics of Petro-violence (Africa Now, 2011).

Obi Cyril, "Oil extraction, dispossession, resistance, and conflict in Nigeria's oil-rich Niger Delta" (2010) 30 Canadian Journal of Development Studies, 219.

Okafor Chinedu Obiora, The African Human Rights System, Activist Forces and International Institutions (Cambridge: Cambridge University Press, 2007).

Saro Wiwa Jr Ken, "We Inherited a Fight: Sweat, Blood and Oil" The Ogoni Chronicles (2009), 2.

SERAP & 10 Ors. v. Federal Republic of Nigeria & 4 Ors [ECW/CCJ/JUD/16/14] ("Case 3").

SERAP Online, "Who We Are" Online: < http://serap-nigeria.org/who-we-are/>.SERAP v. President of Nigeria & 8 Ors [ECW/CCJ/JUD/18/12] ("Case 2").

SERAP v. President of Nigeria & Anor [ECW/CCJ/JUD/07/10] ("Case 1").

SERAP, "Who We Are" http://serap-nigeria.org/who-we-are/.

SERAP, "The Socio-Economic Rights and Accountability Project" (2017).

The Goldman Environmental Prize, "Ken Saro-Wiwa 1995 Goldman Prize Recipient" Online: Goldman Prize http://www.goldmanprize.org/recipient/ken-saro-wiwa/.

Tope Alabi, "Court declares Free Basic Education An Enforceable Right" Informa-tion Nigeria (3 March 2017), http://www.informationng.com/2017/03/court-declares-free-basic-education-enforceable-right.html.

UN Cartagena Protocol on Biosafety, 2000.

UN Committee on Economic Social and Cultural Rights, General Comment No 14 on the Right to the Highest Attainable Standard of Health (art 12) adopted at the Twenty-second Session of the Committee on Economic, Social and Cultural Rights, on 11 August 2000 (Contained in Document E/C.12/2000/4).

UN OHCHR released a fact sheet on forced evictions in 2014 (*UN Habitat Fact Sheet No. 25/Rev.1*).

UNDP, Government of Nigeria, "Niger Delta Biodiversity Project" UNDP Project Document http://www.undp.org/content/dam/undp/documents/pro jects/NGA/.

UNDRIP, Free Prior and Informed Consent https://www.un.org/development/desa/indigenouspeoples/publications/2016/10/free-prior-and-informed-consent-an-indigenous-peoples-right-and-a-good-practice-for-local-communities-fao/.

UNEP Environmental Assessment of Ogoniland, online: Shell http://www.shell.com.ng/sustainability/environment/unep-environmental-assessmen-of-ogoniland.html.

UNHRC, Report of the Special Rapporteur on adequate housing as a component of the right to an adequate standard of living, and on the right to non-discrimination in this context, Miloon Kothari UN doc. A/HRC/7/16 (13 February 2008), para.4.

UNICEF information sheet, "Girls' Education, Nigeria Country Office" (September 2007) <http://www.unicef.org/wcaro/WCARO_Nigeria_Factsheets_GirlsEducation.pd>

United Nations Declaration of the Rights of Indigenous Peoples, 2007.

United Nations Convention on the Elimination of All Forms of Discrimination against Women, 1979.

United Nations Convention on the Rights of the Child, 1989.

United Nations Framework Convention on Climate Change, 1994.

United Nations Guiding Principles on Business and Human Rights, 2011.

United Nations International Convention on Oil Pollution Preparedness, Response and Cooperation, 1990.

United Nations International Covenant on Civil and Political Rights, 1966... 54, 55, 62, 65

United Nations International Covenant on Economic Social and Cultural Rights, 1966.

Universal Declaration of Human Rights, 1948.

UPR, World Evangelical Alliance and Socio-Economic Rights and Accountability Project, "Universal Periodic Review 17th Session of the UPR Working Group (Nigeria)" *Joint Stakeholders Report*. http://www.worldevangelicals.org.

Valentine Ayika v. Republic of Liberia, [ECW/CCJ/APP/07/11].

Vienna Declaration and Programme of Action (VDPA), 1993. WCHR, Vienna, 14 – 25 June 1993, UN Doc A/CONF157/24 (Part I) at 20 (1993), 32 ILM 1661 (1993).

Wikina Ebenezar, "Oil in our Creeks - A Tale of Two Oil Spills: A Story of Rage and Resilience in Ogoniland" (October 2017), *Contrast VR and AJE Online*, http://contrastvr.com/oilinourcreeks/.

CHAPTER 12

Contemporary Developments in Human and Peoples' Rights Protection in Africa: Insights from the African Union

Rhuks Temitope Ako and John Gbodi Ikubaje

1 INTRODUCTION

The Universal Declaration of Human Rights (UDHR) of 1948 that enshrines the universality of human rights principles positively influenced the development of human rights globally. The inherent contribution of the UDHR to human rights is evident in the way that regional and national systems expressly draw inspiration from it in the course of the development of their human rights jurisprudence, laws, policies and institutions. This is not different in Africa where the human rights system also took inspiration from the UDHR. Notably though, Africa has made worthy contributions to international human rights jurisprudence particularly with provisions on 'peoples rights' in addition to 'human rights' as well as the recognition of third-generation rights ahead of other regional systems.

Nevertheless, the state of human rights on the continent remains questionable, especially as focus still remains essentially based on 'cause and effect'. In other words, human rights issues are still primarily within the myopic lenses of abuse and remedies. This perspective tends to limit discussions on human rights in Africa to the enforcement and remedy gaps and considerably less on other factors that highlight positive developments that build on the worthy contributions the continent has made to human rights jurisprudence

R. T. Ako (✉) · J. G. Ikubaje
African Union Commission, Addis Ababa, Ethiopia
e-mail: rhuksako@gmail.com

© The Author(s), under exclusive license to Springer Nature Switzerland AG 2022
A. Adeola and M. W. Mutua (eds.), *The Palgrave Handbook of Democracy, Governance and Justice in Africa*,
https://doi.org/10.1007/978-3-030-74014-6_12

221

globally. These challenges, including poor implementation of relevant Shared Values Instruments, lack of sanctions against non-adherence and compliance with human rights values, norms and decisions by the states; weak human rights institutions and civil society organisations coupled with poor coordination within the African human rights system undoubtedly, hinder the optimal promotion and protection of human and peoples' rights in Africa. These shortcomings not only negatively impact the modest outlook of human rights protection and promotion on the continent, they also portend a serious hindrance to the realisation of African development goals such as Agenda 2063 that aims to promote the general well-being of Africa and its citizens.

This notwithstanding, the African Union (AU) continues to record progress in the advancement of the human rights. This chapter aims to bring to the fore the AU's role and contributions to 'mainstreaming' human rights not only to underscore its governance agenda but also with regard to conflict prevention and post-conflict stabilisation including transitional justice. These initiatives are evidence that the AU not only realises the nexus between and among human rights, conflicts (prevention and resolution) and development, but it also has adopted the human rights-based approach to them. This builds on the trajectory of innovation that the African Charter brought to the global human rights jurisprudence while providing member states the *raison d'etre* to (re)conceptualise human rights nationally, especially integrating human rights-based approaches to governance. Indeed, as experiences across the continent have revealed, human rights violations can be a cause, symptom and/or consequence of violent conflict.

In discussing contemporary developments in the human rights landscape, this chapter is divided into five parts including this introduction section. The following section discusses the evolution of human rights in Africa. By tracing the evolution of human and peoples' rights and highlighting major transformations in the areas of normative and institution development in Africa, the chapter aims to assess the state of human rights jurisprudence and practice on the continent. It advances the position that human rights considerations should extend beyond institutional 'promotion and protection' responsibilities. It argues that a human rights-based approach to organisational programming, again, with specific reference to the AU, contributes to, and has the potential to, advance the cause of human rights on the continent.

2   Evolution of Human Rights in Africa

The official commitment of Africa to human rights promotion and protection dates back to 1963 when the Charter of the Organisation of African Unity (OAU)—the AU's predecessor—was adopted in Addis Ababa, Ethiopia (Article II (e) of the OAU Charter). However, the acknowledgement of the importance of having human rights values was appreciated before this time. For instance, in the early 1960s, the Congress of African Jurists that had been advocating for a continental human rights protection mechanism had also conceived of a document that would establish it. The momentum this effort garnered gained the attention of the Assembly of Heads of States and Government of the OAU, and in 1979, when they met in Monrovia, Liberia, the Secretary-General of the organisation was requested to convene a committee of experts to draft a regional human rights instrument for Africa (Centre for Human Rights 2016, 2).

The outcome document of the Committee of Experts as reviewed and finalised by the OAU organs and subsequently adopted by the OAU Assembly is the African Charter on Human and Peoples' Rights (African Charter). It is noteworthy that the adoption of the African Charter was not simply the hijack of a process of the African jurists by the OAU but one that was in tandem with the provisions of the organisation's Charter: specifically, the Preamble as well as articles 2(1)(d) and (e). The Preamble made express reference to the Heads of States and Governments conviction of the 'inalienable right of all people to control their own destiny...the fact that freedom, equality, justice and dignity are essential objectives for the achievement of the legitimate aspirations of the African peoples' as well as the role of the Charter of the United Nations (UN) and the UDHR to provide 'a solid foundation for peaceful and positive cooperation among States'. The latter provision, restated in article 2(1)(e), references the UDHR as 'the' underpinning instrument on human rights protection and promotion. The provision of sub-section (d) on the eradication of all forms of colonialism from Africa restates the rights of African people to political self-determination and self-governance. In retrospect, this provision is fundamental to the evolution of the 'African' conception of human rights as expressed in the African Charter that recognised the third-generation rights as well as the rights of 'peoples' rather than simply rehashing the existing global rhetoric on human rights.

Arguably, achieving political independence provided a sound foundation to conceptualise post-independence life in Africa in accordance with fundamental values that were inherent in their cultures and traditions that predated colonisation. One of these was the recognition of the right of 'peoples' (collective socio, political and economic rights) in addition to that of the individual. Undoubtedly, the recognition and importance of 'peoples'—comprised of the individual, nuclear family, extended family and community with shared ancestry—are common features of African societies that predate the colonial enterprise. Indeed, for centuries, Africans have practised collective lifestyles wherein properties such as land, houses, farm and traditional titles are communally and/or family owned and managed. In thinking of human rights at a time when colonial authority was waning, it was only natural to insert African ideologies to the emerging normative frameworks. In a nutshell, the adoption of the African Charter was an operationalisation of the OAU Charter that depicted a clear commitment of the OAU Member States to pursue genuinely Afrocentric human rights.

This position runs contrary to some earlier expressed opinions wherein scholars have made the argument that the dearth of express human rights provisions in the OAU Charter was a reflection of the diminutive concerns for and commitment to human rights in Africa at the time (Murrah 2004, 15–20 and Mathews 1984, 49–84). Unarguably, as these authors contend, the OAU in 1963 was more concerned with non-interference in internal affairs of member states, sovereign equality of states, as well as the fight against neo-colonialism and the promotion of self-determination in the context of the nation-state. In their views, the concern of the OAU was focused on the protection of state with issues such as self-determination in the context of colonisation and apartheid in South Africa and not individual rights per se.

While the situation at the time was such that political self-determination was a priority for the OAU and African countries, the conclusion that this was to the detriment and exclusion of the recognition and pursuit of human rights is implausible. Rather, as Aidoo (1992, 703–715) argued, self-determination in Africa during the colonial era marked the beginning of the continent's democratic entitlements while the anti-colonial movement was indeed a struggle for democracy and human rights. There is no gainsaying the fact that as a continent, Africa's priority was to be free from colonial rule. However, to suggest that faced with this priority, there was little or no thought to its citizens' human rights appears far-fetched, especially as the African Charter made express reference to the Charter of the UN and the UDHR, two of the foremost reference instruments regarding human rights.

Indeed, the collective rights of African citizens to political self-determination and self-governance, coupled with the fight against colonialism and apartheid, were part of the justifications for the official codification and appreciation of collective peoples' rights in Africa at the continental level. This human rights development trend has impacted and is still impacting human rights transformation across the globe to date. For example, Africa has introduced a new term and practice 'the peoples' rights' into the global human rights lexicon and this development is today a reference point for comparative lessons and practices in other continents, particularly in Asia. One such example is the ongoing cooperation between the AU and China in the area of the promotion and protection of human and peoples' rights, which comes as a surprise to many. However, the AU and China have been co-hosting an annual Dialogue on Human and Peoples' Rights since 2015 at the request of China, upon the realisation that China and Africa share similar socio-cultural and traditional collective practices and to mutually benefit from each other in the area of the promotion and protection of peoples' rights, in particular as regards to human rights and development and the fight against corruption (Reports of the First and Second African Union and China Human Rights Dialogues, 2016 and 2017).

3 Normative and Institutional Developments of Human and Peoples' Rights in Africa

The normative and institutional frameworks regulating human and peoples' rights in Africa have developed significantly. Broadly, there are two primary factors that precipitated the development of human rights norms and institutions in Africa. The first was the collective conviction of African leaders to promote a vibrant continental human and peoples' rights system that also benefitted from the UN's encouragement that regional human rights mechanisms be established across the globe. Second was the increasing role of civil society and non-governmental organisations (NGOs) as societal watchdogs, especially in lobbying for human and peoples' rights defence, promotion and protection (Centre for Human Rights 2016, 2–6).

Regarding the first element, the consistency in the deliberations, policy decisions and adoption of treaties relevant to human and peoples' rights by the Assemblies of the Heads of State and Government of the OAU/AU since 1963 till date is testamentary to their desire to have a vibrant continental human rights system. For instance, the transformation of the organisation from the OAU to the AU provided an opportunity to emphasise the continuing importance of human rights. While article 3(e) of the AU Constitutive Act re-emphasised the importance of the UN Charter and UDHR, Article 3(h) reinforced the African collective rights. The latter provision states that AU Member States would promote and protect human and peoples' rights in accordance with the African Charter and other relevant human rights instruments. Read concurrently, it is evident that the African leaders were intent on promoting the entire gamut of human rights including the Western notions that emphasise individual civil, political and cultural rights and the African concept that also includes collective socio-economic rights including the rights to the environment and development.

There are some noteworthy developments regarding the appreciation of Africa's human rights normative evolution. First is, as noted previously, the clear indication that African leaders were ready to commit to the human rights agenda at the continental level. In this respect, the African Charter that was adopted by the Assembly on 28 June 1981 came into force on 21 October 1986 and, by 1999, had been ratified by all member states.[1] This is a laudable achievement for Africa and the AU where treaty ratification among its member states has been, and remains, a significant challenge. Second is the fact that the AU Constitutive Act has more provisions on governance and human rights than the OAU Charter. While this may seem to be of little significance, at a theoretical level it does address some of the criticisms against the earlier OAU Charter with regard to having too few human rights provisions. This was for some a reflection that the organisation did not prioritise human rights issues.

---

[1] Except for Morocco that re-joined the AU in 2018.

The adoption of Agenda 2063 (the long-term socio-economic and political development framework), by the AU, is another important milestone by the organisation in the advancement of human and peoples' rights across the continent. Agenda 2063 was developed to galvanise and unite in action all Africans, including those in the diaspora, around the common vision of a peaceful, integrated and prosperous Africa. As an overarching framework, it provides internal coherence to Africa's various frameworks and plans adopted by the OAU and AU as well as providing the normative linkages and coordination of Africa's national and regional frameworks into a common continental transformative drive. Notably, human and peoples' rights is a cut-crossing issue apparent throughout the document. However, Aspiration Three specifically refers to the promotion and protection of human and peoples' rights provided for 'an Africa of good governance, democracy, respect for human rights, justice and the rule of law', while Aspiration Six expressly refers to the promotion of women, youth and children's rights and empowerments.

The AU's commitment to the promotion of women, youth and children's rights is more evident in the AU Assembly's declaration of 2016 as the African year of human rights with emphasis on the rights of women. The aim of this declaration was to assess the past and present commitments of Africa to human and peoples' rights with the aim of appreciating progress made and re-strategising to overcome areas of failure. Moreover, the AU Assembly in July 2016 made a Decade Declaration on human and peoples' rights in Africa and called on all AU organs with a human rights mandate to facilitate the development of a Ten-Year Human and Peoples' Rights Action Plan for Africa. This call is noteworthy particularly when considered on the backdrop of the fact the Year 2016 marked the expiration of the AU Human Rights Strategy. In essence, the AU did not intend for a gap to exist in the recognition of its prioritisation of human and peoples' rights on the continent, even if only from a normative perspective. In essence, the Decade Declaration aims at strengthening the African human rights system and deepening the culture of democracy and human rights in conformity with the objectives of the Constitutive Act of the AU, the African Charter and other relevant African Shared Values instruments, including Agenda 2063, which is expected to shape the AU's work for the next five decades. These normative developments arguably underlie the contemporary idea to mainstream human rights into programming at the continental level.

In addition to the above instruments, there is a plethora of AU instruments that implicate the promotion and protection of human and peoples' rights at the continental and regional levels as well as in AU Member States. Rights implicated by these instruments include civil and political rights, rights of women and children, issues of rights bordering on good governance as enshrined in the Protocol to the African Charter on the Rights of Women in Africa (2003); African Convention on Preventing and Combating Corruption (2003); Africa Charter on Democracy, Election and Governance (2007) (ACDEG); the African Charter on Principle and Practice of Public Service and Administration (2011); and the African Charter on Principles and Practice of Decentralization, Local Governance and Local Development (2014) among others. For example, while the primary aim of the ACDEG is to deepen electoral and democratic governance in Africa, issues of human and peoples' rights are comprehensively and aptly catered for in the instrument. Indeed, reference is made to issues of rights fifteen times; these include respect for human and peoples' rights as one of the AU cardinal principles; respect for the roles and duties of the African Commission on Human and Peoples' Rights and the African Court of Human and Peoples Rights, respectively; respect for corporate entity's rights-political party's rights; respect for women, ethnic minorities, cultural, religious and diversity rights in political processes; etc.

From the above discussion, it is evident that the AU, from the early criticism of having inadequate human rights provisions appearing in continental normative frameworks, has developed a robust set of norms relating to the recognition, protection and promotion of human and peoples' rights. These norms have also directly contributed to the evolution of institutions to advance the cause of human and peoples' rights protection and promotion on the continent. The AU has adopted the following human and peoples' rights treaties leading to establishments of human rights institutions, namely the African Charter, establishing the African Commission on Human and Peoples Rights; the Protocol to the African Charter on the Establishment of an African Court on Human and Peoples' Rights (1998); and the African Charter on the Rights and Welfare of the Child (1990), establishing the African Committee of Experts on the Rights and Welfare of the Child.

These institutions have contributed to both the normative and jurisprudential development of human rights on the continent while impacting the lives of citizens. However, as noted previously, these institutions face fundamental challenges that have affected their optimal performances. Briefly, these include the weak political commitment of AU Member States to commit themselves to the implementation of human and peoples' rights, poor funding and weak institutional capacity to mention a few. Although AU Member States are often quick to voice support and engage in the rhetoric of acknowledging and prioritising human and peoples' rights, the rate of implementation remains relatively low. The situation is not much different with regard to decisions and recommendations taken by the AU organs and institutions with a human rights mandate. Unfortunately, the treaties and protocols that established some of these organs and institutions do not include appropriate mechanisms to follow-up on implementation of previous decisions and adequate enforcement mechanisms aimed at promoting compliance.

Regarding weak institutional capacity, the African Commission on Human and Peoples' Rights, the premier AU organ with a mandate on human and peoples' rights, exemplifies the situation. While the substantive staffing of the institution remains a problem 30 years on, the Commissioners continue to work on a part-time basis meeting only twice annually. This puts pressure on the institution to deliver on its core mandate while creating the impression in the eyes of the public that it does not do much. On the contrary, the Commission has made significant achievements including the development of jurisprudence and making concrete differences in individuals' lives through the various tools and mechanisms at its disposal including its article 58 procedure, urgent appeals or letters of appeal, fact-finding missions, state reporting and thematic and country resolutions. However, the challenges the institution faces greatly impact on its ability to deliver on its core mandate of human and peoples' rights protection and promotion.

In addition to these core human rights institutions, there are other organs of the AU that advance the cause of human rights. These include the African Union Commission (AUC); the African Union Peace and Security Council (AU-PSC); the African Union Advisory Board on Corruption (AU-ABC); the African Peer Review Mechanism (APRM); the Pan African Parliament (PAP); and the African Union Commission on International Law (AUCIL). In other words, in addition to their core mandates, these institutions are also expected, pursuant to the instruments that establish them, to promote and protect human and peoples' rights. The following section will highlight the complementary role that the AUC and the PSC, two organs of the AU, have played recently in promoting human and peoples' rights on the continent. Specifically, it discusses how both organs of the AU have contributed to the advancement of human and peoples' rights by promoting the mainstreaming of human rights into programming, especially at the AUC level. The role of the PSC is considered particularly to showcase how it encourages the integration of human rights into continent's peace and security agenda, an indication of the recognition that rights issues underscore peace and security.

4   New Developments on Human and Peoples Rights in Africa: Mainstreaming Human Rights into Au Programming

This section aims to highlight the roles and contributions of the AU to mainstream human rights into programming through its non-core human rights institutions with particular focus on the Assembly of Heads of States, the AUC and the PSC that are critical institutions to the evolution of norms and programming. It discusses some of the contemporary initiatives from these organs to achieve two broad purposes. First, to aver that human and peoples' rights remain high on the agenda in Africa despite the challenges that have hindered the constellation of the early signs of progress made on the continent. In particular, reference is made to the recognition of peoples' rights in addition to human rights as well as third-generation rights well ahead of the rest of the world. Second is to present an alternative model of assessing human rights in Africa beyond the 'abuse and remedy' framework.

The AU Assembly of Heads of State and Government adopted the 'African Union Ten-Year Action Plan on Human and Peoples' Rights' in 2016. The Plan, after it is finalised and adopted by the AU Assembly, will guide the future direction of the continent on human rights interventions. This long-term plan expectedly will guide the AU's human rights policy direction as well as influence the development of programmes and initiatives that will ensure that human rights issues are continuously integrated into the AU's engagements with member states and African citizens. With regard to the latter, the desire to rebrand the AU as an organisation of citizens will promote respect for human and peoples' rights at member states' level and also at the level of the individual. In the advancement of this decision, the AUC and all the other AU organs with a mandate on human and peoples' rights are currently working with the Pan Africa Lawyers Union (PALU) on the draft Plan.

In addition, the AU and the UN are developing a Human Rights Framework for Africa. The framework is the third in the series of the AU and UN Joint Partnership Agreement. The first framework focuses on 'Development' (effective implementation of the Africa Agenda 2063 and UN Agenda 2030), while the second places premium on the peace and security agenda of the two institutions in Africa. The Joint Framework Agreement, focusing on human rights, will mainstream the principles and practices of human and people's rights of the two institutions into one document, to among other things deepen the culture of human and peoples' rights in Africa. Although this third cardinal pillar of the partnership framework is tagged AU/UN human rights, the RECs and member states will play a primary role on its development and implementation.

The AU Assembly's adoption of the AU Transitional Justice Policy (AUTJP) is another significant development in Africa on human and peoples' rights. The policy adopted on 12 February 2019 during the 32nd Ordinary Session of the AU Assembly in Addis Ababa, Ethiopia, aims at providing guidance to the AU Member States emerging from violent conflict, war and repressive governance. It, among other things, offers guidelines on how to approach and entrench accountability, truth, justice and reconciliation in the aftermath of gross human rights violations in AU Member States. These issues which implicate human and peoples' rights have been appreciated at the Member State level with Gambia and Mali as well as Nigeria's North-East Initiative requesting for and utilising the AUTJP (prior to adoption by the AU Assembly) in support of their various transitional justice initiatives. The uptake from member states in this regard is evidence of the argument that mainstreaming human rights at the continental level can precipitate a theory of change among member states to appreciate human (and peoples') rights beyond the 'cause and effect' perspective.

Related to the AUTJP is the establishment of a new fund—the Africa Transitional Justice Legacy Fund (ATJLF)—primarily to support CSOs participation in transitional justice processes. Two USA-based foundations: the MacArthur and Well-Spring Foundations, established the fund following extensive consultations with stakeholders, including the African Union, ECOWAS and CSOs on the continent. The multi-year, multi-million-dollar fund will initially focus on the following seven West African countries: Cote d'Ivoire, Gambia, Guinea, Liberia, Mali, Nigeria and Sierra Leone and thereafter will be expanded to other countries of the continent. The AUC is finalising a Memorandum of Understanding with the ATJLF. Notably, ECOWAS is developing its transitional justice framework utilising, among other things, the AUTJP. This development further substantiates the argument that mainstreaming human rights into programming at the continental will have a positive spin-off effect on regional institutions as well as member states over time.

Also, the AU is also developing a continental policy on business and human rights based on the UN Guiding Principles on Business and Human Rights. Expectedly, the policy will support the newly adopted Africa Continental Free Trade Area (ACFTA) to entrench the culture of respect for human rights in business activities in Africa. The policy will integrate human and peoples' rights into the business environment to address issues including activities of international conglomerates and investors whose relationships with their host-communities have contributed to the cycle of violent conflicts in various parts of the continent.

Notably, human rights considerations are also being integrated into the peace and security arena. An example from the conflict prevention and (post)-conflict reconstruction and development is highlighted in particular. As noted earlier on, the link between human rights and conflict has been established, at least in theory. In practice, conflict prevention is being redefined to include human rights as an integral factor. In this regard, Conflict Prevention and Early Warning Division tasked with the primary mandate of detecting early signs of conflict on the continent based on data collection and analysis is adopting a human rights-based approach. Specifically, the Division in collaboration with the UN Office of the High Commissioner on Human Rights (OHCHR) and the World Bank Group has carried out extensive review of its working methodology to integrate a human rights-based approach to data (including collection, analysis and reporting). The analyses in the different reports from the Continental Early Warning Systems (CEWS) of CPEWD—including the horizon scanning report to the Peace and Security Council, Early Warning Reports, Conflict Vulnerability and Resilience Assessment (CSVRA) reports—now integrate human rights-based analysis. Furthermore, the Division is in the process of developing data responsibility guidelines to regulate data collection, storage and use. Furthermore, CPEWD has begun disseminating and training on this improved methodology to its partners (including RECs/RMs and CSOs) that feed into and/or use its early warning tools and databases to ensure that the human rights-based approach to data is understood and implemented.

With regard to conflict and post-conflict situations, the AUC recently adopted the methodology of deploying African human rights experts to countries that are experiencing or have recently experienced violent conflicts. The methodology is a specific example of mainstreaming human rights in conflict prevention and/or sustainable resolution. With Mali for example, the 353rd Meeting of the AU-PSC held on 25 January 2013 at the level of AU Assembly decided that both the AU and ECOWAS Commissions deploy, as quickly as possible, civilian observers to monitor the human rights situation in the liberated areas of Mali and to assist the Malian authorities to create the necessary conditions for lasting reconciliation among the different components its population, as well as for the consolidation of peace in the country. The monitors were to be deployed as part of AFISMA with support of the African Commission on Human and People's Rights (ACHPR). Notably, the decision underlined the first AU Human Rights Observation Mission in Africa. The deployment of human rights observers has since been institutionalised with the AU having trained and deployed human rights observers to CAR, Mali, Burundi, DRC, South Sudan and Somalia subsequently. The deployment of human rights observers in these particular circumstances is evidence that the AU recognises the nexus between human rights and conflicts on the one hand and the role human rights play in sustainable conflict mitigation/resolution. Similarly, observers were deployed to the Gambia following the political instability that emanated from the contested 2016 presidential elections. It is interesting that in this case, human rights observers were deployed following the diffusion of the stalemate and settling-in of the new government.

5   Conclusion

Africa's human rights jurisprudence has made considerable contributions to the global repertoire of rights protection; particularly, the recognition of third-generation and peoples' rights contained in the African Charter on Human and Peoples' Rights. However, the state of human rights on the continent has not matched the dynamism attributed to the above notable contributions. A major contributing factor to this state of affairs includes the fact that human rights institutions, with specific attention to continental institutions, face challenges that have inhibited their optimal performance in promoting and protecting the rights enshrined in the ACHPR as well as other continental instruments.

Nonetheless, there are recent developments, both normative and practical, that are noteworthy in that they reveal that human rights remain a topical issue on the continent and particularly to the African Union. These innovative developments have the potential to contribute to the protection and promotion of human rights by contributing to the work done by the more traditional human rights institutions. This chapter concentrates specifically on the role of the AU in the integration (or mainstreaming) of human rights into programming at the AU. Indeed, the role of AU organs outside of the traditional human rights organisations is often understated even though they play fundamental roles and make noteworthy contributions to the development of human rights broadly speaking.

The chapter argues these often unrecognised developments are significant as they present an alternative framing of the state of human rights in Africa that are often discussed within the limited context of 'abuses and remedies'. It highlighted some recent normative and practical developments promoted by the AU that promote the adoption of a human rights-based approaches that integrate human rights concerns into programming. The chapter argues that doing so at the level of the AU precipitates the uptake from regional organisations and AU Member States to instigate a theory of change wherein human rights are inherent considerations rather than within the much narrower 'abuses and remedies' context.

Bibliography

African Charter on Democracy, Elections and Governance (2007).

African Charter on Human and Peoples' Rights (1981).

African Charter on the Establishment of an African Court on Human and Peoples' Rights (1998).

African Charter on Principle and Practice of Public Service and Administration (2011).

African Charter on Principles and Practice of Decentralization, Local Governance and Local Development (2014).

African Charter on the Rights and Welfare of the Child (1990).

African Convention on Preventing and Combating Corruption (2003).

Agenda 2063: The Africa we Want, Popular Version, May 2016 Edition.

Aidoo, A. (1992). *Africa: Democracy without Human Right? HRQ 15*; pp: 703-715.

Centre for Human. (2016). *A Guide to the African Human Rights System*. Pretoria University Press.

Constitutive Act of the African Union (2000).

Kagame, P. (2017). *The Imperative to Strengthen our Nation*.

Mahoney, J. (2006). *The Challenge of Human Rights: Origin, Development, and Significance*. Blackwell Publishing, UK.

Makinda, S. M. (2015). *The African Union: Addressing the Challenges of Peace, Security and Governance*. Second Edition.

Mathews, K. (1984). *The Organization of African Unity*' in D. Mazzeo (ed.), African Regional Organizations. Cambridge: Cambridge University Press; pp: 49–84.

Mubangizi, J. C. (2006). Some Reflections on Recent and Current Trends in the Promotion and Protection of Human Rights in Africa: The Pains and the Gains. *African Human Rights Law Journal*, Vol. 6.

Murithi, T. (2018). African Union, the: Autocracy, Diplomacy and Peacebuilding in Africa.

Murray, R. (2004). *Human Rights in Africa*: From the OAU to the *African* Union. Cambridge University Press.

Network of African National Human Rights Institutions. (2016). *Study on the State National Human Rights Institutions (NHRIs) in Africa.*

Organisation of Africa Union Charter (1963).

Protocol to the African Charter on the Rights of Women in Africa (2003).

CHAPTER 13

Righting the Future from the Past: Four Decades of Human Rights (Illusions) in Zimbabwe

Gift Mwonzora

1 INTRODUCTION

This chapter commences with a critical engagement of the past, reflecting over the last forty years since independence in 1980, on Zimbabwe's human rights record and what measures may be taken in addressing the issues that have emerged over the last four decades. The importance of this scholarly inquiry focusing on Zimbabwe lies in its brave attempt to chronicle the continuities of human rights abuses through different temporal lens. Understanding such has a significance to the empirical and theoretical study of the nature, dynamics and character of political regimes in Africa.

In understanding and cataloguing Zimbabwe's chequered history of human rights violations and deepening authoritarianism, scholars need to understand the various interspersed events post-1980 by looking at different historical moments. I begin my analysis by starting with the first days of Zimbabwe's independence and ending with the post-Mugabe period after the leader was ousted from power in November 2017. There is good reason to include the post-Mugabe phase: many misguidedly thought that once Mugabe had left power, things were going to change. The truth proved far from it: he

G. Mwonzora (✉)
Unit of Zimbabwean Studies, Sociology Department, Rhodes University,
Makhanda, South Africa
e-mail: giftmwonzora@gmail.com

© The Author(s), under exclusive license to Springer Nature
Switzerland AG 2022
A. Adeola and M. W. Mutua (eds.), *The Palgrave Handbook
of Democracy, Governance and Justice in Africa*,
https://doi.org/10.1007/978-3-030-74014-6_13

235

left intact the repressive system—what has been termed by ordinary Zimbabweans as 'Mugabeism'. Hence, the chapter will seek to draw parallels (or trace similarities) with the human rights situation both *during* and *post*-Mugabe rule.

2   Zimbabwe's 1980 Independence: A 'New Baby is Born'

The armed war of liberation between the British settlers led by Ian Smith and the two black armed liberation movements, the Zimbabwe People's Revolutionary Army (ZIPRA) and Zimbabwe African National Liberation Army (ZANLA), came to an end only as a result of protracted negotiations for independence held in London in 1979. Buckling under the economic pressure of the armed liberation war, and under pressure from the United States of America (USA) as well as from apartheid South Africa, Ian Smith, representing the Rhodesian Front Government, joined hands with African nationalists who were viewed as moderates. Ian Smith joined with Bishop Abel Muzorewa, Reverend Ndabaningi Sithole, traditional chiefs, Ndiweni and Chirau into forming the Internal Settlement (Zimbabwe–Rhodesia settlement) of 1978. The settlement did not bring any solution to the war situation as the two liberation fronts (ZANLA and ZIPRA), who were excluded from the transitional arrangement, did not seize hostilities.

Rather, the leadership of the two fronts (ZANLA and ZIPRA) viewed the signatories to the Internal Settlement as quislings of Smith. Following the continued fighting, a solution was eventually found in the Lancaster House Constitutional Conference talks facilitated by the British government. The negotiations were also a result of intense pressure from other African nationalist leaders, inasmuch as they were a response to ending the long-drawn out liberation struggle. Consequently, Zimbabwe went into the 1980 elections. It was from this election that Mugabe emerged the leader, inheriting a country that had been ravaged by a protracted war and was marked by polarisation, fears and insecurity on what the future could hold. Part of these fears and insecurities emanated from the fractured race relations as well as from the unresolved land issue. Considering that the Lancaster House Agreement was a compromise ceasefire agreement, the African nationalist leaders—Robert Mugabe, Joshua Nkomo and others—had agreed on a land reform process with the British government but under a controversial clause of willing buyer-willing seller basis. As enshrined in the Bill of Rights, the new government was obliged to guarantee the land and property rights for a period of 10 years (Dzinesa 2012). This meant that the Zimbabwean government would not be in a position to acquire land if the farm owner (in this case the commercial white farmers) were not willing to relinquish the land under the willing buyer-willing seller basis contained in the agreement. This meant that the land issue remained a ticking time bomb in post-colonial Zimbabwe as will be evidenced in the circumstances that surrounded the 2000 Fast-Track-Land Reform Programme (FTLRP).

In other words, the land question remained a case of unfinished business to the extent that it became a seething cauldron for a violent land seizure two decades later. Despite having a justiciable Bill of Rights, as evident in several clauses that were progressive (e.g. protection from discrimination, freedom of assembly, expression, association and movement, right to personal liberty, right to life as well as freedom from torture and inhuman treatment), the Lancaster House constitution which was a by-product of the Lancaster House Agreement was limited insofar as it did not adequately address the skewed ownership of land contoured along racial lines (Lancaster House Agreement 1979). This deficiency was, however, understandable considering that the Lancaster House constitution was a compromise agreement, little wonder the post-1980 regime of Robert Mugabe had to amend some constitutional provisions.

The coming in of independence in Zimbabwe in 1980, in the aftermath of a violent war, was hailed as a precursor to majority rule, human rights protection and egalitarianism. In a move at the time hailed as a sign of Mugabe's statesmanship, the Prime Minister, Robert Mugabe of the newly named Zimbabwe (the former Southern Rhodesia) extended an olive branch to his erstwhile foes. On the eve of the independence celebrations in 1980, Mugabe, amid pomp and euphoria extended a hand of reconciliation to the white and black races who had been involved in a bitter fight during the entire period of colonial rule. Mugabe's conciliatory efforts helped to steer Zimbabwe on a trajectory of inclusive national development. The fact that he made peace with a racial group that once fought on the opposite side was lauded as a move that created a conducive environment for nation and state-building, post the war of liberation.

In the first decade of independence, Zimbabwe enjoyed a massive boost in terms of international development support, thanks to the goodwill of international partners who supported the initiative. To this end, the country embarked on a massive reconstruction programme of an economy ravaged by the vicissitudes of conflict. During this era, there were commendable policies on the social and economic front, as can be evinced in the progress recorded in the education, social welfare and health sectors ('developmental socialist' policy) (Sachikonye 1995). In this short-lived honeymoon, Mugabe was unfalteringly popular with the majority of Zimbabweans. Fundamental to note is that whilst there was notable progress and when many were still enveloped in the exuberance and pomp of independence, some were already starting to question the democratic credentials of the new leadership. Such questions grew louder after the Mugabe regime started showing signs of establishing a *de jure* one-party state system. Questions on Zimbabwe's democratic experiment also emerged after clear signs that a political culture reminiscent of the colonial era was being perpetuated.

Strictly speaking many envisaged the post-1980 as a new era that was going to be marked by human rights observance, laced with democratic rule and good governance. Little did they knew that the new nationalist leaders emerging from the colonial-rule era would copy and replicate the authoritarian tendencies of their predecessors. This only became evident as the Mugabe-led nationalist government began to spread its authoritarian tentacles on the levers of state power and in the wider political society. In this regard, the initial enthusiasm and hope of democratic rule started to slowly dissipate and faded a few years after independence. The events following the successive elections, post-1980, pointed to signs of a liberation struggle slowly but surely running out of steam.

3   DEFENDING THE (IN) DEFENSIBLE—MUGABE AND THE ONE-PARTY STATE SYSTEM IN ZIMBABWE

In the early 1980s and until the mid-1990s, the ZANU-PF party spiritedly pushed for the establishment of a *de jure* one-party state, to the chagrin of the progressives within the party. Though the one-party system debate remained largely internal, it actually solidified following the convergence of ZANU and ZAPU through the Unity Accord of 1987 which gave birth to ZANU-PF. With ZAPU now part of ZANU, Zimbabwe nearly became a *de jure* one-party state but such was resisted by ZANU's founding Secretary General Edgar Tekere who went on to form the Zimbabwe Unity Movement (ZUM) challenging ZANU-PF in the 1990 General Elections. In spite of the fact that the ZANU-PF party leadership introduced a Leadership Code in 1984 where leaders were supposed to declare their assets, corruption still persisted among the party officials. This became evident in the 1986 National Railways Housing Scandal, the 1988 Willowgate affair and too many others to mention which implicated several top ZANU-PF officials.

On the political front, whilst these developments were unfolding, Edgar Tekere (a liberation war stalwart who had been sacked from ZANU-PF for his outspokenness against growing corruption by what he called a 'vampire class') led a vigorous campaign against the incumbent president's desire to establish a one-party state (Bratton 2016, 60). Students from the University of Zimbabwe also joined in, demanding good governance as well as an end to the emerging trend of state repression.

In this milieu of dissent expressed through demonstrations, Mugabe started to unleash brute force on unarmed and defenceless citizens. This crackdown on protestors proved to be the dominant *modus operandi* of Mugabe's rule to maintain his tenacious grip on power. This period of history is littered with examples of how the regime ill-treated the political opposition and critics who dared challenge the government or those perceived as harbouring ill intent for the country. Most people started to question whether the country had attained only flag and anthem independence. In cementing his rule, Mugabe even adopted and perfected the draconian pieces of legislation inherited from the colonial government.

The new regime, however, believed that it had to keep the repressive legislation intact in order to deal with political opponents and demonstrators. This went against the euphoria that had gripped the nation-state at independence. By this time, the ZANU-PF government had shown its penchant for deploying force to crush dissent.

4   A Chronicle of Human Rights Records Under the Regime

4.1   *The Gukurahundi Massacres (1983–1987)—When a State Turns Against Its Citizens*

Soon after independence, Zimbabwe witnessed one of the worst incidents of violence in the history of the country in what came to be known as the *Gukurahundi* massacres. To provide a brief background, the *Gukurahundi* massacres were primarily driven by an internal conflict between Mugabe's ZANU and Nkomo's ZAPU, however, numerous internal–external dynamics also played a significant role. In this regard, it is largely believed that the apartheid regime in South Africa supported the atrocities (Scarnecchia 2011):

> evidence shows high-ranking ZANU-PF officials negotiated with the South African Defence Force in 1983 to cooperate in their efforts to keep ZAPU from supporting South African ANC operations in Zimbabwe. The 5th Brigade's campaign therefore served the purposes of South Africa, even as ZANU-PF officials rationalized the Gukurahundi violence in international and anti-apartheid circles as a campaign against South African destabilization.

There were also allegations that the apartheid South African regime trained and sponsored the so-called Super-ZAPU and 'pure-ZANU' dissidents who wreaked havoc in the Matebeleland region. Whether true or false, this armed Mugabe with the justification to destroy ZAPU under the aegis of destroying the dissidents (Alexander, McGregor and Ranger 2000). In the same vein, the Cold War relations between Zimbabwe and the UK (former coloniser) provided a concealment for the atrocities and other heinous crimes committed by the armed Fifth Brigade in Matebeleland and Midlands region (Scarnecchia, 2011). This explains why the major international powers including the United States as well as the British government, that had a dominant influence over the new Zimbabwean government, did not act in the face of such human rights abuses. The events which unfolded leading to the massacres are chronicled below.

In the early 1980s, fault lines started to appear between the two former liberation wings, the *Zimbabwe African National Liberation Army* (ZANLA) and the *Zimbabwe People's Revolutionary Army* (ZIPRA). During the war, ZANLA guerrillas had been largely supported by the Chinese whilst ZIPRA was supported by Russia (Simpson and Hawkins 2018). These military wings had been demobilised at the time of independence and members had been integrated into the Zimbabwe National Army. This created a sense of cohesion and unity which was also extended to the leader of PF-ZAPU, Joshua Nkomo, who had also fought alongside Mugabe for the country's liberation. However, the unity between the two did not last for long. In 1982, in what later came to be known as a putsch to oust Nkomo from government, Mugabe deployed the North Korean-trained Fifth Brigade in Matebeleland and Midlands province (Eppel 2005). This was justified on the basis that arms caches had been discovered at Hampton and Escort Farms (operated under Nitram Private Limited) allegedly belonging to ZIPRA—a claim which Joshua Nkomo strenuously disputed and dismissed as a smear campaign. Hence, the validation for deploying forces was to quell an alleged insurrection that was being 'planned' and 'co-ordinated' by Nkomo. Until his death in 2001, Nkomo who was popularly known as ('Father Zimbabwe') strenuously refuted these allegations and dismissed such as a ruse by Mugabe to attack his supporters and to cow him into submission (Nkomo 2001).

With threats on his life, Nkomo managed to flee into exile in the UK. But his escape did not halt the violations, disappearances and extrajudicial killings of civilians. This orgy of violence left a trail of destruction of property and homes, and the loss of an estimated 20 000 innocent civilian lives in what came to be referred to as the *Gukurahundi*[1] massacres (Catholic Commission for Justice and Peace in Zimbabwe 1997). This was only a taste of how a state could become so callous and sadistic that it could butcher its own people in cold blood through a 'soft genocide'. It is important to underscore that long after these atrocities, affected families and victims have failed to attain reparative and restorative justice. To exacerbate the situation, the Zimbabwean government has not owned up to its involvement in the *Gukurahundi*. It has not even condemned the heinous crimes which occurred during this period or even acknowledged its wrongdoings. This is notwithstanding the fact that the 2013 constitution provides for the establishment of a National Peace and Reconciliation Commission (NPRC) to address these and other human rights abuses.

A noticeable trend during the Mugabe era was that his government tried by all means possible to attribute blame to the victims of *Gukurahundi*. This behaviour is akin to victimising the victim. The Mugabe regime even at times brushed aside the entire *Gukurahundi* episode as a moment of 'political madness'. It remains questionable whether such a stance would usher in truth-telling, healing, contrition, reparative justice, closure and reconciliation, even in the post-Mugabe epoch. One could argue that such a tokenistic approach to historical accountability is not enough. The *Gukurahundi* marked the end of the relative peace that had prevailed in the early years of Zimbabwe's independence. The mass killings and torture altered Zimbabwe's political

---

[1] *Gukurahundi* refers to the first rains that wash away the chaff from the previous harvests.

trajectory, judging from the trauma and pain that envelops the nation, specifically in the affected regions of Midlands and Matebeleland (Bratton 2016). The *Gukurahundi* atrocities were a harbinger of further violations that would punctuate the daily lives of the Zimbabwean citizenry as the continuing atrocities attest. In a move aimed at entrenching and consolidating his rule, Mugabe in 1987 amended the constitution to create an executive presidency (Zimbabwe Lawyers for Human Rights, n.d.).

4.2   State Response to the 1998 Food Riots

In the mid to late 1990s, Zimbabwe found itself grappling with a high cost of living and record job losses. This was in part attributed to the adoption of the neo-liberal economic restructuring programme adopted from the twin Bretton Woods institutions—the International Monetary Fund (IMF) and the World Bank. The austerity measures adopted not only in Zimbabwe but in many other African countries had far-reaching implications for the livelihoods of citizens. In Zimbabwe, the Economic Structural Adjustment Programme (ESAP) led to company closures, followed by massive retrenchments, and the privatisation of basic facilities and public assets such as health and education (Potts 2006a). ESAP also heralded the introduction of user fees in hospitals. In general, the structural adjustment programme triggered a spike in the cost of living, increasing the cost of basic commodities like bread and maize meal, among other commodities. To make matters worse, as the structural adjustment programmes (SAPs) were biting, Zimbabwe was also experiencing a series of droughts.

In 1998, Zimbabwe's major cities including Harare witnessed rioters who demonstrated in the streets in what came to be known as the 'food riots' (Zimbabwe Human Rights NGO Forum 1998). Food riots were a manifestation of a two week stay away that was called by the Zimbabwe Congress of Trade Unions (ZCTU)—a labour body under the Secretary Generalship of Morgan Tsvangirai, which in essence was a brewing pro-labour party set to challenge the hegemony of ZANU-PF. Although the ZCTU played a role in galvanising the urban populace to storm the streets, the major trigger for this food riot was the sudden government announcement on price increases of basic foodstuffs, such as mealie meal, cooking oil, and bread (AMANI Trust 1998). As later became the norm for the Zimbabwean government, brute force was used by the Mugabe regime as a countermove to quell the emerging protests. The Zimbabwe Human Rights Forum (and other NGOs) reported that a dozen people were injured during the clashes with the military deployed on unarmed civilians (AMANI Trust 1998).

The deployment of soldiers armed to the teeth and military jets that hovered over Harare, and the proclaimed curfew, was a prologue to the ruthlessness of the Mugabe regime. This deployment of force also underscores the penchant in the resort to the use of what was termed by a prominent scholar, Althusser (1971) as the 'repressive state apparatuses'. Aside from co-ordinating and enforcing election-related violence, torture and abductions, the security elements (in cahoots with the ZANU-PF civilian force war veterans and party-affiliated youth) were also at the forefront of unleashing violence during the era of the 2000 land grabs, as will be discussed in the next section.

4.3 'The Emperor Has no clothes'—The 2000 Land Reform Programme in Zimbabwe

This section discusses the series of human rights violations that ensued following the 2000 land grab which was viewed by many as a noble gesture towards redressing the racially skewed land ownership (Feltoe 2004, 193–223). By 1990, the Lancaster House constitutional clause on land reform had reached its stipulated 10-year period. The Zimbabwean government then made moves to acquire land as the white commercial farmers had shown no interest to implement the willing-seller-willing buyer principle. The amendment of Section 16 of the Lancaster House Constitution, which was followed by the passing of the Land Acquisition Act of 1992, paved the way for the Zimbabwean government to compulsorily acquire land in the commercial farming area for resettlement purposes and this land was designated as rural land (Coldham 1993, 82–88). Such efforts were aimed at addressing the resettlement issue that remained unresolved, stretching back from the Lancaster House constitutional provisions to the Land Acquisition Act of 1985 to the 1992 Land Acquisition Act.

As time went on, the British government explicitly reneged on the willing buyer-willing seller agreement, as evident in its refusal to continue financing the resettlement programme. An impasse between the Mugabe-led government and the British government was inevitable. Clare Short's letter addressed to Kumbirai Kangai (then Zimbabwe's Minister of Lands) says it all. In this letter, Short (then British secretary for International Development) confirms the negation of the pledge and commitment by the UK administration entered into at the Lancaster House Conference. In her letter, Short stated that the election of the Labour government in Britain, which had no responsibility nor colonial interests in Africa, meant that the British government could not continue committing itself to financing the land resettlement exercise in post-colonial Zimbabwe (Baffour 2003). This reneging by the British government on the land resettlement programme then created tensions between the Mugabe administration and the UK government.

In 2000, following the formation of the Movement for Democratic Change (MDC) by the Zimbabwe Congress of Trade Union (ZCTU), women groups and students (Raftopoulos 2001), the liberation war veterans of the 1972–80 era embarked on a chaotic land reform programme. This land grab, which targeted white-owned commercial farms, was dubbed the Fast-Track-Land-Reform-Programme (FTLRP). It is essential to note that the process of violent land acquisition triggered unsettling conversations around issues of social (in)justice and human rights, particularly contestation over the issue of property rights, disregard for court orders, compensation, rule of law and the supremacy of the constitution. In the same vein, it can also be opined that the land reform was an act of last resort by the ZANU-PF after its dismal defeat in the 2000 February Constitutional Referendum which had clauses to do with land compensation.

Hundreds of white farmers were killed in the series of dispossessions (Feltoe 2004). Many suffered huge losses of their crops and property, apart from the violence they endured. Farm workers were also not spared. They were caught in the crossfire of land expropriation, as they lost their only source of livelihood (wage labour) due to the disturbances that occurred on the affected farms. In the following months and years, some became internally displaced and many resorted to eking out livelihoods in informal settlements that started to sprout up near the formerly white-owned farms. It can be posited that when black Zimbabwean farmers seized these farms, the plight of the former farm workers did not get any better; this vulnerable group was further victimised by being forcibly displaced from the settlements on the land where they had previously lived and worked (Sachikonye 2003). The few who were employed at the newly acquired farms were paid a pittance for their hard toil as farm labourers.

To return now to the actual land seizure: in grabbing these farmlands, ZANU-PF framed the narrative that white farmers had no right to own the land in the first place (Rutherford 2001). The argument was that the land formerly belonged to the Africans before being seized from them by the white settler colonialists. Hence, it rightfully belonged to the black Zimbabweans. From their side, the erstwhile white farmers lamented the haphazard nature of the seizures. Not only that, but the disregard for the rule of law, particularly the violation of property rights as well as the human rights that were trampled upon during the exercise. As explained above, many lost their lives and sources of livelihood. By the same token, they maintained that it was unjust for them to be ill-treated for the transgressions (i.e. land grabbing) committed by their forefathers. Many were immigrants who had acquired farmlands and settled in the then Southern-Rhodesia (present-day Zimbabwe). Some had inherited the land and were not part of the land dispossession during the era of colonial settler rule. Land expropriation without compensation opened up an enduring debate (which is far from being settled) over the issue of social (in)justice, race relations and what can be termed as the rise of 'economic nationalism'. This debate is also arising in other countries, particularly in South Africa where the issue of land remains a ticking time bomb (Xaba 2019; James 2007). In response to the violent land grabs that occurred in Zimbabwe during the 2000 era, a few brave farmers stood up, seeking to realise and assert their rights, particularly the right to property. Unfortunately, this was not an easy stroll. Ben Freeth (son-in-law to Mike Campbell now late) fought the dispossession of the latter's farm all the way to the Southern Africa Development Community (SADC) Tribunal. After having been forcibly removed from his farm in Chegutu by the late ZANU-PF national official Nathan Shamuyarira,

Mike Campbell and Ben Freeth approached the SADC Tribunal seeking legal recourse (*The Guardian*, 24 April 2011). This was after having failed to get legal recourse in the Zimbabwean courts. In other words, they had exhausted all domestic legal remedies. The verdict of the tribunal had far-reaching implications within the region, insofar as shaping the rule of law and testing the limits of international law are concerned. But, in response, the Zimbabwean government refused to abide by the ruling, inasmuch as it challenged the jurisdiction of the tribunal. As a corollary, the Mugabe regime opted not to enforce the ruling. Then Minister of State for National Security, Lands, Land Reform, and Resettlement, Didymus Mutasa, had no comforting words for the SADC tribunal, telling a news outlet:

> SADC Tribunal is day-dreaming because we are not going to reverse the land reform exercise. There is nothing special about the 75 farmers and we will take more farms ... "[i]t's not discrimination against farmers, but correcting land imbalances." (IOL News, 1 December 2008).

The above came as no surprise, considering the Mugabe administration's antipathy to international and regional treaties, bodies, and conventions (and in general, to the rule of law). At the height of the land seizure, in a riposte to the accusations that he was dispossessing white-owned commercial farmlands in an act of racial disempowerment, Mugabe uttered: 'If white settlers just took the land from us without paying for it, we can, in a similar way, just take it from them without paying for it' (The Washington Post, 28 April 2016).

In this climate of political pronouncements and executive interference, the bench was tasked to adjudicate. We thus need to understand the context in which the judiciary was operating during the era of the farm invasions. At the height of the 'land reform' programme, numerous white farmers brought several court cases before the bench. But in a cowardly act aimed at intimidating and undermining the autonomy or impartiality of the bench, Mugabe issued thinly veiled attacks on the judiciary. In an incident which clearly exhibited the disdain for the separation of powers principle, a certain Zimbabwean traditional chief noted that the then Chief Justice Antony Gubbay (a white judge) was acting against the government that gave him his job and was paying his salary and as such he should be fired from his position as he was acting against the interests of his paymaster (Feltoe 2004, 206).

Due to these (and other) prevailing and relentless attacks on his person and his office—as well as the intimidation towards him and fellow judges—Antony Gubbay was pressured to resign. This is clear proof of judiciary attack and political overreach by the ZANU-PF and by civilians aligned to the party. As a result, all such actions aided in significantly undermining the principle of supremacy of the law, separation of powers and rule of law in post-independent Zimbabwe. It, therefore, needs no emphasis that, in the context of such threats, amidst heavy executive encroachment in judicial affairs, the bench did not do much in adjudicating on cases regarding the rights violations that accompanied the land reform programme. As Feltoe (2004, 201) further notes, '... by the time of the ZANU-PF Congress in December 2001, the president was really on a warpath against the white farmers'. In this regard he went on to say:

> Our party must continue to strike fear in the heart of the white man, our real enemy ...The courts can do whatever they want, but no judicial decision will stand in our way... My own position is that we should not even be defending our position in the courts. This country is our country and this land is our land (IOL, 14 December 2000).

Hot on the heels of such threats which undermined the rule of law and other attendant human rights of the white farmers, Chenjerai 'Hitler' Hunzvi, then chairman of the dreaded war veterans' association issued chilling threats. In his words, 'we are now fighting for our land and whosoever is killed, it's tough luck' (Feltoe 2004, 201). Even in the midst of such threats and actions, there emerged numerous explanations on the timing of the violent land seizure and the targeting of the whites. One convincing narrative was that the white farmers had supported the rejection of the new constitution on the basis that it had a clause providing for the acquisition of state land without compensation (Feltoe 2004, 201; Rutherford 2001, 635). The facts are as follows: in 2000, Mugabe—characteristic of his loathing of a new people-driven constitution-making process that would water down his executive powers—sponsored the writing of a new constitution containing clause on land expropriation without compensation. He then appointed a commission to undertake the constitution-making process. His efforts failed as the draft constitution produced by these commissioners was rejected by the populace, to the chagrin of Mugabe, through a 'Vote No' campaign during the referendum. The National Constitutional Assembly (NCA) and the newly formed MDC mobilised citizens to reject the draft on the basis that it provided for a weak parliament and a powerful executive, and was weak in guaranteeing fundamental human rights. It is unsurprising that Mugabe had to react by saying the following in reference to the newly formed MDC party and the white commercial farmers:

> 'those who try to cause disunity among our people must watch out because death will befall them' (Feltoe 2004, 197).

It is no secret that the white commercial farmers sponsored the 'Vote No' campaign (i.e. saying 'no' to the draft constitution) by providing financial assistance and ferrying their farm workers to voting stations, confident that they would vote 'No' in the referendum. Such acts drew the ire of the Mugabe regime which went on to initiate the violent land grabs as a backlash against the white farmers. Notably, ZANU-PF always viewed whites as sympathetic to

246 G. MWONZORA

the newly formed opposition MDC party. Some believe it was the strategy of Mugabe and his henchmen to contain the farmers' involvement in opposition politics through stripping them of their source of economic production, the land.

4.4 Enduring Human Rights Violations and Erosion of Democratic Rule

It is significant to note that, from the time of the *Gukurahundi* massacres to the 2000 land invasions, the ZANU-PF regime unwaveringly turned to the systematic use of torture against the pro-democracy movement and citizens. Many people have simply disappeared during Mugabe's reign: a few names that immediately spring to mind are political activists opposed to Mugabe's rule, Paul Chizuzu, Patrick Nabanyama and Itai Dzamara as well as Rashiwe Guzha (former state intelligence secretary) among others. As mentioned earlier, state repression, enforced disappearances and abductions through organised violence and torture were aided and abetted by all key state institutions including the police, army and security forces. In December 2008, Jestina Mukoko, a pro-democracy campaigner and director of the civic organisation— Zimbabwe Peace Project (ZPP), was abducted from her home in Norton suburb and was held incommunicado. She was only released after international condemnation, including the naming and shaming of the Mugabe regime by international human rights organisations as well by the foreign embassies (Howden 2009). As a result, most Zimbabwean citizens lost faith and trust in state institutions as entities that could help and protect them, or promote and uphold fundamental liberties.

As the Mugabe-regime excesses increased, several international human rights organisations—including Human Rights Watch, Amnesty International and Partnership Africa Canada (PAC), along with local human rights groups such as the Crisis in Zimbabwe Coalition (CiZC), Zimbabwe Association of Doctors for Human Rights (ZADHR), Zimbabwe Lawyers for Human Rights (ZLHR), and Zimbabwe Human Rights NGO Forum (the Forum) among others—continued to push for human rights observance and good governance. This was done through actions ranging from advocacy, engagement and holding the state accountable for rights violations through civic mobilisation and class actions. Indeed, Zimbabwe is famed as a country with one of the most formidable and vibrant civil society sectors, alongside others such as Kenya and South Africa. During the tenure of Mugabe, his regime had tried to decimate the civic and trade union movements through trumped-up charges against the civic leaders, arbitrary arrests, intimidation and surveillance, as well as blocking their funding and operations.

It was common to find opposition leaders facing a slew of trumped-up charges including treason or attempts at subverting a constitutionally elected government. Surely, these charges were calculated attempts at emasculating Mugabe's political foes. The MDC's Morgan Tsvangirai and Welshman Ncube and civil society leaders such as Munyaradzi Gwisai found themselves facing serious allegations. In the early years of Mugabe rule, the same fate had befallen liberation war stalwarts such as the late army commander, Lookout Masuku and (also late) Dumiso Dabengwa—an intelligence supremo from the Zimbabwe People's Revolutionary Army (ZIPRA) the military wing of Zimbabwe African People's Union (ZAPU).Both were arrested in 1982 but were acquitted on lack of evidence, only to be re-arrested in 1983 and spending four years in detention.

Such actions were harbingers of the abuse of the rule of law, lack of judicial independence, political interference in executive government and political pressure on the judiciary by the Mugabe regime. Though (the now late) Dabengwa later served in Mugabe's government, he resigned in 2008 bemoaning the deficit of good leadership in ZANU-PF.

4.5   Unleashing Violence Against the Opposition

From 2000 to 2008, Zimbabwean elections have been bloody and violent. This is largely because the incumbent ZANU-PF party has always deployed violent force to thwart the political opposition. The state-sponsored political violence (including torture, beatings, extrajudicial executions and abductions) has continued to stain the country's successive elections. This became evident in the 2008 June run-off election (Human Rights Watch 2008b). Such actions are contrary to the dictates of the Zimbabwean constitution as encapsulated in the Bill of Rights as well as in numerous other regional and international human rights instruments, statutes, covenants and conventions. Human rights violations laced with state-orchestrated violence have been an enduring trend, stemming from the early 1980s. In fact, the Mugabe-led government has been notorious for rights violations of both the top opposition politicians and ordinary citizens (Makumbe 2006, 45–61). In the run up to the 1985 ZANU-PF was sending chilling threats to those who would vote for the opposition. This violence has been an enduring phenomenon in post-2000 Zimbabwe.

On 11 March 2007, the Zimbabwean riot-police descended heavy-handedly on a march by the opposition political leaders who had mobilised under the church-organised Save Zimbabwe Convention. Riot police went around the Highfields high-density suburb beating and torturing citizens in a witch hunt for those who were alleged to have been demonstrating (Human Rights Watch 2007). As a young university student and at the time attached to one of the biggest farm worker trade unions in Zimbabwe (the General Agriculture and Plantation Workers Union of Zimbabwe, GAPWUZ), I had also participated in the demonstration. Along with colleagues, we had to run for cover after the riot police, some on horseback and some with police dogs, swooped on the gathering's venue (the Zimbabwe Grounds) and the entire Highfields suburb, indiscriminately beating people and firing tear gas to disperse the gathered crowd.

The regional and international media quickly picked up this news item after pictures emerged of the bludgeoned leaders of the MDC party, Morgan Tsvangirai and Arthur Mutambara, as well as the leader of the National Constitutional Assembly (NCA) Lovemore Madhuku. Following the broadcasting of these images, Zimbabwe again was placed back into the glare of the regional and international media. The state's heavy handedness drew the attention of the United Nations and, at continental level, the African Union (AU) as well as at regional level the Southern Africa Development Community (SADC). Regional actors were prompted to intervene in halting the human rights violations. After the regional and global criticism and condemnation, the SADC became increasingly involved in trying to solve the Zimbabwean crisis, especially addressing the then-deteriorating human rights situation (Human Rights Watch 2008a).

4.6   From Pillar to Post—Human Rights Violations Under Operation Murambatsvina ('Clear the Filth')

In 2005, the Zimbabwean government embarked on a clean-up campaign ostensibly to destroy illegal structures including housing and small home industries and vending sites (tuck-shops) in an operation code-named 'Operation *Murambatsvina*' (which translates to 'Clear the Filth') (Tibaijuka 2005). The magnitude of human rights violations during the Operation, as recorded by human rights groups, painted a grim picture (Human Rights Watch 2005). It was noted that more than 700,000 people were rendered homeless. To make matters worse, this 'cleanup' was carried out during winter and the affected were exposed to the low temperatures (Potts 2006c).

The destruction of the so-called illegal structures violated a bundle of rights, not only the right to shelter but also the right to health, right to property, children's right to education and the right to a livelihood (Benyera and Nyere 2015; Romero 2007). The last mentioned relates to the fact that many witnessed their small business structures being demolished and they were left with no source of livelihood. As a result of economic collapse, many illegal structures had sprung up, spurred on by the informalisation of the economy. It was these structures, which had become a source of economic livelihood to many, that were razed during the Operation (Howard-Hassmann 2010, 898).

The travesty attracted international scrutiny, and the then United Nations Secretary General Kofi Annan dispatched a UN Special Envoy on Human Settlements Issues (also then Director of UN Habitat) Anna Kajimulo Tibaijuka on a fact-finding visit to Zimbabwe. The UN Habitat produced a damning report detailing the human rights violations that occurred as a result of the Zimbabwe government's policy to demolish settlements in the major cities and also made recommendations to address the situation. As she noted in her report (Tibaijuka 2005):

It is estimated that some 700,000 people in cities across the country have lost either their homes, their source of livelihood or both. Indirectly, a further 2.4 million people have been affected in varying degrees. Hundreds of thousands of women, men and children were made homeless, without access to food, water and sanitation, or health care. Education for thousands of school age children has been disrupted. Many of the sick, including those with HIV and AIDS, no longer have access to care. The vast majority of those directly and indirectly affected are the poor and disadvantaged segments of the population. They are, today, deeper in poverty, deprivation and destitution, and have been rendered more vulnerable.

Some viewed the Operation as a calculated approach by the ZANU-PF regime to dismantle the urban vote which was showing an increasing leaning to the opposition. In this regard scholars contend that the ruling ZANU-PF party anticipated that a strong opposition support base in the urban would provide currency for revolt and protests in case of post-election disputes (Potts 2006b). Therefore, dislocating the urban residents was a mass move to destroy the opposition's constituency (Mlambo 2008). For ZANU-PF, the logic was simple. When the informal-settlement inhabitants were dislocated, where did they go? Back to the rural areas where they originally came from (Potts 2006c) where the power of their votes would be neutralised or swamped by the ZANU-PF supporters there. *Operation Murambatsvina* was a mass violation of human rights and part of Mugabe's machinations to stay in power. This Operation was followed by *Operation Chikhorokhoza Chapera* (End to illegal diamond panning), during which Mugabe's human rights violations and the elite's pillaging of resources, could be said to have reached a climax.

4.7   Discovery of Diamonds and Human Rights Violations

In 2006, after having initially allowed a free-for-all in the Chiadzwa mining community, the Mugabe regime deployed first the police and then the army to clamp down on illegal alluvial-diamond miners. In an initial nod to populist sentiment, the Zimbabwean government had allowed villagers to extract alluvial diamonds in the Chiadzwa/Marange area when they were discovered in 2006. But this later changed when the government entered into a partnership with external diamond-mining companies which led to strict regulation of diamond mining. The state moved into the Marange area and drove out the illegal diamond miners—firstly in an exercise dubbed *Operation Chikhorokhoza Chapera*—End to illegal diamond panning and secondly through an operation code-named *Hakudzokwi*—No Returning Back (Human Rights Watch 2009). The diamond fields were condoned off and securitised and declared no-go areas. In implementing this securitisation initiative, the army and police set dogs on the villagers, shot and killed hundreds of illegal miners, and injured scores more. The state went on to trample on the rights of citizens by forcibly relocating the affected Chiadzwa community against the principles and practice of free-prior-informed consent (FPIC) (Mwonzora 2011). The

250   G. MWONZORA

government even went on to arrest human rights activists like Farai Maguwu who was researching and documenting state abuses around the discovery of diamonds in the Marange area (Human Rights Watch 2010).

4.8   The 2008 Election Violence: A Winter of Agony and Anguish

To suggest that the 2008 election period in Zimbabwe was akin to the Hobbesian state of affairs where life was 'nasty, brutish and short', would not be far off the mark. To this end scholars have branded the violence that marked the June 2008 run-off election as one of the worst episodes in the electoral history of the country since independence (Masunungure 2009). Following Mugabe's defeat in the March 2008 elections, ZANU-PF employed the entire state apparatus as well as the war veterans and paramilitary youth corps popularly known as 'Border Gezis'—a name derived from the late Minister of Youth Border Gezi, who helped in the establishment of this youth wing—to engage in an orgy of violence that left many dead and others internally displaced. The state-sanctioned violence was to punish those who were perceived to have voted for the MDC party in the March 2008 elections, and was dubbed ('Operation *Makavhotera Papi* – Whom did you vote for') (Masunungure 2009; Human Rights Watch 2008b). The scale of the violence was unprecedented and the bloodiest election in post-colonial Zimbabwe.

Leaders of ZANU-PF, starting with Mugabe himself, have always been the ones who fanned political violence during election seasons. At a political rally in 2008, Mugabe opined: 'We fought for this country and a lot of blood was shed... we are not going to give up our country because of a mere X. How can a ballpoint pen fight with a gun?' (IOL News 2008). This message showed his contempt for the ballot and was a call to arms. It was a rallying cry to the party youth and war veterans to engage in political violence—as, according to Mugabe, a vote could not defeat a revolutionary party. Exacerbating the situation was the fact that the police were reluctant to deal with issues of politically motivated violence. This was out of fear of the ZANU-PF political leaders (Human Rights Watch 2008b).

Many rural constituencies were declared no-go zones for the opposition. The declaration of no-go areas was indeed contrary to the notion of freedom of movement, assembly and association, as guaranteed under national and international human rights instruments and statutes. Opposition supporters were beaten and tortured, their houses set ablaze, and some were killed—even thrown into dams (Human Rights Watch 2008b). Rural areas such as Mashonaland East and West, and Manicaland became no-go zones and the same treatment was meted out to opposition supporters and officials in cities and towns (Munyarari 2018). The case of MDC officials and supporters systematically targeted by the acts of violence in areas like Mbare, Dzivarasekwa and Epworth high-density suburbs are only few examples.

This was the situation in Kwekwe situated in Midlands province in Zimbabwe where another militia group going by the moniker Al-Shabaab also targeted opposition supporters and officials (Munyarari 2018). High incidents of political violence and targeted displacements were recorded in the breadth and length of several rural areas. ZANU-PF local party structures comprising of the youth and war veterans set up torture bases, where torture such as 'falanga beating of the feet' became a common trend. (Zimbabwe Human Rights NGO Forum 2009; Human Rights Watch 2008b). These ZANU-PF youth leaders led the dreaded *Chipangano* group, notoriously known for extorting money to fund all ZANU-PF programmes in urban areas. Business people who failed to comply risked having their licences cancelled or their wares confiscated. This all underscores the excesses of a dominant state preoccupied with power interest ahead of upholding human security which has become a key feature of African states.

5   Change and Continuity—Human Rights Violations in the Post-Mugabe Era

Despite the fact that the architects and beneficiary of the military-assisted transition (which some have called a military coup), promised restoration of rule of law and democracy, the human rights situation in Zimbabwe has remained the same, if not worsened, since Mugabe was deposed in November 2017, and replaced with President Emmerson Mnangagwa. The adage 'the more things change, the more they stay the same' has a striking resonance with the human rights status quo in Zimbabwe. In May 2019, the regime arrested five NGO workers who had attended an international conference—Farirai Gumbonzvanda, George Makoni, Gamuchirai Mukura, Tatenda Mombeyarara and Nyasha Frank Mpahlo—on the spurious allegation that they had attended a regime-change meeting to topple Mnangagwa (*Chronicle*, 24 May 2019; eNCA 24 May 2019). In early August, following the July 2018 elections, the fears and suspicions of a rigged election, twinned with the anxiety for change, prompted protestors to storm the streets in Harare demanding a release of the results from the election management body—the Zimbabwe Electoral Commission. In response, the so-called new administration of Mnangagwa (which has been touted within ZANU-PF circles as the 'new dispensation') deployed armed riot police and later soldiers armed with AK-47 rifles, to contain the demonstrations. The 'new dispensation' seemed oblivious to the fact that deployment of soldiers to quell demonstrations has never been a good idea in post-colonial Zimbabwe. In all the cases, where the Zimbabwean military has been involved, they have left a trail of horrifying memories. But again, this depicts an enduring trend which makes one conclude that most regimes in Africa and elsewhere follow a path-dependency route insofar as how they govern state and polity.

The deployment of the army by the 'new-old' administration of Mnangagwa to quell demonstrations by using live ammunition has proven that indeed it is not a picnic site when the army tanks and water cannon roll in the streets and when gun-toting soldiers wielding AK-47 rifles flood the streets. This was evident in the shootings of protesters (in Harare on 1 August 2018) who were agitated over the election results with fears of rigged elections running deep. In a second incident, in mid-January 2019, protesters who were demonstrating over the spike in the petrol price were shot (Human Rights Watch 2019; Amnesty International 2019b; Zimbabwe Human Rights NGO Forum 2019). Following the demonstrations, the army and plain-clothes security agents and suspected ZANU-PF party youth militia went about raiding homes, vandalising property, indiscriminately beating and torturing innocent civilians, and committing acts of rape and sexual abuse as well as extrajudicial killings (Amnesty International 2019a; Amnesty International 2019b; Zimbabwe Human Rights NGO Forum 2009). In the same breadth such acts are similar if not the same during the reign of Mugabe, a clear reflection of the enduring continuities of old habits on the part of Mnangagwa. This trend also underscores how African states often fail to have a break with the past in terms of the human rights record despite a change in leadership.

Considering all these incidents of shootings, abductions, rape, illegal detentions and torture, many have started to label the Mnangagwa administration the 'new error', rather than the self-styled 'new era' it claimed to be. During the current era, the Mnangagwa administration also enforced an internet shutdown, perhaps as a news blackout on the atrocities that were occurring or as a way to demobilise protestors (Amnesty International 2019a). The shutdown of WhatsApp, Facebook, Twitter and other social networking sites meant that it became difficult for protestors to organise, coordinate and circulate information (Human Rights Watch 2019). After deploying soldiers to quash demonstrations, which flouts the new constitution, the Mnangagwa administration went ahead to establish the Kgalema Motlanthe-led Commission of Inquiry into the July 2018 post-election shootings (Commission of Inquiry Report on Post-Election Violence in Zimbabwe 2018). Many are of the opinion that the Commission was put in place not to investigate state violence but to hoodwink the international community. Following the shootings of 1 August 2018, there was mounting pressure by the international community, particularly the EU, the USA and the UK for the government of Zimbabwe to take action by addressing the issue. It can be said that the international community in its different shades and guises strongly condemned the shooting. But even in the wake of such diplomatic pressure, the victims of the shootings and their relatives have not received any remedies for the rights violations despite the Commission making recommendations that should be fulfilled by the state.

Though it is difficult to get verifiable figures, it is believed that countless people lost their lives during the post-election shootings (Human Rights Watch 2019). Such is a clear abrogation of the right to life as enshrined in the Zimbabwean constitution, African Charter on Human and Peoples' Rights (ACHPR), International Covenant on Civil and Political Rights (ICCPR) and Universal Declaration of Human Rights (UDHR) among other human rights instruments and declarations.

The trend of torture, victimisations, arbitrary arrests, illegal detentions, and fast-tracked and manipulated trials has been the persistent trend against human rights activists, human rights defenders, labour activists and trade unionists since the 1 August 2018 protests in Zimbabwe. This has been reflected in the arbitrary arrests, followed by continued incarceration and denial of bail, for trade unionists and civic activists, among them Peter Mutasa and Japhet Moyo of the Zimbabwe Congress of Trade Unions, in the wake of the January 2019 protests (and in some cases sentencing) of protestors (Human Rights Watch 2019; Amnesty International 2019b). This trend has been ongoing as witnessed in the arrests and incarceration of human rights defenders, pro-democracy activists and journalists. The list ranges from: Hopewell Chin'ono, Job Sikhala, Jacob Ngarivhume, Namatai Kwekweza, Vongai Zimudzi and Tsitsi Dangarembga (*Aljazeera* 22 August 2020, *BBC News* 20 July 2020).

6 Reaching Forward from the PAST: ARE There Effective Ways to Re-Write the Future?

Emerging from four decades of human rights abuses and deepening authoritarianism within the Zimbabwean state, there is need to consider the future. Throughout history, it has been shown that not all countries will remain trapped in the past. Some countries emerging from deep seated conflicts and autocratic rule have managed to transition towards a democratic future. One such being South Africa emerging from the apartheid era. This, however, is dependent on the political will and leadership commitment to enhancing democracy and in deepening rule of law.

Viewed in a similar perspective, with the right conditions and political will, Zimbabwe can also adopt a similar trajectory. Just like South Africa and other countries including Ghana that had transitional justice mechanisms—Zimbabwe is in a right path towards building social cohesion. The new constitution promulgated in 2013 provides a window of opportunity for realising several steps that can entrench democracy and deepen rule of law. One such opportunity is the provision and subsequent establishment of the National Peace and Reconciliation Commission (NPRC) which provides for transitional justice mechanisms. The other opportunity lies in the effective functioning of Independent Commissions including the Anti-Corruption, Land, Zimbabwe Electoral, Gender and Human Rights Commission. But it is not enough to have commissions deemed 'independent' on paper but 'not independent' in reality. In this regard, the independent commissions should be free from executive control, domination and interference so that they can discharge their constitutional duties and mandates in a just, fair and impartial manner. In the same vein, the re-writing of Zimbabwe's future is, contingent on historical and state accountability, effective transitional justice mechanisms, respect of the rule of law to break the culture and cycle of impunity. Again, in re-writing Zimbabwe's future there is need to improve state-society inter-actions (engagement of citizens with leadership) without the temptation of always deploying state power (force) in response to citizen disaffection.

7 Conclusion

Over the last four decades, the Zimbabwean state has experienced an authori-tarian streak which saw the erosion of democracy and the violation of human rights. This trend has become part of the political culture, a trend which is not only evident in Zimbabwe alone. It is a trend which is pervasive in most post-colonial states in Africa. In examining this enduring trend in rights viola-tions and in the erosion of democracy, this chapter underscored the role and nexus between agency and structure in conditioning political action and in either entrenching democracy or authoritarianism. Several episodes and inci-dents stretching from the early conflict in Matebeleland which was followed by a culture of impunity, coupled with the Mugabe regime's intent to create one-party state further forestalled efforts at entrenching democracy and social cohesion in the nascent independent state. In years that followed, the ZANU-PF's regime continued on this path. This was evident in how it went on to treat its political foes in the 2000s, how it handled the 2000 fast track land reform programme. All this shows the character and endurance of authoritarian rule in post-colonial African states. Such a trend is further evident in the human rights abuses expressed through the militaristic approach to governance and to electoral politics. The case of the successive state-led *Operations* stemming from the Clean Up Campaign (*Murambatsvina*—'Clear the Filth') which saw the destruction of informal urban structures to the *Operations* in the diamond-mining sector are all clear examples of the deepening militarisation of the Zimbabwean state and society. Coupled with state-sanctioned violence during election times and the closure of the civic and political space, it can be argued that the country has experienced successive decades of misrule and mis-governance. Consequently, this has created a path-dependency syndrome whereby it is proving difficult to break with the past and chart a new way forward. Perhaps, such a trend abounds owing to the limited if not absence of incentives to change or to introduce reforms on the part of the leaders who are at the helm of state power. In this regard, the state has been viewed as a means to an end to gain power which enables one to amass and accumulate resources.

Having examined the human rights landscape and the political economy in Zimbabwe since the 1980s, this chapter also examined ways to re-write the future. In this regard, the analysis established the need for a change in political culture which is, however, not an easy task. This change in political culture and the establishment as well as infusing of political will can enhance the effective work and operations of state institutions. This is a call for an end to the 'state capture' of institutions (Matyszak 2018) in a bid to enhance democratic functioning of state institutions.

Evidently, naming and shaming of the state for human rights abuses have been an effective tool, in some contexts, for building rights-based compliance but the past four decades in Zimbabwe have exposed the limitations of such an approach. This is precisely because states that violates rights can still insulate themselves from external criticism and continue with the same, hiding under the veil of sovereignty and non-interference in their domestic affairs. In this regard, there is need for continued mobilisation and organisation from below and internally by the pro-democracy movement to push and incentivise African regimes to reform. In the end, there is no one-size-fits-all. The context needs to be understood.

BIBLIOGRAPHY

Alexander, Jocelyn, JoAnn McGregor and Terence O Ranger. *Violence and memory: One hundred years in the 'dark forests' of Matabeleland, Zimbabwe*. Heinemann and James Currey, 2000.

Althusser, Luis. *Ideology and ideological state apparatus*. Monthly Review Press, New York, 1971.

Amnesty International, *'Open for Business', Closed for Dissent Crackdown in Zimbabwe During the National Stay-Away 14–16 January 2019*, London: Amnesty International, 2019a. https://www.amnesty.org/download/Documents/AFR4698242019ENGLISH.pdf.

Amnesty International. *Zimbabwe: Ruthless crackdown on freedom of assembly exposes intolerance for dissent*, February 8, 2019b. https://www.amnesty.org/en/latest/news/2019/02/zimbabwe-ruthless-crackdown-on-freedom-of-assembly/

Baffour, Ankomah. "Zimbabwe: The Spark...*Claire Short's letter of November 1997.*" New African, (March. 2003). http://www.swans.com/library/art9/ankomah5.html

Benyera, Everisto, and Chidochashe Nyere. "An exploration of the impact of Zimbabwe's 2005 Operation Murambatsvina on women and children." *Gender and Behaviour* 13, no. 1, (January 2015): 6522–6534.

Bratton, Michael. *Power politics in Zimbabwe*. Kwazulu Natal: University of Kwazulu Natal Press, 2016.

Brooks, Marmon. "36 years after Zimbabwe's independence, the country faces these 4 big questions." *The Washington Post*, April 28, 2016.

Catholic Commission for Justice, Peace in Zimbabwe (CCJP). *Breaking the Silence, Building True Peace: A Report on the Disturbances in Matabeleland and the Midlands, 1980 to 1988*. Harare: Catholic Commission for Justice and Peace in Zimbabwe, 1997.

Chinaka, Chris. "Strike fear in white hearts, urges Mugabe." *IOL News*, December 14, 2000.

Coldham, Simon. "The Land Acquisition Act, 1992 of Zimbabwe." *Journal of African Law*, 37 no.1 (Spring 1993): 82–88.

Commission of Inquiry Report on Post- Election Violence in Zimbabwe, Report of the Commission of Inquiry into the 1st of August Post-election violence—chaired by Kgalema Motlanthe, 2018. http://kubatana.net/wp-content/uploads/2018/12/Final-Report-of-the-Commission-of-Inquiry-18-DEC-18.pdf.

Deborah Potts. "'Restoring Order'? Operation Murambatsvina and the Urban Crisis in Zimbabwe," *Journal of Southern African Studies*, 32:2, 273–291, 2006c.

Dzinesa, Gwinyai A. "Zimbabwe's Constitutional Reform Process: Challenges and Prospects," Wynberg: Institute for Justice and Reconciliation, 2012. http://ijr.org.za/home/wp-content/uploads/2017/05/IJR-Zimbabwe-Constitutional-Reform-OP-WEB.pdf.

Eppel, Shari. "Gukurahundi: The need for truth and reconciliation." In Raftopoulos, Brian and Savage, Tyrone, (eds), *Zimbabwe: Injustice and Political Reconciliation*. Harare: Weaver Press 2005.

Feltoe, Geoffrey. "The onslaught against democracy and rule of law in Zimbabwe in 2000". Harold-Barry, David ed., *Zimbabwe: The Past is the Future, Rethinking Land, State and Nation in the Context of Crisis*. Harare: Weaver Press, 2004, 193–223.

"Four human rights activists held in Zimbabwe: lawyers." *eNCA News*, May 21, 2019.

Herbstein, Denis. "Mike Campbell obituary: White Zimbabwean farmer who took Mugabe to court." *The Guardian*, April 24, 2011.

"Hopewell Chin'ono: Whistleblowing Zimbabwean Journalist arrested." *BBC News*, July 20, 2020.

Howard-Hassmann, Rhode E. "Mugabe's Zimbabwe, 2000–2009: Massive human rights violations and the failure to protect." *Human Rights Quarterly* 32 (January 2010).

Howden, Daniel. "Jestina Mukoko: 'Mugabe's henchmen came for me before dawn." *Independent*, January 17, 2009.

Human Rights Watch. *Zimbabwe: Excessive Force used Against Protesters Investigate, Prosecute Responsible Security Forces, 12 March 2019* https://www.hrw.org/news/2019/03/12/zimbabwe-excessive-force-used-against-protesters.

Human Rights Watch. *"Deliberate Chaos: On-going Human Rights Abuses"* in the *Marange Diamond Fields of Zimbabwe*. 2010, New York: Human Rights Watch, 2010. http://www.hrw.org/reports/2010/06/21/deliberate-chaos-0

Human Rights Watch. *"Diamonds in the Rough: Human Rights Abuses"* in the *Marange Diamond Fields of Zimbabwe*. New York: Human Rights Watch, 2009. http://www.observatori.org/paises/pais_82/documentos/zimbabwe0609web.pdf

Human Rights Watch. *"Our Hands Are Tied" Erosion of the Rule of Law in Zimbabwe*. New York: Human Rights Watch, 2008a. https://www.hrw.org/sites/default/files/reports/zimbabwe1108.pdf

Human Rights Watch. *"Bullets for Each of You" State-Sponsored Violence since Zimbabwe's March 29 Elections"*, 2008b. https://www.hrw.org/reports/2008/zimbabwe0608/zimbabwe0608webwcover.pdf

Human Rights Watch. *"Bashing Dissent Escalating Violence and State Repression"* in *Zimbabwe May 2007 Report*, Volume 19, No. 6(A), (December 2007). https://www.hrw.org/reports/2007/zimbabwe0507/5.htm accessed 2 December 2016.

Human Rights Watch. *"Zimbabwe—Evicted and Forsaken: Internally Displaced Persons"* in the *Aftermath of Operation Murambatsvina*. vol. 17, no. 16(A), (December 2005). http://hrw.org/reports/2005/zim1205/zim1205webwcover.pdf.

Human Rights Watch *"Zimbabwe Not Eligible: The Politicization of Food"* in *Zimbabwe*. Vol. 15, No. 17(A) October 2003, New York: Human Rights Watch, 2003. https://www.hrw.org/sites/default/files/reports/zimbabwe1003.pdf

James, Deborah. *"Gaining ground?: Rights and Property"* in *South African land reform*. London, Routledge, 2007.

Lancaster House Agreement, 21 December 1979. Southern Rhodesia Constitutional Conference Held at Lancaster House, London September—(December 1979). https://sasspace.sas.ac.uk/5847/5/1979_Lancaster_House_Agreement.pdf.

Makumbe, John. "Electoral politics in Zimbabwe: authoritarianism versus the people." *Africa Development* 31, no. 3, (August 2006): 45–61.

Mandaza, Ibbo, and Lloyd M. Sachikonye. *The one-party state and democracy: The Zimbabwe debate*, Harare: Sapes Books, 1991.

Mark Simpson and Tony Hawkins, "The *Primacy of Regime Survival:State Fragility and EconomicDestruction*" *in Zimbabwe*, Cham: Palgrave and Macmillan, 2018.

Masunungure, Eldred V., ed. *Defying the Winds of Change: Zimbabwe's 2008 Elections*, Harare: Weaver Press, 2009.

Matyszak, Derek. "State Capture and Elections in Zimbabwe" in Meirotti, Melanie, and Grant Masterson, (eds), *State Capture in Africa, Old Threats, New Packaging? State Capture*, Johannesburg: EISA, 2018.

Mlambo Alois. 'Historical antecedents to Murambatsvina', in Vambe Maurice Taonezvi (ed). *The Hidden Dimensions of Operation Murambatsvina in Zimbabwe*: Weaver Press, Harare, pp. 9–24, 2008.

"Mugabe mocks the vote." *IOL News,* June 17, 2008.

Munyarari, Tinashe. "Chipangano: vigilantism and Community responses in Mbare District, Zimbabwe, c. 2000–2013." Master's Thesis, Grahamstown: Rhodes University, 2018.

Mwonzora, Gift. "Diamond Rush and the Relocation of the Chiadzwa community in Zimbabwe: A Human Rights Perspective." Masters Research Paper, The Hague: International Institute of Social Studies [ISS]: Erasmus Universiteit Rotterdam, 2011.

Nkomo, Joshua. *Nkomo: The story of my life*. Harare: Sapes Books, 2001.

Potts, Deborah. "'All my hopes and dreams are shattered': Urbanization and migrancy in an imploding African economy–the case of Zimbabwe." *Geoforum* 37, no. 4 (July 2006a):536–551. https://doi.org/10.1016/j.geoforum.2005.11.003.

Potts Deborah. "City Life in Zimbabwe at a Time of Fear and Loathing: Urban Planning, Urban Poverty, and Operation Murambatsvina". In: Murray M.J., Myers G.A. (eds), *Cities in Contemporary Africa*. Palgrave Macmillan, New York, 2006b.

Raftopoulos, Brian. "The Labour Movement and the Emergence of Opposition Politics in Zimbabwe" in Brian Raftopoulos & Lloyd Sachikonye, (eds.), Striking Back: The Labour Movement and the Post- Colonial State in Zimbabwe 1980–2000,(Harare: Weaver Press, 2001), 1–24.

Romero, Sean. "Mass forced evictions and the human right to adequate housing in Zimbabwe." *Northwestern Journal of International Human Rights*, 5, 2 (Spring 2007):271–297.

Rutherford, Blair. "Commercial farm workers and the politics of (dis) placement in Zimbabwe: colonialism, liberation and democracy." *Journal of Agrarian Change* 1, no. 4 (2001): 626–651.

Sachikonye M Lloyd. "From 'equity' and 'participation' to structural adjustment: state and social forces in Zimbabwe" in Moore, David B., and Gerald J. Schmitz, (eds), *Debating Development Discourses: Institutional and Popular Perspectives*. London: Palgrave Macmillan, 1995.

Sachikonye, Lloyd M. "The situation of commercial farm workers after land reform in Zimbabwe." *Harare: Farm Community Trust of Zimbabwe*, 2003.

Scarnecchia, Timothy. "Rationalizing Gukurahundi: cold war and South African foreign relations with Zimbabwe, 1981-1983. *Kronos* 37 no.1, (June 2011): 87–103.
"Suspected coup plotters remanded in custody." *Chronicle*, May 24, 2019.
"They are day-dreaming." *IOL News*, December 1, 2008.
Tibaijuka, Anna Kajumulo. *Report of the fact-finding mission to Zimbabwe to assess the scope and impact of Operation Murambatsvina by the UN Special Envoy on Human Settlements Issues in Zimbabwe.* New York: United Nations, 2005.
Xaba, Mzingaye Brilliant. "The impact of land restitution and resettlement in the Eastern Cape, South Africa: restoring dignity without strengthening livelihoods?." PhD Thesis, Grahamstown: Rhodes University.
Zimbabwe Human Rights NGO Forum. *On the Days of Darkness in Zimbabwe An Updated Report on the Human Rights Violations Committed between 14 January, 2019 to 5 February 2019.* Harare: Zimbabwe Human Rights NGO Forum, 2019a. http://kubatana.net/wp-content/uploads/2019/02/Shutdown-Atrocities-Report-6-February-2019.pdf
Zimbabwe Human Rights NGO Forum. "*'Only bruises on the soles of their feet! Torture and Falanga in Zimbabwe, Report by Zimbabwe Human Rights NGO Forum', February 2009,* 2009b," Harare: Zimbabwe Human Rights NGO Forum, 2009. http://www.hrforumzim.org/wp-content/uploads/2009/02/Torture-and-falanga-in-Zimbabwe1.pdf.
Zimbabwe Human Rights NGO Forum. "A Consolidate Report on the Food Riots 19—23 January 1998 Report compiled by the AMANI Trust on behalf of the Zimbabwe Human Rights NGO Forum, 1998," Harare: Zimbabwe Human Rights NGO Forum, http://hrforumzim.org/wpcontent/uploads/1998/01/con solidatedreportonfood.pdf.
Zimbabwe Lawyers for Human Rights [ZLHR] (n.d). *Amendments to the Constitution of Zimbabwe: A Constant Assault on Democracy and Constitutionalism,* http://hrl ibrary.umn.edu/research/constitution%20statement-sunday%20mirror.pdf.
"Zimbabwe's Opposition M.P Job Sikhala arrested by police: Party." *Aljazeera,* August 22, 2020.

CHAPTER 14

Constitutional Courts as Protection Conduits: The Role of Egypt Supreme Constitutional Court in Advancing Human Rights Protection

Mohamed Abdelaal

1 INTRODUCTION

In 2005, former Secretary-General of the United Nations Kofi Annan highlighted the necessity of sparing no effort in promoting democracy and the rule of law noting that 'while freedom from want and fear are essential they are not enough. All human beings have the right to be treated with dignity and respect' (Annan 2005, 34). One could argue from a liberal point of view that rule of law simply means that law must prevail to the extent that all members of the society, including those who govern, are equally subjected to the law (Al-Sayyid 2013, 211). In fact, the concept of ruling by law carries with it the duty to respect the civility, humanity and dignity of individuals, which together, form the backbone of human rights.

With that being said, one can truly argue that although rule of law and human rights may at first seem different, they are indeed closely related. That is, as long as the principle of human dignity and the respect of civility and humanity are regarded as the acme of human rights, such dignity and respect need to be guaranteed and protected. The good application of the rule of law, which entails the subordination of the ruling and the ruled class to the law as well as limiting arbitrary practices by following a well-defined set of laws, provides such guarantee and protection (Sieder and Schjolden 2005).

M. Abdelaal (✉)
Faculty of Law, Alexandria University, Alexandria, Egypt
e-mail: moha.abdelaal@gmail.com

© The Author(s), under exclusive license to Springer Nature
Switzerland AG 2022
A. Adeola and M. W. Mutua (eds.), *The Palgrave Handbook
of Democracy, Governance and Justice in Africa,*
https://doi.org/10.1007/978-3-030-74014-6_14

259

Since its establishment in 1979, the Egyptian Supreme Constitutional Court ('SCC') has played a pivotal role in Egypt's legal and political life. Given the centrality of the constitutional judiciary in Egypt, whereby the SCC is the sole court that exclusively performs the process of judicial review and decides over the constitutionality of laws, judges and political institutions initially questioned the authority and jurisdiction of the SCC. However, not too long after its establishment, the attitude towards the SCC started to change in that its decisions are regarded with sufficient respect and veneration. The SCC soon became a defiant institutional actor in the interaction process between the government and Egypt's liberals, conservatives and human rights activists.

In Egypt, application of the rule of law witnessed two different phases, pre the 2011 Revolution and post the 2011 Revolution, where the issue of human rights was always of a great concern. In both phases, the SCC was in the forefront of the ongoing intense debate. Advocates of the SCC would argue that its decisions provide the best guarantee for human rights (Moustafa 2014, 281), while critics of the SCC regard the institution as a mere judicial tool to confer legitimacy on the government's political agenda and arbitrary practices at the expense of the well-being of individuals and their most basic human rights (Moustafa 2014, 281).

This view is supported, according to legal analysts, by the claim that the first years of the SCC witnessed its attempt to gain confidence of the legal society by defending individual rights and freedoms (Abu-Odeh 2011, 985–986). After this early stage, especially in the 1990s, the SCC continued to surpass the limit of expectations defying the then ruling regime by liberalising politics and giving great attention to political expression (Moustafa 2009). However, this does not negate the fact that the SCC remained loyal to the regime being reluctant to alter the basic interests of the regime (Moustafa 2014, 106).

In the period that followed the 2011 Revolution, Islamists in Egypt, notably the Muslim Brotherhood and the Salafists, came into power and gradually started to dominate Egypt's political and economic life. The SCC, however, assumed a vocal position against the Muslim Brotherhood, in particular with regard, to how they manage the state affairs. Over the years, the role of the SCC in advancing human rights in Egypt has become notable. Evidently, the position taken by the SCC towards some of the most debatable contemporary legal issues in Egypt proves how a constitutional court can serve as a significant guard (Brown and Waller 2016, 840). In considering how the SCC has engaged in human rights, I will consider some of the Court's notable decisions concerning pertinent issues at the fore of human rights challenges in Egypt, notably, freedom of belief, protest and assembly, women's rights and minorities' rights.

2 CONSTITUTIONAL COURTS AS PROTECTION CONDUITS

Constitutional courts have emerged as important judicial mechanisms that shape societies and entrench the core values of nation-building. According to Donald L. Horowitz Constitutional Courts have the potential to support 'the transition to and consolidation of a stable democratic regime' (Horowitz 2006, 128). Many scholars have validated this point (Henckaerts and van der Jeught 1998, 501; Mayeety and Grosskopf 2004, 464; Mietzner 2010, 399–400).[1] To understand the role of constitutional courts in the consolidation of the rule of law and human rights, I distinguish three main themes that should be taken in account: (1) the stature of the constitutional court in the legal system of a given state, which varies widely according to the difference in the strength and effectiveness of the performed process of judicial review on the constitutionality of the executive and legislative acts; (2) the extent and the efficiency in terms of protecting individual basic rights and freedoms; and (3) the determination of the degree of independence enjoyed by the courts that serve in the constitutional judiciary in terms of their interaction with the various institutions and authorities in the political system.

Firstly, regarding how the process of judicial review affects the stature of the constitutional court in the legal system of a given state, unlike some jurisdictions which perform the process of judicial review in the abstract (i.e. in the absence of an actual case or controversy and before the promulgation of the challenged law),[2] the Egyptian SCC is the sole judicial body that has the power to decide on the constitutionality of laws only in concrete cases or controversies (i.e. after a challenged law has been promulgated, taken effect

---

[1] For example, in 1998, Jean-Marie Henckaerts and Stefaan Van der Jeught asserted that the respective constitutional courts in Western and Eastern Europe new democracies 'have played an active role in ensuring the supremacy of constitutional principles'. Likewise, Nancy Maveety and Anke Grosskopf have argued that the Supreme Court of the Republic of Estonia in adjudicating minority rights and exercising constitutional review has acted 'as a conduit for significant democratic reform'. Further, Marcus Mietzner has claimed that the public support enjoyed by the Indonesian Constitutional Court as well as its effectiveness in enforcing constitutional rights played a major role in the 'diffusion of political power' and the democratic consolidation in Indonesia.

[2] The process of judicial review in the abstract assumes reviewing the constitutionality of laws is essentially a function that ensures the respect of power between the executive branch and the legislature, since the Parliament is not considered the ordinary legislature simply because the constitution has defined certain areas in which it can be exclusively regulated by laws issued by the Parliament. Any other area which is not explicitly reserved by the constitution for the legislature should be regulated by the executive branch. Thus, disagreement between the executive and legislative branch over whether a specific issue falls within the legislative or executive jurisdiction must be solved by the constitutional courts. The French Constitution of 1958 is a good example of legal jurisdictions that adopt judicial review in the abstract. For example, Article 61 of the Constitution requires that Institutional acts, before their promulgation, Private Members' Bills, before they are submitted to referendum, and the Rules of Procedure of the Houses of Parliament, before coming into force, be referred to the Constitutional Council to decide over their conformity with the Constitution. Further, Acts of Parliament may be referred to the Constitutional Council, before their promulgation.

and involved in a specific dispute between litigants). Therefore, if the SCC proves that the legislation violates the constitution, it has the power to refrain from implementing it and rule it unconstitutional.[3]

Secondly, although the position of the Egyptian SCC regarding rule of law and human rights will be discussed based on a case-by-case analysis later in this chapter, in considering the capacity of the Egyptian SCC as a guarantor of the rule of law and individual basic rights and freedoms, one should acknowledge that the fundamental difference between political systems is not related to the legal texts and provisions themselves. If constitutions of different jurisdictions reflect many similarities between them, the vast difference lies in the extent to which these written legal texts are adhered to, in particular enabling citizens to enjoy their basic rights and freedoms. In this sense, the burden of enabling citizens to benefit effectively from their basic rights and freedoms as well as the guarantee of equality between all citizens regardless of their social status lies on the SCC. This function is achieved through the abolition of all laws that violate the constitution or those aimed at reviewing the bulk of these rights. In exercising its jurisdiction regarding judicially reviewing legislative acts, an important aspect of the work of a constitutional court is to provide a remedy where a law or executive ordinance or regulation violate individual basic rights and freedoms.[4]

Thirdly, the question regarding the independence of the Egyptian SCC is in fact a question of the independence of the judiciary as a whole. Although the vast majority of the world constitutions have spoken explicitly about the independence of the judiciary including constitutional and supreme courts, sometimes the reality shows otherwise. It should be noted that any attempt to examine the independence of a given judiciary merits further examination of some important issues such as, the status of the judges themselves, their

---

[3] In addition to the classic functions regarding the process of judicial review and deciding over the constitutionality of laws and regulations, constitutional courts usually have certain other competencies. In German, for example, the Federal Constitutional Court shall maintain the balance between the jurisdiction of the states (Länder) and the jurisdiction of the federal authority (Art. 93(3) of the German Basic Law of 1949). Some other constitutional courts, like that of Thailand, have the power to examine the legality of elections, the validity of Parliament membership, and hearing electoral petitions (Sec(s) 144, 210 of the Thai Constitution of 2017). Further, some constitutional courts have the power to review acts of executive officials and agencies that is, to hear impeachment proceedings against holders of public office and to consider of qualifications of individuals to hold or continue to hold public office. For instance, the Turkish Constitution empowers the constitutional court with the authority to try the President of the Republic, the Speaker of the Grand National Assembly of Turkey, members of the Council of Ministers for offences relating to their official duties (The Turkish Constitution of 1982, art. 148).

[4] For example, in Hungary, since the new constitutional framework came into effect on the 1 January 2012, an ex post review of conformity with the fundamental law can be initiated only by the Government, by one-quarter of the Members of Parliament, by the Commissioner for Fundamental Rights (ombudsman), by the President of the Curia and by the General Prosecutor. Accordingly, a political opposition collation with more than a quarter of parliamentary members may be allowed to use this constitutional right.

qualifications, their financial and moral status, as well as their relationship with the executive authority in a given legal system.

Given the legal and political importance of constitutional courts, the mechanism adopted in appointing constitutional judges is potentially controversial. In this regard, conflicting interests may arise regarding who can be appointed as a constitutional court judge, what are the qualifications a candidate should possess, and most importantly who has the power to appoint. In addressing these issues, practices vary widely across contemporary constitutional systems; however, it seems like different constitutional systems are on agreement that the appointing mechanism of constitutional court judges should be unique in that it should not resemble the mechanism adopted in appointing ordinary judges.

Contemporary constitutional systems have realised that the mechanism of forming their constitutional and supreme courts is one of the most important mechanisms for a better application of the principle of separation of powers as well as maintaining the independence of the constitutional judiciary to the extent that guarantees an effective monitoring of the application of the rule of law and human rights. These constitutional systems realise that the executive branch should not monopolise the power of appointing members of its constitutional and supreme courts. In doing so, these systems require the participation of others actors in the appointment process.[5]

---

[5] Some constitutional systems have required the participation of the legislature along with the executive in the selection and appointment of members of the constitutional courts. For example, by and with the advice and consent of the Senate, the US President appoints the President and members of the Supreme Court. (U.S. Constitution, art. II, § 2, cl. 2). Further, according to the Venezuelan Constitution of 1999, justices of the Supreme Tribunal of Justice are appointed after nomination by the Judicial Nominations Committee and the approval of the National Assembly. (Art. 264). The same paradigm applies when appointing judges of the Czech Constitutional Court, where they are appointed by the President of the Republic with the approval of the Senate. (Art. 84(2) of the Czech Constitution of 1993). Likewise, three of the nine members of the French Constitutional Council are selected by the President of the Republic, three by the Speaker of the National Legislative Council, and three by the President of the Senate. (The French Constitution of 1958, art. 56).

Some other constitutional systems have tried to involve some other parties in the process of appointing members of the constitutional and supreme courts alongside the executive and legislative branches. For example, Article 135 of the Italian Constitution of 1947 stipulates that 'the Constitutional Court shall be composed of 15 judges, one third appointed by the President of the Republic, one third appointed by the Parliament in joint sitting, and a third by the ordinary and administrative supreme Courts'. In a more complex pattern, the Turkish Constitution of 1982 requires that when appointing members of the Supreme Constitutional Court, the Grand National Assembly (Parliament) elects two members from among three candidates nominated by the President of the Republic and the Court of Accountability, and one member from among three candidates nominated by the heads of the Bar Associations. The President of the Republic appoints three members from the Supreme Court of Appeal, two members from the Council of State, one member from the High Military Court of Appeals and one member from the High Military Administrative Court, all three of which are nominated by the respective General Assemblies. Finally, the Constitution of Turkey stipulates that the President of the Republic

264   M. ABDELAAL

According to Article 193 of the Egyptian Constitution of 2014, the SCC 'shall be composed of a President (Chief Justice) and a sufficient number of Vice-Presidents (Deputy Chief Justices)'. In the same context, Article 3 of the Law of the Court No. 48 of 1979[6] stipulates that 'the SCC shall be composed of a President and a sufficient number of members and shall issue its judgments and decisions from seven members and shall be presided over by its President (Chief Justice) or the oldest of its members'.[7]

Regarding the SCC's appointment mechanism, Article 193 of the Egyptian current Constitution of 2014 provides that 'the General Assembly chooses the SCC's President from among the most senior three Vice-Presidents of the court. It also chooses the Vice-Presidents and the members of its Commissioners Authority, who are appointed by a decree from the President of the Republic. The foregoing takes place in the manner defined by the law'. Likewise, according to Article 5 of the SCC Law No. 48 of 1979, the President of the Republic, after the approval of the General Assembly of the Court, shall appoint the President of the Court from among the three most senior Vice-Presidents of the Court. Similarly, the Vice-President of the Court shall be appointed by President of the Republic, after the approval of the General Assembly of the Court.[8]

shall appoint two members of the Constitutional Court of law graduates from among three candidates nominated by the Supreme Education Council. (Art. 146).

However, this does not refute the fact that some of the comparative constitutional regimes preferred to entrust the task of selecting and appointing members of their constitutional courts to one authority, either the legislature or the executive. The German Basic Law of 1949, for example, vests the German Federal Parliament the power to elect members of the Federal Constitutional Court, so that members of the Court shall be elected equally by the two legislative chambers of the Parliament. (Art. 94(1)). On the other hand, some constitutions, like that of Jordan and the United Arab Emirates, have delegated exclusively to the executive branch the task of appointing members of constitutional and supreme courts without the participation of any other actor.

[6] The Supreme Constitutional Court's Law, No. 48 of 1979, 36 Egyptian Official Gazette (Al Gareedah Al Rasmeyah) (6/9/1979).

[7] A careful examination of these two articles reveals that both the constitution and the law of the SCC require the presence of a chief justice to preside over the Court; however, they both refrained from specifying a certain number of justices to act as members of the Court, merely stating that the court should be composed of a sufficient number of members. Nevertheless, Article 3 of the Law of the Court No. 48 of 1979 requires a procedural restriction, that is, for the Court's judgements and decisions to be valid they should be issued by a quorum of at least seven justices. Accordingly, the Egyptian legislator in Article 3 of Law No. 48 of 1979 adopted a policy of setting the minimum limit for the Court's membership, which is the same limit required for the issuance of its judgments and decisions (seven members), without specifying a maximum limit for membership.

[8] It should be noted that the text of Article 5 as it stands today is the product of Article 1 of Decree-Law No. 48 of 2011, which amends certain provisions of the SCC Law No. 48 of 1979. Before being amended, Article 5 authorized the President of the Republic to appoint the President of the Court without any restriction or limitation, as it states that 'the President of the Court shall be appointed by the President of the Republic through a presidential decree issued without the participation of any other party'.

Based on the argument provided above, the role of the Egyptian SCC in the consolidation of the rule of law and human rights is closely related to the degree and extent of its positive intervention in the political life. The effectiveness of such intervention depends largely on the judicial tradition of the court regarding how it introduces itself as a guardian to the individual rights and freedoms as well as the efficiency of the judicial review performed. Further, the court's role in the process of consolidating the rule of law and human rights will always be affected by the political environment in which the court serves. Evidently, a democratic-neutral constitutional court is a worthy objective but not if the process by which we achieve it is tainted with doubts.

3   The SCC and Freedom of Belief

Freedom of belief and practising religious rituals are formally recognised by the current Egyptian Constitution of 2014. Article 64 of the Constitution describes freedom of belief as 'absolute' and freedom of practising religious rituals and establishing places of worship as a 'right' granted only to the 'followers of revealed religions' and to be organised by law.[9] Further, the Constitution in Article 2 specifies Islam as the official religion of the state and designates the 'principles of Islamic Sharia as the main source of legislation'.[10]

Religious constitutionalism found its way in Egypt's first Constitution of 1923 when Article 149 declared that 'the religion of the state is Islam and Arabic is its official language'. Following the Constitution of 1923, Egypt's consecutive constitutions embraced Article 149. However, Egypt's Constitution of 1971 incorporated Article 149 after adding to it a new phrase, that is the new Article read 'Islam is the religion of the state, Arabic is its official language, and the principles of Islamic Sharia are a primary source of legislation'.[11]

Interestingly, Article 2 was the subject of a further amendment in 1980. The amendment maintained Islam as the religion of the state and Arabic as its official language; however, it declared the principles of Islamic Sharia as '*the*' primary source of legislation after being '*a*' primary source of legislation. Article 2 as it stood after the 1980 amendment was incorporated in Egypt's

---

[9] Article 64 of the 2014 Constitution reads 'Freedom of belief is absolute. The freedom of practicing religious rituals and establishing places of worship for the followers of revealed religions is a right organized by law'.

[10] Article 2 of the 2014 Constitution provides that 'Islam is the religion of the state and Arabic is its official language. The principles of Islamic Sharia are the main source of legislation'.

[11] In fact, after President Mohammad Anwar el-Sadat assumed power in Egypt in 1970, he tried to conciliate Egypt's Islamists fearing their influence and power. Thus, his proposal to add the phrase 'and the principles of Islamic Sharia are a primary source of legislation' was a mere attempt to achieve such purpose.

266 M. ABDELAAL

current Constitution of 2014, and it has been the subject of a major constitutional debate regarding whether it serves as a restriction to freedom of religion and belief.

3.1 The SCC on Article 2: Towards a Liberal Interpretation

As mentioned earlier, pursuant to Article 2 of Egypt's current Constitution of 2014, the principles of Islamic Sharia are the primary source of legislation in the state, which means that all legislations must be consistent with the principles of Islamic Sharia to the extent that no law or regulation can violate these principles. This begs the question: What do the principles of Islamic Sharia actually mean?

Islamic Sharia is a broad term that refers to rules derived from the religious precepts of Islam, which includes rules stipulated in the Qur'an as well as rules legislated by Prophet Muhammad by means of revelation (Al-Faruqi and Al-Faruqi 1996, 279). The term Islamic Sharia also accommodates the entire jurisprudential system developed by Islamic scholars (Al-Faruqi and Al-Faruqi 1996, 279). With that being said, listing the principles of Islamic Sharia as the primary source of legislation is something that haunts liberals and Christians in Egypt regarding whether it could be used as a restriction on the freedom of religion and belief.

However, it was indeed the SCC's interpretation to Article 2 that helps in the dispersion of most of the worries of Egypt's liberals and Christians (Abdelaal 2013a, b, 201). Being that it exercises exclusive power to review the constitutionality of laws and regulations and to engage in the process of judicially interpreting laws to remove any alleged ambiguity or vagueness (Abdelaal 2013a, b, 201), the SCC seems to be the perfect forum to guarantee a neutral interpretation to Article 2 out of any religious extremism.

The SCC levelled up to expectations when it came up with a very liberal interpretation in the course of determining the meaning of 'the principles of the Islamic Sharia are the primary source of legislation' that renders Article 2 far from constituting a threat to human rights in Egypt. In 1993, the SCC considered a petition that certain provisions of Law No. 100 of 1985 (EI Alami 1994, 120), which amended some provisions of the Personal Status Law, were unconstitutional since they violated Article 2 (Abdelaal 2013a, b, 39). In rendering its decision, the SCC ruled that 'the principles of Islamic Sharia' that no law should violate are those 'authentic rules' that are inviolable, non-changeable and should not be altered. *Ijtihād*, individual reasoning, has no place to be applied in regard to these authentic rules; however, rules that do not enjoy such authenticity could be changed, altered and construed through *ijtihād* to the extent of maintaining the general purposes of Sharia: religion, life, reason, honour and property.[12]

---

[12] Supreme Constitutional Court, Case no. 7, Judicial Year 8.

A careful examination of the SCC's ruling reveals that it adopted a kind of a secular-liberal interpretation in determining what is meant by 'the principles of Islamic Sharia' that no law should violate. Such secular-liberal interpretation is evident in the SCC's approach in limiting the meaning of 'the principles of Islamic Sharia' to include only those authentic rules in both of its existence and meaning. That is, laws should not violate rules of Islamic Sharia that are beyond doubt regarding their existence and that have only one meaning if interpreted (Stilt 2010, 81). The SCC was of the opinion of examining the meaning of legal texts and maxims embraced in the Sharia's authentic rules and applying this meaning if it is not vague or ambiguous (Lombardi 2006, 186). However, the SCC emphasised, in case the meaning of the religious legal texts is vague or ambiguous, that it will, by itself, carry on the task of interpreting it by performing *ijtihād* without referring the issue to Islamic guilds, which are more equipped to interpret religious texts (Abdelaal 2013a, b, 40).

3.2   Litigating Article 2: Women's Rights and Entitlements

In 1996, the SCC found itself obliged to discuss Article 2 once again; however, this time was in regard to women's rights. A complaint was filed in the SCC challenging the constitutionality of the decision of the Minister of Education, which banned female students wearing the *niqab* [a veil that cover the female's face and hand] from entering schools. A father of two daughters who wore *niqāb* argued that the ministerial decision violated Article 2 of the Egyptian Constitution since it was inconsistent with the principles of the Islamic Sharia.[13]

After citing its previous interpretation of the principles of the Islamic Sharia, the SCC argued that the *Qur'anic* verses undoubtedly commanded women to cover some parts of their bodies; however, those parts that should be covered were not clear enough.[14] The SCC then addressed the fact that no unanimous consensus was found among Islamic jurists that a woman should cover her face and hands by wearing *niqāb*; however, it is indisputable that woman's garments should guarantee decency and dignity.[15] The SCC, therefore, concluded that there is no explicit rule that requires woman to wear *niqāb* and thus the standard would be what the people have agreed about in their community and what is true regarding their habits and customs without contradicting an authentic legal text.[16] Further, the SCC admitted that Islamic

---

[13] Supreme Constitutional Court, Case no. 8, Judicial Year 17.

[14] *Id.*

[15] *Id.*

[16] *Id.*

jurists agreed that wearing *hijāb* is required; however, there is no such agreement regarding *niqāb* and thus *ijtihād* would be allowed to settle this issue in the absence of authentic rules.[17]

The SCC moved on to test the Ministerial decision regarding its consistency with the main purposes of the Sharia, the preservation of mind, reason, honour and property. The SCC argued that these purposes have infinite interest with no limited application. Thus, the achievement of these purposes requires a degree of discretion that entails adhering to 'the established opinions of a certain jurist rather than introducing a new rule by engaging in an individual reasoning (*ijtihād*)'.[18] The SCC found that if covering a woman's face and hand is mandatory it would impose an undue burden that violates the concept of human rights that Islam in fact maintains.[19] Accordingly, the SCC found the ministerial decision constitutional since it is consistent with the main purposes of the Sharia and it does not violate any authentic rule.[20]

Likewise in 2006, the SCC found itself once again in the forefront of defending women's rights and freedoms when it considered a challenge regarding the constitutionality of Article 21 of Law No. 1 of 2000, regarding the regulation of matters of personal status, which provides, '[A] divorce, in case of its denial, cannot be proven except by witnesses and authentication...'. The plaintiff, a woman whom her husband refused to admit that he divorced her, claimed that Article 21 is unconstitutional since it violates Article 2 of the Constitution, after she failed to prove her divorce by witnesses and authentication and refused to comply with an obedience order issued by her husband.[21] In Egypt, an obedience order is a legal order submitted by the husband to his wife ordering her to return to the marital home within 30 days.

The plaintiff argued that the approach taken in Article 21 regarding limiting the possibility of proving the occurrence of divorce to witnesses and authentication without considering other possible legal means to prove such divorce is inconsistent with the principles of Islamic Sharia as the primary source of legislation.[22] In considering such claim, the SCC ruled that limiting the ways to prove a divorce, if one of the spouses denied its occurrence, only to

---

[17] *Id.*

[18] *Id.* There is no doubt that Justices of the Court acknowledged the legitimacy of veiling the woman's hair 'wearing *hijāb*' by following the opinions of the prominent Islamic jurists who agreed on its legitimacy and necessity. However, when the Justices found a disagreement among the jurists regarding the legitimacy of veiling the woman's face and hands 'wearing *niqāb*', they did not adhere to the opinion of a certain jurist; rather, they trigger their own *ijtihādic* skills to reach their decision. Aside from the fact that this decision helps in emphasizing the SCC's position regarding Article 2, this decision, indeed, is a perfect example of how the two intellectual methods, *ijtihād* and *taqlīd*, can work together.

[19] *Id.*

[20] *Id.*

[21] Egyptian Supreme Constitutional Court, Case no. 133, Judicial Year 26.

[22] *Id.*

witnesses and authentication violates the authentic rule of the Islamic Sharia that a divorce could be proven by all methods of proof such as evidence, oaths and recognition.[23] Further, the SCC emphasised that divorce is a kind of mercy from God for both spouses who found it difficult to continue their life together and thus by limiting the ways to prove divorce to witnesses and authentication, the legislator was not successful in triggering its *ijtihādic* skills.[24] Accordingly, the SCC concluded that Article 21 impeded the purposes of Sharia and thus impeded human justice and welfare. For these reasons, Article 21 of Law No. 1 of 2000 was declared unconstitutional.[25]

4 The SCC and Minorities Rights

Egypt's Coptic Christians, being the largest religious minority in Egypt and the entire Middle East and North Africa with a population that makes up around 10% to 15% of Egypt's population of 104 million, continue to face tremendous challenges regarding their religious rights and freedoms (Abdelaal 2013a, b, 43; Stanek 2007). For the purpose of this chapter, I will limit my discussion here to address the position of the SCC regarding the right of Egypt's Coptic Christians to a paid leave from work to perform religious pilgrimage in Jerusalem.

In 1980, Pope Shenouda III of Alexandria and the head of the Holy Synod of the Coptic Orthodox Patriarchate of Alexandria banned Egypt's Coptic from visiting Jerusalem, Bethlehem and other holy sites under the authority of Israel (Sakr Taha 2017). The Pope warned that if Copts breach such ban, they will face excommunication since pilgrimage to Jerusalem is not a religious duty in Christianity. The Pope's decision was in fact a declaration that the Coptic Egyptian Church refuses the normalisation of relationships between Egypt and Israel (Sakr 2017).[26]

On 2 February 2010, Egypt's Administrative Court upheld a decision issued by the Minister of Interior to prevent Egyptian Christians from travelling to Jerusalem, Bethlehem and other holy places under the Israeli jurisdiction. The Administrative Court refused to proceed with the travel procedures of a Coptic citizen who requested to be allowed to travel to these territories after taking part in a tourist trip for this purpose. The Administrative Court stated that the ban imposed on the Coptic Christians by virtue of the decision of the Ministry of Interior is justified by Law No.

[23] *Id.*

[24] *Id.*

[25] *Id.*

[26] The normalisation of relations between Egypt and Israel went into effect in January 1980 following the signing of a peace treaty between the two counties in Camp David in 1979. Pursuant to the normalisation of relations, full diplomatic relations were established between Egypt and Israel, and formal exchange of ambassadors took place.

80/1960, as amended by Law No. 88/2005, regarding the entry and residence of foreigners. Pursuant to this law, the Administrative Court asserted, the Ministry of Interior was given discretion to deny citizens their right to travel if compelling evidence reveals that their travel poses a threat to their personal security or the homeland security.[27]

However, in February 2017, the SCC was called upon to end legal speculations regarding the issue of the Copts' pilgrimage. Specifically, the SCC considered an appeal filled by a Coptic Egyptian woman challenging the constitutionality of Article 71 of Law No. 47 of 1978 regarding Civil Servants of the State, which grants paid leave for pilgrimage only to Muslims.[28] The SCC ruled that since Egypt's successive constitutions have endeavoured to ensure the principle of equality and religious freedoms, including the freedom of belief and the freedom to practice religious rituals in such a way that does not violate public order, the right of Christians to visits religious sites in Jerusalem is a religious ritual that must be respected and guaranteed equally with Muslims' right to pilgrimage.[29] The SCC proceeded to argue that.

> [T]he challenged article did not recognize the right of the Christian employees in having a paid leave for one month and for one time throughout their career to perform pilgrimage and visit Jerusalem, granting such leave to Muslim employees to perform Islamic pilgrimage (Hajj). Thus, the legal protection introduced by the legislator in the challenged article came short and incomplete and failed to embrace the rights and freedoms guaranteed by the Constitution in all of its diameters and aspects. Consequently, Article 71 of Law No. 47 of 1978 regarding Civil Servants of the State stands as a serious breach to the constitutional rights and freedoms, a matter which requires declaring it unconstitutional.[30]

A careful examination of the aforementioned ruling reveals that it constitutes an unprecedented victory and a major step forward towards the elimination of all forms of discrimination based on religion in Egypt. Despite the fact that it is unlikely that the Egyptian Coptic Orthodox Church will abide by the decision of the SCC and will continue to ban its followers from performing pilgrimage

---

[27] Article 4 of Law No. 80/1960, as amended by Law No. 88/2005, regarding the entry and residence of foreigners stipulates that '[T]he entry or exit of the Arab Republic of Egypt may only be from the places specified by the Minister of Interior by a decision issued by him and with the permission of the competent official, by stamping the passport or other alternative document'.

[28] Article 71 of Law No. 47 of 1978 provided that '[T]he employee shall be entitled to a special leave with full pay, which shall not be counted as part of the holidays prescribed in the preceding articles, in the following cases: (1) [T]o perform pilgrimage. [Such leave] shall be for one month and for one time throughout [the employee's] career...'. It is noteworthy that Law No. 47 of 1978 has been replaced by Law of Civil Service No. 81 of 2016, which became the governing law regarding issues of civil servants in the state.

[29] Egyptian Supreme Constitutional Court, Case no. 153, Judicial Year 32.

[30] *Id*.

and visiting Jerusalem, other Christian sects in Egypt such as, followers of the Catholic Church or the Evangelical Church, are now free to ask for a paid leave to perform pilgrimage as a religious duty.

5 The SCC and Civil Liberties (Freedom of Association and Right to Protest)

The Egyptian SCC's judicial jurisprudence is packed with tremendous incidents where it declared its position regarding how to establish the balance between individual rights and freedoms, on the one hand, and the right of the state in maintaining law and order. However, I intend to give attention to two of the SCC's most recent decisions regarding individual rights and freedoms specially freedom of civil association and the right of the citizens to protest.

5.1   Freedom of Association

Over the last two decades, since the emergence of civil society organisations, many scholarly works tried to highlight the important role these organisations can play in the economic and social development of any given country (al-Bayar 2005). These organisations, being charitable organisations, non-governmental organisations, voluntary groups, or trade unions, operate in many different forms on a wide range of issues; however, they all share the advantage of being private, non-profit and that individuals are free to join or support them voluntarily (al-Bayar 2005).

In addressing challenges facing civil society organisations in Egypt, some important factors must be taken in consideration such as, the fact that Egypt is one of the most densely populated countries in the Middle East, a strategic ally of the United States, a regional power that its laws and justice system are most likely to have a great influence on other Arab countries (al-Bayar 2005). With that being said, laws and regulations defining the role to be played by civil society organisations and their practices in Egypt were of a great importance.

In Egypt, for almost 15 years, Law on Associations and Non-Governmental Organizations (No. 84 of 2002) remained the governing law on the work of civil society organisations until it was replaced by Law No. 70 of 2017 on Non-Governmental Organizations. Law No. 84 of 2002 imposed many restrictions on the freedom of associations as well as the work on NGOs in Egypt. The law, for example, listed imprisonment as a punishment, imposed governmental supervision over foreign organisation operating in Egypt, prohibited foreign fund to NGOs, banned NGOs from establishing companies and investment funds, and imposed tremendous restrictions on establishing associations and NGOs in Egypt.

Through its decisions, the Egyptian SCC played a pivotal role in the overthrow of Law No. 84 of 2002 as well as in drawing the attention of the government on how the new law (Law No. 70 of 2017) should be applied. On 2 June 2018, the SCC delivered its decision regarding a petition challenging

272   M. ABDELAAL

the constitutionality of Article 42 of Law No. 84 of 2002 that it grants the competent administrative authority the power to dissolve civil associations and remove their board of directors.[31] In the course of determining the constitutionality of Article 41, the SCC emphasised that civil society organisations are the custodians of the social contract between the individual and the state, which is able to improve the personality of the individual as the basic rule in building the society, by raising awareness and dissemination of knowledge and public culture, and thus educating citizens on the culture of democracy and conciliating a free and constructive dialogue.[32] The SCC went on to state that

> [W]hereas the right to freedom of association has been enshrined in international conventions, such as the Universal Declaration of Human Rights and the International Covenant on Civil and Political Rights, as well as in Egypt's consecutive constitutions from the 1923 Constitution to the current Constitution of 2014, which grants citizens the right to form non-governmental organization on a democratic basis,[33] it is the duty of this Court, therefore, to protect such right and provide its judicial safeguards.[34]

Moreover, the SCC concluded that

> [S]ince the right to freedom of associations is a constituent constitutional right, the independence of these associations from administrative authorities should be maintained to better achieve their goals. This understanding is consistent with Article 75 of the 2014 Constitution which prohibits administrative agency from interfering in the affairs of civil associations and organizations and from dissolving them or their board of directors or trustees. Consequently, Article 42 of Law No. 84 of 2002, in allowing the Minister of Social Solidarity to dissolve civil association, must be ruled unconstitutional.[35]

Although the SCC's ruling was concerned with the constitutionality of Article 42 of Law No. 84 of 2002, which was replaced by Law No. 70 of 2017 on Non-Governmental Organizations, it could be seen as a start to also streamline Law No. 70 of 2017 (which has also been criticised for allowing excessive governmental interventions in the field of community work), in order

---

[31] Article 42 of Law No. 84 of 2002 stipulated that '[T]he dissolution of the association shall be by a reasoned decision to be issued by the Minister of Social Affairs [now the Minister of Social Solidarity], after seeking the opinion of the General Union and after calling the association to hear its statements, in the following cases...'.

[32] Egyptian Supreme Constitutional Court, Case no. 160, Judicial Year 37.

[33] Article 75 of Egypt's current Constitution of 2014 states 'Citizens have the right to form non-governmental organizations and institutions on a democratic basis, which shall acquire legal personality upon notification. They shall be allowed to engage in activities freely. Administrative agencies shall not interfere in the affairs of such organizations, dissolve them, their board of directors, or their board of trustees except by a judicial ruling'.

[34] Egyptian Supreme Constitutional Court, Case no. 160, Judicial Year 37.

[35] *Id.*

to ensure the independence of civil organisations and associations in Egypt. Further, although Law No. 70 of 2002 had been abolished at the time of the SCC's ruling, declaring one of its articles unconstitutional on the basis that it strips civil organisations from its independence will certainly help ensuring the proper application of provisions of Law No. 70 of 2017.

5.2 Right to Protest

The right to protest and assemble is considered to be one of the most important outcomes of the 2011 Revolution in Egypt (Abdelaal 2014, 1115). In 2011, Egyptians used this right demanding economic and social reforms as well as putting an end to emergency laws and police brutality (Abdelaal 2014, 1115). These were a series of demands that resulted in toppling the defiant regime of President Hosni Mubarak who ruled Egypt for almost thirty years (Abdelaal 2014, 1115). Egyptians used their right to protest and assemble once again in 2013 when they gathered in wide demonstrations and sit-ins protesting against the ruling of the Muslim Brotherhood, which led to its overthrow (Abdelaal 2014, 1115).

Moreover, after the fall of Egypt's Muslim Brotherhood regime in 2013, the right to protest and assemble has been used by many Egyptians as a tool to force the government to meet factional demands (Abdelaal 2014, 1115). Specifically, the country witnessed a huge wave of factional demonstrations and sit-ins in: demand for improvements in the standard of living, setting minimum wage rate and achieving transitional justice. However, this right has also been used by supporters of the Muslim Brotherhood that had gathered in many protest movements and sit-ins causing disruption of public facilities and daily life (Kassem 2013, 11).

Consequently, a need has emerged for a new law to regulate the right to protest and assemble. The result was Law No. 107 of 2013 on organising the right to peaceful public meetings, processions and protests, which was signed into law by the then interim President Adly Mansour on 24 November 2013,[36] which has been in force to this day.[37] But ever since it was promulgated, the law has been widely criticised by political activists in Egypt and human rights groups for being a further crackdown on civil liberties and an attempt to ban public protests and assemblies rather than regulating them (Abdelaal 2014, 1114).

In fact, the Egyptian SCC was reluctant to hear legal claims regarding the constitutionality of Law No. 107 of 2013. However, in a case that merits

---

[36] Law No. 107 of 2013, *Al-Jarida Al-Rismiyyah*, 24 Nov. 2013.

[37] It should be noted that beside Law No. 107 of 2013, Egypt's Penal Code (Law No. 58 of 1937) and Anti-Terrorism Law (Law No. 8 of 2015) include provisions that regulate peaceful protest and assembly.

consideration, the SCC in 2016 heard an appeal challenging the constitutionality of four articles of the law (articles 7, 8, 10).[38] Article 10 of Law No. 107 of 2013 authorises the Ministry of Interior or the specialised Director of Security to cancel, postpone, or modify the route of a public meeting, procession, or demonstration in case a serious information or evidence that the assembly would threaten national peace and security has been acquired.[39] The constitutionality of the article has been challenged on the grounds that it violates several articles of the 2014 Constitution.

Egypt's Constitution of 2014 recognises the right of citizens to organise and assemble in all forms of peaceful protests and public meetings (Article 73(1). Likewise, the Constitution emphasises that citizens' rights and freedoms are inalienable and may not be suspended or reduced (Article 92). Further, the Constitution affirms that all institutions of the state are subject to the law and that the rule of law is the basis of governance (Article 94). According to these constitutional directives, the Egyptian SCC found Article 10 of Law No. 107 of 2013 to be unconstitutional.

The SCC grounded its decision on the fact that the Constitution is keen to impose restrictions on both the legislative and executive authorities to guarantee that individual rights and freedoms, principally the right to peaceful assembly and protest, will be maintained.[40] These restrictions serve as a safeguard to curb any authority from interfering within the designated arena protected by the right or freedom with the purpose of preventing its effective exercise.[41]

The SCC went on to argue that according to Egypt's current Constitution of 2014, the legislature is prohibited from choosing any means to regulate the exercise of the right to peaceful assembly and protest other than notification.[42] This notification, according to the SCC, requires the organisers of the peaceful protest or assembly to inform the competent authorities about their intention to protest or assemble without requiring the consent of these authorities.[43] Accordingly, after proper notification, the SCC concluded that any attempt to impede the exercise of the right to peacefully protest and assemble infringes the substance and essence of the right, thus violating the Constitution.[44]

---

[38] Egyptian Supreme Constitutional Court, Case no. 160, Judicial Year 96.

[39] Article 10 of Law No. 107 of 2013 states that 'If serious information or evidence is found before the scheduled time for starting a public meeting, procession, or demonstration, indicating the presence of threats to security of peace, the Minister of Interior of the specialized Director of Security may issue a justified decree prohibiting the public meeting, procession, or demonstrations, or suspending it, or relocating it, or altering the route; the organizers [submitters of the request] should be notified with the decision, at least 24 h prior to the scheduled date'.

[40] Egyptian Supreme Constitutional Court, Case no. 160, Judicial Year 96.

[41] *Id*.

[42] *Id*.

[43] *Id*.

[44] *Id*.

The constitutionality of Article 7 of Law No. 107 of 2013, which prohibits participants in public meetings, processions or protests from disrupting security and order or obstruct production or hamper citizens' interests, or affect the course of justice and public utilities,[45] has been challenged on the grounds that it violates Article 54(1) of the Constitution, which declares that personal freedom is safeguarded and that citizens can only be apprehended, searched, arrested, or have their freedoms restricted by a judicial warrant, expect in cases of flagrante delicto.[46] Moreover, Article 7 was claimed to be inconsistent with Article 92(2) of the Constitution which emphasises that no law that regulates personal rights and freedoms shall restrict them.[47] Further, it has been argued that Article 7 was in conflict with Article 95 of the Constitution regarding the principle of legality, that is penalties are personal and may only be based on law.[48] The case involved a group of young people who have been indicted in a court of law, based on Article 7, for participating in a demonstration without notifying the competent authorities, which resulted in disturbing public security, disrupting the interests of citizens and disrupting traffic.

In assessing these claims, the SCC emphasised that the crime determined in Article 7 is a deliberate crime that cannot be wrongly misrepresented, regardless of its image or degree.[49] The crime is committed only if the act is committed with the knowledge of its nature and the will to inflict it, and that the will of the perpetrator is directed to harm or threaten one of the rights and interests stipulated in the article.[50] According to the SCC, the wording of Article 7 recognises the principle of personal responsibility that whoever

[45] Article 7 of Law No. 107 of 2013 reads 'Participants in public meetings or processions or protests are prohibited to disrupt public security or order or obstruct production, or call for it, or hamper citizens' interests or harm them or subject them to danger or prevent them from exercising their rights and work, or affecting the course of justice, public utilities, or cutting roads or transportation, or road, water, or air transport, or obstructing road traffic or assaulting human life or public or private property or subjecting it to danger'.

[46] Article 54(1) of the 2014 Constitution provides that 'Personal freedom is a natural right which is safeguarded and cannot be infringed upon. Except in cases of in flagrante delicto, citizens may only be apprehended, searched, arrested, or have their freedoms restricted by a causal judicial warrant necessitated by an investigation'.

[47] Article 92(2) of the 2014 Constitution stipulates that 'No law that regulates the exercise of rights and freedoms may restrict them in such a way as infringes upon their essence and foundation'.

[48] Article 95 of the 2014 Constitution reads 'Penalties are personal. Crimes and penalties may only be based on the law, and penalties may only be inflicted by a judicial ruling. Penalties may only be inflicted for acts committed subsequent to the date on which the law enters into effect'.

[49] Egyptian Supreme Constitutional Court, Case no. 160, Judicial Year 36.

[50] *Id.*

commits the crime is the only one to be held responsible.[51] Consequently, the SCC concluded that Article 7 of Law No. 107 of 2013 is constitutional.[52]

With respect to Article 8 (which specifies the means of notification), the SCC found it constitutional on the basis that the Constitution vested the legislature with the power to regulate the notification process prior to public meetings, processions and protests.[53] The SCC emphasised that the legislature in Article 8 regulated the notification process in the most appropriate way that serves the interest of the citizens to exercise their right to protest and assemble, which represents the context for freedom of speech and expression, as well as the interest of the State in maintaining security and order.[54]

This ruling had a major effect in easing the political tension that continued to escalate since the application of Law No. 107 of 2013 in Egypt. Specifically, after large demonstrations against former President Mohamed Morsi on 30 June 2013, and the intervention of the military, President Morsi was overthrown and the ruling of the Muslim Brotherhood came to an end in Egypt. Law No. 107 of 2013 was passed in November 2013 where severe social division in Egypt existed. Instead of easing restrictions on associating and demonstrating, the law imposed further raising serious alarm regarding the view of the new regime towards fundamental rights and freedoms given the fact that the Egyptian society was severely divided between supporters of the new regime and supporters of the Muslim Brotherhood and the Islamists (Hamzawy, 2017, 393).

Following the SCC's ruling, authorities in Egypt started to release some of those detained as a result of violating the protest law. Prior to the SCC's decision, speaker of the Egyptian Parliament proposed a bundle of amendments to the law such as, freeing the law of any prison sentences, easing the procedures required to follow regarding notifying the competent authority before holding a demonstration or a public assembly, curbing the authority of the interior minister and security chiefs in balancing between the right to protest, as a fundamental right, and the interest of maintaining public security and order. However, discussion of these amendments was delayed until after the SCC's ruling (Youngblood and Hamdy, 2016). Now, after the SCC had rendered its decision, it is expected that the idea of amending the protest law will be put forward again.

6   Conclusion

A careful examination of the status quo in Egypt reveals that human rights violations as well as infringements directed towards the rule of law remain a major concern in Egypt. This chapter tried to shed light on the flip side of the

[51] *Id.*

[52] *Id.*

[53] *Id.*

[54] *Id.*

coin—a brighter side that reflects the judiciary efforts in preserving individuals' rights and freedoms and maintaining rule of law. In fact, the jurisprudence of the Egyptian SCC has been extremely influential in the Arab region, not least, in terms of its approaches and methodologies in addressing the constitutionality of legislations, interpreting constitutional provisions and also securing fundamental rights and freedoms. A careful examination of the SCC's conduct in adopting a clear liberal approach in addressing issues related to freedom of belief as a fundamental human right could render many observers to argue that the SCC is eager to enshrine human rights and dignity. However, there are some controversies regarding the attitude of the SCC. For instance, the SCC's conduct in repeatedly refusing to review the constitutionality of the highly controversial Public Protest Law of 2013, which is regarded by many scholars as an attempt to add more restrictions on individual rights and freedoms (Abdelaal 2014, 1114–1124), as well as its decision to validate the agreement between Egypt and Saudi Arabia regarding the case of the Strait of Tiran and Sanafir Island treaty, after being declared void by the Supreme Administrative Court, render many observers and legal analysts to think that the SCC's decisions are still politicised to serve the interest of the government, in some cases of political interests that may have human rights implications.

BIBLIOGRAPHY

Abdelaal, Mohamed. "Egypt's Constitution: What went Wrong?." *Vienna J Int'l Const L 7* (2013): 200–213.

Abdelaal, Mohamed. "Egypt's Public Protest Law 2013: A Boost to Freedom or a Further Restriction?." *US-China L. Rev.* 11, no. 9 (2014): 1114–1124.

Abdelaal, Mohamed. "Religious Constitutionalism in Egypt: A Case Study." *Fletcher F of World Aff* 37 (2013): 35–52.

Abu-Odeh, Lama. "The Supreme Constitutional Court of Egypt: The Limits of Liberal Political Science and CLS Analysis of Law Elsewhere." *Am. J. Comp. L.*. 59 (2011): 985–1007.

Al-Bayar, Karim. "Quanin Al-monazamat ghi'er Al-hokomyyia fi Dowal A'rabyyia Mokhtara [Laws of NGOs in Selected Arab Countries]." Int'l Center for Not-for-Profit Law (ICNL), 2005, http://www.icnl.org/research/library/files/Transn ational/SelectArabStates_AR.pdf

Al-Faruqi, Isma'il. and Al-Faruqi. Louis., *The Cultural Atlas of Islam.* Kazi Publications, (1996): 279.

Annan, Kofi. "In Larger Freedom: Towards Development, Security and Human Rights for All: Report of the Secretary-General," (A/59/2005): 34, https://www.un.org/en/events/pastevents/pdfs/larger_freedom_exec_summary.pdf.

Brown, Nathan J and Waller Julian G. "Constitutional Courts and Political Uncertainty Constitutional Ruptures and the Rule of Judges." *Int'l J. Const. L.* 14 (2016): 817, 840.

El Alami, Dawoud. "Law No. 100 of 1985 Amending Certain Provisions of Egypt's Personal Status Laws." *Islamic Law and Society* 1 (1994): 116–120.

Hamzawy, Amr. "Egypt After the 2013 Military Coup: Law-making in Service of the New Authoritarianism." *Philosophy and Social Criticism* 43 (2017): 392–405.

Henckaerts, Jean-Marie and Van Der Jeught, Stefaan. "Human Rights Protection under the New Constitutions of Central Europe." *Loy. L.A. Int'l & Comp. L. Rev.*. 20 (1998): 475–506.

Horowitz, Donald L. "Constitutional Courts: A Primer for Decision-Makers." *J. Democr.*. 17 (2006): 125–137.

Kassem, Taha. "Non-Governmental Organizations: A Threat to International Law and International Community the Case of Muslim Brotherhood Organization in Egypt." *Int'l J of Political Science, Law & Int'l Relation*. (2013): 9–22.

Lombardi, Clark B. *State Law as Modern Islamic Law in Modern Egypt: The Incorporation of the Sharia into Egyptian Constitutional Law*. Brill Academic Publishers, 2006.

Maveety, Nancy and Grosskopf, Anke. ""Constrained" Constitutional Courts as Conduits for Democratic Consolidation." *Law & Society Rev.*. 38 (2004): 463–488.

Mietzner, Marcus. "Political Conflict Resolution and Democratic Consolidation in Indonesia: The Role of the Constitutional Court." *J. of East Asian Studies* 10 (2010): 397–424.

Moustafa, Tamir. "Law and Courts in Authoritarian Regimes." *Annu. Rev. Law Soc. Sci.*. 10 (2014): 281–299.

Moustafa, Tamir. *The Struggle of the Constitutional Power: Law, Politics, and Economic Development in Egypt*. Cambridge University Press, 2009.

Mustapha Kamel Al-Sayyid, "Rule of Law, Ideology, and Human Rights in Egyptian Courts," In *The Rule of Law, Islam, and Constitutional Politics in Egypt and Iran*, edited by Arjomand S. A. and Brown N. J. New York: State University of New York Press, (2013): 211.

Sakr, Taha. "Will It Be Easy for Coptic Egyptians to go on Pilgrimage to Jerusalem?." *Daily News*, February 15, 2017.

Sieder, Rachel and Schjolden, L and Angell, A. (eds.), *The Judicialization of Politics in Latin America*. Palgrave Macmillan US, 2005.

Stanek, Steve. "Coptic Believers Say Extremists are Driving them out of Egypt." *The Globe and Mail*, July 7, 2007.

Stilt, Kristen. "Islam is the Solution: Constitutional Visions of the Egyptian Muslim Brotherhood." *Tex. J. Int'l. L.* 46 (2010): 73, 108.

Youngblood, Brad and Hamdy, Noor. "Why Is Egypt Amending Its Protest Law Now?." *The Tahrir Institute for Middle East Policy* August 16, 2016, https://timep.org/commentary/analysis/why-is-egypt-amending-its-protest-law-now/

CHAPTER 15

The Media and Freedom of Expression in Democratic Malawi: A Formality or Reality?

Jimmy Kainja

1 INTRODUCTION

Malawi became a one-party dictatorship soon after its independence from Britain in 1964. Hastings Kamuzu Banda, the country's founding president and Malawi Congress Party held absolute power for 31 years, a period marked by human rights violations and lack of civil liberties. In the early 1990s, Banda faced a lot of internal and external pressure, calling for political reforms in the country. This forced him to call for a referendum in which Malawians were to choose between the one-party dictatorship and multiparty democracy, Malawians chose the latter.

Kamuzu Banda lost the resulting election in 1994, paving way for Bakili Muluzi, the winning candidate. The country adopted a new constitution that includes a Bill of Rights with guarantees for civil liberties and human rights. These include freedoms of assembly, association, press and expression, among others. The Bill of Rights aligns the constitution with international instruments and agreements such as the 1991 Windhoek Declaration for the Development of a Free, Independent and Pluralistic Press (Windhoek Declaration), the 1948 United Nations Declaration of Human Rights (Universal Declaration) and the 1981 African Charter on Human and People's Rights (African Charter).

J. Kainja (✉)
University of Malawi, Zomba, Malawi
e-mail: jkainja@unima.ac.mw

© The Author(s), under exclusive license to Springer Nature Switzerland AG 2022
A. Adeola and M. W. Mutua (eds.), *The Palgrave Handbook of Democracy, Governance and Justice in Africa,*
https://doi.org/10.1007/978-3-030-74014-6_15

25 years after Malawi's constitution came into force, evidence shows that media freedoms have largely been guaranteed in principle but not in practice. These freedoms are often denied and violated through undemocratic regulatory and policy environments, in addition to harsh economic conditions in which the mainstream media operates.[1] These regulations have allowed the government to censor and limit media freedom.

Using political economy approach, this chapter discusses the state of media and freedom of expression in Malawi. It takes a historical approach which mostly depends on documentary and literature review, in addition to interviews with media managers in the country. The review of the literature is one way of mapping historical development of the media in the country, which cannot essentially be discussed separately from the country's political history. The chapter further discusses policy, regulatory and legal frameworks in relation to media freedom in the country. Finally, the chapter discusses the economic environment in which the media operates, specifically looking at how the economic environment limits the spectrum of media and freedom in the country.

2   MEDIA AND POLITICAL LANDSCAPE

The history of Malawian media cannot be separated from the country's political history, Croteau and Hoyness (2003) emphasise that this is always the best way to understand functions and operations of the media in every society. There are stark differences between the expectations of media operations in different political systems. For instance, in democratic societies the media are supposed to work in the interest of public; the media are supposed to cater for diversity of views and opinion. This is to ensure that the public has access to diverse information so that they can make informed decisions and participate meaningfully in public affairs. In democracies, the media are also critical in holding those in power to account. On the other hand, media in autocratic states are subservient to the ruling elite and exist solely to serve the interests of the state. Chitsulo and Mang'anda (2011) observe that the history of the Malawian media is marked by 'a three-wave development pattern': colonial period (1895–1950s), dictatorship (1960s–early 1990s) and the current democratic era, which started in the early 1990s.

Reflecting on the nature of political environment of the time, the first two eras were marked by human rights abuses, lack of civil liberties and media freedom. Change of government from colonial administration to self-rule in 1964 did not improve the state of media freedom in Malawi. To the contrary, the relative press freedom of radical publications of the 1950s

---

[1] The harsh economic conditions have also resulted in poor salaries and remuneration for journalists in the country, forcing them into unethical practices in order to supplement their income.

campaigning for the country's independence, such as *Malawi News*, immediately became subjected to state control and censorship after Malawi attained its independence.

Patel (2000) observes that the control of the media was mainly through the 1968 censorship and control of information law, which proved effective in controlling publication and circulation of media in the country. This law criminalised publishing of anything likely to undermine the authority of, or public confidence in, the government. Patel adds that the censorship law included works and writings which had distinct ideological and philosophical base from that of the government. This law did not only curtail media freedom, it also had chilling effect on other human rights, such as freedoms of expression and association in the country.

Thus, controlling media freedom was a matter of state policy in a country that, according to Patel (2000), was to a large extent a police state, with no structures to allow the existence of independent media. For instance, Patel observes that there was no Minister of Information for many years and the President was himself the Director-General of the country's only radio station, Malawi Broadcasting Corporation. Patel's account is collaborated by Mapulanga (2008) who points out that in those days the president's office had the full responsibility for the circulation of information in the country.

These were the hallmarks of the one-party state in which opposition and criticisms were not allowed or tolerated. Journalism meant only covering issues that were permitted by the state. There were no media and journalism training institutions, journalists were trained on the job. Manda (2018) notices that in his public rallies, the State President, Kamuzu Banda, often told the public that journalists were not to be trusted as they were liars. Banda's disdain for journalists could ably explain the lack of trainings institutions for journalists for the 30 years he was in power.

The country had only two newspapers, *Daily Times* and *Malawi News*—both owned and published by Blantyre Print and Packaging Company, which fell under the total control of Kamuzu Banda by 1970. There are disputed accounts on how Kamuzu Banda assumed the ownership of the company. On the one hand, Manda (2018) cites Hall and Ham arguing that Kamuzu Banda bought and consolidated the two newspapers into Blantyre Print and Packaging Company. On the other hand, Patel (2000) asserts that it is unknown how Kamuzu Banda acquired the ownership of the company. It is difficult to deduce from these accounts to discern exactly how the ownership was acquired but Mpasu (2014) observed that Kamuzu Banda's regime had a record of repossessing peoples' private property using the forfeiture law but the true account is not known and may never be known. Banda's security state followed a common trend in post-colonial Africa where government ownership and control of the media were justified on the basis of national unity and development (Nyamnjoh 2004).

Myers (2014) observes that the change in Africa's media landscape emerged with the change in the international political arena, particularly the fall of the

Berlin Wall and the symbolic end of the Cold War. She observes that in 1985, there were only 10 commercial broadcasting services in Africa but as of 2014, there were more than 2,000 commercial and community radio stations and more than 300 independent television stations in sub-Saharan Africa. From one state-owned radio station in 1994, Malawi has issued over 80 broadcasting licences over the last two decades. These licences have been issued for television and three-tier radio broadcasting systems consisting of the public, commercial and community broadcasting.

Kupe (2004) recalls that the liberalisation of the media in Southern Africa followed a push for media reforms by a network of journalists who issued the Windhoek Declaration after a meeting in Namibia in 1991. This gathering discussed press freedom, media diversity and pluralism in Southern Africa; it also led to the declaration of 3rd of May as the World Press Freedom Day by the United Nations. This day has been globally celebrated since 1993. This also led to the establishment of the Media Institute of Southern Africa (MISA) in 1992. MISA's mandate is to promote media diversity, pluralism and media independence, among other things. Kupe observes that these are the developments that were meant to create an enabling environment for the demand of media freedom in most African countries.

At present, African media operates in free and open political environments when compared to what was obtainable in the early 1990s. Yet, Nyamnjoh (2004) sees the state of the media on the continent as that of continuity and not change. African governments effectively remain in control of the media mainly through repressive legal and regulatory frameworks. (Nyamnjoh 2004, p. 123) argues that 'an examination of most legal frameworks in Africa, even after the liberalisation of the 1990s, reveals a craving to control that leaves little doubt of lawmakers perceives journalists as potential troublemakers who must be policed'.

Article 19 (2000)[2] observes that even after attaining multiparty democracy and adopting a new constitution, which provides for Bill of Rights, the Malawi government remained reluctant to fully liberalise the media environment, especially the airwaves. Article 19 (2000, p. 3) asserts, for instance, that in the first five years of democracy (1994–1999), the government only granted two commercial broadcasting licences and one community broadcasting licence. The licences were awarded to politically connected individuals, Alaudin Osman, then a presidential press secretary, and Oscar Thomson, a son to then cabinet minister, Harry Thomson. Without indicating names, Article 19 observes that none of the many other applicants were granted operating licences, 'except for local women's group, which gained UNESCO's support to start a community radio station in the country lakeshore district of Mangochi.'

---

[2] Article 19 is a prominent organisation working in defence and promotion of freedom expression and freedom of information around the world.

Article 19 (2000, p. 3) further observes that while broadcasting licences were proving politically difficult to attain, 'the country had up to 50 newspapers started since early 1990s, although most published only published a few issues and closed'. The contrast in fortunes show that the government was more concerned in controlling the broadcasting sector and not the newspaper industry perhaps because, as Mano (2011) observes, radio has an ability to overcome socioeconomic barriers such as poverty, illiteracy and linguistic diversity, which are prevalent in most African countries. These social and economic factors are among the reasons why most of the newspapers only published few editions before closing down. In addition, Chitsulo and Mang'anda (2011), Patel (2000) and Article 19 (2000) observe that the newspapers were also poorly written, poorly printed and lacked trained management and editorial staff. In addition to this, printing costs in the country were prohibitively high because there were very few newspaper printers in the country, owing to decades of state control on the sector.

The two newspapers that survived and both remain in circulation today did so partly because the owners had political connections. Hastings Kamuzu Banda family owns Times Group, formerly Blantyre Print and Publishing, publishers of *The Daily Times, Malawi News* and *The Sunday Times*. Nation Publication Limited, publishers of *The Nation, Weekend Nation* and *Nation on Sunday*, is owned by a family of Aleke Banda (no relation to Kamuzu Banda), a veteran politician who served in several senior cabinet posts under both Kamuzu Banda and Bakili Muluzi regimes. Manda (2007) observes that the Muluzi government had a practice of placing advertisements in media institutions that were not critical of the government and the ruling party, while denying advertising to media institutions deemed to be critical of it. Manda's observation is collaborated by Article 19 (2000), which also observes that the government's practice of withdrawing advertising from critical media.

This shows that the liberalisation of the media was only on paper as those in power did not allow it in practice. The state of media freedom is best tested when the media are critical of the political status quo, particularly the incumbency and government policies.

3   LEGAL FRAMEWORK

Media freedom in Malawi is guaranteed by Malawi's constitution (1994). Article 34 guarantees freedom of opinion; Article 35 guarantees freedom of expression; Article 36 guarantees freedom of the press; and Article 37 provides for access to information, subject to an enabling Act of Parliament. Getting the access to information legislation through parliament was not easy. Successive political administrations were clearly uninterested in having the legislation, despite heavy lobbying by civil society organisations including MISA. The Access to Information Bill was finally passed into law in 2017 and was operationalised on 30 September 2020 (MISA Malawi 2020) and it's impact on media operations in the country is yet to be felt.

The state of access to information poses a serious restriction on freedom of expression. It is a big problem also because Malawi does not have whistle-blower protection law, which would encourage people to come forward with information, without fearing any possible reprisals. In the end, journalists have to find their own means of getting information that public institutions will not willingly provide. Kanyongolo (2012) notices that access to information is linked to freedom of expression in at least two ways. In the first instance, holders of information must have freedom of expression in order for them to be able to provide information to persons who request them. Secondly, effective enjoyment of free expression requires that people have free access to the widest range of information on which they can then form the opinions and ideas that constitute the content of expression.

This is the open environment that Malawi's constitution envisages. The constitutional provisions are in line with provisions of the Windhoek Declaration (1991) on free and pluralistic media environment. Likewise, Malawi is a party to several international and regional instruments promoting freedoms of the press and expression in Africa. In 2002, the African Commission on Human and Peoples' Rights (African Commission) issued a Declaration of Principles on Freedom of Expression in Africa (African Commission on Human and Peoples' Rights 2002; Rukundo 2018). Principle 2 of the Declaration provides that 'restrictions on freedom of expression shall be provided by law, serve a legitimate interest and be necessary and in a democratic society'. Principle 12 provides that,

1. States should ensure that their laws relating to defamation conform to the following standards:

   - no one shall be found liable for true statements, opinions or statements regarding public figures which it was reasonable to make in the circumstances;
   - public figures shall be required to tolerate a greater degree of criticism; and
   - sanctions shall never be so severe as to inhibit the right to freedom of expression, including by others.

These instruments provide necessary and critical safeguards for media freedom. However, the main issue is ensuring that states adhere to the stipulations of the law. Kanyongolo (2012) points out that it is important to recognise that freedom of expression does not exist in a vacuum, and the big challenge with the Malawian legal framework is that the constitutional provisions were presented in a legal context in which there were many laws which did not reflect the same support for media freedoms as the Malawi constitution. He observes that freedom of expression and its legal restrictions must be understood in terms of the realities of the interactions among state, community and individual interests. According to Kanyongolo (2012,

p. 3), the 'Malawian society is shaped by the realities of poverty and inequality experienced the majority of Malawians'.

This means that majority of Malawians are more occupied with immediate and more pertinent issues of finding food, descent shelter and health care than the somewhat distant issues of freedom expression in comparative terms to their basic needs. Thus, the socio-political context weakens the case to have punitive legislations repealed and amended because it is a minority issue. Yet, sound legislation is the best way of ensuring media freedom, as it sets legal means in which media can operate and restricts the possibility of governmental overreach.

Article 44(2) of the Malawi Constitution provides that 'Laws prescribing restrictions or limitations shall not negate the essential content of the right or freedom in question, and shall be of general application'. However, there are also a number of subordinate laws that contradict the constitutional provisions. In 2016, the African Media Barometer (2016) recorded the following legislations hindering media freedom in Malawi, namely: The Penal Code of 1930, the Protected Flag, Emblems, and Names Act of 1967, the Police Act of 1946, the Official Secrets Act of 1913 and the Censorship and Control of Entertainments Act of 1968.

Similarly, in a 2019 report, MISA Malawi (2019) identified four laws that either need repealing or amending, these are: first, Article 4 of the Protected Flag, Emblems and Names Act, which makes it a crime to 'insult, ridicule or show disrespect to the President'. Second, Article 181 of the Penal Code, which makes it a crime for anyone in any public place to conduct themselves 'in a manner likely to cause a breach of the peace'. Third, the fact that the Minister of Information and Communications needs to set a date for the commencement of the Access to Information Act, which was passed into law in February 2017. This is in accordance with Section 96(1)(g), which gives the Minister responsibility for the implementation and administration of laws. Fourth, the Cyber Security and Electronic Transaction Act, 2016, 'which contains several clauses that are open to abuse, allowing the government to limit online expression'.

These legislations are inconsistent with provisions of Malawi's constitution that guarantees media freedom. Not only do these laws limit media freedoms but these laws also have a chilling effect on the media, which encourages self-censorship (Manda and Kufaine 2013). Manda and Kufaine add that the spirit of crusading journalism in Malawi has died since the beginning of the multiparty era, partly due to heavy fines which the courts have been giving to newspapers. Article 19 (2000) documented a case involving *The Democrat* newspaper, which in 1996 had accused then a Minister of Education, Sam Mpasu of profiting from a purchase of school notebooks from Field York in the UK. *The Democrat* got the story right but it happened that the newspaper was somehow unable to prove its case in court after being sued for defamation. Consequently, Mpasu won the case and the court ruled that *The Democrat* should pay Mpasu K200,000 (approximately $260 today) damages.

286   J. KAINJA

Article 19 (2000, p. 9) points out that failure by *The Democrat* to pay the damages 'effectively resulted in bankruptcy and soon afterwards the closure of a pioneering opposition newspaper'.

4   ECONOMIC ENVIRONMENT

According to the International Monetary Fund (IMF) Country report of May 2017, Malawi's economy is one of the lowest in the world. As of 2016, the country had per capita GNI of just US$320 in 2016, which is one of the lowest in the world. IMF indicates that the 'per capita income has grown at an average of little more than 1.5 percent between 1995 and 2014, below the average of 2.8 percent for non-resource-rich African economies'. These harsh economic conditions make it difficult for investors to invest in the media industry, for the lack of steady capital bus also because industry lack obvious capital returns for investors. The economic environment is one of the reasons Malawi has only two daily newspapers, low access to television and the internet-based media platforms. This has serious limitations on the diversity of the media in the country, a key component of a democratic society.

As with many other societies, advertising revenue is a mainstay of the media industry in Malawi. The Malawi government, through its ministries, departments and statuary corporations, is the main advertiser in the Malawian media, giving the government a huge leverage on the media. This is in addition to government's regulatory powers. Accounts by Gondwe 2010 and Article 19, 2000 indicates that the Malawi government has over the years used this enormous power to control the local media and therefore undermines media freedom in the country. This challenges access to information, and consequently freedom of expression, which Bratton (2019) argues is necessary to ensure a politically active citizenry that are able to communicate with one another and to debate the type of government they desire for themselves. Bratton reminds us that civic discourse can take place in various forms but the most important is the public communications media, both print and electronic. Citizens participation in national issues is critical as it strengthens government's legitimacy.

Withdrawing of advertising from media institutions considered critical of the government and its interests has been a popular means through which the Malawi government restrict silences the media. Manda and Kufaine (2013) refers to Malawi's harsh economic environment as the prime reason most the media institutions are scrambling for government advertisement, as the private sector is too small to sustain the media industry. The newspaper industry, in particular, is a very tough business in Malawi. Price of the newspapers are not enough to cover operational costs. For instance, at MK600 ($0.78) for daily and Sunday newspapers and MK700 ($0.92) for Saturday newspapers; newspapers are way too expensive for an average Malawian whose average daily income is MK900 ($1.18) (Alfred Ntonga, May 2019). Thus, newspaper is a medium only affordable to the privileged few. Further, newspapers in Malawi are largely in the English language, which is mostly spoken in urban areas. Majority of Malawians living in rural areas cannot converse in English, although English is the country's official language. However, Chichewa, Chitumbuka and Chiyao are among the prevalent languages of daily communication across the country.

However, it is important to note that although newspapers have limited circulation; newspaper are the main agenda setters. Where newspapers lead, the rest of the media tend to follow (Kainja 2020). Thus, newspapers remain critical for policymakers. Most of the big stories that matter to the economy and politically originate from the newspapers. This remains the case even in the age of real-time news production and livestreaming facilitated by the new media technologies. The challenges of the internet age, which are reshaping political economy of the media and newsrooms around the world, are yet to have a notable effect on Malawian media due to low internet penetration and usage in the country (Kemp 2020).

Consequently, due to the newspapers' influence on the national policy agenda, the government has a significant interest in the print media. Article 19 (2000) observes that not long after doing away with Kamuzu Banda's dictatorship, the Malawian government adopted a practice of publicly withdrawing advertising from critical media institutions. For example, Article 19 recorded a case in 1998 when former President Bakili Muluzi accused *The Daily Times* of waging war on him and his government. In response, he withdrew advertisement from the accused newspaper, *The Daily Times*. This newspaper is owned by the Kamuzu Banda family, whose political party (Malawi Congress Party) was the main opposition in the country.

The then Minister of Information, Sam Mpasu, justified the withdrawal of advertising by telling Article 19 (2000, p. 10) that 'advertisers, including government, were having qualms about identifying their products and services with newspapers that are sinking low into indecency.' Mpasu added: 'it is a ban [withdrawing advertising], but it is not permanent … We will be able to give advertisements if the papers change. It is happening all over the world: papers have been banned'. *The Daily Times* survived the ban, perhaps because Times Group is a conglomerate with many other interests that could make up for the losses in newspaper revenue.

Similarly, in 2010, former President Bingu wa Mutharika's government resorted to the same tactics of withdrawing advertising from media institutions deemed unfriendly to the government. The deputy Chief Executive Officer (CEO) of Nation Publications Limited (Alfred Ntonga, May 2019) confirmed that this policy was indeed effected. He says it was uncalled for, for the government to behave the way it did, he notices that after all, the government could easily sue the company if it had infringed the laws of Malawi. Ntonga believes that by withdrawing adverting, the government abused its power in fighting a media institution operating on a shoestring budget. Ntonga noted

288 J. KAINJA

that nobody in power likes free press but what the press needs is a room to fight for its right to exist freely.

5   JOURNALISTS' STANDARDS OF LIVING

While the legal frameworks and economic conditions are serious challenges to media freedom in Malawi, what is less discussed, however, are the conditions in which journalists work. The state of the economy makes it difficult for media institutions to pay journalists sufficient wages and remuneration, which leaves journalists vulnerable to receiving bribes. A study on journalists living condition in Malawi by Manda and Kufaine (2013) established that despite being very low, journalists' wages were not different from other professions in the country. This finding was collaborated by Alfred Ntonga who says that newly recruited journalists at Nation Publications Limited are at the same level of remuneration as bank tellers working with the country's top banks (Alfred Ntonga, May 2019). He however notices that although journalists are not an exceptional case in terms of pay, the payment is not enough, this makes journalists susceptible to unethical journalism practices, as they seek to supplement the meagre salary. He observes that the state of the economy means that media institutions are running on shoestring budgets and cannot afford to increase journalists' wages and benefits. Similarly, (Gospel Kazako interview, May 2019), the former CEO of Zodiak Broadcasting Station (ZBS)[3] states that it is difficult to pay journalists enough wages when media institutions are not making enough money in the first place—'you can only pay what you make,' he said.

Random interviews I conducted with journalists indicate that journalists have resorted to supplement their meagre salaries by daily subsistence allowances, locally known by its short form, 'allowances'. These allowances are often paid by news sources looking for journalists to cover their events and conferences. It emerged through the interviews that it has become the norm that journalists expect 'allowances' from function and conference organisers once they have been invited to cover these functions. It is akin to what Knightly (2002) calls embedded journalism, popular with war correspondents, a situation in which journalists travel with the military, often because they have no means of travelling on their own or they cannot guarantee their safety if they do so, so they operate under the custody of the military with expectations from the military that they would report fairly on the war. This clearly has a bearing on the independence of the reports that these journalists are going to produce.

In an interview with Ntonga, he admits that the 'allowance culture', as he calls it, kills the capacity of journalists to think and report independently

[3] According to Malawi Communications Regulatory Authority, ZBS is currently Malawi's biggest radio station, by listenership: https://www.macra.org.mw/wp-content/uploads/2020/08/radio_listenership_2013.pdf.

(Alfred Ntonga, May 2019). A journalist working with a public broadcaster, the Malawi Broadcasting Corporation (MBC), explains the challenges of 'allowance culture' on freedom to report independently: 'it is difficult for you to get to the newsroom and write a critical story of what you saw knowing that you have been treated well' (MBC journalist, May 2019).[4] The journalist said it is expected that if a journalist writes a favourable news story after being given allowances, they are more or less guaranteed that the news source will invite them again to future functions (MBC journalist, May 2019). On the contrary, a critical coverage or failure to produce any coverage guarantees that the journalist will never be invited again. It was also said that in some instances, news sources are able to ask a news editor for specific journalists to cover their events (MBC journalist, May 2019).

The poor remuneration received by journalists is certainly the basis of the problem that is now heavily entrenched within the Malawian journalism, without due regard to integrity and independence of the media. Yet, news organisations are unable to stop the practice knowing that they cannot afford to pay their employees enough wages. It is a case of a helpless victim. (Alfred Ntonga, May 2010) says at Nation Publication Limited has a policy that requires journalists to declared any 'gifts' given to them by news sources. Ntonga added that his organisation has previously sacked journalists for violating the policy but he also admitted that he is aware that even with the policy in place, journalists are still receiving undeclared allowances and 'gifts' from sources while on duty (Alfred Ntonga, May 2019). Ntonga's assertions form part of the company's written policy which is readily accessible on the company's website.[5]

6   ALTERNATIVE MEDIA

Unless the economic fortunes of the country improve, it is very difficult for media freedom to materialise. New ICT-based technologies, especially the internet, have brought some hopes and a possibility that could liberate media institutions from financial burdens, especially as online publishing does not require circulation costs and generally has lower operations costs. However, media institutions in Malawi need to find ways of making significant revenues online given the dominance of existing platforms such as Facebook and Google and the reality that these platforms are already drawing a huge share of online advertising revenue.

For Malawi, the bigger obstacle, at the moment, is the low internet access and usage. At the end of 2018, statistics by the International Telecommunication Union (2019), a United Nations (UN) specialised agency for ICTs, indicates that only 13.9% of Malawi's 17.5 million people had access to the

---

[4] This interview was with a journalist working Malawi Broadcasting Corporation who opted to stay anonymous.

[5] Editorial Policy and Code of Practice: https://www.mwnation.com/editorial-policy/.

internet. A 2019 Freedom House report, *Freedom on the Net*, established that among the key reasons for the low internet usage in Malawi is the lack of state investment in ICT infrastructure and high corporate and value added tax. These lead to high internet prices, which is unaffordable to a majority of Malawians.

These high internet prices reduce the number of people who use the internet and it reduces the amount of time and quality of usage for those that can afford the prices. Consequently, there are not many investors willing to start online media. As of November 2020, Malawi has about four notable online publications, with regular updates but none of these online publications are capable of competing with the traditional media institutions, which dominate the online space. For example, Nation Publications Limited has won MISA Malawi's best online publication of year for three consecutive years (Chunga 2020; Mwale 2019; Pasungwi 2018). In 2017 the award was won by Zodiak Broadcasting Station (M'bwana 2017).

As of November 2020, online media in Malawi has been very limited in reach and impact, and the government is aware of this. In the aftermath of Malawi's disputed 2019 elections, human rights defenders and opposition groups in the country organised a series of public demonstrations. Radio stations engaged in live coverage of these demonstrations, which prompted the country's telecommunication regulator, MACRA to ban live radio broadcasting as well as phone-in programmes, citing a law, which obliges broadcasters to have delay live broadcasting technology (Masina 2019). This technology allows broadcasters to edit 'live' programmes before audiences can listen. Yet, the same regulatory body was not worried about the information being shared on social media platforms, which were left open and unrestricted. This is an indication that the regulator is less worried with the internet-based platforms that are equally capable of providing live updates; it is an indication that the internet is still considered negligible in Malawi, as compared to traditional media.

7   CONCLUSION

It is apparent from this discussion that the Malawian media is much freer today than it was during the colonialism (1891–1961) and one-party doctorship period (1964–1994). Largely this is due to Malawi's Constitution, which guarantees freedom of expression. However, these constitutional guarantees are compromised by the continued existence of other punitive legal provisions such as those in the penal code, the Penal Code of 1930, the Protected Flag, Emblems and Names Act of 1967 and the Official Secrets Act of 1913. In addition to this, the government has the tendency to use its stronghold on the economy to deny the media the much needed advertising revenue, thereby undermining the media's editorial independence, as the media are forced to publish content that is favourable in order to remain operational. Although less discussed, poor salaries and remuneration for journalists also undermine media freedom, as journalists seek to supplement their meagre income by receiving subsistence 'allowances' from news sources, companies and organisations. While the new media has the potential to overcome some of these obstacles, access to the internet in the country remains very low because the internet is very expensive for the majority of Malawians.

At a macro-level, moving beyond formal recognition of media freedom requires significant attention to the social, economic and political environment of the country. Making media freedom a reality, as envisaged by the Malawi constitution, further requires an amendment or repealing of laws that are contrary to the country's Bill of Rights. Also, the Malawi government must recognise the importance of media freedom for the sustenance of democratic legitimacy. Section 12(iii) of the Malawi Constitution (1994) provides that 'the authority to exercise power of state is conditional upon the sustained trust of the people of Malawi and that trust can only be maintained through open, accountable and transparent Government and informed democratic choice'. Integral to the attainment of such 'informed democratic choice' is the media that are free from political and economic interference.

BIBLIOGRAPHY

African Media Barometer. "Malawi 2016" (web page). Friendrich Ebert Stiftung (website), accessed August 8, 2019. http://crm.misa.org/upload/web/malawi-amb-2016.pdf.

African Union. "African Charter on Human and Peoples Rights" (web page). African Union (website), accessed August 8, 2019. http://www.humanrights.se/wp-content/uploads/2012/01/African-Charter-on-Human-and-Peoples-Rights.pdf.

African Commission on Human and Peoples' Rights, 32nd Session, 17–23 October, 2002: Banjul, The Gambia.Manda.

Article 19. "At the Crossroad: Freedom of Expression in Malawi: The Final Report of the 1999 Article 19 Malawi Election Monitoring Project." London: Article 19, 2000.

Bratton, Michael. "Civil Society and Political Transition in Africa, Institute for Development Research Reports" (web page), accessed August 8, 2019. https://www.issuelab.org/resources/19673/19673.pdf.

Chitsulo, Edward and Mang'anda, Gray. "Origins, Development, and Management of Newspaper Industry in Malawi." In *Journalism Practice in Malawi: History, Progress and Prospects*, edited by E.B.Z. Kondowe, Paul Kishindo Paul, and Mkandawire. Lilongwe: UNESCO, 2011.

Chunga, Sam. "NPL Sweeps 2020 MISA Awards" (web page). Nation Publications Limited (website), accessed November 8, 2020. https://www.mwnation.com/npl-sweeps-2020-misa-awards/.

Croteau, David and Hoyness, William. *Media and Society: Industries, Images, and Audiences*. Thousand Oaks. Pine Forge Press, 2003.

Freedom House. "Freedom on the Net" (web page). Freedom House (website), accessed August 6, 2019. https://freedomhouse.org/report/freedom-net/2018/malawi.

Gondwe, Gregory. "JUMA Decries Withdrawal of State Advertising" (web page). Biz Community (website), 2010, accessed November 8, 2020. https://www.bizcommunity.africa/Article/410/12/44506.html.

International Monetary Fund. "IMF Country Report No. 17/184" (web page) IMF (website), accessed August 8, 2019. https://www.imf.org/~/media/Files/Publications/CR/2017/cr17184.ashx.

ITU Country Profile Report (web page), accessed August 9, 2019. https://bit.ly/2VR6faB.

Interview with Nation Publications Limited Deputy Chief Executive Office, Alfred Ntonga, May 2019.

Interview with Zodiak Broadcasting and Chief Executive Officer, Gospel Kazako, May 2019.

Kainja, Jimmy. "How Lack of Access to Information and ICTs has Fueled Disinformation in Malawi" (web page). CIPESA (website) accessed November, 8, 2020 *CIPESA*.

Kanyongolo, Fidelis Edge. "Report on Laws that Restrict Freedom of the Press in Malawi"—A report submitted to MISA Malawi. Chancellor College, Zomba, (2012) (website), accessed August 8, 2019. https://crm.misa.org/upload/web/29-report-on-laws-that-restrict-freedom-of-the-press-in-malawi.pdf.

Kemp, Simon. "Digital 2020: Malawi" (web page). Kepios (website) accessed November 8, 2020.

Knightly, Phillip. *The First Casualty: The War Correspondent as Hero, Propagandist and Myth-Marker from the Crimea to Iraq*. London: The John Hopkins University Press, 2002.

Kupe, Tawana. "Media Policies for Democratising and Developing Countries, 122–128." *African Journalism Studies* 25, no. 1 (2004): 124. https://doi.org/10.1080/025600054.2004.9653283.

The Constitution of Malawi. (Act No. 20 of 1994) Entered into Provisional Operation on May 18, 1994, and Became Fully Operational on May 18, 1995.

Manda, Levi Zeleza. "Challenges Facing Media in Malawi." In *Governance and Politics in Malawi*, edited by Nandini Patel and Lars Svasand. Zomba: Kachere Books, 2007.

Manda, Zeleza Levi. "Journalism Education and Training in Malawi: A Case for a National Policy." *Journal of Development and Communication Studies* 5, no. 2 (July 2018): 38 https://doi.org/10.4314/jdcs.v5i2.3.

Manda, Zeleza Levi, and Kufaine, Noel D. "Starving the Messenger: A Study of Journalists' Conditions of Service in Malawi." *Journal of Development and Communication Studies* 2/3, no. 2 (2013): 308.

Mano, Winston. "Why Radio Is Africa's Medium of Choice in the Global Age." In *Radio in Africa: Publics, Cultures, Communities*, edited by Liz Gunner, Dina Ligaga, and Dumisani Moyo. Johannesburg: Wits University Press, 2011.

Mapulanga, Patrick. "Learning from the Past: Mass Communication and Access to Information in Malawi from 1964–1994." World Library and Information Congress: 74th IFLA General Conference and Council (10–14 August 2008, Quebec Canada).

Masina, Lameck "Malawi Broadcasters, Media freedom Group Citicize Call-in Shows Suspension" (web page). Voice of America (website), 2019, accessed November 11, 2020. https://www.voanews.com/press-freedom/malawi-broadcasters-media-freedom-group-criticize-call-shows-suspension.

M'bwana, Lloyd. "2017 MISA-Malawi Awards: Times Groups Scoops Multiple Awards, Zodiak Retains Best Electronic Media, No Life Time Winner Over Poor Work" (web page) The Maravi Post (website), accessed November 8, 2020. https://www.maravipost.com/2017-misa-malawi-awards-times-groups-scoops-multiple-awards-zodiak-retains-best-electronic-media-no-life-time-winner-poor-work/.

MISA-Malawi. "MISA Malawi Applauds Government on Operationalisation of ATI Act" (web page). MISA Malawi (website), accessed November 8, 2020. https://malawi.misa.org/2020/09/11/misa-malawi-applauds-government-on-operationalization-of-ati-act/.

MISA-Malawi. "Way Forward in 2019: MISA Malawi's Recommendations for Improving Media Freedom, Freedom of Expression and Access to Information" (web page). MISA Malawi (website), accessed August 8, 2019. https://crm.misa.org/upload/web/wayfoward_2019_malawi-1.pdf.

Mpasu, Sam. *Political Prisoner 3/75: A True Story by Sam Mpasu*. Balaka: Montfort Media, 2014.

Mwale, Joseph. "NPL Sweeps MISA Awards" (web page), Nation Publications Limited (website), 2019, accessed November 8, 2020. https://www.mwnation.com/npl-sweeps-misa-awards/.

Myers, Mary. *Africa's Media Boom: The Role of International Aid*. Washington: Centre for International Media Assistance, 2014.

Nyamnjoh, B. Francis. "Media Ownership and Control in Africa in the Age of Globalisation." In *Who Owns the Media?: Global Trends and Local Resistance*, edited by Thomas N. Pradip and Nain Zaharom. London and New York: Zed Books, 2004.

Pasungwi, Jonathan. "NPL Rated Best in 2018 MISA Awards" (web page). Nation Publications Limited (website), accessed November 8, 2020. https://www.mwnation.com/npl-rated-best-2018-misa-awards/.

Patel, Nandini. "Media in the Democratic and Electoral Process." In *Malawi's Second Democratic Elections: Process, Problems, and Prospects*, edited by Martin Ott, Kings Phiri, and Nandini Patel. Blantyre: Kachere Series, 2000.

Rukundo, Solomon. "My President Is a Pair of Buttocks: The Limits of Online Freedom of Expression in Uganda, 252–271." *International Journal of Law and Information Technology* (2018): 26. https://doi.org/10.1093/ijlit/eay009.

The Windhoek Declaration. "Declarations on Promoting Independent and Pluralistic Media - 3 May 1991" (website), accessed August 8, 2019. http://misa.org/wp-content/uploads/2015/06/Windhoek-Declaration.pdf.

CHAPTER 16

The Future in Transition: Realising Respect for Human Rights in the 'New' Gambia

Satang Nabaneh

1   INTRODUCTION

The Gambia, mainland Africa's smallest country and snake-shaped West African nation, is tucked literally inside of Senegal, with just a tiny coastline touching the Atlantic. It has been 22 years since the adoption of the 1997 Constitution of The Gambia. Since that time, The Gambia has witnessed important constitutional developments that enabled dictatorship as well as facilitated the transition to a democratic dispensation (Jammeh 2012).

On 1, December 2016, it became sub-Saharan Africa's newest democracy following twenty-two years of authoritarian rule by former dictator Yahya Jammeh dubbed 'New Gambia'.[1] The opposition coalition candidate Adama Barrow on 26 January 2017 took over the country peacefully following the political crisis with the backing and support of the Economic Community of West African States (ECOWAS). During Jammeh's era, the current 1997 Constitution of the Republic of The Gambia was ushered in.

---

[1] New Gambia is a term coined after the end of dictatorship and the ushering of a democratic one.

S. Nabaneh (✉)
Human Rights Center & School of Law, University of Dayton, Dayton, Ohio, United States of America
e-mail: satang.nabaneh@gmail.com

© The Author(s), under exclusive license to Springer Nature Switzerland AG 2022
A. Adeola and M. W. Mutua (eds.), *The Palgrave Handbook of Democracy, Governance and Justice in Africa,*
https://doi.org/10.1007/978-3-030-74014-6_16

296   S. NABANEH

This chapter takes stock of major developments in the areas of political and civil rights, the changing nature of democratisation in The Gambia, and the intersection between governance and human rights.

2   HUMAN RIGHTS AND GOVERNANCE CHALLENGES IN THE GAMBIA

The concept of constitutionalism within the African context is anchored on the idea that there must be clear limitations on power as well as established mechanisms to enforce such limitations (Fombad 2007, 1–45). Rosenfeld defines it as a 'three-faceted concept' based on the limitation of governmental power, adherence to rule of law, and protection of human rights (Rosenfeld 1994, 3–5, 28). Some of these identified core elements of constitutionalism by scholars include (Gloppen 1997, 23–57)[2] recognition and protection of fundamental rights and freedoms; separation of powers; an independent judiciary for the review of the constitutionality of laws; and control of the amendment process of the constitution.

Based on the abovementioned criteria, this chapter assesses the state of human rights and democratic governance to determine whether constitutional and legislative frameworks and actions by government adhere to these standards.[3]

2.1   *Human Rights in The Gambia: An Assessment*

The 1997 Constitution is the supreme law of the land and is based on the fundamental principles of rule of law, separation of powers, democracy, and fundamental rights and freedoms. It emphasises the principles of democracy and constitutionalism. The Gambia has signed and ratified majority of

---

[2] For a discussion of constitutionalism and its core elements, see, Louis Henkin, Elements of Constitutionalism, Occasional paper series/Center for the Study of Human Rights, Columbia University (1994) (He identifies essential elements: (1) government according to the constitution; (2) separation of power; (3) sovereignty of the people and democratic government; (4) constitutional review; (5) independent judiciary; (6) limited government subject to a bill of individual rights; (7) controlling the police; (8) civilian control of the military; and (9) no state power, or very limited and strictly circumscribed state power, to suspend the operation of some parts of, or the entire, constitution).

[3] This article can never exhaust listing the number of human rights and governance issues and cases that took place between 1994 and 2019. However, an attempt is made to illustrate the precarious environment that prevailed under Jammeh as well as the impact of the continuous existence of draconian laws.

international[4] and regional human rights instruments,[5] which provides a broad range of human rights standards. In terms of the general approach to constitutional interpretation, in *Attorney General v Jobe* (No 2),[6] the Privy Council held that the fundamental human rights chapter should be given a 'generous and purposive construction' (Nabaneh 2016, 78). The preamble recognises that 'the fundamental rights and freedoms enshrined in this Constitution, will ensure for all time respect for and observance of human rights and fundamental freedoms for all, without distinction as to ethnic considerations, gender, language and religion'. The constitutional catalogue of rights and freedoms are provided for under Chapter 4.[7] This section will focus on freedom of speech, press freedom, and assembly.

Freedom of Speech

The Scope of the Right

Section 25(1)(a) of the Constitution provides protection of freedom of expression, which includes protection of the freedom of the press and the media.[8] These rights are not absolute and are subject to lawful limitation pursuant to sections 25(4) and 209 of the Constitution, which are necessary in a democratic society and are required in the interest of national security, public order,

---

[4] These include the International Covenant on Economic, Social, and Cultural Rights ratified on 29 December 1978; International Covenant on Civil and Political Rights ratified on 22 March 1979; Convention on the Elimination of All Forms of Discrimination against Women ratified on 16 April 1993; Convention on the Rights of the Child ratified on 9 August 1990; Minimum Age Convention ratified on 4 September 2000. On 28 September 2018, The Gambia also ratified the Second Optional Protocol to the International Covenant on Civil and Political Rights (ICCPR), the Convention Against Torture and Other Cruel Inhuman or Degrading Treatment or Punishment (CAT), the Convention for the Protection of All Persons from Enforced Disappearance (CED), and the International Convention on the Protection of the Rights of All Migrant Workers and Members of Their Families (CMW).

[5] These include the African Charter On Human And Peoples' Rights ratified on 8 June 1983; African Charter on the Rights and Welfare of the Child ratified on 14 December 2000; Protocol to the African Charter on Human and Peoples' Rights on the Rights of Women in Africa ratified on 25 May 2005 and the African Youth Charter ratified on 30 April 2009.

[6] [1960–1963] GLR 226, p. 241.

[7] These include the right to life (section 18), the right to personal liberty (section 19), protection from slavery and forced labour (section 20), protection from inhuman treatment (section 21), protection from deprivation of property (section 22), the right to privacy (section 23), freedom of speech, conscience, assembly, association, and movement (section 25), political rights (section 26), the right to marry (section 27), rights of women (section 28), rights of children (section 29), the right to education (section 30), rights of the disabled (section 31), culture (section 32), and protection from discrimination (section 33).

[8] Section 207(1) further states that the 'freedom and independence of the press and other information media' are 'guaranteed'.

public morality, and for the purpose of protecting the reputations, rights, and freedoms of others.

While these provisions seem to capture the general essence of the right, it does not adhere to international human rights standards, such as the right to hold opinion and to receive and impart information and does not provide adequate protection against arbitrary interference by the state. Article 19 of the ICCPR guarantees the right to freedom of expression, including the freedom to seek, receive, and impart information and ideas of all kinds. The right to the freedom of expression is likewise protected under article 9 of the African Charter.[9]

Restrictions on this right are bound by a three-part test: the limitation must be (1) provided by law; (2) serve a legitimate aim; and (3) a necessary and proportionate means to achieve the stated aim in a democratic society, that is compatible with the African Charter and international human rights law. For any law that limits the right to freedom of expression, it must be sufficiently precise to enable an individual to assess whether his or her conduct would be in breach of the law and to foresee the likely consequences of any such breach. Section 209 of the Constitution provides that the freedom and independence of the media guaranteed by section 207 is 'subject to laws which are reasonably required in a democratic society in the interests of national security, public order, public morality, and for the purpose of protecting the reputations, rights and freedoms of others'. This provision was broad enough to allow for arbitrary application of the law. Former President Jammeh was able to exploit this for his purposes as the Constitution did not define the precise scope of the lawful limitations allowed with regard to them.

Freedom of the Press and Other Media

Section 25(1)(a) protects the 'freedom of the press and other media'. The freedom and independence of the press and other information media are guaranteed under Section 207(1) of the Constitution. However, under Jammeh's authoritarian regime, this became a sham provision as he attempted to monopolise the provision of information and stifle independent media. Through multiplicity of laws regulating the media, journalists operated in a precarious environment characterised by draconian laws (many of which are still in existence); arbitrary arrests, detentions, and physical assaults against journalists, as well as the closure and burning down of media houses. It is estimated that during Jammeh's rule, 3 journalists were killed in the line of duty; more than a dozen attempts of murder on journalists; at least 89 cases of arrest and detention of journalists occurred, which were mostly arbitrary; an estimated 52 cases of violent attacks were recorded; 15 cases of torture (Gambia Press Union

---

[9] See further African Commission on Human and Peoples' Rights 'Declaration of Principles on Freedom of Expression in Africa' (2002). This declaration is currently under revision to include access to information and developments related to the internet. See Resolution 222 (ACHPR/Res.222 (LI) 2012) and Resolution 362 (ACHPR/Res.362 (LIX) 2016).

2018); 4 cases of arson attacks on media practitioners and media outlets; and 14 instances of arbitrary closure of media outlets.[10]

A catalogue of anti-press measures includes section 52 of the Criminal Code (Amendment) Act 2004, as amended in 2005, which makes any written or verbal statement that is critical of the government an offence. It provides stiff penalties in the form of fines and imprisonment even for first-time offenders, and in some cases, there is not even an option of a fine. A major case involving this law was the trial of US-based Gambian journalist Ms. Fatou Jaw Manneh,[11] who was charged with seditious publication for an interview she gave to a newspaper in 2007 in which she was critical of President Jammeh and the government. *The Point* newspaper reported that on 18 August 2008, Manneh was convicted and sentenced on a four-count charge: sedition, publication of seditious words, publication of false information, and uttering seditious words. She was fined GMD 250,000 (approximately USD 6000) or in default to serve a one-year imprisonment for each of the four charges.

In 2013, Amadou Sanneh (the treasurer of the UDP) and Malang Fatty and his brother Alhaji Sambou Fatty (UDP party members), and Bakary Baldeh (a Commissioner of Oaths) were detained incommunicado for one month at the National Intelligence Agency (NIA) before being tried and found guilty on sedition charges for their involvement in a letter written on UDP letterhead supporting the political asylum application of Malang Fatty (Amnesty International 2012).

In addition, Alagie Abdoulie Ceesay, the manager of Teranga FM, had been in detention since July 2015, charged with 'seditious intention' for allegedly distributing pictures that authorities said were designed to 'raise discontent, hatred, or disaffection among the inhabitants of The Gambia' (The Point 2015). He was refused bail as well as denied visits by his family. The consequences for his health were devastating. After complaining for over a month about stomach pains and difficulties sleeping, he was hospitalised on 13 January 2016. A doctor diagnosed him with an enlarged liver and prescribed pain medication. A month later, he was readmitted to the same hospital for an asthma attack and returned to prison on 1 March.[12] The United Nations

---

[10] Some of these include the closure of Citizen FM Radio in 1998, The Independent newspaper in 2006, as well as The Standard and Daily News in 2012. It has also arbitrarily closed down Teranga FM radio station on at least two occasions without any legal authority. While the Standard and Teranga FM were later allowed to resume operations, The Independent and the Daily News are still closed down.

[11] Fatou Jaw Manneh was arrested at the airport as soon as she landed in The Gambia to pay her respects to her late father.

[12] Amnesty International Press Release, 'Gambia: Free Ailing Journalist—Alhagie Ceesay Arbitrarily Detained for 8 Months', March 9, 2016, http://www.amnestyusa.org/news/press-releases/gambia-free-ailing-journalist-alhagie-ceesay-arbitrarily-detained-for-8-months, accessed June 2, 2019.

Working Group on Arbitrary Detention expressed its concern and acknowledged that the deprivation of liberty of Ceesay was arbitrary (Human Rights Council Working Group on Arbitrary Detention 2015). The group called on The Gambia to release Ceesay, drop all charges against him, and ensure that his rights are respected regardless of his location (OHCHR 2016).

In response to the growing internet activism that was not only highly critical of the government and public officials but also widespread and varied around the world, the National Assembly passed an amendment to the Information Act in April 2013 that provided a 15-year jail term for any person found guilty of using the internet to spread 'false news' about the regime or public officials. The amendment also imposed a fine of 3 million Dalasi (approximately USD 86,000) on persons found guilty of such.

Essentially, these laws and practices limited the capacity of the media to play its rightful role in the promotion of good governance, and holding the government to account, as well as promoting the respect and protection of human rights in the country, a function carved out for the media by The Gambia's Constitution. This was aptly captured by a 2013 study on the 'Plight of Gambian Exiled Journalists' commissioned by the Doha Centre for Media Freedom which stated (Doha Centre for Media Freedom 2013):

> The regular occurrence of threats and attacks against journalists in The Gambia have forced journalists to engage in self-censorship, led their families to pressurize them to abandon the profession because of the imminent dangers, or forced media professionals to go into exile. This fear is given more credence by the prevailing impunity relating to crimes perpetrated against journalists such as murder, disappearances and arson attacks (Doha Centre for Media Freedom 2013, 14).

Following his defeat in the December polls and before his departure, Jammeh continued his crackdown on the media by closing two private radio stations: Teranga FM and Hilltop (BBC 2017).

Interpretation

While limitation on the exercise of freedom of speech is to be applied by an independent body in a manner that is not arbitrary, this has not always been the case in The Gambia as journalists have faced imprisonment for publications made in the course of their work. One of the most notable cases was in 2009 when six journalists were sentenced to imprisonment by the High Court and were only saved from serving time in prison by a Presidential pardon (*The State v Ebrima Sawaneh & Six Others* 2009).

In the new democratic dispensation, the court has made tempered inroads in guaranteeing the right. In the *Bai Emil Touray and Two Others vs. the*

Attorney General (Bai Emil case),[13] the Supreme Court considered the constitutionality of various provisions of the Criminal Code (Cap 10:01) of the Laws of The Gambia and the Information and Communications (Amendment) Act 2013. The plaintiffs in 2017 sought declaration that sections 178 (defining libel), 179 (defining defamatory matter), 180 (defining publication), and 181A of the Criminal Code and section 173(A) (1) (a) & (c) of the Information and Communications (Amendment) Act 2013 (relating to matters committed over the internet) are inconsistent with the abovementioned provisions of the Constitution and therefore void and unconstitutional.

The Court held that sections 78, 179, and 180 of the Criminal Code and sections 173 (A) (1) (a) & (c) the Information and Communications (Amendment) Act 2013 are inconsistent with the rights and freedoms enshrined under sections 25 (freedom of speech including freedom of the press and other media), 207 (freedom and independence of the media and other information media), and 209 (which outlines limitations relative to that guaranteed freedom) of the Constitution.[14] The Court noted that the restrictions placed by these three sections were neither reasonable nor necessary in a democratic society. Subsequently, declaring them *ultra vires* of the Constitution and therefore invalid.[15]

It is important to note that the Court did not deal with sections 181, 182, 183, and 184 of the Criminal Code relating to publication or broadcasting of defamatory matter since their validity was not addressed in the suit. However, these sections derive their premise from sections 178, 179, and 180 of the Criminal Code, which have been declared unconstitutional.

However, the Supreme Court held a contrary decision to the one above relating to section 181A (false publication and broadcasting) in *Gambia Press Union & Two Others v the Attorney General (GPU* case).[16] The *GPU* case was filed in 2014 whereas the plaintiffs argued that various sections of the Criminal Code, in terms of sections 51 (definition of seditious intention); 52 (offence for committing seditious intention); 52A (power to confiscate printing machine on which seditious material is published); 53 (statutory time for initiating prosecution); 54 (require evidence to warrant conviction); 59 (publishing or reproducing statement or rumour or report that is likely to cause fear or alarm to the public or to disturb peace); and 181A (false publication and broadcasting), violated freedom of speech and expression, including freedom of the press and other media.

On 9 May 2018, the Supreme Court held that the protection accorded to the holder of the Office of the President is reasonable and necessary, while the protection accorded to government as an institution is not reasonable

---

[13] SC Civil Suit No: 001/2017, May 9, 2018.

[14] As above, paras 4 & 6.

[15] As above, para 54.

[16] SC Civil Suit No: 1/2014, May 9, 2018.

and not necessary. It thus partially limited the scope of the offence of 'seditious intention' (section 51(a) of the Criminal Code) by removing protection for government as an institution but leaving the protection for the President intact.[17] The Court rejected the argument with little hesitation on the basis that[18]:

> the vicissitudes and trappings of the Office of President and as the Office serves first and foremost as the foundation for national cohesions and stability, coupled with the need for the holder of such office to concentrate on State affairs and not to be unduly distracted, it is reasonable that the holder of such Office is protected. This protection is, in the context of The Gambia and the values attributed to such leadership position in the country consider necessary and thus has a legitimate aim.

While the decision of the Court in limiting the scope of 51(a) of the Criminal Code and consequently the offence of intention is commendable, it retains criminal measures for defamation against the head of state. Put at its simplest—it is contended that the Court did not show that benefit of protecting the stated interest (protecting the President from hatred, contempt, or dissatisfaction) outweighs the harm done by the law (the infringement of freedom of speech). The purpose of this limitation does not contribute to an open and democratic society that is based on human dignity and equality.

Additionally, the rest of the sections were also maintained as they were deemed to be reasonable and necessary in a democratic society for preserving the interest of national security and public order in so far as they do not relate to the severed first limb of section 51(a) (on sedition applying to the government).[19] The Court further upheld section 181A of the Criminal Code, which proscribes the so-called publication or broadcast of 'false news', as well as, section 59. With this stance, the Court missed another opportunity to bring its media laws in line with accepted regional and international standards on free speech, as its limited judgement was directly contrary to the decision made by the ECOWAS Court of Justice in *Federation of African Journalists and Others v. The Republic of The Gambia* (*FAJ* case),[20] three months prior to the *GPU* case.

The Federation of African Journalists and four individual Gambian journalists argued that the state had violated their fundamental rights by failing to protect the rights of citizens in accordance with the international instruments that have been signed by The Gambia, including the ECOWAS Revised Treaty,

---

[17] As above, para 54.

[18] As above, para 52.

[19] As above, paras 55–62.

[20] (ECW/CCJ/JUD/04/18), available from https://www.mediadefence.org/sites/default/files/blog/files/FAJ%20and%20Others%20v%20The%20Gambia%20Judgment.pdf, accessed 9 January 2019.

the African Charter and the ICCPR.[21] It was submitted that security agents of The Gambia arbitrarily arrested, harassed, and detained the journalists under inhumane conditions and forced them into exile for fear of persecution as a consequence of their work.

The Court upheld the claim, finding that The Gambia had violated the journalists' rights to freedom of expression, liberty, and freedom of movement, as well as the prohibition against torture.[22] As such, it awarded six million Dalasi in compensation to the journalists (approximately 21,352 USD). The Court further ordered The Gambia to immediately repeal or amend its laws on criminal defamation (libel), sedition, and false news in line with its obligations under international law.[23] The government is yet to implement the judgement of the ECOWAS Court relating to legislative reform and compensation for the victims.

The Regulation of Assembly

The right to freedom of assembly as guaranteed in section 25(1)(d) of the Constitution includes the right to take part in peaceful demonstrations without arms. In line with the ICCPR, sections 25(4) of the Constitution limits the right and requires that restrictions must be (1) in conformity with the law, (2) in the interests of national security or public safety, public order, the protection of public health or morals, or the protection of the rights and freedoms of others, and (3) necessary in a democratic society.

Due to The Gambian case law's absence of a generous interpretation of the content of this right including the 'peaceful' and 'unarmed' clauses, the state has continuously exploited this requirement, which deters people from organising and participating in such demonstrations.

Limitation of Freedom of Assembly

The Public Order Act of 1961[24] constitutes a significant limitation on the right of assembly. The Act regulates the holding of public gatherings and demonstrations. In section 5(2), the Public Order Act requires any person who wants to form a public procession to first apply for a licence to the appropriate government official authorised by the President who will issue the licence if he or she 'is satisfied that the procession is not likely to cause a breach of the peace'.[25] This requirement for prior application for a licence is not in line with international best practice that requires only prior notification

---

[21] Suit No. ECW/CCJ/APP/36/15.

[22] As above, pp. 60–61.

[23] As above, p. 62.

[24] The 1961 Act came into force on 31 October 1961. It has since been amended by the Amendments Act, 2009 and 2010.

[25] During Jammeh's 22 years of rule, it became impossible to obtain permission to have a public gathering. See, for example, *Peters (Femi) v. the State*, HC 195/10/CR/075/BO (Crim. Appeal).

for a public procession (African Commission on Human and Peoples' Rights 'Guidelines on Freedom of Association and Assembly in Africa 2017). Additionally, requirement for the issuing of licence on the basis that procession is not likely to breach the peace is unclear as it gives officials wide discretion. Thus, the lack of clear guidance on the exercise of freedom of assembly can be viewed as arbitrary. Section 5(4)-(5) of the Public Order Act allows government officers to disperse unlicensed public processions, as well as hold individuals who participate in unlicensed processions liable to imprisonment for a term of three years.

The consequences of unlicensed public processions are real. Under Jammeh's rule, the right of people to protest peacefully and open opposition to the government was met with a consistently repressive response over the years. Section 18 (4) of the Constitution provides:

> Without prejudice to any liability for a contravention of any other law with respect to the use of force in such cases as are hereinafter mentioned, a person shall not be regarded as having been deprived of his or her life in contravention of this section if he or she dies as a result of the use of force to such extent as is reasonably justifiable in the circumstances of the case, that is to say—

> a. for the defence of any person from unlawful violence or for the defence of property;
> b. in order to effect a lawful arrest or to prevent the escape of a person lawfully detained;
> c. *for the purpose of suppressing a riot, insurrection or mutiny*[26];
> d. in order to prevent the commission by that person of a criminal offence, or
> e. if he or she dies as a result of a lawful act of war.

This provision has afforded law enforcement officials with immunity when a person dies under circumstances in which reasonable force was used. For instance, in 2000, during the April 10 and 11 demonstration by students against the alleged murder of a student and the rape of a school girl, 14 people were gunned down including a Red Cross volunteer by the security forces.[27] A Commission of Inquiry, which was established in August 2000, identified security officers as bearing the greatest responsibility for the massacre. However, the recommendations of the Commission including prosecution of the alleged violators were not implemented. Instead, the National Assembly passed an Indemnity Act to absolve the government and its agents of any

---

[26] Emphasis added.

[27] *See Gambia Student's Association v. The Inspector General of Police & Anor.*, 26/04/2000.

liability for their decisions and actions taken in the wake of the April 10 and 11 incidents.[28]

Unquestionably, the case of Solo Sandeng is a clear illustration of the abuse on the regulation of the exercise of freedom of assembly. On 14 April 2016, Solo Sandeng (who was the National Organising Secretary of the main opposition, United Democratic Party (UDP) at the time), alongside other members were arrested for leading a peaceful protest for electoral reforms and demanding for the resignation of President Jammeh (Human Rights Watch 2016). Two days after the arrest, senior members of the UDP, including the leader Ousainou Darboe, confirmed in a press conference the death of Solo Sandeng while in detention. Lawyer Darboe also stated that two detained female protesters were in a coma following their arrest and alleged brutal torture by the security agents. Angered by the harsh treatment meted on the detainees, Darboe, and a group of UPD stalwarts, led a protest march but were swiftly rounded up by The Gambia's security force and arrested. Eyewitnesses said the security agents fired tear gas at the crowd to disperse it (BBC 2016a).

Alarmed by the high-handedness of the authorities, the former United Nations Secretary-General, Mr. Ban Ki-Moon, called 'on the authorities to conduct a prompt, thorough and independent investigation into the circumstances surrounding the deaths' (United Nations 2016). Rights groups such as Amnesty International, Human Rights Watch, and ARTICLE 19 have also called on the government to conduct an independent and impartial investigation into Sandeng's death and to release the protesters. Darboe and his co-defendants were subsequently convicted and sentenced to three years (Sillah 2016). With the new government, they were all released (BBC 2016b).

Notwithstanding, the history of the country and the inhibition of the exercise of freedom of assembly, which criminalised gathering that posed no threat to the security or the protection of other rights, these laws are still in place thereby leading to the same repressive response by the present democratic government. For instance, on 2 June 2017, a protest demanding for the removal of heavy security presence in Foni took place in Kanilai, the birthplace of the former President Jammeh which turned deadly. The clash between the protesters and the ECOWAS Intervention force in The Gambia (ECOMIG) soldiers led to the death of one of the protesters (Sanyang 2017). The Interior Minister in his televised statement to the nation stated that 'you either abide by the law or you will be consumed by the law' (MamosTV n.d.). Following this event, the ECOWAS Commission reaffirmed its commitment to 'stabilize the fragile security situation in the country' which was extended in 2017 during

---

[28] See *Sabally v. Inspector General of Police* Supreme Court, Civil Case No 2, 2001. In a unanimous judgement, the Supreme Court held that the application of the Act to terminate the legal proceedings instituted by the plaintiff at the time constituted a contravention of the provisions against retroactive deprivation of a vested right as provided for by section 100(2)(c) of the Constitution and exceeded the constitutional powers of the National Assembly.

the summit of the ECOWAS Heads of State and Government in Monrovia, Liberia (ECOWAS 2017).

In addition, on June 10, 2017, sports journalist, Baboucarr Sey, was detained and denied bail for holding a protest and press conference over a disputed soccer field claimed by real estate company, Global Properties. His detention was premised on the allegations that he failed to obtain a permit to hold the protest march and subsequent press conference. He was to be indicted with four counts including: conspiracy to commit felony, assembly without a permit, destruction of private property, and unlawful use of banners.

The discretionary use of force by law enforcement and security officials has also been an issue. For instance, on 18 June 2018, a deadly clash between personnel of the Police Intervention Unit (PIU) and the community of Faraba Banta led to the death of two men and the injury of nine others. An outcry led to a swift establishment of a Commission of Inquiry which was mandated to investigate the circumstances, deaths, injuries, destructions, those who may have ordered shootings, those who fired the shots and any possible failure or breakdown in Police chain command that led to the shootings among others.[29]

The Commission was mandated to operate for a period of one month, from 1 July 2018 to 31 July 2018 with a possibility of a one-month extension. The Commission sought an extension and was (by letter dated 31 July 2018) granted an extension of a month to 31 August 2018. The Commission concluded its work on 27 August 2018 and presented its findings and recommendations in the form of a report to the President.[30] The Faraba report is particularly important in that it deals with the duty to investigate human rights violations. Due to the alleged engagements in torture, violence, and human rights violations by the Police Intervention Unit (PIU) personnel during the rule of former President Jammeh, Gambians do not have trust and confidence in the PIU. The Commission held that there was no evidence that the police has taken any steps to vet or screen PIU Officers who have been involved or suspected to have been involved in past human rights abuses nor were they made aware of any programmes in place to train or reorient them in operating under a democratic dispensation.[31] The Commission reiterated the urgent need for a security sector reform. A *White Paper on the Report of the Faraba Banta Commission of Inquiry* has since been published and the

[29] The establishment of the Commission was gazetted on 1 July 2018 and all the Commissioners were sworn before his Excellency on Thursday 5 July 2018.

[30] Report of the Faraba Banta Commission of Inquiry into the events of Monday 18 June 2018 at Faraba Banta, West Coast Region (2018).

[31] As above, p. 59.

government has made an undertaking to use appropriate criminal prosecutions against the perpetrators.[32]

However, it is important to note the unanimous decision of the Supreme Court, which held on 23 November 2017 that the grounds set out in section 25 (4) of the Constitution and section 5 of the Public Order Act were reasonably justifiable in any democratic society. The Supreme Court stated that[33]:

> The right to assembly, as with other individual or collective rights, is usually exercised within the public space. As a result (sic) its exercise by one may conflict with the exercise of the same right by others or with the exercise or enjoyment of other rights by other persons or with the needs for the maintenance of public order and security. Hence the need for some regulation or restrictions on the exercise of the right ... The requirement of a licence from the Inspector General of police for the holding of a public procession ... to prevent a breach of the peace are reasonable limitations on the right to assembly and to free expression.

This freedom of assembly case was brought by Ousainou Darboe who invoked the original jurisdiction of the Supreme Court seeking declarations that section 5 of the Public Order Act was unconstitutional as it violated section 25 of the Constitution which guarantees freedom to assemble and demonstrate peaceably and without arm. The plaintiffs further claimed that the requirement levied on a person to apply for a police permit before holding any public gathering is illegal, unconstitutional, and made in excess of legislative authority.

The Supreme Court's reasoning is contrary to international and regional human rights standards. For instance, as noted above, rule 71 of the African Commission on Human and Peoples' Rights (African Commission) Guidelines on Freedom of Association and Assembly in Africa provides that (African Commission on Human and Peoples' Rights 2017, para 71):

> participating in and organizing assemblies is a right and not a privilege, and thus its exercise does not require the authorization of the state. A system of prior notification may be put in place to allow states to facilitate the exercise of this right and to take the necessary measures to protect public safety and rights of other citizens.

Although the Constitution permits the imposition of restrictions on the exercise of fundamental rights under specified circumstance, the unconstitutionality and undemocratic nature of section 5 of the Act lies in the

---

[32] Gambia Government, "White Paper on the report of the Faraba Banta Commission of Inquiry" Supplement "A" to The Gambia Gazette No. 33 of 28 November 2018, Legal Notice No. 47 of 2018: 11–12.

[33] *Ousainou Darboe v 19 Others IGP & Inspector General of Police, Director General of National Intelligence Agency & the Attorney General*, CML SUIT NO: SC 003/2016, 7–8.

308   S. NABANEH

discretionary or arbitrary nature of the decision of the Inspector General of Police (IGP) to grant or deny a permit. The Coalition Government's 2016 manifesto described the Public Order Act as a law that 'gives too much power to the Inspector General of Police and does fetter freedom of association and assembly'.

Following this immensely unpopular decision of the Supreme Court dismissing claims of unconstitutionality of section 5 of the Public Order Act holding that the section was reasonable and constitutionally legitimate (Nabaneh and Sowe 2018, 99–100), a communication was subsequently submitted to the African Commission.[34] The complainants averred that the Public Order Act, 1961 unlawfully restricts the scope of freedom of expression (article 9(2)); freedom of association (article 10); and freedom of assembly (article 11) as protected under the African Charter on Human and Peoples' Rights (African Charter). They further requested the African Commission to be seized of the communication.[35] The Commission is seized of the matter and the case is now at the admissibility stage.

Governance Challenges

The Gambia's governance challenges were further compounded by total control of state organs and institutions, which rendered them weak and inept (United Nations 2015).[36] Due to the lack of separation of powers, the legislative and judiciary were unable to nurture and consolidate democratic governance as the executive branch played a counter-productive role. For example, one of the powers that Jammeh exerted over the National Assembly, particularly with his party members, was section 91 of the 1997 Constitution, which provides that a parliamentarian may lose his seat if he or she is dismissed from the party. Through this provision, Jammeh was able to control parliamentarians to do his bidding. He had on several occasions, expelled parliamentarians from his party as its chairman.[37]

Similarly, the judicial system in The Gambia suffered large-scale political interference by the former regime, which impacted greatly on their independence. Such interferences came in the form of undue intimidations of judges and magistrates (Nabaneh 2017, 30–32). Further coupled with severe lack of human resources and infrastructures, and under-investment, judicial independence and rule of law were subverted creating an unhealthy climate where the protection of human rights was undermined (Senghore 2010, 215–248).

---

[34] Communication 705/18, *Emil Touray v Saikou Jammeh (represented by IHRDA & Sagar Jahateh) v Republic of The Gambia* (2018), para 4.

[35] As above, para 12.

[36] See UN (2015). Report of the Special Rapporteur on extrajudicial, summary or arbitrary executions: Mission to The Gambia. A/HRC/29/37/Add.2: para 10.

[37] These included Yaya Dibba and Borry Kolley in 2013, Pa Malick Ceesay in 2015, and Kandeh.

3   Democratic Transition: A Scorecard

Since the present government took office in January 2017, it has committed itself to the promotion of democratic rule, respect for human rights, rule of law, and maintaining political stability. To this end, the government is undertaking key constitutional and legal reforms to consolidate the democratic gains made by The Gambia.

3.1   *Equalising the Political Playing Field*

The Jammeh era witnessed major shrinking of the political rights. For instance, the National Assembly, dominated by the then ruling Alliance for Patriotic Reorientation and Construction (APRC), passed the Elections (Amendment) Act 2015, a legislation that dramatically raised the registration posits required for presidential, legislative, mayoral, and local council candidates. Presidential candidates were required to pay GMD 500,000 (approximately USD 12,500), which was raised from GMD 10,000 (approximately USD 250); the fee for candidates for the National Assembly was increased from GMD 5000 (approximately USD 125) to GMD 50,000 (approximately USD 1000) and candidates for local council office were to pay GMD 10,000 (about USD 200). These were considerable sums given the extreme poverty that Gambians live in. Opposition political parties not only regarded the increases as unreasonably high but also as a ploy by the government to drastically limit the participation of the opposition in elections (Nabaneh 2017). The July 2015 election law amendments imposed prohibitive new registration requirements on political parties. Most notably, parties must deposit over $12,000; gather the signatures of 10,000 registered voters, up from 500; ensure that all executive members live in The Gambia; and hold biannual congresses.

In the spirt of re-examination and re-appraisal of the electoral system, the National Assembly passed the Elections (Amendment) Act 2017 to 'encourage the widespread participation of the ordinary citizenry in the new democratisation dispensation'. Thus, reverting the fees back to their initial amounts, i.e. the sum of GMD10,000 for presidential candidates, the sum of GM D5000 for candidates for the National Assembly, and the sums of D2500 and D12500, respectively, for other categories.

3.2   *Accountability and Truth Telling*

Commission of Inquiry
The Constitution gives power to the National Assembly to establish commissions of inquiry. Section 200 of the Constitution outlines how commissions of inquiry can be created. The importance of the establishment of commissions of inquiry was confirmed in The Gambian context in the *State v Abdoulie Conteh* (16):

[w]hen things go wrong in government impartial means are needed for discovering what happened so that those responsible may be called to account. The Commission of Inquiry is a constitutional device that allows techniques of judicial investigation to be applied to investigate serious allegations of corruption or improper conduct in the public service, or to investigate a matter of concern which requires thorough and impartial investigation to allay public anxiety.

The functions and powers of commissions of inquiry are clearly spelt out under section 202 of the Constitution and have the same powers, rights, and privileges of a High Court Judge in ensuring the attendance of witnesses, examination of these witnesses under oath, compelling the production of documents, issuing a commission or request for the examination of witnesses abroad, and making of interim orders.[38]

In a bid to address the atrocities committed under the Jammeh regime, the government has frozen assets suspected of belonging to the former president. Subsequently, the *Commission of Inquiry into the Financial Activities of Public Bodies, Enterprises, and Offices as Regards Their Dealings with Former President Yahya A.J.J Jammeh and Connected Matters* (known as the Jammeh Commission) was established in July 2017.[39] The Commission was mandated to investigate allegations of abuse of office, mismanagement of public funds, and wilful violations of the Constitution by former President Jammeh. The Commission began hearing evidence in public sessions on 10 August 2017, which has seen testimonies from 253 witnesses including former public servants, heads of parastatals, businesspersons, military personnel, managers from commercial and government banks, as well as private citizens.

The final report of the Commission was submitted to the President in April 2019, with the complete report of the investigation made public recently. In his presentation of the report, Minister of Justice, Abubacarr Tambadou noted that the Commission's report exposes the alarming scale of corruption of the former President and his close associates (Statement by Minister of Justice on Janneh Commission Report 2019). For example, it was established that the former President looted more than 300 million USD from public funds (Statement by Minister of Justice on the Janneh Commission Report 2019).

During 22 years of authoritarian rule, there was no effective investigation of human rights violations, and in most cases, perpetrators were not brought to justice. Thus, the Barrow-led government indicated strong commitment to break with past of systematic human rights violations through the enactment of the Truth, Reconciliation, and Reparations Commission (TRRC) Act by the National Assembly on 13 December, which received presidential assent on 13 January 2018.

---

[38] See *AG v Pap Cheyasin Secka* (2002–2008) 2 GLR 88 where it was affirmed that the Commission of Inquiry has the same standing with the High Court.

[39] This is in line with section 200(1) of the Constitution and the Commission of Inquiry Act (CAP. 30:01), Vol. 5 of the Laws of The Gambia.

The Truth, Reparations and Reconciliation Commission (TRRC)

The TRRC Act provides for the establishment of the historical record of the nature, causes, and extent of violations and abuses of human rights committed during the period July 1994 to January 2017 and to consider the granting of reparation of victims. The Commission's mandate includes initiating and coordinating investigations into violations and abuses of human rights; the identity of persons or institutions involved in such violations; identifying the victims; and determining what evidence might have been destroyed to conceal such violations.[40]

The TRRC was launched on 5 October 2018 with the swearing ceremony of the appointed eleven members. The hearings which began on 7 January 2019 serve as an initial first step towards securing justice, truth, and reparations in The Gambia (The Point 2019). The Gambia TRRC provides a foundation, if executed properly, not only to address the structures and causes of violations but also to assure victims of past violations of non-repetition and as such serve as a form of reparation.

3.3   *Constitutional Review Process*

On 11 December 2017, eleven months after the new government took office, the Minister of Justice, Abubacarr Tambadou[41] finally presented the Constitutional Review Commission Bill before the National Assembly. The passing of the Constitutional Review Commission (CRC) Act 2017[42] for the establishment of a commission to draft and guide the process of promulgating a new constitution for The Gambia is a great step in addressing the deficiencies of the 1997 Constitution. The 1997 Constitution lacks legitimacy with Gambians seeing it as an artefact of the Jammeh government.

According to section 6(2)(a), 3 and 4 of the Act, citizens both within the country and abroad will have the opportunity to participate in providing public opinion and proposals to the Commission. Consultations nation-wide and in the diaspora were conducted in which citizens were able to share their views and opinions on a number of issues contained in the CRC's Issues Document. Civil society organisations have also made submissions to the Commission.

Key among the issues that surfaced are citizenship, fundamental rights and freedoms, elections, local government structures, the three branches of government, the need to establish service commissions for health, education, and agriculture and the environment, representation of women, youth, and persons with disabilities, declaration of assets, the use of local languages in the National Assembly, public finance, political party finance, National Youth Service Scheme and security of tenure for the offices of the Auditor General,

---

[40] Sec 14 of the TRRC Act, 2017.

[41] He was Minister of Justice until his appointment on 1 July 2020 as the Registrar of the International Residual Mechanism for Criminal Tribunals (IRMCT).

[42] This was assented to on 11 January 2018 by President Barrow.

Governor of the Central Bank of The Gambia, and chief executives of the Public Enterprises.

The main functions of the CRC are to review and analyse the current 1997 Constitution, draft a new constitution, and prepare a report in relation to the new constitution. The report will provide the reasoning for the provisions contained in the new constitution. Section 21 of the Act empowers the Commission upon submission to the President, to publish the draft constitution and the report in the Gazette and in such other manner as the Commission deems fit. This serves as a safeguard against tampering. The CRC will, therefore, play an indispensable role in efforts to achieve a unified and stable nation and align the new constitution with international standards.

3.4 Building a Culture of Human Rights

In building a culture for the respect, protection, and promotion of human rights, the government of The Gambia recognised the need for a legal and institutional framework to which a human rights culture will be anchored (Nabaneh and Sowe 2018). To this end, a national human rights commission was established. On 13 December 2017, the National Assembly passed the National Human Rights Commission (NHRC) Act and the President assented to it on 13 January 2018. The NHRC Act establishes a Commission for the promotion and protection of human rights in The Gambia. The NHRC is authorised to investigate and consider complaints of human rights violations in The Gambia committed by the state, private persons, and entities. The five commissioners have been approved by the National Assembly and officially appointed by the President as provided by the Act.

In fulfilment of their international human rights obligations, The Gambia became the ninth country on 23 November 2018 to make the declaration under article 34(6) of the Protocol to the African Charter on Human and Peoples' Rights on the Establishment of an African Court on Human and Peoples' Rights (African Court) to allow individual direct access to the Court (African Court on Human and Peoples' Rights 2018). In addition to granting access to individuals, the declaration allows the Court to trigger its jurisdictional competency under article 5(3) to allow for a limited number of access for NGOs.

Ratification of Key UN Human Rights Treaties
The Gambia on 28 September 2018 also ratified important UN human rights treaties including the Second Optional Protocol to the International Covenant on Civil and Political Rights, the Convention Against Torture and Other Cruel Inhuman or Degrading Treatment or Punishment (CAT), the Convention for the Protection of All Persons from Enforced Disappearance (CED), and the International Convention on the Protection of the Rights of All Migrant Workers and Members of Their Families (CMW) (UN International Human Rights Instruments Ratification Status for The Gambia n.d.).

These are good first steps in the fulfilment of The Gambia's human rights obligations including the abolition of the death penalty. The death penalty is still applicable in The Gambia. The last executions were carried out on 27 August 2012, when nine death row inmates—eight men and one woman were executed, allegedly by a firing squad (Report of the Special Rapporteur on extrajudicial, summary, or arbitrary executions 2015, para 25). According to the news report, 'all persons on death row have been tried by The Gambian courts of competent jurisdiction and thereof convicted and sentenced to death in accordance with the law. They have exhausted all their legal rights of appeal as provided by the law' (Nabaneh 2017, 10).

The executions were the first in The Gambia since 1985. The death penalty was abolished in 1993 by the Death Penalty (Abolition) Act 1993 but reinstated in 1995 by Decree No. 52 entitled the Death Penalty (Restoration) Decree, 1995. Among the reasons given for the restoration of the death penalty were that 'since the abolition of the death penalty in The Gambia there has been a steady increase of cases of homicide and treasonable offences which, if not effectively checked, may degenerate into a breakdown of law and order' and that the duty dawned on the 'State to provide adequate mechanisms for the security of life and liberty of its citizenry thereby maintaining law and order and ensuring greater respect for individual human rights'.

While the ratification of CAT is a step in the right direction, The Gambia has not taken any concrete measures towards criminalising torture. The prohibition of torture, inhuman, or degrading punishment or other treatment is enshrined in section 21 of the Constitution. However, the absence of torture as a criminal offence in the Criminal Code inhibits the prosecution of perpetrators of torture under the transitional justice system. There is need to review the Criminal Code to include torture as a criminal offence.

Human Rights Committee's Review of the State of Civil and Political Rights in the Gambia

In July 2018, the Human Rights Committee reviewed the implementation of the ICCPR in The Gambia through the country's response to the list of issues in the absence of the second periodic report (Human Rights Committee 2017). The Committee raised concerns that section 18 of the Constitution and sections 15 (A) and 72 of the Criminal Code allow for a great deal of discretion in the use of force by law enforcement officials, and that section 2 (a) and (b) of the Indemnity Act (as amended in 2001) exonerates all public officials from civil or criminal liability for the exercise of their duties with respect to unlawful assemblies, riotous situations, or public emergencies (Human Rights Committee 2018, para 29). The Committee made recommendations to The Gambia to revise its laws with a view to bringing them in line with international standards (Human Rights Committee 2018, para 30).

While these ratifications are commendable, The Gambia is yet to ensure individual access to a majority of the UN human rights treaty bodies.[43] The Gambia is also yet to withdraw the reservation it made upon ratification of the ICCPR on 22 March 1979 in respect of article 14(3)(d) to the effect that 'for financial reasons free legal assistance for accused persons is limited in our constitution to persons charged with capital offences only' (United Nations Office of the High Commissioner 2019). The spirit of this reservation is reflected in section 24(3)(d) of the Constitution. Despite the reservation, the state established the National Agency for Legal Aid (NALA) through the enactment of the Legal Aid Act in 2008 (Legal Aid Act of The Gambia 2008). The Agency has the mandate to handle civil cases but since its inception it is yet to handle any civil case. To further promote access to justice, The Gambia should take steps to withdraw its reservation to the ICCPR, thus bringing it in conformity with the spirit and intent of the Legal Aid Act 2008 (Institute for Human Rights and Development in Africa 2012).

3.5   *'Gambianization' of the Judiciary*

Given the various assaults on the independence of the judiciary and politicisation, President Barrow's government has taken steps to reform the judiciary by appointing a slate of new judges, including a respected Gambian Chief Justice, Hassan Jallow, former prosecutor of the International Criminal Tribunal for Rwanda in Arusha, Tanzania. Following this, numerous appointments took place including at the level of the Supreme Court. In 2017, 16 superior court judges were appointed including 14 Gambians to the Supreme Court, Court of Appeal, and High Court, respectively (Sowe and Nabaneh 2017, 100–101).

4   Conclusion

The fundamental challenges that The Gambia continue to face are adherence to good governance principles and practices in line with respect for human rights and the rule of law. As noted above, the Supreme Court's approach to the application, interpretation, and limitation of rights in constitutional cases has serious implications for inculcating a culture of human rights restoring the rule of law, and enhancing good governance. The judiciary needs to take bolder stance and summon the courage to give meaning to fundamental human rights in the Constitution.

The change in leadership and President Barrow's commitment to undertake legal reforms to enable greater protection of fundamental rights and freedoms presents an opportunity to revisit existing laws. The Criminal Code is

---

[43] At the moment, individual access to UN Treaty Bodies is only limited to the Human Rights Committee. The 9 June 1988 submitted declaration reads: 'The Government of the Gambia hereby declares that the Gambia recognises the competence of the Human Rights Committee to receive and consider communications to the effect that a State Party claims that another State Party is not fulfilling its obligations under the present Covenant'.

currently under revision. Such revision is critical to expunge provisions that unduly restrict the full enjoyment of human rights including the freedom of expression.

Despite the excitement and enthusiasm that greeted the onset of multiparty democracy following decades of authoritarian rule, The Gambia's democracy remains fragile. While measures have been undertaken by the government to deal with the abuses of the past and to reinstate democratic institutions in the country, there are concerns regarding existing repressive laws that stifle fundamental human rights. More importantly, government should ensure that laws and their interpretations are in conformity with regional and international standards. The Barrow government indeed has a critical opportunity to reengage with constitutional protections and see through its numerous campaign commitments.

BIBLIOGRAPHY

African Charter on Human and Peoples' Rights (ACHPR) OAU Doc. CAB/LEG/67/3 rev. 5, 21 ILM 58 (1982).

African Commission on Human and Peoples' Rights. "Guidelines on Freedom of Association and Assembly in Africa," (2017).

African Court on Human and Peoples' Rights. "The Gambia Becomes the Ninth Country to Allow NGOs and Individuals to Access the African Court Directly," November 23, 2018. Available from http://www.african-court.org/en/index.php/news/press-releases/item/257-the-gambia-becomes-the-ninth-country-to-allow-ngos-and-individuals-to-access-the-african-court-directly. Accessed December 20, 2018.

African Commission on Human and Peoples' Rights. "Declaration of Principles on Freedom of Expression in Africa," (2002).

AG v Pap Cheyasin Secka (2002–2008) 2 GLR 88.

Amnesty International, "The Gambia must Immediately Release Three Opposition Members Convicted of Sedition." December 18, 2012. https://www.amnesty.org/en/latest/news/2013/12/gambia-must-immediately-release-threeopposition-members-convicted-sedition/. Accessed June 8, 2019.

BBC. "Gambian Activist 'Died in Detention." April 16, 2016a. http://www.bbc.com/news/world-africa-36064276. Accessed March 10, 2019.

BBC. "Gambia Opposition Leader Ousainou Darboe Freed on Bail." December 5, 2016b. http://www.bbc.com/news/world-africa-38210873. Accessed March 10, 2019.

BBC. "The Gambia's Teranga FM and Hilltop radio closed." January 2, 2017. http://www.bbc.com/news/worldafrica-38488083. Accessed May 15, 2019.

Communication 705/18. *Emil Touray v Saikou Jammeh (Represented by IHRDA & Sagar Jahateh) v Republic of The Gambia* (2018).

Constitution of the Republic of The Gambia. 1997.

Convention Against Torture and Other Cruel, Inhuman or Degrading Treatment or Punishment (CAT) 10 December 1984, United Nations, Treaty Series, vol. 1465.

Convention on the Elimination of all Forms of Discrimination Against Women (CEDAW).

Criminal Code.

Doha Centre for Media Freedom. "Perils of Being in Exile: The Plight of Gambian Exiled Journalists" (2013).

ECOWAS. "Statement on the Recent Incident Which Occurred in Kanilai (Republic of the Gambia)." 6 June 6, 2017. http://www.ecowas.int/ecowas-statement-on-the-recent-incident-which-occurred-in-kanilai-republic-of-the-gambia/. Accessed June 7, 2019.

Elections Amendment Act, No. 6 of 2015.

Fombad, Charles M. "Challenges to Constitutionalism and Constitutional Rights in Africa and the Enabling Role of Political Parties: Lessons and Perspectives from Southern Africa." *American Journal of Comparative Law* 55, no. 7 (2007): 1–45.

Gambia Government. "White Paper on the Report of the Faraba Banta Commission of Inquiry" Supplement "A" to The Gambia Gazette No. 33 of 28 November 2018, Legal Notice No. 47 of 2018.

Gambia Press Union & Two Others v the Attorney General, SC Civil Suit No: 1/2014, 9 May 2018.

Gambia Student's Association v. The Inspector General of Police & Anor, 26/04/2000.

Gloppen, Siri. *South Africa: The Battle Over the Constitution*. Aldershot, Ashgate, 1997.

Henkin, L. "Elements of Constitutionalism, Occasional Paper Series/Center for the Study of Human Rights, Columbia University," (1994).

Human Rights Committee. "Concluding Observations on the Gambia in the Absence of Its Second Periodic Report." CCPR/C/GMB/CO/2, August 30, 2018.

Human Rights Council. "Replies of the Gambia to the List of Issues." CCPR/C/GMB/Q/2/Add.1, 12 June 2018. See also, Human Rights Committee 'List of Issues in the Absence of the Second Periodic Report of The Gambia' CCPR/C/GMB/Q/2, December 11, 2017.

Human Rights Council Working Group on Arbitrary Detention. "Opinions Adopted by the Working Group on Arbitrary Detention at Its Seventy-Fourth Session, 30 November–4 December 2015 Opinion No. 50/2015 Concerning Alhagie Abdoulie Ceesay (The Gambia)." A/HRC/WGAD/2015, December 16, 2015.

Human Rights Watch. "Gambia: Investigate Death in Custody, Free Protesters." April 18, 2016. https://www.hrw.org/news/2016/04/18/gambia-investigate-death-cus tody-free-protesters. Accessed March 10, 2019.

Institute for Human Rights and Development in Africa (IHRDA) Legal Aid in The Gambia: An Introduction to Law and Practice (2012).https://www.ihrda.org/wp-content/uploads/2012/04/Legal-Aid-in-The-Gambia-layout-2012-website-dow nload.pdf. Accessed February 11, 2019.

International Covenant on Civil and Political Rights (ICCPR).

Jammeh, Ousman. *The Constitutional Law of the Gambia, 1965–2010*. Authorhouse, 2012.

Justice in *Federation of African Journalists and Others v. The Republic of The Gambia* ECW/CCJ/JUD/04/18).

Legal Aid Act of The Gambia, 2008.

Nabaneh, Satang. "The Impact of the African Charter and the Maputo Protocol in The Gambia." In *The Impact of the African Charter and Maputo Protocol in Selected African States*, edited by Victor Ayeni, 75–94. Pretoria: Pretoria University Law Press, 2016.

Nabaneh, Satang. "The Gambia: Commentary." In *Constitutions of the World*, edited by R Wolfrum, R Grote & C Fombad. New York, Oxford University Press, 2017.

Nabaneh, Satang. "New Gambia and the Remaking of the Constitution." ConstitutionNet. March 16, 2017. Available from http://constitutionnet.org/news/new-gambia-and-remaking-constitution. Accessed May 21, 2019.

Nabaneh, Satang and Sowe Gaye (2018). "Gambia." In *The I·CONnect-Clough Center 2018 Global Review of Constitutional Law*, edited by R Albert, D Landau et al.: 107–111.

OHCHR. "UN Expert Group on Arbitrary Detention Urges Gambia to Respect the Rights of Journalist Alhagie Ceesay." May 20, 2016.

Optional Protocol to the Convention on the Elimination of all Forms of Discrimination Against Women Adopted by General Assembly Resolution A/54/4 on 6 October 1999 and Opened for Signature on 10 December 1999 (Human Rights Day); entered into force on 22 December 2000.

Optional Protocol to the International Covenant on Civil and Political Rights Adopted and Opened for Signature, Ratification and Accession by General Assembly Resolution 2200A (XXI) of 16 December 1966; entered into force on 23 March 1976.

Ousman Sabally v. IGP and 2 Others (unreported) SC, Civil Case No 2, 2001.

Ousainou Darboe v 19 Others IGP & Inspector General of Police, Director General of National Intelligence Agency & the Attorney General, CML SUIT NO: SC 003/2016.

Peters (Femi) v. the State, HC 195/10/CR/075/BO (Crim. Appeal).

Phatey, S. "Gambia Arrest, Denies Local Sports Journalist Bail." *SMBC News*. June 9, 2017. https://gambia.smbcgo.com/2017/06/10/gambia-arrest-denies-local-sports-journalist-bail/. Accessed June 7, 2019.

Public Order Act 1961.

Report of the Faraba Banta Commission of Inquiry into the events of Monday 18 June 2018 at Faraba Banta, West Coast Region (2018).

Rosenfeld, Michel. "Modern Constitutionalism as Interplay Between Identity and Diversity." In *Constitutionalism, Identity, Difference and Legitimacy: Theoretical Perspectives*, edited by Michel Rosenfeld, 3–38. Durham and London: Duke University Press, 1994.

Sanyang L. "22 Arrested, 2 Injured & 1 Dead In Kanilai Incident." *The Fatu Network*. 3 June 2017. http://fatunetwork.net/22-arrested-2-injured-1-dead-kanilai-incident/. Accessed June 5, 2019.

Senghore, A.A. "The Judiciary in Governance in The Gambia: The Quest for Autonomy Under the Second Republic." *Journal of Third World Studies*, no. 27 (2010): 215–248.

Senghore, A.A. "Press Freedom and Democratic Governance in The Gambia: A Rights-Based Approach." *African Human Rights Law Journal*, 12, no. 2 (2012): 508–538.

Sillah B. "Darboe & Co Jailed." *Standard Newspaper*. July 21, 2016. http://standard.gm/site/2016/07/21/darboe-co-jailed/. Accessed March 10, 2019.

"Statement by Hon. Mai Ahmad Fatty, Minister of Interior on Kanilai Incident!. *MamosTV*. http://www.mamostv.com/statement-hon-mai-ahmad-fatty-minister-interior-kanilai-incident/. Accessed June 10, 2019.

"Statement by Minister of Justice on Janneh Commission Report." April 8, 2019. Available http://thepoint.gm/africa/gambia/article/statement-by-minister-of-justice-on-janneh-commission-report.

Sowe, Gaye and Satang Nabaneh (2017). "The Gambia: The State of Liberal Democracy." In *The I·CONnect-Clough Center 2017 Global Review of Constitutional Law*, edited by R Albert, D Landau et al.: 100–101.

The State v. Ebrima Sawaneh & Six Others, HC/209/09/CR/046/AO, 2009.

The State v. Ousainou Darboe & Others, High Court Criminal Case No 14, 2000.

UN (2015). Report of the Special Rapporteur on Extrajudicial, Summary or Arbitrary Executions: Mission to The Gambia. A/HRC/29/37/Add.2.

UN International Human Rights Instruments Ratification Status for The Gambia. https://tbinternet.ohchr.org/_layouts/TreatyBodyExternal/Treaty.aspx?CountryID=64&Lang=EN. Accessed January 5, 2019.

United Nations Office of the High Commissioner, Status of Ratification Interactive Dashboard. http://indicators.ohchr.org/. Accessed February 11, 2019.

United Nations (UN). "Gambia: Ban Calls for Release of Detained Protesters After Death of Opposition Members." April 17, 2016. http://www.un.org/apps/news/story.asp?NewsID=53702&utm_source=twitterfeed&utm_medium=twitter#.VxQ1BKQrLIX. Accessed March 10, 2019.

CHAPTER 17

The Psychosocial Well-Being of the African Child in Criminal Proceedings

Emma Charlene Lubaale

1 INTRODUCTION

The child is then cross-examined with the sole purpose of discrediting the child. If the accused is not legally represented, the accused may conduct the cross-examination. The effect of this on the child can be terrifying especially where the accused is an adult relative of the child. The child may agree with questions put by the accused for fear of punishment if he or she disagrees. If the cross-examination is conducted by the legal representative, the child will be taken through his or her evidence in the most minute detail. The cross-examination may bring out facts that were so grotesque that the child could never have imagined being forced to recount them. The child will be taken to task for placing events, often months after they had occurred, out of sequence and for not being able to remember important details concerning the events. In this intimidating and bewildering atmosphere, the child complainant is required to relive and reveal sordid details of the horror that he or she went through. (*Director of Public Prosecution, Transvaal v Minister for Justice & Constitutional Development* 2009, para 105)

This ruling in the case of *Director of Public Prosecution, Transvaal v Minister for Justice & Constitutional Development* could not more succinct in its

E. C. Lubaale (✉)
Faculty of Law, Rhodes University, Makhanda, South Africa
e-mail: e.lubaale@ru.ac.za

© The Author(s), under exclusive license to Springer Nature Switzerland AG 2022
A. Adeola and M. W. Mutua (eds.), *The Palgrave Handbook of Democracy, Governance and Justice in Africa*,
https://doi.org/10.1007/978-3-030-74014-6_17

description of the plight that children endure in their interaction with criminal justice processes. It brings sharply into perspective the theme of this chapter—*the psychological well-being of African children in criminal justice proceedings.*

Crime generally has a devastating effect on victims, with this effect being aggravated when the victims involved are children (United Nations on Drugs and Crime 2019; United Nations Children's Fund 2015; National Research Foundation 2020; Pietro Ferrara et al. 2019; Moffitt and Klaus-Grawe 2013; Margolin and Gordis 2000; Pantell 2017; Stevens and Lubaale 2016). The crimes committed against children are, of themselves, traumatising to them. But when criminal justice systems fail to put in place child-sensitive systems, children are traumatised even further and this impacts negatively on their psychological well-being and ultimately, their survival and development (United Nations on Drugs and Crime 2019; United Nations Children's Fund 2015; National Research Foundation 2020; Pietro Ferrara et al. 2019; Terrie Moffitt and Klaus-Grawe 2013; Margolin and Gordis 2000; Pantell 2017; Stevens and Lubaale 2016). Crime has been an ever-present threat in society, and Africa has not been spared of the challenge. Among those affected are children and globally, it is estimated that up to one billion children between the ages of two and seventeen have suffered some form of violence ranging from sexual and physical abuse to emotional and psychological violence (World Health Organisation 2020). The most prevalent of these include maltreatment, bullying, youth violence, intimate partner violence, sexual violence and psychological violence (Ibid). Children have had to succumb to death, severe injuries, impairment of brain and nervous system, unintended pregnancies and non-communicable diseases as a result of violence (Ibid; National Institute of Justice 2016). In the context of Africa, the impact of crime on children has been exacerbated by factors including poverty, social and cultural norms and the prevalence of conflict in some regions.

Impressively, however, African governments have generally not been aloof to the plight of African children. The increase in crime against children has awakened many criminal justice systems in Africa to action. Those responsible for crimes against children are being prosecuted and inevitably, and African children are increasingly coming into contact with the criminal justice system as witnesses, victims and as accused persons. But amidst this commendable stance by governments, it remains far from clear whether the psychological well-being of children in criminal proceedings is a priority.

Much has been written on the subject of children's experiences in criminal justice processes. For example, there is a plethora of literature on the traumatic effects of cross-examination on children (Fogliati 2014, vii; Lubaale 2015a, 2015b, 1–9; Crump 1992, 103–105). Scholarly work also abounds on methods of reducing trauma against children in judicial proceedings. Notable in this regard are recourse to intermediaries and adoption of inquisitorial approaches (Myklebust 2017, 97–119; Holley 2002, 14–18; Muller and Marowa 2011, 13–24). There is also a proliferation of research on the right to child participation generally (Rap 2019, 299–319; Tolonen 2019, 225–248). Despite such comprehensive research, some scholarly gaps are notable. For example, not much of the literature has located participation and protection of children's psychological well-being in national criminal proceedings within the broader international children's rights framework. Additionally, while country studies have been conducted, with most of these focussing on South Africa (Jonker and Swanzen 2007, 90–113; Bekink 2019, 1–50), hardly any work has discussed South Africa's approach from the wider perspective of African criminal justice responses to child participation and their psychological well-being. Moreover, for quite some time, some scholars have vouched for the inquisitorial approach as a remedy to the psychological trauma that children experience in criminal proceedings (Muller 2001, 1–13). However, no engagement has been conducted on the practice of inquisitorial justice systems such as the Democratic Republic of Congo with a view to critically assessing the limitations of these viewpoints and how current practices in these countries could debunk these proposals. It is these gaps that lend impetus to the analysis in this chapter.

The purpose of this chapter therefore is to critically analyse the law and practice of selected countries in all five of the African blocks namely, the West, East, South, North and Central Africa. Based on this analysis, this chapter assesses whether the procedures currently applicable in these countries guarantee the psychological well-being of African children. It identifies gaps and makes recommendations regarding actions that can be taken to ensure that the psychological well-being of children is guaranteed during their participation in criminal justice processes.

In terms of methodology, this chapter invokes doctrinal and comparative approaches. Relying on the doctrinal method, this chapter critically analyses the national laws of selected countries on the protection afforded to children in criminal trials. In analysing these sources, the various international children's rights standards are relied on as a yardstick against which national criminal justice procedures are gauged. While the chapter does not invoke a purely comparative approach, perspectives from Nigeria, Uganda, South Africa, Egypt and the DRC, representing West, East, South, North and Central Africa, respectively, are explored with a view to offering perspectives from all the five blocks on the African continent. All five of these countries are party to the United Nations Convention on the Rights of the Child. Therefore, they are bound by the standards on child participation in criminal justice as contained in this treaty.

2 INTERNATIONAL CHILDREN'S RIGHTS FRAMEWORK ON PARTICIPATION AND CHILD PSYCHOLOGICAL WELL-BEING IN CRIMINAL JUSTICE PROCESSES

To assess whether criminal justice systems in Africa are giving due regard to the psychological well-being of children, it is important to first get to grips with the particular standards that states are expected to adhere to. It is for this purpose that this section unpacks these standards by engaging with the norms set in selected international instruments relevant to the rights of children in the context of criminal justice. Focus is placed on child participation and protection of children from psychological harm as these two notions feature prominently in children's interaction with criminal justice processes.

The standards set by international law have a major impact on the operations of national criminal justice systems. Regarding international human rights law, treaties remain a major source of law (Statute of the International Court of Justice 1946, Article 38) and by virtue of ratification, states are bound to give effect to the human rights standards that come with such ratification (Vienna Convention on the Law of Treaties 1969, Article 26). In the particular context of children's rights, various international treaties contain provisions that place a mandate on states to ensure that the psychological well-being of children in all spheres including criminal justice proceedings is guaranteed (See generally human rights treaties at the United Nations Level and in the context of Africa, the African Union human rights treaty framework). In addition to these binding legal instruments, over the years, several non-binding instruments have been adopted. Though non-binding, these instruments have played a fundamental role in shaping standards applicable to children's affairs. Mention can be made of the United Nations Guidelines on Justice Matters involving Child Victims and Witnesses of Crime which provides comprehensive guidelines on children's engagement in criminal justice proceedings (United Nations Guidelines on Justice Matters involving Child Victims and Witnesses of Crime 2005).

All considered, these instruments, be they binding or non-binding, constitute a normative framework on issues concerning children including their participation and psychological well-being.

2.1 Participation and Children in Criminal Proceedings

Participation is important to children in all spheres including criminal justice. It fosters personal development, leads to better decision-making, ensures child protection and strengthens accountability (United Nations Committee on the Rights of the Child, General Comment 12 2009). In criminal justice proceedings, participation is a means through which children's right to access justice is guaranteed because in many instances, accountability for crimes against children rests heavily on the evidence of children. Thus, depriving children of the right to participate undermines children's right to access to justice.

The journey to implementing the right to participation for children has not always been a smooth one. Viewing children as rights-holders is an issue that many societies continue to grapple with. Traditionally, children were merely considered as objects of protection and not autonomous individuals in possession of specific rights. In the context of Africa, implementing this right brings with it another layer of challenges on account of some applicable norms. The customary laws applicable in some societies impact on the extent to which the participation rights of children are guaranteed. For example, children's status in family settings and values such as respect for elders have a bearing on children's participation and their recognition as autonomous rights-holders (Amos 2013; Boakye-Boaten 2010, 104–115). But with the development of the international children's regime, the various narratives that undermine children's participation are increasingly being questioned. The international children's rights regime now recognises children as both autonomous beings with rights and individuals in need of protection.

Various global, regional and national human rights instruments now recognise participation as a right and key principle in the advancement of children's rights. The United Nations Convention on the Rights of the Child (UNCRC), one of the most widely ratified treaty, entrenches participation as a right and principle in very strong terms. The central provision on participation under the UNCRC is article 12. In terms of this provision:

1. States Parties shall assure to the child who is capable of forming his or her own views the right to express those views freely in all matters affecting the child, the views of the child being given due weight in accordance with the age and maturity of the child.
2. For this purpose, the child shall in particular be provided the opportunity to be heard in any judicial and administrative proceedings affecting the child, either directly, or through a representative or an appropriate body, in a manner consistent with the procedural rules of national law (United Nations Convention on the Rights of the Child 1989).

While the term participation is neither mentioned nor defined under the UNCRC, the Committee on the Rights of the Child has made recourse to it in its interpretation of article 12. The Committee defines it as an 'ongoing processes, which include information-sharing and dialogue between children and adults based on mutual respect, and in which children can learn how their views and those of adults are taken into account and shape the outcome of such processes' (General Comment 12 2009). The Committee has also provided meaningful content to the phrases used in article 12 and these are instructive to states in ensuring the participation of children in criminal justice processes. For example, the Committee has observed that the phrase *Shall assure,* as used in article 12, 'is a legal term of special strength, which leaves no leeway for State parties' discretion' (Ibid). Based on this articulation, states are under obligation to put in place mechanisms that guarantee children's participation in all matters affecting them. By implication, the processes put in place need to take cognisance of the psychological well-being of children. Practical measures in this regard may entail enacting legislation and policies that foster stress-free participation.

Article 12, read together with other provisions of the UNCRC such as article 19 which mandates states to ensure that children are protected from physical and mental violence, can be interpreted progressively to place obligations on states to ensure that criminal justice processes do not cause trauma and psychological harm to children. Moreover, the Committee has noted that the phrase 'express views freely' means that children should not be placed under any form of pressure (Ibid). It follows from this interpretation that where criminal procedures exert undue stress on children, the same amounts to an affront to the ideal of free expression of views.

Article 12(2) of the UNCRC deals specifically with children's involvement in judicial proceedings, including criminal justice proceedings. To give effect to this right, the Committee calls on states to ensure that the legislative measures in place foster children's participation in judicial proceedings (Ibid). By implication, where legislation at the national level either undermines, or makes no provision for effective and stress-free participation of children in criminal justice processes, the participation rights of children are deemed to be undermined.

Mention here needs to be made of the phrase 'in a manner consistent with the procedural rules of national law' as referred to in article 12(2) of the UNCRC. This phrase could be misinterpreted to suggest that children's participation rights are subject to national legislation even though such legislation is archaic. The Committee has, however, laid to rest such twisted interpretation by underscoring that the phrase 'should not be interpreted as permitting the use of procedural legislation which restricts or prevents the enjoyment of this fundamental right' (Ibid). A skewed interpretation of this phrase is very much possible in the light of the dated nature of many of the criminal procedural laws in Africa. Noteworthy, the criminal laws and procedures of most African states are a remnant of colonialism. Some of the laws and procedures introduced to Africa's justice systems during the colonial era, despite being archaic, remain applicable in current times. It is notable that some of the criminal laws and procedures as introduced in the colonial times were very discriminatory to children and undermined their psychological well-being in criminal justice processes (See generally the rule on mandatory corroboration of the evidence of children on the problematic assumption that their evidence is inherently unreliable. For a commentary on this see Lubaale 2015a, 2015b, 1–15; Lubaale 2020, 149–171; Lubaale 2018, 169–183. This is perhaps less of a surprise in the light of the fact that many of these procedures became law before the international children's regime gained momentum. What is surprising though is the fact despite the prevailing international children's standards that many African states subscribe to, not many of these laws have been revised to reflect these standards (See generally the criminal Codes of African countries including Uganda, Tanzania, Swaziland, Nigeria, Ghana and Kenya).

At the regional level, the African Charter on the Rights and Welfare of the Child (ACRWC) guarantees the participation rights of children in a manner similar to the UNCRC. Under its article 7, 'every child who is capable of communicating his or her own views shall be assured the rights to express his opinions freely in all matters and to disseminate his opinions subject to such restrictions as are prescribed by laws'. One gathers that in comparison to article 12 of the UNCRC, article 7 is not that comprehensive. For example, no specific provision is made for child participation in judicial proceedings. However, in terms of content, similarities including the subjecting of children's right to participation national laws are notable. Article 4(2) places emphasis on the role of child participation with specific focus to judicial proceedings. It underscores, among others, that children should be given an opportunity for their views to be heard in judicial proceedings and for consideration to be given to such views. Traumatic court proceedings are certainly far from being conducive environments for children's views to be heard and taken into consideration. All considered, both the ACRWC and the UNCRC place an obligation on states to ensure that children participate in criminal proceedings in a manner that protects them from psychological harm.

2.2   Children's Psychosocial Well-Being in Criminal Proceedings

Recognition of children as autonomous beings with specific rights does not take away the fact that they are still in need of protection. Children's participation in judicial proceedings should be guaranteed in a manner that ensures that their psychological well-being is taken care of. An approach to criminal justice that undermines the psychological well-being of children would be at odds with the notion of the best interest of children. This principle is the hallmark of children's rights and it finds force in various international instruments including the UNCRC, ACRWC as well as in national constitutions and legislation in Africa (article 3 UNCRC 1989; article 4 ACRWC 1990). The principle has no standard or precise definition (See S v M 2008, paragraph 23, where the court refers to the Best Interest of the Child Principle as indeterminate). However, the UNCRC has observed that 'the full application of the concept of the child's best interests requires the development of a rights-based approach, engaging all actors, to secure the holistic physical, psychological, moral and spiritual integrity of the child and promote his or her human dignity' (Committee on the Rights of the Children, General Comment No. 14 2013, paragraph 1). Generally, in terms of this principle, in all decisions or actions taken concerning children, whether by public or private organs, the best interest of children is to given primary consideration.

Criminal justice processes largely require the involvement of public organs including the judiciary (as an adjudicator), the legislature (as a law maker of children-related laws) and the executive (as the policy maker and implementer of children-related policies). In as far as criminal proceedings are concerned, the Committee on the rights of the Child has underscored that some criminal laws and procedures must give way to procedures that are in the best interest of children (Ibid). By implication, criminal procedures that undermine the psychological well-being of children must give way to procedures that are in the best of children. There are several other rights in the various treaties that lend impetus to the protection of children from psychological harm during criminal proceedings. These are not exhaustible, but some are notable. In terms of article 19 of the UNCRC, states are to take appropriate measures to ensure that children are protected from mental and emotional violence, maltreatment and exploitation. Article 5 of the ACRWC also mandates states to 'ensure, to the maximum extent possible, the survival, protection and development of the child'. The right to dignity as guaranteed in various international instruments also imposes obligations on states to ensure that children are neither maltreated nor psychologically abused during participation in criminal justice processes (African Charter on Human and Peoples' Rights 1981, article 5; United Nations International Covenant on Civil and Political Rights 1966, article 10). The protection guaranteed under these instruments is to be enjoyed by all children be they offenders or victims of crime. As commentators have noted persuasively, children's vulnerable status persists regardless of whether they are offenders or victims of crime (Songca 2019, 316–334). Therefore, in whatever way children come into contact with the criminal justice (i.e. victim or offender), child-sensitive procedures remain critical in ensuring that the prevailing international children's standards are upheld. Moreover, in its General Comment 24 on children's rights in juvenile justice, protection of children as offenders in criminal justice processes is further buttressed. The Committee highlights the need to treat children in conflict with the law with dignity (United Nations Committee on the Rights of the Child, General Comment No. 24 2019). By implication, criminal procedures which undermine children's worth and psychological well-being are an affront to the right to dignity.

Aside from the CRC and the ACRWC, various children's rights treaties entrench provisions placing obligations on states to ensure that children's psychological well-being is protected during criminal proceedings. For example, in terms of article 8 of the Optional protocol to the Convention on the Rights of the Child on the sale of children, child prostitution and child pornography, states are to ensure that the best interest of the children who are victims to crimes under this Protocol is given primary consideration during criminal proceedings (Optional protocol to the Convention on the Rights of the Child on the Sale of Children, Child Prostitution and Child Pornography 2002). States are to implement this by ensuring that the procedures consider the special needs of the individual victims and witnesses. Additionally, with children being major victims and perpetrators of international crimes, their psychological well-being has increasingly come under scrutiny. Accordingly, in terms of the Rules of Procedures and Evidence of the International Criminal Court, the interests of all witnesses including children need to be guaranteed (Rules of Procedures and Evidence of the International Criminal Court 2002, Rule 18). By implication, these interests include protection of children from secondary victimisation and the trauma resulting from criminal justice processes.

While not specific to children's rights, several general treaties entrench provisions whose progressive interpretation places obligation on states to protect the psychological well-being of children in justice processes. Notable are the rights to dignity, equality and no-discrimination guaranteed under various instruments including the African Charter on Human and Peoples' Rights and the United Nations International Covenant on Civil and Political rights (African Charter on Human and Peoples' Rights 1981, article 5 & 3; United Nations International Covenant on Civil and Political Rights 1966, article 10 & 3). In addition to treaties, there are various non-binding instruments with persuasive standards and guidelines on how to ensure the psychological well-being of children in criminal justice processes. The United Nations Guidelines on Justice Matters Involving Child Victims and Witnesses of Crime recognises that children are 'vulnerable and need special protection, assistance appropriate to their age' (United Nations Guidelines on Justice Matters Involving Child Victims and Witnesses of Crime 2005). It is therefore envisaged that some criminal procedures applicable to adults may not be suitable for children. In drafting these guidelines, the United Nations was mindful of the emotional and psychological harm that crime and criminal proceedings can have on children (Ibid). States are therefore implored to treat children with dignity and compassion throughout the criminal justice process (Ibid). Recognising the toll that these processes can have on children, these guidelines implore states to ensure that children are protected from hardship during proceedings. Guidelines on ensuring this include developing child-sensitive procedures and appropriate measures to facilitate children's testimony in court (Ibid).

Furthermore, as consistently alluded to, violence has been so pervasive in society that many children have ended up as victims of crimes. As victims of crime, children fall within the ambit of the protection standards established under the United Nations Declaration of Basic Principles of Justice for Victims of Crime and Abuse of Power. These Principles declare that victims be 'treated with compassion and respect for their dignity' (United Nations Declaration of Basic Principles of Justice for Victims of Crime and Abuse of Power 1985). Criminal justice systems are implored to create an environment that fosters accountability for crimes. This includes provision of proper assistance to victims of crime throughout the criminal justice process. The Unite Nations Guidelines on the role of Prosecutors have also emphasised the message of dignity in dealing with child victims and witnesses of crime (United Nations Guidelines on the Role of Prosecutors 1990).

At the African Union level, Africa's Agenda for Children aspires that by 2040, all children should benefit from child-sensitive criminal justice systems (African Committee of Experts on the Rights and Welfare of the Child, Agenda 2040). Commentators have offered some guidance on fostering child-sensitive approaches including recourse to intermediary mechanisms, pre-recorded testimony and strategies geared towards reduction of direct confrontation between the accused person and the victim (Rap 2019, 299–319; Tolonen 2019, 225–248; Jonker and Swanzen 2007, 90–113; Bekink 2019, 1–50; Muller 2001, 1–13; Myklebust 2017, 97–119; Holley 2002, 14–18; Muller and Marowa 2011, 13–24). This aspiration entails, among others, establishment of systems that respond to the needs of child victims and witnesses. Africa also aspires to an effective child-friendly national legislative, policy and institutional framework across African states (African Committee of Experts on the Rights and Welfare of the Child, Agenda 2040). Also notable is the aspiration on protection on protection of children from all forms of violence including psychological violence (Ibid).

If properly interpreted and applied, these standards, guidelines and aspirations can go a long way in ensuring that the psychological well-being of African children who interact with the criminal justice system is guaranteed. Especially pertinent is the fact that some of these standards are entrenched in international instruments that states have made commitments to by means of ratification. However, it remains to be seen whether African states have adjusted their national criminal procedures with a view to ensuring that the psychological well-being of children who interact with the justice system on a daily basis are guaranteed.

3   National Laws in Africa Vis-A-Viz the International Standards on Participation and Child Psychological Well-Being in Criminal Proceedings

States' ratification of treaties can be an indication of their commitment to align their national laws with the norms entrenched at the international level (See Vienna Convention on the Law of Treaties 1969, article 26 on implementation of treaties in good faith). This, however, may not always be the case. Therefore, this section assesses the national framework of selected states in West, East, North, South and Central Africa against the above international standards with a view to assessing whether the psychological well-being of African children in these states is being guaranteed. Emphasis is placed on the procedure of giving oral evidence because it is by far considered one of the most stressful procedure for children who interact with the criminal justice system as witnesses, victims, or offenders. The section starts by conceptualising the various systems of justice or legal traditions and demonstrates how these impact on the criminal procedures applicable to children. Subsequently, the framework in selected countries is critically analysed.

3.1 Adversarial and Inquisitorial Justice Traditions and Children's Psychological Well-Being in Criminal Proceedings

There are mainly two types of justice systems—the inquisitorial and adversarial systems of justice. The nature of system applicable in each country impacts profoundly on the role the witnesses (including children) play in criminal proceedings and ultimately, the mode of investigation and adjudication of matters in courts. The adversarial system, also known as the accusatorial system, finds its roots in the common law tradition (Bellengere, Theophilopoulos and Palmer 2019, 10–17). In terms of this legal tradition, the defence and the prosecution are adversaries against each other, with the judicial officer generally playing the role of an umpire or referee to ensure fairness during criminal proceedings (Ibid). The nature of this system impacts on the procedure to be followed in the resolution of disputes in court. In terms of evidence and procedure, the system is characterised with rules of exclusion and there is greater emphasis on oral evidence in court (Ibid). Cross-examination is a major feature in the adversarial legal tradition, with some commentators submitting that it is the greatest mechanism ever invented to establish the truth (Wigmore 1940, 29). This assertion has, however, been subject to debate, with some commentators contending that the procedures could in fact distort the truth (Bellengere, Theophilopoulos and Palmer 2019, 335–336).

The inquisitorial system of justice is mainly associated with civil law systems (Bellengere, Theophilopoulos and Palmer 2019, 10–17). As the name suggests, it is more of an inquiry as opposed to the accusatory means to arriving at the truth. Because of the emphasis on inquiry, this system is characterised by comprehensive investigations prior to trial (Ibid). While oral evidence plays a role in the trial process, the emphasis on pre-trial investigations leaves room for greater reliance on non-oral evidence. The rules on exclusion of evidence are not strictly applied, with the judicial officer generally admitting most of the relevant evidence and exercising discretion on how much weight to attach to such evidence (Ibid). The judge plays a more active role in inquisitorial proceedings in comparison to the adversarial judge who wears the hat of a neutral arbiter in engaging with the claims of the defence and the prosecution (Ibid). While traditionally some countries were strictly adversarial or inquisitorial, in recent times, it is hard or close to impossible to have a purely adversarial or inquisitorial system of justice. It is commonplace to have a predominantly adversarial system of justice incorporating inquisitorial features (e.g. despite the notion of confrontation and cross-examination, there are rules of evidence that surmount the strict adversarial practice. Notable are the exceptions to the hearsay rules which may allow a witness not to be available for cross-examination). Similarly, there is evidence of inquisitorial justice systems incorporating adversarial features such as cross-examination in their procedures (e.g. inquisitorial systems such as that of France incorporate aspects of cross-examination despite this being a predominantly adversarial justice feature).

The legal traditions that African justice systems invoke are a remnant of colonialism. The adversarial justice system, which has its roots in the Anglo-American legal tradition, found its way in Africa through British colonialism. The inquisitorial system, which is peculiar to civil law countries such as France, Belgium, and Norway, equally found its way to Africa's justice systems through colonialism, with many Francophone countries generally inclined to towards this legal tradition. Because most African countries are former British colonies, they apply the adversarial system of justice. This makes the notion of orality in the law of evidence and procedures such as cross-examination major features of criminal justice proceedings in these countries. The question that warrants an answer is: Do some of the features of the adversarial justice system impact negatively on the psychological well-being of children?

Cross-examination is one of the ways of challenging evidence of the adverse party in adversarial justice systems. In most of these systems, the right to challenge evidence is trite and is at the core of the right to a fair trial (See generally the right to a fair trial as entrenched in the Constitutions of most, if not all African countries. In terms of this right across Bills of Rights, the right to challenge evidence is entrenched in very strong terms). Despite the centrality of cross-examination in adversarial justice systems, studies have over the years established that this procedure not only undermines the accuracy of children's testimony, but also, causes immense psychological distress to children (Fogliati 2014, vii; Westera and Kaladelfos 2018, 186–195). Studies abound on the psychological hurdles that children have to overcome in order to access justice in adversarial justice systems. Chetty articulates these challenges with regard to child victims of sexual violence (Chetty 2006, 24–45). The author submits that by their very nature, sexual offences are psychologically shattering to children (Ibid). Thus, when criminal justice systems fail to put in place child-sensitive criminal procedures, children are subjected to psychological victimisation for the second time (also referred to as secondary victimisation).

Empirical studies have also been conducted on the effect of adversarial procedures on the accuracy and well-being of children. For example, Fogliati's analysis established cross-examination left most children traumatised, with some recanting true reports of what transpired (Fogliati 2014, vii). The author's study underscored that alternative child-sensitive methods of receiving and assessing children's evidence were more effective in ensuring accuracy in children's evidence as children were in an emotionally stable environment. Fogliati's findings find support in earlier studies by authors like Zajac and Hayne whose study demonstrated the effect of cross-examination on the accuracy and emotional well-being of children (Zajac and Hayne 2012, 181–204; see also Zajac et al. 2003, 199–209). Similar studies by Lamb et al. involving victims of sexual violence established that children contradicted themselves severally when subjected to the confrontational questions typically used during cross-examination (Lamb et al. 2011).

Pantell's (2017) analysis also echoes the above studies in demonstrating that adversarial procedures such as cross-examination cause children to experience anxiety and emotional instability, with most of these effects resulting from the court conventional court surrounding and being confronted by the accused or adverse party. More critically, distressing environments and procedures go to the root of children's right to access to justice. A study conducted by Golding et al. (2003, 1311–1321) established that the traumatised demeanour of child victims and witnesses impacted on the evaluation of their evidence. The emotional breakdown they experience in the course cross-examination and their exposure to child-insensitive environments negatively affect their credibility in the eyes of the presiding officer. By implication, this impacts on the issue of whether or cases involving children are proved beyond reasonable doubt and ultimately, undermines their right to access justice.

Considering the prevalence of crime involving children across the African continent, children are time and again being subjected to this procedure, thus, placing their psychological well-being in jeopardy. These and several similar studies are instructive to criminal justice systems in Africa. Based on these findings, there is need for Africa's national systems to develop procedures which encourage and support children to participate justice processes in a manner cognisant of their psychological well-being. In the light of the well-established international children's standards and guidelines on participation and protection of children from psychological and emotional harm, the work of Africa's national criminal justices seems to be already cut out. What, however, is the actual situation for African children in this regard? The next subsection engages with this issue.

3.2 National Laws and the Psychological Well-Being of Children in Criminal Proceedings

The constitutions, legislation, policies and court decisions at the national level entrench the position of states on a number of issues. They constitute a point of reference in assessing the posture of a given state on the extent to which the various international children's rights standards are implemented. It is for this purpose that this subsection critically analyses the laws, polices and jurisprudence of selected states in West, East, Central, North and Southern Africa on the psychological well-being of children in criminal justice processes.

South Africa
South Africa is one of the countries in Southern Africa. As a former British colony, the Anglo-American adversarial system of justice has had a profound influence on its criminal procedures. While South Africa is a predominantly adversarial system of justice, as already alluded to, in recent times, no system is purely adversarial or inquisitorial. As such, there are features in South Africa's

criminal procedure which echo the procedure in inquisitorial justice systems (See e.g. Section 186 of the Criminal Procedure Act No. 57 1957 of South Africa which provides as follows: 'The court may at any stage of criminal proceedings subpoena or cause to be subpoenaed any person as a witness at such proceedings, and the court shall so subpoena a witness or so cause a witness to be subpoenaed if the evidence of such witness appears to the court essential to the just decision of the case'. This section finds force in South Africa despite the general premise that adversarial judges are merely umpires). With south Africa having one of the highest crime rates on the African continent (Learning Alliance, undated), children have equally suffered the brunt of the devastating effects of crime, thus, constantly placing them in contact with criminal justice processes.

South Africa is party to both the UNCRC and ACRWC. Accordingly, it is bound by the standards on participation contained therein. At the national level, the rights of children are entrenched in very strong terms under South Africa's Constitution of 1996. The Constitution makes specific provision for the rights of children with article 28(1) guaranteeing a number of child-specific rights including the right 'to be protected from maltreatment, neglect, abuse or degradation.' The psychological trauma that children are often subjected to during criminal proceedings could be interpreted to include maltreatment. It could also constitute a transgression of the more general right to dignity which is to be enjoyed by everyone including children. The Constitution considers the best interest of the child to be of paramount importance in all matters concerning children (Constitution of the Republic of South Africa 1996, section 28). The Constitutional Court of South Africa has tried to map out the parameters of this right in various cases including S v M (2008) where it was noted that while the best interest of children is of should be given paramount importance, this should oust or override other considerations. Sloth-Nielsen, however, buttresses the paramountcy of the entrenchment of this principle in the Constitution by underscoring that:

> the inclusion of a general standard ('the best interest of a child') for the protection of children's rights in the Constitution can become a benchmark for review of all proceedings in which decisions are taken regarding children. Courts and administrative authorities will be constitutionally bound to give consideration to the effect their decisions will have on children's lives. (Sloth-Nielsen 1996, 6–25)

In all matters concerning children, the courts in South Africa have, in one way or the other, used the best interest principle as a benchmark. In as far as child witnesses and victims of crime are concerned, the plight of children was duly articulated in *Klink v Regional Magistrate*, where the court highlighted that 'child witnesses experience significant difficulties in dealing with the adversarial environment of a court-room; that a young person may experience difficulty in comprehending the language of legal proceedings and the role of various participants; and that the adversarial procedure involves confrontation and extensive cross-examination' (*Klink v Regional Court Magistrate NO and Others* 1996).

While South Africa applies the adversarial system of justice which, among others, requires that the accused confront the victim of crime in court and assesses their demeanour (*S v Motlala* 1975), when it comes to children, the rules of procedure have been adjusted to respond to the psychological trauma that many of these children are subjected to. Notable mechanisms invoked to afford protection to child witnesses and complainants are: the use of intermediaries, testimony in camera and the use of close circuit television (CCTV). These mechanisms are explicitly provided for under South Africa's Criminal Procedure Act (See e.g. Sections 153, 158 and 170 of the Criminal Procedure Act 57 of 1957). The force of law that these child protection mechanisms enjoy has ensured that that there is an authoritative point of reference for criminal justice practitioners to protect children from trauma and to ensure that they effectively participate in criminal proceedings. In terms of section 153(2) of the Criminal Procedure Act, 'if it appears to any court at criminal proceedings that there is a likelihood that harm might result to any person', the court may direct that the testimony of such a person be received in camera. In addition, while the general rule in adversarial criminal proceedings is that testimony must be received in the physical presence of the accused (Criminal Procedure Act 57 of 1957, section 158(1)). In terms of section 158(2) of the Criminal Procedure Act, 'the court may direct that a witness gives evidence by means of closed-circuit television or similar electronic media.' Section 170A specifically makes for provision of evidence through intermediaries by providing that:

> Whenever criminal proceedings are pending before any court and it appears to such court that it would expose any witness under the biological or mental age of eighteen years to undue mental stress or suffering if he or she testifies at such proceedings, the court may, subject to subsection (4), appoint a competent person as an intermediary in order to enable such witness to give his or her evidence through that intermediary.

By relying on intermediaries, the evidence of a child is relayed to court through a third party (intermediary) who is experienced and offers a supportive environment for the testifying child. The intermediary shields the child from the hostile and intimidating nature of cross-examination and all other forms of questioning.

South Africa's courts have also given detailed meaning to the above provisions, thus, laying to rest some of the controversies pertaining to the scope of their application. In the case of *Director of Public Prosecution, Transvaal v Minister for Justice & Constitutional Development*, the court again recognised that plight of children as witnesses and victims of crime by observing that:

Child complainants in sexual offence cases were required to relive the horror of the crime in open court. The circumstances under which they gave evidence and the mental stress or suffering they went through while giving evidence did not appear to be the concern of the law. And, at times, they were subjected to the most brutal and humiliating treatment by being asked to relate the sordid details of the traumatic experiences that they had gone through. Regrettably, although there were welcome exceptions, the plight of child complainants was seldom the concern of those who required them to testify or those before whom they testified. (*Director of Public Prosecution, Transvaal v Minister for Justice & Constitutional Development* 2009, para 1)

Aligning itself with the United Nations Guidelines on Justice Matters involving Child Victims and Witnesses of Crime, the Court held that 'child complainants and witnesses should receive special protection and assistance that they need in order to prevent hardship and trauma that may arise from their participation in the criminal justice system' (*Director of Public Prosecution, Transvaal v Minister for Justice & Constitutional Development* 2009, para 78). In giving interpretation to section 170(A), the Court held that 'section 170A (1) must therefore be construed so as to give effect to its object to protect child complainants from exposure to undue mental stress or suffering when they give evidence in court' (*Director of Public Prosecution, Transvaal v Minister for Justice & Constitutional Development* 2009, para 98).

All the protective measures under section 153, 158 and 170 prevent the adverse party from confronting the child directly. One could argue that the adverse party's right to a fair trial is undermined. The Constitutional Court, however, set the record straight on this narrative, ruling that: 'these special procedures should not be justifiable limitations on the right to a fair trial, but as measures conducive to a trial that is fair to all' (*Director of Public Prosecution, Transvaal v Minister for Justice & Constitutional Development* 2009, para 116). It is therefore possible to guarantee the participation of children in an emotionally supportive environment without undermining the right to a fair trial. In any case, the Constitutional Court has previously ruled that the right to a fair trial as guaranteed under the Constitution makes provision for challenging evidence of the adverse as opposed to confrontation (S v Ndlovu 1993). While the scope of some of these provisions including section 170A has been criticised on account of leaving the decision to appoint intermediaries to the discretion of the court (Meintjes and Collings 2009, 1–23), all considered, South Africa legislative framework, to a great extent facilitates children's participation and creates an environment for children to testify in light with the international children's rights standards.

Nigeria

Nigeria is a federal state in West Africa bordered by several countries including Cameroon, Chad, Niger, and Benin. It is a former British colony and by implication, inclined towards the adversarial tradition of justice. As consistently alluded to, this inclination has major implication for criminal procedure and more specifically, on the psychological well-being of children in criminal justice processes.

In terms of legal framework, Nigeria is party to both the UNCRC and the ACRWC (Nigeria ratified the UNCRC and ACRWC in 1991 and 2001 respectively). Accordingly, Nigeria is bound by the standards on participation and protection of children from all forms of emotional harm as entrenched in these instruments. The expectation is that Nigeria should enforce the provisions of these treaties in good faith. The Constitution of Nigeria, constituting the supreme law of the land, does not have a section devoted to children's rights. However, in terms of article 17(f), the State aspires to ensuring that 'children, young persons and the age are protected against any exploitation whatsoever, and against moral and material neglect' (The Constitution of the Federal Republic of Nigeria 1999). This aspiration is entrenched under the section: 'Fundamental Objectives and Directive Principles of State Policy.' There has been an ongoing scholarly debate on whether the provisions contained in this section of constitutions is justiciable (Sharmendra 2011; Gebeye 2016; Lubaale 2016, 70–86). While some commentators contend that provisions under this section can be enforced in court (Gebeye 2016), arguably the entrenchment of children's rights would have carried greater weight were they to be located within the substantive sections of Nigeria's Constitution.

In terms of protection of children from psychological harm during criminal proceedings, the Administration of Criminal Justice Act of 2015 of Nigeria comes into play. Section 232 of this Act makes provision for trials in camera for offences including rape, defilement, incest, unnatural offences, offences against the person, indecent assault, offences related to terrorism, financial crimes and offences related to trafficking. To protect the identity of the witness or victim, the court may also receive evidence by video link, permit use of masks and any other appropriate measures.

One gathers from these protective measures that Nigeria's justice framework affords some form of protection to victims and witnesses. This protection extends to all witnesses and victims including children and it can be argued that the international standards on protection of children from psychological harm are being implemented at the national level. It is however notable that the section is more concerned about protection of the identity of a witness as opposed to their psychological well-being. It follows then that where the protection of the identity of the witness is not in issue, protection of children from psychological trauma or mental distress may not be guaranteed. This is an issue of concern because, as demonstrated in the preceding section 2, mental distress remains a major challenge in children's interaction with criminal justice processes.

Moreover, the scope of protective measures listed under section 232 limits the scope of protection that children may enjoy. Notably, section 232 makes provision for receipt of evidence by video link or use of masks. While this protection is a step in the right direction, it does not go far enough in protecting children because the devastating effects of the adversarial trial on children may not be adequately overcome by these measures. For example, the use of masks and video link does not take away the often child-insensitive content of the questions directed at children during cross-examination. In this regard, recourse to intermediaries would have played a key role in ameliorating the traumatic and harmful effect of the questioning. This is because the intermediary formulates the questions directed to the child in a child-appropriate manner. One could, however, interpret the phrase 'any other appropriate measures' as used in section 232 to canvass use of intermediaries. But the fact that such interpretation has since the enactment of the Act never been invoked is testament to the fact that more specific enactments afford better protection to children than general provisions whose interpretation is at the mercy of judicial officers.

Critically too, section 232 applies to a selected number of offences. The implication of this is that other offences are not covered. As such, traumatised and distressed child victims and witnesses for the non-listed offences do not enjoy protection offered by section 232 of the Act. Thus far, however, the courts in Nigeria have demonstrated preparedness to invoke section 232 to protect witnesses where the offences in issue fall within the prescribed list. Thus, the provision could be exploited to protect children. For example, in *Col. Mohammed Sambo Dasuki (Rtd) v Federal Republic of Nigeria* (2018), the Court did not hesitate to invoke the provision in respect of the crime of terrorism which is one of the listed offences under section 232. In addressing the issue before court on the constitutionality of section 232, the Court held that the provision does not conflict with any provision of the Constitution. A similar reasoning was adopted in the subsequent decision in the case of *Chidiebere Onwudiwe v Federal Republic of Nigeria* (2018), where the Court drew on the precedent in the *Col. Mohammed* case to underscore its obligation to protect witnesses in accordance with section 232.

Egypt

Egypt is a former British colony in North Africa. Being a predominantly Muslim country, Sharia law is a source of law and is applicable. In terms of Sharia law, children are not considered to be autonomous beings with rights, and this has implications on their participation (Almihdar 2009). As a former British colony, Egypt follows the adversarial system of justice. By implication, the adversarial procedures of confrontation of the adverse party and cross-examination are part of the country's criminal procedure.

Access to justice for children ranks high on the agenda of Egypt's justice system because of the prevalence of crime against children in the country. Many children experience various forms of violence including inadequate family care, human trafficking, sexual violence and exploitation (UNICEF 2017). The social norms in the country which make cruel disciplinary practices acceptable have also exacerbated violence and crime against children. In a Demographic Health Survey of Egypt, it was revealed that up to 93%

of children in the age between one and fourteen have been subjected to some form of violent disciplinary practices, including physical punishment and psychological aggression (Egypt Demographic and Health Survey 2014). The vulnerability of girls is even higher considering the pervasiveness of female genital mutilation, with over half of both men and women in Egypt in support of its continuation (UNICEF 2020). The prevalence of crime against children in Egypt has therefore made their interaction with the criminal justice system inevitable.

In as far as the legal framework of Egypt is concerned, Egypt is a state party to both the UNCRC and the ACRWC (Egypt ratified the UNCRC in 1990 and the ACRWC in 2001), making the standards entrenched therein applicable to Egypt. At the national level, the Constitution mandates the state to ensure care and protection of children (The Constitution of the Republic of Egypt 2014, Article 11). A specific provision is devoted to children's, with a number of rights guaranteed including the obligation of Egypt to 'care for children and protect them from all forms of violence, abuse, mistreatment' (The Constitution of the Republic of Egypt 2014, Article 80) While the Constitution guarantees those accused the right to a fair trial (The Constitution of the Republic of Egypt 2014, Article 96), a similar measure of protection is afforded to witnesses and victims as is necessary in accordance with the law (The Constitution of the Republic of Egypt 2014, Article 96). The main legislation governing children's issues in Egypt is the Law No. 12 of 1996 (as amended by Law No. 126 of 2008). It is commonly referred to in Egypt as *the Child Law*. Regarding protection of children from all forms of trauma and harm during criminal proceedings, the law provides comprehensive protection which draws on the United Nations Guidelines on Justice for Child Victims and Witnesses of Crime. It provides that:

> Child victims and witnesses of crime, at all stages of arrest, investigation, trial, and implementation, shall have the right to be heard, and to be treated with dignity and sympathy with full respect for their physical, psychological, and moral safety, and shall have the right to protection, to health, social and legal assistance, to rehabilitation, and integration in the society, in accordance with the United Nations Guidelines on Justice for Child Victims and Witnesses of Crime (Law No. 12 of 1996 as amended in 2008, Article 116-bis (d)(49).

As noted in the preceding sections of this chapter, the United Nations Guidelines provide one of the most far-reaching guidelines on protection of children in criminal justice processes. Thus, if the above section is one to go by, Egypt can be commended for having a solid framework on protection of child witnesses and victims of crime. However, the fact that the provision is general, with the measures on protection of children not being explicit and precise, a challenge of implementation and accountability is created. The Guidelines on the protection of child victims and witnesses of crimes in Egypt are underway (UNICEF 2018). It can only be hoped that these guidelines will be more specific, thus, ensuring that criminal justice practitioners easily invoke them to ensure children's participation and psychological well-being.

Despite the seemingly conducive environment for the psychological well-being of children in Egypt to be guaranteed, the plight of children in criminal justice processes seems far from remedied. Reports suggest that this seemingly solid framework has not been accompanied by adequate child protection services (UNICEF 2017). Well-crafted laws including the Law criminalising FGM and the Child Law have not been accompanied by necessary guidelines, resources and measures. This coupled with the lack of training of criminal justice practitioners has left children's psychological stability in criminal justice processes un-ameliorated.

Uganda

Uganda is in the Eastern region of Africa. It is a former British colony and as such, inclined towards the adversarial system of justice. Direct confrontation between adverse parties and cross-examination constitute major features of the justice tradition in Uganda. As with all other African countries, crime against children remains pervasive, thus, placing Ugandan children in constant interaction with criminal justice processes.

Uganda has ratified several international instruments with obligations relevant to protection of children from psychological harm in the course of criminal proceedings. Notable are the UNCRC, the ACRWC and more general treaties such as the ICCPR and the ACHPR (See generally status of ratification of these treaties). At the national level, chapter four constitutes Uganda's Bill of Rights and the rights of children have secured a special slot in this chapter (The Constitution of the Republic of Uganda 1995). Article 34 guarantees several child-specific rights including protection from all forms of exploitation. This provision can be interpreted to encompass protection of children from all kinds of exploitation including psychological distress in criminal justice processes. With Uganda being an adversarial criminal justice system, article 28 which guarantees the right to a fair trial is filled to the brim with provisions giving force to the tenets of an adversarial tradition. Notable is the requirement of the physical presence of the accused in court and the requirement that all adverse witnesses be examined by the accused.

In terms of legislation, the Children's Act constitutes the main legislation on issues concerning children (Children's Act of Uganda 1997 as amended). In terms of section 13 and 14 of this Act, a special court referred to as the Family and Children Court is established. It has jurisdiction over criminal offences committed by children and issues of care and protection pertaining to children. Section 15 of the Act is a provision that could constitute an entry point for the international standards on participation of children as well as protection of their psychological well-being can be advanced in criminal proceedings. In terms of this provision, the Family and Children Court is to be set up a building different from an ordinary court with a view to ensuring that a child-friendly environment is created for children's participation in proceedings. While this is a commendable position in fostering participation and psychologically friendly environment, the protection does not seem to go far enough in affording the protection expected of states in terms of international children's rights. Notably, the fact that criminal proceedings take place in a building different from the ordinary court does not address some of the traumatic effects of the adversarial justice system including confronting the adversary, the intimidating court practitioners as well as the gruelling challenges resulting from cross-examination.

Aside from having proceedings in a separate structure, the Children's Act is silent on alternative means of securing evidence including recourse to intermediaries and CCTV. It is commendable that in terms of section 28(2) of the Constitution, the court may exclude the press or the public from all or any proceedings before it for reasons of morality, public order or national security, as may be necessary in a free and democratic society (Constitution of the Republic of Uganda 1995, article 28(2). However, in principle children, irrespective of age, are expected to attend the main hearing, give oral testimony and be heard directly in court and in the presence of the accused in accordance with the principle of orality under Uganda's law of evidence and procedure.

More generally, section 1 of the Children Act requires the Family and Children Court to apply child-friendly procedures when dealing with cases concerning children. Similarly, section 104(3) of the Children Act provides that 'in any proceedings before the High Court in which a child is involved, the High Court shall have due regard to the child's age and to the provisions of the law relating to the procedure of trials involving children'. Both provisions could be interpreted progressively to give force to the child-friendly procedures envisaged by the various international children's rights instruments. This, however, has not been the case, with children generally being subjected to the same standards and procedures as adult witnesses and victims. The absence of more specific provisions on what child-friendly procedures entail has left the system with no procedure at all and no means of holding the various criminal justice practitioners to account.

Moreover, while the various international children's rights instruments have been unanimous on the need to foster child participation in criminal proceedings, the standards set in these instruments remains a far-reaching goal because of the rules on admissibility of evidence of children in Uganda. Notably, Uganda still applies the archaic rule of evidence inherited from English law the effect that children are inherently unreliable. The rule is applied dogmatically, and convictions cannot be secured where the evidence of children, however credible, is not corroborated or supported by other independent evidence (Lubaale 2015a, 2015b). More advanced systems of justice including those in Africa have since abandoned this dated rule. Even Britain, the country from which Uganda inherited the rule, long struck it down (The rules were abolished by the 1988 and 1991 Criminal Justice Acts of Britain. For a commentary on this, see Wade 1997). However, it remains alive and well in Uganda. The dilemma pertaining to this rule was well-articulated in the

340   E. C. LUBAALE

decision of the court in *Christopher Kizito v Uganda* (1993) where the court held that 'Since the complainant had not given sworn evidence, her evidence alone could not establish the fact that it was the appellant who had committed the offence against her, however truthful she might have been'. Similarly, in *Kizza Samuel v Uganda* (2008), the court held that the uncorroborated evidence of a child complainant was insufficient for a conviction to be secured. With such discriminatory rules on evidence, participation of children and ultimately access to justice is undermined because in the absence corroborative evidence, children are automatically excluded from participating in criminal justice processes.

It is critical to note that the application of this archaic rule remains a chronic challenge across many former British colonies including Nigeria, Ghana and Tanzania. Thus, if reforms are to be made, a continent-wide reform needs to be considered.

Democratic Republic of Congo (DRC)
The DRC, formerly called Zaire, is the largest country, by area, in the central region of Africa. It is a former Belgian colony. Belgium is a civil law country and as such, the DRC was influenced and is currently more inclined towards the inquisitorial tradition of justice. Since the courts in the DRC invoke that inquisitorial system, at the heart of their trials is the discovery of the facts surrounding contentious issues in a case.

Crime has been prevalent in the DRC like all other African countries. However, in the DRC context, this prevalence has been exacerbated by the civil war that has wrecked the country for decades (UNICEF 2017). As a result of the civil war, international crimes were committed, testament of these alleged crimes being the current prosecution of alleged perpetrators before the International Criminal Court. Children have been at the centre of the atrocities committed, both as victims and offenders. This has made children's interaction with the criminal justice system inevitable.

In terms of legal framework, international law finds direct application in the DRC. Profound weight is accorded to international treaties in that upon ratification and publication, a treaty takes precedence over national law (Constitution of the Democratic Republic of Congo 2005, Article 215). The DRC is a party to both the UNCRC and the ACRWC (See status of ratification of these two treaties). It is notable that the DRC only recently (2020) ratified the ACRWC. It may therefore be argued that it is too soon to evaluate the ACRWC's impact on national law and national implementation. Pertinent to note, however, key provisions on child participation under the ACRWC are similar to those contained in the UNCRC which was ratified by the DRC over two decades ago (1990, a year after the UNCRC's entry in force). The mandate in this regard has therefore always been present for the DRC to act. By virtue of article 215 of the DRC Constitution, the norms entrenched in these treaties (including, child participation and protection from psychological harm) take precedence over any other law (Constitution of the Democratic

Republic of Congo 2005). In the absence of any explicit law at the national level, it is expected that recourse can be made to the standards entrenched in these treaties. The DRC Constitution has gone a step further to expressly reaffirm its adherence and attachment to the UNCRC as a yardstick for promotion and protection of children's rights in the DRC (Constitution of the Democratic Republic of Congo 2005, Preamble). Aside from the Constitution's direct reference to the UNCRC, there is a substantive provision devoted to the rights of children. Among the child-specific rights entrenched in the provision is the protection from all forms of violence, which by implication includes protection from psychological violence in criminal justice processes (Constitution of the Democratic Republic of Congo 2005, article 41).

The Constitution also makes provides for instances when trials can be held in camera including public order and public morality (Constitution of the Democratic Republic of Congo 2005, article 20). It is, however, far from clear whether these exceptions accommodate children who, on account of the trauma of criminal justice processes, find it hard to testify. Of note, however, the Sexual Violence Law of the DRC of 2006 makes trials in camera a matter of course in cases of sexual violence (Sexual Violence Law of the DRC 2006). Sadly, however, this protection is limited to cases of sexual violence.

All considered, the fact that the UNCRC takes precedence of national law and has the force of law in the DRC suggests that the country has a solid framework on protection of children form psychological harm and advancement of their participation. This assumes that the norms set by the UNCRC are by implication law in the DRC. However, the fact that the various international norms on child participation and protection are imprecise and not contained in one code could pose challenges of implementation by the relevant criminal justice practitioners. Moreover, with the DRC invoking an inquisitorial approach to criminal justice, one would have expected that the gruelling nature of the trial process is the least of children's worries. However, this is what reports on actual practice have to say:

> Trials are frequently traumatising and alienating experiences for a child victim. According to a study carried out in the United States, approximately 95 percent of child victims of sexual violence report being frightened to testify in court, and many children report that the day they testified was the worst day of their lives. The children also said they feared retaliation by the perpetrator, being sent to jail, being punished for making a mistake, having to prove their innocence, crying on the witness stand, describing the details of the offense(s) in front of strangers, and not understanding the questions being asked. Such traumatic impact on child victims and witnesses is likely to be similar if not greater in a context such as Congo where it is even more difficult to protect victims from renewed violence and where the trauma of family members and communities surrounding the child are also immense. (Kippenberg 2009)

Provision is made for support persons in instances where a child witness might be traumatised. However, despite the DRC being generally inquisitorial, it still applies the mechanism of cross-examination. It is reported that 'the accompanying person may not disturb, hinder or unduly influence the cross-examination and testimony, object to particular questions, or offer advice to the witness' (Fery 2012). One then takes a step back and ponders, with criminal justice systems neither exclusively adversarial or inquisitorial, should reforms towards protection of children's psychological well-being be anchored in a shift towards an inquisitorial approach, or, it should be more about adapting each system in line with current international children's rights standards? The answer to this question is included in the section 4.

Aside from the Constitution, the Child Protection law which came into operation in January 2009 (the 2009 Child Law) has child-specify provisions. This piece of legislation addresses issues of child social protection of the child (Child Protection law 2009, Title II), judicial protection of children (Child Protection law 2009, Title III), and protection of children in criminal proceedings (Child Protection law 2009, Title IV). Social protection in terms of this Act entails, among others, prohibition of the use of a child in armed conflict (Child Protection law 2009, article 71–73). The Act, as alluded to also guarantees protection of children in all judicial proceedings, which by implication include criminal proceedings (Child Protection law 2009, article 84–93). Noteworthy is the fact that the Act prohibits the intentional attack on the life and physical or mental integrity of a child (Child Protection law 2009, article 146–159). Similarly, the Act also protects the child's honour and personal freedom (Child Protection law 2009, article 160–162). Effectively, this mandates the state to ensure children are protected from any form of psychological harm in all contexts including criminal proceedings. Despite being relatively comprehensive, the Act does not make explicit provision of child protection mechanisms in their interaction with the criminal justice systems as victims and witnesses.

4   Children's Psychological Well-Being in Criminal Proceedings: Analysis, Conclusion and Recommendations

This chapter sets out to assess the extent to which the psychological well-being of African children in criminal justice processes is secured. The sections preceding this analysis provided a normative framework on participation of children and their protection from emotional harm in their participation in criminal justice proceedings. This chapter underscored that guaranteeing these rights is part and parcel of children's right to access justice. The chapter has also demonstrated that adversarial justice processes, including the procedure of cross-examination of confrontation of child witnesses and victims by adverse parties are major challenges to children's psychological well-being criminal proceedings. Addressing this challenge remains critical in the light of the pervasiveness of crime by and against African children which inevitably places them into contact with criminal justice systems.

In critically analysing the national framework on participation and protection of child victims in Uganda, Nigeria, South Africa, the DRC and Egypt, the common denominator is that all five of these states are bound by the obligations concerning participation and child protection as contained in treaties such as the UNCRC. However, the manner in which these obligations are implemented at the national level varies, with some affording better protection to children than others. Engaging with all five of these countries has demonstrated that the fact that a country invokes an adversarial tradition or inquisitorial tradition, does not automatically guarantee that children will be protected from psychological trauma and that their participation rights will be advanced in criminal proceedings. Ultimately, the creativeness of the courts and explicit provisions on protection of children in these processes (as the case is for South Africa) plays a critical role in ensuring child participation and protection.

What also stands out clearly from the analysis in this chapter is that some of the impediments to implementing child protection measures are surmountable. For instance, while adversarial criminal justice systems place emphasis on the notion of challenging evidence as part and parcel of the right to a fair trial, a progressive interpretation of this tenet leads to the reasonable conclusion that evidence can still be challenged when protective measures such as intermediaries and CCTV are used, without undermining the right to a fair trial. In fact, having recourse to these child-friendly mechanisms provides children with an emotionally stable conducive to testify truthfully and ultimately contribute to fairness of trial for both the accused and the victim.

Furthermore, while in its purest form, the inquisitorial approach to justice has been vouched for by commentators to be the most suitable in dealing with evidence of children, the fact that a country is inclined towards this system does not guarantee participation of children and their protection from psychological trauma. Reports on the trauma that child victims and witnesses have had to undergo in the inquisitorial system of the DRC is testament to this conclusion. Ultimately, whatever legal tradition a country chooses to invoke, be it inquisitorial or adversarial, there are avenues through which child participation in criminal proceedings can be fostered in manner that guarantees children's psychological well-being. Whether a country invokes an inquisitorial or adversarial, all states must strive towards aligning their laws and practices with current international children's standards on participation and children's psychological well-being. The international and constitutional commitments of all countries in Africa create opportunities for such alignment.

In conclusion, to advance child participation in criminal proceedings in a manner mindful of children's well-being, African countries need to be proactive at the national level. Many are already party to the well-crafted standards set out in both the UNCRC and the ACRWC. The real gap, based on the analysis in section 2, is implementation at the national level. For some states, it may have to take the judiciary striking down the inherited colonial laws consisting of common law and legislation. South Africa has had to take this route in some respects, and it has given way to better protection of children and advancement of their participation in criminal proceedings. Uganda and Nigeria have a lot of work cut out for them in this regard. For ease of reference by criminal justice practitioners, the legislature should enact comprehensive legislation at the national level to guarantee children participation and protection. While ratification is a good starting point, the impreciseness of these international standards leaves the national legal terrain vague and ultimately works to the detriment of children who need the protection entrenched in these instruments.

BIBLIOGRAPHY

Adrian Bellengere, Constantine Theophilopoulos and Robin Palmer, *The Law of Evidence in South Africa* (Oxford 2019).

African Charter on Human and Peoples' Rights 1981.

African Charter on the Rights and Welfare of the Child (ACRWC) 1990.

African Committee of Experts on the Rights and Welfare of the Child, *Agenda 2040: Fostering an Africa Fit for Children* (2016).

Agya Boakye-Boaten, 'Changes in the Concept of Childhood: Implications on Children in Ghana' (2010) 3 *The Journal of International Social Research* 104–115.

Amanda Elizabeth Wade, *The Child Witness and the Criminal Justice Process: A Case Study in Law Reform* (PhD thesis, University of Leeds 1997).

Aoife Daly Stephanie Rap, 'Children's Participation in the Justice System' in Ursula Kilkelly and Ton Liefaard (eds) *International Human Rights of Children* (Springer 2019) 299–319.

Chaudhry Sharmendra, 'Effectiveness of Directive Principles of State Policy' 2011, http://dx.doi.org/10.2139/ssrn.1758849, accessed 25 October 2020.

Chetty Neetu, 'Testimonies of Child-Rape Victims in South African Courts' (2006) 47 *Codicillus* 24–45.

Chidiebere Onwudiwe v Federal Republic of Nigeria (2018) LPELR 43969.

Child Protection Law Which Came into Operation in January 2009, www.leganet.cd, accessed 13 November 2020.

Children's Act of Uganda, 1997 (as amended).

Christopher Kizito v Uganda, Criminal Appeal No. 18/93.

Col. Mohammed Sambo Dasuki (Rtd) v Federal Republic of Nigeria (2018) LPELR 43969 (CA).

Committee on the Rights of the Children, General Comment No. 14 (2013) on the Right of the Child to Have His or Her Best Interests Taken as a Primary Consideration (art. 3, para. 1) (General Comment 14 of 2013).

Committee on the Rights of the Child, General Comment No. 24 (2019), Replacing General Comment No. 10 (2007): Children's Rights in Juvenile Justice.

Congo (Democratic Republic of the)'s Constitution of 2005 with Amendments Through 2011.

Constitution of the Republic of South Africa 1996.

Constitution of the Federal Republic of Nigeria 1999.

Constitution of the Republic of Uganda 1995.

Criminal Procedure Act No. 57 1957 of South Africa.

David Crump, 'Child Victim Testimony, Psychological Trauma, and the Confrontation Clause: What Can the Scientific Literature Tell Us?' (1992) 8 *Journal of Civil Rights and Economic Development* 103–105.

Director of Public Prosecution, Transvaal v Minister for Justice & Constitutional Development 2009 (4) SA 222 (CC).

Egypt Demographic and Health Survey 2014, 'The 2014 EDHS Is the Seventh Full-Scale Demographic and Health Survey Implemented in Egypt; Earlier Surveys Were Conducted in 1988, 1992, 1995, 2000, 2005, and 2008', https://www.unicef.org/egypt/reports/egypt-demographic-and-health-survey-2014, accessed 17 October 2020.

Fery Isabelle, Executive Summary of a Study on the Protection of Victims and Witnesses in D.R. Congo (2012) 8, https://www.protectioninternational.org/wp-content/uploads/2013/08/PI-Summary-Victims-Witnesses-protection-study-DRC-3.08.2012-EN1.pdf, accessed 9 March 2022.

Fogliati Rhiannon, *The Effects of Cross-Examination on Children's Reports* (PhD Thesis, Macquarie University 2014).

Gayla Margolin and Elana Gordis, 'The Effects of Family and Community Violence on Children' (2000) 51 *Annual Review of Psychology* 445–479.

Gebeye Berihun Adugna, 'The Potential of Directive Principles of State Policy for the Judicial Enforcement of Socio-Economic Rights: A Comparative Study of Ethiopia and India' (2016) 5 *Vienna Journal on International Constitutional Law*, https://ssrn.com/abstract=2726836, accessed 13 November 2020.

Gert Jonker and Rika Swanzen, 'Intermediary Services for Child Witnesses Testifying in South African Criminal Courts' (2007) 6, *Sur—International Journal on Human Rights* 90–113.

Golding JM, Fryman HM, Marsil DF and Yozwiak JA, 'Big Girls Don't Cry: The Effect of Child Witness Demeanor on Juror Decisions in a Child Sexual Abuse Trial' (2003) 27 *Child Abuse and Neglect* 1311–1321.

Hannele Tolonen, 'Children's Right to Participate and Their Developing Role in Finnish Proceedings' in Trude Haugli, Anna Nylund, Randi Sigurdsen, and Lena Bendiksen (eds) *Children's Constitutional Rights in the Nordic Countries* (Brill 2019) 225–248.

John Wigmore, *Wigmore on evidence* (Boston: Little Borwn & Co. 1940).

Juliane Kippenberg, Protecting Child Victims in Sexual Violence Trials in the DR Congo: Suggestions for the Way Forward (2009) https://reliefweb.int/report/democratic-republic-congo/protecting-child-victims-sexual-violence-trials-dr-congo, accessed 13 November 2020.

Karen Holley 'Children in Court: The Role and Scope of the Support Person' (2002) 3 *Child Abuse Research A South African Journal* 14–18.

Karen Muller, 'An Inquisitorial Approach to the Evidence of Children' (2001) 4 *Crime Research in South Africa* 1–13.

Karen Muller and Tendai Marowa, 'An Innovative Approach to the Use of Intermediaries: Lessons from Zimbabwe' (2011) 12 *Child Abuse Research A South African Journal* 13–24.

Kizza Samuel v Uganda, Criminal Appeal No. 102 of 2008.

Klink v Regional Court Magistrate NO and Others 1996(3) BCLR 402.

Law No. 12 of 1996 (As Amended by Law No. 126 of 2008) of Egypt.

Learning Alliance, 'Crime Rates and Trends in Africa', http://ella.practicalaction. org/wp-content/uploads/learning/contribution_materials/lea56/Ibadan.%20C rime%20Rates%20and%20Trends%20%20in%20Africa1464715417.pdf, accessed 20 October 2020.

Lubaale Emma Charlene, *Bridging the Justice Gap in the Prosecution of Acquaintance Child Sexual Abuse: A Case of South Africa and Uganda* (PhD Thesis, University of Pretoria 2015a).

Lubaale Emma Charlene, 'Admissibility of Evidence Presented by Children in Sex Abuse Prosecutions in Uganda: The Case for Reforms' (2015b) 5 *African Journal of Law and Criminology* 1–15.

Lubaale Emma Charlene, 'The Need for a Contextual Approach in Identifying Street-Connected Children for Purposes of Intervention' (2016) 11 *International Journal of African Rennaissance Studies* 70–86.

Lubaale Emma Charlene, 'Human Rights Reforms of Criminal Law in Africa' in Addaney M, Nyarko M and Boshoff E (eds) *Governance, Human Rights, and Political Transformation in Africa*. Palgrave Macmillan (2020) 149–171.

Lubaale Emma Charlene, 'Accountability in National Courts for International Crimes Against Children' (2018) 31 *Acta Criminologica: Southern African Journal of Criminology* 169–183.

Michael Lamb David La Rooy Lindsay Malloy and Carmit Katz (eds), *Children's Testimony: A Handbook of Psychological Research and Forensic Practice* (Wiley 2011).

Mildred Bekink, 'The Constitutional Protection Afforded to Child Victims and Child Witnesses while Testifying in Criminal Proceedings in South Africa' (2019) 22 *PER/PELJ* 1–50.

National Institute of Justice, 'Children Exposed to Violence', 21 September 2016, https://nij.ojp.gov/topics/articles/children-exposed-violence#:~:text=%5B1%5D% 20Exposure%20to%20violence%20can,in%20criminal%20behavior%20as%20adults, accessed 20 October 2020

National Research Foundation, 'Effects of Violence on Children' (2020), https:// www.nrf.ac.za/content/effects-violence-children#:~:text=Exposure%20to%20viol ence%20can%20lead,depression, accessed 10 October 2020.

Optional Protocol to the Convention on the Rights of the Child on the Sale of Children, Child Prostitution and Child Pornography 2002.

Patricia Mawusi Amos, 'Parenting and Culture—Evidence from Some African Communities' (2013), https://www.intechopen.com/books/parenting-in-south-american-and-african-contexts/parenting-and-culture-evidence-from-some-african-communities, accessed 20 October 2020.

Philip Stevens and Lubaale Emma Charlene 'Post-traumatic Stress Disorder in Child Sexual Abuse Prosecutions: Gaps and Opportunities' (2016) 17 *Journal Child Abuse Research in South Africa* 1–9.

Pietro Ferrara, Giulia Franceschini, Alberto Villani and Giovanni Corsello, 'Physical, Psychological and Social Impact of School Violence on Children' (2019) 45 *Italian Journal of Pediatrics* 1–4.

Rachel Zajac, Nina Westera and Andy Kaladelfos, 'The "Good Old Days" of Courtroom Questioning: Changes in the Format of Child Cross-Examination Questions Over 60 Years' (2018) 23 *Child Maltreatment* 186–195.

Retha Meintjes and Steven Collings, 'Issues raised by Judge Bertelsmann in Connection with Child Sexual Abuse Victims and Witnesses: The Role and Submission of the South African Professional Society on the Abuse of Children' (2009) 9 *Child Abuse Research* 1–23.

Robert Pantell, 'The Child Witness in the Courtroom' (2017) 137 *Pediatrics* 1–9.

Rules of Procedures and Evidence of the International Criminal Court Adopted by the Assembly of States, First Session New York, 1–10 September 2002, ICC-ASP/1/3 which entered into force in 2002.

Rushiella Songca, 'Children Seeking Justice: Safeguarding the Rights of Child Offenders in South African Criminal Courts' (2019) *De Jure* 316–334.

S v M 2008 (3) SA 232 (CC).

S v Motlala 1975 1 SA 814 TPD (T).

S v Ndlovu 1993 (2) SACR 69.

Sexual Violence Law of the DRC of 2006.

Sloth-Nielsen, 'Chicken Soup or Chainsaws: Some Implications of the Constitutionalisation of Children's Rights in South Africa' (1996) *Acta Juridica* 6–25.

Terrie Moffitt and Klaus-Grawe, 'Childhood Exposure to Violence and Lifelong Health: Clinical Intervention Science and Stress Biology Research Join Forces' (2013) 4 *Dev Psychopathol.* 1–28.

Trond Myklebust, 'The Nordic Model of Handling Children's Testimonies' in Susanna Johansson et al. (eds) *Collaborating Against Child Abuse* (Palgrave Macmillan 2017) 97–119.

United Nations Children's Fund, 'A Familiar Face Violence in the Lives of Children and Adolescents: Egypt' (2017) https://www.unicef.org/egypt/reports/familiar-face, accessed 13 November 2020.

United Nations Children's Fund, 'Child Protection: Egypt' (2017) https://www.unicef.org/egypt/child-protection-0, accessed 13 November 2020.

United Nations Children's Fund, 'Female Genital Mutilation in Egypt: Recent Trends and Projections' (2020) 1–20.

United Nations Children's Fund, 'Judicial Treatment of Children in The Egyptian Law: Egypt' (2018), https://www.unicef.org/egypt/judicial-treatment-children-egyptian-law, accessed 13 November 2020.

United Nations Children's Fund, 'UNICEF Annual Report 2017: Democratic Republic of Congo,' 2017, https://www.unicef.org/about/annualreport/files/DRC_2017_COAR.pdf, accessed 12 November 2020.

United Nations Children's Fund, 'Violence Against Children' (2015), https://data.unicef.org/topic/child-protection/violence/, accessed 12 November 2020.

United Nations Committee on the Rights of the Child, General Comment 12 of 2009 on the Right of the Child to be Heard, CRC/C/GC/12 1 July 2009 (General Comment 12).

United Nations Convention on the Rights of the Child 1989.

United Nations Declaration of Basic Principles of Justice for Victims of Crime and Abuse of Power 1985.

United Nations on Drugs and Crime, 'The Impact of Violence on Children' June 2019, https://www.unodc.org/e4j/en/crime-prevention-criminal-justice/module-12/key-issues/2--the-impact-of-violence-on-children.html, accessed 10 October 2020.

United Nations Guidelines on Justice Matters Involving Child Victims and Witnesses of Crime 2005.

United Nations Guidelines on the Role of Prosecutors 1990.

United Nations International Covenant on Civil and Political Rights 1966.

United Nations Statute of the International Court of Justice, 18 April 1946.

Vienna Convention on the Law of Treaties 1969.

World Health Organisation, 'Violence Against Children', 8 June 2020, https:// www.who.int/news-room/fact-sheets/detail/violence-against-children, accessed 15 October 2020.

Zainah Almihdar, 'Human Rights of Women and Children under the Islamic Law of Personal Status and Its Application in Saudi Arabia' (2009) 5 *Muslim World Journal of Human Rights*, https://doi.org/10.2202/1554-4419.1158.

Zajac O'Neill and Hayne H, 'Disorder in the Courtroom? Child Witnesses Under Cross-Examination' (2012) 32 *Developmental Review* 181–204.

Zajac R, Gross J and Hayne H, 'Asked and Answered: Questioning Children in the Courtroom' (2003) 10 *Psychiatry, Psychology and Law* 199–209.

CHAPTER 18

Taxation as Protection Finance for the African Child

Alexander Ezenagu

1   Introduction

Child protection is one of the most underfunded sectors of the economy in Africa (Save the Children 2019). The quality of childcare received affects the quality of life in adulthood which also affects the overall development of the nation. Addressing this gap is crucial to ensure that the future of the continent is adequately secured. Research has shown that early childhood care and education (ECCE) is a lifelong foundation for learning (Kim and Umayahara 2010). It has a lasting influence on the brain development and the future success of a child in education. In other words, it lays the groundwork for all later learning, behaviour and health. However, some of the challenges currently faced by developing countries impede the adequate and sustainable financing. This article emphasises that taxation can be a significant avenue for responding to the protection imperatives to advance child rights in Africa.

2   Taxes as a Strategy to Finance Child Protection

Tax is the life blood of every society. It makes up one of the major sustainable sources of revenue for most developed countries. However, in many African countries, its full revenue potential is yet to be unlocked, limiting its

A. Ezenagu (✉)
Hamad Bin Khalifa University, Doha, Qatar
e-mail: aezenagu@hbku.edu.qa

© The Author(s), under exclusive license to Springer Nature Switzerland AG 2022
A. Adeola and M. W. Mutua (eds.), *The Palgrave Handbook of Democracy, Governance and Justice in Africa*,
https://doi.org/10.1007/978-3-030-74014-6_18

349

contribution to the overall revenue of states. For decades, financing of government projects in many African countries has historically been from external revenue such as export of natural resources and foreign aid, however, these sources have in recent times been unstable and as such unsustainable. We observe that in recent times, there is shift from external to internal financing, largely from tax revenue, though we note resistance to voluntary tax compliance by taxpayers in many African countries, attributable to a broken social contract (McCulloch et al. 2021). For countries committed to the development and protection of children, tax revenue can play important roles, not just in financing the cost, but in influencing the behaviour of taxpayers and governments, alike.

Thus, there is need for African governments to strengthen their tax system. This can be done by broadening the tax base, exploring missed tax opportunities and by maintaining transparency and accountability. Also, similar to education tax present in some countries, governments can introduce a child tax, specifically designed to fund the development and protection of children. Proper taxation can help the government to fund child protection projects; it can also be used to bring about redistribution of wealth and poverty eradication through progressive tax, repricing/subsidising commodities that are child specific and consumed mostly by children.

Tax can be used as an instrument of wealth *redistribution* if effectively and efficiently administered. This can be achieved through progressive taxation and redistribution of revenue to the poorest and excluded through government budget thereby tackling issues such as inequality, inequity and child poverty. Progressive taxation is tax system that generates sufficient public revenue, while ensuring that this revenue is fairly redistributed and focused on rebalancing economic and gender inequalities (Kumar 2014). It is designed to reduce drastic disparities in income. Hence, higher income individuals pay proportionally higher income tax than lower income individuals. This subsequently increases the income available to low earning families which means more money for essentials like food, clothing and shelter. More available income means a reduction in stress and conflict thereby creating a conducive environment for healthy child development. Social-type expenditure can also be used to raise the income of the poor through investment in child focused sectors education (such as subsidised school fees), health (like free healthcare for children), housing etc.; or even a combination of the two (Tanzi 1974).

Taxation can be used as a tool to *reprice* children related goods and services which are essential to their survival and development such as staple food items and clothing. Repricing is used to adjust the cost of goods and services which do not reflect social and economic or environmental realities. It is usually used to regulate certain behaviours for the general benefit of the society. For example, it could make it expensive to engage in certain activities which are considered undesirable like consumption of alcohol, gambling or cigarettes, to curb addictive and unhealthy habits and making it less expensive to engage in activities regarded as being more valuable to society.

Taxation is potentially the largest source of public revenue to spend on investment in children rights related projects. It is also more predictable and sustainable than other sources of revenue like exportation of natural resources, foreign aid and debt which are more volatile by nature. However, this potential is only partly exploited in Africa as lots of missed tax opportunities undermine efforts to meet these potentials. In a report titled—*The missed taxation opportunities to improve investment in children in Africa*—it is observed that most developing countries generate tax revenues equivalent to 15% of gross domestic product (GDP) or less, compared with two or three times this in other countries (e.g. OECD countries) (Save the Children 2016). Globally, an increase in tax revenue has been linked to an increased investment in children related and child focused services such as education, health and social protection. According to the report by Save the Children (2016, 30).

> By 2013 only 7 countries in Africa had at some point met the Abuja commitment for African governments to allocate at least 15% of their budgets to health, a key child focused sector. Out of the 7 countries, 3 of these countries Rwanda, Malawi, and Madagascar are among the top ten countries in the world with the greatest percentage decline in their under-five mortality rates from 1990- 2011 decreasing by 65.4%, 63.6%, and 61.8% respectively. Markedly, the three countries GDP expanded during this period with an average growth rate of 5.75%, 2.90 % and 3% respectively, a testament of the correlation between increased domestic revenue being invested in key child focused sectors such as health and the resulting positive outcomes for children.

This is in contrast to similar programmes in other countries. For instance, Canada has the Canada Child Benefit (CCB), which replaced the old Canada Child Tax Benefit programme (Stairs 1999; Li and Neborak 2018). The CCB provides monthly payments to eligible families to assist with raising children below the age of 18. Parents with children with disabilities also receive an additional payment under the Child Disability Benefit. Similar programmes can be found in the United States and the Nordic countries (Marcussen 2017).

Summarily, increased tax revenue can be associated with better outcomes in key measures for the survival of children and general wellbeing and would in the long run raise more money to finance public services focused on children.

3   Current Challenges to Effective Tax Regimes

Tax remittance and collection from the informal sector continue to pose a challenge to many African countries. The informal sector makes up a large portion of the African economy. This is composed of small and medium enterprises that operate outside the legal and institutional frameworks that regulate business activities—the economic activity that is not captured in official statistics. They include local market men and women, street vendors and other small business owners. In sub-Saharan Africa, the informal sector is estimated to account for an average of 40% of the GDP.

In Africa, the average size of the shadow economy as a proportion of official GDP was estimated for 2002–2003 at 43% and approximately 16% in the OECD countries. When compared with the 19% in the members of the European Economic and Monetary Union, one gets the impression that the level of tax evasion due to the informal economy in developing economies is about twice that of developed countries. In other words, developing countries miss out on considerable tax from activities in the informal sector. It has been argued that if the informal sector is brought into the tax net, as much as $101 billion could be mobilised.

Others have questioned the accuracy of the claim that the informal sector is able to contribute significantly to the tax revenue of states. The argument is that many of the people involved in the informal sector generally live below the poverty line and as such a significant rise of tax revenue might not occur should the unrecorded become recorded due to the poverty present among this class (Abdel-Kader et al. 2020). However, it is still important to bring the unrecorded informal sector into the formal sector to enhance their legal rights and entitlements to social benefits (Kundt 2017). Also beneficial in crisis situations to ensure palliatives get to them. An unrecorded class may also be a neglected class.

Nevertheless, whether the sector can contribute significantly to the revenue purse, it is the case that the sector contributes considerable cost on public services. Therefore, policy formulation on the formalisation and taxation of the informal sector will be faced with three challenges:

a. Firstly, taxation of the informal economy is potentially regressive because most of the people involved in this sector are usually the poorest in society. On the other hand, to promote development, improve the general standard of living and reduce inequality, the government needs to utilise progressive tax and not regressive tax.
b. Secondly, due to the lack of documentation of players in the sector, their nomadic nature and absence of reliable financial data, it is difficult to identify and track all potential taxpayers.
c. Thirdly, informal sector players have the potential to mobilise collectively against the government and threaten the political survival of politicians. This is every politician's nightmare as such they tread carefully when engaging with people in the informal sector.

Nonetheless, the government needs to find an efficient way to incorporate these informal businesses into the official tax system.

In a study in some African countries, one of the major challenges highlighted by taxpayers was the low human and technical capacity among staffers of tax authorities, alongside lack of modern equipment and the complexity of the system (Sebele-Mpofu et al. 2021). This challenge can be sorted by digitalizing the tax collection process so that it can be automated, and people can pay from the comfort of their homes. The Government also has to employ skilled professionals to handle the administration of tax and where possible, provide easy access to walk in centres. This would make the tax paying process easier and as such encourage more taxpayers to perform their civic duties.

Tax incentive and tax holidays are tactics usually employed by the government of developing nations to encourage and attract foreign investments from multinational corporations. Foreign direct investment is an important source of private external finance for developing countries. It is prized by developing countries for the bundle of assets that are deployed into the economy by multinational enterprises (Save the Children 2015). These assets such as technology, technology, management skills, channels for marketing products internationally, product design, quality characteristics, brand names etc., are intangible and are generally scarce in most developing nations (UN Conference on Trade and Development 2020). It is therefore understandable why there is a competition amongst developing countries to provide the most enticing and generous deals to attract foreign investments.

However, these also deprive developing countries of millions of dollars of tax revenue which could otherwise be invested into childcare services. For example, if not for these kinds of concessions granted in Africa an additional US$30 Million, US$68 Million and US$359 Million annually could have been earned in Tanzania, Ghana and South Africa respectively between 2003 and 2008 from the surge in global prices for metal. Research also shows that if revenue lost by developing countries due to tax evasion and avoidance was spent according to current spending patterns, it could have saved the lives of 86,000 children under 5 each year, or 1.4 million children over the period of the MDGs (2000–2015). The OECD has estimated a financing gap of $62.1 billion annually for achieving the MDGs in middle- and low-income countries where tax collection is usually weak (Save the Children 2014). Pre-COVID the financing gap to achieve the SDGs 2030 for developing countries was estimated to be USD 2.5 trillion in 2019 and expected to increase by USD 1.7 trillion in 2020 and beyond (OECD 2020).

The problem is that these incentives are offered without any clear cost–benefit analysis which result in a race-to-bottom where the countries involved end up losing a substantial amount of potential tax revenue due to these unassessed tax incentives.[1] A link has been drawn between tax incentives and tax evasion as enterprises abuse the loopholes provided by these tax incentives through shifting of profits and abusive transfer pricing (Global Financial Integrity 2014). For example, if company XYZ operates in country A and country B and country A offers more tax incentives, there is a likelihood of mis-invoicing or profit shifting to country A in order to pay less tax thereby depriving county B of potential tax revenue. From the above example, most African countries are not spared from these abusive transfer pricing in key sectors such as mining, telecommunications and tourism (Save the Children

---

[1] Ibid (Save the Children 2015).

2015). Regional intergovernmental bodies in Africa, whose aim is to promote economic integration and cooperation, such as the East African Community (EAC), Southern African Development Community (SADC) and Economic Community of West African States (ECOWAS) could play a key role in harmonising tax policies. This is crucial in order to minimise harmful tax policies amongst countries. In this regard, the Africa wide Tax Administrators Platform could be a useful vehicle to advocate for tax cooperation across Africa (Common African Position on the Post-2015 Development Agenda 2014). In order to deal with this challenge it is important for policymakers in government to conduct a proper cost to benefit analysis and adjust their tax policies to be more beneficial to raise revenue.

Unfortunately, there are no inclusive **intergovernmental mechanisms** in place to fight illicit financial flow at present. Developed countries have however led international initiatives to combat illicit financial flows under structures like the OECD. The United Nations (UN) on the other hand have a Committee of Experts on International Co-operations in Tax Matters that handle all issues on tax. Unfortunately, they are only an expert committee and not an intergovernmental body, so their powers are limited. It has been recommended that governments establish an inclusive, independent and sufficiently resourced intergovernmental body that will spearhead global cooperation on tax matters, where all countries participate on an equal footing.

The 2nd United Nations Conference on Financing for Development held in Doha, 2008 recognised the importance of international cooperation on tax and recommended that the Economic and Social Council to examine the strengthening of institutional arrangements, including the United Nations Committee of Experts on International Cooperation in Tax Matters'. Governments and Civil Society Organizations have hence been advocating that the United Nations Committee of Experts on International Cooperation in Tax Matters be elevated into an intergovernmental body. It would therefore be mandated to 'lead the development of international agreements on tax, which includes the following: multilateral automatic exchange of tax information; committing to and implementing a public register of beneficial ownership information for companies, funds and trust as well as country by country accounting and reporting by companies' (Save the Children 2015).

Corruption is another serious issue affecting the effective and efficient tax mobilisation in many African countries (Global Financial Integrity 2014). These illegal practices are reported from the border post, custom clearance to revenue collection effort. The Corruption Perception index rates the perception of corruption across countries as seen by business people and country analysts between 0 (highly corrupt) and 10 (exceptionally clean). Most African countries perform below average and although it is hard to properly ascertain the potential revenue due to corruption, it is important that states fight corruption by 'establishing transparent tax collection and management system enact supportive laws and policies, ensure the revenue management bodies have the requisite institutional capacities and strengthen oversight and accountability institutions, including parliamentary oversight'. Most Multi-national Corporations (MNC) operate on a global scale through complex networks of subsidiaries, joint ventures, contractors and suppliers. It is there-fore impossible for one single country to successfully fight the practice of illicit financial flows which cost developing countries over US$946.7 billion in 2011 of which trade mis-invoicing accounts for 80% (Global Financial Integrity 2014).[2]

Finally, it is important to consider the **role that private sector businesses** play, the challenges they present and recommendations. The private sector plays a pivotal role in ending global poverty and realizing children's rights. The 2011 Guiding Principles for Business and Human Rights: Implementing the United Nations 'Protect, Respect and Remedy' Framework (Ruggie Prin-ciples) advance knowledge on preventing adverse human rights impacts of human rights operations Although it has been recommended that all private sector players conduct their business in line with the Ruggie Principles; there are still several cases where they engage in acts that undermine the implemen-tation of child rights. These practices include abusive transfer pricing, base erosion and profit sharing and even as far as actions that destroy the envi-ronment such as pollution of water sources. To address this challenge, the Children's Rights and Business Principles (CRBP) was developed by UNICEF, the UN Global Compact and Save the Children. This was 'the first compre-hensive set of principles to guide companies on the full range of actions they can take in the workplace, marketplace and community to respect and support children's rights'. It includes the responsibility to pay tax in full. This is in line with Article 10 of the CRBP which seeks to 'reinforce community and government efforts to protect and fulfil children's rights' (UNICEF 2012). It has also been recommended that MNCs should practise corporate trans-parency. This is especially important in light of the issues of tax evasion and avoidance which are usually perpetuated when companies are not fully trans-parent and accountable on issues concerning their financial record, ownership, profits made, taxes paid and capitalization.

4   POLICY OPTIONS
FOR STRENGTHENING THE TAX REGIME

As tax can serve as a sustainable means of raising revenue in Africa to finance public expenditure and transform the continent, it is important to ensure that issues that impede on its use are addressed. Domestic revenue mobilization through taxation is fundamental to development and sustainably achieving goals. However, this faces serious threats from practices such as base erosion and profit shifting (BEPs), Illicit Financial Flows (IFFs), tax evasion etc., which undermine the growth of the tax base. These missed tax opportunities make it difficult for developing countries to raise sufficient revenue to finance public

[2] Ibid (Global Financial Integrity 2014).

expenditure, especially those related to the protection and development of the child. Most illicit practices are usually possible due to the adoption of poor tax policies which provide 'conducive conditions for base erosion and profit shifting (BEPS) and allow for illicit financial flows (IFFs) to thrive' (Save the Children 2016). In Africa, it has a direct impact on the source of livelihood, thereby denying the citizens of substantial funds which could go a long way in solving fundamental issues like healthcare; basic education; proper nutrition; water and security (International Centre for Tax and Development, n.d.).

According to the Monterrey Consensus on mobilising domestic financial resources for development, it is the responsibility of the government to provide *'an effective, efficient, transparent and accountable system for mobilizing public resources and managing their use'*. Transparency implies that the tax administration process and the budget information are made publicly available and in a timely manner (Koptis and Craig 1998). Although a few African countries like South Africa and Rwanda already make all eight key budget documents (OECD 2009)—ranging from the Pre-Budget Statement to the Citizens Budget—publicly available for its citizens; most other African countries keep these documents for internal use only, making it extremely hard for the public to access these documents by frustrating citizens' efforts, or publishing too late for it to be used for productive civil society engagements and they often lack sufficient detail. According to UNICEF (2017).

> Gaps in the budget information that is publicly available make it difficult for governments seeking to invest in children to plan, enact, execute and oversee budgets in an effective, efficient, equitable and sustainable way. In the absence of such good budgeting practice, parliaments, supreme audit institutions, civil society and others lack the information they need to hold governments to account on their commitments.

In other words, the absence of transparency makes it difficult for the necessary information needed by citizens and other civil society stakeholders to participate in public engagements which in turn denies the government the opportunity to receive valuable input which could help them determine better child policies. Surveys show that most African countries fall short of providing meaningful opportunities for the public to engage in the budget process (Open Budget Survey 2015). Even for those countries (like Kenya) where the introduction of reforms to advance public participation has been made, civil society can act as independent watchdogs and take the place of formal oversight bodies.

In 2015, the average score for legislative strength among those African countries surveyed was 42 out of 100 (International Budget Partnership 2015). This is slightly below the global average of 48. Only seven of the 31 countries scored above 60, a threshold indicating that the legislature has adequate strength to execute its responsibilities. Legislatures in the remaining 24 countries were found to have weak or limited powers to engage in the budget process and fulfil their oversight responsibilities. Legislatures in about a third of the countries have less than six weeks in which to assess and debate the Executive's Budget Proposal. In several African countries, the legislature either has no access to budget research capacity or else must rely on external researchers (International Budget Partnership 2015).

Expanding and reforming the tax base is the next step. The amount of tax that can be collected from a state totally depends on the size of the tax base. Tax collection and management capacity, the volatility of sectors being taxed, and commodity prices are other determinants (United Nations 2014). The tax base of a country is the sum of taxable activities and the total value of assets, properties or income in a certain area or jurisdiction. By broadening the tax base, this means subjecting more gross income taxation by eliminating or curbing tax expenditure such as tax incentives and holiday in the form of deductions, exclusions, credits, exemptions and preferential treatment of capital income over labour income (Economic Policy Institute 2013) (which makes up most of the informal sector). This can be done by: (a) accurately assessing the tax incentives to give smarter incentives in order not to lose too much income to incentives; (b) evaluating tax evasion and illicit financial practices that are made possible by corrupt practices and (c) blocking the leak holes, regulating various sectors and bringing them into the formal tax system.

5 CONCLUSION

Taxes are used for raising revenue for governments in their quest to provide infrastructure for the states they preside over. Beyond raising revenue, taxes possess relevant attributes for child protection. They can be used to reprice commodities and administered in a way to address health and behavioural issues. They can also be used to redistribute wealth, so that the wealth needed for educating and protecting children are available and earmarked for such objectives. However, the right tax regime must be put in place to actualize the benefits of taxation in child protection and advancement.

It should however be noted that raising tax revenue in Africa continues to be threatened by vices such as illicit financial flows, base erosion and profit shifting, among others. African governments therefore need to pay particular attention to these enablers and drivers of illicit financial flows, base erosion and profit shifting for them to strengthen their capacity to mobilise sufficient domestic resources.

BIBLIOGRAPHY

Abdel-Kader, Khaled, de Mooij, Ruud, Gaspar, Vitor and Cerra, Valerie. "Tax Policy and Inclusive Growth)" (2020), IMF Working Paper, Vol. 2020, Iss. 271. https://www.elibrary.imf.org/view/journals/001/2020/271/article-A001-en.xml

CAP (2014). "Common Africa Position (CAP) On the Post 2015 Development Agenda African Union." https://au.int/sites/default/files/documents/32848-doc-common_african_position.pdf

Economic Policy Institute (2013). "Broadening the Tax Base and Raising Top Rates Are Complements, not Substitutes." https://www.epi.org/publication/ib361-bro adening-the-tax-base-and-raising-top-rates/#:~:text=Broadening%20the%20tax%20b ase%20simply,capital%20income%20over%20labor%20income

Global Financial Integrity (2014). "Hiding in Plain Sight." https://secureservercdn. net/45.40.149.159/34n.8bd.myftpupload.com/wp-content/uploads/2014/05/ Hiding_In_Plain_Sight_Report-Final.pdf

International Budget Partnership (2015). "Open Budget Survey 2015." https://www.internationalbudget.org/wp-content/uploads/OBS2015-Executive-Sum mary-English.pdf and https://www.internationalbudget.org/publications/open-budget-survey-2015/

International Centre for Tax and Development. "Taking on Big Business: Does Africa Need One Taxman to Counter Smart Multinationals?" https://www.ictd.ac/ media-coverage/taking-on-big-business-does-africa-need-one-taxman-to-counter-smart-multinationals/

Kim, GJ, Umayahara, M. Early Childhood Care and Education: Building the Foundation for Lifelong Learning and the Future of the Nations of Asia and the Pacific. *ICEP* 4, 1–13 (2010). https://doi.org/https://doi.org/10.1007/2288-6729-4-2-1

Kopits, G and Craig, J (1998). "Transparency in Government Operations." International Monetary Fund (Occasional paper, ISSN 0251–6365; 158 https://www.imf. org/external/pubs/ft/op/158/op158.pdf)

Kumar, C (2014). *Africa Rising? Inequalities and the Essential Role of Fair Taxation.* Christian Aid.

Kundt, TC (2017). *Opportunities and Challenges for Taxing the Informal Economy and Subnational Taxation.* K4D Emerging Issues Report. Brighton, UK: Institute of Development Studies.

Li, Jinyan and Neborak, Jacklyn. "Tax, Race, and Child Poverty: The Case for Improving the Canada Child Benefit Program." *Journal of Law and Social Policy* 28 (2018): 67–96.

Marcussen, Jesper. "Social Protection in the Nordic Countries 2015/2016 Scope, Expenditure and Financing" (2017). Nordic Social Statistical Committee. https://norden.diva-portal.org/smash/get/diva2:1148493/FULLTEXT02.pdf

McCulloch, Neil, Moerenhout, Tom and Yang, Joonseok (2021). Building a Social Contract? Understanding Tax Morale in Nigeria. *The Journal of Development Studies,* 57:2, 226–243. https://doi.org/10.1080/00220388.2020.1797688

OECD (2009). "Budget Transparency Around the World: Results from the 2008 Open Budget Survey." ISSN 1608–7143 OECD Journal on Budgeting Volume 2009/2 https://www.oecd.org/gov/budgeting/45362830.pdf

OECD (2020). "Global Outlook on Financing for Sustainable Development 2021: A New Way to Invest for People and Planet." OECD. https://www.oecd-ilibrary.org/sites/6ea613f4-en/index.html?itemId=/content/component/6ea613f4-en

Save the Children (2014). "Using Taxation to Improve Investment in Children—Policy Brief." https://resourcecentre.savethechildren.net/node/8479/pdf/pb20using20taxation20to20improve20investment20in20children.pdf

Save the Children (2015). "Child Rights Governance: Missed Taxation Opportunities to Improve Investment in Children in Africa: Case Analysis of Kenya, Sierra Leone and Zambia." https://resourcecentre.savethechildren.net/node/9012/pdf/missed20taxation20opportunities20to20improve20iic20in20africa_6.pdf

Save the Children (2016). "Tax and Child Rights Guide." https://resourcecentre.savethechildren.net/node/12128/pdf/tcr_guide_dec_2016_ver_3_0.pdf

Save the Children (2019). "Unprotected: Crisis in Humanitarian Funding for Child Protection." https://reliefweb.int/report/world/unprotected-crisis-humanitarian-funding-child-protection

Sebele-Mpofu, Favourate Yelesedzani, Mashiri, Eukeria and Korera, Patrick. "Transfer Pricing Audit Challenges and Dispute Resolution Effectiveness in Developing Countries with Specific Focus on Zimbabwe" *Accounting, Economics, and Law: A Convivium*, 2021 https://doi.org/10.1515/ael-2021-0026

SOMO (2008). Taxation and Financing for Development, Amsterdam. http://www.bibalex.org/Search4Dev/files/299159/128580.pdf

Stairs, Felicite. "The Canada Child Tax Benefit: Income Support and the Tax System." *Journal of Law and Social Policy* 14 (1999): 123–168

Tanzi, Vito (1974). "Redistributing Income Through the Budget in Latin America." *Banca Nazionale del Lavoro Quarterly Review*. https://www.researchgate.net/publication/288485934_Redistributing_Income_Through_the_Budget_in_Latin_America

UNCTAD (2000). "Foreign Investment in Developing countries: Does it Crowd in Domestic Investment?" No. 146 UNCTAD/OSG/DP/146. https://unctad.org/system/files/official-document/dp_146.en.pdf

UNCTAD (2020). "Economic Development in Africa Report 2020: Tackling Illicit Financial Flows for Sustainable Development in Africa." United Nations: Geneva 2020.

UNICEF (2012). Children's Protection and Business Principles. https://resourcecentre.savethechildren.net/node/5717/pdf/5717.pdf

UNICEF (2017). "Financing Development for Children in Africa: The State of Budget Transparency and Accountability in the Continent." *International Budget Partnership-UNICEF*. https://www.unicef.org/esa/media/2141/file/IBP-UNICEF-2017-Financing-Development-Children-Africa.pdf.

United Nations (2011). "Guiding Principles for Business and Human Rights: Implementing the United Nations 'Protect, Respect and Remedy' Framework"

United Nations (2014). "Report of the Intergovernmental Committee of Experts on Sustainable Development Financing Final Draft." https://www.un.org/ga/search/view_doc.asp?symbol=A/69/315&Lang=E

CHAPTER 19

Protecting 'Climate Refugees' Under the OAU 1969 Refugee Convention

Aderomola Adeola

1 INTRODUCTION

At the 2019 Roundtable on Addressing Root Causes of Forced Displacement and Achieving Durable Solutions in Africa organised by the AU Commission, one of the pertinent summary outcomes was the fact that the 'regional definition in the 1969 OAU Convention may allow decision-makers to recognise refugee status in the context of climate change' (African Union 2019). The expanded 1969 OAU Refugee Convention recognises as a refugee, a person who 'owing to external aggression, occupation, foreign domination or events seriously disturbing public order … is compelled to leave his place of habitual residence in order to seek refuge' (OAU Refugee Convention 1969). The 1969 OAU Refugee Convention does not offer an indication of what might constitute events serious disturbing order. However, it has been argued that an interpretation of this element should reflect the humanitarian outlook of the 1969 OAU Refugee Convention. To what extent the OAU Refugee Convention may apply to persons displaced by climate change is primarily within the optics of this chapter. This chapter argues that while the international legal refugee framework is limited in its scope and application to refugee

---

A. Adeola (✉)
Centre for Refugee Studies, York University, Toronto, Canada
e-mail: romola.adeola@gmail.com

© The Author(s), under exclusive license to Springer Nature
Switzerland AG 2022
A. Adeola and M. W. Mutua (eds.), *The Palgrave Handbook of Democracy, Governance and Justice in Africa*,
https://doi.org/10.1007/978-3-030-74014-6_19

361

362   A. ADEOLA

protection, the 1969 OAU Refugee Convention—through the expanded definition—offers a premise for advancing protection for climate displaced persons in Africa.

2   The Global Regulatory Framework

In international refugee law scholarship, the notion of climate change and refugee protection has been widely contested (Zetter 2010; Wennersten and Robbins 2017; McAdam 2016; Behrman and Kent 2018). The fact that there are persons who will potentially become 'climate change refugees' has become a powerful tool for congregating moral consciousness. The reality shaped in the media that 'there could be 143 million climate change refugees by 2050' (McCarthy 2018), 'Climate change is creating an entirely new kind of refugee' (Hopper 2017) and that 'Even Europe's money can't stop climate change refugees' (Euronews 2017) are powerful headlines that underscore the perplexities of the current state of international refugee law as being incapable of providing adequate protection for all persons who move outside the borders of a state due to reasons other than 'persecution'. In the last few years, these gripping headlines have raised daunting concerns for scholars in the international refugee sphere given that the underlying premise of linking refugee status to climate change cross-border mobility does not consider the set definition of existing international refugee law under the UN Convention Relating to the Status of Refugees (1951) (1951 UN Refugee Convention).[1] Most international refugee scholars do not appear to contest this inadequacy of international refugee law. And even the Human Rights Council, relying on existing scholarship, acknowledges that refugee protection cannot be extended to climate change displaced populations in principle given that such persons may not satisfy the requirement of persecution on the 1951 UN Refugee Convention grounds (UN Human Rights Council 2018, para 69).

However, some scholars have argued for the inclusion of climate displaced populations within the context of international refugee law (Marshall 2011; Alexander and Simon 2015; Gemenne 2015; Scott 2020). Alexander and Simon make this argument essentially on the basis that the 'fundamental lack of basic national protection, rather than persecution … is at the heart of the 1951 Convention' (Alexander and Simon 2015, 573) Gemmene argues that insulating climate change from the discourse on refugee law avoids the rhetoric that climate change needs to be depoliticized (Gemenne 2015, 70). He argues

---

[1] Article 1A(2) of the 1951 UN Refugee Convention defines a refugee as a persons who 'owing to wellfounded fear of being persecuted for reasons of race, religion, nationality, membership of a particular social group or political opinion, is outside the country of his nationality and is unable or, owing to such fear, is unwilling to avail himself of the protection of that country; or who, not having a nationality and being outside the country of his former habitual residence as a result of such events, is unable or, owing to such fear, is unwilling to return to it'. UN 1951 Refugee Convention, art 1; See also 1969 OAU Refugee Convention, art 1(1).

that removing the language from the climate change discourse neglects the fact that climate change is in itself 'a form of persecution against the most vulnerable' (Gemenne 2015, 71). The trend of argument suggests that so long as the 1951 UN Refugee Convention retains jurisdiction over refugee movements, 'it must be responsive to new demands' (Cooper 1988, 528). Contrariwise, McAdam argues that the notion of climate change refugees is conceptually flawed given that 'the relationship between climate change and human mobility is complex'. (McAdam 2016, 520). As with many refugee law scholars opposed to the notion of climate change refugees, McAdam suggests that the international legal definition on refugees under the 1951 Refugee Convention may not apply to persons displaced by climate change for two main reasons: persecution and the five grounds of persecution in article 1A(2) of the 1951 Refugee Convention.

Refugee advocates tend to oppose extending the five Convention grounds to include climate displaced persons for the fear of weakening the status of international refugee law. States are also opposed to this narrative for fear of mass population influx. In 2006, the Maldives proposed amending the 1951 UN Refugee Convention to accommodate climate change, however, the challenge that this could altogether lead to the rejection of the Convention made it less favourable. Indeed, the political temperature in light of current refugee debate makes it less palatable to reopen negotiations on the 1951 UN Refugee Convention given that it is 'set to attract strong resistance from receiving countries' (Islam 2013, 227). The UN Refugee Agency has also taken a similar stance in ruling out the inclusion of climate displaced persons within the context of the 1951 UN Refugee Convention given that the events that occasion displacement require a relational connection between these populations and their states of origin. Scholars such as Jolly and Ahmad, however, argue for the adoption of an additional global protocol on climate refugees (Jolly and Ahmad 2014–2015, 248; Moberg 2009; Islam 2013, 227; Wyman 2013; 342; Ferris 2017, 16; Tetrick 2018; Jayawardhan 2017, 107).

The non-applicability of refugee status to environmental or climate-related issues has been severally articulated in tribunal decisions across Australia and New Zealand (For New Zealand, see: Refugee Status Appeals Authority New Zealand, Refugee Appeal Nos. 72189/2000, 72190/2000, 72191/2000, 72192/2000, 72193/2000, 72194/2000 and 72195/2000 (17 August 2000); For Australia, see: 0907346 (2009) RRTA 1168 (10 December 2009).

In *Ioane Teitiota v The Chief Executive of the Ministry of Business, Innovation and Employment* (*Teitiota* case), there was a clear elucidation of this position by New Zealand courts (2015 NZSC 107). The Supreme Court of New Zealand rejected the appeal of the claimant upholding an earlier decision of the Immigration and Protection Tribunal of New Zealand (the Tribunal) (Immigration and Protection Tribunal New Zealand at Auckland (2013) NZIPT 800413 (Tribunal Decision) supported by the High Court in 2013 (*Ioane Teitiota v The Chief Executive of the Ministry of Business, Innovation and Employment* (2013) NZHC 3125 (High Court Decision) and the

Court of Appeal in 2014 (*Ioane Teitiota v The Chief Executive of the Ministry of Business, Innovation and Employment* (2014) NZCA 173 (Court of Appeal Decision).

In the *Teitiota* case, the applicant argued that he was entitled to refugee status based on the 1951 UN Refugee Convention. The reason for this argument was two-pronged. The applicant argued that there was a real chance of persecution and there was an unwillingness or inability of the Kiribati government to address the factors instituted by climate change which was the source of the persecution. In interpreting 'persecution', the applicant relied on its Latin etymology, emphasising that persecution possesses a passive voice and could contemplate fleeing from something, which in the case was 'climate change because of the serious harm it will do him [Mr. Teitiota] and his family' (Tribunal Decision 2013, para 51). However, the Tribunal rejected this argument on some grounds including that there was no real risk of persecution, and the claim was not premised on any of five Convention grounds. Emphasising the criteria under New Zealand law in light of the 1951 UN Refugee Convention, the Tribunal was emphatic on the need for the applicant to 'establish a real chance of a sustained or systematic violation of a core human right demonstrative of a failure of state protection which has sufficient nexus to a Convention ground' (Tribunal Decision 2013, para 65).

On the issue of persecution, the Tribunal observed that there was no evidence to support the assertion that the environmental conditions faced by the applicant were precarious enough to warrant danger on his life were he to return to Kiribati. Moreover, on the issue of human agency, the Tribunal observed that while there have been variations on this issue in state practice, 'international refugee law has, in recent years, coalesced around the notion that it can emanate from the conduct of either state or non-state actors'. Although the Tribunal did not rule out the possibility that climate change could 'create pathways into the Refugee Convention' (Tribunal Decision 2013, para 59), it did not engage in an interrogation of such pathways beyond acknowledging that the complexities of environmental issues, violent conflict and security could create such pathways (Tribunal Decision 2013, para 59). One might argue that the notion of ascertaining the persecutor in the context of climate change is rather difficult. But if it were to be acknowledged that the 'persecution' was occasioned by industrialised countries emitting greenhouse gases, this perspective tends to reverse the traditional refugee pattern in which the refugee flees his/her country where harm emanates from. This is because, in the context of climate change, the claimant often flees to these industrialised countries where 'persecution' often emanates. In an appeal against the decision of the Tribunal, the High Court categorically emphasised that it was not for it to 'alter the scope of the Refugee Convention' (High Court Decision 2013, para 51). It refrained from accepting the applicant's interpretation which though 'novel and optimistic', had to fail given that 'were they to succeed and be adopted in other jurisdictions, at a stroke, millions of people who are facing medium-term economic deprivation, or the immediate consequences of natural disasters or warfare, or indeed presumptive hardships caused by climate change would be entitled to protection under the Refugee Convention' (High Court Decision 2013, para 51).

In support of the Tribunal on the issue of persecution, the High Court of New Zealand emphasised that the persecution, if one had been established in the instant case was indiscriminate as it was not based on any of the five Convention grounds (High Court Decision 2013, paras 28 and 55). At the Court of Appeal, this position was also supported with the Court emphasising that the applicant, being unable to distinguish himself from the rest of the Kiribati population on any of the Convention grounds did not experience a differential impact (Court of Appeal Decision 2014, para 28). Such differential impact could be where climate change displaced populations flee their countries due to the deliberate act of the state in withholding or hindering assistance in order to victimise them given their membership of one of the stated Convention grounds. However, Kälin argues that 'such cases are likely to be few, and those forcibly displaced across borders by natural disasters are not usually persecuted for any of the relevant reasons listed in the definition' (Kälin 2010, 88).

The Human Rights Council takes a similar view on this point acknowledging that the element of persecution in connection with one of the Convention grounds may be met within the context of climate change in certain conditions. These include where: (a) humanitarian assistance is withheld from certain individuals or groups, (b) government policies are geared towards limiting access to agriculture for groups that survive on these; (c) where a state fails to exercise its protective mandate in safeguarding individuals from the persecution of non-state actors in places affected by slow onset or sudden onset disasters; and (d) where conflict is exacerbated by climate change so that a nexus exists between a well-founded fear of persecution and a Convention ground (Human Rights Council 2018, 70–71).

However, when considering a subsequent communication by Mr. Teitiota, UN Human Rights Committee mentioned that the principle of *non-refoulement* may be violated where individuals are returned to where they may experience harm due to climate change. The Committee emphasised that 'without robust national and international efforts, the effects of climate change in receiving states may expose individuals to a violation of their rights, … thereby triggering the non-refoulement obligations of sending states' (UN Human Rights Committee 2020, para 9.11). Although the Committee decided that New Zealand had not acted arbitrarily in its decision, it nonetheless established a link between climate change and the potential violation of the principle of *non-refoulement* in situations where persons are returned to places where they may experience threat to life. As observed by the UN Human Rights Committee, 'environmental degradation, climate change and unsustainable development constitute some of the most pressing and serious threats to the ability of present and future generations to enjoy the right to life' (UN Human Rights Committee 2020, para 9.4).

Rather than refugee status, the New Zealand tribunal has been more inclined to grant protection to persons affected by climate change based on humanitarian grounds. In *AD Tuvalu*, for instance, the Tribunal emphasised that 'exposure to the impacts of natural disasters can, in general terms, constitute a circumstance of a humanitarian nature' (AD Tuvalu (2014) NZIPT 501370-371, para 27). The Tribunal considered the fact that Tuvalu was susceptible to the negative impacts of climate change given the fact that it was a low-lying island and its low elevation and limited land mass meant that it was at risk of inundation, coastal erosion and flooding. Moreover, there were other anticipated environmental risks such as an increase in 'dengue fever and water borne diseases' (AD Tuvalu 2014, para 8). The increasing human stress due to population growth coupled with the decrease in agricultural production also exacerbated vulnerabilities (AD Tuvalu 2014, para 29).[2] The Tribunal regarded these concerns as 'exceptional circumstances of a humanitarian nature, which would make it unjust or unduly harsh for the appellants to be removed from New Zealand' (AD Tuvalu 2014, para 30). Moreover, the Tribunal was more emphatic on the 'dense network of family relationships' which the appellant had 'spanning three generations in New Zealand' (AD Tuvalu 2014, para 31). This significant connection formed the main consideration for the grant of humanitarian protection. Nonetheless, on the issue of climate change, the Tribunal set a two-pronged criterion for assessing appeals on this basis: (a) a 'broad humanitarian concern' (AD Tuvalu 2014, para 32) must exist which creates (b) 'exceptional circumstances of a humanitarian nature such that it would be unjust or unduly harsh to deport the particular appellant from New Zealand' (AD Tuvalu 2014, para 32). In more recent times, the New Zealand government has sought to adopt this position of granting humanitarian visas to persons affected by climate change as an immigration option (Office of the Minister of Foreign Affairs 2018, 12). In Latin America, countries such as Argentina, Brazil, Peru and Bolivia have made significant strides in granting temporary protection within the context of climate change (de Andrade 2012; Yamamoto 2018, 72; South American Network for Environmental Migrations (RESAMA) 2018).[3]

However, within the African context, the recognition of climate refugees under the OAU 1969 Refugee Convention has been debatable. Some scholars acknowledge that the expanded definition on refugees under the OAU 1969 Refugee Convention has the potential for protecting climate refugees.

---

[2] As above, para 29.

[3] Following the 2010 earthquake in Haiti, Brazil gave temporary protection to Haitians for a period of 5-years on humanitarian grounds. Brazil Normative Resolution 97 (2012); In 2010, Argentina adopted a law that allows temporary protection for persons who cannot return to their countries due to the consequences of natural or environmental disasters. See Argentina Decree No 616 (2010), art 24(h); Peruvian law also grants temporary humanitarian visas due to disasters, see Peru Decree 1236 (2015), art 59(2); Bolivia recognises the admission of climate migrants. Significantly, it is the only Latin American state that significantly regulates migration due to climate change. See Bolivia Law 370 (2013).

Arguably, the provision on events seriously disturbing public order may be interpreted to include populations that are displaced by climate change. Kälin observes, for instance, that it is arguable that sudden onset disasters could seriously disturb public order (Kälin 2010, 88). According to the Human Rights Council, 'this broader understanding of criteria for refugee status could encompass those facing the adverse impacts of climate change, including slow onset events' (UN Human Rights Council 2018, para 72). The next section examines the scope of this expanded definition and argues for an interpretation that considers the object and purpose of the OAU 1969 Refugee Convention.

3 THE 1969 OAU REFUGEE CONVENTION

Article 1(1) of the OAU 1969 Refugee Convention defines refugee in similar terms to the 1951 UN Refugee Convention. However, it goes further in article 1(2) in defining refugees as:

> every person who, owing to external aggression, occupation, foreign domination or *events* seriously disturbing public order in either part or the whole of his country of origin or nationality, is compelled to leave his place of habitual residence in order to seek refuge in another place outside his country of origin or nationality.

This provision, often described as the expanded definition, has been severally described as the 'most celebrated feature' (Okoth-Obbo 2001, 109), 'the most innovative and advanced aspect of the Convention' (Oloka-Onyango 1991, 455) and as establishing 'an important precedent in international law' (Arboleda 1991, 195). In addition to 'well-founded fear of persecution', refugees who are compelled due to violence within the African context are entitled to refugee protection (Aiboni 1978, 35; Gunning 1989, 47). Linked to the altruistic traditions of hospitality prevalent on the continent (D'Orsi 2016, 63), it is trite to conclude that the expanded definition's overarching objective is to provide refuge to displaced populations throwing the net wide for a plethora of circumstances that may occasion these movements. At the time of the development of the OAU 1969 Refugee Convention, African states were mindful of the wide array of challenges associated with the emergence of independent nation-states. And more importantly, the imperative of reflecting on the fluid causes of refugee movement in an emerging continent. Unlike the 1951 UN Refugee Convention, the expanded definition of the OAU 1969 Refugee Convention allows group status-based determination which, given the reality of population displacement in Africa, significantly responds to the regional patterns of population movement. Internal flight alternatives are not also required in refugee status determination within the context of this definition. The flexibility of this definition affords an important space to 'reflect the actual situations which today cause people to flee as refugees in Africa' (Okoth-Obbo 2001, 116).

3.1 Expanding Interpretations: The Place of Climate Change Refugees

While this expanded definition, particularly, _events seriously disturbing public order_ functions as a wide-ranging safety net for potential refugee movement that may not fall strictly within the conventional grounds (Okello 2014, 70), scholarly enterprise on the extent of its reach, significantly within the climate change context, has been divided (Nobel 1982; Rwelamira 1989; Hathaway 1991; Hofmann 1992; Awuku 1995; Republic of South Africa 1998; Edwards 2006; Sharpe 2012; Edwards 2012; Viljoen 2012; Schreier 2014; Wood 2014; Nansen Initiative 2015). It has been argued that events seriously disturbing public order do not relate to climate change and rather an _ejusdem generis_ rule should be applied to interpret the phrase in light of earlier provisions.

However, a consideration of the preamble of OAU Refugee Convention suggests that it is intended as an organic document, and this is suggested both in the emphasis on the 'need for an essentially humanitarian approach towards solving the problems of refugees' (1969 OAU Refugee Convention) and through the evident expression by states that 'all the problems of our continent must be solved in the spirit of the Charter of the Organization of African Unity and in the African context' (1969 OAU Refugee Convention). But there is a pertinent question to be answered as to whether adopting a novel definition in conceptualising public order finds credence in the trajectory of regional thought processes relating to the issue. This evidently seems to be in the affirmative in line with recent decisions of the AU. For instance, at the 2019 regional Roundtable on Addressing Root Causes and Achieving Durable Solutions in Africa organised by the AU Commission, one of the recommendations that emerged from the meeting of stakeholders was the fact that the 'refugee definition in the 1969 OAU Refugee Convention may allow decision-makers to recognize refugee status in the context of climate change' (African Union 2019). Moreover, a literal consideration of the phrase 'events seriously disturbing public order', does not connote an emphasis on the trigger (events) as restricted to the similar patterns mentioned earlier in the provision, i.e. 'external aggression', 'occupation' and 'foreign domination' (1969 OAU Refugee Convention). The use of the word 'events', significantly reflects a wide-ranging term. The ordinary meaning of the word reflects the notion of 'occurrences' or 'happenings'. As to whether these occurrences or happenings are exhaustive is not particularly within the scope of this provision. Rather, what the provision is emphatic about is whether such 'events' seriously disturb public order. To understand this phrase is to fundamentally begin from the premise of defining 'public order'.

An essential starting point from which to begin a discussion on public order is to understand the fact that the notion of 'public order' is polysemic— capable of having more than one meaning. The tension in the meaning of *public order*[4] and *l'ordre public*,[5] explicates this polysemy. The differences in the use of this term in legal traditions, for instance, emerged during the discussion of the phrase in relation to the limitation of rights in the ICCPR. There was a considerable difference in how these notions reflected within national contexts. In the English system, public order was closely connected with the notion of law and order, preventing crime or 'absence of disorder' (Bossuyt 1987, 258). However, there was a different connotation of this term in the Spanish tradition encased in the term *orden publico* which was far more expansive and includes 'the whole body of political, economic and moral principles considered essential to the maintenance of a given social structure'. But this is also different from the usage of the term in the French system where *ordre public* 'denoted a legal concept used as a basis for negating or restricting private agreements, for exercising police power or for voiding the application of foreign law' (Bossuyt 1987, 258). As such, its use in the French context was quite extensive and 'wider than the terms "prevention of disorder or crime"' (Svensson-McCarthy 1998, 165) and as such included 'the general principles governing a democratic society' (Svensson-McCarthy 1998, 165).

In *HKSAR v Ng Kung Sui and another*, the Hong Kong Court of Final Appeal emphasised three pertinent dimensions of the notion of *ordre public*, stating that (1999)

> First, the concept is an imprecise and elusive one. Its boundaries cannot be precisely defined. Secondly, the concept includes what is necessary for the protection of the general welfare or for the interests of the collectivity as a whole. Examples include: prescription for peace and good order; safety; public health; aesthetic and moral considerations and economic order (consumer protection, etc.). Thirdly, the concept must remain a function of time, place and circumstances.

In this sense, *ordre public* was what was understood in the English Common Law System as 'public policy' and not 'public order' as used in the English Common Law System (Svensson-McCarthy 1998, 165). This definition further finds expression in the Siracusa Principles on the Limitation and Derogation Provisions in the International Covenant on Civil and Political Rights. In this text, public order (*ordre public*) is defined as 'the sum of rules which ensure the functioning of society or the set of fundamental principles on which society is founded' (Siracusa Principles on the Limitation and Derogation Provisions in the International Covenant on Civil and Political Rights (1984). The African Commission adopts a similar view in defining public order as 'conditions that ensure the *normal and harmonious functioning* of institutions on the basis of an agreed system of values and principles' (*Scanlen v Holderness* 2009, para 109). The nuances in contextual use of the term have led to the

---

[4] See the English text of the 1969 OAU Refugee Convention (n 2).

[5] See the French text of the OAU Refugee Convention: Convention de l'OUA regissant les aspects propres aux problemes des refugie en Afrique (1969).

description of *ordre public* or public policy as 'wide and malleable' (Villaroman 2015, 258).

These definitional nuances reinforce the fact that the notion of public order is amorphous. However, from the definitional nuances, there are evident truths in the nuances. The notions of *public order* and *l'ordre public* broadly incorporate acts geared towards the preservation of law and order, general societal harmony and the effective functioning of society. And such effective functioning of society may be political, social or economic in nature. However, there is a pertinent question as to whether every climatic event should be regarded as having affected the effective functioning of society. Put differently, what should be the test against which to make such definite assessment. I argue that the provision provides an evident test through the requirement that such events must be of a nature that can be defined as '*seriously disturbing*'. But what is the threshold for defining seriously disturbing? This will evidently be on a case-by-case basis, however, there are specific indices. Applying the ordinary meaning rule of interpretation as expressed in the Vienna Convention on the Law of Treaties (1969) (VCLT), the word 'seriously' may imply 'gravely' or acutely,[6] while the term 'disturbing' may imply an interruption.[7]

However, the pertinent question is: *are climatic events capable of gravely interrupting the effective functioning of society in a political, social or economic manner?* In answering this question, it is relevant to examine the facts. Embedded in the narrative of climate change, is the reality of an emergent crisis. In the 2021 Glasgow Climate Pact, for instance, the Conference of State Parties expressed 'alarm and utmost concern that human activities have caused around 1.1 °C of global warming to date and that impacts are already being felt in every region' (Glasgow Climate Pact 2021, para 3). Moreover, it stressed the 'urgency of enhancing ambition and action in relation to mitigation adaptation and finance in this critical decade to address gaps between current efforts and pathways in pursuit of the ultimate objective of the Convention and its long-term global goals' (Glasgow Climate Pact 2021, para 4). According to the Inter-governmental Panel on Climate Change, '[h]uman-induced climate change is already affecting many weather and climate extremes in every region across the globe. Evidence of observed changes in extremes such as heatwaves, heavy precipitation, droughts, and tropical cyclones, and in particular, their attribution to human influence, has strengthened since AR5 [Fifth Assessment Report]' (Intergovernmental Panel on Climate Change 2021, 8). At the Glasgow Summit, UN Secretary-General emphasised that '[e]ven if the recent pledges were clear and credible—and there are serious questions about some of them—we are still careening towards climate catastrophe' (Sengupta 2021). And human displacement is an evident implication of this catastrophe (Lombrana 2021). At least 30 million were reportedly displaced due to climate disasters in 2020 (Save the Children

[6] 'Seriously' https://www.lexico.com/synonyms/seriously.

[7] 'Disturb' https://www.lexico.com/synonyms/disturb.

2021b). One-third of these were children. In the 2015 Paris Agreement, there is an agreement to keep warming at 1.5 °C above pre-industrial levels while keeping it well below 2 °C (Paris Agreement 2015). However, progressions already indicate a 20% probability that there will be an exceeding of 1.5 °C by the year 2024. Reports indicate that at least 70% of the countries facing the climate crisis are on the African continent (Save the Children 2021a). Evidently, climatic events have the potential of disrupting the effective functioning of societies in severe manners that reach the threshold requirement for the applicability of article 1(2) of the OAU Refugee Convention for persons displaced across borders due to the effect of climate change.

4   Conclusion

While existing scholarship emphasises the fact that the 1951 Refugee Convention does not afford a premise for recognising persons displaced by climate change as refugees, this chapter argues that the definition of the OAU 1969 Refugee Convention affords an expansive space in the phrase: *events seriously disturbing public order*. Within this expansive space, protection for persons displaced across borders by climate change is conceivable given that the definition affords the flexibility of reflecting on contemporary situations of population movement which may not have been contemplated at the time the OAU 1969 Refugee Convention was developed.

The flexibility afforded by the 1969 OAU Refugee Convention must be regarded as a path to responding to specific aspects of refugee problems in Africa. After all, the cornerstone of refugee law is the need to ensure that a protection-oriented approach is given primacy. And this approach is significantly reflected in the cardinal doctrine of *non-refoulement*.

Bibliography

AD Tuvalu (2014) NZIPT 501370-371.

African Union 'Summary conclusions: Roundtable on addressing root causes and achieving durable solutions in Africa' Addis Ababa, Ethiopia (9 February 2019).

Aiboni SA *Protection of refugees in Africa* (Swedish Institute of International Law, 1978).

Alexander H and Simon J '"Unable to return" in the 1951 Refugee Convention: Stateless refugees and climate change' (2015) 26(3) *Florida Journal of International Law* 531–574.

Arboleda E 'Refugee definition in Africa and Latin America: The lessons of pragmatism' (1991) 3 *International Journal of Refugee Law* 185.

Argentina Decree No 616 (2010).

Awuku EO 'Refugee movements in Africa and the OAU Convention on Refugees' (1995) 39(1) *Journal of African Law* 79.

Behrman S and Kent A *'Climate refugees': Beyond the legal impasse* (Routledge, 2018).

Bolivia Law 370 (2013).

Bossuyt MJ *Guide to the "travaux préparatoires" of the International Covenant on Civil and Political Rights* (Martinus Nijhoff Publishers, 1987).

Brazil Normative Resolution 97 (2012).

'Climate crisis – 710 million children live in countries at high risk' *Save the Children* 19 April 2021(a).

'Climate crises force rising numbers of children from their homes every year with no way back' *Save the Children* 29 October 2021 (b).

Cooper JB 'Environmental refugees: meeting the requirements of the refugee definition' (1988) 6 *New York University Environmental Law Journal* 480.

Communication 297/05, *Scanlen v Holderness* (African Commission on Human and Peoples' Rights, 2009), para 109.

'Disturb' https://www.lexico.com/synonyms/disturb.

D'Orsi C *Asylum-seeker and refugee protection in sub-Saharan Africa: The peregrination of a persecuted human being in search of a safe haven* (Routledge, 2016).

Edwards A 'Climate change and international refugee law' in RG Rayfuse and SV Scott (eds) *International Law in the era of climate change* (2012) 58.

Edwards A 'Refugee status determination in Africa' (2006) 14 *African Journal of International and Comparative Law* 204.

'Even Europe's money can't stop climate change refugees: View' *Euronews* 6 December 2017.

Ferris E 'Governance and climate change-induced mobility: International and regional frameworks' in D Manou, A Baldwin, D Cubie, A Mihr and Thorp *Climate change, migration and human rights: law and policy perspectives* (Routledge, 2017) 11.

Gemenne F 'One good reason to speak of "climate refugees"' (2015) 49 *Forced Migration Review* 70.

Glasgow Climate Pact (2021).

Gunning IR 'Expanding the international definition of refugee: A multicultural view' (1989) 13(1) *Fordham International Law Journal* 35.

Hathaway JC *The law of refugee status* (Butterworths, 1991).

HKSAR v Ng Kung Sui and another (1999).

Hofmann R 'Refugee law in the African context' (1992) 52 *Heidelberg Journal of International Law* 318.

Hopper D 'Climate change is creating an entirely new kind of refugee' *Motherboard* 14 July 2017.

Ioane Teitiota v The Chief Executive of the Ministry of Business, Innovation and Employment (2013) NZHC 3125.

Ioane Teitiota v The Chief Executive of the Ministry of Business, Innovation and Employment (2014) NZCA 173.

Ioane Teitiota v The Chief Executive of the Ministry of Business, Innovation and Employment (2015) NZSC 107.

Immigration and Protection Tribunal New Zealand at Auckland (2013) NZIPT 800413.

Intergovernmental Panel on Climate Change *Climate Change 2021: The physical science basis* (2021).

Islam R 'Climate refugees and international refugee law' in R Islam and JH Bhuiyan *An introduction to international refugee law* (Martinus Nijhoff Publishers, 2013).

Jayawardhan S 'Vulnerability and climate change induced human displacement' (2017) 17(1) *Consilience: The Journal of Sustainable Development* 103.

Jolly S and Ahmad N 'Climate refugees under international climate law and international refugee law: Towards addressing the protection gaps and exploring the legal alternatives for criminal justice' (2014–2015) 14 *ISIL Year Book of International Humanitarian and Refugee Law* 216.

Kälin W 'Conceptualising climate-induced displacement' in McAdam (ed) *Climate change and displacement: Multidisciplinary perspectives* (Hart Publishing, 2010).

Lombrana LM 'In 2020, more people displaced by extreme climate than conflict' *Al Jazeera* 25 May 2021.

McAdam J 'Climate change-related displacement of persons' in CP Carlarne, KR Gray and R Tarasofsky (eds) *The Oxford handbook of international climate change law* (Oxford University Press, 2016).

Marshall LW 'Toward a new definition of "refugee": Is the 1951 convention out of date?' (2011) 37 *European Journal of Trauma and Emergency Surgery* 61.

McCarthy J 'There could be 143 million climate change refugees by 2050' *Global Citizen* 21 March 2018.

Moberg KK 'Extending refugee definitions to cover environmentally displaced persons displaces necessary protection' 94 (2009) *Iowa Law Review* 1107.

Nansen Initiative *Agenda for the protection of cross-border displaced persons in the context of disasters and climate change: Volume 1* (2015).

Nobel P 'Refugees, law, and development in Africa' (1982) 3(1) *Michigan Journal of International Law* 255.

OAU Convention Governing the Specific Aspects of Refugee Problems in Africa (1969) 1001 UNTS 45.

OAU Refugee Convention: Convention de l'OUA regissant les aspects propres aux problemes des refugie en Afrique (1969).

Office of the Minister of Foreign Affairs *Pacific climate change-related displacement and migration: A New Zealand action plane* (2018).

Okello JOM 'The 1969 OAU Convention and the continuing challenge for the African Union' (2014) 48 *Forced Migration Review* 70.

Okoth-Obbo G 'Thirty years on: A legal review of the 1969 OAU Refugee Convention Governing the Specific Aspects of Refugee Problems in Africa' (2001) 20(1) *Refugee Survey Quarterly* 79.

Oloka-Onyango J 'Human rights, the OAU Convention and the Refugee crisis in Africa: Forty years after Geneva' (1991) 3 *International Journal of Refugee Law* 453.

Paris Agreement (2015).

Peru Decree 1236 (2015).

Piacentini de Andrade I 'Brazil's draft law for environmental migrants' *Forced Migration Review* 36–37.

Refugee Status Appeals Authority New Zealand, Refugee Appeal Nos. 72189/2000, 72190/2000, 72191/2000, 72192/2000, 72193/2000, 72194/2000 and 72195/2000 (17 August 2000).

Republic of South Africa *Draft Refugee White Paper* (19 June 1998).

Rwelamira MR 'Two decades of the 1969 OAU Convention Governing the Specific Aspects of the Refugee Problem in Africa' (1989) 1(4) *International Journal of Refugee Law* 557.

Schreier T 'The expanded refugee definition' in F Khan and T Schreier (eds) *Refugee law in South Africa* (Juta, 2014) 74.

Scott M *Climate change, disasters, and the Refugee Convention* (Cambridge University Press, 2020).

Sengupta S The U.N. leader warns that the world faces a 'climate catastrophe' *The New York Times* 1 November 2021.

'Seriously' https://www.lexico.com/synonyms/seriously.

Sharpe M 'The 1969 African Refugee Convention: Innovations, Misconceptions, and omissions' (2012) 58(1) *McGill Law Journal* 95.

Siracusa Principles on the Limitation and Derogation Provisions in the International Covenant on Civil and Political Rights (1984).

South American Network for Environmental Migrations (RESAMA) 'Task force on displacement stakeholder meeting: "Recommendations for integrated approaches to avert, minimize and address displacement related to the adverse impacts of climate change"' Château de Bossey Conference Centre, Bogis-Bossey, Switzerland (14–15 May 2018).

Svensson-McCarthy AL *The international law of human rights and states of exception with special reference to the "travaux préparatoires and case-law of the international monitoring organs* (Martinus Nijhoff Publishers, 1998).

Tetrick S 'Climate refugees: Establishing legal responses and US policy possibilities' (2018) 5(2) *Scholarly Horizons: University of Minnesota, Morris Undergraduate Journal* 1

UN Convention Relating to the Status of Refugees (1951).

UN Human Rights Committee Ioane Teitiota v New Zealand UN Doc CCPR/C/127/D/2728/2016 (7 January 2020).

UN Human Rights Council *The slow onset effect of climate change and human rights protection for cross-border migrants* UN Doc A/HRC/37/CRP.4 (22 March 2018).

Villaroman N *Treading on sacred grounds: Places of worship, local planning and religious freedom in Australia* (Brill Nijhoff, 2015) 258.

Viljoen F *International human rights law in Africa* (Oxford University Press, 2012).

Wennersten JR and Robbins D *Rising tides: Climate refugees in the twenty-first century* (Indiana University Press, 2017).

Wood T Expanding protection in Africa? Case studies of the implementation of the 1969 African Refugee Convention's expanded refugee definition (2014) 26(4) *International Journal of Refugee Law* 555.

Wyman KM 'The national immigration policy options: limits and potential' in MB Gerard and GE Wannier *Threatened island nations: Legal implications of rising seas and a changing climate* (Cambridge University Press, 2013) 337.

Yamamoto L 'Human mobility in the context of climate change and disasters: A South American approach' in (2018) 10(1) *International Journal of Climate Change strategies and management* 65.

Zetter R 'Protecting people displaced by climate change: Some conceptual challenges' in J McAdam (ed) *Climate change and displacement: multidisciplinary perspectives* (Hart Publishing, 2010).

0907346 (2009) RRTA 1168 (10 December 2009).

INDEX

A

Africa, 1, 4, 5, 7, 8, 11, 12, 14, 15, 27, 38, 42, 46, 48, 53, 61, 62, 66–71, 75–77, 79, 81, 86, 87, 90, 91, 93, 94, 96–102, 104, 105, 111, 118, 126, 129, 133, 134, 147, 149, 173, 189, 216, 221–232, 235, 242, 246, 251, 254, 281, 282, 284, 295, 307, 320, 322–325, 328, 330–332, 338–340, 343, 349, 351–357, 361, 362, 367, 368, 371

African Union (AU), 5, 7, 14, 15, 36, 38, 62, 63, 65–67, 69–72, 78, 86, 87, 89–93, 95–100, 102–105, 125, 138, 222, 224–232, 248, 322, 328, 361, 368

B

Boko Haram, 134, 141

Burkina Faso, 2, 5, 67, 75, 78–80, 100, 122, 123, 126, 130, 134

C

Cameroon, 4, 5, 35–56, 68, 134, 141, 334

Children, 7, 8, 110–118, 161, 200, 208, 226, 248, 249, 297, 320–344, 350, 351, 353, 355–357, 371

Civil society, 6, 12, 53, 55, 98, 100, 103, 122, 137, 138, 141, 147, 151, 152, 173, 225, 246, 247, 271, 272, 283, 311, 356

Climate change, 8, 361–368, 370, 371

Conflict resolution, 4, 101, 140

Constitutional court, 53, 56, 260–265, 334

Côte d'Ivoire, 6, 99, 100, 122, 124, 126–129, 133–135, 137, 139, 140, 146, 147, 149–165

Criminal proceedings, 7, 8, 320–322, 325–327, 329, 331–333, 335, 337–339, 342–344

D

Democracy, 1–3, 5, 6, 11, 13, 15, 30, 36–38, 41–43, 45, 47, 50, 53, 55, 62, 66, 76, 78, 79, 81, 87, 89, 93, 101, 102, 104, 138, 148, 150–152, 161, 190, 191, 206, 224, 226, 251, 253, 254, 259, 261, 272, 279, 280, 282, 295, 296, 315

Democratic Republic of Congo (DRC), 2, 5, 75, 78, 80, 99, 183, 231, 321, 340–343

© The Editor(s) (if applicable) and The Author(s), under exclusive license to Springer Nature Switzerland AG 2022
A. Adeola and M. W. Mutua (eds.), *The Palgrave Handbook of Democracy, Governance and Justice in Africa*,
https://doi.org/10.1007/978-3-030-74014-6

375

376 INDEX

E

Economic Community of West African States (ECOWAS), 6, 77, 103, 121–127, 129, 131–141, 197, 204, 205, 230, 231, 295, 302, 305, 306, 354

ECOWAS Court, 6, 197–201, 204–207, 210–216, 302, 303

Egypt, 2, 7, 68, 98, 260, 265, 266, 268–274, 276, 277, 321, 336–338, 343

Election, 1–5, 11–30, 35–38, 40–56, 79, 100, 101, 105, 138, 140, 148, 161, 187, 236, 242, 247, 250–252, 254, 279, 290, 309

F

Finance, 28, 311, 351, 353, 355, 370

G

Governance, 1–5, 7, 14, 17, 35, 37–39, 61, 62, 69, 70, 76, 77, 81, 85–87, 89, 91–93, 96–98, 100–105, 122, 123, 126, 129, 132, 138, 141, 152, 161, 187, 189, 191, 206, 222, 225–227, 229, 238, 246, 254, 274, 296, 300, 308, 314

H

Human rights, 2–8, 12–15, 36–39, 41, 43, 45, 47, 49, 50, 52, 55, 66, 76, 79, 87, 93, 97–99, 102, 111, 116, 117, 122, 134, 137, 148, 152–154, 157, 158, 161–163, 175, 176, 178, 186, 187, 189, 197–203, 205–207, 209–216, 221–232, 235–237, 239, 240, 242, 243, 245–255, 259–263, 265, 266, 268, 273, 276, 277, 279, 281, 290, 296–298, 300, 306–315, 322, 323, 355

I

Institutions, 5, 6, 11–14, 16, 17, 28, 29, 36, 38–42, 46–48, 52, 56, 69, 70, 81, 85, 87, 90, 93, 95, 97, 98, 105, 121–127, 131, 132, 136, 138, 140, 141, 146, 155, 214, 215, 221, 222, 225, 227–231, 241, 246, 254, 260, 261, 272, 274, 281, 283, 284, 286–290, 308, 311, 315, 355, 356, 369

J

Journalism, 150, 281, 285, 288, 289

K

Kenya, 2–4, 12, 15–18, 21, 22, 26–30, 39, 42, 48, 53, 62, 67, 98, 101, 110, 145, 146, 246, 325, 356

L

Legitimacy, 4, 6, 11–15, 21, 22, 28–30, 54, 76, 78, 92, 172, 186, 187, 191, 260, 268, 286, 291, 311

M

Malawi, 2, 3, 7, 53, 67, 68, 98, 279–291, 351

Mano River Union (MRU), 6, 121–141

Media, 6, 7, 28, 145–151, 153–165, 214, 248, 280–291, 297–302, 333, 362

Military, 2, 5, 46, 75–81, 124, 127, 130, 131, 133, 141, 148, 173, 177, 183, 185, 190, 202, 205, 239, 241, 247, 251, 276, 288, 296, 310

N

Nigeria, 2, 3, 39, 48, 68, 100, 122, 123, 126, 127, 129–131, 134, 139, 141, 198–203, 205–209, 211, 213–217, 229, 230, 321, 325, 334–336, 340, 343, 344

Norms, 3, 4, 13, 29, 55, 69, 105, 134, 147, 175, 190, 198, 213, 216, 222, 225, 227, 228, 241, 288, 320, 322, 323, 328, 336, 340, 341

P

Pan-African Parliament (PAP), 5, 86–105, 223, 228

Participation, 2, 3, 13–15, 21, 28, 38, 39, 46, 69, 70, 86, 88, 90, 93, 129, 137, 151, 152, 154, 156, 160, 162, 176, 178, 184, 186, 210, 229, 263, 264, 286, 309, 321–326, 331, 332, 334–336, 338–344, 356
Politico-institutions, 121
Presidential term limits, 5, 45, 52, 61, 62, 67–71, 75
Protection, 2–5, 7, 8, 28, 38, 39, 104, 109, 153, 163, 197, 202, 205–207, 209–211, 222–228, 231, 237, 259, 270, 284, 296–298, 300–303, 305, 308, 312, 314, 315, 321–323, 325–328, 331–344, 349–351, 356, 357, 362, 364–367, 369, 371
Psychological well-being, 7, 8, 320–322, 324–328, 330, 331, 335, 338, 342, 343

R
Reform, 7, 21, 22, 26, 28, 30, 35, 45, 55, 67–69, 72, 118, 136, 137, 149, 160, 161, 175, 188, 198, 236, 242–245, 254, 255, 261, 273, 279, 282, 303, 305, 306, 309, 314, 340, 342, 356
Refugees, 8, 134, 362, 363, 366–368, 371

Rule of law, 12, 14, 15, 47, 69, 72, 76, 87, 93, 97, 153, 161, 175, 226, 243–245, 247, 251, 253, 259–263, 265, 274, 276, 277, 296, 308, 309, 314
Rwanda, 6, 67, 98, 171–191, 314, 351, 356

S
Social justice, 213, 216
State sovereignty, 5, 62–67, 72, 105

T
Taxation, 8, 349–352, 355, 357
Technology, 3–5, 12, 13, 15–22, 24–30, 154, 287, 289, 290, 353
The Gambia, 2, 7, 46, 76, 101, 122, 123, 231, 295–297, 299, 300, 302, 303, 305, 307–309, 311–315
Third-termism, 5, 75, 78, 80, 81
Transitional justice (TJ), 4, 6, 145–147, 149, 150, 152, 153, 156, 158–165, 175, 176, 179, 186, 191, 222, 229, 230, 253, 273, 313

W
West Africa, 6, 121–126, 128–131, 133–139, 141, 198, 199, 201, 215, 216, 334

Printed in the United States
by Baker & Taylor Publisher Services